KT-457-635

Schott's
Almanac

2010

LIBER PRAETERITORUM ET POSTERITATIS CARMEN

A man should keep his little brain attic stocked with all the
furniture that he is likely to use, and the rest he can put away in
the lumber room of his library, where he can get it if he wants it.
— ARTHUR CONAN DOYLE (1856–1930)

Schott's Almanac 2010 ™ · Schott's Almanac ™
Schott's Annual Astrometer ™ © 2009

© BEN SCHOTT 2009 · All rights reserved

Published by Bloomsbury Publishing Plc., 36 Soho Square, London, W1D 3QY, UK

www.benschott.com

1 2 3 4 5 6 7 8 9 10

The moral right of Ben Schott to be identified as the author
of this work has been asserted by him in accordance with
the Copyright, Designs and Patents Act, 1988.

No part of this publication may be reproduced, transmitted, or stored in a retrieval system, in any form, or by any means, without permission in writing from the publisher. This book is sold subject to the condition that it shall not, by way of trade or otherwise, be lent, hired out, resold, or otherwise circulated without the publisher's prior consent in any form of binding or cover other than that in which it is published, and without a similar condition being imposed on the subsequent purchaser. ❦ All trademarks and copyrights are acknowledged. ❦ Crown Copyright material is reproduced with the permission of the Controller of HMSO and the Queen's Printer for Scotland.

Cover illustration by Alison Lang. © Ben Schott 2009. All rights reserved.
Portraits by Chris Lyon. © Ben Schott 2006–09. All rights reserved.
The table of PMs on pp.264–65 was first published in *The Times*; grateful thanks are extended to *Facts About the British Prime Ministers*, Englefield, Seaton, & White (The H.W. Wilson Co., NY). The 'Twittergraphy' piece on p.334 as well as a number of other entries throughout the book were first published in *The New York Times* and on the *Schott's Vocab* blog on nytimes.com. The *Catch It, Bin It, Kill It* logo used on p.23 is © Crown copyright 2007. Other illustrations © Ben Schott 2009. All rights reserved.

NOTE · Information included within is believed to be correct at the time of going to press. Neither the author nor the publisher can accept any responsibility for any error or subsequent changes.

The paper this book is printed on is certified by the © 1996 Forest Stewardship Council A.C. (FSC). It is ancient-forest friendly. The printer holds FSC chain of custody SGS-COC-2061

FSC
Mixed Sources
Product group from well-managed
forests and other controlled sources
Cert no. SGS-COC-2061
www.fsc.org
© 1996 Forest Stewardship Council

ISBN 978-0-7475-9842-8

A CIP catalogue record for this book is available from the British Library. Designed & typeset by BEN SCHOTT Printed in Great Britain by CLAYS Ltd, ST IVES Plc.

Also by BEN SCHOTT

Schott's Original Miscellany
Schott's Food & Drink Miscellany
Schott's Sporting, Gaming, & Idling Miscellany
Schott's Miscellany Diary (with Smythson)

Schott's Almanac

2010

LIBER PRAETERITORUM · ET · POSTERITATIS CARMEN

· *The book of things past and the song of the future* ·

Conceived, edited, and designed by

BEN SCHOTT

Series Editor · Claire Cock-Starkey

Assistant Editor · Bess Lovejoy
Researcher · Iona Macdonald

BLOOMSBURY
LONDON · BERLIN · NEW YORK

Preface

A calendar, a calendar! look in the almanack;
find out moonshine, find out moonshine.
— A Midsummer Night's Dream, III i

Completely revised and updated, *Schott's Almanac 2010* is the fifth annual edition in the series [see p.5]. The American writer and patron of the arts, Gertrude Stein (1874–1946), once commented that 'everybody gets so much information all day long that they lose their common sense'. *Schott's Almanac* aspires to step back from the overwhelm of daily news and speculation to select and assess the events, ideas, people, and opinions that truly define the year. For if what Stein said was accurate before the Second World War, how much more relevant is her observation now? ❦ The C21st almanac is necessarily different from some of its distinguished predecessors, which were published in times when the year was defined by considerations astronomical, ecclesiastical, or aristocratic. By exploring high art and pop culture, geopolitics and gossip, scientific discovery and sporting achievement, *Schott's Almanac* endeavours to describe the year as it is lived, in all its complexity and curiosity.

— *Schott's* is an almanac written to be read.

THE ALMANAC'S YEAR

In order to be as inclusive as possible, the *Schott's Almanac* year runs until mid-September.

Data cited in *Schott's Almanac* are taken from the latest sources available at the time of writing.

ERRORS & OMISSIONS

Every effort has been made to ensure that the information contained within *Schott's Almanac* is both accurate and up-to-date, and grateful acknowledgement is made to the various sources used. However, as Goethe once said: 'error is to truth as sleep is to waking'. Consequently, the author would be pleased to be informed of any errors, inaccuracies, or omissions that might help improve future editions.

Please send all comments or suggestions to the author, care of:

Bloomsbury Publishing Plc, 36 Soho Square, London, W1D 3QY
or email *editor@schottsalmanac.com*

The author is grateful to the readers who sent in comments on the 2009 edition. Notable corrections and clarifications are included in the Errata section on p.352.

FIVE YEARS OF SCHOTT'S ALMANAC

	Person of the year	Object of the year	Words of the year	Substance of the year
2009–10	Peter Mandelson: New Labour's midwife & mortician	The tweets of Twitter: the rise (and fall?) of a social networking fad	FLIPPING *MPs on the make and on the take* SAVED THE WORLD *Gordon Brown's Freudian slip/boast* CATCH IT, BIN IT, KILL IT *The NHS's low-fi advice for H1N1*	H_2O: droughts, deluges, water wars, & taps running dry
2008–09	Hu Jintao: Beijing's triumphant games & Sichuan's tragic quake	The hand: Iraqi voting stains, iPhone gestures, & historic handshakes	THE N.I.C.E. DECADE IS OVER *'Non-Inflationary Consistent Expansion'* WIDOW SIX SEVEN *Prince Harry's code name in Afghanistan* CRASH GORDON *Brown's nickname as the economy soured*	Honey: the curious & concerning decline of the honey bee
2007–08	Vladimir Putin: the resurgence of Russia on the world stage	The demise of the incandescent light bulb & the vital 'wife test'	SURGE *Bush's deployment of 21,500 troops to Iraq* MORAL COMPASS *Gordon Brown's statement of values* SMEATONATOR *John Smeaton, the hero of the Glasgow airport terror attack*	Polonium 210 & the strange death of Alexander Litvinenko
2006–07	M. Ahmadinejad & the provocative realpolitik of Iran	The St George Cross: football, fascism, & an icon of England	YO BLAIR! *George W. Bush's friendly/patronising greeting to Tony* THE LONG WAR *The preferred term for the war on terror* BROWNSPLOITATION *The profusion of Dan Brown rip-offs*	Oseltamivir phosphate –Tamiflu & the threat of avian flu H5N1
2005–06	Saparmurat Niyazov & Turkmenistan's final years of bizarre rule	Camera phones: citizen reporters & the end of photo-journalism?	SANTO SUBITO *Chanted after the death of John Paul II* HAPPY SLAPPING *Capturing assaults on mobile phones* TURKEY TWIZZLER *The curious kids' food targeted by Jamie Oliver*	Sudan 1: a ubiquitous red dye at the centre of a mass food scare

Contents

Chronicle

Men talk of killing time, while time quietly kills them.
— DIONYSIUS LARDNER BOURSIQUOT (1820–90)

─────────── SOME AWARDS OF NOTE ───────────

Time magazine Person of the Year [2008] · BARACK OBAMA

*His arrival on the scene feels like a step into the next century – his genome is
global, his mind is innovative, his world is networked, and his spirit is democratic.
Perhaps it takes a new face to see the promise in a future that now looks dark.*

Tipperary International Peace Prize . . . . The Cluster Munition Coalition
Woodrow Wilson Award for Public Service . . . . Luiz Inácio Lula da Silva
Robert Burns Humanitarian Award . . . . Guy Willoughby
Australian of the Year . . . . Professor Michael Dodson AM
BP Portrait Award . . . . Peter Monkman
Car of the Year [*What Car?*] . . . . Ford Fiesta
Prison Officer of the Year [HM Prison Service] . . . . Senior Officer Dom Chapman
International Engine of the Year . . . . Volkswagen 1·4-litre TSI Twincharger
Whisky of the Year . . . . Ardbeg Uigeadail
Shed of the Year . . . . The Kite Cabin, Wales
Charity Awards · overall winner . . . . Leap Confronting Conflict
Sandwich Designer of the Year . . . . Thomas Allen · Buckingham Foods
Barrister of the Year [*The Lawyer*] . . . . Dinah Rose QC, Blackstone Chambers
Annual Ernest Hemingway Look-Alike Award . . . . David Douglas
Slimming World Man of the Year . . . . Roberto Enrieu [lost 159kg · 25st]
Pet Slimmer of the Year . . . . Keano the Labrador [lost 10·2kg · 1·6st]
Lollipop Person of the Year [Kwik Fit · 2008] . . . . Heather Day
Rears of the Year . . . . Rachel Stevens · Russell Watson
Pier of the Year . . . . Saltburn Pier
Airline of the Year [Skytrax] . . . . Cathay Pacific
Pantone Colour of the Year . . . . Mimosa [see p.182]
Celebrity Mum of the Year [Tesco] . . . . Nell McAndrew
Best British Cuppa [UK Tea Council] . . . . The Bridge Tea Rooms, Wiltshire

─────────── PLAIN ENGLISH CAMPAIGN · 2008 ───────────

The PEC honoured former president George W. Bush with a 'Foot in Mouth Lifetime Achievement Award for his services to gobbledygook', citing such examples as:

I hope you leave here and walk out and say, 'what did he say?'

————— MISC. LISTS OF 2009 ————— | —2010 WORDS—

THE NATION'S FAVOURITE SWEETS
according to a Marks & Spencer poll

Fizzy cola bottles
Cola bottles
Rhubarb and custards
Wine gums · Black jacks
Jelly babies · Bon bons
Chocolate raisins

GREATEST RUSSIANS
voted for by the Russian public on Rossiya TV

Alexander Nevsky
Peter Stolypin
Joseph Stalin
Alexander Pushkin
Tsar Peter the Great
Vladimir Lenin

MOST DANGEROUS BISCUITS
according to research into biscuit-related injuries by Mindlab International

Custard cream · Cookie
Chocolate biscuit bar
Wafer · Rich tea
Bourbon · Oat biscuit

BRITONS' TOP TEN GUILTY PLEASURES
according to beauty firm Montagne Jeunesse

1. watching daytime TV
2. staying in pyjamas
3. raiding the fridge
4. squeezing spots
5. picking nose
6. cheesy music
7. burping
8. talking to yourself
9. stealing chips off partner's plate
10. watching kids' TV

TOP TEN UK SUPERBRANDS
according to a survey by Superbrands UK/The Centre for Brand Analysis

1 .... Microsoft
2 .... Rolex
3 .... Google
4 .... British Airways
5 .... BBC
6 .... Mercedes-Benz
7 .... Coca Cola
8 .... Lego
9 .... Apple
10. . Encyclopaedia Brit.

FAVOURITE BRITISH 'CURVACEOUS' PEOPLE
according to a onepoll.com survey

Dawn French
Fern Britton · Peter Kay
Chris Moyles
Johnny Vegas
Nigella Lawson
Jo Brand · Beth Ditto
Charlotte Church
Cheryl Fergison

WORDS CULLED FROM COLLINS DICTIONARY
in March 2009

Abstergent – *scouring*
Caducity – *senility*
Caliginosity – *dimness*
Embrangle – *confuse*
Exuviate – *to shed (skin or similar outer layer)*
Fatidical – *prophetic*
Griseous – *greyish*
Malison – *a curse*
Mansuetude – *mildness*
Niddering – *cowardly*
Nitid – *glistening*
Olid – *foul-smelling*
Oppugnant – *contrary*

2010 WORDS

The following words celebrate anniversaries in 2010, based upon the earliest cited use traced by the venerable *Oxford English Dictionary*:

{1510} *cheesemonger* (one who trafficks in cheese) · *nipple* (external projection of the mammary glands) · {1610} *rhyme* (a composition 'in which the consonance of terminal sounds is observed') · *watchdog* (seemingly neologised by Shakespeare) · {1710} *speech-maker* (a public orator) · *Tangerine* (a native of Tangier) · {1810} *moo-cow* (childish term for a cow, or the noise the animal makes) · {1910} *cripes* (ejaculation of surprise, a 'vulgar perversion of Christ', according to the OED) · *melt-in-the-mouth* (description of especially light and effervescent foodstuffs) · {1920} *Chopinesque* (resembling the style of Frédéric Chopin, 1810–49) · {1930} *go-slow* (industrial protest) {1940} *baby blues* (colloquial phrase for post-natal depression) · {1950} *bar-hopping* (peripatetic imbibing) · {1960} *Pinteresque* (reminiscent of Harold Pinter, 1930–2008, notably 'implications of threat and strong feeling produced through colloquial language, apparent triviality, and long pauses' … …)

——————— SOME SURVEY RESULTS OF NOTE · 2008–09 ———————

%	*of British adults, unless stated*	*source & month*
94	of English teenagers say they need better career advice	[Equality & H. Rights Com.; Jun]
90	store fresh food in the wrong place (e.g., tomatoes in the fridge)	[Morrisons; May]
86	of 6–12s would give up pocket money to help recession-hit parents	[BBC; Apr]
84	think the British banking system needs to be reformed	[Which?; Feb]
84	consider themselves to be good listeners	[Siemens Hearing Instruments; May]
82	cannot recite any poem in its entirety by heart	[BBC; May]
82	have ordered a dish while abroad without knowing what it was	[TripAdvisor; Aug]
79	would prefer extra sleep to having sex	[Edinburgh Sleep Centre/GMTV; Mar]
77	of students (11–16) plan to go on to higher education	[Sutton Trust; Jul]
77	find the world more frightening now than it was in 1999	[Mental Health Fdtn.; Apr]
75	of Londoners are pleased to be hosting the 2012 Olympics	[London Councils; Jun]
75	of Glaswegians admit to exercising fewer than 3× a week	[Nuffield Health; Aug]
72	of kids do not take the advised daily hour of post-school exercise	[Change4Life; Apr]
67	know someone who has been made redundant during the recession	[BBC; Jul]
67	would tell the police if they knew someone was going to drive drunk	[AA; Dec '08]
62	did not know the parable of the Prodigal Son	[Nat. Biblical Literacy Survey; Jul]
62	believe 'religion has an important role to play in public life'	[ComRes; Feb]
59	of Welsh people think there should be a monarchy	[BBC Wales; Jun]
58	did not know that excessive drinking can hinder sleep	[Know Your Limits; Aug]
53	feel the media portrays boys too negatively [see p.96]	[ICM; Nov 08]
53	believe in life after death	[Theos; Apr]
49	of teachers make assumptions based upon a pupil's name	[Bounty.com; Sep]
40	are unaware of the calories in a glass of wine or a pint of beer	[Drinkaware; Apr]
39	of mothers said they identified most with their eldest child	[netmums.com; Jun]
37	think the recession will focus people less on possessions	[Charities Aid Fdtn; Mar]
37	of women will wear uncomfortable shoes if they are fashionable	[SCP; Sep]
35	of dogs in Scotland are obese	[PDSA; Jul]
32	of English children (10–15) worry about their bodies	[Ofsted; Oct '08]
31	of parents wished their children had a shorter summer holiday	[TDA; Jul]
30	think single women should not be allowed to adopt children	[ICM; Nov '08]
30	say they are kept awake by their partner's snoring	[NetDoctor; Oct '08]
29	have been splashed by hot drinks while dunking biscuits [see p.8]	[Mindlab/Rocky; Sep]
29	said they had no savings whatsoever	[EuroDirect; Feb]
27	of teens tell grandparents things they can't tell their parents	[Grandparents Plus; Sep]
25	believe Charles Darwin's theory of evolution is 'definitely true'	[*Guardian*; Feb]
25	of men eat more to reassure their pregnant partner about weight	[Onepoll; May]
23	would vote in favour of joining the euro	[BBC; Jan]
19	of >18s have personal experience of drug addiction	[ICM; Jul]
16	in N Ireland would mind having a mentally ill neighbour	[Equality Commission; Jun]
15	believe in fortune telling or Tarot card readings	[Theos; Apr]
13	of mothers think lullabies are too old-fashioned	[The Baby Website; Dec '08]
8	of 16–17s say they drink at least once a week out of boredom	[Drinkaware; Aug]
6	of UK streets contain rubber bands dropped by postal workers	[Keep Britain Tidy; Jun]
4	would be happy for Britain to withdraw from the Commonwealth	[YouGov; Mar]
2	of 6–12s carry a weapon because of their fears about crime	[BBC; Apr]

—————————— WORDS OF THE YEAR ——————————

FLIPPING · where MPs switch the homes they nominate as their secondary residence to claim expenses for more than one property. *Also* GHOST MORTGAGES · those claimed by MPs that have already been paid off [see p.18].

McPOISON · [see p.251].

SUICIDE WATCH · the fear that some MPs might take their lives when their expenses were made public [see p.18].

TOGETHER FOR EVER · the name given to a suicide pact between a couple – often where one is terminally or chronically ill [see p.94].

PM FOR PM · the suggestion that Peter Mandelson might renounce his peerage and become Prime Minister. *Also* KINDLY PUSSYCAT · 'I don't really see myself as a big beast', Mandelson told *The Guardian*, 'more as a kindly pussycat'. (Ed Miliband called him a 'BENIGN UNCLE'.) [see p.38].

LIKE GOING TO A SPA · bizarre analogy for soliciting International Monetary Fund financing, used by a Cabinet Minister, that some suspect was part of a political 'de-stigmatisation strategy'.

BUDGETARY INFINITY · describing the 'feeling of audacity' among US politicians during the banking collapse, David Brooks noted in *The New York Times*: 'Zeros have lost their meanings. The amount of consideration once devoted to a proposal costing $3 billion is now devoted to a proposal costing $300 billion. Americans have entered the age of budgetary infinity.'

MOMSHELL · a 'hot' mother [mom + bombshell] – e.g., Michelle Obama.

SWINE FLU · the common name for the A(H1N1) virus [see p.23]. Israel's Deputy Health Minister argued that A(H1N1) be renamed MEXICAN INFLUENZA in deference to Muslim and Jewish sensitivities towards pork. Some in the EU advocated NOVEL FLU, and World Animal Health proposed (the curiously specific) NORTH AMERICAN FLU. One US charity named the disease KILLER MEXICAN FLU, and a British expert, warning that swine flu could combine with avian flu, warned of an ARMA-GEDDON VIRUS. Satirical website *The Spoof* suggested that, to reassure tourists, the virus be called MISS PIGGY FLU – which was disturbingly close to *The Sun's* headline, PIGGIES IN THE MUDDLE. In America, to arrest the spread of the flu, schools taught the DRACULA SNEEZE – catching sneezes in the crook of one's arm. In Britain, the NHS publicised the slogan CATCH IT, BIN IT, KILL IT. Others, however, decided that OINKMENT was required for the APORKALYPSE. *Also* SWINE FLU PARTIES · social gatherings reportedly (but not actually?) staged to spread A (H1N1), with the aim of contracting the virus before it becomes more virulent.

HYACINTH BUCKET SYNDROME · the middle-class desire to keep up pre-recessionary appearances at any cost.

NEWS SANDWICH · see p.253.

SUFFRA-JETS · activists protesting against the expansion of Heathrow [see p.214] who, to attract media attention, sported the red sash of the Suffragettes.

SOVIET BOROUGHS · areas of Britain where more than 40% of workers are employed in the public sector. (In Castle Morpeth, Northumberland, the rate is 57·1%.)

——————— WORDS OF THE YEAR cont. ———————

OCTOMEL · Mel Gibson's self-created nickname, alluding to the news that he was expecting his eighth child.

LESSER SPOTTED KATE · press nickname for Kate Middleton, based upon her (relatively) low profile.

STEALTH STARBUCKS · 'unbranded' US Starbucks outlets, designed to look like neighbourhood coffee shops.

TWITTERDEAD · celebrities whose deaths have been erroneously reported online (e.g., Jeff Goldblum). *Also* OBITUTAINMENT · entertainment provided by celebrity deaths (e.g., Michael Jackson) [see p.142]. *Also* MOURNGASM · morbid delight at a celebrity death.

SILVER CRIME · crime committed by senior citizens (during the recession).

GOVERNMENT MOTORS · the latest nickname for troubled US car giant General Motors (GM used to be called Generous Motors, because of its benefits policy).

FOREVER GENERATION · A cohort of British youth who, because of a dearth of savings, face working 'forever'.

MILK · Michael Jackson's nickname for the anaesthetic propofol, to which he may have been addicted [see p.142].

NEGOTIATION FATIGUE · lassitude and cynicism induced by the repeated failure of Middle East peace talks.

GLAM-MAS · hands-off grannies reluctant to care for their grandchildren.

DIRT & DUST · Mahmoud Ahmadinejad's term for those protesting against the Iranian election results [see p.30].

ECO-KOSHER · the trend among some kosher-keeping Jews to eat only food that has been ethically, sustainably, and, where possible, locally sourced. *Similarly* SUSTAINABLE SHABBATS.

DIAL-A-FATWA · nickname for an Islamic phone line that offers religious advice. (*The Columbia World Dictionary of Islam* states 'It is a vulgar error to suppose that a *Fatwa* is a "sentence of death"'. Rather, 'A *Fatwa* (Arabic plural *Fatawa*) is nothing more or less than the answer to a question on a matter of religion put to a person qualified to deliver answers to such questions, who is known as a *mufti*'.)

MANSCAPING · male grooming.

KEY MAN RISK · The (corporate) danger of over-reliance on one or a few individuals, e.g., Warren Buffet, Steve Jobs.

KETTLING · a police strategy of crowd control through containment [see p.34].

NAG WAGs · the Wives And Girlfriends of jockeys. Indeed.

AMORTALITY · a state of hopeful agelessness wherein one acts the same from adolescence to the grave.

MANTIQUES · antiques that appeal to men (e.g., weaponry, tools, cars, &c.).

FIRE FATIGUE · exhaustion of Australians fleeing bushfire (threats) [see p.33].

HA-HA-RARE · a darkly ironic name for Zimbabwe's capital, Harare, which is gripped by disease and economic ruin.

COPPER STANDARD · speculation that China is stockpiling copper, and other metals, in an attempt to diminish its reliance on the US dollar.

---------- WORDS OF THE YEAR cont. ----------

POPE INVISIBLE · critical assessment of Benedict XVI's insular papacy. *Also* CLOUDS OF EVIL · the Pope's description of man's wrongdoing, including: war, tribalism, drugs, sexual irresponsibility, divorce, and abortion. *Also* OPERATION WHITE ROBE · codename for the security surrounding Pope Benedict XVI's May visit to Israel.

PLURAL CITIES · cities in which there is no single majority ethnic group. (Leicester is predicted to become Britain's first plural city by *c.*2019; Birmingham by *c.*2024.)

PET-ERNITY LEAVE · the domestic animal equivalent of maternity leave.

BUFFLING · business waffling [see p.253].

SOMALIA-WITH-NUKES · one assessment of what Pakistan might become if the country is overtaken by extremists.

QUEEN BEES · nickname for the army vehicles that transport the Queen's belongings from p(a)lace to p(a)lace.

SKIPS · expats who flee Dubai because of unemployment or debt.

FLEECE REVOLUTION · anti-establishment (and fleece-clad) movement in Iceland, protesting the country's economic collapse. *The Times* noted: 'The revolution has different names – the HOUSEHOLD REVOLUTION, the SAUCEPAN REVOLUTION [because of the pots and pans banged], the FLEECE REVOLUTION – choose your brand' [see p.31].

ALOHA ZEN · a description of Barack Obama's laid-back presidential style.

FIT NOTE · sick notes that detail the tasks an unwell worker is capable of.

COLD PROGRESSION · when taxes rise faster than real-term incomes, because tax rate thresholds are not adjusted for inflation: a form of STEALTH TAX known also as BRACKET CREEP.

PALLYWOOD · the controversial allegation that some media organisations and Palestinian groups employ 'Hollywood' techniques of manipulation and fabrication to present Israel in a negative light. *Similarly* HEZBOLLYWOOD.

ZIL LANES · roads reserved for VIP cars – named after the Zil limos driven by the Soviet nomenklatura. Now used to describe the dedicated routes insisted upon by the Olympic organisers.

L.G.B.T.Q.Q.I · Lesbian, Gay, Bisexual, Transsexual, Queer Question(ing) & Intersex · a novel initialism for the gamut of non-heterosexual identities.

CHAIWAN · a portmanteau of China and Taiwan, reflecting improved economic relations between the powers.

SIMPLES! · catchphrase of Aleksandr Orlov from CompareTheMeerkat.com (not to be confused with CompareTheMarket.com).

M.D.F. · 'My Daddy's Famous' · Jasper Gerard's term for the children of celebrities who seem to expect (and receive) the same adulation as their parents.

STRAWBERRY FIELDS · CIA term for Guantánamo, inspired by the Beatles, because inmates would stay 'forever'.

ZOMBIE HOUSEHOLDS · property owners who are dangerously indebted while still in possession of their homes.

(See also p.80, pp.200–1, pp.232–33, & p.252)

—————— OBJECT OF THE YEAR · TWEETS ——————

Twitter is a social networking site that simply asks: 'What are you doing?' Once registered, users can respond to this question via computer or text message, and their answers ('tweets') are immediately visible either to a selected group or to the universe online. The only restriction (profanity is permitted) is that tweets can be no longer than 140 characters [see p.334]. Users can 'follow' the tweets of others and gain followers for their own tweets. Launched in 2006, Twitter now boasts *c.*35m users but, because the service is free, the company admits 'we spend more money than we make'. ❧ The twecting of tweets was an inescapable part of 2009. In January, Twitter users posted the first images of the Hudson River plane crash [see p.46]. In February, Lance Armstrong tweeted for help to recover a stolen bicycle, and Stephen Fry tweeted that he was stuck in a lift ('arse, poo and widdle'). In March, Google's CEO called Twitter 'a poor man's email system', but in April rumours flew that Google was looking to buy it. In May, a US astronaut sent the first ever tweets from space, and China blocked Twitter, and other sites, in the days before the anniversary of Tiananmen Square. In June, eyewitness tweets describing post-election protests and violence in Iran [see p.30] circumvented censorship and galvanised local and world opinion. In July, Buckingham Palace said that news of the Royal family would henceforth be tweeted, and David Cameron apologised for saying on live radio, 'the trouble with Twitter, the instantness of it, too many twits might make a twat'. In August, Sara Williams, the wife of Twitter's CEO, tweeted throughout giving birth; and Gordon Brown joined millions in tweeting his support for the NHS. In September, it was reported that Twitter was 'worth' $1bn. ❧ Twitter's appeal lies in its limitation. Restricting posts to 140 characters can test a writer's pith and poise; more significantly, it guarantees the reader a bitesize read. As the flood of data becomes unnavigable, Twitter's assurance of brevity is more than just charming, it can come as a relief. (The founders of the Webby Awards came to the same conclusion when they limited winners' speeches to five words [see p.204].) Yet, the overwhelming morass of tweets are quotidian and banal (40% are 'gibberish', according to an August survey). And Twitter's much-vaunted role in 'citizen journalism' is as prone to error and abuse as any other unverified reporting (as evinced by the contradictory tweets during the 2008 Mumbai attack [see p.16]). In their breathless reporting of tweets, the media seem to forget that the bad guys can Twitter too. ❧ Recent research [see p.141] found that 10% of Twitter users accounted for 90% of all tweets, and that the average user tweets just once. Clearly, many join Twitter only to follow stars such as Ashton Kutcher (>3·1m followers) and Britney Spears (>2·7m), and it may be that Twitter's fate is to become another vehicle for marketing celebrity [see p.124]. ❧ Twitter has many of the features of a fad: it exploded out of nowhere, was embraced by the fashionable, and serves, for most people, no useful function. At its best, Twitter is a novel mode of communication, spun to recognise that some people love the sound of their own voice, others like to eavesdrop on the famous, and everyone's attention span is rapidly contracting.

————————————SIGNIFICA · 2009————————————

Some (in)significa(nt) footnotes to the year. ❦ According to *The Telegraph*, the Driver and Vehicle Licensing Agency has refused to approve licence plates that could be read as words that promote terrorism, alcohol, sex, or racial hatred. Banned licence plates include HE580LA (Hezbollah), BU580MB (bus bomb), MO56LEM (Muslim), and B004ZZY (boozy). ❦ A California businesswoman opened a shop where individuals irate about the economy, their jobs, or their relationships can smash fragile valuables. At 'Sarah's Smash Shack' customers pay $15–$50 to destroy china, wine glasses, and brightly coloured vases inside specially sound-proofed 'break rooms'. ❦ Debenhams reported a 35% rise in sales of Y-fronts over the 6 months preceding April 2009. A store spokesperson attributed the increase to the need for 'a greater sense of security' during the recession. ❦ A survey of 1,200 schoolchildren aged 11–16, conducted by the London Jewish Cultural Centre, found that *c.*8% thought Auschwitz was a country bordering Germany, and 2% thought it was a brand of beer. ❦ Barack Obama's campaign proved inspirational during Israel's February 2009 presidential elections: Tzipi Livni's supporters handed out T-shirts emblazoned with the word *Believni*, and Benjamin Netanyahu's distributed shirts that read, *No, She Can't.* ❦ A pair of Malaysian identical twins convicted of trafficking marijuana and opium were spared execution after police admitted they couldn't be certain which brother had committed the crime. A month later, German authorities were forced to release another set of identical twins, linked to a jewellery heist, for the same reason. ❦ In March 2009, an artist slipped past security at Ireland's National Gallery and hung two nude portraits of the Irish PM, Brian Cowen. In one picture, Cowen was holding a roll of toilet paper; in the other he was holding a pair of pants. ❦ Frustrated after receiving 20 letters reminding his dead father to attend kidney treatment, a British man presented his father's ashes to the hospital that had sent the letters. ❦ A German scientific journal, *MaxPlanckForschung*, was embarrassed to discover that the Chinese text it used on the cover of a special China issue was not a classical poem, but rather an advert for a Macau brothel promising 'hot housewives'. ❦ A New Jersey family drew international attention after a local shop refused to inscribe a birthday cake for their three-year-old son, 'Adolf Hitler'. The child was later removed from the family's home, along with his younger sisters 'JoyceLynn Aryan Nation' and 'Honszlynn Hinler [sic] Jeannie'. Officials stressed the children were not removed because of their names. ❦ Amnesty International reported on a witchcraft crackdown in Gambia, where 1,000 people were reportedly detained as potential sorcerers and sent to detention camps. The action apparently began after the President of Gambia said that witchcraft had been responsible for the death of his aunt. ❦ A Turkish television station announced plans for a reality series titled *Penitents Compete*, in which a Greek Orthodox priest, a Buddhist monk, a rabbi, and an imam will vie to convert ten atheists to their religion. At the end of the show, nonbelievers who claim to have found God will be given a free trip to a pilgrimage site sacred to their new faith. ❦ Campaigners in Riga, Latvia, held a 'blonde weekend' to cheer up the country during the recession. Highlights included a blonde golf tournament and a 'blonde parade' with hundreds of blondes

—————————SIGNIFICA · 2009 cont.—————————

dressed in pink. ❦ A report published in *The Lancet* revealed that the annual global spending on luxury cosmetics ($25bn) and pet food ($40bn) could comfortably fund basic social services for all low-income countries. ❦ A coalition of women's groups in Kenya asked the wives of top politicians to withhold sex until their husbands stopped bickering and start cooperating with the country's coalition government; prostitutes were also enjoined to enforce the ban. ❦ Russia provided $30m to rescue manufacturers of the country's iconic nesting dolls, sales of which plummeted during the recession. ❦ A bishop of the Open Episcopal Church in Britain announced a new service to deliver pre-consecrated Communion wafers by mail. Designed for those who can't or won't attend the Eucharist, the delivery service is, splendidly, called 'Host in the Post'. ❦ A police academy in Bangladesh hired one of the country's leading beauticians to lecture recruits on cosmetics, etiquette, and choosing clothes in coordinated colours. The head of the academy said the lessons would help recruits become 'world class police leaders'. ❦ Lewes District Council in East Sussex agreed to a new policy banning 'aesthetically unsuitable' street names and those 'capable of deliberate misinterpretation', like Hoare Road or Typple Avenue. The town already has a Juggs Road and a Cockshut Road. ❦ In honour of World Metrology Day (20/5), the UK's National Physical Laboratory revealed some of the measurements it has been asked to calculate. These include analysing which location in the world has the bluest sky (Rio de Janeiro), how much a Concorde jet weighs (78,700kg without fuel), and how many fist-sized plastic balls can fit inside a Smart car (3,441). ❦ The BBC reported on the rise of 'bet dieting', in which would-be slimmers agree to donate money to charity if they fail to reach certain weight goals. At the time of writing, >1,000 Britons had joined bet dieting websites. ❦ In September 2009, Samoa switched from driving on the right to driving on the left, thereby becoming the first nation to make such a change in *c*.40 years. To ease the inevitable confusion, the government declared a two-day national holiday and restricted sales of alcohol. ❦ A Serbian textile union leader, angry over unpaid wages, chopped off his left little finger and ate it to show how desperate his workers were for food. ❦ Amid fears about swine flu, Afghanistan quarantined the country's only pig – Khanzir – which is kept at the Kabul Zoo. ❦ Malaysia's National Fatwa Council issued a ruling forbidding the country's Muslims from practising yoga, claiming the exercise incorporated Hindu elements that might 'destroy the faith of a Muslim'. ❦ After a rash of reported mermaid sightings, the Israeli town council of Kirvat Yam announced a $1m prize to anyone who could prove the existence of the mythical creature off the city's shores. The town was later threatened with legal action by a spoof group calling itself the Mermaid Medical

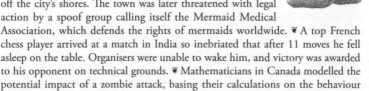

Association, which defends the rights of mermaids worldwide. ❦ A top French chess player arrived at a match in India so inebriated that after 11 moves he fell asleep on the table. Organisers were unable to wake him, and victory was awarded to his opponent on technical grounds. ❦ Mathematicians in Canada modelled the potential impact of a zombie attack, basing their calculations on the behaviour of the undead depicted in zombie movies. They concluded that only a series of quick and increasingly aggressive attacks could save humanity from zombie doom.

—— MUMBAI ATTACKS ——

In November 2008, Mumbai was hit by a series of terror attacks that rank among the worst in India's history. At 8:30pm on 26/11, 10 heavily-armed men arrived in Mumbai by boat from Pakistan. After splitting into teams, two stormed the city's largest railway station, Chhatrapati Shivaji Terminus, where they shot and killed 58 people. Two others attacked the Café Leopold, killing 10, before attacking the Taj Mahal hotel. At *c*.10pm, terrorists simultaneously attacked the Taj Mahal, the Oberoi Trident hotel, and the Jewish centre Nariman House. Hostages were taken at all three sites, and Indian police and military launched brutal counter-attacks to free them. Fighting at the Oberoi Trident ended on the morning of 28/11: *c*.33 had died (including 2 terrorists), and 160 hostages were freed. The Nariman House attack ended on the evening of 28/11, with 14 hostages freed and 10 killed, including the US couple who ran the centre, and 2 terrorists. The most prolonged violence took place at the Taj Mahal hotel, which ended on 29/11: *c*.50 were killed (including 3 terrorists), and *c*.450 rescued. In total, *c*.173 were killed and *c*.308 wounded in the attacks, including casualties from street shootings and two taxi bombings. The attacks strained India's already fraught relationship with Pakistan which, after initially denying involvement, admitted the violence was planned on its soil. According to Indian officials, the attackers were all Pakistani members of Lashkar-e-Taiba, a group fighting for control of Kashmir. At the time of writing, the sole terrorist taken alive was on trial in India, and cities around the world were pondering what their response might be to a similar 'full frontal' suicide terror attack.

—— SRI LANKA & LTTE ——

In May 2009, the Sri Lankan government declared victory over the Liberation Tigers of Tamil Eelam (LTTE), ending one of the longest civil wars in Asia. Founded in the 1970s, the Tamil Tigers fought a brutal insurgency against the country's ethnic Sinhalese majority, with the aim of establishing a separate homeland for the Tamil minority. The war lasted 26 years, and resulted in *c*.80,000 deaths. In January 2008, the Sri Lankan military launched an offensive designed finally to defeat the Tigers. By March 2009, the rebels had been flushed from the country's west coast and isolated in a tiny corner of the country's north-east. On 18/5, the military announced that the leader of the Tigers, Velupillai Prabhakaran, had been killed, along with his senior command. Sri Lankan President Mahinda Rajapaksa declared the country 'liberated' from the 'clutches of terrorism', and Sri Lankans celebrated throughout the nation. Yet while some countries offered their congratulations, others expressed concern over the war's civilian toll. According to the UN, 7,000 civilians were killed between January–May 2009, and a *Times* investigation estimated that >20,000 civilians had died in the war's final weeks. At the time of writing, *c*.300,000 Tamils were being held in abysmal refugee camps. The Sri Lankan government said that resettlement was being delayed while the camps were screened for fighters, yet human rights groups argued that a protracted humanitarian crisis will impede efforts towards peace. It remains to be seen whether such peace is possible: in August 2009, the government arrested a new Tiger leader, and elections held days later showed significant Tiger support, suggesting that many Tamils are not yet ready to give up their fight.

——— GAZA CONFLICT · 'OPERATION CAST LEAD' ———

On 19/12/08, a tentative six-month truce between Israel and Hamas expired, and attacks along the Gazan border escalated and intensified. Israel warned Hamas to halt its rocket attacks, and on 27/12 launched a series of air raids on the strip. Palestinian health officials reported that >195 Palestinians were killed and >250 wounded in the deadliest attack on Gaza since 1967. Over the following days Israel continued to target Hamas and its supply tunnels. Yet, because of Gaza's population density (*c.*1·5m people in 138 mi²), and Hamas's tactic of operating from within residential areas, civilian deaths were inevitable and numerous. By 29/12, Gaza's hospitals were reportedly rebuffing all but the most seriously injured. The UN Sec. Gen. and the British government were among those who called for a ceasefire, but the outgoing Bush administration made its allegiance clear: 'In order for the violence to stop', the White House said, 'Hamas must stop firing rockets into Israel and agree to respect a sustainable and durable ceasefire'. On 31/12, long-range Hamas missiles reached the Israeli city of Beersheba for the first time, putting >10% of the Israeli population at risk from rocket attacks. On 3/1/09, Israeli troops began a ground offensive and engaged in heavy street fighting. Hamas responded with further rocket attacks into Israel. The UN warned of a humanitarian disaster as supplies of food, fuel, medicines, and water all ran low. On 6/1, >40 Palestinians died when Israel attacked a UN school in which they were seeking shelter. On 9/1, the UN Security Council finally agreed the wording for Resolution 1860, which called for an immediate ceasefire; the US abstained, and the fighting continued. On 18/1, Israeli PM Ehud Olmert announced that Israel had achieved its goals, and declared a ceasefire. Hamas followed suit, and called for the removal of all Israeli troops. *The New York Times* noted that the ceasefire was 'grudging and unilateral' and said 'the immediate challenge is to find ways to make it more stable'. ❧ The UN estimated that 50,000 homes, 200 schools, and 39 mosques had been damaged or destroyed during the 22-day war. The number of Palestinian fatalities was disputed: Israel counted 1,166, the majority of whom, it said, were combatants. However, the Israeli human rights group B'Tselem said 1,387 died, over half of whom, it claimed, were civilians, including 252 children. 13 Israelis were killed: 10 soldiers and 3 civilians. ❧ As international aid organisations and media returned to Gaza, accusations of human rights abuses surfaced. The UN, Human Rights Watch, and Amnesty all claimed that Israel had indiscriminately used white phosphorus, a tactic prohibited by international law. Israel denied it had employed such munitions illegally. Both Hamas and Israel also denied using civilians as human shields. ❧ Despite Olmert stating 'we won', Israel achieved few of its war aims: it did not destroy, dethrone, or disarm Hamas; it did not rescue Cpl Gilad Shalit (seized in 2006); and it did not restore confidence in its forces, dented in the 2008 Lebanon war. ❧ Despite Hamas's Gazan leader, Ismail Haniyeh, claiming a 'great victory', his forces made almost no impact on Israel's military, and clearly shared culpability in the death of so many civilians.

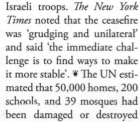

--- 'EXPENSEGATE' ---

The issue of MPs' pay and expenses has ebbed and flowed for decades – based on the expedient logic that if the public would not accept the 'private sector' salaries parliamentarians thought were their due, MPs would supplement their income via the liberal interpretation of a generous expenses regime. In addition to a salary of *c*.£64,000 (>2× the national mean), in 2007–08 MPs claimed, on average, £144,176 each on a variety of expenses, from IT equipment and travel to staffing and the second home allowance [see p.258]. ❦ Usually, public ire was only piqued by egregious breaches – such as in March 2009, when it emerged that the Home Secretary Jacqui Smith had 'mistakenly' claimed for two pornographic films enjoyed by her husband. However, the fragile trust between MPs and the public was destroyed in May 2009, when *The Daily Telegraph* published leaked details of individual MPs' uncensored expense claims between 2004–08. (These expenses were to have been published anyway, after Parliament failed to block a Freedom of Information application. But, significantly, when they were released in June the receipts were 'redacted' to remove nearly all of the most damaging details.) Day by day, as *The Telegraph* scoured and cross-referenced thousands of receipts, story after story hit the headlines. Some of the reports were trivial and embarrassing, since almost any claim for living expenses can be reduced to the absurd if examined in forensic detail (an 88p bath plug). Other reports suggested possible fraud, not least when MPs were discovered to have claimed for nonexistent 'ghost' mortgages. ❦ Some of the most damaging allegations concerned 'flipping' – whereby MPs switched the homes they nominated as their second residence to claim expenses for more than one property. Flipping was used by MPs to refurbish and improve properties at the taxpayers' expense and, it seems, to circumvent capital gains tax on property sales. ❦ Below are just a few of the myriad 'Expensegate' stories:

The Telegraph reported a host of bizarre and shaming expenses, including claims for: a trouser press, a glitter lavatory seat, a ride-on lawn-mower, 70p-a-bag manure, a chocolate Santa, dog food, swimming pool cleaning, hedge-trimming around a helipad, and even clearance of a moat. Not all of these claims were thought to follow the letter or the spirit of the Green Book rules which state that all expenses be '*wholly, exclusively and necessarily incurred when staying overnight away from their main UK residence … for the purpose of performing Parliamentary duties*'. Perhaps the most iconic image of the scandal was a £1,645 'floating duck island' which formed part of Tory MP Sir Peter Viggers *c*.£30,000 claims for gardening.

Although the Commons Fees Office disallowed his duck refuge, Viggers announced he would retire at the next election, admitting: 'I have made a ridiculous and grave error of judgment. I am ashamed and humiliated and I apologise.' ❦ The public were shocked to discover that MPs could claim £400 a month for food, without any receipts, even when Parliament was not sitting. One Labour MP reportedly claimed £18,800 for food over 4 years. ❦ Although she denied any wrongdoing, the then Communities Secretary Hazel Blears publicly displayed a £13,332 cheque she had written in lieu of unpaid capital gains tax. ❦ On 14/5/09, during a recording of *Question Time* in Grimsby, MPs were heckled and jeered by the studio

––––––––––––––––– 'EXPENSEGATE' cont. –––––––––––––––––

audience with such intensity that the show's editor later admitted 'the programme was teetering on the edge of trouble'. ❦ The Labour MP Elliot Morley announced he would resign after it was revealed that he had claimed £16,000 for interest payments on a mortgage that had already been paid off. Morley denied wrongdoing but apologised 'unreservedly', blaming 'sloppy accounting'. A handful of other MPs were alleged also to have claimed for mortgages that had been paid off, although all denied wrongdoing. ❦ Public concern surrounding the expense claims of Luton South MP Margaret Moran prompted the TV presenter Esther Rantzen to announce that she would challenge her at the next election. Moran subsequently announced her resignation, although she denied wrongdoing or dishonesty. ❦ Keen to

note that not every MP was on the take, *The Telegraph* listed a handful of 'honest politicians', including Martin Salter, the Labour member for Reading West: 'His total additional costs allowance claim between 2001–08, covering the cost of staying away from home, was zero.' ❦ *The Telegraph*'s circulation rose *c.*2·3% during its scoop. The paper refused to say whether it had paid for the leaked data, which, according to one MP, were touted for *c.*£300,000. Steven Glover wrote in *The Independent*, '*The Times* was offered the disk. So too, on two occasions, was *The Sun*. (Oddly, the *Daily Mail* was not). The two Murdoch-owned newspapers turned it down not, I think, principally for reasons [of] money, but because they did not want to be accused of planting a bomb under the House of Commons'. Indeed, some suggested that by failing properly to distinguish between the trivial and the possibly criminal, *The Telegraph* had unduly damaged parliament.

When the magnitude of the scandal and the depth of public anger became clear, party leaders rushed to apologise, announce reviews, and discipline the most serious offenders. Many MPs were astonished at the vitriol they faced. The refrain that their claims were 'within the rules' and 'approved by the Fees Office' seemed only to inflame the situation, not least because MPs had created these rules themselves. (The Fees Office noted that it was not its job to police 'honourable members'.) As politicians queued up to refund claims while admitting only 'errors', the press mused upon what criminal sanctions the public might face in a similar situation. When the police were called in to investigate the leak – not the claims – many commentators responded that MPs just did not 'get it'. ❦ The full consequences of Expensegate will not be known until at least the next election. Since so many MPs have announced they will quit, and many more will be challenged by 'anti-sleaze' candidates, the next parliament is guaranteed a sea of fresh faces. Depending on one's view, this promises either a transfusion of uncorrupted new blood or the triumph of professional hacks. ❦ In August, the Tory MP Alan Duncan was castigated after he was covertly taped warning that 'no one who's done anything in the outside world … will ever come into [parliament] ever again', complaining, 'it's been nationalised, you have to live on rations, and they treat you like shit'. This outburst encapsulated the divide between the public and parliamentarians. The public want honest, independent, and talented MPs, but do not necessarily appreciate the cost of running both a constituency and a Westminster home. MPs have been happy to tolerate (and abuse) a disreputable expenses system rather than make the case for higher wages. ❦ At the time of writing, the future of MPs' pay and expenses was unresolved.

———————LOCAL & EUROPEAN ELECTIONS · 2009———————

On 4/6/09, elections were held for 27 county councils and 7 unitary authorities, the mayors of Doncaster, Hartlepool, and N Tyneside, and the European Parliament.

Labour's disastrous showing in the local elections came as little surprise, not least after the last-minute Cabinet resignations of Jacqui Smith and Hazel Blears. Labour lost control of all of the councils contested, as well as 291 councillors, to come third behind the Lib Dems.

Councils		party	Councillors	
No.	±		No.	±
30	+7	Conservative	1,531	+244
1	–1	Lib. Dem.	484	–2
0	–4	Labour	178	–291
0	0	Independents	97	+6
0	0	Green	18	+8
0	0	Residents Assoc.	9	+2
0	0	UKIP	7	+7
0	0	Mebyon Kernow	3	0
0	0	BNP	3	+3
0	0	Liberal	2	0
0	0	Others	30	+15
3	–2	No Overall Control	·	·

The Tories won in a number of key areas, taking Lancashire, Derbyshire, and Staffordshire from Labour and Devon and Somerset from the Lib Dems. David Cameron called the results 'remarkable' and noted that the Conservatives were 'winning in every part of the country'. Labour turned in on itself: John Prescott said his party's election organisers were 'resigned to defeat', and Alastair Campbell bemoaned the lack of a 'clear and strong campaign'. The BNP won three council seats. ❦ In the three mayoralty elections: Hartlepool's independent mayor (and former football mascot H'Angus the Monkey) Stuart Drummond won a third term; the nationalist English Democrat candidate Peter Davies beat Labour in Doncaster; and in North Tyneside the Tory candidate Linda Arkley beat the incumbent Labour mayor John Harrison.

Although Britain's Euro elections were held on Thursday 4 June, the results were not announced until the following Sunday to synchronise with voting in the other 26 member states [see p.271]. The intervening days were febrile for Brown, who suffered yet further resignations [see p.21] and was forced to bring forward his Cabinet reshuffle [see p.255]. To some extent this activity softened the blow of the results which, when they came, saw Labour again pushed into third place, this time by UKIP.

Party	% of vote	±%	MEPs	±
Conservative	27·7	+1·0	26	+1
UKIP	16·5	+0·3	13	+1
Labour	15·7	–6·9	13	–5
Lib. Dem.	13·7	–1·2	11	+1
Green	8·6	+2·4	2	0
BNP	6·2	+1·3	2	+2
SNP	2·1	+0·7	2	0
Plaid Cymru	0·8	–0·1	1	0
Sinn Féin	·	·	1	0
DUP	·	·	1	0

As the BBC's David Thompson noted, there was 'pain for Labour in almost every part of the country': it was beaten in Scotland by the SNP, beaten in Wales by the Tories, beaten in the SE and SW of England by the Greens, and beaten in Cornwall by the Cornish nationalists. Neither the Tories nor the Lib Dems distinguished themselves, mainly because of the dramatic performance of UKIP. For many, the most concerning result was the election of 2 British National Party MEPs – including the party's leader, Nick Griffin. The BNP's success was helped by the collapse of Labour's vote, but in the post-Expensegate landscape, all the major parties shared some of the responsibility.

— GORDON BROWN'S YEAR —

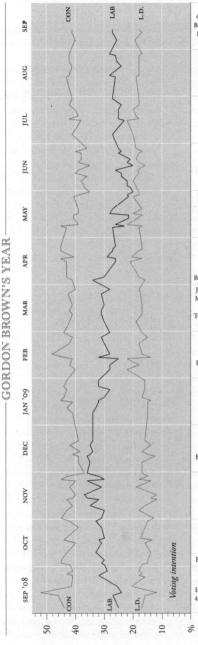

SEP

The Cabinet began discussing future spending cuts.
48% said 'literally anyone' in Labour could outperform Brown.
Brown admitted 'cuts' needed; Tories leaked Treasury 'cuts' plans.
Brown faced further questions over Megrahi and a Libya 'deal'.
Eric Joyce resigned over Britain's Afghanistan strategy.

AUG

Brown held talks with Israeli PM, Binyamin Netanyahu.
Whitehall mandarins criticised New Labour's governing style.
Lockerbie bomber Abdelbaset al-Megrahi released [see p.37].
The 200th British soldier was killed in Afghanistan.
Cabinet ministers jostled for position while Brown holidayed.

JUL

The Chilcot inquiry into the Iraq conflict opened [see p.24].
Leadership speculation emerged during summer break.
The Tories won the Norwich North by-election.
Brown was criticised for lack of army helicopters [see p.25].
Eight British soldiers killed in one day in Afghanistan.

JUN

Brown reshuffled his Cabinet [see p.255].
Local & Euro elections [see p.20]; James Purnell resigned.
Senior ministers left government, including Geoff Hoon.
Hazel Blears & Caroline Flint resigned from the Cabinet.
Home Sec. Jacqui Smith announced she would resign.

MAY

Record numbers of Labour MPs applied for peerages.
Speaker Martin resigned; many MPs announced retirement.
Brown apologised on behalf of all MPs for Expensegate.
The Telegraph's Expensegate revelations overwhelmed politics.
Hazel Blears launched a thinly veiled attack on Brown.

APR

Brown defeated in a parliamentary vote on Gurkha residency.
In his Budget, the Chancellor announced a 50% tax rate.
Brown posted a bizarre YouTube clip on MPs' expenses.
McBride & Draper 'Smeargate'; Brown belatedly apologised.
Brown hosted G20 Summit in London; $1·1tr package unveiled.

MAR

Jacqui Smith apologised for claiming pornography on expenses.
Mervyn King warned 2nd round of fiscal stimulus unaffordable.
Brown 'deeply saddened' by news of Jade Goody's death.
Two soldiers killed in N Ireland: Real IRA claimed responsibility.
Brown became 1st European leader to visit President Obama.

FEB

Brown criticised Sir Fred Goodwin's pension [see p.31].
Binyam Mohamed arrived back in the UK.
FSA deputy chairman Sir James Crosby resigned.
Former bank bosses apologised before the Treasury Committee.
Nicolas Sarkozy publicly criticised Brown's VAT cut.

JAN '09

Brown's phone rang while he was giving a speech in Davos.
Britain officially entered recession.
Brown reversed plans to keep MPs' expenses secret.
Brown and Darling announced new bank bailout plan.
The Bank of English cut interest rates to 1·5%.

DEC

Brown called for an Israel/Gaza ceasefire [see p.17].
Brown ruled out early 2009 general election.
Brown announced UK troops would leave Iraq by July 2009.
Brown warned Pakistan 75% of UK terror plots originate there.
Brown claimed to have 'saved the world' [see p.252].

NOV

Tory MP Damian Green arrested [see p.32].
Pre-Budget report temporarily cut VAT to 15%.
Brown & Cameron clashed at PMQs over Baby P [see p.31].
Labour won the Glenrothes by-election.
45 Labour MPs rebelled over trade union vote.

OCT

Brown urged banks to keep lending to small businesses.
Brown admitted Britain faced a recession; the £ fell.
The Government part-nationalised three banks.
The Government dropped its plans for 42-day detention.
Brown amazed many by returning Peter Mandelson to Cabinet.

SEP '08

Bradford & Bingley nationalised by the government.
Ruth Kelly announced she would resign as SoS for Transport.
In his Conference speech, Brown warned: 'no time for a novice'.
4 ministers quit or were sacked in <1 week for criticising Brown.
Charles Clarke warned Labour was heading for disaster.

Voting intention from PollingReport.co.uk
(Multiple polls on the same day have been averaged.)

──────── NOTABLE EVENTS IN THE BANKING CRISIS ────────

01·09·08	The Pound fell to a record low against the euro
07·09·08	The US government rescued mortgage lenders Freddie Mac & Fannie Mae
15·09·08	Lehman Brothers, the 4th-largest US investment bank, filed for bankruptcy
15·09·08	Bank of America announced it had agreed to buy Merrill Lynch
16·09·08	The US Fed agreed to an $85bn rescue package for insurance firm AIG
17·09·08	Lloyds TSB announced it would take over HBOS
29·09·08	The UK government confirmed it would nationalise Bradford & Bingley
03·10·08	The US Congress approved a $700bn 'bailout' plan
06·10·08	The FTSE 100 closed down 391·1 – the worst ever one-day points fall
08·10·08	The UK government announced a £500bn bank 'bailout' plan
13·10·08	The UK government 'bailed out' RBS, Lloyds TSB, and HBOS
06·11·08	The Bank of England cut interest rates by 1·5% to 3·0%
24·11·08	Darling announced a temporary 2·5% cut in VAT to stimulate spending
04·12·08	The Bank of England cut interest rates by 1·0% to 2·0%
11·12·08	Bernard Madoff was accused of a multi-billion-dollar fraud [see p.32]
16·12·08	The US Federal Reserve cut interest rates to 0%–0·25%
31·12·08	The FTSE 100 recorded its largest annual loss: 31·3%
08·01·09	The Bank of England cut interest rates by 0·5% to 1·5%
23·01·09	Britain officially entered a recession
05·02·09	The Bank of England cut interest rates by 0·5% to 1·0%
13·02·09	The US Congress approved a $787bn stimulus package
05·03·09	The Bank of England cut interest rates by 0·5% to 0·5%
02·04·09	G20 leaders pledged $1·1tr in fiscal stimulus [see p.34]
22·04·09	Alistair Darling announced his 'austerity' Budget [see p.234]
30·04·09	The FTSE 100 registered a monthly gain of 8·1%, the highest since 2003
07·05·09	B of E announced it would inject a further £50 billion into the economy
01·06·09	General Motors filed for bankruptcy protection
24·07·09	It was reported that the UK economy had contracted 5·6% in 12 months
03·08·09	Barclays reported six-month pre-tax profits of £2·98bn
14·09·09	The FTSE 100 registered its highest close of 2009: 5,018·85
15·09·09	Mervyn King announced that economic growth had 'resumed'
16·09·09	UK unemployment reached 2·47 million [see p.28]
18·09·09	Gold spot prices hit an 18-month high of $1,023·85 an ounce

─────── 2009 A(H1N1) 'SWINE FLU' PANDEMIC ───────

In June 2009, the World Health Organization declared A(H1N1) swine flu to be a global pandemic – the first in 41 years. The virus emerged in mid-April 2009, when authorities observed an unusual cluster of illnesses in Veracruz, Mexico. While the symptoms matched seasonal flu, the cases resulted in an unusually high rate of hospitalisation among healthy young adults. Laboratory analysis confirmed that A(H1N1) was a new strain of flu that combined genetic material from swine, avian, and human viruses. Because few people around the world had any immunity to this novel strain, epidemiologists soon raised the spectre of a global pandemic. ❦ Infections first spiked in Mexico in late April, leading authorities to close schools and businesses for weeks. The virus next spread in N America, prompting the WHO to raise its pandemic alert level to 5, on 29/4. In the following weeks, A(H1N1) was reported in Europe, Japan, China, and Australia. On 11/6, the WHO declared swine flu a global pandemic [see p.64]. ❦ Around the world, responses ranged from stoical to hysterical. Many nations advised their citizens to adopt protective behaviour: New York students were told to avoid giving high-fives; Spaniards were advised to abandon cheek-kiss greetings; and Argentinians were warned not to accept communion wafers. Other countries imposed more sweeping measures: China quarantined any feverish passenger arriving from a swine flu-stricken country, while several nations issued travel advisories and alerts for pork products. However, as the summer wore on, swine flu proved less lethal than first feared. Although highly contagious, A(H1N1) caused few

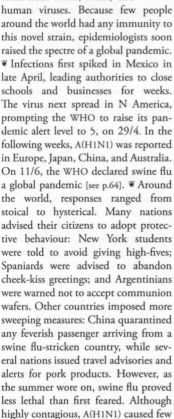

'CATCH IT, BIN IT, KILL IT' – NHS

deaths outside of those with underlying medical conditions. Yet, concerns remained that A(H1N1) could mutate into a deadlier strain. At the time of writing, *c.*3,486 deaths had been reported, and many nations were braced for an autumnal 'second wave'. ❦ The first UK cases of A(H1N1) were confirmed on 27/4. By early May, several schools had closed, and the government had delivered to every home a leaflet explaining swine flu and emphasising the importance of elementary hygiene: *'Catch it, Bin it, Kill it'.* The number of new UK infections grew in May, escalated in June, and rose sharply in July. On 23/7, with 110,600 cases of A(H1N1) suspected, the NHS launched the National Pandemic Flu Service, to allow people whose symptoms matched those of swine flu to access antivirals without a GP. This service proved popular (500,000 packs of Tamiflu were given out in the first 2 weeks). However, the medicating of otherwise healthy adults proved controversial, as did mixed messages on the safety of antivirals for children and pregnant women, and the adequacy of the government's Tamiflu supplies. In August, new UK infections fell sharply and by September, the predicted worst-case death toll for winter 2009/10 had been cut from 65,000 to 19,000. ❦ At the time of writing, 78 UK deaths had been attributed to A(H1N1). Efforts were focused on immunising *c.*13m in the most susceptible groups during the autumn, when it was feared that the new school year could trigger a fresh and more fatal outbreak. It remains to be seen whether A(H1N1) will become the 'big one', or will remain a 'dry run' for the catastrophic pandemic that many epidemiologists fear is inevitable.

———————————— BRITAIN & IRAQ ————————————

On 30/4/09, a ceremony transferred control of Basra airport to the US army, and marked the end of British combat operations in Iraq – six years after the 2003 invasion. Brigadier Tom Beckett, Commander of 20th Armoured Brigade, said: 'We are sad to leave our Iraqi friends, but we leave knowing we have done our job, and done it well. We leave with our heads held high'. Gordon Brown said, 'Today Iraq is a success story. We owe much of that to the efforts of British troops. Our mission has not always been an easy one, many have said that we would fail. Britain can be proud of our legacy that we leave there'. ❦ Below are the Ministry of Defence statistics for the UK military and civilians injured or killed during the course of Operation Telic:

CASUALTIES	222
very seriously injured/wounded	*73*
seriously injured/wounded	*149*
FIELD HOSPITAL ADMISSIONS	3,598
wounded in action	*315*
disease or non-battle injury	*3,283*
AEROMED EVACUATIONS	1,971
FATALITIES	179
killed in action	*111*
died of wounds	*25*
other	*43*
Service: Army	77%
Royal Air Force	12%
Royal Navy	4%
Royal Marines	6%
Age: ≤19	8%
20–29	54%
30–39	30%
≥40	7%
not released	1%

[Sources: MoD & BBC]

According to the BBC, the total cost of UK operations in Iraq was £6·44bn, and £744m was spent on reconstruction. However, as Deborah Haynes reported for *The Times*, 'The aftermath of Britain's involvement in Iraq bears little resemblance to its two previous occupations over the past century, which left behind railways, bridges, hospitals and refineries'. ❦ In the first few months of his presidency, Barack Obama announced, 'Let me say this as plainly as I can, by August 31, 2010, our combat mission in Iraq will end'. To this end, on 30/6/09, US troops in Iraq withdrew from urban areas, handing over control of the cities to Iraqi forces. Although c.130,000 US troops remained in his country, and the security situation showed little sign of stabilising, Iraqi PM Nuri al-Maliki declared 30 June to be 'National Sovereignty Day'. ❦ On 15/6/09, Brown announced that the promised independent inquiry into the Iraq war would be chaired by Sir John Chilcot and would report in the summer of 2010. The inquiry will explore the period from 2001–09, when the invasion was planned, presented, and prosecuted. Immediately, critics seized upon the secrecy and timing of Brown's plan. As Nick Clegg noted: 'He says the inquiry has to be in private to protect national security. But it looks suspiciously like he wants to protect his reputation and that of his predecessor, not Britain. Why else would he want it to report after the general election?' In the following weeks, the government performed a series of U-turns, as a consequence of which the Chilcot inquiry will hear much of its evidence in public, be free to apportion blame, and be able to call upon expert legal and military advice. However, it may not now report until late 2010, or even 2011.

BRITAIN & AFGHANISTAN

Support for Britain's presence in Afghanistan was tested in 2009 by a spike in fatalities, controversy over how British forces were equipped, and allegations of mission creep. Two symbolic milestones sharpened attention to the toll of the conflict: in July, the number of British deaths in Afghanistan outstripped that in Iraq; and in August, the 200th British soldier died in Afghanistan. ❦ Below are the UK military and civilian casualties from Operation Herrick [as of 20/9/09 · Source: MoD]:

CASUALTIES	265
very seriously injured/wounded	*122*
seriously injured/wounded	*143*
FIELD HOSPITAL ADMISSIONS	2,864
wounded in action	*850*
disease or non-battle injury	*2,014*
AEROMED EVACUATIONS	2,531
FATALITIES (as at 16/9/09)	216
killed in action	*185*
died of wounds	*31*

Fatalities 7/10/01–16/9/09

	'01	'02	'03	'04	'05	'06	'07	'08	'09
	0	3	0	1	1	39	42	51	79

As fatalities rose, the Wiltshire town of Wootton Bassett became the focus of public remembrance, and hundreds regularly paid their respects as the bodies of the fallen were driven from RAF Lyneham. A July ComRes poll showed that 58% of Britons thought the war in Afghanistan was 'unwinnable', 52% thought Britain should withdraw immediately, and 75% thought that British troops lacked the necessary equipment. This last figure reflected growing concern that the military was under-resourced. In July, the outgoing head of the Army, General Sir Richard Dannatt, proposed a 'shopping list' of equipment and troops he needed, and travelled across Afghanistan in a US Black Hawk, which spotlighted the dearth of British helicopters in theatre. The issue of the 'military covenant' (under which the civilian government is morally bound to support the forces) quickly became a political issue, and the supply of helicopters and other equipment was the subject of heated Commons debate. ❦ In August 2009, the Commons Foreign Affairs Cmte said the government 'should re-focus its wide-ranging objectives in Afghanistan and concentrate … on one priority, namely security', noting 'the UK has experienced mission creep from its initial goal of supporting the US in countering international terrorism, far into the realms of counter-insurgency, counter-narcotics, protection of human rights and state building'. ❦ On 20/8/09, Afghans went to the polls to vote for a president and provincial council. The fact that the elections were marred by widespread violence, and allegations of intimidation, fraud, and ballot stuffing did little to reassure the British public that 9 years of military engagement had been worth the 'blood and treasure'. At the time of writing, preliminary results indicated that presidential incumbent Hamid Karzai had *c.*54% of the vote – over the 50% threshold required to avoid a run-off. However, the UN-backed Electoral Complaints Commission had ordered *c.*850,000 suspicious ballots to be recounted – which could trigger a second round of voting.

─────── ONE & OTHER · THE FOURTH PLINTH ───────

For 100 days between 6 July and 14 October 2009, an extraordinary experiment in public art was conducted on the empty 'fourth plinth' in Trafalgar Square, London, as 2,400 individuals seamlessly inhabited the space, alone, for an hour apiece. The project – entitled *One & Other* – was conceived by Antony Gormley (most famous for *The Angel of the North*), who said of the spectacle: 'In the context of Trafalgar Square with its military, valedictory and male historical statues to specific individuals, this elevation of everyday life to the position formerly occupied by monumental art allows us to reflect on the diversity, vulnerability and particularity of the individual in contemporary society'. ❧ Applications to appear on the plinth were received from across the country (the project even featured on Radio 4's *The Archers*). Successful candidates, chosen at random, were required to be over 16, occupy the plinth alone, stay for the whole hour, bring onto the plinth only what they could carry, and comply with the law. ❧ The first 'plinther' to be hoisted into place by JCB (after an anti-smoking protester briefly stormed the stage and stole the limelight) was 35-year-old Lincolnshire housewife Rachel Wardell, who spent her hour holding a giant lollipop advertising Childline. Thereafter, hour upon hour, a rota of British eccentrics and extroverts took to the fourth plinth and performed an eclectic range of activities, including: knitting; praying; sculpting bread (and balloons); singing; dancing; reading; writing; teaching aerobics; sketching; painting; trimming hedges; idling morosely; playing the bassoon; reading poetry through a megaphone;

Antony Gormley

practising golf; performing burlesque; sleeping; sewing; releasing balloons; acting; skipping; telling jokes; eating; drinking; trampolining; juggling; drumming; miming; hula hooping; space hopping; blowing bubbles; advertising bog snorkelling; dressing up; stripping off; and, of course, playing Swingball while dressed as Godzilla. ❧ *One & Other* caught the imagination of many. Millions around the world watched live webcasts of the (in)action, and a constant stream of tweets commented on each plinther, at least initially. ❧ The critics, however, were less than impressed. In *The Telegraph* Rupert Christiansen sighed, 'I fear that within nine hours the Fourth Plinth has already become a bore'. Tim Lott in the *Independent on Sunday* complained, 'Virtually nobody has made any kind of effort or put any kind of thought into what is a once-in-a-lifetime opportunity'. And, the former editor of *The Sun*, Kelvin MacKenzie observed, 'there's a lot of weirdos out there, and most of them seem to be on that plinth'. In *The Guardian*, Jonathan Jones wondered, 'Did Gormley measure the plinth before he had the idea? It's far too big for the work. How can it be a democratic living artwork when the people sitting up there are so far away from the crowds below? You can't talk to them and they can't talk to you. They just while away their hour up there, and the flurry of interest when the forklift raises a new participant to the heights soon dissipates'. In *The Evening Standard*, Brian Sewell simply dismissed *One & Other* as a 'puerile attempt to amuse us with look-at-me nincompoops on what should be an empty plinth'.

ENGLAND'S 2009 ASHES VICTORY

1st Test · Cardiff
8–12 Jul 2009
England won the toss

England	435 all out
Australia	674 for 6 (dec)
England	252 for 9

match drawn

MOTM · Ricky Ponting

What looked like a solid English score of 435 was soon surpassed by an impressive display of Australian batting. Ponting led the way with 150, and was one of 4 Australian centurions. The Aussies declared in the hope of bowling England out quickly, but rain delayed play. Bowlers Panesar and Anderson tenaciously blocked out the innings (with what some Australians criticised as delaying tactics) and secured the draw.

2nd Test · Lord's
16–20 Jul 2009
England won the toss

England	425 all out
Australia	215 all out
England	311 for 6 (dec)
Australia	406 all out

England won by 115 runs

MOTM · Andrew Flintoff

Flintoff's announcement that he would retire from Test cricket at the end of the Ashes series seemed to inspire England's bowlers. They took 6 wickets for 49 runs in 15 overs on day two, and the Aussies collapsed for 215. Strauss declared on 311 to chase victory. Flintoff took 3 of the 5 wickets needed on the final day and England secured victory over Australia at Lord's for the first time in 75 years.

3rd Test · Edgbaston
30 Jul–3 Aug 2009
Australia won the toss

Australia	263 all out
England	376 all out
Australia	375 for 5

match drawn

MOTM · Michael Clarke

After taking a first innings lead of 113 runs, England looked on course to go two up in the series until rain stopped an entire day's play. Excitement grew as England went into the final day requiring just 8 wickets. Anderson and Swann worked tirelessly to dislodge the dogged Australian batsmen, but to no avail. Michael Clarke and Marcus North held fast to score 185 runs between them, and secured Australia's revenge for Cardiff.

4th Test · Headingley
7–9 Aug 2009
England won the toss

England	102 all out
Australia	445 all out
England	263 all out

Australia won by an innings and 80 runs

MOTM · Marcus North

England suffered an embarrassing defeat at Headingley. They were dismissed for a paltry 102 before Australia proved there was nothing wrong with the pitch by scoring 445. England's middle-order batting raised some eyebrows as Bopara, Bell, and Collingwood all failed to reach double figures in either innings. After inflicting such a demoralising defeat, Australia looked set to take the series.

5th Test · The Oval
20–23 Aug 2009
England won the toss

England	332 all out
Australia	160 all out
England	373 for 9 (dec)
Australia	348 all out

England won by 197 runs

MOTS · Andrew Strauss & Michael Clarke

England looked nervous after they scored 332 on a wicket that seemed to favour batsmen. But Swann and Broad worked their magic to limit Australia to 160 all out. Trott, on his England debut, scored an impressive 119 in the second innings, allowing Strauss to declare. Flintoff brilliantly ran out Ponting to set the tone for a glorious English victory.

--------- UK ECONOMIC INDICATORS ---------

The latest data from the Office of National Statistics (ONS) revealed that unemployment increased by 210,000 in the three months to July 2009, to total 2·47m – or 7·9%. In August, 1·61m people were claiming unemployment benefit, the greatest number since May 1997. Below is a breakdown of unemployment by sex:

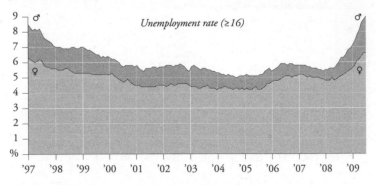

Unemployment rate (≥16)

The ONS also reported that productivity across the whole economy (measured by output per worker) fell by 4·2% in the first quarter of 2009 compared with 2008:

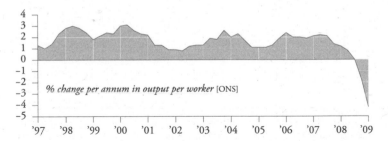

% change per annum in output per worker [ONS]

Below is the public sector net debt, expressed as a % of Gross Domestic Product:

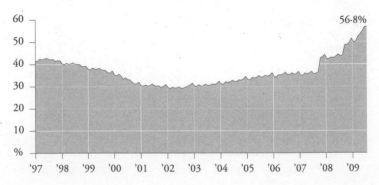

56·8%

——————— UK ECONOMIC INDICATORS cont. ———————

The precipitous collapse of house prices during 2008–09 was caused both by the unwillingness of banks to issue mortgages to any but the most secure of borrowers, and by a general sense of unease about the market and the state of the economy:

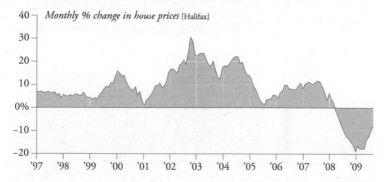

As the Bank of England base rate fell to historic lows [see p.238], so mortgage rates declined, though not as dramatically. Below are the average quoted household rates:

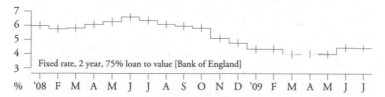

At the time of writing, some confidence seemed to be creeping back into the housing market. However, in September, Ernst & Young's Item Club called this a 'false dawn', and predicted that prices will not return to their 2007 high for at least 5 years. Charted below are Halifax data for average national house prices, average national earnings, and (in parentheses) the price-to-earnings ratio, for 1997–2009:

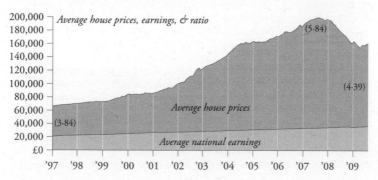

————— IRANIAN ELECTION & PROTESTS —————

In June 2009, demonstrations over Iran's presidential election grew into the nation's largest uprising since the 1979 revolution, when massive unrest forced out the secular monarchy in favour of an Islamic Republic. Below is an outline of the key events:

On 12/6/09, Iranians went to the polls in record numbers to elect a president. After a hard-fought campaign, notable for mass rallies in support of the moderate candidate Mir Hossein Mousavi – the primary opponent of incumbent Mahmoud Ahmadinejad – many expected the result to be close. However, on 13/6 officials declared that Ahmadinejad had won with 63% of the votes. Mousavi rejected this result and alleged widespread electoral fraud. As soon as Ahmadinejad's victory was announced, thousands of Iranians (many sporting the bright green of Mousavi's campaign) took to the streets. Over the next few days these demonstrations intensified, and although many were peaceful, others escalated into violent street battles during which police and Basij (state-sponsored religious militia, often in plain clothes) beat and shot protesters. In total, *c*.30 were killed and >1,000 arrested. Under the cover of night, Iranians took to their rooftops to chant *Allah O Akbar* [God is great] – deliberately echoing the dissent of 1979. ❧ After Iran banned foreign media from the streets and withdrew journalists' credentials, independent reporting became all but impossible. Instead, the world was forced to rely on emails, Twitter posts, and amateur video uploaded by protesters themselves. The defining image of the uprising was of the death of 26-year-old Neda Agha-Soltan, who died on a Tehran street after being shot, apparently by a Basij militiaman. Grainy mobile phone footage of Neda's

M. Ahmadinejad

final moments flashed across the internet, galvanising opinion in Iran and around the world. ❧ Iran's Supreme Leader Ayatollah Khamenei endorsed the election results, and on 19/6 blamed foreign agents, notably Britain, for fomenting the unrest. In late June, Iran expelled 2 British diplomats and arrested 9 Iranians who worked at the British Embassy in Tehran. Ahmadinejad dismissed the protesters as 'dirt and dust' and compared them to disappointed football fans. ❧ As the protests continued, Khamenei appeared to soften and he asked Iran's Guardian Council to review the results. However, on 29/6, having recounted just 10% of the votes, the Council certified the results, and on 5/8 Ahmadinejad was sworn in for a second term. ❧ At the time of writing, Iran was conducting a trial of >100 opposition leaders accused of inciting the uprising, and had begun publishing 'confessions'. Ahmadinejad had shrugged aside criticisms from clerics and political opponents, and was restating Iran's nuclear ambitions. ❧ It is tempting to describe Iran's summer of 2009 as the first uprising of the social network age. Facebook and Google rushed out Farsi translation tools to help information flow in and out of Iran, and the US government asked Twitter to delay maintenance that would have interrupted the service at the height of the violence. Yet, for all the emails, tweets, and raw footage that escaped Iran's censors, the uprising was crushed by a regime that cared more about power than PR.

OTHER MAJOR STORIES IN BRIEF

Iceland

In the autumn of 2008, Iceland came perilously close to bankruptcy after its soaring economy untethered from reality. (At the height of the boom, Iceland's banks were 'worth' >10× the country's GDP.) From late Sep 2008, the Icelandic government took control of the country's 3 largest banks, and raised interest rates by 6% to 18%; in November, the IMF approved a $2·1bn loan, as inflation hit 17%; and in January, facing a barrage of demonstrations, Iceland's PM, Geir Haarde, quit along with his government. As Icelanders reacted with shock and fury to the immolation of their economy, British savers with money in Icelandic banks (including dozens of local authorities) were stunned to learn that their deposits had been frozen and might not be guaranteed. In a move that outraged Icelanders, Britain invoked the Anti-terrorism, Crime & Security Act 2001 to seize assets held in Britain by the online Icelandic bank Icesave, which had c.300,000 UK accounts. ❦ In April, Icelandic voters swept to power a centre-left coalition led by Johanna Sigurdardottir, the country's first female PM and the world's first openly homosexual head of state. Sigurdardottir said, 'The people are calling for a change of ethics. That is why they have voted for us.' In July, Iceland applied to join the EU, and in August agreed to repay >$5bn lost by British and Dutch savers in Icelandic banks.

City Bonuses & Fred 'The Shred'

As the recession deepened and tax revenues were injected into failing banks, [see p.22] the issue of City salaries and bonuses became more than usually toxic. Fairly or not, the banker Sir Fred 'The Shred' Goodwin came to personify this issue. (His nickname derived from a ruthless approach to cost- and job-cutting.) Appointed CEO of Royal Bank of Scotland in March 2000, Goodwin had presided over the bank's spectacular, if controversial, expansion by acquisition. However, in late 2008, RBS came close to collapse when its exposure to subprime mortgages emerged, and inter-bank lending froze. In October, as RBS shares sank and Goodwin announced his retirement, the government injected £20bn into the bank. A month later, the government injected a further £15bn, in return for a 58% stake. Anger at this bailout reached incandescence when it was revealed that Sir Fred (also nicknamed 'the worst banker in the world') had, quite legitimately, amassed a pension pot of c.£16·6m and an annual income of c.£555,000. Pundits and politicians lambasted these figures. The deputy Labour leader Harriet Harman called it 'money for nothing', and warned that 'the court of public opinion' would step in. And it did. In June 2009, after months of criticism – and vandalistic attacks on his car and home – Goodwin agreed to cut his annual pension to £342,500. ❦ At the time of writing, City remuneration was vexing politicians in a number of countries, who were jostling to be tough on 'fat cats' while recognising that punitive measures would drive talent and businesses abroad. In June, as Goldman Sachs, Credit Suisse, Deutsche Bank, Barclays Capital, JP Morgan, &c. predicted bumper profits, *The Guardian* reported on a new city buzzword: BAB, or 'Bonuses Are Back'.

The Death of Baby Peter

On 3/8/07, a 17-month-old boy, first identified as 'Baby P' and then as 'Peter', died at his home in Tottenham, London. A post-mortem revealed a

──────────── OTHER MAJOR STORIES IN BRIEF cont. ────────────

horrific catalogue of 22 injuries, including: several broken ribs and a broken back; bruises, cuts, and lacerations (possibly dog bites); a damaged finger and missing nails; and an absent front tooth discovered, having been swallowed, in his colon. ❦ In 11/08, Peter's mother Tracey Connelly (27), her boyfriend Steven Barker (32), and his brother Jason Owen (36) were found not guilty of murder. However, Connelly pleaded guilty to causing or allowing Peter's death, and Barker and Owen were found guilty of the same offence. ❦ In the following months, details of Peter's abuse were revealed in harrowing detail, as were the repeated failings of Haringey Council and the numerous agencies to whom Peter was known (he was on the 'at risk' register). The case prompted unprecedented public revulsion and press condemnation, and a *Sun* petition calling for the sacking of all the social workers involved attracted >1m signatures. Yet, while Peter's death led to the resignation of senior Haringey officials, the dismissal of social services managers, and the suspension of a GP who had seen Peter 14 times, few were convinced that a similar tragedy could not happen again. In July 2009, an Ofsted report into Haringey Council concluded, 'not all children are adequately safeguarded'.

The Arrest of Damian Green MP

In the wake of a series of leaks embarrassing to the Home Office, on 27/11/08 the Tory shadow immigration minister Damian Green MP was arrested on suspicion of 'conspiring to commit misconduct in a public office', and 'aiding and abetting, counselling or procuring misconduct in a public office'. Police searched his parliamentary office and Kent home, and he was held for 9 hours before being bailed. Green's arrest came a week after a Home Office civil servant, Christopher Galley, had been arrested on similar charges. Both men denied any wrongdoing. ❦ The arrest of an MP and the search of his offices angered members across the House, and questions were asked as to how an MP's Westminster office could be searched by police without a warrant. The Home Sec. Jacqui Smith defended the police's right to investigate leaks that could threaten national security. However, on 16/4/09, the Director of Public Prosecutions announced that there was insufficient evidence to proceed against Galley or Green, noting 'the information leaked was not secret information or information affecting national security ... moreover, some of the information leaked undoubtedly touched on matters of legitimate public interest'. On 24/4/09, Galley was dismissed from the civil service, although he maintained, 'I actually did this as a public servant for the actual country'. ❦ The chaos surrounding Green's arrest damaged the independence of parliament, and undermined confidence in the Home Secretary and the Speaker – both of whom resigned within months.

Bernie Madoff

On 11/12/08, one of the largest frauds in history unravelled when 'star' financier Bernard L. Madoff was arrested in New York after admitting that his investment empire was simply a 'giant Ponzi scheme' [see p.246]. To gathering outrage, details emerged of a fraud in which new investors paid the returns of existing clients while Madoff faked investment activity. Authorities estimated the total client losses at $65bn. On 12/3/09, Madoff pleaded guilty to 11 charges, including securities fraud,

———————— OTHER MAJOR STORIES IN BRIEF cont. ————————

money laundering, and perjury. On 29/6/09, he was sentenced to 150 years for crimes the judge called 'extraordinarily evil'. ❦ Madoff cultivated an air of exclusivity and financial sagacity, first working his connections among the Jewish elite and then in the wider community of big money. Investors were reassured by his credentials as a former NASDAQ chairman and by the consistent returns he reported even in turbulent times. His fraud destroyed companies and charities, wiped out life savings, and has been implicated in at least two suicides. ❦ The scandal prompted calls for wholesale reform of financial regulation, not least when it emerged that the US Securities & Exchange Commission had investigated Madoff 8 times in 16 years without finding any evidence of impropriety.

Barack Obama's Impact

The inauguration of Barack Obama in January 2009 [see p.267] could hardly have been greeted with greater optimism. Yet with America in the midst of a deep recession, delivering 'change you can believe in' was always going to be tough. Obama's first year was packed with announcements, including: setting a timetable for partial withdrawal from Iraq; lifting restrictions on stem cell research; ordering the closure of CIA 'black site prisons', and the Guantánamo Bay detention camp; repealing restrictions on federal funding of organisations that promote abortions overseas; sending c.21,000 more troops to Afghanistan; easing certain sanctions with Cuba; setting strict limits on car exhaust emissions; and planning education reforms, including performance-related pay for teachers. Unsurprisingly, the economy proved to be the most contentious issue, and Obama's stimulus package, auto industry bailout, and plans to secure homeowners were simultaneously criticised for being too generous and not going far enough. Equally controversial were Obama's plans for health care reform, which resulted in angry town-hall meetings, and the comparison, by some, of Obama to Hitler. ❦ Faced with the realities of governing, it was not surprising that Obama's approval rating fell from c.69% in February to c.52% in August. Internationally, Obama's impact was less ambiguous. A July 2009 survey by the Pew Global Attitudes Project revealed that America's image had 'improved markedly in most parts of the world' under Obama. Below are the responses to the question, 'How much confidence do you have in the US President?' comparing George W. Bush in 2008 with Obama in 2009:

Confidence	'08	'09	+%				
Argentina	7	61	54	Jordan	7	31	24
Brazil	17	76	59	Kenya†	72	94	22
Britain	16	86	70	Lebanon	33	46	13
Canada†	28	88	60	Mexico	16	55	39
China	30	62	32	Nigeria	55	88	33
Egypt	11	42	31	Pakistan	7	13	6
France	13	91	78	Palest. Ter.†	8	23	15
Germany	14	93	79	Poland	41	62	21
India	55	77	22	Russia	22	37	15
Indonesia	23	71	48	Spain	8	72	64
Israel†	57	56	-1	Turkey	2	33	31
Japan	25	85	60	USA	37	74	37
				(† data from 2007)			

Australian Bush Fires – 'Black Saturday'

On 7/2/09, hundreds of wildfires blazed across the southern Australian state of Victoria, killing >200 people, destroying c.1,834 homes, and razing 4,130km². The flames were encouraged both by record temperatures and by the country's ongoing drought [see p.186], although arson was suspected in several cases. In August 2009, a preliminary report of the Royal Commission convened to investigate the fires found that the public had been inadequately

――――――― OTHER MAJOR STORIES IN BRIEF cont. ―――――――

warned of the danger, and that the risk of staying to defend homes was poorly communicated. A full report into the tragedy is due in July 2010.

Josef Fritzl & others

The March 2009 trial of 73-year-old Josef Fritzl on charges of murder, incest, and incomprehensible cruelty stunned his native Austria, and the world. In 1984, after years of abuse, Fritzl lured his 18-year-old daughter Elisabeth into the cellar of their house in Amstetten where he imprisoned her. Over the next 24 years, Fritzl enslaved, assaulted, abused, and raped Elisabeth, fathering seven children by her: one he murdered by neglect and incinerated, three he brought out of the dungeon, and three he imprisoned alongside Elisabeth. The cellar was dark, damp, and cramped, and the children were warned they would be gassed or electrocuted if they attempted escape. The three children saw daylight for the first time in their lives only when they were rescued. ❦ At the start of his trial, Fritzl pleaded guilty to rape, incest, coercion, and deprivation of liberty, but denied enslavement and murder. However, after watching hours of videotaped testimony from Elisabeth, he changed his plea to guilty on all charges, and was sentenced to life. ❦ Tragically, the Fritzl case was not the only story of abuse to hit the news. In November 2008, an unnamed 56-year-old British man was given 25 life sentences for abusing his two daughters over a 30-year period: he made them pregnant 19 times, and fathered 9 children by them. In August 2009, Jaycee Lee Dugard – who had been abducted in 1991, aged 11, near South Lake Tahoe – was reunited, aged 29, with her mother. It was reported that she had been held for 18 years in a ramshackle complex of tents in the Californian yard of a convicted sex offender, who fathered 2 children by her.

London G20 Summit & Ian Tomlinson

London's April G20 summit was billed (by George Soros) as a 'make-or-break' event for the world's financial system. Brown called on his fellow leaders to inject 'the oxygen of confidence' into the global economy – and, to a large extent, they did. On 2/4/09, in addition to agreements on tighter financial regulation, a $1·1tr package was unveiled which promised to boost world trade, increase the purse and power of the IMF, and ensure that finance and aid were available to the poorest nations. Although some argued that the G20 had not gone far enough, the agreement was hailed as 'historic' by Barack Obama, and the world's markets spiked in agreement. ❦ The summit was widely perceived as a victory for Brown (described in the media as 'the world's chancellor') whose poll ratings received a temporary fillip [see p.21]. ❦ In keeping with most econo-political gatherings, the G20 was the focus of a range of protests concerning globalisation, climate change, poverty, jobs, trade, and aid. Despite a few skirmishes, some of them violent, the majority of demonstrations were peaceful. Yet the police were criticised for their heavy-handedness and their use of 'kettling' – a technique of crowd control via containment where protesters and passers-by are forcibly corralled for hours on end and denied access to food, water, or lavatories. Although a number of complaints were made against the police, the incident that attracted the most publicity involved the death of Ian Tomlinson – a 47-year-old newspaper vendor, apparently unconnected with the protests, who died after

——————— OTHER MAJOR STORIES IN BRIEF cont. ———————

being pushed to the ground by a policeman. ❦ At the time of writing, three post-mortems had been performed on Tomlinson, a policeman had been suspended and questioned on suspicion of manslaughter, and the Independent Police Complaints Commission had yet to release reports into the death and allegations of a cover-up by the police.

Piracy in Somalia

Pirate attacks off Somalia's coast continued to escalate in late 2008 and 2009, with several dramatic incidents drawing worldwide attention. According to the International Maritime Bureau (IMB), pirates attacked a record 240 times worldwide in the first half of 2009, compared to 114 times in the same period in 2008. In both years, the vast majority of attacks were by Somalis. ❦ On 25/9/08, pirates captured the MV *Faina*, a Ukrainian freighter loaded with heavy weapons, as she sailed the Gulf of Aden. The vessel was held for 4 months, until a £2·3m ransom was delivered on 5/2/09. On 15/11/08, pirates captured their largest ship yet, the Saudi supertanker MV *Sirius Star*, which was carrying $100m of oil to the US. The ship was held until 9/1/09, when a reported £1·95m ransom was paid. On 8/4/09, pirates attacked their first US-flagged ship, the *Maersk Alabama*. While the crew managed to retake the ship within hours, the captain was held hostage in a lifeboat for 5 days, and freed only when US Navy snipers shot and killed his captors. ❦ Many of Somalia's 9m people have been starving since the government collapsed in 1991, and piracy has emerged as one of the few viable livelihoods. Indeed, some Somali pirates see themselves as guardians of the country's coast, which environmental groups say is a destination for toxic waste dumping and illegal fishing. On 17/12/08, the UN Security Council ruled that countries could pursue pirates on Somali land as well as at sea, and *c*.15 international vessels now patrol the Gulf of Arden. According to the IMB, the pirates have adapted by extending their hijackings further out into the open ocean.

L'Aquila Earthquake

On 6/4/09, at 3:32am local time, a 6·3 Richter earthquake shook the Abruzzo region of central Italy. The worst devastation occurred in the medieval town of L'Aquila, the quake's epicentre. *c*.300 people were killed, 65,000 left homeless, and 28,000 forced to seek temporary shelter. >10,000 buildings were damaged in L'Aquila, where the extent of the devastation prompted an investigation into whether builders had followed seismic safety codes. The Italian government pledged to help the reconstruction, and allocated €100m in aid. ❦ 10/4/09 was declared a day of national mourning, and a funeral mass was held for 205 of the victims. The quake was the deadliest in Italy since a 6·9 Richter earthquake struck Eboli in 1980.

Rugby Union & 'Bloodgate'

On 12/4/09, during a Heineken Cup quarter-final against Leinster, Harlequins winger Tom Williams left the field with blood pouring from his mouth. Rumours soon circulated that Williams had faked the incident to enable a key substitution, and the European Rugby Cup (ERC) launched an investigation. In July, Williams told an ERC hearing that he, acting alone, had feigned injury using a capsule of fake blood procured from a Clapham joke shop. But after he was handed a potentially career-ending 12-month

─────────── OTHER MAJOR STORIES IN BRIEF cont. ───────────

ban, he agreed to give a full account of the incident, and received a lighter punishment. In August, Williams revealed that the Harlequins director of rugby, Dean Richards, had orchestrated the deceit. Williams was offered an extension to his contract if he took the blame. Richards quickly admitted responsibility, apologised for his actions, and resigned from the club. He was banned from coaching for 3 years. Harlequins was fined £260,000, and further resignations followed. It remains to be seen whether this bloodletting can restore Harlequins' reputation.

Swat Valley Offensive

In late April 2009, after bowing to US pressure to escalate the fight against Islamic extremists, Pakistan began a campaign to seize control of the Swat Valley from the Taliban. Throughout May, *c*.30,000 Pakistani troops fought *c*.5,000 Taliban and al-Qaeda-affiliated militants, eventually retaking control of most of the valley. According to analysts, the militants largely disappeared without fighting major battles, though the finality of their defeat is far from clear. Aid agencies warned that the conflict had caused a humanitarian crisis, and thousands of civilians were trapped with dwindling access to food and supplies. *c*.2·3m refugees were forced to flee the area in the largest regional migration since the 1947 India–Pakistan partition. Many of those who fled were forced into squalid camps, which some feared could breed further extremism. ❦ At the time of writing, a tripartite plan to repatriate refugees was in place, and *c*.1·6m had returned to the Swat Valley. However, many of the region's most prosperous inhabitants were staying away, another sign the area's troubles may be far from over.

Joanna Lumley & the Gurkhas

Gordon Brown suffered a humiliating defeat in May 2009, when the actress Joanna Lumley spearheaded a popular campaign to allow all Gurkha veterans with ≥4 years' service the right to settle in the UK. The government's existing policy denied residency to *c*.36,000 Gurkhas who had left the army prior to 1997. Despite this position being challenged by an April parliamentary vote, immigration officials remained intransigent. Lumley, whose father had been a Gurkha officer, was widely credited with out-charming and outmanoeuvring both Brown and his immigration minister Phil Woolas. Eventually, the Home Sec. Jacqui Smith was forced to declare she was 'proud to offer this country's welcome to all who have served in the brigade of Gurkhas'.

Ethnic Violence in Xinjiang

In July 2009, China saw the most deadly incident of ethnic violence in a decade, after fighting erupted between Uighurs and Han Chinese in the restive western province of Urumqi, Xinjiang. The Uighurs, a Turkic Muslim minority group, have long begrudged rule by China's dominant ethnic group, the Han. Tensions boiled over on 25/6, when a riot broke out between Uighur and Han workers at a toy factory in Shaoguan, Guangdong Province, and 2 Uighurs were killed. On 5/7, hundreds of Uighurs, angry about the lack of an investigation into the factory riot, took to the streets in Urumqi. When police confronted the protesters, the group turned violent and, by evening, *c*.1,000 Uighurs had begun a rampage against the Han through the streets of Urumqi; Han reprisals continued for several days thereafter. In all, *c*.197 were killed and *c*.1,721 injured, with both groups

──────── OTHER MAJOR STORIES IN BRIEF cont. ────────

claiming a majority of the victims. The Chinese government arrested *c*.718, and blamed the acts on Uighur separatists and foreign agents. At the time of writing, >200 were facing trial for the July attacks, while early September saw a fresh round of Han demonstrations over new reported Uighur attacks.

Silvio Berlusconi

The colourful (in both senses) PM of Italy was again assailed by controversy in 2009, not least in May, when his wife Veronica Lario announced she planned to divorce him. Berlusconi vigorously denied lurid allegations of inappropriate relationships with younger women, telling the press in August: 'the premier has no skeletons in the closet and cannot be blackmailed by anybody.' Yet, when asked why his poll ratings had remained strong, the 72-year-old boasted: 'I think most Italians privately wish they could be like me and recognise themselves in me and the way I behave.'

Aung San Suu Kyi

On 11/8/09, a Burmese court sentenced the pro-democracy activist and Nobel laureate Aung San Suu Kyi to 18 months' house arrest. Suu Kyi was charged with violating the terms of her previous house arrest, after a 53-year-old American, John Yettaw, swam uninvited to her house on 3/5/09. (Yettaw later claimed he was attempting to save Suu Kyi from assassins he had seen in a 'vision'.) The court initially sentenced Suu Kyi to 3 years hard labour, but moments later, in a coup de théâtre, read an order from the country's military leader, Than Shwe, commuting the sentence. World leaders condemned the trial and its verdict and, at the time of writing, Suu Kyi had launched an appeal. ❦ Yettaw was sentenced to 7 years in prison,

including 4 years hard labour. However, in August 2009, US Senator Jim Webb travelled to Burma, and secured his release. ❦ Suu Kyi's detention was due to expire shortly after Yettaw's bizarre visit. Many noted that this new conviction would keep the figurehead of Burma's democracy movement usefully out of sight during the 2010 elections.

Abdelbaset Ali al-Megrahi

On 20/8/09, Abdelbaset Ali al-Megrahi was freed from Greenock Prison in Scotland and flown home to Libya. He had served <8 years of his life sentence. Megrahi was the only man convicted of the 1988 bombing of Pan Am Flight 103, which exploded over Lockerbie, killing 270. He was released by the Scottish government on compassionate grounds, after his prostate cancer was diagnosed as imminently fatal. Critics of the decision, most vocally the victims' families in Scotland and America, argued that Megrahi had never shown any compassion himself, and had only dropped his appeal in order to be eligible for medical release. ❦ The controversy surrounding Megrahi's release was exacerbated by the hero's welcome he received in Tripoli, and by suggestions that it formed part of wider political and commercial negotiations with Libya, not least concerning the exploitation of the country's significant oil reserves. Barack Obama called the release a 'mistake', and the director of the FBI said he was 'outraged at [the] decision, blithely defended on the grounds of "compassion"'. Gordon Brown denied his government had been involved in the Scottish decision, and said he was 'angry' and 'repulsed' by Megrahi's reception in Libya. However, at the time of writing, many speculated about the possible existence of a realpolitik deal.

———— PERSON OF THE YEAR · PETER MANDELSON ————

Gordon Brown's October 2008 decision to return his 'nemesis' Peter Mandelson to the Cabinet stunned British politics. But even then no one imagined the role 'Mandy' would play in securing Brown's reign, or the grip on power he would establish. ❧ At 10pm on 4/6/09, as the polls closed for the local and Euro elections [see p.20], James Purnell became the latest and most significant minister to quit and call on Brown to go. According to reports, had Mandelson not been in No. 10 at the time and able to persuade key Cabinet Blairites to keep the faith, Brown might not have lasted the week. Mandy's reward came in the next day's reshuffle which established him as the de facto deputy PM [see p.255], and vindicated his much-mocked 2001 claim to be 'a fighter not a quitter'. William Hague observed, 'His title now adds up to, *The Right Hon. the Baron Mandelson of Foy in the county of Herefordshire and Hartlepool in the county of Durham, First Secretary of State, Lord President of the Privy Council and Secretary of State for Business, Innovation, and Skills.* It would be no surprise to wake up in the morning and find that he had become an archbishop.' ❧ Mandelson was born in 1953. A youthful dalliance with Communism ended at St Catherine's, Oxford, and in 1979 he was elected to Lambeth's Labour council. In 1982, he became a TV producer, only to return to politics in 1985 as Neil Kinnock's director of communications. In 1992, he became MP for Hartlepool and formed a triumvirate with two young MPs – Gordon Brown and Tony Blair. ❧ The process by which Blair bested Brown after John Smith's death in 1994 lies at the ineffable core of New Labour. Yet Mandelson's rejection of Gordon in favour of Tony led to the former's enmity and the latter's loyalty – evinced in Mandelson's appointment as Minister Without Portfolio (in charge of the Millennium Dome) in Blair's first Cabinet. In July 1998, Mandelson was made Trade Secretary, but quit in December when it emerged he had taken a £373,000 home loan from a colleague. In October 1999, he returned to the Cabinet as N Ireland Sec., but in January 2001 resigned over (denied) claims that he had intervened in a passport application by one of the Hinduja brothers. (He was later cleared of any impropriety.) In 2004, Blair backed Mandelson to become EU Trade Cmsnr – a post he held until his rapprochement with Brown. ❧ In 2009, Mandelson parlayed his political re-rehabilitation into real power. He currently attends 35 of the 43 Cabinet committees (as Blair's deputy, John Prescott attended 17), and by taking the fight to the Tories he has injected confidence into Brown's lacklustre reign. In an August *Guardian* profile, Mandelson exuded unabashed glee at being back in the game, protesting that New Labour's 'hit man' was now 'a kindly pussycat'. ❧ Summer headlines mooting 'PM for PM' were patently whimsical, but they were encouraged by a sense that anything is possible with 'the prince of darkness' – who remains one of the most compelling figures of the Blairite age and, in the *Economist*'s words, 'the Great High Giver of Good Copy'. ❧ If, as seems likely, Brown loses the 2010 general election, or quits before, then Mandelson will have been New Labour's midwife and mortician – and, against all the odds, will himself have survived.

— SCHEMATIC · WORLD EVENTS OF NOTE · 2008–09 —

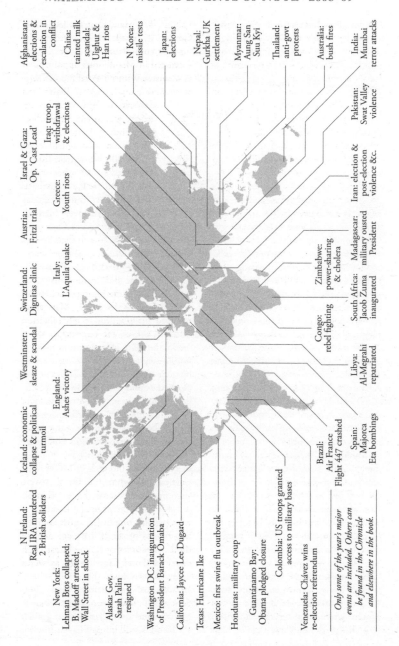

Afghanistan: elections & escalation in conflict

China: tainted milk scandal; Uighur & Han riots

N Korea: missile tests

Japan: elections

Nepal: Gurkha UK settlement

Myanmar: Aung San Suu Kyi

Thailand: anti-govt protests

Australia: bush fires

India: Mumbai terror attacks

Iraq: troop withdrawal & elections

Israel & Gaza: Op. 'Cast Lead'

Greece: Youth riots

Austria: Fritzl trial

Pakistan: Swat Valley violence

Iran: election & post-election violence &c.

Madagascar: military ousted President

Switzerland: Dignitas clinic

Italy: L'Aquila quake

Zimbabwe: power-sharing & cholera

South Africa: Jacob Zuma inaugurated

Westminster: sleaze & scandal

England: Ashes victory

Congo: rebel fighting

Libya: Al-Megrahi repatriated

Iceland: economic collapse & political turmoil

Brazil: Air France Flight 447 crashed

Spain: Majorca Eta bombings

N Ireland: Real IRA murdered 2 British soliders

New York: Lehman Bros collapsed; B. Madoff arrested; Wall Street in shock

Alaska: Gov. Sarah Palin resigned

Washington DC: inauguration of President Barack Omaba

California: Jaycee Lee Dugard

Texas: Hurricane Ike

Mexico: first swine flu outbreak

Honduras: military coup

Guantánamo Bay: Obama pledged closure

Colombia: US troops granted access to military bases

Venezuela: Chávez wins re-election referendum

Only some of the year's major events are included. Others can be found in the Chronicle and elsewhere in the book.

———— IN BRIEF · SEPTEMBER – OCTOBER 2008 ————

The daily chronicle below picks up from the 2009 edition of Schott's Almanac.

SEPTEMBER 2008 · {13} Texas declared a disaster zone in the wake of Hurricane Ike. ❦ Joan Ryan MP was sacked as Labour Party Vice Chair after calling for a leadership contest. {14} Lehman Bros, America's 4th largest investment bank, began insolvency proceedings after Barclays pulled out of talks to buy it. {15} World markets were thrown into flux as Lehman Bros filed for bankruptcy protection and rumours suggested that AIG, the world's largest insurer, could fall. ❦ A power-sharing deal between Robert Mugabe and Morgan Tsvangirai was signed in Harare. {16} Government minister David Cairns resigned after calling for a leadership challenge to Gordon Brown. {17} Lloyds TSB and HBOS merged. ❦ >16 died in a car bomb attack on the US Embassy in Yemen. {19} In China, 4 children died and >6,000 were taken ill after drinking milk contaminated with melamine; Chinese milk products were recalled across the world. ❦ Scientists closed the Large Hadron Collider after a helium leak; it was announced the device would be out of action for months. {20} >40 died when a car bomb exploded at the Marriott hotel in Islamabad, Pakistan. ❦ S African President Thabo Mbeki announced he would resign after the ANC called for him to step down for allegedly interfering in a corruption case against his rival Jacob Zuma. {21} >13,000 children were treated in hospital in China after drinking tainted milk. ❦ The US beat Europe in the Ryder

George W. Bush

Cup. {23} Brown made a key speech at a Labour conference in Manchester, stating 'this is no time for a novice'; this line was spun as an attack on two Davids: Cameron and Miliband. ❦ A 22-year-old man burst into a catering college in Kauhajoki, Finland, and killed 10 before turning the gun on himself. {24} Transport Sec. Ruth Kelly announced she would stand down to spend more time with her family. {25} The US Congress agreed to a $700bn bail-out for US financial institutions to stabilise world markets; Obama, McCain, & Bush held talks on the details. {26} The US bail-out faltered as discussions between Bush and Congress ended in a 'shouting match'. ❦ HSBC announced the loss of 1,100 jobs. {27} Bradford & Bingley was nationalised [see p.22]. ❦ RIP @ 83, Paul Newman [see p.61]. {28} Spanish bank Santander acquired the savings business of Bradford & Bingley. {29} The US House of Representatives rejected a $700bn rescue package for Wall St; world markets fell. ❦ >100 died in a stampede at a Hindu temple in Jodhpur. ❦ Tesco announced £1·43bn profits. ❦ A 45-year-old man died of head injuries after intervening in the assault of 2 people in Norwich.

> *The idea of financial innovation has come back to bite us.*
> – DAVID PATERSON, NY State Govnr.

OCTOBER · {1} David Cameron made a key speech at the Conservative party conference, claiming he was 'a man with a plan'. {2} Met Police Chief Sir Ian Blair was forced to stand down after London Mayor Boris Johnson refused to back him. ❦ The wreckage of Steve Fossett's plane was found in a remote part of E California; the adventurer had gone missing while on a solo flight in Sep '07. {3} The US

IN BRIEF · OCTOBER 2008

House of Reps voted in favour of a re-worked $700bn rescue package. ❦ Brown returned Peter Mandelson to the Cabinet [see p.255]. ❦ 9 died in Pakistan after a US missile attack. ❦ The Financial Services Authority (FSA) announced that British bank deposits would be guaranteed to £50,000. {4} N Korean leader Kim Jong-il made his first public appearance since reports suggested he had suffered a stroke. {5} Germany appeared to guarantee *all* bank deposits, sending European markets into further turmoil; Chancellor Darling called on Europe to cooperate and resist unilateralism. {6} The FTSE100 fell 391·1 points. ❦ The German government used a €50bn rescue package to save mortgage lender Hypo Real Estate. ❦ Iceland was forced to pass emergency legislation to prevent national bankruptcy [see p.31]. {7} Stocks in Asia and Europe continued to fall as the banking crisis deepened. ❦ Troops took to the streets in Bangkok in a bid for order after violent anti-government protests broke out. {8} 6 central banks across the world (including the BoE) cut interest rates in an attempt to stabilise the economy. ❦ The UK government announced a £500bn package to rescue the British banking system. {10} In one of the worst day's trading in 30 years, stocks fell sharply across the globe. {11} Mugabe gave key government posts to his Zanu-PF colleagues in contravention of the power-sharing agreement. {12} Eurozone leaders agreed to a deal protecting savings until the end of 2009. {13} After 2008's marking crisis, Children's Sec. Ed Balls announced that Sats for 14-year-olds would be scrapped. {14} The US govt announced a $250bn

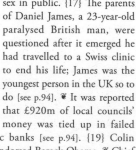

Kim Jong-il

package to secure the banking sector. {15} UK unemployment hit 1·79m; the highest rate for 17 years. ❦ After months of speculation, Madonna and Guy Ritchie confirmed their separation. {16} In Dubai, a British man and woman were jailed for 3 months for having sex in public. {17} The parents of Daniel James, a 23-year-old paralysed British man, were questioned after it emerged he had travelled to a Swiss clinic to end his life; James was the youngest person in the UK so to do [see p.94]. ❦ It was reported that £920m of local councils' money was tied up in failed Icelandic banks [see p.94]. {19} Colin Powell endorsed Barack Obama. ❦ Chief Sec. to the Treasury Yvette Cooper urged banks to make home repossessions a last resort after it emerged that (nationalised) Northern Rock was repossessing 50% more homes than the average. {20} British aid worker Gayle Williams was shot dead in Kabul; the Taliban claimed responsibility. ❦ Figures showed that government borrowing had reached a record £8bn in September 2008. {21} Ex-Thai PM Thaksin Shinawatra was found guilty of corruption in his absence, and sentenced to 2 years in jail. ❦ The Governor of the BoE, Mervyn King, warned that the UK was headed for a recession in 2009 – a prognostication that caused

It now seems likely that the UK economy is entering a recession.
– MERVYN KING

stocks to waver and the £ to fall against the $. {22} Brown admitted that the current economic downturn could cause a recession. ❦ India successfully launched its first space mission to the moon, the unmanned *Chandrayaan 1* spacecraft [see p.205]. {24} Official figures showed that the economy shrank for the first time in 16 years, between Jul–Sep 2008. {26} A

—— IN BRIEF · OCTOBER – NOVEMBER 2008 ——

US raid near the Syrian border with Iraq killed 8; the Syrian government reacted angrily. {27} The BBC apologised to Andrew Sachs for telephone calls made to him by Russell Brand and Jonathan Ross and broadcast on Radio 2 [see p.129]. {28} Iceland's central bank raised interest rates from 12% to 18% to stave off financial collapse. ❦ Rudy Hermann Guede was found guilty of murdering British student Meredith Kercher in Perugia, Italy; he was sentenced to 30 years. ❦ Fighting between rebel Tutsis and government forces in E Congo raged, causing thousands to flee. {29} >300 were feared dead after an earthquake struck the Balochistan region of Pakistan. ❦ Multiple sclerosis sufferer Debbie Purdy lost her high court challenge to have the laws on assisted suicide clarified [see p.94]. ❦ The US Federal Reserve reduced its key US interest rate from 1·5% to 1%; the lowest level since 2004. ❦ German airline Lufthansa announced it was taking over BMI. {30} Radio 2 controller Lesley Douglas resigned and Jonathan Ross was suspended without pay for 3 months in the wake of 'Sachsgate' [see p.129]. {31} Chaos continued in the Congo as aid agencies struggled to reach thousands of displaced people. ❦ >20 died in US missile attacks on Pakistan.

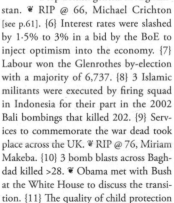

Jonathan Ross

that the British National Party had attempted to form an electoral pact with UKIP at the European elections; UKIP rejected the offer. {4} Americans went to the polls after a tense and dramatic election campaign. ❦ 6 Palestinians died after the first Israeli incursion into Gaza since the June 2008 ceasefire [see p.17]. {5} Barack Obama swept to power in a historic victory; world leaders were quick to welcome the first black US President (elect) [see p.267]. ❦ Corporal Daniel James was found guilty of spying for Iran while working as a translator for a top British general in Afghanistan. ❦ RIP @ 66, Michael Crichton [see p.61]. {6} Interest rates were slashed by 1·5% to 3% in a bid by the BoE to inject optimism into the economy. {7} Labour won the Glenrothes by-election with a majority of 6,737. {8} 3 Islamic militants were executed by firing squad in Indonesia for their part in the 2002 Bali bombings that killed 202. {9} Services to commemorate the war dead took place across the UK. ❦ RIP @ 76, Miriam Makeba. {10} 3 bomb blasts across Baghdad killed >28. ❦ Obama met with Bush at the White House to discuss the transition. {11} The quality of child protection services in the London Borough of Haringey was questioned after it was reported that a 17-month-old boy, referred to as Baby P, died after months of abuse [see p.31]. {12} The BoE announced that the UK had probably entered a recession that would continue into 2009. ❦ The government ordered a review into the death of Baby P. {13} Haringey council said it was 'truly sorry' for Baby P's death. {14} The Eurozone officially entered a recession. {15} RIP @ 92, Reg Varney. {17}

I hope this is the first of many.
– LEWIS HAMILTON

NOVEMBER · {1} David Miliband announced that UK troops were not expected to join UN troops in the Congo. {2} Lewis Hamilton became the youngest ever Formula One world champion, after securing the title with a 5th place finish in Brazil. {3} A UN aid convoy arrived in the Congo as a tentative ceasefire was established. ❦ It was revealed

——— IN BRIEF · NOVEMBER – DECEMBER 2008 ———

Somali pirates hijacked a Saudi oil tanker, the *Sirius Star*, off the coast of Kenya; the 25 crew, including 2 Britons, were said to be well. {18} Building firm Wolseley cut 2,300 jobs. ❦ Consumer inflation fell from 5·2% to 4·5% in October. {19} A BNP membership list was leaked onto the internet. ❦ Foreign Sec. Miliband called for the immediate release of the British hostages held on the *Sirius Star*. ❦ 'Dancing Pig' John Sergeant quit *Strictly Come Dancing* fearing he might actually win the show which, he said, would be 'a joke too far' [see p.122]. {20} Oil prices fell below $50 a barrel. ❦ The UN agreed to send 3,000 additional troops to DR Congo, after fighting intensified. {21} It was reported that the pirates holding the *Sirius Star* were demanding a $25m ransom. ❦ The death toll from a cholera outbreak in Zimbabwe hit >300. {22} An alleged British militant, Rashid Rauf, was killed by a targeted US airstrike in Pakistan. {23} 4 policemen died in a road crash in N Ireland. {24} In his pre-Budget Report, Chancellor Darling cut VAT from 17·5% to 15% for 13 months but warned of tax rises in 2010; the Tories criticised the rise in government debt and accused Labour of taking 'huge risks'. ❦ RIP @ 60, conductor Richard Hickox. {25} A 56-year-old Sheffield man was jailed for life for the repeated rape of his two daughters, with whom he fathered 9 children. {26} >80 died in a series of terrorist attacks on hotels and bars in Mumbai, India [see p.16]. ❦ >30,000 jobs were threatened after Woolworths announced it was entering into administration. ❦ Protests continued in Bangkok; anti-government activists blockaded the airport. {27} Indian troops fought with

David Miliband

I was astonished to have spent more than nine hours today under arrest for doing my job. – DAMIAN GREEN

terrorists holding hostages in 2 Mumbai hotels; the death toll rose to *c*.119. ❦ Conservative immigration spokesman, Damian Green MP, was arrested and questioned over leaks from the Home Office; he denied wrongdoing and the police action was strongly criticised by senior Tories [see p.32]. {28} The Indian army announced it had regained control of the Oberoi-Trident hotel in Mumbai; 93 hostages were escorted to safety after a 36-hour siege. It was thought at least one gunman remained at large in the Taj Mahal Palace hotel. ❦ The number of cases of measles in Britain exceeded 1,000 for the first time since 1995. {29} The Indian army announced it had killed the last gunman occupying the Taj Mahal Palace hotel. {30} Britain urged Thailand to assist hundreds of Brits stranded as anti-government protesters continued to occupy Bangkok's airports.

DECEMBER · {1} Royal Bank of Scotland announced it would allow those defaulting on their mortgage repayments 6 months' grace before proceeding with repossession. ❦ The Speaker of the House of Commons, Michael Martin, came under pressure to explain how police were able to search Green's parliamentary office. {2} A Thai court ruled that PM Somchai Wongsawat should step down over alleged election fraud; Wongsawat accepted the ruling, raising hopes that the political crisis might soon end. ❦ Radical preacher Abu Qatada was sent back to jail for breaching his bail conditions. ❦ Peter Tobin was jailed for >30 years for the 1991 murder of Vicky Hamilton. ❦ The coroner investigating the death of

─────── IN BRIEF · DECEMBER 2008 ───────

Jean Charles de Menezes ruled that the inquest jury would not be allowed to return a verdict of unlawful killing. {3} Brown unveiled a package of measures designed to help those defaulting on mortgage payments. ❦ Speaker Martin revealed that the police did not have a warrant to search Green's parliamentary office. {4} Karen Matthews and Michael Donovan were found guilty of kidnapping and imprisoning Shannon Matthews in a plot to earn the £50,000 reward. ❦ The BoE cut interest rates to 2%, the lowest rate since 1951. ❦ As cholera continued to blight Zimbabwe, Kenyan PM Raila Odinga urged African leaders to unite against Mugabe. {5} It was reported that 533,000 Americans lost their jobs in November 2008, the greatest loss since 1974. ❦ O. J. Simpson was sentenced to 33 years in prison for his part in an armed robbery. {6} Pork products from Ireland were recalled after dioxins were found in Irish pigs. {7} Uncertainty over the position of Speaker Martin continued. {8} Many flights were delayed or cancelled as climate change protesters occupied Stansted's runways. ❦ Young people continued to riot across Greece after a 15-year-old boy was shot dead by policeman. {9} RIP @ 83, Oliver Postgate [see p.61]. {10} Brown was ridiculed in the Commons after accidentally claiming to have 'saved the world' [see p.252]. {11} The £ reached a record low against the € – 1·1236. ❦ 14 alleged al-Qaeda suspects were arrested in Belgium, hours before an EU summit. ❦ Mugabe claimed the cholera outbreak was over, as aid agencies warned the situation was deteriorating. {12} A $14bn US bail-out package for car-makers failed to clear the

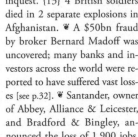

Gordon Brown

I am happy we are being assisted by others and we have arrested cholera.
— ROBERT MUGABE

Senate, leading to fears that the country's car industry could collapse. ❦ Brown announced a unified EU recovery package worth €200bn. ❦ RIP @ 85, 50s pin-up, Bettie Page. {12} Jurors returned an open verdict at the Jean Charles de Menezes inquest. {13} 4 British soldiers died in 2 separate explosions in Afghanistan. ❦ A $50bn fraud by broker Bernard Madoff was uncovered; many banks and investors across the world were reported to have suffered vast losses [see p.32]. ❦ Santander, owner of Abbey, Alliance & Leicester, and Bradford & Bingley, announced the loss of 1,900 jobs. ❦ Alexandra Burke won *The X Factor* [see p.122]. {14} An Iraqi journalist threw his shoes at President Bush in disgust, during a press conference in Iraq [see p.262]. ❦ Chris Hoy was named BBC Sports Personality of the Year [see p.315]. ❦ RIP @ 80, Kathy Staff. {15} It was reported that >1,000 had died from cholera in Zimbabwe. {17} It was announced that all 807 Woolworths stores would close in January 2009, with the loss of 27,000 jobs. ❦ Brown said that UK troops would leave Iraq by July '09. ❦ OPEC cut oil production by 2·2m barrels a day as oil prices continued to fall. {17} Bilal Abdulla was sentenced to life in prison for conspiring to murder; in 2007, Abdulla, an NHS doctor, planted car bombs in London's West End before launching an attack on Glasgow airport. {18} Robert Napper pleaded guilty to the manslaughter on the grounds of diminished responsibility of Rachel Nickell, who was killed on Wimbledon Common in 1992. {19} RIP @ 95, Mark Felt, a.k.a. Watergate's 'Deep Throat'. ❦ The US government announced it would give $17·4bn in

──── IN BRIEF · DECEMBER 2008 – JANUARY 2009 ────

loans to GM and Chrysler. ❦ 1,400 jobs were lost as furniture retailer MFI closed. {20} Actor Tom Chambers beat Rachel Stevens to win *Strictly Come Dancing* [see p.122]. {23} 4 animal rights protesters were found guilty of harassing firms supplying Huntingdon Life Sciences. {24} Music, games, and DVD retail chain Zavvi was put into administration. ❦ RIP @ 78, Harold Pinter [see p.61]. {25} RIP @ 81, Eartha Kitt. ❦ Israel warned Hamas to stop firing rockets into Israel, claiming >50 rockets had been launched since the 6-month ceasefire ended. ❦ Conjoined twin Faith Williams died 23 days after the death of her sister, Hope. {27} >255 Palestinians died after Israel launched an attack on Gaza. {28} Air raids on Gaza continued; Israel vowed to fight until rocket attacks ceased. ❦ >30 died in a car bomb attack in NW Pakistan. {29} >350 Palestinians were reported dead as Israel continued its barrage of air raids; 4 Israelis were reported dead after being hit by Hamas rockets. Brown and Ban Ki Moon urged an immediate ceasefire. {31} The UN convened to discuss the ongoing violence in Gaza, as calls for a ceasefire grew.

Kate Winslet

reported that >500 Palestinians had been killed and *c*.2,500 wounded since the fighting began. ❦ Waterford Wedgwood went into administration. {6} A number of European countries reported problems with their gas supplies after Russia cut its supply to Ukraine. ❦ Freezing weather across the UK continued; in some areas, temperatures dropped to –10°C. ❦ The final 200 Woolworths stores closed. [7] The UN Security Council struggled to find a consensus in its response to the Gaza crisis; Israel allowed a 3-hour truce to let aid into Gaza. ❦ 1,230 jobs were lost at Marks & Spencer. ❦ England cricket captain Kevin Pietersen resigned after a dispute with the English Cricket Board concerning coach Peter Moores. {8} The BoE cut interest rates to 1·5%, the lowest-ever rate. ❦ The UN suspended operations in Gaza after 2 of its staff were killed by Israeli bombs. ❦ Rockets were fired from Lebanon into Israel sparking fears that the conflict might spread. ❦ 1,200 jobs were lost at the Nissan plant in Wearside [see p.207]. {9} The UN resumed aid operations in Gaza after Israel guaranteed their safety. ❦ The Saudi tanker *Sirius Star* was released by Somali pirates after a ransom was dropped onto the ship by parachute. ❦ RIP @ 65, 60s popstar Dave Dee. {10} Israel dropped leaflets across the Gaza strip warning that attacks on the area were set to intensify. ❦ A video from 2006 emerged, in which Prince Harry used racist language when describing his fellow soldiers; the Prince issued an immediate apology [see p.276]. {11} Kate Winslet won Best Actress and Best Supporting Actress awards at the Golden Globes. {12} Israeli ground troops moved

JANUARY 2009 · {1} Air strikes on Gaza continued; the UN warned of an impending humanitarian crisis as vital supplies to the Palestinians were blocked. ❦ Russia cut off the gas supply to Ukraine citing a financial dispute. {3} The Israeli army began ground attacks on Gaza. {4} A British journalist was freed after being held for a month by Somali pirates. {5} Israel vowed to maintain its offensive against Gaza despite the toll of civilian deaths; it was

Israel must abide by its humanitarian obligations.
– DAVID MILIBAND

IN BRIEF · JANUARY 2009

further into Gaza; it was reported that, of the >900 Palestinians killed, >400 were women and children. ❦ RIP @ 73, David Vine. {13} Russia reported that it had resumed gas supplies to Ukraine, but that Kiev had blocked the flow to the rest of Europe. ❦ Barclays announced it would cut 2,100 jobs. {14} The government approved the controversial 3rd runway at Heathrow [see p.214]. ❦ RIP @ 80, Patrick McGoohan. ❦ >1,000 Palestinians were reported to have died since the conflict with Israel began. ❦ The European Cmsn warned it might sue Russia and Ukraine over the disruption of gas supplies. {16} A plane carrying 155 people made an emergency landing on the Hudson River in New York after hitting a flock of geese; all the passengers and crew survived, and the pilot, Chesley Sullenberger, was hailed as a hero. ❦ The trial of Amanda Knox and Raffaele Sollecito, accused of murdering British student Meredith Kercher, began in Italy. ❦ Honda announced it was extending the closure of its Swindon plant until May. ❦ An investigation was launched into the deaths of 2 British servicemen in Afghanistan amid reports that they were killed by 'friendly fire'. ❦ RIP @ 85, John Mortimer [see p.61].

{17} Israel announced it would declare a ceasefire in Gaza. {18} Cameron announced

Barack Obama

We now have a governmental crisis on top of the economic one.
– GEIR HAARDE, Iceland's PM

Ken Clarke would become shadow business secretary, pitting him against Peter Mandelson. ❦ Hamas announced a week-long ceasefire to allow Israeli troops to withdraw. ❦ RIP @ 83, Tony Hart [see p.61]. {19} The government unveiled a package of measures to encourage banks to resume lending; the move gave the government a greater stake in some banks,

and a *c.*70% stake in RBS. ❦ The UN said that >50,000 Gazans were homeless as a result of the Israeli conflict. {20} Obama was sworn in as US President [see p.267]. ❦ The £ hit its lowest value against the $ since 2001: $1·40. {21} UK unemployment hit 1·92m. {22} Fulfilling his campaign promise Obama ordered the (planned) closure of the Guantánamo Bay prison. ❦ Ministers announced that, under Freedom of Information laws, MPs would have to publish receipts for their expenses dating back to 2004 [see p.18]. {23} Official figures confirmed that the UK was in a recession. ❦ Rwandan forces arrested Congolese rebel leader General Laurent Nkunda, leading to hope that a peace deal in DR Congo could become possible. ❦ The BBC was criticised for its decision not to screen a Disasters Emergency Committee (DEC) appeal for humanitarian aid for Gaza. {25} The steelmaker Corus announced it would cut 2,500 UK jobs. ❦ There were calls for an inquiry after it was alleged that 4 Labour peers had discussed taking payment to make amendments to laws. ❦ Sri Lankan troops gained control of Mullaitivu, the last major town held by Tamil Tigers. ❦ Despite numerous complaints and pressure from MPs the BBC stood by its decision not to show the DEC's Gaza appeal; Sky also declined to show the appeal. {26} Cannabis was reclassified as a Class B drug in England and Wales. ❦ At his trial in the Hague [see p.269], Congolese 'warlord' Thomas Lubanga pleaded not guilty to charges of using child soldiers. ❦ Icelandic PM Geir Haarde and his entire cabinet resigned in response to the economic crisis [see p.31]. {27} Sir Paul Stephenson

─────── IN BRIEF · JANUARY – FEBRUARY 2009 ───────

was named the new Met. Police Cmsnr. ❦ RIP @ 76, John Updike [see p.61]. ❦ The government promised £2·3bn in loans and training to help the British car industry [see p.207]. ❦ Israel launched an airstrike against Gaza after Palestinian militants broke the ceasefire and killed an Israeli soldier. {28} The International Monetary Fund (IMF) warned that the UK's economy would shrink by 2·8% in '09; the worst outlook among developed nations. ❦ MSPs rejected the Scottish budget. {29} Workers at the Total refinery in Lincolnshire struck after an Italian firm contracted by Total used Italian workers. {30} Energy workers across Britain struck in support of the Total workers. {31} Thousands of Iraqis voted in largely peaceful provincial elections.

Morgan Tsvangirai

Workers at the Total refinery agreed to return to work after ACAS negotiated a guarantee that over half the disputed jobs would go to British workers. ❦ Jade Goody revealed that her cervical cancer had spread and that doctors were no longer looking for a cure [see p.127]. {5} The BoE cut interest rates to 1%. ❦ 5,000 schools closed in England and Wales as more snow fell. {6} Sarkozy publicly criticised Brown's VAT cut, to the irritation of No.10. {7} Darling announced an inquiry into the management of banks to counteract public anger over large bonus payouts [see p.31]. ❦ >25 died after wildfires ripped through S Australia [see p.33]. {8} >108 were reported dead after the wildfires in S Australia intensified; this was the highest wildfire death toll in the country's history. ❦ Darling warned RBS not to give large bonuses to poorly performing bankers, but conceded that some high-flyers may receive sizable payments [see p.31]. {9} British artists won many of the top awards at the Grammys; British film *Slumdog Millionaire* took top honours at the Baftas. ❦ Britain prepared for yet more snow as councils warned they were running out of salt and grit. ❦ Australian fire crews resumed the search for bodies as the wildfire death toll of 178 was predicted to rise. {10} Obama's $838bn economic stimulus package was passed by the Senate. {11} A Dutch MP was banned from entering Britain to attend the screening of a short film about Islam. ❦ After months of negotiation, Morgan Tsvangirai was sworn in as PM of Zimbabwe. {13} >50 were killed when a plane crashed into a house in Buffalo, New York. {14} Lloyds banking group

F EBRUARY · {1} Severe weather warnings were issued as heavy snow fell across the UK. ❦ Israeli forces bombed militant targets in Gaza after fresh rocket attacks on Israel. {2} Airports closed across Britain as heavy snow choked the country. ❦ Wildcat strikes continued across Britain as nuclear workers at Sellafield joined the protests against foreign workers. {3} 100s of schools throughout Britain remained closed due to the snow. ❦ Carol Thatcher was dropped as roving reporter for the BBC's *One Show* after reportedly referring to a tennis player as a 'golliwog' off-screen; her spokesman said 'Carol never intended any racist comment'. {4} Two judges alleged that America had threatened to stop sharing intelligence with the UK if accounts of the alleged torture of Guantánamo prisoner Binyam Mohamed were made public. ❦

This is of a level of horror that few of us anticipated.
– KEVIN RUDD, Australian PM

─────── IN BRIEF · FEBRUARY – MARCH 2009 ───────

defended a decision to award >£120m in bonuses. {15} 3 soldiers died in a car crash in Pembrokeshire. {16} 850 jobs were lost at the Mini factory in Cowley, Oxford. ❦ An Australian man was charged with arson after allegedly setting a fire that killed 11 in Churchill, Victoria. ❦ Hugo Chávez won a controversial referendum that allowed him to stand for re-election in 2012. ❦ >8 were killed when a US drone targeted militants in Pakistan's tribal region. ❦ The Royal Navy admitted that a British and a French nuclear submarine had collided under the Atlantic; the MoD insisted that nuclear security had not been compromised. {17} Obama signed into law the $787bn economic stimulus plan. ❦ Sir Allen Stanford was charged with an $8bn investment fraud; he denied wrongdoing. ❦ 17,000 extra US troops were deployed to Afghanistan. {18} The Law Lords announced radical cleric Abu Qatada could be deported to Jordan. {19} US authorities searched for Sir Allen Stanford, who had apparently gone to ground. {20} The FBI located Stanford; meanwhile, the English Cricket Board severed all links with the billionaire. {21} >100,000 protested in Dublin over the Irish government's handling of the economy. {22} Australia held a day of mourning for the >200 bushfire victims. ❦ Brown called for banks to stop giving 100% mortgages. ❦ >73 died in an explosion at a mine in Shanxi, China. ❦ Northern Rock announced it was reviving its mortgage-lending business. {23} *Slumdog Millionaire* won 8 Oscars [see p.156]. {23} Freed Guantánamo prisoner Binyam Mohamed arrived back in the UK as investigations continued into

Fred Goodwin

his claims of torture. {24} Postal workers staged a protest in Westminster over government plans to sell 30% of the Royal Mail. ❦ Jack Straw vetoed the release of the minutes from key meetings held in the run-up to the Iraq invasion. {25} David Cameron's 6-year-old son Ivan died; he had been suffering from severe epilepsy and cerebral palsy. ❦ 4 British soldiers died in Afghanistan. ❦ A row erupted after the size of former RBS CEO Sir Fred Goodwin's pension was revealed [see p.31]. {26} Treasury Minister Lord Myners urged Goodwin to voluntarily surrender some of his pension. ❦ The government admitted that, contrary to previous denials, 2 suspects arrested in Iraq had been handed to the US, sparking claims that the British government was complicit in extraordinary rendition. ❦ RIP @ 65, actress Wendy Richard [see p.62]. {27} >200 Bangladeshi border guards were arrested after a 2-day mutiny in which >40 were killed. ❦ Obama announced that US troops would be withdrawn from Iraq by August 2010. ❦ The Land Registry reported that UK house prices had fallen 15·1% year on year. {28} Brown criticised the size of Goodwin's pension.

Let me say this as plainly as I can: by August 31, 2010, our combat mission in Iraq will end. – BARACK OBAMA

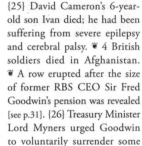

MARCH · {1} An EU summit rejected a Hungarian proposal for a £160bn aid package for E Europe; unity across Europe was urged as the recession tempted governments into protectionism. ❦ Man U beat Tottenham 4–1 on penalties in the Carling Cup final [see p.318]. {2} The President of Guinea-Bissau Joao Bernardo Vieira was shot dead by renegade soldiers. ❦ Stock markets around the world fell

── IN BRIEF · MARCH 2009 ──

dramatically; the Dow Jones dipped below 7,000 for the first time since 1997 and the FTSE closed at a 6-year low. ❦ The winning University Challenge team Corpus Christi was disqualified after fielding an ineligible team member; runners-up Manchester University were handed the trophy. ❦ $4·5bn was pledged by international donors to re-build Gaza. {3} 5 Pakistani policemen were killed and 7 Sri Lankan cricketers were injured after gunmen attacked the team bus as it journeyed to Lahore, Pakistan. ❦ Brown arrived in Washington for his first meeting with President Obama. ❦ Northern Rock posted losses of £1·4bn. {4} The International Criminal Court issued an arrest warrant for Sudanese President Omar al-Bashir in relation to accusations of war crimes in Darfur; the Sudanese government dismissed the warrant and expelled foreign aid agencies. ❦ ITV announced it was shedding 600 jobs and cutting its drama budget. {5} The BoE announced it would cut interest rates to 0·5%, and implement 'quantitative easing' (QE) – whereby £75bn of new money would be created in an attempt to kickstart the economy. ❦ Michael Jackson announced a 10-date residency at the O2 arena, London. {6} An eco-campaigner threw green custard over Mandelson in a protest against Heathrow's 3rd runway [see p.214]. ❦ The government agreed to insure £260bn of Lloyds Bank's loans in return for a 60% stake in the company. ❦ Zimbabwean PM Morgan Tsvangirai was injured and his wife killed after a car crash with a US aid convoy. {7} 2 British soldiers were killed and 2 pizza deliverymen injured in a shooting at an army barracks

Bernard Madoff

in Massereene, N Ireland; they were the first British soldiers to die in N Ireland since 1997. ❦ 2,300 jobs were placed in jeopardy when no buyer could be found for the clothing retailer Principles. {8} The Real IRA claimed responsibility for the Massereene killings; Brown condemned the attack and pledged it would not jeopardise the peace process. ❦ 28 were killed by a suicide bomber at a police academy in Baghdad. {9} Obama lifted restrictions on federal funding for stem cell research. ❦ *YouTube* blocked access to premium music video content for British users after it failed to come to a royalty agreement with the Performing Rights Society. {10} A 48-year-old policeman, Stephen Carroll, was shot dead in Craigavon, County Armagh, N Ireland; the Continuity IRA claimed responsibility. ❦ >33 died in a suicide attack at a reconciliation conference in Baghdad. ❦ A small group of anti-war activists and Muslims protested as British soldiers returning from Iraq paraded through Luton. {11} A 17-year-old boy and a 37-year-old man were arrested in connection with the murder of Constable Stephen Carroll. ❦ 15 died after a German teenager, Tim Kretschmer, went on the rampage in Winnenden before turning the gun on himself. ❦ Rallies were held across N Ireland to protest against the recent murders. {12} Madoff pleaded guilty to all charges against him [see p.32]. {14} After weeks of unrest in Madagascar, opposition leader Andry Rajoelina warned President Marc Ravalomanana to step down or be overthrown. ❦ The Comic Relief telethon raised a record £57m. {15} Pakistan's PM Yousaf Raza Gilani announced the

> *America is not just the indispensable nation, you are the irrepressible nation.*
> – GORDON BROWN

IN BRIEF · MARCH 2009

supreme court chief justice would be reinstated in an effort to prevent further protests from opposition parties. {16} The trial of Josef Fritzl opened in Austria [see p.34]. ✤ Soldiers seized one of the presidential palaces in Madagascar in part of an attempted coup. {17} Actress Natasha Richardson suffered serious brain injuries after a skiing accident in Canada. ✤ Madagascar's military gave 'its backing to opposition leader Andry Rajoelina as he took control of the country after the President stepped down. ✤ The Pope rejected condoms as a solution to the AIDS crisis in Africa, much

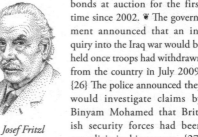

Josef Fritzl

to the dismay of aid agencies. {18} Fritzl changed his plea to guilty on all charges [see p.34]. ✤ UK unemployment topped 2m for the first time since 1997. ✤ Sean Hodgson was released from prison after his conviction for the murder of Teresa de Simone was quashed; he had served 27 years in jail. {19} Fritzl was sentenced to life in prison. ✤ RIP @ 45, Natasha Richardson [see p.62]. {20} UK car production fell 59% in February, the 5th successive monthly fall. {21} Ireland won the rugby Grand Slam for the first time in 61 years, and with it the Six Nations [see p.304]. ✤ A video of 5 British hostages kidnapped in Iraq in 2007 was released, reviving hopes that they were alive and might be freed. ✤ >100,000 Italians took part in an anti-Mafia march in Naples. {22} RIP @ 27, Jade Goody [see p.127]. {23} The *Daily Mail* and General Trust cut 1,000 jobs as advertising revenue slumped. {24} The RPI fell to 0% in February, for the first time in 49 years, leading analysts to suggest that Britain faced a prolonged period of deflation. ✤ A 17-year-old boy and a 37-year-old man

were charged with the murder of Stephen Carroll. {25} The Edinburgh home of former RBS boss Sir Fred Goodwin was attacked by vandals [see p.31]. ✤ Analysts expressed concerns over the UK economy after the government failed to sell all its bonds at auction for the first time since 2002. ✤ The government announced that an inquiry into the Iraq war would be held once troops had withdrawn from the country in July 2009. {26} The police announced they would investigate claims by Binyam Mohamed that British security forces had been complicit in his torture. {27} A man was charged with the murder of 2 army officers outside their barracks in Antrim. ✤ A 19-year-old man was found guilty of the murder of teenager Jimmy Mizen in a bakery in SE London. {28} The Dunfermline Building Society was put up for sale. ✤ Thousands attended a peaceful march in London ahead of the G20; protesters were marching over climate change, jobs, and global poverty. ✤ Violence broke out between Polish and N Irish football fans after their World Cup qualifier in Belfast. {29} The husband of Home Sec. Jacqui Smith apologised after it was revealed that she had claimed on her parliamentary expenses for 'adult' films he had watched [see p.18]. ✤ The Conservative party expelled millionaire Stuart Wheeler after he donated £100,000 to UKIP. {30} 11 were killed at a police training academy in Lahore, Pakistan, after militants stormed the building. ✤ 22 died in a stampede after an international football match in the Ivory Coast. ✤ Nationwide took over the Dunfermline Building Society. ✤ Dissident republicans in N Ireland caused

> *I am really sorry for any embarrassment I have caused Jacqui* [Smith].
> – RICHARD TIMNEY (her husband)

—— IN BRIEF · MARCH – APRIL 2009 ——

chaos across the province by phoning in a number of hoax bomb warnings; First Minister Peter Robinson condemned those trying to reignite the Troubles, stating that 'those who would try to destabilise and destroy N Ireland will fail. We won't be going back'. {31} Labour MP Stuart Bell alleged that details of MPs' expenses had been offered for sale to the press for £300,000; the Commons Estimates Committee launched an investigation. ❦ The British military began to withdraw from Iraq; bases in S Iraq were handed over to US control. ❦ World leaders gathered in London for the G20 summit.

Madonna

A PRIL {1} As the G20 summit began, thousands congregated in London to protest on a range of issues from climate change to globalisation [see p.34]. ❦ 16 were killed when a helicopter carrying oil workers crashed off the coast of Aberdeen. {2} At the close of the G20 summit, world leaders announced a $1·1tr package to ameliorate the downturn. {3} A Malawian court ruled that Madonna could not adopt a second child from the country due to residency issues. {4} Ofcom fined the BBC £150,000 over 'Sachsgate' [see p.129]. ❦ The funeral of Jade Goody was held; thousands gathered to pay their respects [see p.127]. {5} N Korea launched a test missile; the UN Security Council was quick to convene but was unable to agree on a response; Japan called for 'clear, firm and unified' action, but China warned any response should be 'cautious and proportionate'. {6} >150 were killed when a 6·3 earthquake struck the Abruzzo region of Italy; whole

villages were flattened and thousands were left homeless. Much of the worst damage centred on the medieval city of L'Aquila [see p.35]. ❦ Two Manchester gang leaders – Colin Joyce, 29, and Lee Amos, 33 – were found guilty of murder; police revealed that since their arrest, shootings in the area had fallen by 92%. ❦ Corruption charges against ANC leader Jacob Zuma were dropped. {7} Rescuers dug through the rubble searching for survivors of the L'Aquila earthquake as the death toll rose to >179. ❦ 2 brothers aged 10 and 11 were charged with attempted murder and robbery after an attack on a 9- and 11-year-old in Edlington, near Doncaster. ❦ Video footage was released which appeared to show that a man who had died during G20 protests in London had been pushed to the ground by police. The film was handed over to the Independent Police Complaints Commission. ❦ RBS announced the loss of a further 9,000 jobs. {8} 12 people were arrested during a police anti-terror raid in NW England; the raid had been brought forward after Assistant Commissioner (and anti-terror chief) Bob Quick was photographed carrying in plain sight a top secret document outlining plans for the operation. ❦ US crew members of the *Maersk Alabama* managed to recapture their ship from Somali pirates after an attack, but the captain of the ship Richard Phillips was taken hostage in a lifeboat. {9} Bob Quick resigned. {10} It was revealed that 10 of the 12 suspects arrested in the NW England anti-terror raids were Pakistanis who had entered Britain on student visas. ❦ A state funeral was held in Italy for the victims of the L'Aquila earthquake. ❦ A

> *Hands reached out,*
> *they grabbed me, and I got out.*
> – GUIDO MARIANI, L'Aquila survivor

──────── IN BRIEF · APRIL 2009 ────────

French man died when French forces attacked Somali pirates holding him and his family captive; 3 other adults and a child were rescued. ❧ Richard Phillips attempted to escape from his Somali captors by diving into the sea, but a pirate snatched him from the water before US forces could intervene. {11} Senior Labour advisor Damian McBride resigned after emails were published in which he discussed circulating unfounded smears about senior Tories and their families [see p.251]. ❧ A summit of Asian leaders was abandoned after Thai anti-government protesters stormed the venue. {12} The US Navy announced it had freed Richard Phillips during a dramatic rescue in which 3 Somali pirates were killed. ❧ Cameron demanded an apology from Brown over the McBride email scandal. ❧ 2 were killed as anti-government protests took place in Bangkok and troops struggled to regain order. ❧ Angel Cabrera won the US Masters [see p.303]. {13} Phil Spector was found guilty of the murder of actress Lana Clarkson. ❧ The Thai government announced Bangkok was back 'under control' after days of protests. ❧ >100 environmental campaigners were arrested in connection with a plot to disable a power station. {14} N Korea announced it would withdraw from international talks over its nuclear programme after the UN criticised the country's recent rocket launch. ❧ Further video footage emerged from the London G20 protests which appeared to show a police officer assaulting a woman [see p.34]. ❧ French fishing boats blocked the Channel in a dispute over fishing quotas. {15} Thousands of football fans visited Anfield to commemorate

Damian McBride

the 20th anniversary of the Hillsborough disaster. {16} It was announced that Damian Green would not face charges over a series of Home Office leaks [see p.32]. ❧ RIP @ 84, Clement Freud [see p.62]. ❧ Brown belatedly apologised for the McBride email 'smears', after critics accused him of being unable to say 'sorry'. ❧ French fishermen lifted their blockade of Channel ports after the French government agreed to give them €4m in aid. {17} A Swedish court sentenced the 4 founders of the internet file-sharing website 'The Pirate Bay' to a year in prison for copyright infringement. ❧ RIP @ 78, J.G. Ballard [see p.62]. ❧ Obama released 4 previously secret memos that revealed the extent of torture used by the US; one suspect, Khalid Sheikh Mohammed, suffered waterboarding 183 times. {18} Thousands of Sri Lankans fled from heavy fighting as government troops broke into the last Tamil Tiger stronghold in N Sri Lanka. ❧ After a one-day trial, an Iranian court jailed Iranian-American journalist Roxana Saberi for 8 years; Obama expressed his 'disappointment'. {20} In London, Tamil protesters attempting to draw attention to the ongoing crisis in Sri Lanka broke through police lines and blocked many of the roads around Westminster. ❧ Diplomats walked out of a UN anti-racism conference in Geneva when Iranian President Ahmadinejad made an inflammatory speech accusing Israel of being 'totally racist'. {21} The RPI was negative for the first time since 1960 [see p.243]. ❧ The Tamil Tigers accused the Sri Lankan government of shelling civilians; Sri Lanka denied the accusations. ❧ Tesco announced record

There is no need of a ceasefire. They must surrender. That is it.
— G. RAJAPAKSA, Sri Lankan Defence Sec.

—————— IN BRIEF · APRIL – MAY 2009 ——————

profits of £3·13bn. ❦ The IMF warned that the global economic crisis would cost $4tr, and take years to repair. ❦ All 12 men arrested in NW England over a suspected terrorist bomb plot were released without charge; 11 were handed over to the UK Borders Agency. {22} Darling unveiled his Budget [see p.234]. {23} >76 were killed when suicide bombers launched separate attacks in Baghdad and Baquba, Iraq. {24} >60 were reported to have died in Mexico after contracting a deadly strain of swine flu, A(H1N1) [see p.23]. {25} The UN warned that the A(H1N1) outbreak had the potential to become a pandemic as >81 died in Mexico and reports emerged that the virus had spread to the US. ❦ RIP @ 86, *Golden Girls* star Bea Arthur. {26} The Tamil Tigers' call for a unilateral ceasefire was rejected by the Sri Lankan government. ❦ Pakistani forces launched attacks on the Taliban occupying positions near the Swat Valley. {27} 2 Scottish cases of A(H1N1) were confirmed in a couple returning from honeymoon in Mexico; other possible cases were identified in Canada, America, New Zealand, France, Spain, and Israel; the death toll in Mexico rose to >100. ❦ General Motors announced it would shed another 21,000 jobs. {28} The WHO raised its pandemic threat level to 4; 2 points away from a pandemic [see p.64]. ❦ After a retrial, 3 men were cleared of helping to plan the 7/7 London bomb attacks; prosecutors admitted that it was unlikely anyone would be brought to justice for the attacks. {29} The WHO raised its pandemic alert level to 5 as it was confirmed that 5 Britons had contracted the virus after visiting Mexico. ❦ Brown

We stick to our guns and say equal rights for the Gurkhas.
– JOANNA LUMLEY

suffered an embarrassing Commons defeat over Gurkha resettlement [see p.36]. ❦ Obama marked 100 days in office. ❦ Van maker LDV announced it would go into administration unless a buyer could be found. {30} A ceremony was held in Basra to mark the end of UK military involvement in Iraq. ❦ 8 Britons were confirmed to have A(H1N1). ❦ US car maker Chrysler confirmed a rescue deal with Fiat.

Alistair Darling

MAY · {1} Carol Ann Duffy became the first female poet laureate [see p.164]. ❦ Mexico announced it would shut down parts of its economy for 5 days in an effort to stem A(H1N1). ❦ The 32-year-old boyfriend of Baby P's mother was jailed for life for raping a 2-year-old girl. {2} Communities Sec Hazel Blears attacked her own party's inability to communicate its message. ❦ >91 died after the Sri Lankan government shelled a hospital inside the so-called 'safe zone' in Tamil Tiger territory. {3} Senior members of the Cabinet backed Brown as rumours surfaced of another leadership challenge. ❦ The Mexican health minister announced that A(H1N1) had peaked. {4} A 5th school closed in Britain as 9 further cases of A(H1N1) were confirmed; in total, the UK had 27 known cases of the disease. {5} An American woman from Texas became the first person outside Mexico to die from A(H1N1). ❦ The government provided a £5m bridging loan to enable Malaysian company Weststar to take over LDV. {6} Joanna Lumley met with Brown to discuss the resettlement of Gurkhas [see p.36]. {7} Government policy on the Gurkhas was called a 'shambles' as Lumley pressed

— IN BRIEF · MAY 2009 —

Immigration Minister Phil Woolas for a solution. ❦ 4 British soldiers were killed in Helmand, Afghanistan. {8} *The Telegraph* published details of some Cabinet members' expenses including claims made by Gordon Brown for the cleaning of his flat [see p.18]; all denied any wrongdoing. ❦ A 24-year-old US soldier was found guilty of raping and killing a 14-year-old Iraqi girl and murdering her family. {9} *The Telegraph* revealed further embarrassing details of MPs' expenses. ❦ Jacob Zuma was inaugurated as President of S Africa. ❦ Pakistan launched further attacks on militants in the Swat Valley in an effort to purge the Taliban. {10} David Cameron said MPs must apologise for their expenses, as the *Telegraph* published details of Tory claims. ❦ The Sri Lankan government continued to deny it had been shelling N Sri Lanka, despite reports that >378 had been killed in the area. {11} Brown apologised 'on behalf of all parties' for the expenses scandal. ❦ Iranian-American journalist Roxana Saberi was released from an Iranian jail after her sentence for spying was cut; commentators interpreted the move as a thawing of relations between Iran and the West. ❦ 65 cases of A(H1N1) were confirmed in the UK. {12} Unemployment rose to 2·22m in the first 3 months of 2009. ❦ Cameron demanded Tory MPs pay back any 'excessive' expenses, as party leaders vied to seize the initiative. {13} >50 died when the Sri Lankan government shelled a Tamil hospital. ❦ Tory MP Douglas Carswell tabled a motion of no confidence in Commons Speaker Michael Martin. {14} The Foreign Office warned Sri Lanka it could face war crimes charges over their

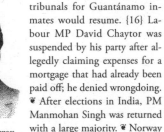

David Cameron

treatment of the Tamils. ❦ Burmese opposition leader Aung San Suu Kyi was jailed on spurious charges just as her house arrest was set to expire [see p.37]. {15} After failing to find a viable alternative, Obama announced that military tribunals for Guantánamo inmates would resume. {16} Labour MP David Chaytor was suspended by his party after allegedly claiming expenses for a mortgage that had already been paid off; he denied wrongdoing. ❦ After elections in India, PM Manmohan Singh was returned with a large majority. ❦ Norway won the Eurovision Song Contest [see p.146]. ❦ The Sri Lankan army claimed victory over the Tamil Tigers, bringing to an end 26 years of conflict. {17} 14 further cases of A(H1N1) were confirmed in Britain, bringing the total number infected to 101. {18} Speaker Martin resisted calls for his resignation. ❦ Tamil Tiger leader Velupillai Prabhakaran was reported to have been killed. {19} Speaker Martin announced he would stand down [see p.254]. {20} The US Senate blocked Obama's plans to move prisoners from Guantánamo Bay and refused to release funds to close it down. ❦ Lord Truscott and Lord Taylor of Blackburn were suspended from the Lords for 6 months over allegations of 'cash for amendments' to legislation. {21} All

In order that unity can be maintained I have decided I will relinquish the office of Speaker. – MICHAEL MARTIN

Gurkhas who served >4 years in the British army won the right to settle in the UK [see p.36]. {22} British Airways announced an annual pre-tax loss of £401m. {23} Andrew MacKay became the 4th Tory MP to announce he would stand down at the next election over the expenses scandal; 2 Labour MPs had made similar announcements [see p.18]. {25} N Korea staged a

─────── IN BRIEF · MAY – JUNE 2009 ───────

successful nuclear test, prompting immediate international condemnation. ❦ 2 further Tory MPs, Sir Nicholas and Ann Winterton, announced they would stand down at the next election. {26} N Korea fired 2 more test missiles as the international community struggled to find consensus to censure the 'rogue state'. ❦ 44 new cases of A(H1N1) were confirmed at a school in Birmingham, bringing the total number of UK cases to 184. ❦ Ruth Padel resigned as Oxford Professor of Poetry just days after accepting the post [see p.166]. {27} >23 were killed and hundreds injured in a bomb attack in Lahore, Pakistan; the Taliban were blamed for the atrocity. ❦ Barcelona beat Man Utd 2–0 in the Champions League final [see p.301]. ❦ N Korea announced it was ending its truce with S Korea after the South joined a US-led initiative to search N Korean ships for nuclear weapons. {28} Tory MP Julie Kirkbride and Labour MP Margaret Moran both announced they would stand down at the next election after revelations about their expenses claims. {29} It was reported that >35,000 new cars had been ordered in association with the government's car scrappage scheme since its April launch. {30} Dance troupe Diversity beat Susan Boyle to win *Britain's Got Talent*. {31} It was reported that Susan Boyle had entered The Priory to recuperate from the pressure of instant world fame.

J UNE · {1} Air France Flight 447 disappeared en route from Brazil to France; 228 were aboard. ❦ In the largest industrial failure in US history, General Motors filed for bankruptcy

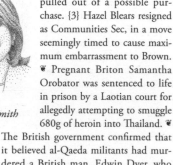

Jacqui Smith

protection. ❦ RIP @ 81, Danny La Rue [see p.62]. {2} Rescuers began searching for the wreckage of Flight 447. ❦ Jacqui Smith announced she would stand down as Home Sec. at the next reshuffle. ❦ LDV was forced into administration after the Malaysian firm Weststar pulled out of a possible purchase. {3} Hazel Blears resigned as Communities Sec, in a move seemingly timed to cause maximum embarrassment to Brown. ❦ Pregnant Briton Samantha Orobator was sentenced to life in prison by a Laotian court for allegedly attempting to smuggle 680g of heroin into Thailand. ❦ The British government confirmed that it believed al-Qaeda militants had murdered a British man, Edwin Dyer, who had been held captive in Mali. {4} Britons went to the polls for the European and local elections [see p.20]. As the polls closed, Work and Pensions Sec. James Purnell resigned from the government and called on Brown to stand down 'to give our Party a fighting chance of winning'. ❦ Dano Sonnex and Nigel Farmer were jailed for life for the horrifically sadistic murder of French students Gabriel Ferez, 23, and Laurent Bonomo, 23. London's chief probation officer resigned after it emerged that a series of probation blunders had left Sonnex free to commit the crime. ❦ Obama made a speech in Cairo reaching out to the Muslim world. ❦ RIP @ 72, Kung Fu actor David Carradine. {5} Brown admitted that Labour had suffered a 'painful defeat' in the elections but he exerted his authority with a bold Cabinet reshuffle [see p.255]; Geoff Hoon and John Hutton resigned from the Cabinet. ❦ The number of UK A(H1N1) cases was reported at close to

I continue to believe that Gordon Brown is the best man for the job.
– ALAN JOHNSON

———————— IN BRIEF · JUNE 2009 ————————

500. {6} Bodies of passengers on Air France Flight 447 were recovered from the ocean. {7} Roger Federer triumphed at the French Open, taking the one title that had previously eluded him [see p.313]. {8} Labour slumped to 3rd place in the European elections; the Tories came first, and UKIP second; the BNP secured 2 seats in the North [see p.20]. ✻ RIP @ 73, Omar Bongo Ondimba, President of Gabon [see p.62]. {9} Brown suffered another blow when Environment Minister Jane Kennedy resigned after admitting she would not back Brown as leader. ✻ LDV went into administration; >850 jobs were expected to go. {10} A female nursery worker from Plymouth was charged with 4 counts of sexual assault and 3 counts relating to the distribution of indecent images of children. {11} After an emergency meeting, the WHO declared that A(H1N1) was a global pandemic; >30,000 cases had been reported in a total of 74 countries. ✻ 3 young men were found guilty of stabbing to death 16-year-old Ben Kinsella. ✻ Man Utd confirmed it had accepted a record £80m bid from Real Madrid for Cristiano Ronaldo [see p.302]. {12} Iranians went to the polls. ✻ Madonna won an appeal that allowed her to adopt a second child from Malawi. {13} Ahmadinejad was named winner of Iran's election, but thousands of protesters clashed with police as doubts about the veracity of the result were raised; Ahmadinejad's opponent Mir Hossein Mousavi called the poll 'a charade' [see p.30]. {14} In a keynote speech, Israeli PM Benjamin Netanyahu made his first references to accepting a demilitarised Palestinian state. ✻ The first

Andy Murray

UK A(H1N1) death was reported; the unidentified Scottish victim was said to have had an underlying medical condition. ✻ Andy Murray beat James Blake 7–5, 6–4 to become the first Brit in 71 years to take the title at Queens. {15} Mir Hossein Mousavi called for the Iranian election result to be annulled, as Iran's government continued to crack down on public protests. ✻ Brown announced that the promised inquiry into the Iraq war would be held in secret [see p.24]. {16} Iran's Guardian Council announced there would be a partial electoral recount, after 7 were killed in protests [see p.30]. ✻ >100 Romanians were forced from their homes in N Ireland after attacks by a gang of racists. {17} Treasury Minister Kitty Ussher resigned from the government after further revelations connected to her expenses; she denied any wrongdoing. {18} MPs' expenses were published online but with many crucial details redacted; freedom of information campaigners denounced this as 'censorship' [see p.18]. {19} *c*.900 oil workers at Total's plant in Lincolnshire were sacked after unofficial strike action over redundancies. ✻ Police announced they would investigate the expenses claims of a number of MPs. {20} 2 bodies were handed over to the British embassy in Iraq; it was feared that they were the bodies of 2 of the 5 Britons held captive by militants. ✻ Police again clashed with demonstrators in Iran, as thousands of protestors continued to take to the streets. {21} The 2 bodies recovered in Iraq were identified as missing security guards Jason Swindlehurst and Jason Creswell. ✻ Iran reported that >10 had died after recent protests. ✻ England's

Some claim there has been fraud. Where are the irregularities?
– MAHMOUD AHMADINEJAD

women beat New Zealand, and Pakistan's men beat Sri Lanka in the finals of the Twenty20 Cricket World Cup [see p.299]. ❦ A video appeared online showing the dying moments of a young Iranian woman, Neda Agha-Soltan, after she had been shot during the ongoing protests in Tehran [see p.30]. {22} Tory MP John Bercow was elected the new Speaker of the Commons [see p.254]. ❦ Most of the >100 Romanians who fled their homes after racist attacks in Belfast returned to Romania. ❦ Iran's Guardian Council ruled that the election would not be annulled, despite admissions that in some areas more votes had been cast than there were eligible voters. {23} Satellite broadcaster Setanta went into administration; >200 jobs were lost. {24} >43 died in a US drone attack on a Taliban stronghold in Pakistan. {25} RIP @ 62, Farrah Fawcett [see p.62]. ❦ Top BBC executives published details of their pay and expenses; many were criticised by the media. ❦ At a court appearance in America, Sir Allen Stanford pleaded not guilty to charges of fraud. ❦ >2,000 British jobs were cut by Corus. ❦ British Airways announced that >800 of its staff had volunteered to work for no pay for up to a month to aid the struggling carrier. {26} RIP @ 50, Michael Jackson [see p.142]. {27} The US government estimated there had been >1m cases of A(H1N1) in America, and *c.*127 associated deaths. ❦ An autopsy on Jackson showed no foul play, but further toxicology tests were ordered. {28} 9 Iranian staff from the British embassy in Tehran were arrested on charges of abetting anti-government demonstrations; the Foreign Office demanded their

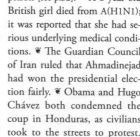

John Bercow

immediate release. ❦ Honduran President Manuel Zelaya was ousted in a military coup, and exiled to Costa Rica in his pyjamas. {29} 5 of the Iranian staff from the British embassy in Tehran were released. ❦ Madoff was sentenced to 150 years in prison [see p.32]. ❦ A 6-year-old British girl died from A(H1N1); it was reported that she had serious underlying medical conditions. ❦ The Guardian Council of Iran ruled that Ahmadinejad had won the presidential election fairly. ❦ Obama and Hugo Chávez both condemned the coup in Honduras, as civilians took to the streets to protest. {30} Many Iraqis celebrated as US forces began withdrawing.

JULY · {1} Jack Straw refused to grant parole to 'Great Train Robber' Ronnie Biggs. ❦ RIP @ 86, Mollie Sugden [see p.63]. {2} Lt Col Rupert Thorneloe, of the 1st Battalion Welsh Guards, was killed in Afghanistan; he was the highest-ranking British soldier to die in conflict since the Falklands. ❦ The British government announced that A(H1N1) could not be contained. {3} 3 children and 3 adults died in a fire at a tower block in SE London. {4} Serena Williams beat her sister Venus to take her 3rd Wimbledon title [see p.312]. {5} Questions were asked when it emerged that the wife of Sir John Sawers, the next head of MI6, had posted family details onto Facebook. ❦ Roger Federer beat Andy Roddick in an epic Wimbledon final [see p.312]. ❦ President Zelaya attempted to return to Honduras, but his plane was prevented from landing by the military. {6} >140 were killed and hundreds injured in clashes between state

Let me return in peace.
Let calm return to Honduras.
– ousted President MANUEL ZELAYA

—————— IN BRIEF · JULY 2009 ——————

police and Uighurs in Xinjiang province of China; the violence was caused by increasing tensions between Han Chinese and Uighurs [see p.36]. ❦ Presidents Obama and Medvedev agreed to cut nuclear stockpiles. {7} A televised memorial service for Michael Jackson was held in LA [see p.142]. ❦ The Lords rejected a motion to change the law on assisted death in England and Wales [see p.94]. {8} The 7th British soldier died in 7 days of fighting in Afghanistan. ❦ G8 leaders reached an agreement on new climate change targets; Ban Ki-moon criticised the agreement's timidity. {9} A teacher was arrested on suspicion of attempted murder after seriously injuring a 14-year-old pupil. ❦ *The Guardian* alleged that *The News of the World* had tapped the mobile phones of 100s of politicians and celebrities; the police said insufficient evidence existed to bring charges. {10} 2 British soldiers were killed in Helmand, Afghanistan. {12} S Korean sources claimed that N Korean leader Kim Jong-il had pancreatic cancer. ❦ An apparently healthy 6-year-old girl and a GP from Bedfordshire died of A(H1N1), raising fears that the virus was more virulent than seasonal flu. {13} A memorial service was held in Afghanistan to commemorate the lives of 8 British soldiers who had died in a 24-hour period. {15} A 19-year-old British backpacker, Jamie Neale, who had been missing for 12 days in the Australian bush, was found alive and well. ❦ During a heated PMQs, Brown strongly denied that the army lacked helicopters in Afghanistan [see p.25]. {16} The death toll from A(H1N1) in Britain rose to 29. {17} Head of the British army Sir

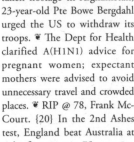

Ban Ki-moon

Richard Dannatt said that British troops in Afghanistan needed more equipment. ❦ >9 died after 2 luxury hotels in Jakarta, Indonesia were bombed. {18} RIP @ 113, Henry Allingham [see p.63]. {19} A video emerged of an American soldier taken hostage in Afghanistan; 23-year-old Pte Bowe Bergdahl urged the US to withdraw its troops. ❦ The Dept for Health clarified A(H1N1) advice for pregnant women; expectant mothers were advised to avoid unnecessary travel and crowded places. ❦ RIP @ 78, Frank McCourt. {20} In the 2nd Ashes test, England beat Australia at Lord's for the first time in 75 years [see p.27]. {21} The 18th British soldier to die in July was killed in S Afghanistan. ❦ A watered-down version of the MPs' expenses clean-up bill was passed. {23} The government launched the National Flu Service – a call centre and website to diagnose A(H1N1) and dispense Tamiflu. ❦ Voters went to the polls in the Norwich North by-election. {24} The Tories took Norwich North with a majority of >7,000. ❦ RIP @ 88, cartoonist and creator of *Captain Pugwash*, John Ryan. {25} RIP @ 111, Harry Patch [see p.63]. ❦ Lifeguards successfully rescued 36 children and 4 adults after a sandbank collapsed in Tenby, Pembrokeshire. {26} >100 died after Islamists attacked multiple targets in N Nigeria. {28} It was reported that 2 hostages held in Iraq for 2 years, Alan McMenemy and Alec MacLachlan, were most likely dead; it was hoped that a 3rd hostage, Peter Moore, might still be alive. {29} 16 families from Corby won a legal fight against the local council whom they accused of negligence; children from the 16 families were born

It is completely wrong to say the loss of life is due to the absence of helicopters.
— GORDON BROWN

—— IN BRIEF · JULY – AUGUST 2009 ——

with birth defects after their mothers had inhaled toxic fumes from the reclamation of a steel works. {30} 2 Civil Guards were killed in a car bomb attack in Majorca; ETA was blamed. ☞ MS sufferer Debbie Purdy won her legal challenge to clarify the law on assisted suicide [see p.94]. {31} British Airways reported a £148m loss in the 3 months to the end of June. ☞ RIP @ 76, Sir Bobby Robson.

Aᴜɢᴜsᴛ · {1} >100 people were put on trial in Iran for participating in pro-democracy demos; opposition leaders called it a 'laughable show trial'. {3} 4 people were arrested in Melbourne, Australia, for allegedly plotting a suicide bomb attack on an army barracks. ☞ Ahmadinejad was formally endorsed as the winner of Iran's disputed presidential elections. ☞ 2 US reporters, Laura Ling and Euna Lee, who had been jailed for 12 years with hard labour for entering N Korea illegally were released after a dramatic intervention by Bill Clinton. {4} Northern Rock posted losses of £724·2m. {6} Private detectives searching for Madeline McCann released an e-fit of a woman they were searching for. ☞ ITV sold *Friends Reunited* for £25m; it bought the company for £175m in 2005. {7} RIP @ 59, John Hughes [see p.63]. ☞ 'Great Train Robber' Ronnie Biggs was released from prison on compassionate grounds. {9} A British security guard shot and killed 2 colleagues after a drunken argument in the Green Zone in Baghdad. ☞ 3 bombs exploded in Majorca, no one was injured; ETA was thought responsible. {10} >40 were killed and >200 injured after 4 bombs exploded in Baghdad and Mosul. ☞ Research

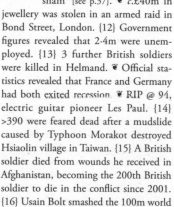

Aung San Suu Kyi

Our justice system demands that justice be imposed but compassion be available.
– KENNY MACASKILL, Scot. Justice Sec.

published in the *BMJ* suggested that antiviral drugs such as Tamiflu were unlikely to help children who caught A(H1N1). {11} Those involved in the death of Baby P were named after a court order protecting their anonymity expired. ☞ Typhoon Morakot battered China and Taiwan causing numerous buildings to collapse and killing hundreds of people. ☞ Burma's pro-democracy leader Aung San Suu Kyi was sentenced to a further 18 months' house arrest for breaking the conditions of her previous detention; Gordon Brown denounced the trial as a 'sham' [see p.37]. ☞ *c.*£40m in jewellery was stolen in an armed raid in Bond Street, London. {12} Government figures revealed that 2·4m were unemployed. {13} 3 further British soldiers were killed in Helmand. ☞ Official statistics revealed that France and Germany had both exited recession. ☞ RIP @ 94, electric guitar pioneer Les Paul. {14} >390 were feared dead after a mudslide caused by Typhoon Morakot destroyed Hsiaolin village in Taiwan. {15} A British soldier died from wounds he received in Afghanistan, becoming the 200th British soldier to die in the conflict since 2001. {16} Usain Bolt smashed the 100m world record in Berlin; his time was 9·58s [see p.298]. {17} Japan announced it had exited recession. {19} >85 were killed and >500 injured in bombs across Baghdad. {20} The Scottish Justice Sec. announced the release of Megrahi [see p.37]; President Obama called the move 'a mistake'. ☞ The Afghan presidential elections were held [see p.25]. ☞ Usain Bolt smashed another world record in Berlin; he ran the 200m in 19·19s. {21} Relatives of those killed in Lockerbie reacted with

——————— IN BRIEF · AUGUST – SEPTEMBER 2009 ———————

disgust at the hero's welcome Megrahi received in Tripoli. {22} Election monitors reported that the Afghan election was 'generally fair' despite 'intimidation' and 'fraud'. {23} England regained the Ashes after beating Australia in the final test at the Oval [see p.27]. {24} Leaked court documents revealed that Michael Jackson had lethal levels of the drug propofol in his body when he died. {25} >40 died when a car bomb exploded in Kandahar, Afghanistan. {26} RIP @ 77, Edward Kennedy [see p.63]. {27} The population of Britain hit 61m. {28} An American girl abducted in 1991, at the age of 11, reappeared and confirmed her identity to police; Jaycee Lee Dugard had reportedly borne 2 children by her kidnapper [see p.34]. {29} A US coroner ruled that Jackson's death was homicide due to 'acute anaesthetic intoxication'. {30} It was revealed that, in 2007, Justice Sec. Jack Straw had agreed that Megrahi would not be excluded from any prisoner transfer deals because of 'overwhelming national interests'. ❦ The Democratic Party of Japan won an landslide majority in Japan's general election, ending >50 years of Liberal Democratic Party rule. ❦ RIP @ 74, Simon Dee [see p.63]. {31} 2 British soldiers were killed while on foot patrol in Helmand.

Al-Megrahi

At times I didn't think we were going to get there, but that makes it more special. – ANDREW STRAUSS

SEPTEMBER · {1} Libya began elaborate celebrations to mark 40 years since Muammar Gaddafi seized power. {2} As questions continued to be asked about the release of Megrahi, Brown insisted there had been 'no cover-up'. {3} Defence secretary aide Eric Joyce resigned over Britain's Afghanistan strategy. ❦ 2 brothers aged 10 and 12 admitted to causing grievous bodily harm with intent to 2 boys aged 9 and 11 during a brutal attack in Edlington, Yorkshire. ❦ The body of British hostage Alec MacLachlan was handed to Iraqi authorities. {4} >90 were killed in N Afghanistan after Nato forces destroyed 2 fuel tankers hijacked by the Taliban. ❦ RIP @ 80, Keith Waterhouse [see p.351]. {5} Apprentice jockeys, Jamie Kyne (18) and Jan Wilson (19) died in a fire in N Yorkshire; arson was suspected. {6} After initially declining to help, Brown announced the government would support IRA victims' claims for compensation from Libya, which reportedly supplied the IRA with the Semtex. {7} 3 British men, Abdulla Ahmed Ali, 28, Tanvir Hussain, 28, and Assad Sarwar, 29, were found guilty at Woolwich Crown Court of plotting to blow up aircraft using bombs hidden in drink containers. ❦ Israel approved the building of >450 new homes in occupied areas of the West Bank. {8} A 600lb bomb was discovered close to the Irish border in S Armagh; the device, thought to be planted by dissident Republicans, was safely defused. {9} Liverpool FC fan Michael Shields was granted a Royal Pardon; he had spent 4 years in jail for the attempted murder of a Bulgarian barman. The Justice Sec. Jack Straw, said Shields was 'morally and technically innocent'. ❦ A British soldier and an Afghan interpreter were killed during a mission to rescue a British journalist held captive by the Taliban. {10} GM Motors announced the sale of Vauxhall and Opel to the Canadian parts manufacturer Magna.

The daily chronicle will continue in the 2011 edition of Schott's Almanac.

───────── SOME GREAT LIVES IN BRIEF ─────────

PAUL NEWMAN
26·1·1925–26·9·2008 (83)

For 50 years as one of Hollywood's leading leading men, Newman's nuanced interpretations of anti-hcrocs earned him critical acclaim, and his boyish charm delighted female fans. A fixture of the silver screen in the 1960s and '70s, Newman finally won an Oscar in 1986 for *The Colour of Money*. Off-screen, his passions included motor sport and philanthropy: his 'Newman's Own' range of foodstuffs and sauces raised >$200m for charity.

MICHAEL CRICHTON
23·10·1942–4·11·2008 (66)

Crichton wrote some of the most successful thrillers of the past 40 years, crafting high-tech novels that had a knack of translating into blockbuster films (*Jurassic Park* may be his greatest contribution to pop culture). He also found success in TV, not least as the creator of *ER*. In later years, he caused a ripple of controversy by questioning mankind's role in global warming.

OLIVER POSTGATE
12·4·1925–8·12·2008 (83)

Postgate used his remarkable skills as an author, animator, and puppeteer to revolutionise children's TV. Millions of Britons fondly remember *Bagpuss*, *The Pogles*, *Noggin the Nog*, *Ivor the Engine*, and *The Clangers* – and the continuing DVD sales of these low-fi classics mean that Postgate's work is likely to entertain many more generations to come.

HAROLD PINTER
10·10·1930–24·12·2008 (78)

Pinter exploded the conventions of theatre to create his own dramatic universe, one instantly recognisable for its preoccupation with power, control, and incipient violence. In 29 plays and 27 screenplays – from his early 'comedies of menace' to later works exploring political oppression – Pinter drew controversy, acclaim, and a host of awards – most notably the 2005 Nobel for literature, which he used to deliver a scathing attack on US foreign policy.

JOHN MORTIMER
21·4·1923–16·1·2009 (85)

Mortimer's fame as the creator of *Rumpole of the Bailey* (one of the few popular lawyers in fiction, or elsewhere) overshadowed his other writing and his work as a barrister. In the 1960s and '70s, when the public's decency was permanently outraged, Mortimer defended a host of contentious cases from *Oz* magazine to The Sex Pistols. But combining careers in fiction and fact was not easy: 'Rumpole would have got me off', complained one of Mortimer's legal clients.

TONY HART
15·10·1925–18·1·2009 (83)

Few artists did more than Hart to instil in children a love of art and a sense of its possibilities. On TV programmes such as *Blue Peter*, *Vision On*, *Take Hart*, and *Hart Beat*, Hart demonstrated that art could be made on any scale and with any material – not least plasticine, from which Hart's trusty, if hapless, sidekick Morph was fashioned.

JOHN UPDIKE
18·3·1932–27·1·2009 (76)

One of the greatest American writers of the C20th, Updike explored the beauty and banality of small-town, middle-class, white America. He will best be remembered for his *Rabbit* pentalogy – five novels that chronicled the quotidian adventures of car salesman 'Rabbit' Angstrom. On occasion, critics found

─────────── SOME GREAT LIVES IN BRIEF cont. ───────────

Updike's work devoid of deeper meaning; he claimed that his aim was merely 'to give the mundane its beautiful due'.

WENDY RICHARD
20·7·1943–26·2·2009 (65)

Although Richard acted in a wide variety of parts, she found fame in two long-running and much loved roles: the cocky Cockney junior Miss Shirley Brahms in *Are You Being Served?*, and the salt of the earth and down to earth matriarch Pauline Fowler in *EastEnders*. In 2000, Richard was awarded an MBE for services to television drama.

NATASHA RICHARDSON
11·5·1963–18·3·2009 (45)

The granddaughter of Sir Michael Redgrave and the daughter of Vanessa Redgrave, Richardson was born into British theatrical royalty. Yet it was in America that she made her mark, both in Hollywood (first in art-house films and later in more commercial roles) and on Broadway (where she earned a Tony for *Cabaret* in 1988). Her premature and unexpected death after a skiing accident dismayed her many fans.

CLEMENT FREUD
24·4·1924–15·4·2009 (84)

Journalist and author, chef and food critic, politician and pundit, gambler and racehorse owner, speaker and raconteur, Freud was a man of many talents. His manner, inevitably described as 'lugubrious', matched well his hangdog expression, and his ready, deadpan wit served him well – not least as a favourite fixture on Radio 4's *Just a Minute*.

J.G. BALLARD
15·11·1930–19·4·2009 (78)

Ballard navigated the psychological undercurrents of the C20th to write bleak and bizarre tales of modernity gone awry. He achieved notoriety with his 1973 novel *Crash*, and mainstream success with 1984's *Empire of the Sun*, but much of his wide output was boundary-pushing. The adjective 'Ballardian' entered the language to describe his uniquely dystopian aesthetic.

DANNY LA RUE (Daniel Patrick Carroll)
26·7·1927–31·5·2009 (81)

A self-described 'comic in a frock', la Rue made female impersonation so acceptable that, in 2002, he was awarded the OBE. La Rue would walk on stage, in sequins and diamonds, and break the spell with a very masculine 'Wotcha, mates!' 'Sleazy impersonators get their laughs by having people laugh at them', la Rue once observed. 'I do the reverse. I love laughter, glitter, and glamour'.

OMAR BONGO
30·12·1935–8·6·2009 (73)

Africa's longest-serving leader, Bongo ruled the small, oil-rich African nation of Gabon for 41 years. Despite accusations of trading resources for political support, his reign was recognised as largely peaceful. At his death, Bongo was one of the richest heads of state in the world – maintaining 39 properties in France, as well as his 30 children.

FARRAH FAWCETT
2·2·1947–25·6·2009 (62)

Fawcett's wide smile and blonde mane helped make her the 'face of the 1970s', first in *Charlie's Angels* and then beaming out from an iconic poster that decked the bedrooms of millions of adolescent American boys. Yet the queen of 'jiggle TV' was determined to be something more, and in the 1980s she took on demanding roles that finally earned her critical respect, notably as

──────── SOME GREAT LIVES IN BRIEF cont. ────────

the victim of male violence in *The Burning Bed* (1984) and *Extremities* (1986).

MOLLIE SUGDEN
21·7·1922–1·7·2009 (86)

A graduate of the Guildhall School of Music and Drama and a talented repertory player, Sugden achieved cult status as Betty Slocombe, the elaborately coiffured and innuendo-prone co-star of *Are You Being Served?* No episode of this britcom was complete without a reference to Mrs Slocombe's pussy, and few actresses could deliver with Sugden's poise lines such as, 'Captain Peacock, I do not respond to any man's finger!'

HENRY ALLINGHAM
6·6·1896–18·7·2009 (113)
HARRY PATCH
17·6·1898–25·7·2009 (111)

At his death, Allingham was the oldest-known man in the world, and the oldest surviving veteran of WWI. He joined the Royal Naval Air Service in 1915, serving as a mechanic and a bomber, and he witnessed the Battle of Jutland. In 1918, he became a founding member of the RAF. After a postwar career in the motor industry, Allingham devoted his retirement to speaking about the war in the hope that future generations would never forget the sacrifice of his comrades. ❦ Patch was the last surviving British soldier to have fought in the trenches. He was wounded at the Battle of Passchendaele in 1917, in which he was a machine gunner. Yet he demurred from speaking about his service until the age of 100. Patch never gloried in his status as 'the last fighting Tommy', famously calling war 'organised murder … and nothing else'. ❦ The deaths of Allingham and Patch within just days of one another closed a tragic chapter in British history and highlighted the inestimable power of personal testimony.

JOHN HUGHES
18·2·1950–6·8·2009 (59)

The 'bard of teen angst', Hughes wrote and directed bittersweet comedies such as *Sixteen Candles* (1984), *The Breakfast Club* (1985), and *Ferris Bueller's Day Off* (1986). He later turned his hand to slapstick, including *Home Alone* (1990), before vanishing from Hollywood, leaving his signature on pop culture. As he had Ferris Bueller say: 'Life moves pretty fast – you don't stop and look around once in a while, you could miss it.'

EDWARD KENNEDY
22·2·1932–25·8·2009 (77)

Kennedy laboured in the shadow of his brothers John and Robert before becoming himself one of the most respected Congressional Democrats – renowned for a passionate advocacy of civil rights, education, and health-care. Blessed with the Kennedy charisma, he could not escape the family 'curse', and the 1969 'Chappaquiddick incident', in which 28-year-old Mary Jo Kopechne died as a result of his driving, dogged him all the way to a disastrous presidential run in 1980. Nevertheless, his long record of service may have been the fullest flowering of the Kennedy dream.

SIMON DEE
28·7·1935–29·8·2009 (74)

As a DJ and a chatshow host, Dee was an icon of the Swinging '60s, and the model for Austin Powers. Yet, his moment in the limelight was as dazzling as his fall from fame was breakneck; from a suave playboy whose TV show garnered 18m viewers he became an eccentric and indebted recluse – a journey since dubbed 'Simon Dee Syndrome'.

The World

Let the great world spin forever down the ringing grooves of change.
— ALFRED TENNYSON (1809–92)

PANDEMIC ALERT PHASES

On 11 June, 2009, the World Health Organisation escalated its pandemic alert level to 6, declaring swine flu to be a global pandemic [see p.23]. The WHO's alert levels – developed in 2005 amidst concern over avian flu H5N1 – are designed to help governments, business, and the pharmaceutical industry prepare for and respond to epidemics. Broadly speaking, phases 1 through 3 signal a focus on preparation, phase 4 signals a focus on containment, and phases 5 and 6 signal a focus on reduction and mitigation. A simplified outline of the alert phases appears below[†]:

Level	pandemic probability	description
1	Uncertain	*no human infections from viruses circulating in animals*
2	Uncertain	*an animal virus has caused a human infection and is considered a specific potential pandemic threat*
3	Uncertain	*sporadic cases or small clusters of an animal or human-animal virus in humans, but no human-to-human community-level outbreaks*
4	Medium–High	*community-level outbreaks of an animal or human-animal virus, created by human-to-human transmission*
5	High–Certain	*community-level outbreaks in >2 nations in a WHO region[‡]*
6	Pandemic Underway	*community-level outbreaks in 2 WHO regions[‡]*

The UK maintains its own system of alerts that are designed to be used once the WHO has declared an alert level of 6. The UK's system of pandemic alerts is:

Level	description	organisations advised to …
1	No UK cases	*focus on preparation*
2	Virus isolated in UK	*investigate cases and slow contagion; those who are ill advised to stay home*
3	Outbreaks in UK	*ensure access to care, maintain supplies, adapt services to surge capacity, strengthen infection control*
4	Widespread in UK	*maintain essential services, minimise social disruptions, enhance monitoring, develop vaccine*

† During the swine flu outbreak, some government health officials said the declaration of a level 6 alert had created undue panic, and they criticised the WHO alert levels for focusing solely on geographic spread while failing to take into account disease severity (thus far, swine flu has proved relatively mild). The WHO admitted that the phases had been designed for the deadlier avian flu, and in May, announced it would reconsider its criteria for declaring level 6. ‡ The WHO is organised into six regions: Africa, the Americas, the Eastern Mediterranean, Europe, South-East Asia, and the Western Pacific.

———————————— CLIMATE REFUGEES ————————————

As the effects of climate change have become more severe, a new class of displaced person has emerged: the 'climate refugee'. The Intergovernmental Panel on Climate Change (IPCC) has estimated that, by 2050, 150m such refugees could be moving across the globe – a process known as 'climigration'. A 2008 report by the Norwegian Refugee Council outlined some of the ways climigration could increase:

Sudden disasters, such as floods and storms, force people to flee
'Slow-onset disasters', such as drought and desertification, force
people to move elsewhere in search of jobs and resources
Increased competition for resources leads to conflict and war
Rising sea levels cause some parts of the
world to disappear altogether[†]

Climigration is already a fact in many parts of the world. The thousands displaced by Hurricane Katrina in 2005 have been called 'the first documented mass movement of climate refugees', and the UN Environmental Program has said that climigration helped ignite the conflict in Darfur. Other reports of climate refugees appear below:

In 1995, >500,000 people were forced to evacuate Bhola Island in Bangladesh after rising sea levels caused the island to flood. ❦ In 2008, the President of the Maldives, the lowest-lying nation in the world, announced a trust fund to buy a new homeland, if necessary. ❦ The government of Tuvalu has appealed to Australia and New Zealand to accept its citizens as refugees, amid fears the island nation could become uninhabitable by 2050. ❦ The President of Kiribati has also asked Australia and New Zealand to consider taking in refugees; two of the nation's islands have already been submerged. ❦ On the Carteret Islands in Papua New Guinea, a government resettlement programme is already under way; some reports estimate that the islands will be under water by 2015. ❦ Citizens of the village of Newtok, Alaska, voted in 2009 to move their settlement 9 miles inland because of flooding and melting permafrost.

[†] In 2009, the UN Environmental Program reported that new studies had shown a probable global sea level rise of *c*.1 metre over the coming century. Such an increase would displace *c*.100m people in Asia (mostly E China, Bangladesh, and Vietnam); 14m in Europe; and 8m in both Africa and South America. A June 2009 study found that 40 island nations could disappear if the seas rise by 2 metres.

———————— INTERNALLY DISPLACED MIGRANTS ————————

26m people around the world were 'internally displaced' at the end of 2008 – that is, they had been forced from their homes due to conflict or violence but had not crossed an international border. Below are the countries with the most internally displaced migrants, according to the Internal Displacement Monitoring Centre:

Sudan	4,900,000 people	DR Congo	1,400,000
Colombia	2,650,000–4,360,000	Somalia	1,300,000
Iraq	2,840,000	[See p.73]	

GLOBAL POPULATION GROWTH

7bn people will inhabit the globe by 2012, according to UN estimates. By 2050, the number could exceed 9bn. The bulk of this increase is set to occur in the developing world, where the population will rise from 5·6bn in 2009 to 7·9bn in 2050. The population of the developed world, however, is likely to stabilise. Below are the 10 most populous countries as of 2009 and 2050, according to UN estimates:

Country	2009 pop. (m)	rank	2050 pop. (m)	country
China	1,346	1	1,614	India
India	1,198	2	1,417	China
US	315	3	404	US
Indonesia	230	4	335	Pakistan
Brazil	194	5	289	Nigeria
Pakistan	181	6	288	Indonesia
Bangladesh	162	7	222	Bangladesh
Nigeria	155	8	219	Brazil
Russia	141	9	174	Ethiopia
Japan	127	10	148	DR Congo

POPULATION BY CONTINENT

Year	World	Africa	N America	S America	Asia	Europe	Oceania
Millions							
1980	4,438	482	254	240	2,623	693	23
1990	5,290	639	283	296	3,179	721	27
2000	6,115	819	319	347	3,698	727	31
2010	6,909	1,033	352	393	4,167	733	36
2020	7,675	1,277	383	430	4,596	733	40
2030	8,309	1,524	410	458	4,917	723	45
2040	8,801	1,770	431	475	5,125	708	48
2050	9,150	1,998	448	483	5,231	691	51

WORLD BIRTH & DEATH RATES

Births	time unit	deaths	change
134,434,533	*per* YEAR	56,622,740	+77,811,793
11,202,878	*per* MONTH	4,718,562	+6,484,316
368,314	*per* DAY	155,131	+213,183
15,346	*per* HOUR	6,464	+8,883
256	*per* MINUTE	108	+148
4·3	*per* SECOND	1·8	+2·5

[Source: US Census Bureau, 2009 · Figures may not add up to totals because of rounding]

———————— WORLD ENVIRONMENTAL OPINION ————————

Only 22% of people around the globe rate the condition of the world's environment 'excellent' or 'good', according to the market information group TNS. In 2008, the company surveyed people in 17 countries about their views on the environment, asking them to rate its condition in their own country, and across the Earth as a whole. The survey also asked respondents to name the environmental problem that caused them the most concern. Lastly, respondents were asked whether they had changed their behaviour to help improve the environment – 40% claimed they had.

%	World environ. rated 'excellent or good'	Country environ. rated 'excellent or good'	Top environmental concern	Changed behaviour to benefit environ.
Argentina	9	21	water pollution	67
Australia	29	58	air pollution	53
Brazil	8	17	water pollution	65
France	8	27	air pollution	37
Germany	13	43	air pollution	28
Hong Kong	35	33	air pollution	33
Italy	14	24	air pollution	37
Japan	7	22	air pollution	34
Korea	15	29	air pollution	19
Malaysia	25	40	air pollution	45
Mexico	11	11	water pollution	74
Russia	10	12	air pollution	29
Singapore	36	81	air pollution	49
Spain	20	47	air pollution	55
Thailand	37	35	air pollution	68
UK	29	51	air poll./over-development[†]	51
USA	36	51	air pollution	36
WORLD	22	38	air pollution	40

† Air pollution and over-development tied at 24% of the vote in the UK. 23% said deforestation, 7% nuclear waste, 7% toxic waste, 5% water pollution, and the rest said 'something else' or 'nothing'.

———————— UK CLIMATE PREDICTIONS 2009 ————————

In June 2009, the Met Office Hadley Centre released a collection of online resources to help decision-makers understand how the climate might change in their region. While some scientists criticised the methodology underlying these projections, most agreed with their overall thrust: i.e., the weather in the UK looks set to change significantly over the coming century. According to the projections, in the 2080s, London's weather will be 3°C warmer in the winter and 3.9°C warmer in the summer, as well as 20% wetter in the winter and 22% drier in the summer (compared to 1961–1990 averages). Potential consequences include water shortages, wildfires, storm surges, crop failures, and the need to replace the Thames Barrier by 2070.

———————— MOST WAR-PRONE COUNTRIES ————————

In October 2008, the Human Security Report Project at Simon Fraser University in Canada released the *miniAtlas of Human Security*, a collection of statistics on war and armed conflict across the globe between 1946–2005. According to the report, the UK has engaged in more international armed conflicts than any other country in this period (see below), though Israel has spent the most *time* in armed conflict:

Most international armed conflicts[†]	*Most years spent in armed conflict*[‡]
UK 22	Israel 58
France 19	Myanmar 57
United States 17	Philippines 50
Australia 8	UK 49
Netherlands 8	India 48
Portugal 8	Ethiopia 44
Chad 7	Colombia 43
Russia (USSR) 7	Indonesia 41
Spain 7	Iraq 41

(Pre-1991 data for Russia include the entire Soviet Union; 1991–2005 data include only the Russian Federation.) † International conflicts and civil wars involving external military forces. ‡ Any conflict involving government forces. In both columns, only conflicts with ≥25 battle deaths were included.

The United Kingdom's count of 22 conflicts included those with >25 casualties in:

Israel 1946	Brunei 1962	Al-Qaeda 2001–
Albania 1946	Indonesia/Malaysia	Iraq 2003
Malaysia 1948–57	1963–66	Afghanistan 2003–
N Korea 1949–53	Yemen 1964–67	Iraq (insurgents) 2004–
Egypt 1951–52	Northern Ireland........	
Kenya 1952–56	1971–91, 1998	[Source: Centre for the Study
Cyprus 1955–59	Oman 1972–75	of Civil Wars, International
Suez 1956	Argentina 1982	Peace Research Institute,
Oman 1957	Yugoslavia 1999	Oslo and the Uppsala
Malaysia 1958–60	Sierra Leone 2000	Conflict Data Program]

———————— VIOLENCE AGAINST AID WORKERS ————————

122 humanitarian aid workers were killed in 2008, the highest total since records began 12 years ago, according to the Overseas Development Institute. Violence was concentrated in Somalia, Afghanistan, and Sudan, which together accounted for 60% of serious incidents. A summary of 2008's aid-worker attacks is given below:

Total victims 260	UN victims 65	Donor/other victims .. 4
Total killed 122	Red Cross victims..... 4	
Total injured 76	IFRC[†] victims......... 1	† Intl. Fed. of Red Cross and
Total kidnapped......62	NGO victims 185	Red Crescent Societies

————————— NOBEL PEACE PRIZE —————————

The 2008 Nobel Peace Prize was awarded to MARTTI AHTISAARI (1937–)

*for his important efforts, on several continents and over more
than three decades, to resolve international conflicts*

Martti Oiva Kalevi Ahtisaari was born in 1937 in Viipuri, Finland. In 1940 Viipuri was ceded to Russia as part of the peace treaty that ended the Soviet-Finnish War, and the town's residents were forced to evacuate. Ahtisaari has said that this early experience of displacement influenced his later life as a negotiator for peace. However, Ahtisaari's first ambition was not diplomacy, but to be a primary school teacher. On completing his teacher training in 1959, he moved to Karachi to work on an educational project. While in Pakistan, he developed a taste for international politics and, in 1965, joined Finland's Ministry of Foreign Affairs. ❦ Ahtisaari's first major accomplishments came in Namibia, which was involved in a protracted struggle for independence from South Africa. Ahtisaari furthered Namibia's independence in a variety of posts. First, he worked as the Finnish ambassador to Tanzania, Zambia, Somalia, and Mozambique, during which time he developed contacts with local liberation organisations. After he was appointed as the UN Commissioner for Namibia in 1977, he oversaw dialogue between liberation groups, the UN, and the Organization of African Unity. Finally, as the Special Representative for the UN's Transition Assistance Group for Namibia, Ahtisaari supervised the country's transition to self-rule and, in 1989, its first democratic elections. As a reward for his work, he was made an honorary Namibian

Martti Ahtisaari

citizen; today, Ahtisaari is not an uncommon first name among Namibian children. ❦ In 1994, Ahtisaari was elected to the first and only political office of his career: the Finnish presidency. In this post, in addition to supporting Finland's 1995 entry into the EU, he strove to create a pivotal role for his country in foreign affairs, travelling so often that he earned the nickname *Matka-Mara* or 'Travel-Mara' (Mara is a diminutive form of Martti). As president, Ahtisaari also worked as a behind-the-scenes negotiator in Kosovo, and in 1999 he succeeded in convincing Slobodan Milošević to accept a peace plan for the region. ❦ After his presidential term ended in 2000, Ahtisaari formed the independent Crisis Management Initiative. This organisation was instrumental in facilitating talks between rebel groups and the government in the Indonesian territory of Aceh, leading to the 2005 peace agreement that ended a 30-year war. Ahtisaari also served as a weapons inspector in N Ireland in 2001, helped mediate conflicts in the Horn of Africa from 2002, and arranged meetings between Iraqi Sunnis and Shiites in 2008. ❦ Many interpreted Ahtisaari's award as a return by the Nobel committee to recognising more traditional peacemaking, after recent prizes had rewarded work on poverty and the environment. In his acceptance speech, Ahtisaari said that 'peace is a question of will', and argued that 'all crises, including the one in the Middle East, can be resolved'.

———————————— POLITICAL TERROR SCALE ————————————

The Political Terror Scale (PTS) measures the extent of political violence, terror, and repression that a country's citizens experience in a given year. Developed by political science academics at the University of North Carolina and the human rights watchdog Freedom House, the PTS assigns countries one of the following ratings:

5	*terror affects entire population, leaders use any means to pursue their goals*
4	*rights violations affect many; murders, disappearances, and torture are common*
3	*extensive political imprisonment (or recent history of such), political murders and brutality common, unlimited detention, with or without trial*
2	*limited imprisonment for nonviolent political activity (but few affected), torture and beatings exceptional, political murder rare*
1	*secure rule of law, no imprisonment for political views, torture rare, political murders extremely rare*

Ratings are based on assessments of annual reports from Amnesty International, and the US State Department's Country Reports on Human Rights Practices. In 2008, the following countries were given PTS ratings of 5, based on conditions in 2007:

Afghanistan · DR Congo · Iraq · Myanmar · Somalia · Sri Lanka · Sudan

The following countries scored the highest average PTS ratings during 1976–2006:

Iraq ....4·64	Iran ....4·07	DR of the Congo ..3·96
Afghanistan ....4·62	Sudan ....4·04	Angola ....3·93
Colombia ....4·34	Ethiopia ....4·01	Uganda ....3·92
North Korea ....4·34	Myanmar ....3·97	Guatemala ....3·88

The UK was rated 2 in 2008; the US was rated 3 – based only on data from Amnesty International.

———————————————— UNION REPRESSION ————————————————

91 workers around the world were murdered in 2007 for participation in trade union activities, according to the International Trade Union Confederation (ITUC). The organisation's 2008 Annual Survey of Trade Union Rights Violations found that Latin America was the most dangerous continent for union members: Colombia was the most dangerous country (39 workers lost their lives there in 2007); Guinea was the second most dangerous (30 were killed). Union workers were also murdered in:

Argentina · Brazil · Cambodia · Chile · El Salvador · Ethiopia · Iraq · Mexico
Mozambique · Saudi Arabia · Panama · Peru · the Philippines · Zimbabwe

The ITUC also found that 73 union workers were imprisoned in 2007 (40 in Iran, 14 in Morocco, and 7 in Myanmar); 63 countries engaged in 'serious and systemic' harassment of union workers; and 15 countries passed new rules restricting union membership (most in Asia). A total of 183 countries were surveyed for the report.

—————————— PRESIDENTIAL MEDAL OF FREEDOM ——————————

In August 2009, President Obama presented the Medal of Freedom, the nation's highest civilian honour, to 16 'agents of change' – men and women who 'discovered new theories, launched new initiatives, and opened minds to new possibilities'. The Medal of Freedom was established by Harry Truman to honour those who served with merit in WWII, and was re-established by JFK in 1963 as a peacetime award for meritorious service. Because the medal is the sole gift of the President, recipients tend to reflect the vision of the Oval Office's occupant. Obama awarded medals to:

Nancy Brinker .... *breast cancer activist; founded Susan G. Komen for the Cure*
Pedro José Greer, Jr .... *doctor who provides medical care to the poor in Miami*
Stephen Hawking .... *renowned theoretical physicist and author*
Jack Kemp [posthumous] .... *former Republican senator and advocate for the poor*
Edward Kennedy .... *respected Democratic senator, champion of numerous causes*
Billie Jean King .... *tennis star and one of the first openly gay sports figures*
Rev. Joseph Lowery .... *civil rights leader in the US since the 1950s*
Joe Medicine Crow .... *last living Plains Indian war chief, and author*
Harvey Milk [posthumous] .... *politician and gay rights activist; murdered in 1977*
Sandra Day O'Connor .... *the first female Supreme Court justice*
Sidney Poitier .... *first major African-American movie star*
Chita Rivera .... *groundbreaking Hispanic actress, singer, and dancer*
Mary Robinson .... *first female President of Ireland*
Janet Davison Rowley .... *human geneticist and cancer researcher*
Desmond Tutu .... *leader of the anti-apartheid campaign in South Africa*
Muhammad Yunus .... *economist who pioneered the use of micro-finance*

—————————— WORLD'S WORST DICTATORS ——————————

The weekly magazine *Parade* publishes an annual list of the world's worst dictators, based on their record of human rights abuse. The 2009 top ten [facial hair added, Ed.]:

# ('08)	dictator	age	country	years' reign	facial hair?
1 (6)	Robert Mugabe	85	Zimbabwe	29	Hitler-esque
2 (2)	Omar al-Bashir	65	Sudan	20	goatee
3 (1)	Kim Jong-il	67	North Korea	15	none
4 (3)	Than Shwe	76	Myanmar	17	none
5 (4)	King Abdullah	85	Saudi Arabia	14	cavalier beard
6 (5)	Hu Jintao	66	China	7	none
7 (7)	Sayyid Ali Khamenei	69	Iran	20	bushy beard
8 (10)	Isayas Afewerki	63	Eritrea	18	full moustache
9 (–)	G. Berdymuhammedov†	51	Turkmenistan	3	none
10 (11)	Muammar al-Qaddafi	66	Libya	40	none

† 2009 marked Gurbanguly Berdymuhammedov's first appearance on *Parade*'s list. Since taking power in 2006, he has discontinued some of the most outrageous excesses of his predecessor, Saparmurat Niyazov, although Turkmenistan remains a one-party state with rigid controls on media and religion.

———————————————— BRIBERY INDEX ————————————————

In December 2008, a survey by Transparency International measured the extent of bribery (or perceptions of bribery) in 22 of the world's largest economies. 2,742 senior executives were asked to assess the level of bribery they perceived in countries in which they did business. (Executives were not asked to rate their own country.) Below are the countries said to be the most and least likely to require palm-greasing:

Least likely to engage in bribery	Most likely to engage in bribery
1 ....Belgium & Canada [tie]	1 .... Russia
3 ..... Netherlands & Switzerland [tie]	2 ....China
5 ....Germany, Japan, & UK [tie]	3 .... Mexico

Public works, real estate, and oil and gas were the sectors said to involve most bribes worldwide. · 53% thought the private sector was corrupt, according to another '09 survey by Transparency International.

———————————————— MEGA-DISASTERS ————————————————

'Mega-disasters' are those that kill >10,000 people or cause losses worth >$10bn, according to the UN International Strategy for Disaster Reduction. Below are the most fatal and costly disasters to occur between 1975–2008, according to the UN:

Disaster	fatalities	Disaster	total loss ($bn)
1983 *Ethiopian drought*	300,000	2005 *Hurricane Katrina*	125
1976 *Tangshan quake, China*	242,000	1995 *Kobe earthquake, Japan*	100
2004 *Indian Ocean tsunami*	226,408	2008 *Sichuan earthquake, China*	30
1983 *Sudan drought*	150,000	1998 *Yangtze flood, China*	30
1991 *Cyclone Gorky*	138,866	2004 *Chuetsu earthquake, Japan*	28

———————————————— YOUTH MURDER RATES ————————————————

Young people are statistically more likely to be murdered in Latin America than anywhere else in the world, according to a November 2008 report by the Latin American Technological Information Network. After comparing murder rates collected between 2002–06 in 83 countries, researchers discovered that a youth aged 15–24 is *c.*30 times more likely to be murdered in Latin America than in Europe. Researchers blamed the high murder rates on the prevalence of youth gangs, and on 'injustices derived from the concentration of income and wealth' in the region. Below are the the nations with the highest youth murder rates, and rates for some nations of note:

Rank	youth murder rates per 100,000		
1 ...... El Salvador................. 92·3	17..... USA......................... 12·9
2 ...... Colombia .... 73·4	19..... Mexico...................... 10·4
3 ...... Venezuela .... 64·2	41..... Canada....................... 2·5
4 ...... Guatemala .... 55·4	58..... Italy .... 1·3
5 ...... Brazil......................... 51·6	67..... UK .... 0·7
	76..... Japan .... 0·3

DEVELOPMENT AID · 2008

In 2008, development aid contributed by the Development Assistance Committee (a group of the world's major donors) rose to the highest total ever recorded: $119·8bn in net aid, according to the Organisation for Economic Co-operation and Development. The largest increases came from the US, UK, Spain, Germany, Japan, and Canada. Yet, only 5 of the 22 donors contributed the UN target of 0·7% of their gross national income. A breakdown of 2008 development aid appears below:

Country	aid $m	% income†		Country	aid $m	% income†
US	26,008	0·18		Australia	3,166	0·34
Germany	13,910	0·38		Denmark	2,800	0·82
UK	11,409	0·43		Belgium	2,381	0·47
France	10,957	0·39		Switzerland	2,016	0·41
Japan	9,362	0·18		Austria	1,681	0·42
Netherlands	6,993	0·80		Ireland	1,325	0·58
Spain	6,686	0·43		Finland	1,139	0·43
Sweden	4,730	0·98		Greece	693	0·20
Canada	4,725	0·32		Portugal	614	0·27
Italy	4,444	0·20		Luxembourg	409	0·92
Norway	3,967	0·88		New Zealand	346	0·30

† % of gross national income

Top recipients of UK aid			
India	$510·5m	Afghanistan	268·7	Pakistan	197·8
Ethiopia	291·5	Bangladesh	245·6	Uganda	167·2
Nigeria	286·0	Tanzania	231·8	China	162·4
		Sudan	206·2	[2007 data; most recent available]

ASYLUM LEVELS & TRENDS · 2008

Global asylum applications (those seeking formal refugee status) rose 12% between 2007–08, led by a surge in applicants from Afghanistan and Somalia, according to the UN High Commissioner for Refugees. The top 2008 countries of origin for refugees were:

Origin†	applications	'07–'08 ±%		Origin†	applications	'07–'08 ±%
Iraq	40,483	−10		Serbia	15,204	−5
Somalia	21,823	+77		Nigeria	13,708	+71
Russian Fed.	20,477	+9		Pakistan	13,268	−8
Afghanistan	18,459	+85		Eritrea	12,309	+34
China	17,428	+1		Mexico	12,169	+27
				All countries	382,670	+12

Below are the nations that received the most applicants, with the change since 2007:

Destination	apps	±%				
US	49,020	−3	Canada	36,900	+30	Italy	31,160	+122
			France	35,160	+20	UK	30,550	+8

† Data on individual countries of origin are based on applications submitted to 44 industrialised countries. The total listed in 'all countries' is based on data from all 51 countries monitored by the UN.

———————————————— POLAR ICE ————————————————

In April 2009, an Antarctic 'ice bridge' that connected the Wilkins ice shelf to two nearby islands collapsed – potentially precipitating the disintegration of the 10,300 km² Wilkins ice shelf itself. ❦ Ice shelves are thick lips of frozen water that extend from grounded ice sheets out over the ocean. Because they rest on water rather than frozen rock, ice shelves respond more quickly to the effects of climate change than other forms of polar ice. Although scientists predict that the disintegration of the Wilkins shelf will not contribute to a rise in sea levels (since the shelf already floats on water) the collapse of other shelves could cause glaciers and ice streams to empty out into the sea. Already, six Antarctic ice shelves have collapsed in the past 30 years. The largest remaining Antarctic ice shelves are listed below:

Ross	472,960 km²	Fimbul	41,060 km²
Ronne-Filchner	422,420 km²	Shackleton	33,820 km²
Amery	62,620 km²	George VI	23,880 km²
Larsen C	48,600 km²	West	16,370 km²
Riiser-Larsen	48,180 km²	Wilkins	13,680 km²

Polar ice in the Arctic has been declining for the past 30 years, at a rate of *c.*4% per decade. In September 2007, the extent of the ice was at a 30-year low. Recent measurements of sea ice, taken each September at its annual minimum, are listed below:

Year	size of sea ice (km²)	% ± avg†	Year	size of sea ice (km²)	% ± avg†
2008	4·67m	–33·6	2005	5·57m	–20·9
2007‡	4·28m	–39·2	2004	6·04m	–14·2
2006	5·89m	–16·3	2003	6·15m	–12·6
			2002	5·96m	–15·3

† Average 1979–2000. ‡ Record 30-year low. [Sources: National Snow & Ice Data Center; UNEP]

———————————— THE MONACO DECLARATION ————————————

The acidification of the world's oceans is a serious threat to marine ecosystems, according to the Monaco Declaration signed by 155 scientists in October 2008. The Declaration states that, largely as a result of CO_2 created by humans, ocean acidity has increased by 30% since the C18th, which translates to a drop of approximately 0·1 units on the pH scale. Overly acidic water causes a number of problems, not least hampering the ability of marine organisms to build shells and skeletons, which in turn retards the development of fish stocks and coral reefs. If current trends continue, most of the world's waters will be inhospitable to coral reefs by 2050 – exposing shorelines to erosion, and potentially costing billions of dollars in lost tourism. As a result of these concerns, the Monaco Declaration called for further research, better coordination between scientists and policy-makers, and 'urgent plans to cut emissions drastically' at the 2009 UN Climate Change Conference in Copenhagen.

In October 2008, researchers at the US Monterey Bay Aquarium showed that rising ocean acidity has also made the seas noisier, which could disrupt communication between marine animals.

───────ENDANGERED MIGRATORY SPECIES───────

In December 2008, 21 species were granted increased protection under the UN-administered Convention of Migratory Species of Wild Animals. Since 1979, the Convention has protected endangered wild mammals, birds, reptiles and fish that roam across national boundaries. By signing up to the convention, countries are required to conserve habitats, remove obstacles to migration, and ban hunting of animals protected by the treaty. Species are protected under two lists: Appendix I lists species threatened with extinction, and Appendix II lists animals with 'unfavourable conservation status'. The following species were added to the lists in 2008:

Appendix I	Appendix II
Bottlenose dolphin (Black Sea pop.)	*Harbour porpoise (NW African pop.)*
Irrawaddy dolphin · Atlantic humpback	*Risso's dolphin (Mediterranean pop.)*
dolphin · Cheetah · W Afr. manatee	*Bottlenose dolphin (Mediterranean pop.)*
Barbary sheep · Baer's pochard	*Clymene dolphin (W African pop.)*
Egyptian vulture · Saker falcon	*African wild dog · Saiga*
Peruvian tern · Yellow-breasted bunting	*Maccoa duck · African skimmer*
Cerulean warbler · Streaked reed-warbler	*Mako sharks · Porbeagle · Spiny dogfish*

Since 2006, the Convention's Secretariat has chosen one species or issue per year on which to focus its conservation efforts. 2006 was the Year of the Turtle; 2007–08 was the Year of the Dolphin; 2009 was the Year of the Gorilla; 2010 is the Year of Biodiversity; and 2011 is set to be the Year of the Bat.

───────────THE RED LIST · 2008───────────

The World Conservation Union (IUCN) publishes an annual 'Red List' of plant and animal species under threat – classifying them according to the following scheme:

Least Concern (LC) → *Near Threatened (NT)* → *Vulnerable (VU)* → *Endangered (EN)*
  → *Critically Endangered (CR)* → *Extinct in the Wild (EW)* → *Extinct (EX)*

44,838 species were included on the 2008 Red List, of which 16,928 (38%) were considered threatened with extinction. Of these, 8,912 were listed as Vulnerable, 4,770 as Endangered, and 3,246 as Critically Endangered. Below are some of the species whose status declined since the 2007 list, and the threats these species face:

Species	status change	threatened by
Tasmanian Devil	LC→EN	fatal infectious facial cancer
The Fishing cat	VU→EN	habitat loss in wetlands
Caspian seal	VU→EN	unsustainable hunting & habitat degradation
Holdridge's toad	CR→EX	likely chytridiomycosis[†] and climate change
The Cuban crocodile	EN→CR	illicit hunting for its meat and its skin

The IUCN is currently working on a tool to track overall extinction risk within a taxonomic group, based on a sample of *c.*1,500 species – a measurement it says will be the 'Dow Jones Index' of biodiversity. † A fungal skin infection that kills amphibians, linked to frog extinctions over the last 15 years.

———————————— DEADLY DOZEN DISEASES ————————————

In October 2008, the Wildlife Conservation Society released a list of twelve deadly diseases that are likely to spread as a result of climate change. The Society called for the establishment of wildlife monitoring networks to identify signs of these diseases in animal populations, before they spread to humans. According to scientists, the warmer weather and disrupted rainfall patterns of climate change are responsible for the increased spread of many diseases, including the dozen tabulated below:

Disease	climate change concerns
Avian influenza	*disrupted flight patterns may see wild and domestic birds mingle*
Babesiosis	*spread by ticks, which may multiply due to climate change*
Cholera	*highly temperature dependent, widespread outbreaks expected*
Ebola	*outbreaks linked to disruptions in rainfall patterns*
Parasites	*changes in temperature and rainfall will help parasites spread*
Lyme disease	*spread by ticks, which may multiply in warmer weather*
Plague	*spread by rodents and fleas, which may multiply in warmer weather*
Red tides [algal bloom]	*temperature changes thought to have an unpredictable effect*
Rift Valley fever	*outbreaks follow heavy rainfalls; can be spread by mosquitoes*
Sleeping sickness	*transmitted by the tsetse fly, whose distributions are changing*
Tuberculosis	*less water causes livestock to drink at the same spots as infected animals*
Yellow fever	*carried by mosquitoes, which are spreading into new areas*

———————————— TRIANGLES OF DEATH ————————————

The US military returned control of Iraq's so-called *Triangle of Death* to Iraqi forces in October 2008. The triangle is located in central Iraq and defined by Mahmudiyah to the north, Yusufiyah to the west, and Iskandariyah to the south. Between 2004–07, the area was home to a simmering Sunni insurgency that launched hundreds of terrorist attacks. Strangely, the area is not the world's only triangle to contain more than its fair share of sinister activity – of both terrestrial and other-worldly varieties:

The *Bermuda Triangle* in the North Atlantic is bounded by Florida, Puerto Rico, and Bermuda. According to some authors, more than 50 ships and 20 planes have vanished in this triangle. (The most famous mystery concerns Flight 19 – when five US Navy bomber planes simply disappeared during a training mission off Florida in 1945.) Marine experts note frequent storms and strong currents which batter the region, while occultists have seized on the idea that the triangle lies near the lost city of Atlantis, where powerful 'fire crystals' wreak havoc with technical equipment. ❦ The *Bridgewater Triangle* in Massachusetts, USA, is the location of countless reports of UFOs, prehistoric beasts, and 'Bigfoot'. ❦ The *Golden Triangle* includes parts of Myanmar, Laos, and Thailand, and is one of Asia's primary centres of opium production. ❦ The *Michigan Triangle*, located in central Lake Michigan, is famous for sightings of sea monsters and ghost ships. ❦ The *Dragon's Triangle* of the Pacific, including parts of Japan, Guam, and Taiwan, is said to contain lost vessels and ghost ships, and to explain the 1937 disappearance of Amelia Earhart.

———— UK ENVIRONMENTAL INDICATORS ————

As part of its mission to protect the air, land, and water of England and Wales, the Environment Agency keeps track of thirty indicators that reveal how the natural environment has been responding to various pressures. Recent trends for each of these indicators, based on the latest information from the Agency, are listed below:

Aerial emissions from industrial processes[†]	reduced over the past decade
Air pollution	reduced 1993–2002, but particles and ozone remain a problem
Bathing water quality	major improvement since 1990
Dangerous substances in water	considerable decrease since 1990
Electricity from renewable sources	increase since 1988
Energy consumption	overall increase since 1980
	(industry use has been decreasing, but transport use is up)
Flood levels in rivers	some increase in frequency of peak river levels
Greenhouse gas emissions	fell 12·8% 1990–2000, now slower decrease
Groundwater levels	low in 1992, 1996, and 1997; maximum levels 2000–01
Household waste & recycling	increase in waste, but also recycling, since 1996
Hazardous waste arisings	no clear trend, annual variation
Household water use	risen 70% over the past 30 years [see p.186]
Nuclear industry discharges	decrease in air & water discharges in past 20 years
Nutrients in rivers	phosphate in English rivers increased since 1995 (decreased in Wales); nitrate in England/Wales increased 1995–2000, but now decreasing
Otter occurrence[‡]	significant increase over past 25 years
Pesticide use in agriculture/horticulture	declined in early 1990s, constant since
Pesticides in fresh waters	no clear trend, depends on the chemical
Pollution incidents	long-term decrease in water pollution incidents
Quality of surroundings	householders have reported litter, rubbish and graffiti less frequently since 1992; noise complaints have remained constant
Radioactive waste stocks	stores are steadily increasing
Rainfall in summer and winter	increase in total precipitation over past 40 years
River flows	annual fluctuation, no clear trend
Rivers of good quality	significant improvement since 1990
Sea level change	a rise of c.1mm per year (from various sites starting 1830–c.1900)
Soil loss to development	c.7,200 hectares developed each year 1985–96, but a decrease 2000–02
Temperature in central England	warmed c.0·6°C during C20th
Thames Barrier closures against tidal surges [§]	before 1990, 1–2 closures per year; since 1990, an average of 4 per year
Waste arisings and management	increase since 1998
Water taken from freshwater sources	more water taken for public supply since 1970, but less taken for industry
Wild bird pop.	declining since mid–1970s; woodland birds may be recovering

† Of the 1,600 industrial processes regulated by the Agency. ‡ According to the Agency, otters are a good indicator of river quality because they thrive with clean water, abundant food sources, and lush vegetation. § The Agency noted that, because climate change is likely to increase flooding, and the Thames Barrier is closed against floods, the closures could be a useful indicator of climate change.

——————— WORLD'S BEST CITIES ———————

In 2009, Citi Private Bank and the London-based property consultancy Knight Frank ranked the world's top cities based on measures of economic activity, political power, intellectual influence, and quality of life (see below). The ranking was designed to guide wealthy individuals choosing sites for their first or second homes. Below are the top-ranked locations, and how each city ranked in the four categories:

Rank		Economic activity	Political power	Intellectual influence	Quality of life
1	London	2	4	1	3
2	New York	1	2	2	8
3	Paris	4	5	5	2
4	Tokyo	3	6	4	7
5	Los Angeles	11	16	6	9
6	Brussels	16	3	15	14
7	Singapore	6	15	7	22
8	Toronto	22	22	9	1
9	Washington	30	1	10	13
10	Chicago	12	19	8	15

Rankings based on: *Economic activity* – economic output, income per head, market activity and share, and number of international business HQs. *Political power* – number of national political headquarters, international NGOs, embassies, and think tanks. *Intellectual influence* – educational levels and international market share of local media; number of leading educational facilities and media organisations. *Quality of life* – measures of freedom, security, health, public services, leisure, and other factors.

——————— MASDAR & ECO-CITIES ———————

In Autumn 2009, the first residents were scheduled to arrive in the 'world's greenest city' – Masdar City, in Abu Dhabi. Masdar aims to be both zero-carbon and zero-waste, generating all of its power on-site from renewable resources and re-using all waste water and solids. Cars have been banned, in favour of driverless electric vehicles which will run underground. The city has been designed by British architect Norman Foster in a style inspired by traditional medinas and souks, and it will eventually be home to 50,000 people and 1,500 businesses, many focused on green technology. Masdar is not the only 'eco-city' under development: *Sonoma Mountain Village* in California is planned as a zero-waste, zero-carbon community of 1,900 homes, each a 5-minute walk from shops. *The Gateway City* of Ras al Khaimah in the UAE is being designed by Rem Koolhaas using local materials and solar technology; it will house *c*.150,000 by 2012. *Logroño Montecorvo Eco City* in La Rioja, Spain, will include 3,000 carbon-neutral homes, powered by photovoltaic cells and wind turbines. (At least one eco-city has thus far proved more hype than reality: in 2009 the press reported that builders had yet to break ground on an ambitious Chinese eco-city called *Dongtan*, which was to be completed by 2010, and house 500,000.)

——————————— AN AVERAGE DAY ———————————

Figures released by the Organisation for Economic Co-operation and Development (OECD) in 2009 showed the percentage of time devoted to various activities by people in 18 OECD countries (the data are from various years, but primarily 2006):

(% of an average 24 hours)	Leisure	Personal care	Paid work/study	Unpaid work	Unspecified
Mexico	15·8	42·7	20·3	20·6	0·7
Japan	18·0	46·1	20·7	13·0	2·2
France	18·4	49·2	14·9	14·9	2·5
New Zealand	18·7	48·3	15·6	16·7	0·7
Turkey	18·7	46·7	13·1	16·0	5·4
Australia	19·6	45·6	15·7	17·6	1·5
Italy	21·1	46·8	15·2	16·1	0·8
Poland	21·4	45·4	15·3	17·4	0·5
Korea	21·6	44·8	21·6	10·2	1·7
United States	21·7	45·0	17·0	14·8	1·5
Spain	21·7	46·4	16·6	14·9	0·3
Canada	23·1	43·3	18·3	14·7	0·6
United Kingdom	23·4	44·0	15·9	15·8	0·9
Sweden	23·7	43·4	17·4	14·4	1·0
Belgium	24·7	45·7	12·8	14·4	2·4
Germany	25·0	45·1	13·6	15·2	1·1
Finland	25·0	43·8	15·4	14·5	1·3
Norway	26·5	42·8	16·6	13·8	0·3
AVERAGE	21·6	45·3	16·5	15·3	1·4

Leisure includes time spent on hobbies, games, television viewing, computer use, recreational gardening, sports, socialising, &c. *Personal care* includes time spent sleeping, eating and drinking, and on other household, medical, and personal services (hygiene, doctor visits, &c.).

Paid work includes full-time and part-time jobs, workplace breaks, commuting to work/school, time looking for work, and time spent on paid work at home. *Unpaid work* includes all household work – including chores, cooking, caring for children/others, shopping, &c.

Other OECD stats show the total hours spent on leisure and work in an average *year*:

Hours spent on ...	work	leisure		work	leisure
United States	1,896	6,864	Ireland	1,543	7,217
Hungary	1,889	6,872	Italy	1,536	7,224
Poland	1,806	6,954	United Kingdom	1,530	7,230
Greece	1,783	6,977	Germany	1,478	7,282
Australia	1,733	7,027	Belgium	1,461	7,299
Portugal	1,675	7,085	France	1,459	7,301
Switzerland	1,618	7,142	Sweden	1,386	7,374
Spain	1,601	7,159	Denmark	1,367	7,393
Canada	1,579	7,181	Netherlands	1,325	7,435
			Norway	1,290	7,470

——— INTERNATIONAL VOCABULARY OF NOTE ———

Bulletins from some of the year's less-reported stories, and the memorable vocabulary attached. ❦ In Haiti, the UN expressed concern over *restaveks*, poor children sent to live with wealthier families where they risk being exploited or abused (the term derives from the French '*rester avec*', 'stay with'). ❦ In Uganda, the press released a list of senior military officers on *katebe* – a type of forced retirement in which officers are not deployed, yet retain a salary. ❦ In Turkey, the government launched a plan to destroy all illegally constructed buildings, which are known as *gecekondu* (literally, 'constructed overnight'). ❦ In Somalia, the press reported that some pirates prefer to be called *badaadinta badah*, or 'saviours of the sea' [see p.35]. ❦ In Japan, Google Earth came under fire for using old maps that labelled some areas *eta*, a derogatory term, meaning 'filthy mass', that was once applied to settlements of *burakumin*, Japan's ancient 'untouchable' caste. ❦ In France, a film about a man teaching a Kurdish refugee to swim renewed a national debate on a law – *délit de solidarité*, or the 'offence of solidarity' – that criminalises giving assistance to illegal immigrants. ❦ In China, reports focused on the plight of the *liushou ertong*, or 'left behind' – children whose migrant worker parents have gone to work in the city. ❦ In Tanzania, a report on HIV slang noted that emaciated AIDS sufferers are said to be *amesimamia msumari*, or 'standing on a nail'. ❦ In Greece, a group of violent protesters attacking banks and other buildings became known as the *koukouloforoi*, or 'hooded ones', because of their tendency to disguise their faces. ❦ In Melbourne, Australia, a series of violent attacks against Indian students were dubbed *curry bashings* by the media, which warned such assaults could threaten the country's $12·2bn international education sector. ❦ In Kenya, the word for flour – *unga* – became a rallying cry for the country's poor, and the title of a popular protest song. ❦ In India, the press reported on the construction of *elephant flyovers* – concrete bridges that span roads and railways where elephants are at risk of being run over. ❦ In Liberia, the government began electronically tagging trees in order to confound *pit sawers* – small-scale, illegal loggers who hack planks from trees with chainsaws, &c. ❦ In Germany, a court upheld a ban on couples combining their names to form interminably long surnames; known as the *Hadschi Halef Omar Ban*, the ruling is named after a character invented by the writer Karl May called 'Hadschi Halef Omar Ben Hadschi Abul Abbas Ibn Hadschi Dawuhd al Gossarah'. ❦ In Cairo, the government slaughtered 350,000 pigs owned by the *Zabaleen*, or 'garbage people' – a group of (mainly) Coptic Christians who sort through Cairo's refuse for items to recycle and re-sell. The pigs had munched rotting food, and were sold for additional income, but were culled over H1N1 fears. ❦ In S Korea, the press reported on the rise of *instead-men* who are hired to perform odd jobs, from delivering food to killing cockroaches; their employers are called *can't-botherists*. ❦ In Brazil, voters mounted a *greve de bigode* – or moustache strike – to target Brazil's embattled President of the Senate, José Sarney, who is famed for his facial hair.

Further details on these, and other, stories can be found at http://schott.blogs.nytimes.com.

———————— TOP TEN NEW CHINESE PHRASES ————————

18 December 2008 was the 30th anniversary of the Chinese Communist Party's decision to begin the evolution of socialism by 'opening up' China to the global economy. To mark this occasion, 15 Chinese newspapers and internet portals asked their readers and users to select the 10 best new words and phrases introduced into Chinese during these three decades. Below are the winners, in order of popularity:

Xiahai (going to do business) · Literally, 'jumping into the sea'. As economic policies relaxed in the 1980s, a swell of Chinese began to start their own businesses – giving up their 'iron rice bowl' jobs for the chance to sink or swim.

Xiagang zaijiuye (to be laid off and to find a new job) · The restructuring of state-owned enterprises in the 1990s led to massive unemployment – so much so that, for a time, the traditional greeting 'Have you eaten?' was replaced by 'Have you been sacked?' However, the government soon instituted a major re-employment project, including occupational re-training and new policies to encourage small businesses.

Nongmingong (rural migrant workers) · Agricultural privatisation freed millions from farm jobs, and new policies encouraged migrant labourers to stream to cities. The influx began in earnest in the early 1990s, though some Chinese claim that the *nongmingong* have yet to enjoy the same rights as their city brethren.

A cat that catches mice is a good one, be it black or white · Deng Xiaoping's pragmatic observation, employed to overcome debate about whether a given reform was capitalist or socialist.

Shangwang (surfing the internet) · The internet has become hugely popular in China since it was introduced in the mid-1990s, and the country now boasts more internet users than the US.

Gaige kaifang (reform and opening up) · In 1978, 18 villagers in the province of Anhui decided secretly to abandon the collective system and divide farmland among their houses. Deng praised the move and adopted the plan as a nationwide model, ushering in 30 years of reform and expansion. In 2007 China's GDP was fourth in the world.

Beijing aoyun (Beijing Olympic Games) · Despite protests during the torch relay, the Games were seen as a major success and a national 'coming-out party'. China also topped the list of most gold medals, with a haul of 51.

Chaogu (stock market speculation) · China opened its first stock market in Shanghai in 1990, and the nation has anxiously followed its cycles ever since – despite the fact that stock markets used to be decried as a capitalist evil.

Zhongguo tese (Chinese characteristics) · To quell criticism of his reforms, Deng said he was creating 'socialism with Chinese characteristics'. Today the phrase *zhongguo tese* is used to describe something that is neither Marxist nor capitalist, but uniquely Chinese.

Xiongqi (rise to the challenge) · First shouted by Sichuan football fans in the 1990s, then used off the field to encourage the populace to keep their peckers up. *Sichuan, Xiongqi!* became a nationwide slogan after the 2008 Sichuan quake that killed *c.*70,000.

—————————————— THE PLANETS ——————————————

Symbol	Name	Diameter km	No. of moons	Surface gravity m/s²	Rings?	Distance from Sun ×10⁶ km	Mean temp. °C	Day length hours
☿	Mercury	4,879	0	3·7	N	57·9	167	4,222·6
♀	Venus	12,104	0	8·9	N	108·2	457	2,802·0
⊕	Earth	12,756	1	9·8	N	149·6	15	24·0
♂	Mars	6,794	2	3·7	N	227·9	−63	24·6
♃	Jupiter	142,984	63	23·1	Y	778·4	−110	9·9
♄	Saturn	120,536	60	9·0	Y	1,426·7	−140	10·7
♅	Uranus	51,118	27	8·7	Y	2,871·0	−195	17·2
♆	Neptune	49,532	13	11·0	Y	4,498·3	−200	16·1

In 2009, the legislature of Illinois declared Pluto would be awarded 'full planetary status' as it passed over the skies of the US state, regardless of the opinion of the International Astronomical Union.

—————————————— PLANETARY MNEMONIC ——————————————

Many **V**ery **E**ducated **M**en **J**ustify **S**tealing **U**nique **N**inth
Mercury Venus Earth Mars Jupiter Saturn Uranus Neptune

—————————————— THE CONTINENTS ——————————————

Continent	area km²	est. population	population density
Asia	44,579,000	3,959m	88·8
Africa	30,065,000	910m	30·3
North America	24,256,000	331m	13·6
South America	17,819,000	561m	31·5
Antarctica	13,209,000	(Summer: 20k tourists & 3k scientists; winter: 1k scientists)	
Europe	9,938,000	729m	73·4
Australia	7,687,000	33m	4·3

—————————————— THE OCEANS ——————————————

Oceans make up *c.*70% of the globe's surface. The five oceans are detailed below:

Ocean	area km²	greatest known depth at	depth
Pacific	155,557,000	Mariana Trench	11,033m
Atlantic	76,762,000	Puerto Rico Trench	8,605m
Indian	68,556,000	Java Trench	7,258m
Southern	20,327,000	South Sandwich Trench	7,235m
Arctic	14,056,000	Fram Basin	4,665m

─────────── A WORLD OF SUPERLATIVES ───────────

Highest capital city	La Paz, Bolivia	3,636m
Highest mountain	Everest, Nepal/Tibet	8,850m
Highest volcano	Ojos del Salado, Chile	6,908m
Highest dam	Nurek, Tajikistan	300m
Highest waterfall	Angel Falls, Venezuela	979m
Biggest waterfall (volume)	Inga, Dem. Rep. of Congo	43,000m³/s
Lowest point	Dead Sea, Israel/Jordan	c.-400m
Deepest point	Challenger Deep, Mariana Trench	c.-11,033m
Deepest ocean	Pacific	average depth -4,300m
Deepest freshwater lake	Baikal, Russia	1,637m
Largest lake	Caspian Sea	370,886km²
Largest desert	Sahara	9,065,000km²
Largest island	Greenland	2,166,086km²
Largest country	Russia	17,075,200km²
Largest population	China	1·3bn
Largest monolith	Uluru, Australia	345m high; 9·4km base
Largest landmass	Eurasia	c.54,000,000km²
Largest river (volume)	Amazon	28bn gal/min
Largest peninsula	Arabian	2,590,000km²
Largest rainforest	Amazon, South America	1·2bn acres
Largest forest	Northern Russia	2·7bn acres
Largest atoll	Kwajalein, Marshall Islands	16km²
Largest glacier	Lambert Glacier, Antarctica	c.1,000,000km²
Largest concrete artichoke	Castroville, USA	6m×4m
Largest archipelago	Indonesia	17,508 islands
Largest lake in a lake	Manitou, on an island in Lake Huron	104km²
Largest city by area	Mount Isa, Australia	40,977km²
Smallest country	Vatican City	0·44km²
Smallest population	Vatican City	824 people
Smallest republic	Republic of Nauru	21km²
Longest coastline	Canada	202,080km
Longest mountain range	Andes	c.8,900km
Longest suspension bridge	Akashi-Kaikyo, Japan	1,990m
Longest rail tunnel	Seikan, Japan	53·8km
Longest road tunnel	Lærdal, Norway	24·5km
Longest river	Nile	6,695km
Tallest inhabited building	Burj Dubai, UAE	688m
Tallest structure	KVLY-TV Mast, USA	629m
Most land borders	China & Russia	14 countries
Most populated urban area	Tokyo, Japan	35·2m
Most remote place	Tibetan plateau	3 weeks to nearest city
Least populous capital city	San Marino, San Marino	pop. 4,482
Warmest sea	Red Sea	Average temp. c.25°C
Longest bay	Bay of Bengal	c.2,000km
Largest banknote	Brobdingnagian bills, Philippines	14"×8½"

Unsurprisingly, a degree of uncertainty and debate surrounds some of these entries and their specifications.

—————— NATIONS WITH A POSITIVE INFLUENCE ——————

Germany has a more positive impact on the world than any other country, according to a 2009 BBC World Service poll of citizens in 21 countries. Respondents were asked whether the influence of a country was 'mainly positive' or 'mainly negative'; the global average of those saying 'mainly positive' for some key countries is below:

Country	*% mainly positive*	Country	
Germany	61	China	39
UK	58	India	38
Canada	57	South Africa	34
Japan	56	Russia	30
EU	51	Israel	21
France	51	North Korea	20
Brazil	44	Pakistan	17
US [see p.33]	40	Iran	17

————————————— POVERTY RATES —————————————

Below are the percentages of the working-age population (18–65) living below the poverty line[†] in various nations, according to data released by the OECD in 2009:

Mexico	15%	New Zealand	11	Slovak Rep.	8	Norway	7
US	15	Portugal	11	Austria	7	Switzerland	7
Turkey	14	Spain	11	Belgium	7	UK	7
Poland	14	Australia	10	Finland	7	Sweden	6
Canada	12	Germany	10	France	7	Czech Rep.	5
Ireland	12	Italy	10	Hungary	7	Denmark	5
Japan	12	Greece	9	Iceland	7		
Korea	12	Luxembourg	8	Netherlands	7	OECD avg	9

† The poverty line is defined as 50% of the median household disposable income in each country.

————————————— GLOBAL HUNGER INDEX —————————————

In October 2008, the International Food Policy Research Institute released the 2008 Global Hunger Index (GHI), ranking levels of hunger in 88 countries. Three indicators were used to rank countries on a 0–100 scale: the percentage of the population who did not consume sufficient calories; infant mortality rates; and the prevalence of underweight children under five years old. While the report showed significant improvement in certain countries compared to 1990 (notably Kuwait, Peru, Syria, Turkey, and Mexico), levels of hunger in Sub-Saharan Africa remain severe. Seven countries with values exceeding 30 displayed 'extremely alarming' rates of hunger:

Country	*hunger level*				
DR Congo	42·7	Burundi	38·3	Liberia	31·8
Eritrea	39·0	Niger	32·4	Ethiopia	31·0
		Sierra Leone	32·2	[2001–06 data]	

—DEVELOPMENT INDEX—

The UN Human Development Index annually ranks 179 countries by health, life expectancy, income, education, and environment. The 2008 ranking was:

Most developed	Least developed
1 .. Iceland [see p.31]	179 .... Sierra Leone
2 .... Norway	178 .. C African Rep
3 .... Canada	177 ..... DR Congo
4 .... Australia	176 .... Liberia
5 .... Ireland	175 ... Mozambique
6 ...... Netherlands	174 .... Niger
7. .... Sweden	173 ... Burkina Faso
8 .... Japan	172 ...... Burundi
9 ..... Luxembourg	171 .. Guinea-Bissau
10 ..... Switzerland	170 .... Chad

——— PEACE INDEX ———

The Global Peace Index, calculated by the Economist Intelligence Unit, ranks 144 countries on 23 qualitative and quantitative indicators, including military spending, homicide rates, jail populations, and international relations. According to the Index, the most and least peaceful countries in 2009 were:

Most peaceful	Least peaceful
1 ..... New Zealand	144 .... Iraq
2 .... Denmark	143 .... Afghanistan
3 .... Norway	142 .... Somalia
4 .... Iceland	141 .... Israel
5 .... Austria	140 .... Sudan
6 .... Sweden	139 ..... DR Congo

——— NOTES TO THE GAZETTEER ———

The gazetteer on the following pages is designed to allow comparisons to be made between countries around the world. As might be expected, some of the data are tentative and open to debate. A range of sources has been consulted, including the CIA's *World Factbook*, Amnesty International, HM Revenue and Customs, &c.

Size km²	*sum of all land and water areas delimited by international boundaries and coastlines*
Population	*July 2009 estimate*
Flying time	*approximate travelling time from London Heathrow to capital city; will vary depending on route and connecting flight, as well as direction travelled, &c.*
GMT	*based on capital city; varies across some countries; varies with daylight saving*
Life expectancy at birth	*in years; 2009 estimate*
Infant mortality	*deaths of infants <1, per 1,000 live births, per year; 2009 estimate*
Median age	*in years; 2009 estimate*
Birth & death rates	*average per 1,000 persons in the population at midyear; 2009 estimate*
Fertility rate	*average theoretical number of children per woman; 2009 estimate*
HIV rate	*percentage of adults (15–49) living with HIV/AIDS; mainly 2007 estimate*
Literacy rate	*%; definition (especially of target age) varies; mainly 2003 estimate*
Exchange rate	*as at September 2009 (HM Revenue & Customs)*
GDP per capita	*($) GDP on purchasing power parity basis/population; from 2008*
Inflation	*annual % change in consumer prices; years vary, generally from 2008*
Unemployment	*% of labour force without jobs; years vary, generally from 2008*
Voting age	*voting age; (U)niversal; (C)ompulsory for at least one election; entitlement varies*
Military service	*age, length of service, sex and/or religion required to serve vary*
Death penalty	*(N) no death penalty; (N*) death penalty not used in practice; (Y) death penalty for common crimes; (Y*) death penalty for exceptional crimes only*
National Day	*some countries have more than one; not all are universally recognised*

—— GAZETTEER · ALGERIA – SOUTH KOREA · [1/4] ——

Country	Size (km2)	Population (m)	Capital city	Phone access code	Phone country code	Flying time (h)	GMT
United Kingdom	244,820	61·1	London	00	44	—	n/a
United States	9,826,630	307·2	Washington, DC	011	1	7h50	−5
Algeria	2,381,740	34·2	Algiers	00	213	2h45	+1
Argentina	2,766,890	40·9	Buenos Aires	00	54	15h45	−3
Australia	7,686,850	21·3	Canberra	0011	61	25h	+10
Austria	83,870	8·2	Vienna	00	43	2h20	+1
Belarus	207,600	9·6	Minsk	810	375	4h40	+2
Belgium	30,528	10·4	Brussels	00	32	1h	+1
Brazil	8,511,965	198·7	Brasilia	0014	55	16h	−3
Bulgaria	110,910	7·2	Sofia	00	359	3h	+2
Burma/Myanmar	678,500	48·1	Rangoon	00	95	13h	+6½
Cambodia	181,040	14·5	Phnom Penh	001	855	14h	+7
Canada	9,984,670	33·5	Ottawa	011	1	7h45	−5
Chile	756,950	16·6	Santiago	00	56	17h	−4
China	9,596,960	1·3bn	Beijing	00	86	10h	+8
Colombia	1,138,910	45·6	Bogota	009	57	13h	−5
Cuba	110,860	11·5	Havana	119	53	12h	−5
Czech Republic	78,866	10·2	Prague	00	420	1h50	+1
Denmark	43,094	5·5	Copenhagen	00	45	1h50	+1
Egypt	1,001,450	83·1	Cairo	00	20	4h45	+2
Estonia	45,226	1·3	Tallinn	00	372	4h	+2
Finland	338,145	5·3	Helsinki	00	358	3h	+2
France	547,030	64·1	Paris	00	33	50m	+1
Germany	357,021	82·3	Berlin	00	49	1h40	+1
Greece	131,940	10·7	Athens	00	30	3h45m	+2
Haiti	27,750	9·0	Port-au-Prince	00	509	20h30	−5
Hong Kong	1,092	7·1	—	001	852	12h	+8
Hungary	93,030	9·9	Budapest	00	36	2h25	+1
India	3,287,590	1·2bn	New Delhi	00	91	8h30	+5½
Indonesia	1,919,440	240·3	Jakarta	001	62	16h	+7
Iran	1,648,000	66·4	Tehran	00	98	6h	+3½
Iraq	437,072	28·9	Baghdad	00	964	14h30	+3
Ireland	70,280	4·2	Dublin	00	353	1h	0
Israel	20,770	7·2	Jerusalem/Tel Aviv	00	972	5h	+2
Italy	301,230	58·1	Rome	00	39	2h20	+1
Japan	377,835	127·1	Tokyo	010	81	11h30	+9
Jordan	92,300	6·3	Amman	00	962	6h	+2
Kazakhstan	2,717,300	15·4	Astana	810	7	8h15	+6
Kenya	582,650	39·0	Nairobi	000	254	8h20	+3
Korea, North	120,540	22·7	Pyongyang	00	850	13h45	+9
Korea, South	98,480	48·5	Seoul	001	82	11h	+9

—————— GAZETTEER · KUWAIT – ZIMBABWE · [1/4] ——————

Country	Size (km2)	Population (m)	Capital city	Phone access code	Phone country code	Flying time (h)	GMT
United Kingdom	244,820	61·1	London	00	44	—	n/a
United States	9,826,630	307·2	Washington, DC	011	1	7h50	−5
Kuwait	17,820	2·7	Kuwait City	00	965	6h	+3
Latvia	64,589	2·2	Riga	00	371	2h45	+2
Lebanon	10,400	4·0	Beirut	00	961	4h45	+2
Liberia	111,370	3·4	Monrovia	00	231	12h	0
Lithuania	65,300	3·6	Vilnius	00	370	4h	+2
Malaysia	329,750	25·7	Kuala Lumpur	00	60	12h25	+8
Mexico	1,972,550	111·2	Mexico City	00	52	11h15	−6
Monaco	1·95	33·0k	Monaco	00	377	2h	+1
Morocco	446,550	34·9	Rabat	00	212	5h45	0
Netherlands	41,526	16·7	Amsterdam	00	31	1h15	+1
New Zealand	268,680	4·2	Wellington	00	64	28h	+12
Nigeria	923,768	149·2	Abuja	009	234	6h15	+1
Norway	323,802	4·7	Oslo	00	47	2h	+1
Pakistan	803,940	176·2	Islamabad	00	92	10h	+5
Peru	1,285,220	29·5	Lima	00	51	15h15	−5
Philippines	300,000	98·0	Manila	00	63	15h	+8
Poland	312,679	38·5	Warsaw	00	48	2h20	+1
Portugal	92,391	10·7	Lisbon	00	351	2h30	0
Romania	237,500	22·2	Bucharest	00	40	3h15	+2
Russia	17,075,200	140·0	Moscow	810	7	4h	+3
Rwanda	26,338	10·5	Kigali	00	250	11h20	+2
Saudi Arabia	2,149,690	28·7	Riyadh	00	966	6h15	+3
Singapore	692·7	4·7	Singapore	001	65	12h45	+8
Slovakia	48,845	5·5	Bratislava	00	421	3h30	+1
Slovenia	20,273	2·0	Ljubljana	00	386	3h30	+1
Somalia	637,657	9·8	Mogadishu	00	252	12h45	+3
South Africa	1,219,912	49·1	Pretoria/Tshwane	00	27	11h	+2
Spain	504,782	40·5	Madrid	00	34	2h20	+1
Sudan	2,505,810	41·1	Khartoum	00	249	12h	+3
Sweden	449,964	9·1	Stockholm	00	46	2h30	+1
Switzerland	41,290	7·6	Bern	00	41	2h	+1
Syria	185,180	20·2	Damascus	00	963	6h30	+2
Taiwan	35,980	23·0	Taipei	002	886	14h30	+8
Thailand	514,000	65·9	Bangkok	001	66	14h20	+7
Turkey	780,580	76·8	Ankara	00	90	5h15	+2
Ukraine	603,700	45·7	Kiev/Kyiv	810	380	3h25	+2
Venezuela	912,050	26·8	Caracas	00	58	11h30	−4½
Vietnam	329,560	87·0	Hanoi	00	84	13h45	+7
Zimbabwe	390,580	11·4	Harare	00	263	12h50	+2

―――― GAZETTEER · ALGERIA – SOUTH KOREA · [2/4] ――――

Country	Male life expectancy	Female life expectancy	difference	Infant mortality	Median age	Birth rate	Death rate	Fertility rate	Adult HIV rate	Literacy
United Kingdom	76·5	81·6	–5·1	4·9	40·2	10·7	10·0	1·7	0·2	99
United States	75·7	80·7	–5·0	6·3	36·7	13·8	8·4	2·1	0·6	99
Algeria	72·4	75·8	–3·4	27·7	22·6	16·9	4·6	1·8	0·1	70
Argentina	73·3	80·0	–6·7	11·4	30·0	17·9	7·4	2·4	0·5	97
Australia	79·3	84·1	–4·8	4·8	37·3	12·5	6·7	1·8	0·2	99
Austria	76·6	82·6	–6·0	4·4	42·2	8·7	10·0	1·4	0·2	98
Belarus	65·0	76·7	–11·7	6·4	38·6	9·7	13·9	1·2	0·2	100
Belgium	76·1	82·5	–6·4	4·4	41·7	10·2	10·4	1·7	0·2	99
Brazil	68·4	75·7	–7·3	22·6	28·6	18·4	6·4	2·2	0·6	89
Bulgaria	69·5	76·9	–7·4	17·9	41·4	9·5	14·3	1·4	0·1	98
Burma/Myanmar	61·2	65·7	–4·5	47·6	28·2	17·0	9·1	1·9	0·7	90
Cambodia	60·0	64·3	–4·3	54·8	22·1	25·7	8·1	3·0	0·8	74
Canada	78·7	83·9	–5·2	5·0	40·4	10·3	7·7	1·6	0·4	99
Chile	74·1	80·8	–6·7	7·7	31·4	14·6	5·8	1·9	0·3	96
China	71·6	75·5	–3·9	20·3	34·1	14·0	7·1	1·8	0·1	91
Colombia	69·0	76·8	–7·8	18·9	27·1	19·6	5·5	2·5	0·6	90
Cuba	75·2	79·9	–4·7	5·8	37·3	11·1	7·2	1·6	0·1	100
Czech Republic	73·5	80·3	–6·8	3·8	40·1	8·8	10·7	1·2	0·1	99
Denmark	76·0	80·8	–4·8	4·3	40·5	10·5	10·2	1·7	0·2	99
Egypt	69·6	74·8	–5·2	27·3	24·8	21·7	5·1	2·7	0·1	71
Estonia	67·5	78·5	–11·0	7·3	39·9	10·4	13·4	1·4	1·3	100
Finland	75·5	82·6	–7·1	3·5	42·1	10·4	10·1	1·7	0·1	100
France	77·8	84·3	–6·5	3·3	39·4	12·6	8·6	2·0	0·4	99
Germany	76·3	82·4	–6·1	4·0	43·8	8·2	10·9	1·4	0·1	99
Greece	77·1	82·4	–5·3	5·2	41·8	9·5	10·5	1·4	0·2	96
Haiti	59·1	62·5	–3·4	59·7	20·2	29·1	8·7	3·8	2·2	53
Hong Kong	79·2	84·8	–5·6	2·9	42·3	7·4	6·8	1·0	0·1	94
Hungary	69·3	77·9	–8·6	7·9	39·4	9·5	12·9	1·4	0·1	99
India	67·5	72·6	–5·1	30·2	25·3	21·8	6·2	2·7	0·3	61
Indonesia	68·3	73·4	–5·1	30·0	27·6	18·8	6·3	2·4	0·2	90
Iran	69·7	72·7	–3·0	35·8	27·0	17·2	5·7	1·7	0·2	77
Iraq	68·6	71·3	–2·7	43·8	20·4	31·0	5·0	3·9	0·1	74
Ireland	75·6	81·1	–5·5	5·1	35·0	14·2	7·8	1·9	0·2	99
Israel	78·6	83·0	–4·4	4·2	29·1	19·8	5·4	2·8	0·1	97
Italy	77·3	83·3	–6·0	5·5	43·3	8·2	10·7	1·3	0·4	98
Japan	78·8	85·6	–6·8	2·8	44·2	7·6	9·5	1·2	0·1	99
Jordan	76·3	81·6	–5·3	15·0	24·3	19·6	2·8	2·4	0·1	90
Kazakhstan	62·6	73·5	–10·9	25·7	29·6	16·6	9·4	1·9	0·1	100
Kenya	57·5	58·2	–0·7	54·7	18·7	36·6	9·7	4·6	6·7	85
Korea, North	61·2	66·5	–5·3	51·3	33·5	14·8	10·5	2·0	—	99
Korea, South	75·5	82·2	–6·7	4·3	37·3	8·9	5·9	1·2	0·1	98

———— GAZETTEER · KUWAIT – ZIMBABWE · [2/4] ————

Country	Male life expectancy	Female life expectancy	difference	Infant mortality	Median age	Birth rate	Death rate	Fertility rate	Adult HIV rate	Literacy
United Kingdom	76·5	81·6	−5·1	4·9	40·2	10·7	10·0	1·7	0·2	99
United States	75·7	80·7	−5·0	6·3	36·7	13·8	8·4	2·1	0·6	99
Kuwait	76·5	79·0	−2·5	9·0	26·2	21·8	2·4	2·8	0·1	93
Latvia	67·0	77·6	−10·6	8·8	40·1	9·8	13·6	1·3	0·8	100
Lebanon	71·2	76·3	−5·1	21·8	29·3	17·1	6·0	1·9	0·1	87
Liberia	40·7	43·0	−2·3	138·2	18·0	42·3	20·7	5·8	1·7	58
Lithuania	70·0	80·1	−10·1	6·5	39·3	9·1	11·2	1·2	0·1	100
Malaysia	70·6	76·2	−5·6	15·9	24·9	22·2	5·0	3·0	0·5	89
Mexico	73·3	79·0	−5·7	18·4	26·3	19·7	4·8	2·3	0·3	91
Monaco	76·3	84·1	−7·8	5·0	45·7	9·1	12·7	1·8	—	99
Morocco	69·4	74·3	−4·9	36·9	25·0	21·0	5·5	2·5	0·1	52
Netherlands	76·8	82·1	−5·3	4·7	40·4	10·4	8·7	1·7	0·2	99
New Zealand	78·4	82·4	−4·0	4·9	36·6	13·9	7·1	2·1	0·1	99
Nigeria	46·2	47·8	−1·6	94·4	19·0	36·7	16·6	4·9	3·1	68
Norway	77·3	82·7	−5·4	3·6	39·4	11·0	9·3	1·8	0·1	100
Pakistan	63·4	65·6	−2·2	65·1	20·8	27·6	7·7	3·6	0·1	50
Peru	68·9	72·7	−3·8	28·6	26·1	19·4	6·1	2·4	0·5	93
Philippines	68·2	74·2	−6·0	20·6	22·5	26·0	5·1	3·3	0·1	93
Poland	71·7	79·9	−8·2	6·8	37·9	10·0	10·1	1·3	0·1	100
Portugal	75·0	81·7	−6·7	4·8	39·4	10·3	10·7	1·5	0·5	93
Romania	69·0	76·2	−7·2	23·0	37·7	10·5	11·9	1·4	0·1	97
Russia	59·3	73·1	−13·8	10·6	38·4	11·1	16·1	1·4	1·1	99
Rwanda	49·3	51·8	−2·5	81·6	18·7	39·7	14·0	5·3	2·8	70
Saudi Arabia	74·2	78·5	−4·3	11·6	21·6	28·6	2·5	3·8	0·01	79
Singapore	79·4	84·8	−5·4	2·3	39·0	8·8	4·7	1·1	0·2	93
Slovakia	71·5	79·5	−8·0	6·8	36·9	10·6	9·5	1·4	0·1	100
Slovenia	73·3	80·8	−7·5	4·3	41·7	9·0	10·6	1·3	0·1	100
Somalia	47·8	51·5	−3·7	109·2	17·5	43·7	15·6	6·5	0·5	38
South Africa	49·8	48·1	1·7	44·4	24·4	19·9	17·0	2·4	18·1	86
Spain	76·7	83·6	−6·9	4·2	41·1	9·7	10·0	1·3	0·5	98
Sudan	50·5	52·4	−1·9	82·4	19·1	33·7	12·9	4·5	1·4	61
Sweden	78·6	83·3	−4·7	2·8	41·5	10·1	10·2	1·7	0·1	99
Switzerland	78·0	83·8	−5·8	4·2	41·0	9·6	8·6	1·5	0·6	99
Syria	69·8	72·7	−2·9	25·9	21·7	25·9	4·6	3·1	0·1	80
Taiwan	75·1	81·1	−6·0	5·4	36·5	9·0	6·8	1·1	—	96
Thailand	70·7	75·6	−4·9	17·6	33·3	13·4	7·3	1·7	1·4	93
Turkey	70·1	73·9	−3·8	25·8	27·7	18·7	6·1	2·2	0·1	87
Ukraine	62·4	74·5	−12·1	9·0	39·5	9·6	15·8	1·3	1·6	99
Venezuela	70·5	76·8	−6·3	21·5	25·5	20·6	5·1	2·5	0·7	93
Vietnam	68·8	74·6	−5·8	22·9	27·4	16·3	6·2	1·8	0·5	90
Zimbabwe	46·4	45·2	1·2	32·3	17·6	31·5	16·2	3·7	15·3	91

—— GAZETTEER · ALGERIA – SOUTH KOREA · [3/4] ——

Country	Currency	Currency code	£1 =	GDP per capita $	Inflation %	Unemployment %	Fiscal year end
United Kingdom	Pound=100 Pence	GBP	—	36,600	3·8	5·5	5 Apr
United States	Dollar=100 Cents	USD	1·6	47,000	4·2	7·2	30 Sep
Algeria	Dinar=100 Centimes	DZD	120·4	7,000	3·6	12·9	31 Dec
Argentina	Peso=10,000 Australes	ARS	6·3	14,200	22·0	7·8	31 Dec
Australia	Dollar=100 Cents	AUD	2·0	38,100	4·7	4·5	30 Jun
Austria	euro=100 cent	EUR	1·2	39,200	3·7	3·7	31 Dec
Belarus	Ruble=100 Kopecks	BYR	4,686·4	11,800	15·5	1·6	31 Dec
Belgium	euro=100 cent	EUR	1·2	37,500	4·5	6·5	31 Dec
Brazil	Real=100 Centavos	BRL	3·1	10,100	5·8	8·0	31 Dec
Bulgaria	Lev=100 Stotinki	BGN	2·3	12,900	7·8	6·3	31 Dec
Burma/Myanmar	Kyat=100 Pyas	MMK	10·6	1,200	27·3	9·4	31 Mar
Cambodia	Riel=100 Sen	KHR	6,779·2	2,000	20·2	3·5	31 Dec
Canada	Dollar=100 Cents	CAD	1·8	39,300	1·0	6·1	31 Mar
Chile	Peso=100 Centavos	CLP	914·9	14,900	8·8	7·5	31 Dec
China	Renminbi Yuan=100 Fen	CNY	11·3	6,000	6·0	c.9·0	31 Dec
Colombia	Peso=100 Centavos	COP	3332·4	8,900	7·7	11·8	31 Dec
Cuba	Peso=100 Centavos	CUP/C	1·7	9,500	4·2	1·8	31 Dec
Czech Republic	Koruna=100 Haléru	CZK	29·9	26,100	3·6	6·0	31 Dec
Denmark	Krone=100 Øre	DKK	8·6	37,400	3·5	2·0	31 Dec
Egypt	Pound=100 Piastres	EGP	9·2	5,400	18·0	8·7	30 Jun
Estonia	Kroon=100 Sents	EEK	18·2	21,200	10·4	6·2	31 Dec
Finland	euro=100 cent	EUR	1·2	37,200	4·1	6·4	31 Dec
France	euro=100 cent	EUR	1·2	32,700	1·0	7·4	31 Dec
Germany	euro=100 cent	EUR	1·2	34,800	2·8	10·8	31 Dec
Greece	euro=100 cent	EUR	1·2	32,000	4·4	8·0	31 Dec
Haiti	Gourde=100 Centimes	HTG	65·7	1,300	15·8	c.65	30 Sep
Hong Kong	HK Dollar=100 Cents	HKD	12·8	43,800	2·1	4·1	31 Mar
Hungary	Forint=100 Fillér	HUF	315·5	19,800	6·1	8·0	31 Dec
India	Rupee=100 Paise	INR	80·5	2,800	7·8	6·8	31 Mar
Indonesia	Rupiah=100 Sen	IDR	16,414·8	3,900	11·1	8·4	31 Dec
Iran	Rial(=100 Dinars)	IRR	16,489·2	12,800	28·0	12·5	20 Mar
Iraq	New Iraqi Dinar	NID	1901·1	4,000	6·8	c.30·0	31 Dec
Ireland	euro=100 cent	EUR	1·2	46,200	4·0	6·2	31 Dec
Israel	Shekel=100 Agorot	ILS	6·4	28,200	4·7	6·1	31 Dec
Italy	euro=100 cent	EUR	1·2	31,000	3·6	6·8	31 Dec
Japan	Yen=100 Sen	JPY	154·7	34,200	1·8	4·2	31 Mar
Jordan	Dinar=1,000 Fils	JOD	1·2	5,000	14·9	12·9	31 Dec
Kazakhstan	Tenge=100 Tiyn	KZT	249·3	11,500	18·6	6·9	31 Dec
Kenya	Shilling=100 Cents	KES	125·9	1,600	25·5	40·0	30 Jun
Korea, North	NK Won=100 Chon	KPW	236·5	1,700	—	—	31 Dec
Korea, South	SK Won=100 Chon	KRW	2,072·0	26,000	4·7	3·2	31 Dec

——————— GAZETTEER · KUWAIT – ZIMBABWE · [3/4] ———————

Country	Currency	Currency code	£1 =	GDP per capita $	Inflation %	Unemployment %	Fiscal year end
United Kingdom	Pound=100 Pence	GBP	—	36,600	3·8	5·5	5 Apr
United States	Dollar=100 Cents	USD	1·6	47,000	4·2	7·2	30 Sep
Kuwait	Dinar=1,000 Fils	KWD	0·5	57,400	11·7	2·2	31 Mar
Latvia	Lats=100 Santims	LVL	0·8	17,800	10·5	5·5	31 Dec
Lebanon	Pound=100 Piastres	LBP	2,483·7	11,100	10·0	9·2	31 Dec
Liberia	Dollar=100 Cents	LRD	1·6	500	11·2	85·0	31 Dec
Lithuania	Litas=100 Centas	LTL	4·0	17,700	11·0	5·7	31 Dec
Malaysia	Ringgit=100 Sen	MYR	5·9	15,300	5·8	3·7	31 Dec
Mexico	Peso=100 Centavos	MXN	21·3	14,200	6·2	4·1	31 Dec
Monaco	euro=100 cent	EUR	1·2	30,000	1·9	—	31 Dec
Morocco	Dirham=100 Centimes	MAD	13·1	4,000	4·6	10·0	31 Dec
Netherlands	euro=100 cent	EUR	1·2	40,300	1·5	4·5	31 Dec
New Zealand	Dollar=100 Cents	NZD	2·5	27,900	4·3	4·0	31 Mar
Nigeria	Naira=100 Kobo	NGN	259·3	2,300	10·6	4·9	31 Dec
Norway	Krone=100 Øre	NOK	10·0	55,200	3·6	2·6	31 Dec
Pakistan	Rupee=100 Paisa	PKR	136·4	2,600	20·8	7·4	30 Jun
Peru	New Sol=100 Centimos	PEN	4·9	8,400	6·7	8·4	31 Dec
Philippines	Peso=100 Centavos	PHP	80·0	3,300	9·3	7·4	31 Dec
Poland	Zloty=100 Groszy	PLN	4·8	17,300	4·3	9·7	31 Dec
Portugal	euro=100 cent	EUR	1·2	22,000	2·9	7·6	31 Dec
Romania	Leu=100 Bani	RON	4·9	12,200	7·8	3·6	31 Dec
Russia	Ruble=100 Kopecks	RUB	52·3	15,800	13·9	6·2	31 Dec
Rwanda	Franc=100 Centimes	RWF	939·0	900	9·5	—	31 Dec
Saudi Arabia	Riyal=100 Halala	SAR	6·2	20,700	10·3	c.25·0	31 Dec
Singapore	Dollar=100 Cents	SGD	2·4	52,000	4·3	2·3	31 Mar
Slovakia	euro=100 cent	EUR	1·2	21,900	4·6	8·4	31 Dec
Slovenia	euro=100 cent	EUR	1·2	29,500	6·0	6·7	31 Dec
Somalia	Shilling=100 Cents	SOS	2,272·9	600	—	—	—
South Africa	Rand=100 Cents	ZAR	13·3	10,000	11·3	21·7	31 Mar
Spain	euro=100 cent	EUR	1·2	34,600	1·4	13·9	31 Dec
Sudan	Pound=100 Piastres	SDG	3·9	2,200	16·5	18·7	31 Dec
Sweden	Krona=100 Øre	SEK	11·9	38,500	1·6	6·4	31 Dec
Switzerland	Franc=100 Centimes	CHF	1·7	40,900	2·4	3·0	31 Dec
Syria	Pound=100 Piastres	SYP	76·0	4,800	14·9	9·0	31 Dec
Taiwan	Dollar=100 Cents	TWD	54·5	31,900	3·7	4·1	31 Dec
Thailand	Baht=100 Satang	THB	56·2	8,500	5·5	1·2	30 Sep
Turkey	Lira=100 Kurus	TRY	2·5	12,000	10·2	7·9	31 Dec
Ukraine	Hryvnia=100 Kopiykas	UAH	13·9	6,900	25·0	3·0	31 Dec
Venezuela	Bolívar=100 Centimos	VEB	3·6	13,500	31·0	8·5	31 Dec
Vietnam	Dong=100 Xu	VND	2,9454·0	2,800	24·5	4·9	31 Dec
Zimbabwe	Dollar=100 Cents	ZWD	598·6	200	11·2m	80·0	31 Dec

—— GAZETTEER · ALGERIA – SOUTH KOREA · [4/4] ——

Country	Voting age	Driving side	UN vehicle code	Internet country code	Military service	Death penalty	National Day
United Kingdom	18 U	L	GB	.uk	N	N	—
United States	18 U	R	USA	.us	N	Y	4 Jul
Algeria	18 U	R	DZ	.dz	Y	N*	1 Nov
Argentina	18 UC	R	RA	.ar	N	N	25 May
Australia	18 UC	L	AUS	.au	N	N	26 Jan
Austria	16 U	R	A	.at	Y	N	26 Oct
Belarus	18 U	R	BY	.by	Y	Y	3 Jul
Belgium	18 UC	R	B	.be	N	N	21 Jul
Brazil	16 U	R	BR	.br	Y	Y*	7 Sep
Bulgaria	18 U	R	BG	.bg	N	N	3 Mar
Burma/Myanmar	18 U	R	BUR	.mm	N	N	4 Jan
Cambodia	18 U	R	K	.kh	Y	N	9 Nov
Canada	18 U	R	CDN	.ca	N	N	1 Jul
Chile	18 UC	R	RCH	.cl	Y	Y*	18 Sep
China	18 U	R	RC	.cn	Y	Y	1 Oct
Colombia	18 U	R	CO	.co	Y	N	20 Jul
Cuba	16 U	R	CU	.cu	Y	Y	1 Jan
Czech Republic	18 U	R	CZ	.cz	Y	N	28 Oct
Denmark	18 U	R	DK	.dk	Y	N	5 Jun
Egypt	18 UC	R	ET	.eg	Y	Y	23 Jul
Estonia	18 U	R	EST	.ee	Y	N	24 Feb
Finland	18 U	R	FIN	.fi	Y	N	6 Dec
France	18 U	R	F	.fr	N	N	14 Jul
Germany	18 U	R	D	.de	Y	N	3 Oct
Greece	18 UC	R	GR	.gr	Y	N	25 Mar
Haiti	18 U	R	RH	.ht	N	N	1 Jan
Hong Kong	18 U	L	—	.hk	N	N	1 Oct
Hungary	18 U	R	H	.hu	N	N	20 Aug
India	18 U	L	IND	.in	N	Y	26 Jan
Indonesia	17 U	L	RI	.id	Y	Y	17 Aug
Iran	18 U	R	IR	.ir	Y	Y	1 Apr
Iraq	18 U	R	IRQ	.iq	N	Y	14 Jul
Ireland	18 U	L	IRL	.ie	N	N	17 Mar
Israel	18 U	R	IL	.il	Y	Y*	14 May
Italy	18 U	R	I	.it	N	N	2 Jun
Japan	20 U	L	J	.jp	N	Y	23 Dec
Jordan	18 U	R	HKJ	.jo	N	Y	25 May
Kazakhstan	18 U	R	KZ	.kz	Y	Y*	16 Dec
Kenya	18 U	L	EAK	.ke	N	N*	12 Dec
Korea, North	17 U	R	—	.kp	Y	Y	9 Sep
Korea, South	19 U	R	ROK	.kr	Y	N*	15 Aug

──────── GAZETTEER · KUWAIT – ZIMBABWE · [4/4] ────────

Country	Voting age	Driving side	UN vehicle code	Internet country code	Military service	Death penalty	National Day
United Kingdom	18 U	L	GB	.uk	N	N	—
United States	18 U	R	USA	.us	N	Y	4 Jul
Kuwait	21 U	R	KWT	.kw	Y	Y	25 Feb
Latvia	18 U	R	LV	.lv	N	Y*	18 Nov
Lebanon	21 C	R	RL	.lb	N	Y	22 Nov
Liberia	18 U	R	LB	.lr	N	N*	26 Jul
Lithuania	18 U	R	LT	.lt	Y	N	16 Feb
Malaysia	21 U	L	MAL	.my	N	Y	31 Aug
Mexico	18 UC	R	MEX	.mx	Y	N	16 Sep
Monaco	18 U	R	MC	.mc	—	N	19 Nov
Morocco	18 U	R	MA	.ma	Y	N*	30 Jul
Netherlands	18 U	R	NL	.nl	N	N	30 Apr
New Zealand	18 U	L	NZ	.nz	N	N	6 Feb
Nigeria	18 U	R	WAN	.ng	N	Y	1 Oct
Norway	18 U	R	N	.no	Y	N	17 May
Pakistan	18 U	L	PK	.pk	N	Y	23 Mar
Peru	18 UC	R	PE	.pe	N	Y*	28 Jul
Philippines	18 U	R	RP	.ph	Y	N	12 Jun
Poland	18 U	R	PL	.pl	Y	N	3 May
Portugal	18 U	R	P	.pt	N	N	10 Jun
Romania	18 U	R	RO	.ro	N	N	1 Dec
Russia	18 U	R	RUS	.ru	Y	N*	12 Jun
Rwanda	18 U	R	RWA	.rw	N	N	1 Jul
Saudi Arabia	21	R	SA	.sa	N	Y	23 Sep
Singapore	21 UC	L	SGP	.sg	Y	Y	9 Aug
Slovakia	18 U	R	SK	.sk	N	N	1 Sep
Slovenia	18 U	R	SLO	.si	N	N	25 Jun
Somalia	18 U	R	SO	.so	N	Y	1 Jul
South Africa	18 U	L	ZA	.za	N	N	27 Apr
Spain	18 U	R	E	.es	N	N	12 Oct
Sudan	17 U	R	SUD	.sd	Y	Y	1 Jan
Sweden	18 U	R	S	.se	Y	N	6 Jun
Switzerland	18 U	R	CH	.ch	Y	N	1 Aug
Syria	18 U	R	SYR	.sy	Y	Y	17 Apr
Taiwan	20 U	R	—	.tw	Y	Y	10 Oct
Thailand	18 UC	L	T	.th	Y	Y	5 Dec
Turkey	18 U	R	TR	.tr	Y	N	29 Oct
Ukraine	18 U	R	UA	.ua	Y	N	24 Aug
Venezuela	18 U	R	YV	.ve	Y	N	5 Jul
Vietnam	18 U	R	VN	.vn	Y	Y	2 Sep
Zimbabwe	18 U	L	ZW	.zw	Y	Y	18 Apr

Society & Health

Your prayers should be for a healthy mind in a healthy body. — JUVENAL

──────────── ASSISTED SUICIDE ────────────

A series of high-profile deaths and legal decisions in 2008–09 intensified the debate over assisted suicide. In September 2008, Daniel James (23), who had been paralysed playing rugby but was not terminally ill, took his life at the Swiss 'suicide clinic', Dignitas. Two months later, the Director of Public Prosecutions (DPP) said that no charges would be brought against James's parents, who had gone with him to the clinic. In December,

Debbie Purdy

Sky broadcast the moment Craig Ewert (59), who had been suffering from motor neurone disease, took his life at Dignitas while listening to Beethoven's 9th. In February 2009, Peter Duff (80) and his wife Penelope (70) became the first terminally ill British couple to die together at Dignitas. In July, the conductor Sir Edward Downes (85) and his wife Joan (74) took their lives at Dignitas; even though Sir Edward was not terminally ill, he chose not to live without his wife, who had cancer. ❧ The most significant event took place in July, when MS sufferer Debbie Purdy (46) won a long legal battle to clarify whether her husband would be prosecuted if he accompanied her to Dignitas to help her die. In a landmark decision, the House of Lords ruled that the European Convention on Human Rights gave Purdy the right to choose how she died and, significantly, the Law Lords called on the DPP to clarify the circumstances in which charges for assisting a suicide would be brought. (Under the 1961 Suicide Act, anyone who 'aids, abets, counsels or procures the suicide of another' is liable to ≤14 years in jail.) In response, the DPP promised an interim policy by September 2009 and, after consultation, a final policy by spring 2010. Speaking to *The Telegraph*, the DPP confirmed that his guidance would cover assisted suicides in Britain as well as abroad, but acknowledged the difficulty of allowing such a controversial issue to be decided by the judiciary: 'Parliament has to speak'. ❧ If this trend of decriminalisation continues, it seems likely that assisted suicide will move from the margins of medical care towards the mainstream, and perhaps from clinics abroad to facilities in Britain. That said, assisted suicide will continue to face vigorous resistance from those opposed on religious or moral grounds, and from those who fear that the old and ill will feel obliged to end their lives. ❧ In 2008, the founder of Dignitas, Ludwig A. Minelli, observed that c.70% of those given a 'green light' (i.e., confirmation that a doctor was prepared to write them a fatal prescription) never contacted his clinic again: 'For them, simply knowing that there is an emergency exit available, should they need it, is so comforting that they have a good chance of living until their life's "natural end".'

─────────── UK BIRTHS & DEATHS ───────────

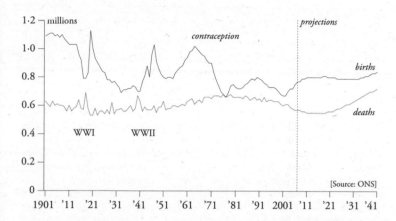

─────── SENSE OF BELONGING BY ETHNIC GROUP ───────

The proportion of people who feel they belong strongly to their neighbourhood and to Great Britain, by ethnicity (April–September 2008), is tabulated below:

Belong strongly to their neighbourhood %	ethnicity	Belong strongly to Great Britain %
83	Pakistani	91
83	Bangladeshi	89
81	Black Caribbean	84
78	Indian	90
76	White	83
73	Mixed race	86
71	Black African	81
70	Chinese or other	82

[Source: *Citizenship Survey* Apr–Sep 2008, England · Communities & Local Government, Jan 2009]

─────── BRITISH NATIONAL CHARACTER DEFINED ───────

5,000 Britons were asked by onepoll.com in November 2008 to select traits that define the British national character. The top British characteristics are, it seems:

1 .... talking about the weather	6 .... a love of bargains
2 .... queueing [see p.211]	7 .... curtain twitching
3 .... sarcasm [yeah, right]	8 .... stiff upper lip
4 .... watching soaps	9 .... love of all television
5 .... getting drunk	10 .... moaning

——————— BRITISH POPULATION AGED 90 & OVER ———————

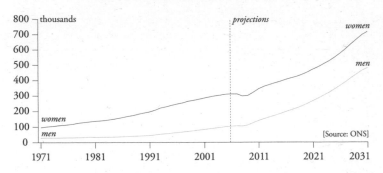

——————— PARENTS & INFLUENCES ON GIRLS ———————

39% of parents said that 'sex and relationships' was the topic they found hardest to discuss with their daughters, according to a survey by the Girls' School Association in January 2009. Despite this, 35% reported discussing the subject often or very often. When asked about the issues that worried them, 28% of parents said they were most concerned about the quality of their daughters' education; 24% said drink and drugs; and 11% said sex. 33% of mothers said that they spent >2 hours a day at weekends chatting alone with their daughters. Parents were also asked what they thought were the most positive and negative influences on their daughters:

Most positive influences	*Most negative influences*
family	WAGs
friends	'It' Girls
teachers	celebrity magazines
Olympians	reality TV stars
businesswomen	politicians

The authors of the report warned that girls were being bombarded by a culture of 'high heels and low IQs' that encouraged the abandonment of intellectual pursuits in favour of chasing fame.

——————— ATTITUDES TOWARDS CHILDREN ———————

54% of Britons think children are starting to behave 'like animals', according to a November 2008 poll by the children's charity Barnardo's. The survey, which suggested that society had a very negative and intolerant view of children, also found:

49% .... agree that children are increasingly 'a danger to each other and to adults'
43% ....agree that something needs to be done to 'protect us' from children
35% .... think the streets are 'infested' with children
49% .... disagree that children who get into trouble are often misunderstood
45% ....think people refer to children as 'feral' because they behave that way

———————— CHILDREN & THEIR WORRIES ————————

69% of British children aged 8–16 said they felt happy about life, according to the latest annual Ofsted survey, released in September 2008. However the pressures of exams and what to do in later life were two of the top issues concerning those still at school. Ofsted asked 148,988 children what most worried them; the results were:

Worry	%		
Exams	57	Money	28
My future	49	Being bullied	27
Friendships	34	Getting into trouble	27
My body	32	Crime	27
School work	31	Girlfriend/boyfriend/sex‡	26
My parents or family	30	Something else	11
Being healthy†	30	Nothing	5
		Don't know	3

† A July 2009 child health study was sabotaged by wily participants who tied pedometers intended to test their levels of activity to the collars of their pet dogs. ‡ Year 8 & 10 only. [Source: TellUs3]

———————— MOST POPULAR NAMES · 2008 ————————

In September 2009, the Office for National Statistics published a list of the most popular baby names in 2008. 708,711 live births were registered in England and Wales during 2008: 26,815 different boys' names and 34,043 different girls' names:

Jack	*nickname for John*	1	*? feminine version of Oliver*	Olivia
Oliver	*? from Latin for 'olive tree'*	2	*from the gemstone*	Ruby
Thomas	*Greek form of Aramaic for 'twin'*	3	*from the Latin Aemilia*	Emily
Harry	*pet form of Henry*	4	*from the Latin Gratia*	Grace
Joshua	*Jehova saves*	5	*allegedly created by Shakespeare*	Jessica
Alfie	*pet form of Alfred*	6	*Greek for 'young green shoot'*	Chloe
Charlie	*pet form of Charles*	7	*French form of Sophia*	Sophie
Daniel	*from Hebrew for 'God is my judge'*	8	*flower, symbol of purity*	Lily
James	*English form of Jacomus & Jacob*	9	*blend of medieval Emilia & Amalia*	Amelia
William	*from German for 'protector'*	10	*pet form of Eve*	Evie

According to Experian, the most common surnames in the UK in 2008 were:

Surname	number				
Smith	545,707	Taylor	253,481	Johnson	151,429
Jones	418,534	Davies	214,263		
Williams	294,865	Wilson	194,940	The incidence of the Chinese	
Brown	264,052	Evans	172,166	name Zhang has grown	
		Thomas	159,402	by 4,718% since 1996.	

TheBabyWebsite.com revealed a list of some of the most unfortunate names in Britain after analysing online telephone records in February 2009. The quirky names included: Justin Case, Terry Bull, Barb Dwyer, Paige Turner, Anna Sasin, Pearl Button, Jo King, Barry Cade, Carrie Oakey, and Tim Burr.

———————— SCHOOLCHILDREN & THE MEDIA ————————

86% of teachers said they believed TV programmes had a negative effect on the behaviour of their pupils, according to a 2009 poll by the Association of Teachers and Lecturers. The survey asked which media adversely influenced pupil behaviour:

Media	%				
Television	40	Social networking	17	Other	2
Computer games	28	Films/DVDs	9	Magazines	1
		Internet	5	Radio	0·1

Teachers were asked to list which television shows they thought caused pupils to adopt bad or inappropriate behaviour; below are the most commonly cited shows:

Big Brother [see p.122]	66%	*Hollyoaks*	36	*The Simpsons*	20
Little Britain	61	*Skins*	33	*Coronation Street*	17
EastEnders	43	*Waterloo Road*	26	*Gossip Girl*	12

When asked to specify the various types of inappropriate behaviour caused by watching such television shows, 88% of teachers thought 'general rudeness' (such as answering back or mimicking character catchphrases) was the most common problem; 82% said that some television programmes encouraged swearing or inappropriate language; 74% cited aggressive behaviour; and 43% sexually inappropriate behaviour.

More than 5 weeks a year are wasted at secondary schools in Britain due to bad behaviour, according to a survey by the NASUWT teaching union, released in April 2009. Researchers estimated that, on average, 50 minutes of lesson time are wasted each day as a consequence of pupil disruption.

———————— INTENTION TO STAY IN SCHOOL ————————

Children are less likely to want to stay in school (or to actually do so) if their parents are in 'routine' jobs, according to 2005 figures from England published in Social Trends 2009. Children aged 14–15 were asked if they would remain in school beyond 16, and were then tracked to see whether they did so. The results below are tabulated according to the socio-economic classification of the parents:

Intended to stay in school (%)	profession of parent	actually stayed in school	difference %
94	Higher professional	86	–8
89	Lower professional	81	–8
85	Intermediate	71	–14
77	Lower supervisory	63	–14
75	Routine	62	–13
84	Other	62	–22
84	All	72	–12

2009 research by Kent University and the London School of Economics suggested that those who had attended a private school earn on average 30% more than those who had attended a state school.

—————————— MATHS & SCIENCE ——————————

English children are the best in Europe at maths and science according to a 4-yearly Trends in International Mathematics and Science Study, published in December 2008. However, the study, which assessed the skills of pupils aged 10–14 in 60 countries, suggested that although English pupils are performing well in maths and science they are not actually enjoying these lessons, raising concerns that many will simply drop the subjects. ❦ Below are the top ten countries in maths and science:

#	Maths · *age 10*	Science · *age 10*	Maths · *age 14*	Science · *age 14*
1	Hong Kong	Singapore	Taiwan	Singapore
2	Singapore	Taiwan	South Korea	Taiwan
3	Taiwan	Hong Kong	Singapore	Japan
4	Japan	Japan	Hong Kong	South Korea
5	Kazakhstan	Russia	Japan	England
6	Russia	Latvia	Hungary	Hungary
7	England	England	England	Czech Rep.
8	Latvia	USA	Russia	Slovenia
9	Netherlands	Hungary	USA	Hong Kong
10	Lithuania	Italy	Lithuania	Russia

———— ENGLISH PARENTS · HELPING WITH HOMEWORK ————

The table below reveals how confident parents feel when helping with homework:

Level of confidence	school year of child (%)			
	years 1–2	years 3–6	years 7–9	years 10–12
Always confident	59	38	19	17
Never confident	1	1	2	3

[Source: ONS Social Trends 39, 2009 · data from 2007, England]

———————— STUDENTS IN HIGHER EDUCATION ————————

The number of students in higher education (2006/07) by subject and sex is below:

Subject %	♂	♀	all	Subject %	♂	♀	all
Business studies	15·8	11·2	13·1	Law	3·7	4·0	3·8
Education	5·4	12·0	9·2	Physical sciences	4·8	2·6	3·6
Social studies	7·5	9·3	8·5	Medicine & dentistry	2·6	2·7	2·7
Biological sciences	5·9	7·7	7·0	Architecture/planning	4·1	1·4	2·6
Arts & design	6·2	7·2	6·8	Mass communication	2·0	2·1	2·0
Engineering & tech	11·7	1·7	5·9	Mathematical sciences	2·1	0·9	1·4
Languages	4·5	7·0	5·9	Agriculture	0·6	0·7	0·7
Computer science	8·3	1·7	4·5	Veterinary science	0·1	0·3	0·2
History/philosophy	4·6	4·2	4·4				

[Source: Higher Education Statistics Agency]

———————— SEX & SEXUALITY ————————

76% of Britons are satisfied with their sex life, according to *The Observer*'s October 2008 'Sex Poll'. The survey revealed that the average Briton lost their virginity between the ages of 16–17 – although it seems that, as might be expected, Britons are increasingly losing their virginity at a younger age: on average, those aged >65 lost their virginity at 19; those aged 16–24 lost their virginity at 15. Men admitted (boasted?) an average of 11 sexual partners, whereas women reported (admitted?) an average of just under 7 partners. Further results from this survey are listed below:

How do you define your sexuality?	%
Heterosexual	92
Homosexual	4
Bisexual	2
Don't know	2

In an average month, how many times do you currently have sex?				%
None	25	11–15		11
1	4	16–20		6
2	5	21–25		3
3	5	26–30		1
4	8	>31		2
5	5			
6–10	25	*Average*		6·7

On a scale of 1–5, how would you rate your sex drive?		%
1	(very low)	12
2	(low)	12
3	(average)	32
4	(high)	25
5	(very high)	19
	Average = 3·3	

On a scale of 1–5, how would you rate the sexual performance of…		
%	*yourself*	*your partner*
1 – very poor	2	3
2 – poor	3	5
3 – average	40	33
4 – good	31	31
5 – very good	24	28
Average rating	3·73	3·77

Have you ever been unfaithful to your current partner?			%
Yes	18	No	82

Which of the following best describes how frequently you were unfaithful?	%
Regularly	10
Occasionally	32
Rarely	29
Only once	29

Have you ever been unfaithful with a friend of your partner?			%
Yes	56	No	44

Other findings from the survey indicated that: 68% are currently in a stable relationship. ❦ 45% admitted to using sex toys. ❦ 49% had experienced a one-night stand. ❦ 21% had slept with someone whose name they did not know. ❦ 79% believe that monogamy is *desirable*, but only 70% believe it is *natural*. ❦ 59% said that trust was the most important aspect of a successful relationship; only 5% said that money was. ❦ 12% of those in a stable relationship thought their partner had cheated on them. ❦ 48% thought it was possible to maintain a happy relationship or marriage without sex. ❦ 13% have had sexual contact with someone of the same sex as them. ❦ 26% had slept with a work colleague. ❦ 13% had made love at their place of work. ❦ 9% had visited a prostitute. ❦ 22% of those in full-time work said that they would have sex in order to further their career. ❦ 13% would consider having sex for a large amount of money. ❦ 86% of men reported that they were content with the size of their penis. [Source: *The Observer* Sex Poll 2008 · ICM Research]

SUMMARY OF MARRIAGES 1981–2007

231,450 couples were married in England and Wales in 2007, a fall of 3·3% from 2006, and the fewest weddings since 1895, according to a 2009 Office for National Statistics report. Marriages hit a peak in 1972 when 480,285 couples got hitched, but since then there has been a steady decline. Only 62% of all marriages in 2007 were first marriages for both parties; in 1940, this figure peaked at 91%. Below is a summary of marriage statistics from England and Wales for the period 1981–2007:

	1981	1991	2001	2007
TOTAL MARRIAGES	351,973	306,756	249,227	231,450
Civil ceremonies	172,514	151,333	160,238	153,960
Religious ceremonies	179,459	155,423	88,989	77,490
Of which · C of E	118,435	102,840	60,878	55,890
· Roman Catholic	26,097	19,551	10,518	8,750
· Nonconformist	29,017	25,472	11,163	6,680
· other Christian bodies	4,422	5,597	4,047	3,420
· other	1,488	1,963	2,383	2,750
Previous marital status · first for both	227,713	192,238	148,642	143,440
· first for one	67,048	63,159	55,943	46,970
· remarriage for both	57,212	51,359	44,642	41,040

ARGUING COUPLES

British couples spend nearly ten days a year not speaking to one another after a row, according to a March 2009 survey by OnePoll. On average, couples have two arguments a week, after which sulking normally lasts for two hours and 14 minutes. 60% admitted they would rather sulk than quickly kiss and make up, and 55% admitted that they would hold a grudge against their loved one even once they had forgotten what the argument was about. The top reasons for not speaking are:

1 .... saying the wrong thing
2 ....taking each other for granted
3 .... money
4 ...... being unable to find something
5 ...... disagreement over child-raising
6 .... getting lost on car journey
7 .... never going out as a couple
8 ...... being shunned in the bedroom
9 .... hogging the television
10 .... jealousy over friendships

THE WAY TO WOO A WOMAN

British men are some of the world's least romantic, according to Professor Richard Wiseman who conducted an international study of >6,500 people in July 2009. According to the women questioned by Wiseman, the best ways to woo them are:

Give her a lovely surprise	Tell her she is the most wonderful
Take her on a weekend away	woman you have ever met
Write a poem or song about her	Run her a bath after a bad day

———————————— GENERATIONS ————————————

Journalists and sociologists have long enjoyed dividing British and American society into generational cohorts with catchy nicknames and supposedly defining characteristics. Below are thumbnail sketches of some UK generations of note:

The Lost Generation · the men lost in WWI – therefore, not a generation so much as a lack of one. Some claim that war casualties were disproportionately heavy among the elite (because they possessed the physical and financial resources to fight); thus the war robbed the nation of a generation of leaders.

Baby Boomers · those born after WWII who came of age during the countercultural movements of the 1960s. Known for making marketeers weak at the knees by their sheer number and (until recently) spending power.

The Windrush Generation · Caribbean immigrants who came to Britain in the 1940s and 1950s; named after the *Empire Windrush*, the ship from Jamaica that brought the first wave of immigrants in 1948.

The Me Generation · young, upwardly mobile, and materialistic Thatcherites who came of age in the 1980s. The term developed from the 'me decade', coined by American writer Tom Wolfe to describe the narcissistic 1970s.

Generation X · the term coined by the Canadian writer Douglas Coupland for those born in the 1960s and '70s. *Gen X* is characterised as cynical, apathetic, and aimless.

Generation Y · one of many terms used to define the group born after *Generation X*, between 1979–1994. Also called *Echo Boomers*, *Generation Y* is primarily the progeny of the original Boomers. Also known as the *Millennium Generation*, the *Net Generation*, and *Generation O* (for those in the US who helped sweep Obama to power).

Recent economic woes have inspired new generational nicknames: *Babygloomers* are those stuck supporting their children and their parents; the *Bungee Brood Generation* are young adults who still rely on their parents financially; and the *Boomerang Generation* refers to adult children who have moved back in with their parents. In the *FT*, Gideon Rachman described *Generation L*, the 'lucky generation' that (until recently, perhaps) had enjoyed a 'holiday from history' by escaping war and recession.

———————— EXPERIENCE OF FAMILY EVENTS BY AGE 25 ————————

Below are the results of an ONS study of British women aged 25–59 that explored which 'family events' various generations had experienced by the time they were 25:

% experienced	age† 25–29	30–34	35–39	40–44	45–49	50–54	55–59
Marriage	24	33	45	56	65	72	75
Birth of child	30	29	33	34	39	44	51
Cohabitation	21	16	12	7	4	2	1
Marriage breakdown	13	13	14	14	11	7	6

† Age at time of interview [Source: ONS Social Trends 39, 2009 · data from 2001–03]

———————— ADULTS LIVING WITH THEIR PARENTS ————————

The prohibitive cost of housing has been blamed for the number of young adults living at home with their parents. A 2007 Eurobarometer survey found that 44% of Britons aged 15–30 believed young adults could not leave home because of a lack of affordable housing, and 38% thought it was because they could not afford to live independently. The data below, from Social Trends 2009, reveal the increasing number of young people still living with their parents, most notably young males:

(thousands)	age 20–24		age 25–29		age 30–34	
Year	♂	♀	♂	♀	♂	♀
2001	949	624	454	220	208	75
2002	996	638	390	193	213	68
2003	969	641	416	184	216	84
2004	1,054	675	434	201	203	89
2005	1,079	685	432	211	194	66
2006	1,103	733	438	210	185	64
2007	1,085	747	445	232	178	63
2008	1,086	745	486	245	180	70

———————————— THE PINK LIST 2009 ————————————

The Independent on Sunday annually compiles a 'Pink List' of the most influential gay and lesbian people in British society. Listed below are 2009's Pink List top ten:

1 . . Peter Mandelson [see p.38] . politician
2 . . Stephen Fry . . . . polymath
3 . . Sir Ian McKellen . . . . actor
4 . . David Starkey . . . . historian
5 . . Beth Ditto . . . . singer
6 . . . Alan Bennett . . . . writer
7 . . . Phyllida Lloyd . . film/stage director
8 . . . Ben Bradshaw . . . . MP
9 . . . Carol Ann Duffy . . . . poet
10 . . Nick Bowles . . . . political strategist

———————————— MEMORABLE EVENTS ————————————

Recent global events can be more memorable than personal milestones, according to March 2009 research by UKTV. The study suggested that a larger proportion of adults could recall in great detail the events of 9/11 than could remember the birth of their first child. The attack on the World Trade Center in 2001 was the event best remembered by respondents, 82% of whom recalled the disaster in detail. 81% remembered who told them about 9/11, 84% could pinpoint when they heard about the attacks, 92% knew where they were, and 71% could remember what they were doing at the time. The most remembered historical and personal events are below:

Historical event	% remembered	Personal event	% remembered
The 9/11 attacks	82	Death of a close relative	81
Death of Diana, Princess of Wales	62	Passing driving test	79
July 7 London bombings	58	First date with partner	76

──────── VIEWS ON DOMESTIC VIOLENCE & RAPE ────────

Attitudes to domestic violence were examined by a Home Office survey released in March 2009. Men and women were asked how acceptable they thought it was for a man to hit or slap his wife or girlfriend in a variety of different situations, viz:

Situation (%)	acceptable	sometimes acceptable†	never acceptable
Her nagging or constantly moaning at him	2	14	82
Her flirting with other men	3	10	86
Her being dressed in sexy/revealing clothes in public	6	14	79
Her having an affair/cheating on him	1	7	90
Her not treating him with respect	2	9	88

37% reported that they personally knew a woman who had suffered domestic violence at the hands of a man. 93% said they would take action if they thought a female family member was suffering domestic violence, 87% would take action if it was a female friend, and 81% a neighbour. 54% who suspected a family member was being abused would contact the police; 44% would offer advice or support; and 25% would confront the abuser and ask him to stop. ❦ The survey also explored attitudes to rape. Respondents were asked whether a woman should be held responsible for being raped or sexually assaulted in the following circumstances:

If the woman is ...	be held responsible	be partly held responsible	never be held responsible
Drunk	11	25	62
Wearing sexy or revealing clothes	6	20	72
Not clearly saying 'no' to the man	10	39	48
Using drugs	15	27	56
Flirting heavily with man beforehand	10	33	55
Out walking alone at night	4	10	84
Working as a prostitute	17	30	52

† Actually phrased as 'acceptable in some circumstances but not in others'. Respondents were aged >18 and living in England or Wales. [Source: Home Office Ipsos Mori Poll, March 2009] ❦ Research by South Africa's Medical Research Council (MRC) in June 2009 revealed that one in four South African men admitted they had raped somebody. 73% of those who admitted committing rape said that the attack had taken place when they were under the age of 20. Nearly half of those who had carried out a rape admitted they had done so more than once. In an interview with the BBC on these disturbing findings, Professor Rachel Jewkes of the MRC said, 'We know that we have a higher prevalence of rape in South Africa than there is in other countries. And it's partly rooted in our incredibly disturbed past and the way that South African men over the centuries have been socialised into forms of masculinity that are predicated on the idea of being strong and tough and the use of force to assert dominance and control over women, as well as other men'. ❦ In the United Kingdom, only 6·5% of all reported rapes currently lead to a criminal conviction. In an effort to improve this conviction rate, judges are to begin advising juries to ignore some of the many myths surrounding rape. The guidelines, promoted by Solicitor General Vera Baird QC, include the advice that juries should not presume a victim was 'asking for it' by dressing or behaving in a provocative fashion.

————————— ETHNICITY & FAMILY —————————

One in ten British children is now part of a mixed-race family, according to a January 2009 report, *Ethnicity & Family*, from the Equality and Human Rights Commission. The researchers noted that Britain's youngest generation has a significantly higher proportion of ethnic minorities – 20% of under-16s are from an ethnic minority background, compared to 15% of the total population. The white British population has the oldest age profile; nearly 24% are over 60 years old. Tabulated below are the average ages of various ethnic groups within the UK:

Ethnic group	*average age*		
White British	40	Other Asian 31	Mixed white/African. 19
Other white	39	Other black 28	Mixed white/Asian... 18
Black Caribbean	35	Black African 26	Mixed white/Carib... 16
Indian	33	Pakistani 26	
Chinese	32	Bangladeshi 24	
		Other mixed 23	ALL GROUPS 39

The report suggested that inter-racial relationships were most prevalent among the young – only 4% of men aged >60 in a relationship had a partner from a different ethnic background, compared to 10% of men aged 16–29. Below are the partnership patterns of British men and women aged 16–29 who are in a relationship:

♂ w. partner of same ethnicity	♂ w. partner of different ethnicity	ethnicity %	♀ w. partner of different ethnicity	♀ w. partner of same ethnicity
95	5	White British	5	95
75	25	Other White	34	66
84	16	Indian	11	89
94	6	Pakistani	3	97
86	14	Bangladeshi	4	96
38	62	Black Caribbean	51	49
74	26	Black African	20	80
87	13	Chinese	37	63

[Source: *Ethnicity and Family: Relationships Within and Between Ethnic Groups*
January 2009 · Figures from Labour Force Survey Oct–Dec 2004 – Apr–Jun 2008]

————————— CHILDLESS WOMEN —————————

Childless women are more likely to be employed in 'professional' or 'managerial' positions, according to research released in June 2009 by the Office for National Statistics. Researchers analysed long-term statistical data to explore lifelong childlessness, and noted that of the sample group (women born between 1956–60), 17% remained childless in their early forties. The absence of a partner was (unsurprisingly) one of the main causes of childlessness – although 68% of childless women had been married or had cohabited with a man at some point during the study. The ONS noted that childlessness had become a 'choice' for women during the 1980s, whereas previously it was mainly a consequence of poverty and poor nutrition.

———————————— FEAR & ANXIETY ————————————

77% of adults in the UK think that the world has become a more frightening place during the last ten years, according to April 2009 research by the Mental Health Foundation. 61% reported that they felt anxious some of the time, and 11% of women said they felt frightened or anxious a lot of the time. 29% admitted that fear had stopped them from doing something they wanted to. Respondents were asked what they personally became frightened or anxious about; the results are below:

Fear	(%)	♂	♀		♂	♀
Money/finance/debt		43	66	Losing their job	26	23
Death of a loved one		36	66	Terrorism	19	29
Threat of crime		30	38	Being isolated	15	31
Welfare of their children		28	40	Losing their home	18	23
Developing serious illness		26	39	Climate change	15	21
Getting old		21	33	Threat of war	9	19
				Losing social status	7	5

———————————— SWEARING ————————————

The average Briton swears 14 times a day, according to a survey by Australian company Nulon. 87% admitted swearing every day, and 92% claimed they were not offended by swearing in an adult context. Below are the five most common curses:

Profanity	% saying in previous week		
Shit	90	Bastard	86
Fuck	88	Twat	83
		Bollocks	81

The average child hears its parents swear at least 6 times a week, according to a survey by youngpoll. com. 86% of 11-year-olds said that their parents' profanities, and foul language by celebrities such as Gordon Ramsay, set a bad example. 1 in 3 said they had asked their parents to stop swearing. ❧ A July 2009 study by Keele University suggested that swearing can help to reduce pain. Researchers asked volunteers to submerge their hands in a bowl of freezing water for as long as they could stand while repeating a swear word of their choice. The volunteers were then asked to retake the exercise while repeating any innocuous word they would use to describe a table. On average, volunteers could keep their hands in the freezing water for nearly 2 minutes while swearing but for only 1 minute 15 seconds when being polite. The researchers suggested that swearing triggered the body's fight-or-flight mechanism and warned that, to preserve its effect, people should not swear too often.

———————— PROBABILITY OF SURVIVING TO AGE 75 ————————

Women in England and Wales have a 78% chance of living until they are 75, according to ONS data from 2005–07, released in July 2009. Men have only a 67% chance of living to this age. The scale of health inequalities across the region was illustrated by the variations in this indicator. Women and men in east Dorset had an 86% and 77% respectively chance of seeing 75. However, the probability for women in Blaenau Gwent was 68%, and for men in Manchester it was just 53%.

———— BURIALS, CREMATIONS & CEMETERIES ————

A pilot scheme to create more space in Britain's overcrowded cemeteries was launched in January 2009. Under new government proposals, graves >100 years old may be re-used to create space-saving 'double-decker' plots. According to a 2007 Department of Justice report, there are some 9,747 burial grounds across England and Wales, the majority of which (70%) are run by the Church of England. 11% of local authority burial grounds are currently closed to new burials; 12% are open only to new burials in existing graves. This crisis in capacity is particularly acute in London, where only 50% of cemeteries have space for new burials. The table below shows the estimated usable area for new burials in local authority cemeteries:

Region	AREA OCCUPIED BY GRAVES		UNUSED AREA		av. predicted life of cemetery
	hectares	% of total	hectares	% of total	
North East	489	81	117	19	41 years
North West	692	86	112	14	38
Yorkshire	455	78	125	22	50
East Midlands	352	75	117	25	52
West Midlands	462	79	123	21	33
East of England	337	76	107	24	38
London	562	86	88	14	37
South East	413	77	120	23	50
South West	279	75	94	25	44
Wales	257	77	76	23	53
TOTAL	4,298	80	1,079	20	45

According to the Cremation Society of Great Britain, Britain has one of the highest cremation rates in the world: 72% of all deaths were cremated in 2006. There are currently 254 crematoria in the UK which, in 2007, performed a total of 417,920 cremations. The regions performing the greatest number of cremations in 2007 were:

Region	crematoria	cremations			
London	24	35,806	Greater Manchester	13	19,130
Scotland	25	34,557	Yorkshire West	11	15,835
West Midlands	12	21,183	Essex	8	15,721
Wales	13	20,331	Kent	8	12,770
			Merseyside	6	12,403

During the early C19th, inner-London graveyards became severely overcrowded and, as the urban population grew, the tradition of burying bodies in small local churchyards became unsustainable. In 1832, the government enacted legislation to encourage the construction of large private cemeteries on the outskirts of London. The resulting cemeteries – which became known as the 'Magnificent Seven' – are:

Kensal Green [*founded in* 1832] · West Norwood [1837] · Highgate [1839]
Abney Park [1840] · Nunhead [1840] · Brompton [1840] · Tower Hamlets [1841]

Highgate is renowned for its interred celebrities (not least Karl Marx), but Kensal Green has many celebrated burials, including Charles Babbage (1791–1871), and Isambard Kingdom Brunel (1806–89).

────────── DRINKING HABITS ──────────

The government recommends that men should not regularly drink more than 3 or 4 units of alcohol a day† and women not more than 2 or 3 units. However, 37% of British adults admit to exceeding this benchmark. Figures from the General Household Survey, released in January 2009, showed that 20% of adults consumed more than double the recommended amount on their heaviest drinking day of the week. Below is the average weekly consumption of different types of alcohol, by sex:

Men %	*type of alcoholic drink consumed* (2008)	*women %*
44	normal strength beer, lager or cider	12
28	wine	59
13	strong beer, lager or cider	5
12	spirits	16
2	alcopops	5
1	fortified wine	3

According to the survey, men were 7% more likely than women to exceed the daily guidelines for regular drinking, 41% compared to 34%. Those in 'managerial and professional' households were more likely (43%) to exceed daily limits on their heaviest drinking day of the week than those in 'routine and manual' households (31%). Below are self-reported drinking frequencies, by sex and age, for 2008:

%	16–24 ♂	16–24 ♀	25–44 ♂	25–44 ♀	45–64 ♂	45–64 ♀	>65 ♂	>65 ♀	total ♂	total ♀
Frequency of drinking										
Almost every day	8	2	5	4	18	7	22	14	13	7
5 or 6 days a week	2	1	5	2	4	5	3	5	4	3
3 or 4 days a week	13	4	19	10	20	11	14	7	18	9
Once or twice a week	35	30	36	29	29	28	19	17	30	26
Once or twice a month	18	28	13	19	7	15	10	10	11	17
Once every few months	3	9	5	10	4	10	4	7	4	9
Once or twice a year	10	5	3	7	6	11	8	16	6	10
Not at all in last year	12	21	14	18	11	14	20	24	14	18

According to 2007 NHS data, 6,541 deaths in England were directly related to alcohol consumption. Since 2001, the number of deaths attributed to alcohol has risen by 19%. In 2007–08 there were 863,300 hospital admissions related to alcohol; of these, 4,700 were children aged under 16. Those aged 45–54 were most likely to be admitted to hospital owing to alcohol. The NHS estimates that the total annual cost to the service of alcohol misuse (in 2006–07 prices) is £2,704·1m.

† The government previously advised women not to exceed 14 units a week, and men not to exceed 21; however concerns over binge drinking changed the focus to daily consumption. 1 pint of strong lager=3 units; 1 pint of ordinary lager, bitter or cider, or glass of wine=2; 1 alcopop=1·5; 1 measure of spirits=1. [Source: Drinking: Adults Behaviour and Knowledge in 2008 · ONS] ❦ Research by the University of the West of England in March 2009 indicated that British teenagers were among the heaviest drinkers in Europe. Teenagers aged 15 and 16 were asked if they had been drunk in the last 30 days; the percentage admitting to binge drinking was: Denmark, 49%; UK, 33%; Ireland, 26%.

—— INCIDENCE & MORTALITY OF MAJOR CANCERS ——

Roughly one-third of the British population will develop cancer at some point in their lives. Since 1998, prostate cancer has overtaken lung cancer to become the most commonly diagnosed cancer in men. Breast cancer is the most commonly diagnosed cancer in women. Below are the incidence rates of major cancers, by sex:

Men · England			*Women · England*		
Cancer	1996	2006	Cancer	1996	2006
Lung	20,200	18,000	Breast	31,500	38,000
Prostate	19,900	30,000	Lung	11,400	13,100
Colorectal	14,800	16,400	Colorectal	13,600	13,500
Bladder	7,700	5,900	Ovary	5,400	5,300
Stomach	5,300	4,000	Uterus	4,000	5,600

Mortality rates (measured as rates per 100,000 population) for lung cancer in men were reduced considerably between 1995–2004, but in women the rate remained roughly the same. Mortality rates for major cancers by sex in the UK are below:

♂ · Cancer	1995	2004	♀ · Cancer	1995	2004
Lung	76	56	Breast	38	29
Prostate	31	27	Lung	31	30
Colorectal	30	24	Colorectal	19	15

[Source: ONS Social Trends 39, 2009]

———————— RISING OBESITY RATES ————————

22% of all English adults are obese and 61% are overweight – according to the latest figures released by the NHS Information Centre in February 2009, which used the Body Mass Index (BMI)[†] as a yardstick. As the population gets fatter, so the number of people admitted to hospital with a primary diagnosis of obesity increases. Below is a breakdown of such admissions by gender between 1996–2008:

Obesity admissions	♂	♀	*total*		♂	♀	*total*
1996/97	225	507	738	2003/04	498	1,213	1,711
1997/98	217	536	756	2004/05	589	1,442	2,035
1998/99	270	682	954	2005/06	746	1,786	2,564
1999/00	275	704	979	2006/07	1,047	2,807	3,862
2000/01	309	741	1,054	2007/08	1,405	3,613	5,018
2001/02	427	731	1,019				
2002/03	427	848	1,275				

[Source: Hospital Episode Statistics, the NHS Information Centre]

The statistics also showed a rise in the number of people who underwent bariatric surgery, i.e., procedures to aid weight loss, including stomach stapling or gastric bypass. In 2007/08 there were 2,724 Finished Consultant Episodes for bariatric surgery (598 for males and 2,126 for females), an increase of 40% since 2006/07. † Those with a BMI >25 are classified as overweight; >30 as obese.

———————— TEENAGERS & DRUG TREATMENT ————————

23,905 children under the age of 18 were treated for drug and alcohol problems in 2007–08, according to a January 2009 report by the National Treatment Agency. The NTA claimed that although the number of children in the UK using drugs was falling, greater numbers were able to access treatment services. Below are the numbers of children accessing help, by age and primary substance abused:

Substance (No.)	age <12	12–13	13–14	14–15	15–16	16–17	17–18
Heroin/opiates	10	–	16	21	46	172	382
Amphetamines	–	–	12	32	69	88	140
Cocaine	–	–	7	60	164	226	344
Crack	–	0	5	6	25	33	85
Ecstasy	–	–	18	47	100	146	123
Cannabis	102	230	745	1,884	3,114	3,035	2,911
Solvents	22	23	49	75	71	32	33
Alcohol	57	169	565	1,244	1,970	2,131	2,453
Other	–	–	15	30	44	61	85
TOTAL	202	436	1,432	3,399	5,603	5,924	6,556

49% of those treated received only 'psychosocial intervention' – i.e., specialist counselling and mentoring to bring about behavioural change. 14% of these interventions involved 'harm reduction', such as advice on preventing overdose, needle exchanges, &c. Only 9 teenagers attended residential rehabilitation facilities in 2007–08. Below are the outcomes for young people accessing these services, 2005/06–2007/08:

Outcome (%)	2005/06	2006/07	2007/08
Completed	48	50	57
Referred on	7	6	7
Dropped out/left	29	25	18
Prison	2	2	2
Treatment declined	0	2	5
Other	14	14	11

———————— SMOKING STATISTICS OF NOTE ————————

39% ....of the British population were smokers in 1980
22% ....of the English population were smokers in 2006
23% .... of the Welsh population were smokers in 2006
26% .... of the Scottish population were smokers in 2006
39% ....started smoking aged under 16
34% .... of male smokers smoked hand-rolled cigarettes
17% .... of mothers reported smoking throughout their pregnancy
34% .... of smokers are divorced or separated
13·5................................the average number of cigarettes smoked a day

[Source: Statistics on Smoking, England 2008 – released October 2008]

―――――――――――――― EUROPE & DRUGS ――――――――――――――

Cannabis is the most commonly consumed drug in Europe: 71m (or 22%) of all European adults aged 15–64 admitted to using cannabis at least once in their lifetime. According to the European Monitoring Centre for Drugs and Drug Addiction's 2008 annual report, released in November, it is estimated that there are 7,000–8,000 drug-induced deaths across Europe each year (80% of which are associated with the abuse of opiates). In 2005–06, drug-induced deaths accounted for 3·5% of all deaths of Europeans aged 15–39. ❧ Tabulated below is the prevalence of lifetime drug use in the general European population (aged 15–64):

	cannabis	*amphetamines*	*cocaine*
Estimated number of European users	71·5m	11m	12m
European average	21·8%	3·3%	3·6%
Lowest prevalence	Romania (1·7%)	Greece (0·1%)	Romania (0·4%)
	Malta (3·5%)	Romania (0·2%)	Malta (0·4%)
	Bulgaria (4·4%)	Malta (0·4%)	Lithuania (0·4%)
Highest prevalence	Denmark (36·5%)	UK (11·9%)	UK (7·7%)
	France (30·6%)	Denmark (6·9%)	Spain (7·0%)
	UK (30·1%)	Norway (3·6%)	Italy (6·6%)

―――――――――――― EUROPEAN HEALTH LEAGUE ――――――――――――

The Swedish think tank Health Consumer Powerhouse produces an annual index of the quality of health care across Europe. Released in November 2008, the latest index ranks health care providers on a range of measures including: MRSA deaths; 5-year cancer survival rates; waiting times; patients' rights; and childhood vaccination rates. Since 2007, the UK has risen 4 places to 13th. The top 20 in 2008 were:

1.... Netherlands	6....... Germany	11........ Estonia	16 =.. Czech Rep.
2....... Denmark	7..... Switzerland	12...... Belgium	16 =.........Italy
3.........Austria	8........Norway	13.............UK	18..........Spain
4...Luxembourg	9........ Finland	14......Hungary	19........ Greece
5......... Sweden	10........ France	15.........Ireland	20.......Slovenia

―――――――――――――― BAFFLED BY ANATOMY ――――――――――――――

Many Britons cannot identify the location of major body organs, according to research undertaken at King's College London in May 2009. Respondents were shown a series of cards depicting outlines of the human body with various organs placed in different positions. Respondents were then asked to identify the card that showed the correct location. 85% of respondents knew where the intestines were, but less than 50% could correctly locate the heart, and only 46% could pinpoint the kidneys. Comparing these results to a similar study undertaken in 1970, the researchers found that, despite advances in education and the advent of the internet, no significant improvement in anatomical knowledge was discernible.

———————————— HEAT WAVE WARNING LEVEL ————————————

In 2009, the Met Office and the government established Heat-Health Watch – a colour-coded alert system to monitor summertime temperatures between 1 June and 15 September, and dispense appropriate advice. Below are the regional temperature thresholds that must be achieved before a heat wave is officially declared:

Region	(°C)	day	night
North East		28	15
North West		30	15
Yorkshire & Humber		29	15
East Midlands		30	15
West Midlands		30	15
East of England		30	15

South East	31	16
London	32	18
South West	30	15
Wales	30	15

These temperatures can damage health if hit on two consecutive days and the intervening night.

Below are the colour-coded warning levels, and the associated government actions:

Level	colour	actions
1	GREEN	*minimum state of vigilance, background preparations*
2	YELLOW	*≥60% risk that threshold temps could be reached in ≥1 regions over consecutive days, health care services in readiness*
3	AMBER	*threshold temps met for 1 day and night in ≥1 region, 90% chance of high temps the following day; health care advice targeted at high-risk groups such as elderly and infirm*
4	RED	*emergency – heat wave so prolonged/severe that effects can harm infrastructure and endanger the fit and healthy. Stay out of the sun*

Climate change is forecast to increase the frequency of British heat waves. It is predicted that heat waves similar in severity to that experienced in 2003 will occur every summer by the 2080s. [See p.77]

———————————— ORGAN TRANSPLANTS ————————————

3,235 people had their lives saved or improved by an organ transplant in 2007–08, and 2,488 people had their sight restored after a cornea transplant. Below are some other transplant statistics of note, from the Transplant Activity Report 2007–08:

No. listed as actively waiting for a transplant (as of March 2008) 7,655
No. on the NHS Organ Donor Register (as of March 2008) 15,140,826
No. receiving an organ from a deceased donor 2,381
No. receiving an organ from a living donor 854
% rise in living donors from 2006–07 to 2007–08 .... 22%
% of deceased donors giving a kidney 98%
% of deceased donors giving more than one organ 81%
Mean age of deceased organ donors, 2007–08 .... 45·8

In February 2009 it was disclosed that 23% of all liver transplants in the United Kingdom in 2007–08 went to recipients with alcohol-related liver disease, an increase of 60% over the last decade.

─────── SNAPSHOT OF ENGLAND'S HEALTH ───────

The Health Profile of England is compiled annually to provide a snapshot of the nation's well-being. The 2008 report, published in January 2009, revealed declining mortality rates from circulatory disease, all types of cancer, and suicide, and showed that life expectancy was at a record high and infant mortality at a record low. However, rates of diabetes and chlamydia rose, as did the levels of obesity in adults and children [see p.109]. Below is a snapshot of health and well-being in England, showing how key indicators of health have changed over the previous five years:

Indicator	year	%	5 yrs ago (%)	±%
People who smoke · ♀	2006	21	25	−4
People who smoke · ♂	2006	23	28	−5
Smoking cessation · 4-week quitters	2007/08	52	53	−1
Drinking · excessive† · ♀	2006	20	n/a	−
Drinking · excessive† · ♂	2006	31	n/a	−
Binge drinking‡ · ♀	2006	15	n/a	−
Binge drinking‡ · ♂	2006	23	n/a	−
Healthy eating · fruit/veg 5-a-day · ♀	2007	31	26	+5
Healthy eating · fruit/veg 5-a-day · ♂	2007	27	22	+5
Physically active§ · ♀	2006	28	24	+4
Physically active§ · ♂	2006	40	36	+4
Obese · ♀	2007	24·4	23·0	+1·4
Obese · ♂	2007	23·6	22·2	+1·4
Adults misusing any drugs	2007/08	9·3	12·2	−2·9
Adults misusing Class A drugs	2007/08	3·0	3·3	−0·3

† Exceeding government guidelines of 14 units a week for a woman and 21 for a man. ‡ Drinking >6 units on at least one day a week for women and 8 for men. § Achieving a minimum of 30 mins or more moderate-intensity activity 5 days a week. [Source: Health Profile of England 2008]

─────── PROTECTING THE NHS ───────

90% of the British public fear that the recession will lead to cuts in NHS funding, according to a June 2009 survey by the BMA. Further findings are below:

Statement	% agree
Cuts should be made in other government departments to protect NHS	77
Taxes should increase to maintain growth of NHS funding	40
The recession could cause NHS to charge for some services	85
NHS should prioritise its funding for the most important services	80
Private involvement in the NHS is a good thing	59
The NHS internal market should be abolished	55
Patients and public should have greater say in how NHS delivers services	77
There should be less political involvement in the running of the NHS	73
The government cannot safeguard the NHS in the current climate	40
Doctors and nurses can safeguard the NHS in the current climate	95

———————SOME HEALTH STORIES OF NOTE———————

{OCT 2008} · The British Association of Dermatologists warned of 'mobile phone dermatitis', the symptoms of which include a red, itchy rash on the ear or cheek caused by an allergic reaction to the nickel used to manufacture mobiles. {NOV} · Research by a group of scientists at Emory University suggested that the daily rhythms of cells could explain why many succumb to heart attacks and strokes in the early hours of the morning. The scientists discovered that the cells which maintain blood vessels were at their least active at this time. {DEC} · A Dutch study suggested that babies born by Caesarean section were 80% more likely to develop asthma than those delivered naturally. {JAN 2009} · A study published in *The Lancet Neurology* warned against the long-term prescription of anti-psychotic drugs to patients with dementia. The research suggested that those on such drugs long-term had an increased mortality. ❦ Research by Consensus Action on Salt and Health revealed that many restaurant meals contain very high levels of salt. The organisation analysed dishes from 16 high-street restaurant chains and found that 6 served main courses containing more than 6g of salt – the entire adult daily recommended intake. {FEB} · Researchers at the University of Oxford suggested that daily supplements of vitamin D could help to prevent multiple sclerosis. Their investigations indicated that insufficient vitamin D during pregnancy and in childhood could lead to a susceptibility to the disease. ❦ A successful trial at Addenbrooke's Hospital, Cambridge, has given hope for a cure for nut allergies. Children were given very small doses of peanut flour over a 6-month period to build up tolerance. At the end of the study many children could eat up to 12 peanuts a day without suffering anaphylaxis [do not try this at home]. ❦ A study published in the journal *Cancer* indicated that frequent or long-term use of marijuana could increase the risk of testicular cancer. {MAR} · A British study published in *Thorax* suggested that children who spend ≥2 hours a day watching television doubled their risk of developing asthma. It was thought TV viewing was symptomatic of a sedentary lifestyle, rather than a direct cause of the disease. ❦ An American study in *Archives of Internal Medicine* suggested that eating large quantities of red or processed meat was damaging to health. Those who ate the most red meat were at highest risk of death, especially from cancers. ❦ Drinking scalding hot tea can increase the risk of developing cancer of the oesophagus, according to research in the *British Medical Journal*. Those who drank tea hotter than 70°C increased their risk of cancer eightfold. ❦ A study by researchers at the University of Michigan suggested that adults who suffer from chronic sleep problems might be more likely to attempt suicide. ❦ Initial results from the Indian Polycap Study suggested that healthy people who took a daily 'polypill' (which combines a statin, aspirin, and drugs to lower blood pressure) could halve their risk of heart attack or stroke. {APR} · Research by scientists at Harvard indicated that women who live close to major roads are more likely to suffer from rheumatoid arthritis. ❦ Scientists from Queen Mary College, University of London, suggested a link between

─────────── SOME HEALTH STORIES OF NOTE cont. ───────────

mouth cancer and exposure to nicotine. The study proposed that those using nicotine gum, lozenges, or inhalers to help them quit smoking may still be at risk of contracting cancer. ❧ Researchers in Finland suggested that many children who exhibit symptoms of ADHD may in fact be overtired. The study published in *Pediatrics* found that children who slept ≤8 hours a night were the most hyperactive. {MAY} · A study suggested that postponing retirement could help combat early onset dementia. The research by Cardiff University and King's College London examined the retirement age of a selection of men with Alzheimer's and discovered that those who put off retirement delayed the symptoms of the disease by up to 6 weeks for every additional year worked. ❧ Researchers at the World Cancer Research Fund suggested that *c.*19,000 British people a year are diagnosed with cancer that could have been prevented if they had a healthy Body Mass Index (of 18·5–25). Obesity is linked to cancers of the breast, bowel, kidney, and oesophagus. ❧ The Health Protection Agency (HPA) analysed 63,000 tonsil tissue samples and concluded that far fewer people in the UK may have the human form of 'mad cow disease' than was initially feared. Since 1995, 168 definite or probable cases of Variant Creutzfeldt-Jakob disease (vCJD) have been reported, which led researchers to estimate that many thousands could be incubating the disease. The HPA called their results 'reassuring'. {JUN} · Scientists at Newcastle University suggested that cooking carrots whole boosted their health benefits. The researchers discovered that boiled whole carrots contained 25% more of the anti-cancer compound falcarinol than carrots that had been sliced before cooking. ❧ A study by doctors from Italy's Pavia University indicated that music can be used to stimulate or calm patients: crescendos in classical music can cause an increase in blood pressure, heart, and respiratory rates, whereas diminuendos can aid relaxation, lowering blood pressure and slowing the heart rate. {JUL} · A mouse study at the University of South Florida indicated that 500mg of caffeine a day (equivalent to three large espresso-based coffees or 15 cups of tea) can delay the onset of Alzheimer's. The mice given daily doses of caffeine showed a 50% reduction in levels of the sticky protein aggregates in the brain that impair cognitive function. ❧ A 20-year monkey study published in *Science* suggested that counting calories can delay the ageing process. The research revealed that monkeys who were not placed on a restricted diet were nearly 3× more likely to die than those on a calorie-controlled diet. {AUG} · A study by Northern California Cancer Center at Berkeley suggested that 'apple shaped' women (those with a waist >88cm) might have a higher risk of developing asthma. {SEP} · According to a study by the US National Academy of Science, using a shower can cause lung disease. Researchers took samples from >50 shower heads across America, and discovered that 30% harboured the potentially harmful *Mycobacterium avium*. ❧ A study in the *British Medical Journal* suggested that middle-aged men with high blood pressure and raised cholesterol might be reducing their life expectancy by up to 10 years.

―――――――――――― WOMEN & CRIME ――――――――――――

In England and Wales, crimes by girls aged 10–17 have increased by 22% in four years, according to a January 2009 report from the Ministry of Justice, *Statistics on Women and the Criminal Justice System*. The number of girls and women arrested also reached a record high. Although men were 5 times more likely than women to be arrested in 2007, and 11 times more likely to go to prison, the recent increase in female crime is illustrated by the fact that, in 1994, men were 21 times more likely to be imprisoned than women. Below is the representation of women and men at different stages of the criminal justice process in England and Wales during 2006–07:

	♀	♂
General population (age >10)	♀ · 51%	♂ · 49%
Self-reported offending	40	60
Arrests	17	83
Cautions, warnings, reprimands	28	72
Proceeded against for indictable offence	14	86
Sentenced to custody	8	92
Prison population	6	94

Between 2002/03 and 2006/07, the number of arrests increased for both sexes – although the increase was greater for women. For both sexes, violence against the person was the most common reason for arrest. Tabulated below are arrests for notifiable offences and offence categories by sex in England and Wales for 2006–07:

♂ number	%	offence/ offence category	%	♀ number
400,900	33	violence against the person	35	87,200
263,400	21	theft & handling stolen goods	32	80,200
145,800	12	criminal damage	9	22,100
77,100	6	drugs	5	12,100
21,600	2	fraud & forgery	3	7,800
92,100	7	burglary	3	8,800
36,400	3	robbery	2	4,400
31,200	3	sexual	<1	900
162,100	13	other	11	28,100

The report suggests that although men commit far more crimes than women, the courts treat the sexes with relative parity. The table below shows the percentage found guilty in all courts (as a proportion of those proceeded against) by sex, 2007:

Offence (% found guilty)	♀	♂
Sexual offences	52	59
Robbery	68	62
Other	57	64
Violence vs person	67	69
Criminal damage	77	75
Burglary	70	77
Fraud & forgery	85	81
Theft/handling	88	87
Drugs offences	88	91
ALL OFFENCES	78	77

SCOTTISH POLICE DIVERSITY HANDBOOK

In April 2009, the Association of Chief Police Officers in Scotland (ACPOS) distributed a 140-page 'Diversity Handbook' to every police force in Scotland. The publication was intended as a practical guide to dealing with sensitive issues surrounding age, gender, religion and disability, and crimes where cultural sensitivity is important, such as 'honour' killings. Alongside a significant quantity of helpful advice, the handbook included a few pointers that some thought a little obvious:

Advice for dealing with ...

DISABLED PEOPLE · Avoid behaviour that could be seen as patronising or impatient, e.g. finishing sentences for someone with speech impairment, leaning on a person's wheelchair, or moving someone's walking stick without asking. ~ Don't use words like cripple, retarded, defective, handicapped, affliction, or incapable, etc. ~ Don't use phrases like blind as a bat, deaf and dumb, victim, mentally deficient, etc. ~ If you see someone wearing a hearing aid, do not assume they can hear you. FACIAL DISFIGUREMENT · Concentrate on what they are saying and respond naturally, ignoring any curiosity you may have. Don't ask 'What happened to you?'

TRANSGENDER PEOPLE · So long as a person has their genitals covered, it is completely legal for them to wear clothing and accessories of any gender in public. Going out in public partially or completely cross-dressed is no offence. ~ A transgender person is not breaking any laws by using the opposite gender toilet facilities from the gender they were labelled at birth. PROSTITUTION · When dealing with a street sex worker, it is important that sufficient evidence is gained to support a caution/charge under Section 46. Simply dressing in such a manner as to stereotypically look like a street sex worker is not enough, nor is standing still in the street paying attention to passing vehicles.

The Taxpayers' Alliance said: 'This is not only a waste of taxpayers' money but also completely patronising ... every police officer and every normal person would take this sort of thing for granted.'

DEATHS FOLLOWING POLICE CONTACT

Figures from the Independent Police Complaints Commission (IPCC) released in July 2008 revealed the number and nature of deaths following police contact:

Incident	2004/05	2005/06	2006/07	2007/08
Road traffic fatalities	44	48	36	23
Fatal shootings	3	5	1	5
Deaths in/following custody	36	28	27	21
Deaths due to other police contact	24	39	20	26
Total deaths	107	120	84	75

In April 2009, the IPCC was called in after a man died during the G20 protests in London [see p.34] ❦ Further IPCC statistics revealed that in 2008, 131 police left the force after allegations of misconduct: 44 were dismissed, 87 were ordered to resign, 15 officers were demoted, and 147 fined.

─────────── YOUNG PEOPLE & CRIME ───────────

In a wide-ranging survey for the Youth Justice Board, published in March 2009, young people (aged 11–16) in mainstream education were asked about their experiences of crime. 23% admitted to committing an offence in the last 12 months, down from 27% admitting the same during the last survey in 2005. Notably, crimes involving mobile phones (such as 'happy slapping') were mentioned in the survey for the first time. Some of the most common offences committed in 2008 were:

Offence	*% of 11–16s admitting committing in last 12 months*
Travelled on bus/train without paying	53
Stole something from a shop/supermarket	45
Hurt someone (but they did not need medical treatment)	42
Damaged or destroyed something belonging to someone else	39
Wrote or sprayed graffiti	33
Threatened/assaulted others in public	31
Sent a voicemail/text to scare, threaten, or harass someone	22
Bought drugs	21
Used a mobile to film an assault ('happy slapping')	16

Of those who had committed an offence in the last 12 months: 64% admitted they did so with friends; 20% were on their own; and 2% were with a sibling. The most common reason given for committing a first offence was 'for fun' (43%), followed by a low chance of being caught (23%), boredom (23%), and peer pressure (20%). Of those who had been caught by the police, 48% said that being caught would not stop them from offending again, and 65% admitted that they had re-offended after being caught by the police. 31% confessed that they had carried a weapon in the last year, reflecting the rise in knife crime. The types of weapons carried were:

Pen knife	17%	Other type of knife	3
BB-gun	15	Real/loaded firearm	3
Flick knife	6	Other type of gun	3
Airgun	5	Replica firearm	2
Kitchen knife	4	None of the above	47

32% of those admitting to carrying a knife did so for use in hobbies, activities, or sports, however 30% admitted carrying a knife to protect themselves. While 39% of those carrying a gun did so for hobbies, activities, or sports, only 8% said they did so to protect themselves, 4% in case they got in a fight, and 2% to threaten others.

[Source: Youth Justice Board · Mori Youth Survey 2008: Young people in mainstream education] ❦ Figures released by the Home Office in July 2009 revealed that a high-profile government campaign to tackle knife crime in England's largest cities had failed to stem the number of fatal stabbings. The number of teenagers murdered as a result of knife crime remained unchanged since 2007–08 at 23. The number of adults aged over 20 fatally stabbed went up by 7, to 103. Despite these depressing headline figures, the £3m campaign could boast some successes: between July 2008 and March 2009 the number of violent incidents involving those under 19 had fallen by 17%, and hospital admissions for stabbing injuries in the ten English cities targeted by the campaign had fallen by 32%.

———————— BRITISH CRIME STATISTICS ————————

Recorded crime in England and Wales fell by 5% from 2007/08–2008/09, according to the Home Office, though the overall risk of being a victim of crime rose from 22% to 23% – the first significant rise since 1994. Violent crime fell by 6%, and gun crime by 17%. Additionally, there were only 648 murders and manslaughters during 2008/09: 136 fewer than the previous year, and a 20-year low. However, 12,165 women were raped, an increase of 5%, and attempted murders with knives rose by 11%. ❧ Domestic burglary rose by 1%, shoplifting rose by 10%, and thefts from the person (e.g. pickpocketing and bag-snatching) rose by 25% – all three were interpreted by the media as indicators that the economic situation was fuelling 'cash reward' criminality. ❧ Tabulated below are Home Office data for the incidence of some of the more unusual crimes recorded by the police during 2008/09:

Offence	No. of offences recorded
Corporate manslaughter	2
Endangering life at sea	8
Abandoning a child aged <2	23
Procuring illegal abortion	5
Incest or familial sexual offence	1,045
Theft of mail	3,729
Dishonest use of electricity	1,779
False accounting	145
Forgery or use of false drug prescription	448
Arson endangering life	3,629
Arson not endangering life	31,212
Concealing an infant death close to birth	8
Bigamy	65
Blackmail	1,366
Kidnapping	2,034
Riot	3
Perjury	179
Aiding suicide [see p.94]	7
Perverting the course of justice	8,402
Absconding from lawful custody	649
Health and Safety offences	16
Obscene publications, &c. and protected sexual material	2,734
Trade descriptions, &c.	1,139
Adulteration of food	14
Public health offences	115
Planning law	1

———————— TERRORISM ARRESTS & OUTCOMES ————————

In May 2009, the Home Office revealed that 1,471 people had been arrested in Britain in connection with terrorism between 11 September 2001 and 31 March 2008. Of these arrests, just 521 (35%) resulted in a charge connected to terrorism. The main charges under terrorism legislation since 9/11 are tabulated below:

	% of those charged
Possession of an article for terrorist purposes	32
Fundraising for terrorist purposes	15
Membership of a proscribed organisation	14
Provision of information relating to a terrorist investigation	9
Collection of information useful for a terrorist act	7
Other offences under terrorist legislation	23

46% of those arrested under section 41 of the Terrorism Act 2000 were held in pre-charge detention for <1 day; 66% for <2 days. Since 2006, when the maximum pre-charge detention time was increased to 28 days, 6 people were detained for this period – of which 3 were then charged, and 3 released.

Media & Celebrity

Success has ruined many a man.
— BENJAMIN FRANKLIN, *Poor Richard's Almanack*, 1752

─────────── HELLO! vs OK! COVER STARS ───────────

Date	Hello!	OK!
06·01·09	Jamie & Louise Redknapp	Cheryl Cole
13·01·09	Kylie Minogue	Amanda Holden marries Chris Hughes
20·01·09	Kylie Minogue	Kerry Katona
27·01·08	Lisa Marie Presley & baby twins	Jordan
03·02·09	President Barack Obama	Charlotte Church, Gavin Henson & baby
10·02·09	Prince Harry & Chelsy Davy	Cheryl Cole & Victoria Beckham
17·02·09	Sienna Miller	Kerry Katona & daughter Molly
24·02·09	Cheryl Cole	Kate Garraway
03·03·09	Kate Winslet	Jade Goody marries Jack Tweed
10·03·09	Michelle Obama	Jade & Jack's wedding
17·03·09	Mel C & baby Scarlet	Jade & family
24·03·09	Prince William	Jade Goody tribute issue†
31·03·09	Natasha Richardson & Liam Neeson	Jade Goody
07·04·09	Jade Goody	Jack Tweed
14·04·09	Jade Goody's funeral	Jade's funeral
21·04·09	Eamonn Holmes & Ruth Langsford	Jade Goody
28·04·09	Roger Federer marries Mirka Vavrinec	Kerry Katona
05·05·09	Cheryl Cole	Patsy Kensit marries Jeremy Healy
12·05·09	Natascha McElhone	Cheryl Cole
19·05·09	Cheryl Cole	Kian Egan marries Jodie Albert
26·05·09	Prince William & Kate Middleton	Jordan
02·06·09	Brad Pitt & Angelina Jolie	Samantha Janus's wedding
09·06·09	Charlotte Church & Gavin Henson	Jordan & Kerry Katona
16·06·09	Queen Rania of Jordan	Cheryl & Ashley Cole
23·06·09	Boris Becker marries Lilly Kerssenberg	Jordan
30·06·09	Joe Cole marries Carly Zucker	Wes Brown marries Leanne Wassell
07·07·09	Michael Jackson	Michael Jackson
14·07·09	Michael Jackson	Michael Jackson
21·07·09	Michael Jackson's children	Michael Jackson
28·07·09	Ulrika Jonsson	Kerry Katona
04·08·09	Noel Edmonds marries Liz Davies	Jordan
11·08·09	Zara Phillips & Mike Tindall	Cheryl Cole
18·08·09	Cindy Crawford	Rachel Stevens marries Alex Bourne

† Jade was not yet dead when this issue was published, leading media pundits to deplore its release and >60 readers to complain to the PCC. Goody's family expressed support for the magazine [see p.127].

———SOME HATCHED, MATCHED, & DISPATCHED———

HATCHED

Winston James *to* .... Billie Piper & Laurence Fox
Bronx Mowgli† *to* ....Ashlee Simpson-Wentz & Pete Wentz
Beau *to* ....Jamie & Louise Redknapp
Dexter Lloyd *to* .... Charlotte Church & Gavin Henson
Seraphina Rose Elizabeth *to* .... Jennifer Garner & Ben Affleck
Rayn Lee Amethyst‡ *to* ....Lee Ryan & Sammi Millar
Kit Valentine *to* ....Sophie Ellis-Bextor & Richard Jones
Petal Blossom Rainbow *to* ....Jamie & Jools Oliver
Amber Isabella *to*..Tess Daly & Vernon Kay
Sparrow James Midnight *to*......................... Nicole Richie & Joel Madden

MATCHED

Salma Hayek & François-Henri Pinault ....Paris, France & Venice, Italy
Fergie & Josh Duhamel.. Malibu, California
Gisele Bündchen & Tom Brady............Santa Monica, California & Costa Rica
Denise Van Outen & Lee Mead...Seychelles
Spencer Pratt & Heidi Montag..California
Maggie Gyllenhaal & Peter Sarsgaard...................................Brindisi, Italy
Kian Egan & Jodi Albert ....Barbados
Joe Cole & Carly Zucker..London
Rachel Stevens & Alex Bourne...London

DISPATCHED

Madonna & Guy Ritchie (*married for* 8 years) .... divorced
Peaches Geldof & Max Drummey (186 days) ....divorcing
Mel & Robyn Gibson (28 years)..divorcing
Katie Price & Peter Andre (3½ years)...................................... divorced
Amy Winehouse & Blake Fielder-Civil (2 years) .... divorced
Kelis & Nas (6 years) ....divorcing

† Wentz declined to reveal the full inspiration behind his son's name but did admit that '*The Jungle Book* was something that me and Ashlee bonded over'. ‡ When explaining to *Hello!* how he came up with the unusual name Lee Ryan helpfully pointed out 'It's an anagram of Ryan. And Amethyst came about because we wanted a precious stone in there. If we ever have a girl, she'll be called Rose Quartz'.

———— MOST ENVIABLE BODY————

Celebrities with the most enviable bodies according to a July 2009 *Heat* survey:

1 ....Megan Fox†	6 ......Jennifer Aniston	† When asked by
2 .... Cheryl Cole	7 .... Jessica Alba	*Entertainment Weekly* in July
3 ....Kelly Brook	8 ....Jennifer Lopez	2009 if she thought she was
4 ....Beyoncé	9 ....Katie Price	good-looking, Fox replied,
5 ....Angelina Jolie	10...............Rihanna	'Well, I'm clearly not ugly'.

—— STRICTLY ——

Strictly Come Dancing courted controversy in 2008 – first with the furore surrounding John 'the dancing pig' Sergeant, who quit the show when it became obvious that the public were not going to vote him off despite his patent lack of dancing talent. Then, the semi-finals were dogged by a complicated voting scandal which meant that three couples progressed to the final instead of the usual two. The contestants were voted off in the following order:

16	Phil Daniels
15	Gillian Taylforth
14	Gary Rhodes
13	Jessie Wallace
12	Don Warrington
11	Mark Foster
10	Andrew Castle
9	Heather Small
8	Cherie Lunghi
7	John Sergeant (quit)
6	Jodie Kidd
5	Christine Bleakley
4	Austin Healey
3	Lisa Snowdon
RUNNER-UP	Rachel Stevens
WINNER	Tom Chambers

—— X FACTOR ——

14·6m watched Alexandra Burke beat boyband JLS to win 2008's *X Factor*. Cheryl Cole's appointment as the fourth judge (in place of Sharon Osbourne) dominated the watercooler gossip, and the nation quickly embraced the Girls Aloud singer's easy tears, fighting spirit, and enviable wardrobe. (Indeed, Burke's victory was doubtless helped by the fact that Cole, the nation's new sweetheart, was her mentor.) The acts were eliminated from the show in the following order:

12	Bad Lashes
11	Girlband
10	Scott Bruton
9	Austin Drage
8	Laura White
7	Daniel Evans
6	Rachel Hylton
5	Ruth Lorenzo
4	Diana Vickers
3	Eoghan Quigg
RUNNERS-UP	JLS
WINNER	Alexandra Burke

Guest stars included: Mariah Carey, Take That, Girls Aloud, Miley Cyrus and Britney Spears.

—— THE END OF BIG BROTHER ——

In August 2009, Channel 4 announced that the next series of *Big Brother* would be the last. Director of television at C4, Kevin Lygo echoed the thoughts of many when he said the show 'had reached a natural end point on Channel 4 and it's time to move on'. Viewing figures for the show had fallen considerably in recent years, and even tabloid interest had waned. Average viewers for the 10 series are below:

Series	year	ratings (m)	winner
1	2000	4·5	Craig Phillips
2	2001	4·5	Brian Dowling
3	2002	5·8	Kate Lawler
4	2003	4·6	Cameron Stout
5	2004	5·1	Nadia Almada
6	2005	4·6	Anthony Hutton
7	2006	4·7	Pete Bennett
8	2007	3·9	Brian Belo
9	2008	3·6	Rachel Rice
10	2009	2·4	Sophie Reade

Celebrity BB4 (non-celeb Chantelle Houghton won) was the highest rated series with 5·9m.

THE WORLD'S MOST POWERFUL CELEBRITIES

Angelina Jolie unseated the queen of American media, Oprah Winfrey, to top *Forbes*'s list of the World's 100 most powerful celebrities. The June 2009 ranking was calculated by measuring a celebrity's earning power and their exposure across the media. J.K. Rowling and Johnny Depp both exited the list, due to a paucity of new material. The top ten most powerful celebrities in 2009 are listed below:

Rank	celebrity	earnings[†] ($m)	web rank	press rank	TV rank
1	Angelina Jolie	27	3	5	3
2	Oprah Winfrey	275	4	8	2
3	Madonna	110	9	6	8
4	Beyoncé	87	2	20	16
5	Tiger Woods	110	54	4	4
6	Bruce Springsteen	70	32	19	25
7	Steven Spielberg	150	48	26	48
8	Jennifer Aniston	25	6	30	21
9	Brad Pitt	28	11	7	6
10	Kobe Bryant[‡]	45	53	10	15

[†] Earnings in the previous 12 months. [‡] Professional basketball player for Los Angeles Lakers.

BEST & WORST MALE CELEBRITY HAIRSTYLES

The best and worst male celeb hairstyles were judged in a May 2009 poll by Optima:

Best barnet	*Worst barnet*
Robert Peston (BBC's business editor)	Russell Brand
Daniel Craig	Jonathan Ross
George Clooney	Laurence Llewlyn-Bowen
Brad Pitt	Christiano Ronaldo
David Beckham	Donald Trump

SEXIEST MEN & WOMEN · 2009

FHM's 'sexiest' women		*Company*'s most eligible bachelors
Megan Fox	1	Prince Harry
Jessica Alba	2	George Lamb
Keeley Hazell	3	Robert Pattinson
Elisha Cuthbert	4	Noel Fielding
Hayden Panettiere	5	Paul Sculfor
Scarlett Johansson	6	Ed Westwick
Cheryl Cole	7	Guy Ritchie
Hilary Duff	8	Jack Penate
Angelina Jolie	9	Sam Branson
Keira Knightley	10	Jamie Dornan

——————— TWITTERING CELEBRITIES ———————

Twitter replaced Myspace as the chosen celebrity mouthpiece in 2009, with a host of stars updating fans on the minutiae of their daily lives. Gossip site Holy Moly ranked celebrity Twitterers in March 2009, by comparing their followers-to-followed ratio. Unsurprisingly, this wildly unscientific measure of the 'most narcissistic' celebrity Twitterers revealed that most stars spent so much time tweeting to their vast audience they had little time to follow anyone else. The most narcissistic were:

[1] Russell Brand [2] Katy Perry [3] Lily Allen
[4] Ashton Kutcher [5] Chris Moyles

Below are some 2009 tweets from a smorgasbord of celebrity Twitter users:

rustyrockets/Russell Brand
'If we detach ourselves from the material we will become enlightened and live in perpetual, blissful, endless orgasm – but imagine the mess.'

aplusk/Ashton Kutcher
'Oh no! My stunt double waxed his chest. Oh good god nooooo! I'm in the middle of a debate as to how to avoid doing the same.'

Wossy/Jonathan Ross
'One of the dogs threw up last night and is making weird faces. Will take him to the vet. Might get myself checked out while I'm there.'

stephenfry/Stephen Fry
'Mm. Uploaded new profile picture. Thought looking away from camera was less arsey. Now think it might be MORE arsey. Oh dear. So self-conscious.'

lilyroseallen/Lily Allen
'The travelling has caught up with me. I've got a really painful spot on my back, guess I'm run down.'

Hammer/MC Hammer
'I sought to impact the world on a positive level (did it), see the world (saw it), change the world (helped) … now I live to help you see it.'

lancearmstrong/Lance Armstrong
'I'm alive! Broken clavicle (right). Hurts like hell for now. Surgery in a couple of days.'

katyperry/Katy Perry
'I wish I had someone to eat the orange & yellow starbursts, I only like the red & pink. I ate them all at the end. oops.'

ztnewetep/Pete Wentz
'Should the stage be a confessional or a place where you play a character? been going back and forth in my head.'

In March 2009, the *New York Times* reported that some celebrities who are just too busy to Twitter employ minions to tweet for them. Recognising the marketing opportunities offered by Twitter, celebrities such as 50 Cent reportedly employ 'ghost-twitterers' to create online content on their behalf. ❦ Gossip magazine *Star* reported in March 2009 that Jennifer Aniston ended her relationship with John Mayer because of his Twitter addiction. The singer had allegedly been too busy to call Aniston and yet found the time to repeatedly update his Twitter page. Mayer supposedly posted the rather telling tweet, 'This heart didn't come with instructions', just after the break-up. ❦ P Diddy's tweets are the most 'negative', according to experts who analysed the language used by celeb twitterers.

——— CELEBRITY INTRIGUE ———

{OCT 2008} · Kerry Katona made a shambolic appearance on *This Morning* in which she seemed to slur her words. She denied she had been drinking and claimed her performance was a result of medication she was taking for bipolar disorder. ❦ Russell Brand resigned from Radio 2 and Jonathan Ross was suspended without pay for 3 months after making lewd phone calls to Andrew Sachs [see p.129]. {NOV} · Amy Winehouse's husband Blake Fielder-Civil was released from prison on the condition that he attend rehab. {DEC} · Blake Fielder-Civil was sent back to jail after failing a drug test. {JAN 2009} · Boy George was jailed for 15 months for falsely imprisoning a male escort at his London flat. ❦ Kelly Osbourne was admitted to rehab for the third time. ❦ Ashlee Simpson-Wentz raced to defend her sister Jessica after magazines criticised her recent weight gain: 'A week after the inauguration and with such a feeling of hope in the air for our country, I find it completely embarrassing and belittling to all women to read about a woman's weight or figure.' {FEB} Christian Bale's 3-minute expletive-ridden rant at a director of photography during the filming of *Terminator: Salvation* was leaked onto the internet. Bale later apologised for his 'inexcusable' tirade. ❦ American R&B star Chris Brown was arrested for allegedly assaulting his girlfriend Rihanna. {MAR} Chris Moyles was criticised by Ofcom after he adopted a high-pitched voice to mimic the singer Will Young. Moyles sang to the tune of Young's hit *Leave Right Now*:

Katie Price

'When you saw me years ago you didn't know, but now I'm the gayest fella you probably know. Mmm I like to wear a silly hat, I get camper by the hour, oh would you look at the muck in here. I'm Will Young and I'm gay.' {APR} · After numerous reports of rows, Lindsay Lohan confirmed she had split from girlfriend Samantha Ronson. {MAY} · Katie Price released a statement claiming to be 'devastated' after Peter Andre started divorce proceedings against her. Price said, 'Pete is the love of my life – and my life. We have children together and I am devastated and disappointed by his decision to separate and divorce me, as I married him for life'. {JUN} Katie Price was pictured enjoying the party island of Ibiza with a bevy of male models. {JUL} · Mischa Barton was reportedly placed under 'involuntary psychiatric hold' at a LA hospital after police were called to her home to assist with an unspecified 'medical issue'. {AUG} · Chris Brown was sentenced to 180 days' community labour and 5 years' probation for assaulting Rihanna. ❦ After a video emerged allegedly showing Kerry Katona snorting white powder, she was dropped as a face of Iceland supermarkets. {SEP} During the MTV Video Music Awards, Kanye West climbed on stage and interrupted Taylor Swift's acceptance speech for Best Female Video: 'I'm sorry, but Beyoncé had one of the best videos of all time,' Kanye protested. Later, when Beyoncé won for Best Video, she graciously invited Swift to have 'her moment'. Later still, Kanye apologised.

> *Mmm I like to wear a silly hat,*
> *I get camper by the hour …*
> – CHRIS MOYLES as Will Young

—CELEBRITY QUOTES—

LADY GAGA (to *Rolling Stone*) · The truth is, the psychotic woman that I truly am comes out when I'm not working. ❦ JENNIFER LOVE HEWITT (to *Maxim*) · My new thing is that I always take my bubble baths wearing a tiara; I am a grown-up who bathes in a tiara. One that I got from Disneyland. ❦ OPRAH WINFREY (in a speech at Duke University) · It's great to have a private jet. Anyone that tells you that having your own private jet isn't great is lying to you. ❦ BONO (to *Q*) · I own up to being a spoiled-rotten rock star ... It would be really wrong for me to try to pretend to be something I'm not. ❦ SIMON COWELL (to the *Daily Mail*) · If I went to a psychiatrist, it would be a very long session. ❦ JOAQUIN PHOENIX (on quitting acting for hip hop) · It simply doesn't excite me anymore, there is nothing left for me to discover. ❦ KATY PERRY (in *FemaleFirst*) · Every night, when I play a show, I pick one girl and I kiss her. I've kissed about 50 and I'm not worried about swine flu. Or herpes. ❦ HUGH JACKMAN (on his greatest fear, in WENN) · When dolls come to life in films, that just freaks me out, I just can't stand that. Chucky? Forget that. ❦ JONATHAN RHYS MEYERS (in *Contact Music*) · I think people would like to think I'm a hell of a lot naughtier than I am actually. I am actually quite a boring guy. I spent the last week and a half playing bloody golf. ❦ KATE WINSLET (to *The Sunday Express*) · There's always going to be a part of me that worries about not looking as slim as other actresses. ❦ DUFFY (to *The Western Mail*) · I have sold my soul and I'm no longer anonymous, but I have to remember that the majority of people are good.

Lady Gaga

❦ LILY ALLEN (to *The Sun*) · Now guys are really nice when they're breaking up with me because they don't want to end up on a song. ❦ SETH ROGAN (to *Playboy*) · I have seen more guys lately who kind of look like me ... I created a new look for rotund Jews. It's an easily attainable look. ❦ CHRISTIAN BALE (to *Entertainment Weekly*) · People were telling me, 'Christian, you're too good for *Terminator*.' And I'm thinking, I'm too good? I'm not a snob. I really fucking enjoy watching a good action movie. Who do you think I am?! ❦ RUSSELL BRAND (on the word 'shag', to *The Sydney Morning Herald*) · I continue to live as a single man might but I certainly don't do anything as vulgar as shagging. ❦ PEACHES GELDOF (on her marriage, to *Grazia*) · Max and I are really good friends ... We were just too young. That's all it was ... I still love the idea that we did it. ❦ CHERYL COLE (on celebrity parties, to *Now*) · It's all such bullshit, because you don't really know the people there. It's like waving across the room: 'Hello. I'm famous, you're famous.' ❦ MARTIN SCORSESE (on working with Michael Jackson on the video for *Bad*, to MTV) · Every step he took was absolutely precise and fluid at the same time. It was like watching quicksilver in motion. ❦ JOHNNY DEPP (to *Total Film*) · I love it when I see youngsters dressing up as Jack Sparrow from *Pirates of the Caribbean*, but that's not vanity, it's because we've fired their imaginations – and imagination is such a vital thing for them. ❦ JESSICA SIMPSON (to fans at a US concert, reacting to criticism about her weight) · I feel like in our world today we focus on so many things that are completely pointless.

JADE GOODY · 1981–2009

Jade Goody, the villain and heroine of reality TV, died on 22 March 2009, aged 27. Her very public battle with cervical cancer had obsessed and shocked the nation in equal measure, and the media had spun itself into a frenzy, dissecting every aspect of its own overblown coverage. ❦ Goody first entered the public's consciousness in 2002, when she became a housemate on *Big Brother 3*. Initially, the almost proud ignorance of this 21-year-old Essex dental nurse amazed and amused the audience. (Goody thought 'Pistachio' painted the Mona Lisa, and wondered if the eyes on peacocks' feathers were real.) Quickly, though, the humour soured as the tabloids turned against her, urging their readers to 'vote out the pig'. The public was not entirely swayed by this witch-hunt, but by the time Goody was evicted, in 4th place, genuine concern was expressed for her mental and physical well-being. Against the odds, Goody carved out a niche for her anti-talent; her 'ordinary' looks and extraordinary utterances appealing to audiences tired of over-spun celebrity. Goody amassed a reported £2–4m fortune from magazine deals, an autobiography [see p.165], a fitness DVD, a perfume ('*Shh …*'), and further reality TV appearances. But then, as the narrative of celebrity demands, Goody fell from grace. In 2007, she became a housemate on *Celebrity Big Brother 5*, but was quickly evicted in a storm of public anger over her racist bullying of the Indian actress Shilpa Shetty. Calling Shetty 'Poppadom' and 'Fuckawalla', Goody showed her ignorance was not so innocent, and the media rushed to vilify her. In August 2008, in an attempt at redemption, Goody joined the Indian version of *Big Brother* (*Bigg Boss*) but after a few days she received a diagnosis of cervical cancer and flew home. As her cancer spread, Goody told *The News of the World*, 'I've lived in front of the cameras and maybe I'll die in front of them'. And so began a very public death. The media covered every moment of Goody's decline, from her radiotherapy and hair loss to her marriage to Jack Tweed, whose post-assault curfew was relaxed for the wedding. Throughout her decline, Goody was adamant that her motive was to secure a financial future for her two young sons. Yet one unexpected outcome of the blanket coverage of Goody's demise was to encourage thousands of women to attend screenings for cervical cancer.

OTHER REALITY TV SHOWS OF NOTE · 2009

Show	winner	prize
Big Brother	Sophie Reade	£71,320
I'm a Celebrity [2008]	Joe Swash	a crown
Celebrity Masterchef	Jayne Middlemiss	a trophy
Britain's Got Talent	Diversity	£100,000 & Royal Variety Show gig
Dancing on Ice	Ray Quinn	a trophy
The Apprentice	Yasmina Siadatan	£100,000-a-year job
Hell's Kitchen	Linda Evans	a bouquet

TYPES OF TELEVISION VIEWED BY AGE

Below are the genres of television watched by various age groups during 2006/7:

Genre	(age) 16–24	25–34	35–44	45–64	>65	All
News	48%	63	70	74	81	69
Films	76	71	68	64	57	66
Comedy	71	63	60	53	48	58
Live sport	50	49	52	52	53	52
Wildlife	28	40	46	59	67	51
Soaps	55	45	40	40	48	45
Food and cookery	21	35	35	40	38	35
Quiz shows	28	26	26	35	45	33
Current affairs/politics	13	25	29	38	40	31
Home and DIY	19	31	36	34	21	29
Gardening	5	13	22	37	48	28
Reality TV	40	35	27	15	8	23
Pop music programmes	42	27	22	15	10	21

Television viewers have recently suffered a resurgence of programming intended for the whole family. Dubbed 3GTV – because three generations of the family can watch together – the genre is characterised by Saturday night prime-time shows such as *Doctor Who* and *Ant and Dec's Saturday Night Takeaway*. [Source: Taking Part: The National Survey of Culture, Leisure and Sport, England · DCMS]

MOST-WATCHED TV PROGRAMMES

The Christmas Day premiere, on BBC1, of Wallace and Gromit's latest adventures, *A Matter of Loaf and Death*, was the most-watched television programme of 2008, according to audience researchers BARB. The most-watched shows in 2008 were:

Show	channel	viewers (million)
A Matter of Loaf and Death	BBC1	16·15
The X Factor Results	ITV1	14·06
Britain's Got Talent Final Result	ITV1	13·88
The X Factor	ITV1	13·77
Doctor Who Christmas episode	BBC1	13·10
Coronation Street†	ITV1	13·02
Strictly Come Dancing	BBC1	12·97
Dancing on Ice	ITV1	12·08
Britain's Got Talent	ITV1	11·86
EastEnders‡	BBC1	11·73

† Featured the death of much-loved character Vera Duckworth who had been a resident of the Street for 33 years. Unlike the usual macabre soap death, Vera was revealed to have died peacefully in her sleep from heart failure. ‡ The second episode in a story arc that saw philandering Max Branning buried alive by wife Tanya (who then relented and dug him up, still alive). The BBC received >600 complaints about the storyline; many viewers objected to such grisly fare before the watershed.

—— A BRIEF HISTORY OF SWEARING ON TELEVISION ——

{1965} Theatre critic Kenneth Tynan became the first person to say 'fuck' on British television, during a live late-night debate on the BBC's *BBC-3* programme. Tynan was asked if he thought it appropriate for sexual intercourse to be enacted on stage. He replied, 'Oh, I think so, certainly. I doubt if there are any rational people to whom the word "fuck" would be particularly diabolical, revolting or totally forbidden.' As a result of the furore, the BBC issued a formal apology, and the House of Commons set down four separate motions signed by 133 MPs. ❦ {1973} *The Daily Telegraph* columnist Peregrine Worsthorne became the second person to utter the F-word on TV. When asked on BBC's *Nationwide* what he thought the public would think about a Tory politician being found in bed with a prostitute, Worsthorne replied, '{the public} will not give ... there is only one word for it ... will not give a fuck'. Worsthorne was suspended by *The Telegraph* from broadcasting for a few months. ❦ {1976} The Sex Pistols swore repeatedly during an early evening broadcast of Thames Television's *Today* programme. Host Bill Grundy flirted openly with Siouxsie Sioux, causing Steve Jones to call Grundy a 'dirty sod', a 'dirty bastard', a 'dirty fucker', and a 'fucking rotter'. The episode brought huge attention to the Sex Pistols and made front-page news, including *The Daily Mirror*'s famous headline: 'The Filth and the Fury!' ❦ {1987} *The Tube* was taken off air for 3 weeks after Jools Holland said 'groovy fucker' during a trailer for the show. ❦ {2004} In a live edition of *I'm a Celebrity Get Me Out of Here*, John Lydon called the British public 'fucking cunts' for not voting him out of the show. Of the >10m watching the programme *c.*100 complained. ❦ {2005} >50,000 complained after the BBC screened *Jerry Springer: The Opera* (which features *c.*174 swearwords), making the broadcast the most complained-about on UK television.

—— RUSSELL BRAND, JONATHAN ROSS, & 'SACHSGATE' ——

On 16/10/08, during the recording of his Radio 2 show, Russell Brand and his guest Jonathan Ross left a series of obscene messages on the answerphone of the *Fawlty Towers* actor Andrew Sachs, who had been scheduled as an interviewee. Alluding to Brand's claim of a relationship with Sachs's granddaughter, Georgina Baillie, Ross said, 'He fucked your granddaughter ... I'm sorry, I apologise. Andrew, I apologise ...' Brand made up a song: 'I said some things I didn't of oughta, like I had sex with your granddaughter'. Despite some confusion as to whether Sachs had consented to the broadcast, the show was approved, and aired on 18/10. Initially, only two complaints were received, but after *The Mail on Sunday* splashed the story on 26/10, 'Sachsgate' exploded. Over the next few days, politicians weighed in, apologies flew, and the number of complaints soared (by 30/10, the total was >37,500). On 29/10, Brand quit his show; the next day, the controller of Radio 2 resigned, and Ross was suspended for 3 months without pay. Criticism of the BBC's editorial lapse was compounded by anger at the money spent on 'talent' such as Ross (who is said to earn £6m a year). On 21/11, a BBC Trust report called the incident a 'deplorable intrusion with no editorial justification'. On 3/4/09, Ofcom fined the BBC £150,000.

WORST TV ADVERTS · 2008

The ten worst television adverts of 2008, according to *Campaign* magazine, were:

Rank	brand	featuring
1	Gillette	Thierry Henry, Roger Federer, & Tiger Woods
2	Specsavers	footage of Édith Piaf dubbed to say company catchphrase
3	Renault	very badly dubbed European actors
4	Warburtons	Asian businessman seeing the Warburtons brand everywhere
5	Country Life	John Lydon pushing 'best of British' butter
6	Kellogg's	wooden performance by Dame Kelly Holmes
7	Orangina	sexually inappropriate animated animals
8	Premier Inn	bad jokes from Lenny Henry
9	Samsung	dull Chelsea players in suits
10	DFS	'normal' people miming to the Nickelback song *Rockstar*

MOST COMPLAINED-ABOUT ADVERTS

The Advertising Standards Authority (ASA) received 26,433 complaints in 2008, which resulted in 2,475 ads being changed or withdrawn. The ASA's 2008 annual report listed the broadcast adverts that drew the most complaints. The top 6 were:

BARNARDO'S

Graphic adverts raising awareness of domestic child abuse. Complainants said that scenes of drug-taking and violence were upsetting and inappropriate for transmission at times when children might be watching.

840 complaints · Not upheld

VOLKSWAGEN

The advert featured a dog that sang happily while inside a car but cowered and shook when outside. Viewers were mostly worried about the animal's welfare during filming of the advert.

743 complaints · Not investigated

AG BARR

An Orangina advert featuring 'sexy' animated, dancing animals. The voice-over proclaimed, 'Orangina ... Life is juicy'. Most complainants said that the advert was overly sexualised and demeaning to women.

286 complaints · Not investigated

HEINZ

A mayonnaise advert featuring a burly, unshaven Italian-American man identified as 'mum' making sandwiches. At the end of the advert 'mum' kissed 'dad' goodbye. Viewers complained about two men kissing pre-watershed.

215 complaints · Not investigated

DEPARTMENT OF HEALTH

An anti-smoking campaign featuring children mimicking their parents, with the warning 'If you smoke, your children are more likely to smoke'. Viewers were concerned the depiction of children smoking could encourage kids who misunderstood the advert to smoke.

205 complaints · Not upheld

TISCALI

A light-hearted advert themed around sleeping with your neighbour. Complainants said the advert trivialised adultery.

159 complaints · Not investigated

―――― SHARE OF GLOBAL ADVERTISING BY SECTOR ――――

Advertising in newspapers has declined as advertising on the internet has grown, according to figures from PricewaterhouseCoopers published by the World Association for Newspapers in 2008. The shifting share of global advertising spend by media sector since 2002 is shown below, alongside the estimated share in 2011:

Advertising medium	(%)	2002	2005	2008	(est) 2011
Television		36·9	37·6	37·9	37·1
Newspapers		31·5	29·6	26·5	25·0
Internet		2·8	6·0	10·8	13·8
Magazines		14·2	13·4	12·4	12·0
Radio		8·9	8·3	7·5	7·3
Billboards		5·7	5·7	5·8	6·0

―――――― MOST-WATCHED TV PRESENTERS · 2008 ――――――

Adrian Chiles was seen by a total audience of 1·04bn people in 2008, making him the most-watched TV presenter in the UK. This calculation, by media agency MPG, was made by taking the average audience for each show Chiles presented and multiplying it by the number of episodes. The most-watched TV presenters were:

Presenter	shows presented	audience
Adrian Chiles	One Show, MOTD 2, The Apprentice, Olympics	1·04bn
Phillip Schofield	This Morning, Mr & Mrs, Dancing on Ice	677·6m
Noel Edmonds	Deal or No Deal	611·7m
Fern Britton	This Morning, Mr & Mrs	494·2m
Davina McCall	Big Brother	403·5m
Dermot O'Leary	The X Factor	358·5m
Ant & Dec	I'm a Celebrity, Britain's Got Talent	314·6m
Gary Lineker	MOTD, Ryder Cup highlights	302·3m
Holly Willoughby	The Xtra Factor, Celebrity Juice, Dancing on Ice	249·8m

――――――――――― TV ON DEMAND ―――――――――――

Analysis by Entertainment Media Research in June 2009 revealed that most consumers were reluctant to pay for television on-demand content delivered online:

Content	% interested	% definitely consider paying
New movies just released in cinema	80	20
Top movies only just released on DVD	79	12
Recent movies not yet out on DVD	78	14
TV comedy programmes	76	5
TV drama programmes	73	4

49% admitted they didn't know how to link their television to their PC, or considered it too difficult.

—————————— THE TV BAFTAS · 2009 ——————————

Best actor.................Stephen Dillane · *The Shooting of Thomas Hurndall* [C4]
Best actress.........................Anna Maxwell Martin · *Poppy Shakespeare* [C4]
Entertainment performance.............Harry Hill · *Harry Hill's TV Burp* [ITV1]
Comedy performance..........................David Mitchell · *Peep Show* [C4]
Single drama...*White Girl* [BBC2]
Drama serial...*Criminal Justice* [BBC1]
Drama series...*Wallander* [BBC1]
Continuing drama...*The Bill* [ITV1]
Feature...*The Choir: Boys Don't Sing* [BBC2]
Factual series.......................................*Amazon with Bruce Parry* [BBC2]
Specialist factual...*Life in Cold Blood* [BBC1]
Single documentary..*Chosen* [C4]
Sport..*F1: Brazilian Grand Prix* [ITV1]
News coverage...........................*News at Ten – Chinese Earthquake* [ITV1]
Current affairs.................*Saving Africa's Witch Children – Dispatches* [C4]
Best interactivity......................................*Embarrassing Bodies Online* [C4]
Entertainment..*The X Factor* [ITV1]
Sitcom...*The IT Crowd* [C4]
International...*Mad Men* [BBC4]
Comedy programme or series..............................*Harry and Paul* [BBC1]
Audience award for programme of the year..............................*Skins* [E4]
Special award...Jane Tranter
BAFTA Fellowship............................Dawn French and Jennifer Saunders

BAFTA IN QUOTES

GRAHAM NORTON [host, referring to Jonathan Ross's three-month suspension for making lewd phone calls to Andrew Sachs] · I'm looking around the room at everyone who contributed to a great 12 months of television – nine months if you are Jonathan. ❦ DAVID ATTENBOROUGH · Thanks go to spitting cobras, axolotls, golden frogs, dwarf chameleons, those happy tortoises. ❦ HARRY HILL · I never thought I'd get three Baftas for a clip show. Ridiculous. ❦ JENNIFER SAUNDERS · It's kind of like the cherry on the icing on the cake. ❦ KENNETH BRANAGH · Bloody marvellous.

—————————— AGEISM & THE MEDIA ——————————

The BBC received >1,369 complaints in July 2009 after its decision to replace 66-year-old Arlene Phillips with 30-year-old Alesha Dixon as a judge on *Strictly Come Dancing*. The BBC's decision was seen as a crude attempt to boost ratings for its flagship Saturday night entertainment show, and emulate the success of ITV's *X Factor*, which was reinvigorated by the introduction of 26-year-old Cheryl Cole as a judge (who, incidentally, replaced 56-year-old Sharon Osbourne). Equalities Minister Harriet Harman was moved to call the episode 'absolutely shocking', and she called on the BBC to reinstate Phillips. The saga reignited the issue of ageism in the media that had been highlighted by (58-year-old) Selina Scott who, in 2008, settled out of court with Five after she was seemingly passed over for a younger presenter.

———— INTERNATIONAL TELEVISION INDUSTRY ————

Ofcom's November 2008 *International Communications Market* report included a comparative study of the TV industry across Europe, North America, and Japan. Some key statistics provide an overview of the industry in various countries in 2007:

Benchmark	UK	FRA	GER	ITA	USA	CAN	JPN
Income £bn (ads, subscription, pub funds)	10·4	7·0	9·3	6·3	66·6	4·4	17·7
Revenue per head (£)	172	109	113	109	221	135	139
– from advertising (£)	58	38	36	55	110	34	67
– from subscription (£)	71	52	37	35	111	86	48
– from public funding (£)	43	20	39	19	1	14	25
Annual licence fee (£)	140	79	140	73	–	–	108
Largest TV platform†	DTT	DTT	ACab	ATT	DCab	ACab	DSat
– percent of homes (%)	37	29	50	40	33	35	36
ATT channels	5	7	13	9	5	7	7
Viewing per head (mins per day)	218	207	208	230	272	223	unav.
Share of largest channel (%)	22	31	13	22	8	9	19
Share of the 3 largest channels	50	63	38	54	22	18	53
Digital TV penetration (%)	86	66	32	56	70	53	65
Digital switchover date	2012	2011	2009	2012	2009	2011	2011

2% of British homes migrated to pay TV in 2006–07, showing the steady growth of subscription-based TV. Pay versus free-to-view television in 2007 is charted below:

Country	proportion of households %		CAN	86	14
UK	47 Pay	53 Free	JAP	46	54
FRA	56	45	ESP	27	73
GER	69	31	NED	99	1
ITA	22	78	SWE	91	9
USA	86	14	IRL	76	24

Across Europe, most public service broadcasters (PSBs‡) produce a significant quantity of original programming: on average, 49% of all hours broadcast on European PSBs are first-run original programmes. The breakdown below illustrates the percentage of PSB first-run programmes that are original versus those that are acquired (purchased from other sources), as well as the overall percentage of shows that are repeats:

	% first-run		%			
Country	orig.	acquired	repeats	Poland	33	22	45
UK	53	5	41	Spain	60	15	25
France	51	23	26	Sweden	31	19	51
Germany	54	9	37	Ireland	23	30	47
Italy	63	15	22	AVERAGE	49	15	36

† DTT = digital terrestrial television; ACab = analogue cable; ATT = analogue terrestrial television; DCab = digital cable; DSat = digital satellite. ‡ In Britain, the PSBs include BBC1, BBC2, ITV1, Channel 4, and S4C. ❦ On average, viewers in Europe watch 3·4 hours of TV each day.

———————————— POLITICAL JOURNALISM ————————————

A November 2008 report by the Committee on Standards in Public Life revealed a general mistrust of political journalism in tabloid newspapers – as shown below:

% agreeing that the media	broadsheets	tabloids	TV news	radio news
Do a good job of keeping politicians accountable for their conduct	55	37	61	31
Are generally fair in their representation of politicians	51	10	62	43
Help the public learn about what is happening in politics	60	26	78	51
Look for any excuse to tarnish the name of politicians	19	86	18	10
Focus on negative stories about politics and politicians	24	83	31	18
Are more interested in getting a story than telling the truth	19	89	20	10

———————————— TEENAGERS & THE MEDIA ————————————

The majority of teenagers feel that they are negatively stereotyped by the media, according to a report undertaken by young people for the National Children's Bureau in December 2008. An analysis of media coverage during 2007 indicated that only 23% of stories about young people were positive, 29% were neutral, and 48% were negative. When broken down by media type, 45% of the stories in broadsheets were positive, compared to 24% in tabloids, and 10% of broadcast news coverage. When young people were questioned, 78% said they believed there was more negative coverage of teenagers in the press than positive; 76% thought knife crime was the most prevalent story about young people; 22·4% thought gun crime was. The researchers also interviewed a number of journalists – most of whom admitted that coverage of teenagers was unduly negative, and explained this by arguing that sensationalised bad news 'sells'. 88% of the teenagers questioned agreed that the media should report on more positive stories about young people.

———————————— BRITISH PRESS AWARDS · 2009 ————————————

Newspaper .... *The Times*
Journalist of the year.................................... Gillian Tett · *Financial Times*
Political journalist... Quentin Letts · *Daily Mail*
Show business............................... James Desborough · *News of the World*
Columnist.. Charlie Brooker · *The Guardian*
Interviewer .... Decca Aitkenhead · *The Guardian*
Sports journalist.................................... Matthew Syed · *The Times*
Reporter..................................... Christopher Leake · *Mail on Sunday*
Scoop.................. 'Ross & Brand' · Miles Goslett · *Mail on Sunday* [see p.129]

─────── DECLINING NEWSPAPER READERSHIP ───────

The proportion of Britons aged ≥15 reading a (purchased) daily national newspaper has almost halved since 1978, probably because of the growth of free newspapers and the ease of accessing news online. Readership of daily national papers is below:

Paper (%)	1978	1988	1998	2008
The Sun	29	25	21	16
Daily Mail	13	10	11	11
Daily Mirror	28	20	14	8
The Daily Telegraph	8	6	5	4
The Times	2	2	4	4
Daily Express	16	10	6	3
Daily Star	–	8	4	3
The Guardian	2	3	3	2
The Independent	–	2	2	1
Financial Times	2	2	1	1
Any national daily	72	67	56	44

[Source: National Readership Survey]

─────── DECLINE OF AMERICAN NEWSPAPERS ───────

2009 was an especially bleak year for American newspapers, as round after round of layoffs, bankruptcies, and closures battered the industry. At the time of writing, LA, Philadelphia, Boston, Detroit, San Francisco, Miami, and Denver were said to be in danger of losing all their daily print newspapers. According to some analysts, the financial crisis has helped weaken papers already depressed by the migration of readers to the internet – a forum to which most papers post content without any idea of how to make money. As print circulation has declined, so too has print advertising and, so far, online advertising has failed to fill the void. (Between 2006–08, total advertising revenue for the entire newspaper industry fell by 23%.) Listed below are notable US newspaper closures and bankruptcies in late 2008 and 2009:

Paper or parent company	est.	closure or bankruptcy
The Tribune Company†	1847	filed for bankruptcy 8/12/08
Minneapolis Star-Tribune	1867	filed for bankruptcy 15/1/09
Journal Register Company†	1990	filed for bankruptcy 21/2/09
Philadelphia Newspapers†	2006	filed for bankruptcy 22/2/09
Rocky Mountain News	1859	published last issue 27/2/09
Seattle Post-Intelligencer	1863	published last print issue 17/3/09
Christian Science Monitor	1908	published last weekday print issue 27/3/09
Tucson Citizen	1870	published last print issue 16/5/09

† The Tribune Company publishes the *Los Angeles Times*, *Chicago Tribune*, *Baltimore Sun* and *Hartford Courant*, among other papers. The Journal Register Company publishes a total of 20 daily newspapers. Philadelphia Newspapers LLC publishes *The Philadelphia Inquirer* and the *Philadelphia Daily News*.

——————————— PRESS FREEDOM ———————————

Only 17% of the world's population live in a country with a free press, according to the 2009 *Freedom of the Press* report, by Freedom House. For the seventh year in a row, press freedom around the world has declined. Of the 195 countries classified by the report, 36% are rated FREE, 31% PARTLY FREE, and 33% NOT FREE. Listed below are the countries with the freest and least free presses:

Most free press	*Least free press*
Iceland · Finland · Norway · Denmark	North Korea · Turkmenistan · Burma
Sweden · Belgium · Luxembourg	Libya · Eritrea · Cuba · Uzbekistan
Andorra · Netherlands · Switzerland	Belarus · Eq. Guinea · Zimbabwe

All countries in western Europe are classed as having 'free' press except for Turkey and Italy – the latter was recently demoted to 'partly free' after free speech was limited by the courts, journalists were intimidated by organised crime groups, and concerns grew over the concentration of media ownership. ❦ In March 2009, Freedom House produced an assessment of freedom online. It concluded that of the 15 countries examined, all suffered some degree of internet censorship, but four of the countries – Estonia, UK, South Africa, and Brazil – were classed as having 'free' internet. Repressive internet censorship in Iran, Tunisia, Cuba, and China meant these countries were classified as 'not free'.

——————— TIME SPENT READING NEWSPAPERS ———————

The average *Telegraph* reader spends 52 minutes perusing their paper, compared to the average *Star* reader's 30 minutes, according to the National Readership Survey. Below are the average number of minutes spent reading daily national newspapers:

Daily newspaper *(minutes)*	<5	c.5	c.15	c.30	c.60	c.120	c.180	*Avg*
The Sun	2%	8%	31%	40%	16%	2%	1%	31mins
Daily Mail	1	4	18	39	28	6	2	43
Daily Mirror	1	6	25	36	25	5	1	39
The Daily Telegraph	1	3	14	31	34	12	3	52
The Times	2	3	15	33	34	9	3	49
Daily Express	2	4	21	35	28	7	1	43
Daily Record	1	3	30	51	13	1	–	30
Daily Star	2	10	33	37	14	2	1	30
The Guardian	1	4	14	34	32	11	1	48
The Independent	1	5	19	37	29	6	2	43
Financial Times	3	8	27	32	22	6	1	36
Metro	5	15	47	27	6	1	–	21

Sunday Times readers spent longest on their Sunday newspaper – on average, 102 minutes. At just 35 minutes, *The Daily Star Sunday* had the shortest average read. Data from January–December 2007. ❦ ABC figures from May 2009 revealed that, at the height of Expensegate [see p.18], *The Daily Telegraph*'s sales were boosted by an average of 18,718 a day. Combined sales of *The Daily Telegraph* and *Sunday Telegraph* since the expenses scandal erupted on 8/5/09 showed *c.*1m extra copies were sold [see p.19]. Only the *Daily Star* saw better year-on-year figures after it cut its cover price to 20p.

MAJOR BRITISH NEWSPAPERS

Title	editorial address	phone	editor	circulation	readership	cost	owner	founded
Sun	1 Virginia St, Wapping, London E98 1SN	020 7782 4000	Dominic Mohan	3,121,407	7,870,000	20p	N	1911
Daily Mail	Northcliffe Ho., 2 Derry St, London W8 5TT	020 7938 6000	Paul Dacre	2,178,640	4,949,000	50p	A	1896
Daily Mirror	1 Canada Sq., Canary Wharf, London E14 5AP	020 7293 3000	Richard Wallace	1,340,028	3,489,000	45p	T	1903
Daily Telegraph	111 Buckingham Palace Rd, London SW1W 0DT	020 7931 2000	Will Lewis	818,937	1,887,000	90p	H	1855
Daily Star	10 Lower Thames St, London EC3R 6EN	020 8612 7000	Dawn Neesom	887,106	1,451,000	20p	S	1978
Daily Express	10 Lower Thames St, London EC3R 6EN	020 8612 7000	Peter Hill	734,045	1,557,000	25p	S	1900
Times	1 Virginia St, Wapping, London E98 1XY	020 7782 5000	James Harding	580,483	1,770,000	90p	N	1785
Financial Times	1 Southwark Bridge, London SE1 9HL	020 7873 3000	Lionel Barber	397,600	417,000	200p	P	1888
Guardian	Kings Place, 90 York Way, London N1 9GU	020 3353 2000	Alan Rusbridger	328,773	1,206,00	90p	G	1821
Evening Standard	2 Derry St, London W8 5TT	020 3367 7000	Geordie Greig	236,075	613,000	50p	E	1827
Independent	2 Derry St, London W8 5HF	020 7305 2000	Roger Alton	189,013	649,000	100p	I	1986
News of the World	1 Virginia St, Wapping, London E98 1SN	020 7782 1001	Colin Myler	3,104,205	7,808,000	100p	N	1843
Mail on Sunday	Northcliffe Ho., 2 Derry St, London W8 5TT	020 7938 6000	Peter Wright	2,040,939	5,589,000	150p	A	1982
Sunday Mirror	1 Canada Sq., Canary Wharf, London E14 5AP	020 7293 3000	Tina Weaver	1,248,613	3,919,000	100p	T	1915
Sunday Times	1 Virginia St, Wapping, London E93 1XY	020 7782 5000	John Witherow	1,190,936	3,175,000	200p	N	1821
Sunday Express	10 Lower Thames St, London EC3R 6EN	020 8612 7000	Martin Townsend	645,342	1,676,000	130p	S	1918
People	1 Canada Sq., Canary Wharf, London E14 5AP	020 7293 3000	Lloyd Embley	594,759	1,458,000	95p	T	1881
Sunday Telegraph	111 Buckingham Palace Rd, London SW1W 0DT	020 7931 2000	Ian MacGregor	602,495	1,675,000	190p	H	1961
Observer	119 Farringdon Rd, London EC1R 3ER	020 3353 2000	John Mulholland	398,330	1,370,000	200p	G	1791
Daily Star Sunday	10 Lower Thames St, London EC3R 6EN	020 8612 7000	Gareth Morgan	414,533	857,000	90p	S	2002
Independent on Sun.	2 Derry St, London W8 5HF	020 7005 2000	John Mullin	160,395	676,000	180p	I	1990
Scotland on Sunday	108 Holyrood Rd, Edinburgh EH8 8AS	0131 620 8620	Ian Stewart	56,738	228,000	150p	J	1988

Ownership: [N]ews Corporation · [I]ndependent News & Media · Press [H]oldings Ltd · [A]ssociated Newspapers · [G]uardian Media Group · [J]ohnston Press · [T]rinity Mirror · [E]vening Press Ltd · Northern & [S]hell Media · [P]earson · Circulation: ABC [Jul 2(09] · Readership: NRS [June 2008] · Founded dates relate to the paper's earliest incarnation.

―――――――――――― UK RADIO HALL OF FAME ――――――――――――

The Radio Academy Hall of Fame pays tribute to 'those legendary voices who make and have made an outstanding contribution to the sound of British radio and to British cultural life'. In 2008, the following voices were inducted to the Hall of Fame:

Emperor Rosko · James Naughtie · Ken Bruce · Simon Bates

―――――――――――― RADIO LISTENERSHIP BOOM ――――――――――――

90·2% of the UK population (aged ≥15) now listens to the radio at least once a week, according to May 2009 RAJAR data. This is the highest rate of listenership ever recorded. The growth of digital technology, which allows people to listen to the radio via DAB (12·7%), on their mobile phones (13%), over digital TV (3·4%), or on the internet (2·2%) has boosted radio's reach. RAJAR data below from the first quarter of 2009 revealed the most popular national radio stations:

Station	*reach (000s)*	*reach* (%)	*avg hours/listener*
BBC Radio 2	13,457	27	12·10
BBC Radio 1	11,072	22	9·60
BBC Radio 4	9,982	20	12·80
BBC Radio 5 Live	6,211	12	7·80
Classic FM	5,414	11	7·00
talkSPORT	2,416	5	7·50
BBC Radio 3	1,992	4	5·80
BBC World Service	1,470	3	5·30
The Hits	1,300	3	3·30
Smash Hits	996	2	3·50
BBC7	984	2	5·20

Chris Moyles' Radio 1 morning show drew 7·7m listeners in Q1 2009; 80,000 behind Terry Wogan's Radio 2 morning show. In September, Wogan announced his retirement; Chris Evans will replace him.

―――――――――――― THE SONY AWARDS · 2009 ――――――――――――

Since 1983, the Sony Radio Academy has rewarded excellence in British radio with bronze, silver, and gold awards. Some of the 2009 golds are listed below:

Breakfast show	5 Live Breakfast [BBC Radio 5 Live]
Music radio personality of the year	Chris Evans [BBC Radio 2]
Music broadcaster of the year	Mark Radcliffe [BBC Radio 2]
Entertainment award	Chris Evans Drivetime [BBC Radio 2]
Speech broadcaster	Nick Ferrari [LBC 97·3]
News journalist	Gavin Lee [BBC Radio 5 Live]
Digital station of the year	Fun Kids
Station of the year UK	BBC Radio 3

NOTABLE DESERT ISLAND DISCS · 2008/09

Castaway	luxury	favourite Desert Island Disc
David Davis	a magic wine cellar that never runs out	*Un Bel Di* (Puccini)
Janet Street-Porter	a notebook and pens	*Always on My Mind* (Pet Shop Boys)
Michael Eavis	a mouth organ with instruction manual	*How Great Thou Art* (Elvis Presley)
Marcus du Sautoy	his trumpet	*Parsifal* (Wagner)
Michael Deeley	200 cases of vintage wine	*I'd Do Anything for Love (But I Won't Do That)* (Meat Loaf)
James Nesbitt	a chilled bottle of Sancerre for every night	*Come Fly with Me* (Frank Sinatra)
Haleh Afshar	a rose bush	*Cello Suite No.1* (Bach)
Simon Murray	lots of paper, a pencil and a pencil sharpener	*O Soave Fanciulla* (Puccini)
Ruth Padel	a lot of paper and pencils	*E Voi Ridere?* (Mozart)
Vince Cable	an Aston Martin	*La Ci Darem La Mano* (Mozart)
David Suchet	his clarinet and an unlimited supply of reeds	*When I Fall in Love* (Nat King Cole)
Richard Madeley	a guitar	*Summertime* (Ella Fitzgerald)
Sebastian Faulks	a wicket, a cricket bat, a net, an endless supply of balls and a bowling machine that can be set to replicate the style of any bowler	*Miles* (Miles Davis)
Whoopi Goldberg	Wise potato chips	*Lovely Day* (Bill Withers)
Barry Humphries	his paints	*Songs of Sunset* (Delius)
Piers Morgan	his cricket bat	*Mambo Italiano* (Dean Martin)
Denis Healey	a very big box of chocolates including nougat	*String Quartet No.13 in B flat major* (Beethoven)
Martin Shaw	a synthesiser to make up his own music	*The Messiah* (Handel)
Harvey Goldsmith	a piano	*Sing, Sing, Sing (with a Swing)* (Benny Goodman)
Hugh Pennington	a brass microscope	*Sonata in D minor* (Bach)
David Mitchell	DVDs of sitcoms and a DVD player	*Rainbow Connection* (Jim Henson as Kermit)
Hugh Fearnley-Whittingstall	a full set of scuba gear	*Love Reign O'er Me* (The Who)
Nicky Haslam	a large C18th picture	*You're Just in Love* (Ethel Merman & Dick Haymes)
Joan Bakewell	an abundance of paper and pencils	*String Quintet in C major* (Schubert)
Roberto Alagna	a guitar	*Dagli Immortali Vertici* (Verdi)

TRUST & ONLINE NEWS

Online news sites are the most trusted news source in the United Kingdom, according to a TNS survey released in December 2008. Tabulated below are the percentage of people who said they 'highly trusted' various sources of information:

Information source	% highly trusting		
Recommendations by friends	45	Newspapers	23
Online news	40	Industry magazines	22
TV news	38	User forums	20
Product comparison sites	30	Company websites	20
Industry expert reviews	27	Free newspapers	16
Wikipedia	24	Company brochures	14
		Private blogs	6

Trust in online news varies around the world; below are those expressing *high trust*:

Finland	54%	Canada	41	Korea	37
China	48	Italy	41	Australia	36
Netherlands	45	UK	40	Germany	34
Japan	43	USA	38	France	28

PROFILE OF BLOGGERS

According to Technorati's 2008 *State of the Blogosphere* report, the average blogger is male, 25–34, has a university degree, and has a higher than average salary. Some key blogger demographics:

Aged: 18–24	13
· 25–34	36
· 35–44	27
· 45–54	15
· >55	8
Have a university degree	70
Have household income >£45k	40
Are parents	44
Live in North America	48

Profile	% of global bloggers
Male	66
Female	34

SWINE FLU & INTERNET SEARCHES

1 in every 260 UK internet searches during the week ending 2·5·09 included the words 'swine flu', according to Hitwise, a statistic that illustrates the extent to which Britons now rely on the internet as a source of key information. There were >23,000 variations in the terms used to search for information on swine flu. The top five most popular internet searches related to A(H1N1) [see p.23] during May 2009 were:

Search term	% searches
Swine flu	36·6
Swine flu symptoms	6·8
Symptoms of swine flu	2·5
Swine flu more condition_symptoms	1·4
Swine flu jokes	1·2

Wikipedia was the greatest recipient of traffic for UK searches relating to H1N1. In May 2009, Pew Research reported that 49% of Americans turned to the web for swine flu information.

———————————— TWITTER USERS ————————————

Research by Harvard Business School, released in May 2009, provided insight into how the micro-blogging site Twitter [see p.13] is used. The researchers found that only 10% of all users account for 90% of all tweets, suggesting that Twitter is less of a two-way social networking tool and more of a 'one-way, one-to-many publishing service'. On a traditional social networking site such as Facebook, the top 10% of users account for 30% of all content, indicating a much greater level of interactivity. The researchers pointed out that Twitter's usage patterns were much more like those of Wikipedia – where the top 15% of prolific editors are responsible for 90% of all edits. Typically, Twitter users contribute very rarely: the average lifetime tweets per member is just 1, and >50% of all users produce just 1 tweet every 74 days. It seems that many users sign up to follow high-profile Twitterers such as Ashton Kutcher (the site's most popular user, with >3m followers) or Stephen Fry (640,000 followers, at the time of writing), rather than to write tweets themselves. The study also revealed that although there are a greater number of female users (55%) than male (45%), the average male user is almost twice as likely to follow other male users than to follow women. This finding is in direct contrast to social networking sites, where women are by far the most popular users – both men and women are more likely to follow content produced by other women.

————————— TOP SOCIAL NETWORKING SITES —————————

Facebook continues to be the UK's most popular social networking site, and it is the UK's second most-visited website after google.co.uk, according to Hitwise. The top ten most popular social networking websites in the UK in May 2009 were:

Rank	domain	market share %
1	Facebook	42·08
2	YouTube	17·56
3	Bebo	6·08
4	MySpace	3·61
5	Twitter	1·58
6	Yahoo! Answers	1·17
7	Tagged	0·79
8	Windows Live Home	0·64
9	Nasza Klasa†	0·63
10	BBC Forums	0·58

† The Polish equivalent of Friends Reunited, which translates as 'our class'.

————————— ORWELL PRIZE FOR BLOGS —————————

In 2009, the Orwell Prizes for political writing added a £3,000 prize for blogs alongside those for books and journalism. The inaugural prize was awarded to *Night Jack – An English Detective*, a pseudonymous blog by a policeman. The judges said, 'the insight into the everyday life of the police that Jack Night's wonderful blog offered was – everybody felt – something which only a blog could deliver, and he delivered it brilliantly'. In June 2009 the *Times* published Night Jack's real identity (Detective Constable Richard Horton of Lancashire Police) after a test case in which Justice Eady refused to grant an injunction to the blogger to protect his anonymity. At the time of writing, the *Night Jack* blog was unavailable online.

Music & Cinema

'We are out of our joy. He is out of his pain.'
— REV JESSE JACKSON on the death of Michael Jackson

─────── R.I.P. THE 'KING OF POP' ───────

Michael Jackson was pronounced dead at 2:26pm on 25/6/09 – hours after suffering a cardiac arrest at his LA home. On 28/8/09, the county coroner ruled Jackson's death a homicide caused by a combination of Propofol (an anaesthetic) and Lorazepam (an anti-anxietal). In the weeks prior to his demise, Jackson had been rehearsing for a gruelling 'comeback' tour due to start at London's O2 arena in July; his death plunged fans around the world into shock. Billions scrambled to the net (crashing Twitter, Wikipedia, and latimes.com) and crowds gathered spontaneously at the Hollywood Walk of Fame, NYC's Apollo Theatre, Trafalgar Square, and in smaller vigils from Australia to Zimbabwe. A memorial service on 7/7, attended by 11,000 and watched by *c.*1bn, opened with Jackson's gilded coffin wheeled on-stage by his brothers, each wearing a single sequined glove. The service continued with messages of condolence from Nelson Mandela, Brooke Shields, and Magic Johnson; a poem written by Maya Angelou; and performances by stars including Stevie Wonder and Mariah Carey. Al Sharpton received a standing ovation when he told Jackson's children, 'There wasn't nothing strange about your daddy. What was strange was what your daddy had to deal with'. ❦ Born the seventh of nine children in Gary, Indiana, on 28/8/58, Jackson entered showbiz as the youngest member of the Jackson 5. The R&B group's first four singles – *I Want You Back, ABC, The Love You Save,* and *I'll be There* – all hit No. 1: a first in pop history. Yet it was as a solo performer that Jackson reached the celebrity stratosphere. In 1982, aged just 24, he released *Thriller* – a ground-breaking mix of disco and R&B that won 8 Grammys on its way to becoming the best-selling album of all time. *Bad* (1987) and *Dangerous* (1991) were also smash hits, but soon Jackson's reputation was overshadowed by a 1993 child abuse scandal. *HIStory* (1995) and *Invincible* (2001) failed to reach the (unreachable) highs of his earlier albums, and in 2005 Jackson found himself again defending child abuse charges, this time in court. ❦ In later years, Jackson was portrayed by the tabloids as 'Wacko Jacko' – an immature eccentric who blurred racial and gender boundaries, slept with a chimpanzee, and outfitted his 'Neverland' ranch with juvenile amusements. Yet regardless of his personal demons, speculation as to the paternity and maternity of his children, and the Elvis-esque rumours that dog his death, Jackson will be remembered as one of the greatest entertainers of the C20th, and one of only a handful of people who achieved truly global fame.

———————— MUSIC TASTES & PERSONALITY ————————

The stereotypical image of heavy metal fans as rowdy, head-banging lunks was challenged by a September 2008 study. Prof. Adrian North of Heriot-Watt University questioned >36,000 people from around the world about their character and their musical tastes to create a list of typical personality traits for various music genres:

Music genre	typical personality traits
Blues	*high self-esteem, creative, outgoing, gentle, at ease*
Classical music	*high self-esteem, creative, introvert, at ease*
Rap	*high self-esteem, outgoing*
Opera	*high self-esteem, creative, gentle*
Country & Western	*hardworking, outgoing*
Reggae	*high self-esteem, creative, not hardworking, outgoing, gentle*
Indie	*low self-esteem, creative, not hardworking, not gentle*
Heavy metal	*low self-esteem, creative, not hardworking, not outgoing, gentle, at ease*
Chart pop	*high self-esteem, not creative, hardworking, outgoing, not at ease*
Soul	*high self-esteem, creative, outgoing, gentle, at ease*

Research by American PhD student Virgil Griffith in March 2009 suggested that fans of hip hop artist Lil Wayne may not be the sharpest tools in the box. Griffith's somewhat curious findings came from a study of average exam results cross-referenced with students' favourite music (as listed on Facebook). By this method, Griffith deduced that those with the highest exam results tended to enjoy artists such as Beethoven, Radiohead, or Bob Dylan, whereas those languishing at the lower end of the academic spectrum were more likely to be fans of Beyoncé, Lil Wayne, or Aerosmith.

———————— BRITAIN'S MOST-PLAYED SONGS ————————

Procul Harum's *A Whiter Shade of Pale* was the most-played song in Britain over the last 75 years, according to statistics released by PPL in April 2009. (PPL licenses recorded music on behalf of thousands of record companies for play on the radio, at public events, or over pub jukeboxes.) The 10 most-played songs since 1934 are:

No. song	artist	released	weeks at No. 1
1 .. *A Whiter Shade of Pale*	Procul Harum	1967	6
2 .. *Bohemian Rhapsody*	Queen	1975	9 ('75) & 5 ('91)
3 .. *All I Have to do is Dream*	Everly Brothers	1958	7
4 .. *Love is All Around*	Wet Wet Wet	1994	15
5 .. *(Everything I Do) I Do It for You*	Bryan Adams	1991	16
6 .. *Angels* [†]	Robbie Williams	1997	–
7 .. *All Shook Up*	Elvis Presley	1957	7
8 .. *Dancing Queen*	Abba	1976	6
9 .. *Magic Moments*	Perry Como	1958	8
10. *White Christmas* [‡]	Bing Crosby	1942	–

[†] Despite the enduring popularity of *Angels* (it was named as most popular karaoke song by PRS in 1998) the song only ever peaked at No. 4 in the UK charts. [‡] Official UK chart started in 1952.

THE BRIT AWARDS · 2009

Pop princess Kylie Minogue and comedians Matt Horne and James Corden formed the presenting triumvirate of the 2009 Brit Awards – but few could doubt it was Duffy's night. While critics lamented the show's lack of 'edge' and frequently feeble jokes, all eyes were on the platinum-haired soul singer, who swept aside Grammy-award-winning rivals Adele and Estelle to take three top prizes. The Pet Shop Boys closed the evening with a medley of their hits accompanied, in flamboyant style, by Brandon Flowers of the Killers and rising star Lady Gaga. And the winners were:

British male solo artist .... Paul Weller
British female solo artist .... Duffy
British group .... Elbow
British album .... Duffy · *Rockferry*
British single[1] .... Girls Aloud · *The Promise*
British live act[2] .... Iron Maiden
British breakthrough act[3] .... Duffy
International male solo artist .... Kanye West
International female solo artist .... Katy Perry
International album .... Kings of Leon · *Only By The Night*
International group .... Kings of Leon
Critics' choice .... Florence and the Machine
Outstanding contribution to music .... Pet Shop Boys

[1] Live public vote that night. [2] Voted for by Radio 2 listeners. [3] Voted for by Radio 1 listeners.

IN QUOTES: DUFFY · It's a real honour to be here. British female – I don't know what that means, but it's a good job my mum didn't have a boy. ❧ KATY PERRY · I'm so sick right now, but they said to show up to the Brits because something special might happen. ❧ SARAH HARDING (Girls Aloud) · It's about time … I think I've just wet myself. ❧ JARED FOLLOWILL (Kings of Leon) · If it wasn't for England, Kings of Leon wouldn't be here right now. You created Kings of Leon, good luck getting rid of us.

CHRISTMAS NUMBER ONE · 2008

The battle for Christmas No. 1 pitted against each other three versions of Leonard Cohen's 1981 song *Hallelujah*. 'Real' music fans across the UK, united by their disdain for talent shows, attempted to prevent *X Factor* winner Alexandra Burke's version from taking the top spot by purchasing Jeff Buckley's more 'credible' 1994 cover. (The plan backfired when it was revealed that *X Factor* puppetmaster Simon Cowell owned the rights to both versions of the song, and was reportedly earning £250,000 a day as a result.) Burke ultimately triumphed, selling 576,000 copies and beating Jeff Buckley (who sold 81,000 copies) into second place. It was the first time in *c*.52 years that the same song claimed the top two chart positions. (In 1957, Tommy Steele and Guy Mitchell held the top two spots with their versions of *Singing the Blues*.) Leonard Cohen himself also entered the chart, at No. 36, with his original version of *Hallelujah*. Previous *X Factor* winner Leona Lewis took the No. 3 spot with *Run*.

———————— TOP-GROSSING TOURS 2008 ————————

The top-grossing worldwide tours in 2008, according to music magazine *Billboard*:

Artist	total attendance	total capacity	gigs	sellouts	total gross ($)
Bon Jovi	2,157,675	2,157,675	99	99	210,650,974
Bruce Springsteen	2,094,851	2,181,839	82	46	204,513,630
Madonna	1,357,906	1,369,452	39	38	185,696,018
The Police	1,468,705	1,492,947	78	71	149,623,800
Celine Dion	738,947	755,710	44	36	91,006,221
Kenny Chesney	1,187,622	1,252,227	46	25	86,306,618
Neil Diamond	834,689	834,689	61	61	81,206,383
Spice Girls	581,066	595,220	45	34	70,123,272
Eagles	427,231	436,075	34	27	56,625,336
Rascal Flatts	941,827	967,726	65	58	55,863,364

Reported period: Nov 2007–Nov 2008; some tours, such as Madonna's, had not yet been completed. The Spice Girls' 17 sell-out concerts at the O2 arena, London, in December 2007–January 2008 grossed £16,637,563, making them the most profitable series of concerts at one venue in 2008. ☞ PRS data revealed in April 2009 that live music revenues outperformed sales of recorded music in Britain for the first time. Tours generated £1·28bn in 2008 compared to recorded music receipts of £1·24bn. This shift towards live music was confirmed by news that the Glastonbury, Reading, and Leeds festivals sold out by April 2009 and Take That's Circus Tour sold 600,000 tickets in just 5 hours.

———————— YOUTUBE & MUSIC VIDEOS ————————

More British 15–24s watch music videos on YouTube than on dedicated music video TV channels, according to March 2009 research by Ipsos MediaCT. The percentage who had watched YouTube music videos in the past 12 months was:

Age	%				
15–24	57	35–44	24	All adults · ♂	27
25–34	30	45–54	25	All adults · ♀	20
		≥55	3	TOTAL	23

50% of adults who watched a YouTube music video subsequently spent money on that artist. Below are those who bought items after watching YouTube videos:

Purchased ...	%		
CD	36	DVD/Blu-ray	5
Paid download of music video	15	Ringtones	3
Ticket for live performance	7	Merchandise	2
		Total buying any item	50

YouTube is by far the dominant internet site for watching music videos. Among those who had watched any music video online in the last 12 months, 91% did so on YouTube. 53% of adults viewing YouTube music videos in the last year watched one or more a week, while 9% watched music videos every day. ☞ In September 2009, YouTube ended a 6-month block on British users accessing thousands of music videos, after settling a dispute over fees with the Performing Right Society (PRS).

THE EUROVISION SONG CONTEST · 2009

As the 2008 Eurovision Song Contest drew to a close, Britain's Eurovision future was in crisis. Years of poor results and accusations of East European 'block voting' had taken their toll. Legendary host Terry Wogan quit after 35 years, observing, 'It has always been an event, but at least the voting used to be about the songs. Now it's really about national prejudices'. However, the spirit of Eurovision could not be crushed and, undaunted by 2008's controversies, Sir Andrew Lloyd Webber announced he would compose the UK entry and help the BBC search for a singer. Graham Norton took over Wogan's duties, and the UK began its quest for Eurovision glory with the series *Your Country Needs You*. The acts competing were:

The Twins · Emperors of Soul · Charlotte · Jade · Damien · Mark

In February 2009, after weeks of competition, Britain chose Jade Ewen to represent the country's hopes and dreams by singing Lloyd Webber's *My Time* in Moscow.

Paddy Power's odds for Eurovision winner
Norway 6/5 · Greece 4/1 · Turkey 8/1 · Azerbaijan 10/1 · UK 12/1

THE FINAL · 16·05·09 · MOSCOW, RUSSIA

The kitsch and glitz of Moscow's Eurovision finals were overshadowed somewhat by the heavy-handedness of the Russian hosts. The Georgian entry (*We Don't Wanna Put In*) was barred from the contest for daring to include veiled criticisms of Vladimir Putin, and >30 gay rights activists, including Britain's Peter Tatchell, were arrested during a gay pride march timed to coincide with the event. The competition itself maintained its high levels of high camp, offering the now obligatory mix of Europop, obscure ethnic instruments, and the odd preposterous key-change. The voting system, overhauled to prevent block-voting, combined a fifty-fifty mix of public votes and judging panel scores. Eventually, Norway's Alexander Rybak scooped a record 387 points to win with his gypsy violin song, *Fairytale*. Jade Ewen came a creditable fifth, in Britain's best showing since 2002. The top three acts were:

Country	artist	song	score
Norway	Alexander Rybak	*Fairytale*	387
Iceland	Yohanna	*Is It True?*	218
Azerbaijan	AySel & Arash	*Always*	207

SONG LYRICS OF MERIT

NORWAY · *I'm in love with a fairytale, Even though it hurts. 'Cause I don't care if I lose my mind; I'm already cursed.* ❦ AZERBAIJAN · *I believe I'm addicted to you, In your eyes I see dreams coming true, Finally I have found you and now, I will never let you go, No.* ❦ UNITED KINGDOM · *There's nothing I'm afraid of, I'll show you what I'm made of, Show you all, It's my time now.* ❦ ICELAND · *Did you tell me you would never leave me this way? Is it true? Is it over? Did I throw it away?* ❦ LITHUANIA · *If you really love, The love you say you love (really love), Then surely that love would love … Then surely that love would love to love you back.* ❦ GERMANY · *Do the dee dee hi hey sing dee dee hi hey, Do the de de de he do the de de de he, Do the skiddle de skiddle de boom.*

OTHER NOTABLE MUSIC AWARDS · 2009

Awards	prize	*winner*
	Best British band	Bullet For My Valentine
Kerrang!	*Hall of fame*	Limp Bizkit
	Best live band	Slipknot
	Best British band	Oasis
	Best solo artist	Pete Doherty
NME	*Best new band*	MGMT
	Best album	Kings of Leon · *Only by the Night*
	God-like genius award	The Cure
	Best female video	Taylor Swift · *You Belong With Me*
MTV	*Best male video*	T.I. · *Live Your Life*
	Best pop video	Britney Spears · *Womanizer*
	Record of the year	Robert Plant & Alison Krauss *Please Read the Letter*
Grammys	*Album of the year*	Robert Plant & Alison Krauss · *Raising Sand*
	Song of the year	Coldplay · *Viva la Vida*
	Best New Age album	Jack DeJohnette · *Peace Time*
	Best song	Elbow · *One Day Like This*
Ivor Novello	*Songwriter of the year*	Eg White
	Most performed work	Duffy · *Mercy*
	Best contemporary song	Elbow · *Grounds for Divorce*
	Best UK male	Dizzee Rascal
	Best UK female	Estelle
MOBO [2008]	*Best R&B/soul*	Chris Brown
	Best hip hop	Lil Wayne
	Best African act	9ice
	Icon award	Phil Lynott
Mojo	*Maverick*	Manic Street Preachers
	Song of the year	Elbow · *One Day Like This*

THE MERCURY MUSIC PRIZE · 2009

The 2009 Mercury Music Prize was won by Speech Debelle, a relatively unknown 26-year-old hip-hop artist from S London. Her debut album, *Speech Therapy*, sold just 2,763 copies when it was released in June 2009, but subsequently hit No. 1 on the Amazon UK download chart. After her win, Debelle said: 'Hopefully people will hear [my] album and realise they don't have to make music that sounds the same.'

The 2009 Mercury nominees

Florence and the Machine....... *Lungs*
Kasabian..............................
    West Ryder Pauper Lunatic Asylum
Bat for Lashes................ *Two Suns*
La Roux.........................*La Roux*
Glasvegas.....................*Glasvegas*

Speech Debelle..........*Speech Therapy*
Friendly Fires.............*Friendly Fires*
The Horrors...........*Primary Colours*
Lisa Hannigan ....*Sea Sew*
The Invisible ....*The Invisible*
Led Bib...................*Sensible Shoes*
Sweet Billy Pilgrim.... *Twice Born Men*

————————— UK NUMBER ONES · 2008–09 —————————

W/ending	weeks	artist	song
20·09·08	3	Kings of Leon	*Sex on Fire*
11·10·08	3	Pink	*So What*
01·11·08	1	Girls Aloud	*Promise*
08·11·08	3	X Factor Finalists 2008	*Hero*
29·11·08	1	Beyoncé	*If I Were a Boy*
06·12·08	1	Take That	*Greatest Day*
13·12·08	2	Leona Lewis	*Run*
27·12·08	3	Alexandra Burke	*Hallelujah*
17·01·09	3	Lady Gaga	*Just Dance*
07·02·09	4	Lily Allen	*The Fear*
07·03·09	1	Kelly Clarkson	*My Life Would Suck Without You*
14·03·09	1	Flo Rida	*Right Round*
21·03·09	1	Jenkins, West, Jones, Gibb	*Islands In The Stream*
28·03·09	3	Lady Gaga	*Poker Face*
18·04·09	2	Calvin Harris	*I'm Not Alone*
02·05·09	3	Tinchy Stryder feat. N-dubz	*Number 1*
23·05·09	1	Black Eyed Peas	*Boom Boom Pow*
30·05·09	2	Dizzee Rascal, Armand Van Helden	*Bonkers*
13·06·09	1	Black Eyed Peas	*Boom Boom Pow*
20·06·09	1	Pixie Lott	*Mama Do*
27·06·09	1	David Guetta feat. Kelly Rowland	*When Love Takes Over*
04·07·09	1	La Roux	*Bulletproof*
11·07·09	2	Cascada	*Evacuate The Dancefloor*
25·07·09	2	JLS	*Beat Again*
08·08·09	1	Black Eyed Peas	*I Gotta Feeling*
15·08·09	1	Tinchy Stryder feat. Amelle	*Never Leave You*
22·08·09	1	Black Eyed Peas	*I Gotta Feeling*

——————— GLOBAL BEST-SELLING ALBUMS · 2008 ———————

Album	artist
Viva La Vida Or Death And All His Friends	Coldplay
Black Ice	AC/DC
Mamma Mia! The Movie Soundtrack	Various
Rockferry	Duffy
Death Magnetic	Metallica
Spirit	Leona Lewis
Back To Black	Amy Winehouse
High School Musical 3: Senior Year†	Various
Tha Carter III	Lil Wayne
Good Girl Gone Bad	Rihanna

[Sources: IFPI · Physical albums & downloads] † All three High School Musical soundtracks have made it into the top ten global best-selling albums, but the previous two both topped the chart.

———————— GLOBAL DIGITAL MUSIC SALES ————————

Digital music accounted for 20% of all global music sales in 2008, according to the latest Digital Music Report by the IFPI. America is the largest digital market, accounting for 39% of all digital music sold. Japan is the second largest market (19%), followed by the UK (16%). The best-selling digital singles in 2008 were:

Rank	artist	song	sales (m)
1	Lil Wayne	*Lollipop*	9·1
2	Thelma Aoyama[†]	*Sobaniirune*	8·2
3	Flo Rida feat. T-Pain	*Low*	8·0
4	Leona Lewis	*Bleeding Love*	7·7
5	Timbaland	*Apologize*	6·2
6	Greeeen[‡]	*Kiseki*	6·2
7	Katy Perry	*I Kissed a Girl*	5·7
8	Alicia Keys	*No One*	5·6
9	Usher feat. Young Jeezy	*Love In This Club*	5·6
10	Chris Brown	*With You*	5·5

The report also discussed the increasing influence of the internet, and noted the number of bands using social networking to promote their music. Below are the number of musical acts (signed and unsigned) on MySpace, as of December 2008:

Musical genre	no. acts				
Hip Hop	2·5m	Pop	723,000	Reggae	314,000
Rap	2·4m	Metal	611,000		
Rock	1·8m	Punk	468,000	Some acts may have been
R&B	1·6m	Electronica	413,000	registered under more than
		Techno	335,000	one musical genre.

† Japanese R&B artist. ‡ Four-piece Japanese band who never show their faces in public lest it harm their aspiration to become dentists. In April 2008, it was revealed that two of the band members had passed their dentistry exams, however their identity will remain secret until all four are wielding drills.

———————— TEENAGERS & FILESHARING ————————

26% of 14–18-year-olds confessed to filesharing music illegally in January 2009, down from 42% in December 2007, according to a July 2009 report by Music Ally. The report indicated that illegal filesharing may be giving way to streaming music over the internet via sites such as Spotify and YouTube [see p.145]. 65% of teenagers questioned said they streamed music regularly, and 31% said they streamed music on their computer every day. This trend should mollify music executives who have struggled to find a way to sell music to tech-savvy teenagers who are now used to getting all the music they want online, for free. Of all music fans (aged 14–64) questioned for the survey, 19% regularly paid to download singles compared to 17% who regularly file-shared singles. However more people regularly file-shared entire albums (13%) than legally purchased them digitally (10%) which suggests that the music industry has some way to go to reorganise its money-making model.

———————————————— MUSIC & GAMING ————————————————

Currently, some of the most popular computer games are those such as *Rock Band* and *Guitar Hero* in which virtual interaction with music is a key part of play. And increasingly, such games are a key source of revenue for record labels contending with plummeting CD sales. Indeed, in 2008, Warner Music UK stated that games were its second-highest source of licensing revenue, and *The Economist* reported that Aerosmith earned more from *Guitar Hero: Aerosmith* than from any of their albums. Below are some notable recent collaborations between bands and gaming:

In September 2008, Metallica released the album *Death Magnetic* as a premium download on *Guitar Hero 3* on the same day as album's general release. (Oddly, some fans said the *Guitar Hero* version sounded better.) ❦ In September 2008, Guns N' Roses released its first new single in 14 years, *Shackler's Revenge*, on *Rock Band 2*. ❦ In May 2009, Activision confirmed the development of *Guitar Hero: Van Halen*. Also in May, *Guitar Hero: Metallica* was released in Europe. ❦ *The Beatles: Rock Band* was unveiled on 9/9/2009. The game features tracks from the Fab 4's catalogue as well as previously unreleased material. This much-anticipated release was the first time the Beatles have allowed their music to be used in a computer game.

———————————————— GREATEST VOICES IN ROCK ————————————————

The top ten greatest voices in rock, according to Planet Rock in January 2009, are:

1	Robert Plant	*Led Zeppelin*	6	David Coverdale	*Whitesnake*
2	Freddie Mercury	*Queen*	7	Axl Rose	*Guns N' Roses*
3	Paul Rodgers	*Free/Bad Company*	8	Bruce Dickinson	*Iron Maiden*
4	Ian Gillan	*Deep Purple*	9	Mick Jagger	*Rolling Stones*
5	Roger Daltrey	*The Who*	10	Bon Scott	*AC/DC*

———————————————— MUSIC & THE LONG TAIL THEORY ————————————————

According to a theory popularised by Chris Anderson's influential 2006 book *The Long Tail*, the internet offers such a vast choice to consumers that niche markets flourish. Anderson used figures from an American online music retailer to support his theory, creating a model for the internet economy that moved away from a *few mainstream* products towards *many niche* markets. However, the 'long tail' theory was challenged in December 2008 by Will Page of the MCPS–PRS Alliance, a not-for-profit royalty collection society. After assessing online sales data, Page revealed that 80% of all online music revenue originated from just 52,000 singles, and although 1·23m albums were available for sale online, only 173,000 were ever bought – i.e., 85% of all albums garnered no sales whatsoever. Anderson admitted to *The Times* that Page had 'found a dataset where [the long tail] doesn't work' but he maintained 'there is a reason why the "long tail" has become a fixture in the technology world over the past five years – it fits countless phenomena we see every day'.

QUEEN'S MEDAL FOR MUSIC

The Queen's Medal for Music is awarded annually to those who have had 'a major influence on the musical life of the nation'. The nomination process is overseen by a committee under the chairmanship of the Master of The Queen's Music†, currently Sir Peter Maxwell Davies. Established in 2005, the first award was presented to the conductor Sir Charles Mackerras. Welsh opera singer Bryn Terfel was honoured in 2006, and composer Judith Weir was the winner in 2007. The next award was presented in 2009, when Northumbrian folk musician KATHRYN TICKELL was honoured. ❦ Tickell developed a fascination with the music of the North-east at an early age, and started playing the Northumbrian smallpipes when she was nine years old. After winning all the traditional open smallpipes competitions, Tickell released her first album, *On Kielderside*, at the age of 16. This album proved to be just the first in a series of accomplishments, that included 12 more albums, world tours, collaborations with The Chieftains, Alan Parsons, and Sting, a series of programmes for Radio 2 and Channel 4 Schools, and the 2005 Musician of the Year award at the Radio 2 Folk Awards. ❦ Tickell has also focused on enriching the musical traditions of the North-east by encouraging its next generation of musicians. In 1997, she founded The Young Musicians Fund, which awards grants to young musicians; in 1999, she was named to the founding staff of the new degree course in folk and traditional music at Newcastle University; and in 2002, she founded The Sage Gateshead's youth folk ensemble, Folkestra, which has performed around the country and as part of 2008's first-ever BBC Proms Folk Day. ❦ Announcing the award, Sir Peter said, '[Tickell] has put the pipes and the music of her own part of England back among the public where it belongs, and is also spreading a love of this music throughout the whole world'.

† Committee members include: *The Times'* critic Richard Morrison; composer Michael Berkeley; MD of the Barbican Nicholas Kenyon; and former chair of the Royal Opera House, Lord Moser.

BEST CHRISTMAS CAROLS

In the Bleak Midwinter was voted the best Christmas carol in a November 2008 poll of directors of music by *BBC Music* magazine. The top ten festive songs were:

1	*In the Bleak Midwinter*	6	*Tomorrow Shall be My Dancing Day*
2	*In Dulci Jubilo*†	7	*There is No Rose*
3	*A Spotless Rose*	8	*O Come All Ye Faithful*
4	*Bethlehem Down*‡	9	*Of the Father's Heart Begotten*
5	*Lully, Lulla*	10	*What Sweeter Music*

† An instrumental version by Mike Oldfield of the 1837 translation of the carol by Robert Lucas de Pearsall (1795–1856) reached No. 4 in the charts in 1976. ‡ Written in 1927 by Peter Warlock (1894–1930) and journalist Bruce Blunt (1899–1957), the composition won the *Daily Telegraph's* carol contest in 1927, and as a result helped to finance the indebted pair's Christmas revelries.

———————————— STRADIVARIUS CELLOS ————————————

Despite a record-breaking bid of $1·35m, a world-renowned Stradivarius cello – known as 'the Fleming' – failed to meet its (undisclosed) reserve price in the first-ever online auction of a Strad, held in November 2008. Crafted in 1717 by maestro luthier Antonio Stradivari, the Fleming was slightly damaged in the 1750s and lovingly restored by the famed Spanish instrument maker Joseph Contreras. ❦ Stradivari was born in Cremona, Italy, in 1644. He established his own workshop in 1680 and, until his death in 1737, manufactured >1,100 instruments including harps, guitars, violins, violas, and cellos, of which *c*.650 have survived. Recent research attributes the superior sound of Strads to the uncommonly dense wood from which they were crafted. This wood, according to dendrochronologists at the University of Tennessee, may have grown during a 'mini ice age' in 1645–1715. ❦ Strads can be identified by the Latin inscription *Antonius Stradivarius Cremonensis Faciebat Anno* ___ [Antonio Stradivari, Cremona, made in the year ___], and his instruments are generally named after their most famous owner. Hence the Fleming was named after the late Amaryllis Fleming (1925–99), a respected British cellist and the half-sister of James Bond's creator, Ian Fleming. Amaryllis was said to adore her cello's sumptuous tone. ❦ Other famous Stradivarius cellos include:

Name	*made*	*named after*	*recently played by*
Davidov	1712	Karl Davidov (1838–89)	Yo-Yo Ma
Duport	1711	Jean-Pierre Duport (1714–1818)	Mstislav Rostropovich
Barjansky	1690	Alexandre Barjansky (C20th)	Julian Lloyd Webber
Du Pré	1673	Jacqueline Du Pré (1945–87)	Lynn Harrell
Bonjour†	1696	Abel Bonjour (C19th)	Soo Bae
Servais	1701	Adrien François Servais (1807–66)	Anner Bylsma
Piatti	1720	Carlo Alfredo Piatti (1822–1901)	Carlos Prieto

† The Bonjour is the world's most expensive cello – it was bought for $1·03m at auction in 1999.

———————————— CLASSIC FM HALL OF FAME · 2009 ————————————

In 2009, the top six entries in the *Classic FM* 'Hall of Fame' remained unchanged from 2008. The chart is compiled yearly, and reflects the 300 favourite pieces of the radio station's listeners. The 2009 top ten (with 2008 places in brackets) were:

1 ..... [1] ... Ralph Vaughan Williams .... *The Lark Ascending*
2 ..... [2] ... Sergei Rachmaninov .... *Piano Concerto No. 2 in C minor*
3 ..... [3] ... Ralph Vaughan Williams .... *Fantasia on a Theme by Thomas Tallis*
4 ..... [4] ... Ludwig van Beethoven ...... *Piano Concerto No. 5 in E flat (Emperor)*
5 ..... [5] ... Ludwig van Beethoven .... *Symphony No. 6 (Pastoral)*
6 ..... [6] ... Wolfgang Amadeus Mozart .... *Clarinet Concerto in A*
7 ..... [8] ... Max Bruch .... *Violin Concerto No. 1*
8 ..... [7] ... Edward Elgar .... *Cello Concerto*
9 .... [10] .. Ludwig van Beethoven .... *Symphony No. 9 (Choral)*
10 .... [9] ... Edward Elgar .... *Enigma Variations*

———————— BBC PROMS · 2009 ————————

Highlights of the 2009 Proms included: the first Bollywood Prom, a celebration of Darwin's anniversary [see p.190], 12 BBC commissions, 15 premieres, and an exploration of 1934 – the year in which Frederick Delius, Edward Elgar, and Gustav Holst all died, and Sir Harrison Birtwistle and Sir Peter Maxwell Davies were both born.

PROM 76 · THE LAST NIGHT OF THE PROMS · 12·9·2009

Oliver Knussen..*Flourish with Fireworks*
Henry Purcell (arr. Henry Wood) ....*New Suite*
Henry Purcell .... *Dido and Aeneas, 'Thy hand, Belinda ...When I am laid in earth'*
'With drooping wings ye cupids come'
Joseph Haydn.....................................*Trumpet Concerto in E flat major*
Gustav Mahler..*Lieder eines fahrenden Gesellen*
Heitor Villa-Lobos................................*Chôros No. 10, 'Rasga o Coração'*
Malcolm Arnold ....*A Grand, Grand Overture*
Albert William Ketèlbey..*In a Monastery Garden*
Astor Piazzolla ....*Libertango*
G. Gershwin (arr. Barry Forgie) ...*Shall We Dance, 'They can't take that away from me'*
BBC Proms Inspire Young Composers ....*Fireworks Fanfares*
George Frideric Handel ....*Music for the Royal Fireworks*
Thomas Arne (arr. Malcolm Sargent) ....*Rule, Britannia!*
Hubert Parry (orch. Edward Elgar) ....*Jerusalem*
Edward Elgar.......*Pomp and Circumstance March No. 1, 'Land of Hope and Glory'*
Henry Wood (arr.)...*The National Anthem*

———————— THE CLASSICAL BRITS · 2009 ————————

Best album .... The Royal Scots Dragoon Guards · *Spirit of the Glen: Journey*
Female artist of the year ....Alison Balsom
Male artist of the year ....Gustavo Dudamel
Young British classical performer or group ....Alina Ibragimova
Lifetime achievement award..José Carreras

———————— SOME CLASSICAL ANNIVERSARIES · 2010 ————————

2010 marks a number of significant milestones for Romantic composers, including the 200th anniversary of the birth of FRÉDÉRIC CHOPIN (1·3·1810) and ROBERT ALEXANDER SCHUMANN (8·6·1810), as well as the 150th anniversary of the birth of GUSTAV MAHLER (7·5·1860). Other notable classical anniversaries in 2010 are:

b.1660..............Alessandro Scarlatti	*d*.1910................... Mily Balakirev
b.1710.......Thomas Augustine Arne†	*d*.1935....Sir Alexander C. Mackenzie
b.1810........................Ole Bull	*d*.1960..............Rutland Boughton
b.1860......................Hugo Wolf	
b.1860.........Ignacy Jan Paderewski	† Composer of *Rule, Britannia!* in 1740.

———— 'CELLO SCROTUM' & MUSICAL MALADIES————

In January 2009, the rather unlikely affliction of 'cello scrotum' was unmasked as a hoax. According to its perpetrator, Baroness Elaine Murphy, the ruse began in 1974, when Murphy and her then husband John read a letter in the *British Medical Journal* describing 'guitar nipple', a condition in which the instrument was said to irritate the breast. Finding this malady highly implausible, Murphy convinced her husband to sign a letter describing the similarly painful condition 'cello scrotum', purportedly caused by 'irritation from the body of the cello'. Much to their surprise, the letter was published and the condition has been cited in medical literature over the years. In January, Baroness Murphy (a cross-bench Peer and former professor of psychiatry) was finally moved to admit that the condition was a hoax after it was again discussed in the *BMJ*'s Christmas 2008 issue[†]. Fortunately, the venerable journal took the deception with good grace: editor Fiona Godlee said 'It seems the *BMJ* has been deliciously hoaxed', while a *BMJ* spokesman said that while the journal may have to print a retraction, 'it all adds to the gaiety of life'.

[†] Author Sarah Bache cited the condition in her article 'A symphony of maladies', alongside: *fiddler's neck* (a brown mark caused by sensitisation and pressure), *flautist's chin* (similar skin issue caused by friction and saliva), *pianist's hand* (a type of focal dystonia characterised by muscle contractions), and *Satchmo's syndrome* (a rupture of the orbicularis oris, named for Louis 'Satchelmouth' Armstrong). While these ailments are seldom fatal, it is possible to die because of one's instrument: in 1687 composer Jean-Baptiste Lully died of blood poisoning after striking himself on the foot with the staff he was using to conduct a French performance of *Te Deum*, a Latin hymn of thanksgiving to God.

———— THE WORLD'S BEST ORCHESTRAS————

The world's best orchestras were ranked by an international team of music critics who attempted to ensure their selections were neither 'patriotic' nor 'parochial'. Below is their orchestra top ten, as published in *Gramophone* in November 2008:

1 ....Royal Concertgebouw Orchestra[†]	6 .... Bavarian Radio Symphony
2 ....Berlin Philharmonic Orchestra	7 .... Cleveland Orchestra
3 ..... Vienna Philharmonic Orchestra	8 ....Los Angeles Philharmonic
4 ....London Symphony Orchestra	9 .... Budapest Festival Orchestra
5 .... Chicago Symphony Orchestra	10 ....Dresden Staatskapelle

[†] Based in Amsterdam, the Netherlands, the Royal Concertgebouw Orchestra was founded in 1888.

———— ROYAL PHILHARMONIC SOCIETY AWARDS · 2009————

Chamber-scale composition................	Harrison Birtwistle · *The Tree of Strings*
Large-scale composition	George Benjamin · *Into the Little Hill*
Conductor	Valery Gergiev
Instrumentalist......................................	Janine Jansen
Singer..	Susan Bullock

——————— UK TOP GROSSING FILMS · 2008 ———————

Film	UK box office gross (£m)	Director
Mamma Mia!	69·2	Phyllida Lloyd
Quantum of Solace	51·1	Marc Forster
The Dark Knight	48·8	Christopher Nolan
Indiana Jones: Kingdom of the Crystal Skull	40·3	Steven Spielberg
Sex and the City	26·4	Michael Patrick King
Hancock	24·7	Peter Berg
Madagascar: Escape 2 Africa	23·0	Eric Darnell & Tom McGrath
WALL·E	22·9	Andrew Stanton
High School Musical 3: Senior Year	22·8	Kenny Ortega
Kung Fu Panda	20·2	M. Osborne & J. Stevenson

[Source: Nielsen EDI, RSU · Box office gross as at 22·2·09]

——————— SOME MOVIE TAGLINES OF NOTE · 2009 ———————

I was born under unusual circumstances...... *The Curious Case of Benjamin Button*
How far would you go to protect a secret? .... *The Reader*
Here comes the bribe .... *The Proposal*
A basterd's work is never done .... *Inglourious Basterds*
To find her son, she did what no one else dared .... *Changeling*
Evil never looked so good .... *G.I. Joe: The Rise of Cobra*
Revenge is coming.............................. *Transformers: Revenge of the Fallen*
Passion. Ambition. Butter. Do you have what it takes?................. *Julie & Julia*
The world needs bigger heroes .... *G-Force*
The future begins .... *Star Trek*
Oooze gonna save us?... *Monsters vs Aliens*
Outwit. Outspy. Outsmart. Outplay. Then get out .... *Duplicity*

——————— TOP-SELLING DVDS OF ALL TIME ———————

Mamma Mia became the top-selling DVD of all time in January 2009 – after >5m copies had been sold. The Abba-thon also became the highest grossing movie in UK history (overtaking *Titanic* to earn >£69m) and it produced a best-selling soundtrack. Second-placed DVD *Pirates of the Caribbean: The Curse of the Black Pearl* was the only other DVD to sell >4m copies. Below are the top ten all-time (1998–2008) best-selling DVDs in the UK, according to the Official Chart Company:

1	*Mamma Mia!*	5	*Casino Royale*
2	*Pirates of the Caribbean: Curse of the Black Pearl*	6	*Pirates of Carib.: Dead Man's Chest*
3	*Lord of the Rings: Fellowship of the Ring*	7	*The Shawshank Redemption*
		8	*Gladiator*
4	*Lord of the Rings: The Two Towers*	9	*Lord of the Rings: Return of the King*
		10	*Shrek 2*

———81ST ACADEMY AWARD WINNERS · 2009———

Slumdog Millionaire was the star of the 81st Oscars, taking home eight awards including Best Picture. After 2008's record slump in viewing figures, Australian actor Hugh Jackman was drafted in as host to inject some glitz. Jackman, who promised 'more show, less biz', enlivened the ceremony with some fancy musical numbers (with a little help from Beyoncé), and received mainly favourable reviews for his efforts. The awards essentially followed form; the only surprise came when Sean Penn took Best Actor from the much-tipped Mickey Rourke. And the Oscars went to ...

Leading actor.. Sean Penn · *Milk*

Leading actress ....Kate Winslet · *The Reader*

Supporting actor.....................................Heath Ledger · *The Dark Knight*

Supporting actress ....Penélope Cruz · *Vicky Cristina Barcelona*

Best picture.. *Slumdog Millionaire*

Directing ....Danny Boyle · *Slumdog Millionaire*

Animated feature... Andrew Stanton · *Wall-E*

Art direction .... Donald Graham Burt & Victor J. Zolfo
The Curious Case of Benjamin Button

Cinematography ....Anthony Dod Mantle · *Slumdog Millionaire*

Costume design....................................Michael O'Connor · *The Duchess*

Doc. feature...........................James Marsh & Simon Chinn · *Man on Wire*

Doc. short subject.......................................Megan Mylan · *Smile Pinki*

Film editing .... Chris Dickens · *Slumdog Millionaire*

Foreign language film...............................Yojiro Takita · *Departures*

Make-up...................... Greg Cannom · *The Curious Case of Benjamin Button*

Music (score)...............................A. R. Rahman · *Slumdog Millionaire*

Music (song) ....A. R. Rahman · *Jai Ho* · *Slumdog Millionaire*

Short film (animated)........................ Kunio Kato · *La Maison en Petits Cubes*

Short film (live) .... Jochen Alexander Freydank · *Spielzeugland*

Sound mixing ... Ian Tapp, Richard Pryke & Resul Pookutty · *Slumdog Millionaire*

Sound editing..Richard King · *The Dark Knight*

Visual effects ....Eric Barba, Steve Preeg, Burt Dalton & Craig Barron
The Curious Case of Benjamin Button

Screenplay (adapted).......................... Simon Beaufoy · *Slumdog Millionaire*

Screenplay (original).....................................Dustin Lance Black · *Milk*

QUOTES ❦ KATE WINSLET · I'd be lying if I said I haven't made a version of this speech before. I think I was probably 8 years old and staring into the bathroom mirror, and this would have been a shampoo bottle. Well, it's not a shampoo bottle now. ❦ HUGH JACKMAN · Here's Brad and Angelina. I don't have a joke for them, I'm just contractually obliged to mention them at least five times in the show. ❦ PENÉLOPE CRUZ · It's not going to be 45 seconds, I can say that right now. Has anybody ever fainted here because I might be the first one. ❦ SEAN PENN · You commie, homo-loving, sons-of-guns! ❦ DANNY BOYLE (bouncing up and down as he received award) · My kids are too old to remember this now but, when they were much younger, I swore to them if this miracle ever happened, I would receive it in the spirit of Tigger from Winnie the Pooh, and that's what that was. ❦

—————————— OSCAR NIGHT FASHION · 2009 ——————————

Star	dress	*designer*
Kate Winslet	*pewter satin, one-shouldered, lace detail*	Yves Saint Laurent
Penélope Cruz	*cream, silver embroidery, strapless, full skirt*	vintage Balmain
Tilda Swinton	*beige draped top with black draped column skirt*	Lanvin
Angelina Jolie	*black, plunging sweet-heart neckline, strapless*	Elie Saab
Miley Cyrus	*nude, beaded, scallop-layered full skirt*	Zuhair Murad
Amy Adams	*crimson strapless bodice, draped chiffon skirt*	Carolina Herrera
Anne Hathaway	*pearlescent cream, beaded, strapless*	Armani Privé
Meryl Streep	*off-the-shoulder, dove grey, long sleeved*	Alberta Ferretti
Freida Pinto	*royal blue, single beaded net sleeve*	Galliano
Natalie Portman	*lilac tulle, strapless, Grecian drapes*	Rodarte
Marisa Tomei	*silver satin, one-shoulder, multi-pleated skirt*	Versace

—————————— WHERE'S OSCAR? ——————————

Oscar winners are often asked about the location of their statuettes: whether they have given them pride of place on the mantelpiece or, more modestly, have stowed them somewhere more private. Below, recent winners reveal the fate of their Oscars:

Many winners admit to keeping their trophies in the lavatory, including Emma Thompson ('It matches the fixtures perfectly'), Juliette Binoche, Rachel Weisz ('It's one of the biggest rooms in my house'), and Susan Sarandon, who keeps so many awards in one loo that her children call it the 'famous bathroom'. Jodie Foster once kept her Oscars in the lavatory ('because they looked good with the faucets'), until the bottom of the awards became so corroded she had to move them to the den. ❦ Cate Blanchett keeps her Oscar on her grand piano (sometimes); Anthony Hopkins placed his near the TV; and Christopher Walken keeps his inside a blue slipcover, so that it does not fade. ❦ Some stars go even further: Jennifer Hudson apparently keeps hers on a lighted pedestal and doesn't allow people to touch it, while Morgan Freeman has a custom-built cabinet. (According to Freeman, a friend constructed the cabinet long before Freeman's 2005 Oscar win, and placed a sign saying 'No Parking: Oscar Only' on the top shelf.) ❦ Other celebrities decide to part with their statuettes entirely: Nicole Kidman gave her Oscar to her mother, Jamie Foxx has given his to his manager, and Tilda Swinton says she gave hers to her agent. Jon Voight also gave his 1979 award to his mother, who long used it as the centrepiece inside her aquarium, surrounded by fish.

An unusual quandary arose when Heath Ledger (1979–2008) won Best Supporting Actor at the 81st Academy Awards for his role in *The Dark Knight*. Academy rules state that posthumously awarded Oscars should go to the deceased's spouse or child of legal age, yet Ledger had neither (he never married actress Michelle Williams, the mother of his 3-year-old daughter Matilda). Eventually, an agreement was reached that allows Williams to hold the statue in trust until her daughter turns 18.

———————————— UK FILM WORLDWIDE ————————————

In 2008, 15% of cinema tickets sold around the world were for UK-made films, according to the UK Film Council. Below are the global box office totals from 2002 to 2008, and the share of those amounts spent on UK films (see definition below):

	Global box office	UK films	% UK				
2002	$19·8bn	$1·8bn	9·1	2005	23·1	3·6	15·5
2003	20·1	1·4	6·9	2006	25·5	2·2	8·5
2004	24·9	2·9	11·5	2007	26·7	3·3	12·4
				2008	28·1	4·2	14·9

The share of the national box office spent on UK films in some countries of note:

UK share of box office, 2008 (%)			
New Zealand	26·2	Spain	17·5
Australia	21·7	North America	16·3
Chile	19·9	Mexico	15·8
Germany	19·6	Brazil	15·5
Argentina	19·3	France	10·7

[Source: UK Film Counci]

'UK films' are generally those that have been certified as such by the UK Secretary of State for Culture, Media and Sport and have thus passed the 'Cultural Test' (see *Schott's Almanac 2008*); those that have been produced under a co-production agreement with the UK or the European Convention on Cinematic Co-production; or those which are 'obviously British' on the basis of talent, funding, &c.

———————————— TOP ADAPTATIONS ————————————

Screenplays based on British story material accounted for 30 of the 200 top-grossing films that were produced between 2001–2007, according to the UK Film Council. Below are the 15 top-grossing films adapted from British books during those years:

Title	box office gross	based on novel by ...
The Lord of the Rings: The Return of the King	$1,119m	J.R.R. Tolkien
Harry Potter and the Philosopher's Stone	970	J.K. Rowling
Harry Potter and the Order of the Phoenix	937	J.K. Rowling
The Lord of the Rings: The Two Towers	923	J.R.R. Tolkien
Harry Potter and the Goblet of Fire	892	J.K. Rowling
Harry Potter and the Chamber of Secrets	877	J.K. Rowling
The Lord of the Rings: The Fellowship of the Ring	868	J.R.R. Tolkien
Harry Potter and the Prisoner of Azkaban	790	J.K. Rowling
The Chronicles of Narnia: The Lion ... &c.	749	C.S. Lewis
The War of the Worlds	596	H.G. Wells
Casino Royale	589	Ian Fleming
Charlie and the Chocolate Factory	473	Roald Dahl
Die Another Day	432	Ian Fleming (series)
The Golden Compass	350	Philip Pullman
Bridget Jones: The Edge of Reason	261	Helen Fielding

MOVIE AWARDS OF NOTE

BAFTAs 2009 · *bafta.org*

Best film..*Slumdog Millionaire*
Outstanding British film ....*Man on Wire*
Best actor in a leading role...........................Mickey Rourke · *The Wrestler*
Best actress in a leading role.............................Kate Winslet · *The Reader*
Best actor in a supporting role....................Heath Ledger · *The Dark Knight*
Best actress in a supporting role..........Penélope Cruz · *Vicky Cristina Barcelona*

MTV MOVIE AWARDS 2009 · *mtv.com*

Best male performance.............Zac Efron · *High School Musical 3: Senior Year*
Best female performance ....Kristen Stewart · *Twilight*
Best movie..*Twilight*
Best villain ....Heath Ledger · *The Dark Knight*
Best fight.............................Robert Pattinson *vs.* Cam Gigandet · *Twilight*

GOLDEN GLOBES 2009 · *hfpa.org*

Best dramatic film ....*Slumdog Millionaire*
Best dramatic actor ....Mickey Rourke · *The Wrestler*
Best dramatic actress...........................Kate Winslet · *Revolutionary Road*
Best director..Danny Boyle · *Slumdog Millionaire*
Best actor in musical or comedy...........................Colin Farrell · *In Bruges*
Best actress in musical or comedy................Sally Hawkins · *Happy-Go-Lucky*

BRITISH INDEPENDENT FILM AWARDS 2008 · *bifa.org.uk*

Best British independent film....................................*Slumdog Millionaire*
Best actor...Michael Fassbender · *Hunger*
Best actress ....Vera Farmiga · *The Boy in the Striped Pyjamas*
Richard Harris award for outstanding contribution.................David Thewlis

GOLDEN RASPBERRIES 2009 · *razzies.com*

Worst picture ....*The Love Guru*
Worst actor...Mike Myers · *The Love Guru*
Worst actress ....Paris Hilton · *The Hottie & the Nottie*

EMPIRE AWARDS 2009 · *empireonline.com*

Best actor..Christian Bale · *The Dark Knight*
Best actress ....Helena Bonham Carter · *Sweeney Todd*
Best director...................................Christopher Nolan · *The Dark Knight*
Best British film..*RocknRolla*
Best film..*The Dark Knight*

EVENING STANDARD BRITISH FILM AWARDS 2009

Best film...*Hunger*
Best actor..............Michael Sheen · *Frost/Nixon* shared with Pat Shortt · *Garage*
Best actress ....Tilda Swinton · *Julia*
Most promising newcomer......................Joanna Hogg (director) · *Unrelated*

WORST FILMS OF 2008

The ten worst films of 2008 – as judged by *The New York Post* – were as follows:

10	*Beverly Hills Chihuahua*	5	*10,000 B.C.*
9	*Witless Protection*	4	*What Happens in Vegas*
8	*Rambo*	3	*Mad Money*
7	*You Don't Mess With the Zohan*	2	*The Hottie & The Nottie*
6	*Babylon A.D.*	1	*The Love Guru*†

† *The Love Guru* flopped in the US, taking just $14m on its opening weekend. The *New York Times* said of the movie: 'To say that the movie is not funny is merely to affirm the obvious. The word "unfunny" surely applies to Mr. Myers's obnoxious attempts to find mirth in physical and cultural differences but does not quite capture the strenuous unpleasantness of his performance. No, *The Love Guru* is downright antifunny, an experience that makes you wonder if you will ever laugh again'.

MOST MISQUOTED FILM PHRASE

The phrase 'Luke, I am your father' has been mimicked by many a film fan in homage to the famous scene in *The Empire Strikes Back*. Unfortunately, the line never appeared in the film, and it tops the list of the most frequently misquoted film phrases compiled by LOVEFiLM.com in May 2009. The top movie misquotes were:

Misquoted line	movie (year)
Luke, I am your father	*The Empire Strikes Back* (1980)
Mirror, mirror on the wall, who is the fairest of them all?	*Snow White* (1937)
Do you feel lucky, punk?	*Dirty Harry* (1971)
Play it again, Sam	*Casablanca* (1942)
Hello, Clarice	*Silence of the Lambs* (1991)
Beam me up, Scotty!	*Star Trek: The Motion Picture* (1979)
Frankly, Scarlett, I don't give a damn	*Gone with the Wind* (1939)
If you build it, they will come	*Field of Dreams* (1989)
I don't think we're in Kansas anymore, Toto	*The Wizard of Oz* (1939)
Mrs Robinson, are you trying to seduce me?	*The Graduate* (1967)

BEST CHILDREN'S FILM

Onepoll asked adults to name the best children's film ever made; the top ten were:

1	*Shrek*†	8	*Monsters Inc.*
2	*Pirates of the Caribbean*	9	*Ice Age*
3	*Finding Nemo*†	10	*Wallace & Gromit:*
4	*Toy Story*		*Curse of the Were-Rabbit*†
5	*Harry Potter & Philosopher's Stone*		
6	*The Lion King*		[† Won Oscar for best animated feature.
7	*Mrs Doubtfire*		Source: Onepoll.com · January 2009]

─────── DUBBING IN FILM ───────

Ever since the advent of 'talkies' in the 1930s, film companies have had to choose whether to subtitle or dub foreign films. While subtitles are cheaper to produce and can offer a more 'authentic' experience, some find the experience of reading on-screen irksome. Dubbing, though expensive, makes watching a film more fluid and adds layers of humour and irony that are difficult to achieve with text alone. Preferences for each technique vary across the globe, reflecting everything from economic to nationalistic concerns. Below are the favoured methods in various countries:

Countries that usually dub	*Countries that usually subtitle*
Austria · China · France · Germany†	Australia · Canada · Denmark
India · Iran · Italy† · Mexico	Finland · Greece · Japan
Pakistan · Russia · Spain†	Norway · Philippines · Poland
Switzerland (German-speaking parts)	Portugal · Romania · Sweden
Thailand · Vietnam · *also* Quebec	UK · US

In countries that use dubbing, studios sometimes repeatedly employ the same actor as the voice of a foreign star, cementing associations that can create lucrative side careers. For example, Irina von Bentheim, the German voice of Carrie Bradshaw in *Sex and the City*, so 'embodied' her character that she followed the show by giving sex and relationship advice on radio programmes. Dubbing artists who have become known in their home countries as the 'voice of' an English-speaking star include:

Dubbing artist	voice of ...
Ernesto Aura [Spain]	*Arnold Schwarzenegger, Tommy Lee Jones*
Françoise Cadol [France]	*Angelina Jolie, Gong Li, Sandra Bullock*
Richard Darbois [France]	*Harrison Ford, Richard Gere, Patrick Swayze*
Gert Günther Hoffmann [Germany]	*Sean Connery, William Shatner, Paul Newman*
Pawan Kalra [India]	*Arnold Schwarzenegger*
Oreste Lionello [Italy]	*Woody Allen, Peter Sellers, Jerry Lewis*
Claudia Motta [Mexico]	*Kirsten Dunst*
Giuseppe Rinaldi [Italy]	*Marlon Brando, Rock Hudson, Robert Redford*
Ren Wei [China]	*Tom Cruise*

† The prevalence of dubbing in Italy, Spain, and Germany arose out of the political context of those countries in the 1930s, when fascist dictators restricted foreign languages for ideological reasons. (Preferences listed above are for films for adults; children generally have a hard time with subtitles.)

─────── MOST PROFITABLE FILMS & ACTORS · 2008 ───────

Juno was the most profitable film between 1 December 2007 and 1 December 2008, earning $15·40 for every $1 spent on the production, according to *Forbes*. *Mamma Mia!* was the second most profitable film, earning $5·50 for every $1. The most profitable actor was Robert Downey Jr for his role in *Iron Man*. Downey generated $52·60 for every dollar that was spent on his salary. Meryl Streep was the most profitable actress, bringing in $12 for every dollar for her role in *Mamma Mia!*

———————————— FILM FESTIVAL PRIZES · 2009 ————————————

Sundance · World Cinema Dramatic [JAN]............. *The Maid* · Sebastian Silva
Berlin · Golden Bear [FEB]..................... *The Milk Of Sorrow* · Claudia Llosa
Tribeca · Best Narrative Feature [APR].................*About Elly* · Asghar Farhadi
Cannes · Palme d'Or [MAY].................. *The White Ribbon* · Michael Haneke
Moscow · Golden St George [JUN].....*Pete on the way to Heaven* · Nikolai Dostal
Edinburgh · Audience Award [JUN]............. *The Secret of Kells* · Tomm Moore
Montreal · Grand Prize of the Americas [AUG].............*Freedom* · Tony Gatlif
Venice · Golden Lion [SEP]...............................*Lebanon* · Samuel Maoz
Toronto · People's Choice Award [SEP] ....*Precious* · Lee Daniels
London · Sutherland Trophy [OCT '08]................*Tulpan* · Sergey Dvortsevoy

———————————— ALTERNATIVE MOVIE TITLES ————————————

UK title   Also known as ...
Airplane! (1980)....................................*Flying High!* (New Zealand, Philippines)
Annie Hall (1977).......*Der Stadtneurotiker* ('The urban neurotic', Austria, West Germany)
Cruel Intentions (1999)......*The Temptation More Beautiful Than a Love* (South Korea)
The Deer Hunter (1978)..........*Die durch die Hölle gehen* ('Those who go through hell',
                                                                    Austria, West Germany)
The French Connection (1971) ....*Focus Brooklyn* (Germany)
The Hideaways (1973)....*From the Mixed-Up Files of Mrs Basil E. Frankweiler* (USA)
Gone With the Wind (1939)....................................*Lo que el viento se llevó*
                                        ('What the wind blew away', Spanish-speaking countries)
Never Been Kissed (1999)......................................*College Attitude* (France)
Pulp Fiction (1994)...*Kriminale* (Bulgaria)
Snakes on a Plane (2006)...*Snake Flight* (Japan)
The Sound of Music (1965)................. *Sonrisas y Lágrimas* ('Smiles and tears', Spain)
                             Tutti insieme appassionatamente ('All together passionately', Italy)
A View To a Kill (1985)....................................*The Beautiful Prey* (Japan)
Wild Things (1998).......................................*Sex Crimes* (France, Belgium)

———————————— WORLDWIDE FILM ADMISSIONS ————————————

Americans see the most films per person per year, whereas Germans see relatively
few, according to 2009 statistics for several countries from the UK Film Council:

Film admissions per person ...	2003	2004	2005	2006	2007	±'03–'07
USA	5·4	5·2	4·7	4·8	4·6	–0·8
Australia	4·5	4·5	4·	4·1	4·1	–0·4
France	2·9	3·2	2·9	3·1	2·9	0
UK	2·8	2·9	2·7	2·6	2·7	–0·1
Spain	3·3	3·4	2·9	2·7	2·6	–0·7
Italy	1·5	1·7	1·6	1·6	1·8	+0·3
Germany	1·8	1·9	1·5	1·7	1·5	–0·3

FILM SCRIPT REVISIONS & COLOUR CODE

The final draft of a film script is rarely that, and revisions are constantly made during production. To ensure that everyone on set is working from the same script, filmmakers have developed a meticulous method of version control that involves both numbers and colours. The system begins with numbers: when the screenplay has been finalised, each scene is numbered in order. Once the scene numbers have been allocated they are never changed, so any additions to the script are managed by adding a letter to the scene number. For example, if a new scene is to be slotted between scenes 8 and 9, the new scene would be scene 8a. If a scene is to be deleted, the scene number remains but the word 'omitted' is typed next to it. When scripts are revised on set, a colour coding system is also included. The first draft is always white, but as revisions are made the altered pages are printed on new colours of paper and added back into the script. A typical colour cycle, as described by Eve Light Honthaner in *The Complete Film Production Handbook*, is shown below:

WHITE → BLUE → PINK → YELLOW → GREEN → GOLD → BUFF
→ SALMON → CHERRY → TAN → GREY → IVORY

Once every colour has been used, the cycle begins again. The script then becomes known as 'double white', then 'double blue', and so on. By the end of filming, most scripts are 'rainbow-coloured'. Once a movie has completed filming, a final, final script – known as the 'continuity script' – is printed. This contains the dialogue and action as it occurs in the director's cut of the film, and is used for distribution purposes.

A standard film script is usually 100–120 pages long – roughly one page per minute of film action.

FILMS FOR FUTURE GENERATIONS

As part of its 75th anniversary celebrations in 2008, the BFI asked 75 notables which films they most wanted to share with future generations; the films included:

Juliette Binoche .... *The Sacrifice*	Nicholas Hytner ...... *The Band Wagon*
Cate Blanchett .... *Stalker*	Matt Lucas .... *Billy Elliot*
Melvyn Bragg .... *The Seventh Seal*	Bill Nighy .... *Mississippi Burning*
Gurinder Chadha .... *Tokyo Story*	Simon Pegg .... *Raising Arizona*
Greg Dyke .... *Cabaret*	Jason Solomons .... *This is England*
Mike Figgis .... *Bonnie & Clyde*	Ken Russell .... *Metropolis*
Chiwetel Ejifor .... *Dr Strangelove*	Leslie Phillips .... *Empire of the Sun*
Stephen Frears .... *The Third Man*	Roger Moore .... *Lawrence of Arabia*
Paul Greengrass ... *The Battle of Algiers*	James Christopher .... *Blade Runner*

In April 2009, Turner Classic Movies created a list of the 15 most influential classic movies of all time (in chronological order): *The Birth of a Nation* (1915) · *Battleship Potemkin* (1925) · *Metropolis* (1927) · *42nd Street* (1933) · *It Happened One Night* (1934) · *Snow White and the Seven Dwarfs* (1937) · *Gone with the Wind* (1939) · *Stagecoach* (1939) · *Citizen Kane* (1941) · *The Bicycle Thieves* (1947) · *Rashomon* (1950) · *The Searchers* (1956) · *Breathless* (1959) · *Psycho* (1960) · *Star Wars* (1977).

Books & Arts

*Art is the imposing of a pattern on experience, and our aesthetic enjoyment
is recognition of the pattern.* — A.N. WHITEHEAD (1861–1947)

POET LAUREATE · CAROL ANN DUFFY

In May 2009, Carol Ann Duffy became the first female poet laureate in the 341-year history of the post. ❦ Duffy was born in Glasgow in 1955, to a solidly working-class family. The eldest of five, she grew up in Stafford in a household with few books. A love of language was fed by the stories and rhymes imagined by her mother, the effect of which Duffy celebrated in her poem *The Way My Mother Speaks*. Duffy's early talent was spotted and encouraged first by one, then another, English teacher – who instilled in her a passionate appreciation of the importance of education. At ten, Duffy began composing her first poems; by sixteen, she had a pamphlet of poetry published. Her first anthology, *Standing Female Nude*, was released in 1985 to considerable acclaim. Duffy's popularity grew as her body of work developed and attracted the attention of prize judges: she won the Dylan Thomas Prize in 1989, the Forward and Whitbread Prizes in 1993 (for *Mean Time*), and the T.S. Eliot Prize (for *Rapture*) in 2005. Duffy quickly became known for her ability to inhabit a wide range of characters, a talent showcased in *The World's Wife*, in which she ponders what Queen Kong or Mrs Icarus might have thought of their husbands. In 2008, Duffy's poem *Education for Literature* was removed from the AQA

GCSE syllabus after an invigilator, Mrs Schofield, complained that it glorified knife crime. In a typically elegant and witty response, Duffy penned *Mrs Schofield's GCSE*, a poem highlighting the numerous stabbings in the works of William Shakespeare. ❦ The post of Poet Laureate has been described as a millstone by a number of incumbents and, at the time of Duffy's appointment, her predecessor Andrew Motion was open about his ambivalent relationship with the honour. Yet Duffy sees a future in the ten-year post: 'I believe that the continuance of the laureateship acknowledges that poetry is vital to the imagining of what Britain has been, what it is and what it might yet become'. ❦ Much was made of suggestions that Duffy was vetoed for the post in 1999 because politicians thought that middle England would be intolerant of an openly gay laureate. Duffy dismissed these rumours, claiming that Britain had 'grown up' in its attitudes to sexuality, while maintaining that her private life would remain just that. Illustrating her passion for promoting poetry, Duffy asked for her modest £5,760 annual stipend to be given to the Poetry Society to fund a new prize. She also requested that the laureate's traditional 'butt of sack' (600 bottles of sherry) be paid up-front, as Motion had reportedly yet to receive any of his.

———————— CELEBRITY MEMOIRS ————————

Hannah Montana star Miley Cyrus announced in October 2008 that – at the age of 15 – she was ready to pen her first memoir (reportedly, for a seven-figure sum). Below are the ages at which a range of celebrities felt it time to take stock of life:

Celebrity	book title	age at release
Charlotte Church	*Voice of an Angel, My Life (So Far)* (2001)	15
Wayne Rooney	*My Story So Far* (2006)	21
Lewis Hamilton	*My Story* (2007)	22
Billie Piper	*Growing Pains* (2006)	24
Jade Goody	*My Autobiography* (2006)	25
Katie Price	*Being Jordan* (2004)	26
Kerry Katona	*Too Much, Too Young* (2006)	26
Chris Moyles	*The Gospel According to Chris Moyles* (2006)	32
Peter Kay	*The Sound of Laughter* (2006)	33
Michael Parkinson	*Parky: My Autobiography* (2008)	73
Harry Patch [see p.63]	*The Last Fighting Tommy* (2007)	109

———————— BAD SEX IN FICTION PRIZE · 2008 ————————

Each year the *Literary Review* awards its 'Bad Sex in Fiction' prize to a novel featuring the most 'inept, embarrassing, and unnecessary' sex scene. Rachel (sister of Boris) Johnson was awarded the 2008 prize for her novel *Shire Hell*. She described her victory as an 'absolute honour'. Below is the prizewinning extract:

Almost screaming after five agonizingly pleasurable minutes, I make a grab, to put him, now angrily slapping against both our bellies, inside, but he holds both my arms down, and puts his tongue to my core, like a cat lapping up a dish of cream so as not to miss a single drop. I find myself gripping his ears and tugging at the locks curling over them, beside myself, and a strange animal noise escapes from me as the mounting, Wagnerian crescendo overtakes me. I really do hope at this point that all the Spodders are, as requested, attending the meeting about slug clearance or whatever it is.

———————— THE OLDEST WORDS ————————

A study of the evolution of language by researchers from Reading University proposed a list of words that modern Britons might have in common with Stone Age cavemen. Dr Mark Pagel tracked the evolutionary history of Indo-European languages by comparing words in different languages and tracing common ancestors. In February 2009, he suggested that the following words were some of the oldest:

I · WHO · THOU · WE · TWO · THREE · FIVE

The researchers suggested that the following rapidly evolving words are likely, over time, to disappear: dirty, squeeze, bad, because, guts, push [verb], smell [verb], stab, stick [verb], turn [verb], wipe.

─────────── BOOKS WE PRETEND TO HAVE READ ───────────

65% of people admitted to lying about which books they had read, according to a March 2009 survey for World Book Day. Most said that they had lied to seem more impressive. Below are the top ten books people pretended that they had read:

[1] *1984* · George Orwell (42%) [2] *War & Peace* · Leo Tolstoy (31%)
[3] *Ulysses* · James Joyce (25%) [4] *The Bible* (24%)
[5] *Madame Bovary* · Gustave Flaubert (16%)
[6] *A Brief History of Time* · Stephen Hawking (15%)
[7] *Midnight's Children* · Salman Rushdie (14%)
[8] *In Remembrance of Things Past* · Marcel Proust (9%)
[9] *Dreams From My Father* · Barack Obama (6%)
[10] *The Selfish Gene* · Richard Dawkins (6%)

─────── OXFORD UNIVERSITY'S PROFESSOR OF POETRY ───────

On 22 January 2009, Oxford University began its search for a new Professor of Poetry, to replace Christopher Ricks. The five-year position, founded in 1708, entails giving a number of public lectures, judging some of Oxford's literary prizes, and encouraging 'the art of poetry in the university'. Previous holders include Matthew Arnold, W. H. Auden, and Seamus Heaney. ❦ After Andrew Motion ruled himself out of consideration in February, the poet Ruth Padel emerged as front-runner. In the following weeks, St Lucia-born Nobel laureate Derek Walcott and Indian poet Arvind Krishna Mehrotra both joined the race. Yet just days before the May election, reports surfaced that allegations of sexual harassment against Walcott had been posted anonymously to Oxford academics. Walcott withdrew from the race, claiming it had 'degenerated into a low and degrading attempt at character assassination'. Padel, who denied any involvement in this 'smear campaign', was elected to the professorship on 16 May. Just nine days later, however, Padel resigned after it transpired that she had alerted journalists to allegations of misconduct by Walcott. ❦ At the time of writing, Oxford University had yet to schedule fresh elections.

─────────── ODDEST BOOK TITLE OF THE YEAR · 2008 ───────────

The Diagram Group's prize for the Oddest Title of the Year is administered by *The Bookseller*, and voted on by the book trade. The 2008 winner and runners-up were:

The 2009–2014 World Outlook for 60-milligram Containers of Fromage Frais
Professor Philip M. Parker – WINNER

RUNNERS-UP: *Baboon Metaphysics*.....Dorothy L. Cheney & Robert M. Seyfarth
Curbside Consultation of the Colon .... Brooks D. Cash
Strip and Knit with Style.. Mark Hordyszynski
The Large Sieve and its Applications............................ Emmanuel Kowalski
Techniques for Corrosion Monitoring...Lietai Yang

--------- NOBEL PRIZE IN LITERATURE ---------

The 2008 Nobel in Literature was awarded to Jean-Marie Gustave Le Clézio (1940–),

author of new departures, poetic adventure and sensual ecstasy,
explorer of a humanity beyond and below the reigning civilization

Despite near-anonymity in the English-speaking world, Le Clézio is considered a major writer in France, where he has published more than 40 books exploring themes of exile, self-discovery, and cultural collision. His first novel, *Le Procès-Verbal* [1963], written at age 23, was seen as an ambitious debut, and won France's prestigious Renaudot prize. In 1980, Le Clézio published what many consider his breakthrough – *Désert*. The story of a young Sudanese immigrant in Europe, the book was praised for its imagination and relevance. ❦ Le Clézio's selection prompted charges of deliberate obscurantism on the part of the Nobel committee, and revived the ongoing dispute over the dearth of American winners. However, with his globe-trotting background, Le Clézio would seem well-placed to fend off claims of Eurocentricity; indeed Nicolas Sarkozy called him 'a citizen of the world, son of all continents and cultures'. In his Nobel lecture, Le Clézio focused on the need to bring to a wider audience writing from disadvantaged parts of the world, so that literature can become a means for 'listening to the concert of humankind, in all the rich variety of its themes and modulations'.

--------- WORLD BOOK CAPITAL ---------

Each year since 2001, UNESCO has named one city the World Book Capital. The title is awarded to the city that presents the best plan for a year of programming devoted to books and reading. The honour lasts from one World Book and Copyright Day† (23 April) until the next. In 2010, Ljubljana, Slovenia, will be capital. Below are the World Book Capitals named since the beginning of the programme:

City (year as capital)	highlights
Madrid (2001)	*'book mountain' constructed around the Puerta de Alcalá*
Alexandria (2002)	*opening of the New Library of Alexandria*
New Delhi (2003)	*literacy campaigns, book fairs, and exhibitions*
Antwerp (2004)	*a project on the 26 letters of the alphabet*
Montreal (2005)	*literary tour of Montreal; international copyright symposium*
Turin & Rome (2006)	*tour from Sicily to Turin in the footsteps of famous travellers*
Bogotá (2007)	*selection of the 39 most important Latin American writers under 39*
Amsterdam (2008)	*quotes by writers on houses across the city; 'Spinoza Day'*
Beirut (2009)	*projects on four themes: book culture, the professions of the book, the promotion of reading and writing, youth literacy*

† World Book Day originated in Catalonia where, by tradition, a free rose is presented with each book sold on 23 April, or St George's Day. This date is also fitting because it marks the death, in 1616, of William Shakespeare, Spain's Miguel de Cervantes, and Peru's 'El Inca' Garcilaso de la Vega.

──── CHILDREN'S LAUREATES' FAVOURITE BOOKS ────

To celebrate the 10th anniversary of the creation of the Children's Laureate, the 5 authors to have held the post were asked to reveal their 7 favourite children's books.

QUENTIN BLAKE (1999–2001)
Little Tim and the Brave Sea Captain – Edward Ardizzone · *Queenie the Bantam* – Bob Graham · *The Box of Delights* – John Masefield · *Rose Blanche* – Ian McEwan & Roberto Innocenti · *Five Children and It* – E. Nesbit · *Snow White* – Josephine Poole · *Stuart Little* – E. B. White

ANNE FINE (2001–03)
The Wolves of Willoughby Chase – Joan Aiken · *Absolute Zero* – Helen Cresswell · *Just William* – Richmal Crompton · *Journey to the River Sea* – Eva Ibbotson · *Lavender's Blue* – Kathleen Lines · *A Child's Garden of Verses* – Robert Louis Stevenson *The Sword in the Stone* – T. H. White

MICHAEL MORPURGO (2003–05)
Five Go to Smuggler's Top – Enid Blyton · *Mike Mulligan and his Steam Shovel* – Virginia Lee Burton

Oliver Twist – Charles Dickens · *Just So Stories* – Rudyard Kipling · *A Book of Nonsense* – Edward Lear · *Treasure Island* – Robert Louis Stevenson *The Happy Prince* – Oscar Wilde

JACQUELINE WILSON (2005–07)
Little Women – Louisa May Alcott *A Little Princess* – Frances Hodgson Burnett · *What Katy Did* – Susan Coolidge · *The Family from One End Street* – Eve Garnett · *The Railway Children* – E. Nesbit · *Ballet Shoes* – Noel Streatfeild · *Mary Poppins* – P. L. Travers

MICHAEL ROSEN (2007–09)
Clown – Quentin Blake · *The Diary of a Young Girl* – Anne Frank · *Emil and the Detectives* – Erich Kästner · *Not Now, Bernard* – David McKee · *Fairy Tales* – Terry Jones · *Mr Gum and the Dancing Bear* – Andy Stanton *Daz 4 Zoe* – Robert Swindells

In June 2009, illustrator Anthony Browne was named as the new Children's Laureate. Browne's most famous creation is *Gorilla* (1983), the story of a girl taken on a trip to the zoo by her toy gorilla.

──────── MOST BORROWED BOOKS ────────

The most borrowed books from UK libraries, according to Public Lending Right:

[1] *Harry Potter and the Deathly Hallows* · J. K. Rowling
[2] *The House at Riverton* · Kate Morton
[3] *The Memory Keeper's Daughter* · Kim Edwards [4] *Relentless* · Simon Kernick
[5] *The Other Side of the Bridge* · Mary Lawson [6] *The Quickie* · James Patterson
& Michael Ledwidge [7] *The 6th Target* · James Patterson & Maxine Paetro
[8] *The Savage Garden* · Mark Mills [9] *Cross* · James Patterson
[10] *Step on a Crack* · James Patterson & Michael Ledwidge

[Books lent between June 2007–June 2008.] According to a February 2009 survey of independent bookshops by *The Times*, the book most often stolen from UK bookshops is the *London A–Z*.

MOST MISQUOTED PHRASES

A February 2009 survey by the hearing aid retailer Amplifon revealed the phrases that are most frequently misquoted by the British public. Below are the top ten:

Misquote	*actual phrase*	origin
A damp squid	a damp squib	*a squib is a small explosive*
On tender hooks	on tenterhooks	*tenterhooks used to stretch/dry cloth*
Nip it in the butt	nip it in the bud	*pruning a flower*
Champing at the bit	chomping at the bit	*a horse chewing its harness*
A mute point	a moot point	*moot was an Anglo-Saxon meeting*
One foul swoop	one fell swoop	*falconry; first recorded use in Macbeth*
All that glitters is not gold	all that glisters ...	*from* The Merchant of Venice
Adverse to	averse to	*averse means to actively dislike*
Batting down the hatches	battening ...	*C19th nautical term*
Find a penny pick it up	find a pin and ...	*from* The Real Mother Goose

OTHER BOOK PRIZES OF NOTE · 2009

Carnegie Medal	Siobhan Dowd · *Bog Child*
Kate Greenaway Medal	Catherine Rayner · *Harris Finds His Feet*
Commonwealth Writers' Prize	Christos Tsiolkas · *The Slap*
Forward Prize: best poetry collection [2008]	Mick Imlah · *The Lost Leader*
Guardian children's fiction [2008]	Patrick Ness · *The Knife of Letting Go*
First book award	Alex Ross · *The Rest Is Noise*
Orange prize	Marilynne Robinson · *Home*
Samuel Johnson Prize for non-fiction	Philip Hoare · *Leviathan or, The Whale*
T.S. Eliot Prize for poetry [2008]	Jen Hadfield · *Nigh-No-Place*
Costa Book of the Year [2008]	Sebastian Barry · *The Secret Scripture*
Children's prize	Michelle Magorian · *Just Henry*
Biography	Diana Athill · *Somewhere Towards the End*
Poetry	Adam Foulds · *The Broken Word*
First Novel	Sadie Jones · *The Outcast*
Blue Peter Book Awards:	
Book I couldn't put down	Matt Haig · *Shadow Forest*
Best book with facts	Anita Ganeri · *Planet in Peril*
Most fun story with pictures	Andy Stanton · *Mr Gum and the Dancing Bear*
British Book Awards: Author of the year	Aravind Adiga
Book of the year	Kate Summerscale · *The Suspicions of Mr Whicher*
New writer of the year	Tom Rob Smith · *Child 44*
Crime thriller of the year	Stieg Larsson · *The Girl with the Dragon Tattoo*

In October 2008, Aravind Adiga won the £50,000 Man Booker Prize for Fiction for his debut novel *The White Tiger* (Atlantic). In May 2009 Canadian short-story writer Alice Munro was awarded the £60,000 biennial Man Booker Prize International. The International prize is bestowed on an author whose body of work has 'contributed to an achievement in fiction on the world stage'.

DAILY ROUTINES OF WRITERS

On his fascinating blog *Daily Routines*, Mason Currey collects schedules once kept by notable writers, artists, and thinkers. A sample of these quotidian routines is below:

IMMANUEL KANT

Wake at 5 am. Drink one or two cups weak tea, smoke pipe, meditate. Prepare lectures and books until 7 am. Lecture 7–11 am. Write until lunch. Walk. Spend rest of afternoon with friend. Light work and reading. [Source: Manfred Kuehn, *Kant: A Biography*]

FRANZ KAFKA

Work at office 8:30 am–2:30 pm. Lunch until 3:30 pm. Sleep until 7:30 pm. Exercise. Family dinner. At 11 pm, begin work, letter- and diary-writing 'until one, two, or three o'clock', followed by 'every imaginable effort to go to sleep'. [*The New York Review of Books*, 17 July, 2008]

HARUKI MURAKAMI

Wake at 4 am. Work for five to six hours. Run for 10km or swim for 1,500m (or both). Read, listen to music. In bed at 9 pm. [*The Paris Review*, Summer 2004]

P. G. WODEHOUSE

Wake at 7:30 am. Perform calisthenics. Breakfast with a 'breakfast book' (perhaps a mystery). First pipe of the day. Short walk with dogs. Work 9am–1pm. Lunch at 1. Walk. Soap opera. Tea with wife. Nap. Bath. More work. Cocktail. Sun parlour. Dinner. Reading, occasional game of bridge. [Source: Robert McCrum, *Wodehouse: A Life*]

CHARLES DARWIN

Wake at 7am. Breakfast at 7:45am. Work 8–9:30am. Letters until 10:30am. Work 10:30–12. Walk. Lunch at 12:45pm. Read *The Times*. Answer letters. Rest, smoke. Listen to light literature read by wife. Walk. Work. Rest. Listen to reading aloud again at 6. Light high tea at 7:30. Games of backgammon if no guests present. Read, listen to piano. In bed by 10:30pm. [Source: R.B. Freeman, *Charles Darwin: A Companion*]

[Collected at: dailyroutines.typepad.com]

J.G. Ballard, the author of *Crash* (1973) and *Empire of the Sun* (1984) who died on 19/4/09 [see p.62], described his routine in a 2007 *Guardian* article: 'I work for three or four hours a day, in the late morning and early afternoon. Then I go out for a walk and come back in time for a large gin and tonic'.

BULWER-LYTTON FICTION CONTEST

In 1982, the Department of English and Comparative Literature at San José State University created a literary contest in honour of E.G.E. Bulwer-Lytton (1803–73), who opened his book *Paul Clifford* with 'It was a dark and stormy night'. The contest rewards the best 'bad' opening line to an imaginary novel. 2009's winner was 55-year-old David McKenzie from Federal Way, Washington, whose entry was:

Folks say that if you listen real close at the height of the full moon, when the wind is blowin' off Nantucket Sound from the nor' east and the dogs are howlin' for no earthly reason, you can hear the awful screams of the crew of the "Ellie May," a sturdy whaler Captained by John McTavish; for it was on just such a night when the rum was flowin' and, Davey Jones be damned, big John brought his men on deck for the first of several screaming contests.

THE TURNER PRIZE · 2008

Founded in 1984, the Turner Prize is awarded each year to a British artist (defined, somewhat loosely, as an artist working in Britain or a British artist working abroad) under 50, for an outstanding exhibition or other presentation in the twelve months prior to each May. The winner receives £25,000 – and three runners-up £5,000.

Mark Leckey won the 2008 Turner Prize for two solo exhibitions: *Industrial Light & Magic* at Le Consortium, Dijon, and *Resident* at Kölnischer Kunstverein, Cologne. Leckey's body of multi-media work defies simple classification. He has been variously described as a magpie, a subjective anthropologist, and a *flâneur* – reflecting his use of film, performance, and music to create art that is as concerned with process as the works themselves. ❦ Born in 1964 in Birkenhead, Leckey attended Newcastle Polytechnic in the early 1990s, where his immersion in the vibrant rave scene informed his later work.

Mark Leckey

Leckey currently combines his artistic endeavours with a part-time role as professor of film studies at Frankfurt's Städelschule. ❦ Film plays a central part in Leckey's winning piece, *Cinema-in-the-round* – a video installation in which the artist is shown giving a lecture on the relationship between film and popular culture, cogitating on everything from Homer Simpson to James Cameron's film *Titanic*. Leckey's preoccupation with modern culture is revealed by his exploration of visual overload – a bombardment of the senses designed to stimulate questions rather than provide answers. The judges said that Leckey 'celebrates the imagination of the individual and our potential to inhabit, reclaim or animate an idea, a space, or an object'. ❦ After years of deriding the Turner for deliberately courting controversy, many critics pronounced the 2008 shortlist 'dull'. Richard Dorment in the *Telegraph* lamented that it was just 'a bad year'; Michael Glover in the *Independent* wrote, 'It has been a dismal year for the Turner Prize – and all that can be said for Mark Leckey's piece is that it is the least uninteresting of the lot'. Nodding at artists such as Banksy and Damien Hirst, Leckey said 'I'd like people to realise that art isn't just about spectacle and not just about a direct urge to shock and unsettle'.

Year	winner				
'91	Anish Kapoor	'96	Douglas Gordon	'02	Keith Tyson
'92	Grenville Davey	'97	Gillian Wearing	'03	Grayson Perry
'93	Rachel Whiteread	'98	Chris Ofili	'04	Jeremy Deller
'94	Antony Gormley	'99	Steve McQueen	'05	Simon Starling
'95	Damien Hirst	'00	Wolfgang Tillmans	'06	Tomma Abts
		'01	Martin Creed	'07	Mark Wallinger

It was announced in April 2009 that the following four artists were shortlisted for the 2009 Turner Prize, the winner of which will be announced on 7 December:

sculptor Roger Hiorns · *painter* Richard Wright
contemporary surrealist Enrico David · *artist* Lucy Skaer

———————————— WORLD DIGITAL LIBRARY ————————————

The World Digital Library is an online collection of maps, manuscripts, prints and recordings from cultures around the globe, unveiled by the United Nations Educational, Scientific and Cultural Organization (UNESCO) in April 2009. The website aims to enhance inter-cultural understanding and scholarly research by presenting historically and culturally significant documents from UNESCO's 193 member countries. At its unveiling, the library's collection included digitalisations of *c*.1,250 items, alongside explanations and background material in Arabic, Chinese, English, French, Portuguese, Russian, and Spanish. Some of the highlights of the World Digital Library, which can be viewed at wdl.org, are below:

The Tale of Genji · a 1654 edition of the 4,000-page C11th Japanese book
which is said to be the world's first novel

Declaration of Intention for Albert Einstein · the US citizenship
papers filed by Einstein in 1936 after he fled from the Nazis

The Codex Gigas (Devil's Bible) · a C13th Bible from Bohemia, said to be Europe's
largest surviving manuscript, which includes a full-page portrait of the Devil

Scenes from Lourdes, France · selections from some of the world's first film footage,
shot by the Lumière brothers in 1897

Boke of the Fayt of Armes and of Chyualrye · guide to proper conduct for a knight,
written in *c*.1410 by Christine de Pisan, one of Europe's first female authors

———————————— TOP EXHIBITIONS · 2008 ————————————

For the third year in a row, a Japanese show topped the *Art Newspaper*'s list of the most popular art exhibitions in the world. Below are the most popular art exhibitions of 2008 around the world – and in London – by the number of daily visitors:

GLOBAL TOP FIVE

2008 exhibition	*museum*	*daily attendance*
Shoso-in Treasures	Nara National Museum	17,926
Treasures from Yakushi-ji Temple	Tokyo National Museum	12,762
Images in the Night	Grand Palais Nave	10,357
Highlights of Japanese Artists	Tokyo National Museum	9,531
Treasures by Rinpa Masters	Tokyo National Museum	8,735

LONDON TOP FIVE

From Russia†	Royal Academy of Arts	4,627
China's Terracotta Army	British Museum	4,190
Tutankhamun	O2 Millennium Dome	3,781
Gallery Pavilion by Frank Gehry	Serpentine Gallery	2,665
Hadrian: Empire and Conflict	British Museum	2,569

† Britain was forced to expedite anti-seizure legislation to ensure that this exhibition went ahead. The Russian authorities refused to lend paintings expropriated by the Communists after the 1917 Bolshevik Revolution to countries where they might be impounded by descendants of previous owners.

—————————— INTANGIBLE CULTURAL HERITAGE ——————————

90 cultural 'elements' were added to the UNESCO Representative List of the Intangible Cultural Heritage of Humanity in November 2008. According to the 2003 Convention for the Safeguarding of the Intangible Cultural Heritage (ICH), ICH can include: oral traditions and expressions; performing arts; social practices, rituals and festive events; knowledge and practices concerning nature and the universe; and traditional craftmanship. The list is intended to safeguard ICH and encourage continuing creativity. New elements are added to the list each year. In November 2008, the ICH list integrated 26 new Asia Pacific elements, 20 European, 19 Latin American, 18 African, and 7 Arab; some examples are below:

Region	element
Albania	*folk iso-polyphonic music*
Belgium	*the carnival of Binche*
Bhutan	*the Mask dance of the drums from Drametse*
Brazil	*the Samba de Roda of Recôncavo of Bahia*
Cambodia	*Sbek Thom, Khmer shadow theatre*
Central African Rep.	*the Polyphonic Singing of the Aka Pygmies of Central Africa*
China	*Kun Qu Opera*
Côte d'Ivoire	*the Gbofe of Afounkaha – the music of the Transverse Trumps of the Tagbana community*
Egypt	*the Al-Sirah Al-Hilaliyyah epic*
India	*Ramlila – the traditional performance of the Ramayana*
Indonesia	*the Wayang puppet theatre*
Italy	*Canto a tenore, Sardinian pastoral songs*
Japan	*Kabuki Theatre*
Kyrgyzstan	*the art of Akyns, Kyrgyz epic tellers*
Malawi	*the Vimbuza healing dance*
Mexico	*the indigenous festivity dedicated to the dead*
Nigeria	*the Ifa divination system*
Spain	*the mystery play of Elche*
Tonga	*the Lakalaka, dances and sung speeches of Tonga*
Vietnam	*Nha Nhac, Vietnamese court music*

The European Parliament proposed that the Mediterranean diet be added to the list of Intangible Cultural Heritage. MEPs argued that the famously healthy diet is one of the 'various elements of the European cultural model helping to survive against globalization and American foods'. The success of this bid (and of the 111 other applications from 35 countries) will be revealed in autumn 2009.

————————————— THE ART FUND PRIZE · 2009 —————————————

The £100,000 Art Fund Prize (formerly the Gulbenkian Prize) celebrates 'original-ity and excellence' in UK museums and galleries. In 2009, the prize was awarded to *The Wedgwood Museum*, Barlaston, Stoke-on-Trent. The other award finalists were: *Orleans House Gallery*, Twickenham; *Ruthin Craft Centre*, Denbighshire; and '*The Centre of New Enlightenment*', Kelvingrove Art Gallery & Museum, Glasgow.

———————————— ART AFTER DEATH ————————————

In December 2008, a photograph of the painter Francis Bacon snapped a few hours after his death was displayed at his favourite Soho haunt, the Colony Room Club. The photo, taken in a Spanish mortuary by Bacon's friend Catherine Shakespeare Lane, showed Bacon in a plastic body bag atop a background image of offal, flanked by images of Salvador Dali. While some found the work gruesome, it seems to have been in keeping with Bacon's notoriously macabre world view: 'we are potential carcasses', he once observed. Below are some other artists who have given their bodies to art:

From July until November 2008, the skull of the pianist André Tchaikowsky was used by the Royal Shakespeare Company in 22 performances of the 'Alas, poor Yorick' scene in *Hamlet*. Tchaikowsky donated his skull to the RSC upon his death in 1982, because he felt the company should have a real skull for use in performances. ❧ Though not yet dead, the American artist Alan Sonfist has promised his body to the Museum of Modern Art in New York. Sonfist's work is concerned with natural processes, and he reportedly intends the decay of his body to be seen as another such artwork. ❧ The French multimedia artist Orlan is known for using her body as a medium: in one ongoing 'performance', she reshaped her face using plastic surgery. Orlan has also said she plans to donate her body to a museum after her death, with the request that it be mummified and displayed. ❧ In 2004, the German artist Karl Friedrich Lentze wrote to zoos asking that his body be fed to piranhas after death. At least one zoo responded that piranhas generally prefer live food. ❧ The American performance artist Bob Flanagan, who died in 1996, left a variety of instructions for art projects involving his body after death. One included training a video camera upon his corpse to document its decay; fortunately, the project was never undertaken. ❧ The past decade has seen two travelling exhibits of preserved human bodies: *Body Worlds*, created in 1995 by German anatomist Gunther von Hagens, and *Bodies... The Exhibition*, which opened in Florida in 2005 (both continue to travel around the world).

Philosopher Jeremy Bentham (1748–1832) also believed in preserving the body after death. In his will, Bentham asked that his corpse be dissected in a private lecture, his head mummified in 'the style of the New Zealanders', and his skeleton stuffed and dressed in a suit of his clothes and seated on one of his favourite chairs. Bentham's creation, which he called his 'Auto-Icon', was later donated to University College London, where it can be seen today. At the school's centenary and sesquicentenary, Bentham was brought to the College Committee meeting and recorded as 'present but not voting'.

————————— TOP FIVE ARTISTS BY REVENUE · 2008 —————————

Artprice annually ranks artists based on sales generated by their works at auction:

Rank artist *('07 rank)*	2008 sales ($)
1 .... Pablo Picasso (2) 262m	4 .... Damien Hirst (15) 230m
2 .... Francis Bacon (3) 256m	5 .... Claude Monet (5) 174m
3 .... Andy Warhol (1) 236m	The total revenue for the 2008 market's Top 10 artists was $1·7bn, $100m lower than in 2007.

CORPORATE ART COLLECTIONS

In April 2009, auctioneers Christie's announced the establishment of a new department focusing solely on sales of corporate art collections. Although banks and other businesses are not always foremost in mind as guardians of fine art, corporations have been collecting and displaying artworks since the 1960s, when the practice became popular as a way to project a positive image and stimulate employees. Unfortunately, the credit crunch may imperil some of the world's finest collections; for example, the fate of 3,500 precious artworks owned by the financial services firm Lehman Brothers is currently in doubt. While Christie's would not reveal the name of its prospective clients, it was said to be in talks with a dozen US and European firms looking to sell off their art. ❦ Some of the world's important corporate art collections are:

DEUTSCHE BANK
Est. 1979 · >56,000 works
Includes pieces by Vassily Kandinsky, Piet Mondrian, Joseph Beuys, Marc Chagall, Pablo Picasso, and Damien Hirst. The largest corporate art collection in the world.

MICROSOFT
Est. 1987 · *c.*5,000 works
Includes pieces by Cindy Sherman, Takashi Murakami, Sol LeWitt, Chuck Close. Focuses on artists from the US Northwest.

JPMORGAN CHASE
Est. 1959 · >30,000 works
Includes pieces by Roy Lichtenstein, Jasper Johns, Keith Haring, Julian Schnabel, and Jeff Koons. Said to be the first major corporate art collection.

PROGRESSIVE INSURANCE (US)
Est. 1974 · >6,500 works
Includes pieces by Cindy Sherman, Kara Walker, Gregory Crewdson, and Andy Warhol.

UBS
Est. 2004 · >40,000 works
Includes pieces by Jean-Michel Basquiat, Louise Bourgeois, Christo, Willem de Kooning. Launched formally in 2004, as an outgrowth of several collections.

SIMMONS & SIMMONS
Est. 1993 · *c.*400
Includes pieces by Damien Hirst, Sarah Lucas, Tracey Emin, Gary Hume, and Wolfgang Tillmans. Legal firm that collects contemporary British art, sometimes in exchange for legal services given to artists.

THE MOST POWERFUL PEOPLE IN ART

Damien Hirst was the most powerful figure in contemporary art in 2008, according to *ArtReview* magazine. Among other exploits, in September 2008 Hirst became the first artist to bring his work directly to auction, earning an unprecedented £111m in sales at Sotheby's London. The magazine's top ten most powerful were:

1 .. Damien Hirst .... *artist*	6 .. Jay Jopling .... *dealer/gallerist*
2 .. Larry Gagosian ...... *dealer/gallerist*	7 .. David Zwirner .... *dealer/gallerist*
3 .. Kathy Halbreich .. *museum director*	8 .. François Pinault.. *owner of Christie's*
4 .. Nicholas Serota ... *museum director*	9 .. Jasper Johns .... *artist*
5 .. Iwan Wirth .... *gallerist*	10. Eli Broad .... *collector*

THE CRITICAL YEAR · 2008–09

{SEPT 2008} · *Rain Man* at the Apollo, London, starring Josh Hartnett, was according to Michael Billington of *The Guardian* 'thin stuff. 'It manages to take a movie that Anthony Lane accurately described as "rancid corn" and somehow make it even cornier', he added. {OCT} · The Royal Academy of Arts *Byzantium 330–1453* was billed as an epic exhibition, but Brian Sewell in the *Evening Standard* felt it did not even brush the surface: 'For me, it has taken a lifetime to acquire only a nodding acquaintance with Byzantine art and architecture ... How can the Academy claim, with only some 320 exhibits ... to offer a didactic introduction to the art of a thousand years spread over a

Sleeping Beauty

thousand thousand miles of territory?' In *The Times*, Waldemar Januszczak disagreed, arguing, 'Anyone can put the whole lot in front of you and say: "Make sense of that." A harder ask is to identify the milestones and the turning points, and to construct a telling journey between them'. {NOV} · Michael Billington in *The Guardian* decried the 'orgy of overacting' in *Treasure Island* at the Theatre Royal, Haymarket: the 'assault on the eardrums' is lessened only by Keith Allen's portrayal of Long John Silver, which he plays with 'refreshing restraint'. {DEC} · The English National Ballet's production of *Sleeping Beauty* at the Coliseum was praised for its magical staging. Zoë Anderson in *The Independent* said 'If you want Christmas ballet, with tutus and lavish scenery, this is lovely. If you want a faithful, intelligent staging of a 19th-century classic, here it is, too'. {JAN 2009} · Nicholas Hytner's famous production of Mozart's *Magic Flute* was again revived at the London Coliseum. Critics praised the humour of the production, but found many of the main players lacking. Roderick Williams as Papageno gained widespread praise, as David Gutman in *The Stage* noted: 'Only Papageno is truly world class. The role is one that Roderick Williams has made very much his own and his freshness and warmth save a musically unremarkable evening'. ❦ Richard Dreyfuss's prompt-providing earpiece gained much coverage for *Complicit* at the Old Vic, but it was the play that bothered Benedict Nightingale of *The Times*: 'Altogether, Sutton's attack on America stripping away liberty in the name of liberty seems badly in need of updating'. {FEB} · The cartoonish portrayal of immigration in the East End of London in Richard Bean's *England People Very Nice* at the Olivier garnered mixed reviews. In the *Evening Standard*, Nicholas de Jongh described his dislike of how the play handled a sensitive subject: 'I hated this gross, cartoon history of English reaction to four centuries of refugees arriving in London's East End'. However, in *The Times*, Benedict Nightingale applauded the controversy: 'Will the Thames "run with blood", to repeat a quote frequently cited in the play? It's the sort of question a genuinely "national" theatre should be asking'. ❦ The much anticipated, and long overdue, retrospective *Picasso: Challenging the Past* at the National Gallery received warm praise. However, Alistair Smart in *The Telegraph* believed its premise was flawed, 'but if it makes for a fine soliloquy, the show works less well as a dialogue between Picasso and his

THE CRITICAL YEAR · 2008–09 cont.

artistic ancestors. Where the old-master comparisons were overdrawn and often random in Paris, they are under-drawn to the point of being literally invisible here'. {MAR} · *Priscilla, Queen of the Desert*, at the Palace Theatre, London, was full of sumptuous costumes and roaring tunes but critics grumbled at the low humour. Simon Edge of *The Express* summed up the general feeling: 'Loud, lewd and lavish, it's about as subtle as a smack in the teeth with a didgeridoo, but who cares when it's this much fun?' ❦ The problem with the V&A's *Baroque: Style in the Age of Magnificence* was that 'its greatest works are not going anywhere since they are monumental sculpture or architecture, mostly abroad'. So said Stephen Bayley in the *Observer*. He went on to remark 'To the contemporary eye, most of what is on show is gag-makingly hideous, begging questions about a great art museum's role in promoting beauty'. {APR} · The American Ballet Theater production of *Swan Lake* at the Coliseum was greeted with disappointment. Mark Monahan of *The Telegraph* lamented the poor casting of the lead and summed up the production as 'a lovingly prepared soufflé that almost completely fails to rise'. {MAY} · *Waiting for Godot* at the Haymarket, London, starring Ian McKellen, Patrick Stewart, and Simon Callow was generally well received. In *The Times*, Benedict Nightingale praised the acting of McKellen and Stewart, stating they were 'subtle and commanding, touching and funny, vulnerable and dignified and just about everything we could expect Vladimir and Estragon to be'. {JUN} · Jude Law's depiction of Hamlet, at Wyndham's,

Ian McKellen

London, won much praise but suffered in comparison to David Tennant's recent command of the role. In the *Evening Standard*, Henry Hitchings said 'Law's performance is detailed and powerful', and in *The Telegraph* Charles Spencer noted that 'Law's boyish Hamlet is often on the brink of tears, but there is also no mistaking the intelligence of his mind or the nobility of his heart as he confides in the audience in soliloquies that allow us to follow every fleeting thought, every quicksilver change of mood'. ❦ *Futurism* at Tate Modern was perfectly summed up by Joanna Pitman of *The Times* thus: 'To a modern audience, accustomed to regular revolutions in the speed of travel and of the spread of information, our eyes are no longer astonished by the artistic fireworks of the Futurists. But the impact of their collective work has in no way been diminished, and the Tate has put together an exhibition that successfully reassesses the movement and remains astonishing on many levels'. {JUL} · The critics applauded Rachel Weisz's portrayal of the iconic Blanche DuBois in *A Streetcar Named Desire* at the Donmar. In *The Guardian*, Michael Billington reflected that, 'what Weisz brings to the role is a quality of desperate solitude touched with grace'. {AUG} · Ricky Gervais's new show *Science* premiered in Edinburgh and was greeted with little enthusiasm. Many critics blamed Gervais's recent Stateside success; the comments of Julian Hall in *The Independent* were typical: 'Perhaps Hollywood, the reason why Gervais's stock has risen lately, is also why his latest stand up offering is his most disappointing.'

UNDERSTUDIES

Understudy Edward Bennett was thrust literally into the spotlight in December 2008, when a back injury prevented David Tennant from appearing in the title role of the Royal Shakespeare Company's production of *Hamlet*. Bennett, who had been playing Laertes, was given just a few hours' notice that he would be taking Tennant's place, but he received a standing ovation for his performance and warm critical praise. Michael Billington wrote in *The Guardian*, 'Bennett's Hamlet is very different in tone and style, as you might expect, from Tennant's ... but this is a more robustly traditional reading of the part which marks Bennett down as an actor to watch'. Below are some other understudies who were launched to fame:

Actor	understudy for	production (year)
Shirley MacLaine	Carol Haney	*The Pajama Game* (1954)
Albert Finney	Laurence Olivier	*Coriolanus* (1959)
Anthony Hopkins	Laurence Olivier	*The Dance of Death* (1967)
Catherine Zeta Jones	*not known*	*42nd Street* (1984)
Jeremy Northam	Daniel Day-Lewis	*Hamlet* (1989)
Natalie Portman	Laura Bell Bundy	*Ruthless!* (1993)
Laura Michelle Kelly	Martine McCutcheon	*My Fair Lady* (2001)

LAURENCE OLIVIER AWARDS OF NOTE · 2009

Best actor..Derek Jacobi · *Twelfth Night*
Best actress......................................Margaret Tyzack · *The Chalk Garden*
Best performance in a supporting role....................Patrick Stewart · *Hamlet*
Best new play ....*Black Watch* · Gregory Burke
Best new musical..*Jersey Boys*
Best actor (musical)..........................Douglas Hodge · *La Cage Aux Folles*
Best actress (musical) ....Elena Roger · *Piaf*
Best new comedy ....*God of Carnage* · Yasmina Reza
Best director..John Tiffany · *Black Watch*

THEATRE CATS

The actors' union Equity launched a campaign in July 2009 to return cats to London's theatres – both to improve the morale of actors and to control vermin. Theatre cats used to be a common sight backstage. It is thought the tradition dates back centuries to when out-of-work sailors began working as backstage riggers, bringing with them their marine felines. However, in recent years, fewer establishments have kept up this custom. One of the most famous theatre cats was Beerbohm – a tabby who stalked the aisles of the Gielgud Theatre from the 1970s to the early 1990s, when he retired. Beerbohm frequently wandered nonchalantly onto the stage mid-performance, yet actors held him in such high esteem that his passing in 1995 received a front-page obituary in *The Stage*. More recently Boy Cat, who resided at The Albery, enlivened a gala performance by eating Princess Margaret's bouquet.

―――――――――― CELEBRITY-INSPIRED SHOWS ――――――――――

In February 2009, the Royal Opera House announced it would stage a work based on the turbulent and tragic life of Anna Nicole Smith, written by Mark-Anthony Turnage. Other recent stage shows inspired by modern celebrity include:

Title	by	artform
Jerry Springer: The Opera (2003)	Stewart Lee & Richard Thomas	opera
Diana The Princess (2005)	Peter Schaufuss	ballet
I, Keano (Roy Keane) (2005)	Paul Woodfall	musical
Meltdown: Britney Spears (2008)	Rambert Dance Company	modern dance
Big (Big Boi of Outcast) (2008)	Atlanta Ballet	ballet
Shane Warne: The Musical (2008)	Eddie Perfect	musical

――――――― MOST POWERFUL WOMEN IN THEATRE ―――――――

In March 2009, *Harper's Bazaar* named the twenty most powerful women in British theatre. The list (which was ranked in no particular order) is given below:

Bola Agbaje (27) playwright · Gillian Anderson (40) actor
Miriam Buether (39) set & costume designer · Caryl Churchill (70) playwright
Paule Constable (42) lighting designer · Dame Judi Dench (74) actor
Michelle Dockery (27) actor
Maxine Doyle (38) choreographer & associate director, Punchdrunk
Sonia Friedman (43) producer · Sally Greene (52) impresario & producer
Kathryn Hunter (52) actor & director · Lisa Makin (43) casting agent & producer
Dame Helen Mirren (63) actor · Katie Mitchell (44) director
Rosamund Pike (30) actor · Emma Rice (41) artistic director, Kneehigh Theatre
Fiona Shaw (50) actor & director · Polly Stenham (22) playwright
Summer Strallen (24) musical theatre actor · Rachel Weisz (38) actress

――――――――― THE TONY AWARDS 2009 ―――――――――

Best play	*God of Carnage* · Yasmina Reza
Best musical	*Billy Elliot, The Musical*
Best leading actor in a play	Geoffrey Rush · *Exit the King*
Best leading actress in a play	Marcia Gay Harden · *God of Carnage*
Best leading actor in a musical	David Alvarez, Trent Kowalik, & Kiril Kulish · *Billy Elliot*
Best leading actress in a musical	Alice Ripley · *Next to Normal*
Best featured actress in a play	Angela Lansbury · *Blithe Spirit*
Best direction of a play	Matthew Warchus · *God of Carnage*
Best direction of a musical	Stephen Daldry · *Billy Elliot*

In 2009, journalists and critics were dropped from the judging panel for the Tonys, ostensibly to avoid conflicts of interest. Incensed critics complained that the awards had become an 'infomercial'.

———————— CHANGING DANCING POSITIONS ————————

An academic study of ballerinas, published in May 2009, revealed that modern dancers employ more extreme postures than their predecessors. The study, led by Elena Daprati and her colleagues at University College London, examined photos and videos of dancers performing the Rose Adagio from Act One of *The Sleeping Beauty* between 1946–2004. From their research it became clear that the angle of the leg raises, known as extensions, has increased in recent times. The researchers suggested that this reflected the modern taste for more extreme and unnatural body postures. To confirm these findings, the old and new dance positions were recreated as stick drawings for the public to assess. Twelve non-ballet fans shown the drawings all declared a preference for the more elaborate modern positions.

———————— NATIONAL DANCE AWARDS · 2008 ————————

The Critics' Circle National Dance Awards are judged and presented by the critics and journalists involved in reviewing dance productions. The awards aim to celebrate the diversity of dance in Great Britain. The winners in 2008 included:

Outstanding achievement . . . . Richard Alston
Best male dancer . . . . Edward Watson · *The Royal Ballet*
Best female dancer . . . . Agnes Oaks · *English National Ballet*
Dance UK industry award . . . . Janet Smith · *Scottish Dance Theatre*
Best choreography: classical . . . . Christopher Wheeldon · *Electric Counterpoint*
– modern . . . . Hofesh Shechter · *In Your Rooms*
Spotlight Awards: male classical dancer . . . . Martin Harvey · *The Royal Ballet*
– female classical dancer . . . . Yuhui Choe · *The Royal Ballet*
– male modern dancer . . . . Anh Ngoc Nguyen · *Random Dance*
– female modern dancer . . . . Kate Coyne · *Michael Clark Company & freelance*
Outstanding company . . . . *English National Ballet*
Best foreign dance company . . . . *New York City Ballet*
Working Title *Billy Elliot* award . . . . Michael Guihot-Jouffray
Patron's award . . . . *Northern Ballet Theatre*

———————— BOYS & DANCING ————————

In March 2009, both the *Guardian* and *Telegraph* ran articles reporting that boys have become more interested in dance classes as a result of the BBC1 show *Strictly Come Dancing*. The articles pointed to role models such as Darren Gough, the cricketer who was the first male winner on *Strictly*, and included quotes from teachers who said it was now 'cool' to dance in their schools. Government figures agree: the number of schoolchildren taking dance classes rose 83% in the past four years, according to the Arts Council, with boys comprising a third of that rise. The number of dance GSCEs taken has also risen, from 7,003 in 2001 to 18,666 in 2007. Nor is this phenomenon confined to the UK: in 2008, Australian paper *The Age* reported on the number of boys taking ballet classes there – called the 'Billy Elliot effect'.

———— EDINBURGH FRINGE COMEDY AWARDS · 2009 ————

Edinburgh Fringe's comedy awards went ahead in August 2009 despite lacking a corporate sponsor. The £8,000 prize was awarded to stand-up poet Tim Key for his show, *The Slutcracker*. Jonny Sweet was named Best Newcomer for his first solo show.

WINNER & NOMINEES 2008

TIM KEY	*The Slutcracker*
Idiots of Ants	*This Is War*
John Bishop	*Elvis Has Left The Building*
Jon Richardson	*This Guy at Night*
Russell Kane	*Human Dressage*
Tom Wrigglesworth	*Open Return Letter to Richard Branson*

———————— UK'S FAVOURITE COMEDIAN ————————

The top ten in a November 2008 poll to find the nation's favourite comedians:

1 .... Peter Kay	5 .... Dawn French	9 .... Eddie Izzard
2 .... Lee Evans	6 ...... Rowan Atkinson	10 .... Frankie Boyle
3 .... Alan Carr	7 .... Al Murray	
4 .... Catherine Tate	8 .... Jack Dee	[Source: Smile]

In 2009, Michael McIntyre's *Live And Laughing* became the fastest-selling debut comedy DVD ever. ♥ After extensive research, evolutionary theorist Alastair Clarke concluded in March 2009 that all jokes fall into the following eight categories: POSITIVE REPETITION – *use of catchphrases*; SCALE – *exaggerating the size of something*; QUALITATIVE RECONTEXTUALISATION – *when something familiar is changed*; APPLICATION – *words having a double meaning*; COMPLETION – *audience needs to guess to complete a phrase or scenario*; QUALIFICATION – *when a familiar word is pronounced in an unfamiliar fashion*; DIVISION – *when a joke is told in parts, by different people*; and OPPOSITION – *sarcasm*.

———————— BRITISH COMEDY AWARDS · 2008 ————————

Best TV comedy actor	Ricky Gervais · *Extras Christmas Special*
Best TV comedy actress	Sharon Horgan · *Pulling*
Best TV comedy	*Gavin and Stacey*
Best comedy entertainment programme	*Harry Hill's TV Burp*
Best male comedy newcomer	Simon Bird · *The Inbetweeners*
Best female comedy newcomer	Katy Brand · *Katy's Big Ass Show*
Best new British TV comedy	*The Inbetweeners*
Best TV comedy drama	*Drop Dead Gorgeous*
Best live stand-up	*Russell Brand*
Best comedy panel show	*QI*
Ronnie Barker writer of the year	David Renwick
Lifetime achievement award	Jasper Carrott
Outstanding contribution to comedy	Geoffrey Perkins

———————————— COLOUR FORECASTS ————————————

Colour forecasters scan emerging colour trends to predict the hues consumers will soon see in their clothing, cosmetics, houses, and cars. These forecasters constantly monitor street styles, lifestyle trends, social issues, and even upcoming movies and art exhibits in an attempt to discover which colours are likely to dominate over the coming years[†]. The forecasters meet within an international network of colour forecasting groups, where they compare swatches and photographs, debate trends, and then forecast a palette of promising shades. The palettes are used by everyone from fashion and graphic designers to product manufacturers. According to industry textbooks, designers for women's lines are often the first to adopt the most new and daring colours, while manufacturers of other products wait longer to see which shades will gain acceptance. A simplified version of the colour acceptance cycle as outlined in the 2003 book *Color in Three-Dimensional Design* by Jeanne Kopacz:

Women's fashion and cosmetics ⇢ men and children's fashion
⇢ graphic design and product packaging ⇢ home furnishings
⇢ automobiles ⇢ architecture and interior design

Major colour forecasting groups include the British Textile Colour Group, Intercolor, the International Colour Authority, the Color Association of the United States, and the Color Marketing Group, although a variety of other groups exist. A selection of forecasts available to the public for 2010 and beyond appears below:

International Colour Authority · '*A refined palette with organic origins, inspired by a hi-tech thrust for sustainability*', including *Pantone 18-1441 TC* (a heathery purple), *Pantone 14-0636 TC* (pale yellow-green), and *Pantone 15-6313 TC* (mid-seafoam green)
[Autumn/Winter 2010/11, womenswear]

Interfilière · '*stars of the season: the greens. Guests of honour: nuances of red and soft and refined pinks, mauves and neutrals in full evolution*' including *Young Shoot* (pale bamboo green), *Grenadine* (bright pink) and *Turkish Delight* (pale rose pink) [2010 Spring/Summer, focused on lingerie/beachwear]

Clariant · *a palette focused on 'reinventing happiness*', including '*Goldiva – brown enriched with gold, giving a sensation of warmth and luxury*' and '*Spring Fling – light and fresh turquoise, expressing optimism in our chaotic world*' [2010, focused on plastics]

TFL · *Pantone TPX 15-6310* (pale taupe), *Pantone TPX 18-3949* (vibrant medium blue), *Pantone TPX 16-1632* (light watermelon), *Pantone TPX 13-3820* (pale lilac), *Pantone TPX 16-1362* (cantaloupe) [Spring/Summer 2010, focused on leather]

† Some of the social trends that have influenced popular colours, according to various textbooks and interviews with colour forecasters: the popularity of metallic fabrics in the 1970s apparently stemmed from the King Tut artefacts then touring the US; the acid colours of the 80s were influenced by the psychedelic drugs that were then popular in clubs; the ecru fad of the early 90s was due to a renewed interest in the Middle East; the popularity of greens in the mid-90s reflected a focus on environmental concerns; the dominance of pink in 2003–05 was a reaction to 9/11; and the current craze for bright apple green is apparently due to the verdant hue of the animated ogre in the *Shrek* film series.

READY-TO-WEAR FASHION WEEKS

NEW YORK
February & September
Who shows: *Ralph Lauren, Vera Wang,
Diane Von Furstenberg, Calvin Klein,
Zac Posen, Oscar de la Renta,
Michael Kors, Donna Karan*

MILAN
February & September/October
Who shows: *Gucci, Armani, Prada,
Dolce & Gabbana, Moschino, Versace,
Roberto Cavalli, Max Mara,
Burberry Prorsum, Fendi*

LONDON
February & September
Who shows: *Aquascutum, Erdem,
Paul Smith, Nicole Farhi,
Jasper Conran, Betty Jackson,
Marios Schwab, House of Holland*

PARIS
February/March & October
Who shows: *Stella McCartney, Chanel,
Vivienne Westwood, Jean Paul Gaultier,
John Galliano, Issey Miyake,
Christian Dior, Chloé, Lanvin*

According to *Vogue*, some key trends for Autumn/Winter 2009/10 include: shades of teal; over-the-knee boots; razor-sharp tailoring; urban-styled tweed; jewel-toned velvet; over-sized shoulders; leather dresses and skirt suits; romantic drapes; homage to the eighties; austere silhouette; statement shoes.

TOP FASHION CITIES

Global Language Monitor uses an algorithm to trawl the print media, internet and blogosphere for mentions of 'fashion forward' cities. The 2008 top ten cities were (2007 position in parenthesis):

1 (1) .. New York	6 (6) Los Angeles
2 (2) ...... Rome	7 (12).... Sydney
3 (3)........Paris	8 (9) .. Las Vegas
4 (5) ...... Milan	9 (11)..... Berlin
5 (4) .... London	10 (6)..... Tokyo

Dubai shot up the ranking from 24th to 12th.

ELLE STYLE AWARDS

Best	*winner*
Actor	Mickey Rourke
Actress	Freida Pinto
Music	Kings of Leon
Style icon	Sienna Miller
Woman of the year	Courtney Love
Model	Rosie Huntington Whitley
British designer	Christopher Kane
Fashion future	Erdem
H&M style visionary	Viktor & Rolf
TV star	Alexa Chung
TV series	Gavin & Stacey
Jewellery designer	Lara Bohinc

BRITISH FASHION AWARDS · 2008

Designer of the year	Luella Bartley
Emerging talent	Louise Goldin
Designer brand	Jimmy Choo
Menswear designer	Christopher Bailey for Burberry
Accessory designer	Rupert Sanderson
Red carpet designer	Matthew Williamson
Model of the year	Jourdan Dunn
Outstanding achievement in fashion	Stephen Jones

——————————— CONSERVATION AREAS AT RISK ———————————

According to English Heritage, 727 of England's 9,300 conservation areas are at risk of neglect, decay, or inappropriate change. Conservation areas are designated by local councils keen to protect the unique character of buildings in the area. In June 2009 English Heritage carried out a survey of councils to discover the condition of conservation areas around England. The survey indicated that the top threats are:

Threat *conservation areas affected* %	
Plastic windows and doors 83	Effects of traffic calming.............36
Poorly maintained roads.............60	Alterations to the fronts, roofs
Street clutter 45	and chimneys 34
Loss of garden walls/hedges 43	Unsympathetic extensions...........31
Unsightly satellite dishes.............38	Impact of advertisement boards.....23
	Neglected green spaces 18

English Heritage maintains the Heritage at Risk register. In 2009, 5,094 sites were on this register, including: Crystal Palace park, London; the battlefield at Stamford Bridge, Yorkshire, where King Harold defeated the Norwegian army in 1066; the Town Square conservation area of Stevenage; the late-medieval Bellasis bridge in Northumberland; and the C13th Gleaston Castle in Cumbria.

——————————— 'CONSTRUCTION FOR SEDUCTION' ———————————

The Roman baths in Bath topped an online poll by the Royal Institute of British Architects (RIBA) to uncover the most romantic building in Britain. The light-hearted survey – designed to celebrate RIBA's 175th anniversary – invited the public to vote from a shortlist of 14 'constructions for seduction'. The top 3 were:

[1] Roman baths, Bath · 41%
[2] Warwick Castle · 11% [3] Royal Pavilion, Brighton · 9%

——————————— THE STIRLING PRIZE · 2008 ———————————

Accordia, a modern concept of high-density housing in Cambridge, won the 13th annual RIBA Stirling prize in October 2008. (The £20,000 prize was jointly awarded to Feilden Clegg Bradley Studios, Alison Brooks Architects, and Maccreanor Lavington.) The judges said, 'the development proves that good modern housing sells, that a committed local authority can have a very positive influence on the design, that a masterplan with a range of architects can be successful and that the very best architecture does not need to rely on gimmicks'. The other nominees were:

Nominated building	*architect*
Amsterdam Bijlmer Arena Station ....Grimshaw and Arcadis	
Manchester Civil Justice Centre........................... Denton Corker Marshall	
Nord Park Cable Railway, Innsbruck, Austria........................... Zaha Hadid	
Royal Festival Hall, London....................................Allies and Morrison	
Westminster Academy, London....................Allford Hall Monaghan Morris	

—————— THE ARCHAEOLOGICAL YEAR 2008–09 ——————

{OCT 2008} · Archaeologists excavating at Khirbat al-Nahas, Jordan, suggested that the ancient copper mines they had uncovered could be the legendary mines of King Solomon. Soil samples indicated that the mine was in use as early as the C9th BC, when Solomon reigned. {NOV} · The world's oldest grave of a shaman was unearthed in N Israel. The 12,000-year-old 'Natufian grave' held the remains of an elderly woman, a human foot, and animal parts – a collection of 'grave goods' that some archaeologists claim are consistent with shamanism. {DEC} · The oldest-known stash of marijuana was discovered in the 2,700-year-old grave of a shaman in Xinjiang Province, China. ❦ Archaeologists excavating at York University uncovered a skull containing the remains of brain tissue. The find, thought to date back to 300 BC, is very unusual, since brain tissue normally decomposes quickly. {JAN 2009} · The mummified remains of Queen Sheshestet, who ruled Egypt *c.*4,300 years ago, were unearthed in Saqqara. ❦ Research published in the *Proceedings of the National Academy of Sciences* questioned the theory that the impact of a giant comet 13,000 years ago caused the extinction of woolly mammoths. Analysis of charcoal and pollen layers from the period do not show evidence of the widespread wildfires that the comet theory suggests. {FEB} · Examination of Henry VIII's armour allowed researchers at the Royal Armouries at Leeds to estimate the king's growing dimensions. As a young man, the 6'1" Henry VIII had a 32" waist and a 39" chest; by his mid-fifties the portly monarch had ballooned to a 52" waist and 53" chest. {MAR} · Archaeologists

Ida: the 'missing link'?

discovered the remains of a huge sea creature off Svalbard, Norway. The beast, dubbed *Predator X*, had a head twice as big as a *Tyrannosaurus rex* and a bite with four times its force. *Predator X* would have been the ultimate sea creature; at least 15m long and weighing 45 tonnes [see p.190]. {APR} · Archaeologists in Scotland unearthed flints that suggested Scotland was colonised *c.*4,000 years earlier than previously thought. The finds, at Biggar in South Lanarkshire, are similar to tools dating from 12,000 BC found in the Netherlands. {MAY} · A 47m-year-old fossilised lemur-like creature grabbed headlines around the world after it was described as the 'missing link' in human evolution. The fossil, nicknamed Ida, had been kept in storage for >20 years by a private collector before it was purchased by the Natural History Museum in Oslo, who identified its significance. However, some scientists remain sceptical of the 'missing-link' claims, and are demanding further scrutiny. {JUN} · Pottery excavated in a cave in Yuchanyan, China, could be the oldest known to science. Fragments of the find were radio-carbon-dated to be 17,500–18,300 years old. {JUL} · Bone fragments discovered in the tomb of St Paul in Rome have been carbon-dated to somewhere between the 1st and 2nd centuries AD. Pope Benedict XVI announced the findings and stated that this evidence proves the remains are indeed those of St Paul. {AUG} · An ancient letter penned by an Assyrian leader begging for reinforcements as Babylonian invaders advanced was excavated in south-east Turkey. The tablet, dated to 630 BC is 30 lines long and written in cuneiform.

Sci, Tech, Net

A virus is only doing its job.
— DAVID CRONENBERG (1943–)

─────────── SUBSTANCE OF THE YEAR · WATER ───────────

Water (two hydrogen atoms bonded to an atom of oxygen: H_2O) is one of the most ubiquitous substances: it covers 70% of the Earth's surface, comprises 65% of the human body, and is essential to all forms of life. ❦ For some time, reports have warned of an imminent 'water crisis' – but only in recent years has this threat been taken seriously at a policy level. At the World Water Forum in March 2009, government representatives signed the Istanbul Water Consensus, pledging to 'shift water security higher in national and international policy priorities', while the UN Under-Secretary-General stressed the urgent need to make water security a priority at the December 2009 climate change talks in Copenhagen. ❦ The total quantity of water on Earth remains constant at $1.4bn$ km^3. However, water demand increased six-fold during the C20th as a consequence of population growth, industrialisation, and urbanisation. Climate change has also threatened water security – drying up supplies in some areas while deluging others in 'extreme water events'. The UN estimates that 700m people currently live in 'water stressed' countries; by 2025, this number could reach 3bn. ❦ The increased burden on water resources is evident around the world: in China, the three rivers that supply half the country's water (the Hai, Huai, and Huang) are being depleted at twice their rate of replenishment; in America, seven states have been haggling over the rights to the dwindling Colorado River; in Mexico City, buildings are sinking as aquifers below the capital become over-exploited; in Australia, the Murray-Darling Basin is in the midst of a seven-year drought; and along the Nile, diversions for irrigation mean that this mighty river no longer reaches the sea. ❦ The tension between finite supply and insatiable demand has led many to predict 'water wars'. Famously, in 1995, the World Bank's Ismail Serageldin warned: 'Many of the wars of the C20th were about oil, but wars of the C21st will be over water'. That said, a 2001 study of 1,831 international water-related events since 1948 found only 37 examples of violent conflict (30 involved Israel). And co-operation will be key to managing future water scarcity, whether via trade or through technological fixes such as desalination or wastewater recycling. ❦ It is tempting for 'first worlders' to see water shortages as a foreign problem; images of Africans carrying well-water spring easily to mind. But few of us are aware of how much water we use – in the UK, 150 litres a day each, just for household washing and drinking. Fewer still would be able to survive for longer than a day or so if the taps ran dry.

——————— 'SEED' MAGAZINE SCIENTIST SURVEY ———————

In December 2008, *Seed* magazine released the results of a survey that interviewed 1,000 scientists from the public and private sectors in the UK, US, France, and Germany on the state of their field. Their answers to selected questions are below:

What do you see as the primary inhibitor of scientific progress? %

Lack of funds	36
Lack of time	25
Political interference	11
Lack of knowledge	10
Lack of technology	7
Lack of collaborators	6
Lack of fundamental theory	6

Are scientists obliged to ... ? % agree

Teach others about science	90
Be environmentally conscious	83
Make their work freely available	83
Address the biggest challenges facing humanity	80
Take an active role in social and civic issues	77
Inform policy-makers	74
Speak with journalists	61

How would you describe your interaction with the media? %

No interaction	65
Positive	26
Negative	9

Do you feel you are well-respected by the media? %

No	89
Yes	11

Do you feel you are well-respected by the government? %

No	91
Yes	9

Intriguingly, scientists working in the United States were twice as likely as those in the other countries to say they had the respect of both the media and the government.

——————— 'EDGE' ANNUAL QUESTION · 2009 ———————

Each year, the online science and culture magazine *Edge* invites scientists, philosophers and others to answer one thought-provoking question. In 2008, the question was, 'What will change everything? What game-changing scientific ideas and developments do you expect to live to see?' Some notable answers appear below:

John D. Barrow (physicist)	*a very, very good battery*
Gregory Cochran (physicist, anthropologist)	*better measurements*
Keith Devlin (mathematician)	*the mobile phone*
Freeman Dyson (physicist)	*'radiotelepathy', the direct communication of feelings and thought from brain to brain*
J. Enriquez (CEO, Biotechonomy)	*human speciation – an ever-faster accumulation of small, useful improvements that eventually turn homo sapiens into a new hominid*
Lawrence Krauss (physicist)	*the use of nuclear weapons against a civilian population*
Ian McEwan (novelist)	*the full flourishing of solar technology*
David Myers (editor, Wired)	*cheap, powerful, ubiquitous artificial intelligence*
James J. O'Donnell (classicist)	*Africa*
Gino Segré (physicist)	*the existence of additional space-time dimensions*
Sherry Turkle (psychologist)	*the robotic movement* [see p.199]

—————— NOBEL PRIZES IN SCIENCE · 2008 ——————

THE NOBEL PRIZE IN PHYSICS

Yoichiro Nambu, *Enrico Fermi Inst.*

'for the discovery of the mechanism
of spontaneous broken symmetry
in subatomic physics'

One half jointly to Makoto Kobayashi,
KEK, Japan, and Toshihide Maskawa,
Kyoto Sangyo University/YITP, Japan

'for the discovery of the origin of
the broken symmetry which
predicts the existence of at least
three families of quarks in nature'

THE NOBEL PRIZE IN CHEMISTRY

Osamu Shimomura,
*Marine Biological Laboratory/Boston
University Medical School*
Martin Chalfie, *Columbia University*
Roger Y. Tsien, *U of Calif. San Diego*

'for the discovery and development of
the green fluorescent protein, GFP'

THE NOBEL PRIZE IN
PHYSIOLOGY OR MEDICINE

Harald zur Hausen,
German Cancer Research Centre

'for his discovery of human papilloma
viruses causing cervical cancer'

One half jointly to Françoise Barré-
Sinoussi, *Institut Pasteur*
and Luc Montagnier, *World Foundation
for AIDS Research and Prevention*

'for their discovery of human
immunodeficiency virus'

In the 1960s, Nambu formulated a mathematical description for the phenomenon known as spontaneous broken symmetry, which helped refine the Standard Model in particle physics. In 1972, Kobayashi and Maskawa posited the existence of three generations of quarks (only two generations were known at the time), as a way of explaining symmetry violations that had recently been observed in experiments. The existence of all three generations of quarks was later confirmed, and has helped scientists work towards understanding why the universe is full of matter and not antimatter.

The work of Shimomura, Chalfie, and Tsien has allowed scientists to harness the green flourescent protein (GFP) from *Aequorea victoria* jellyfish for use as a tagging mechanism, which makes the movements of otherwise invisible proteins visible. By inserting the gene for GFP into various proteins, scientists have been able to watch glowing maps of interactions inside and between cells, yielding insights into a range of diseases, from cancer to Alzheimer's.

In the 1970s, zur Hausen proposed that human papilloma viruses (HPV) caused cervical cancer, even though herpes was then thought to be the culprit. In the 1980s, zur Hausen proved the link after discovering HPV in cervical cancer biopsies. His work allowed vaccines to be developed against HPV. In 1983, Barré-Sinoussi and Montagnier discovered the virus that came to be called human immunodeficiency virus (HIV), two years after cases of what we now call AIDS were first reported. Their work paved the way both for HIV blood tests and for anti-retroviral drugs.

——— ABEL PRIZE ———

The Abel Prize, awarded by the Norwegian Academy of Science and Letters for extraordinary contributions in the mathematical sciences, was presented in 2009 to Mikhail Leonidovich Gromov of New York University and the Institut des Hautes Études Scientifiques. Gromov won the *c*.£600,000 prize for 'his revolutionary contributions to geometry', which have led recent developments in the field.

——— COPLEY MEDAL ———

The Copley Medal, presented by the British Royal Society, is the world's oldest prize for scientific achievement (it has been awarded since 1731). The 2008 award was given to Sir Roger Penrose for his 'beautiful and original insights into many areas of mathematics and mathematical physics'. The prize, now worth £5,000, has been previously awarded to Charles Darwin, Albert Einstein, and Stephen Hawking.

——— Ig NOBEL PRIZES ———

Ig Nobel prizes are awarded for scientific 'achievements that cannot or should not be reproduced'. Below are some notable honours presented at the 2008 ceremony:

ARCHAEOLOGY · Astolfo G. Mello Araujo and José Carlos Marcelino (Universidade de São Paulo, Brazil) *for measuring how the course of history, or at least the contents of an archaeological dig site, can be scrambled by the actions of a live armadillo.*

CHEMISTRY · Sharee A. Umpierre (University of Puerto Rico), Joseph A. Hill (The Fertility Centers of New England, USA), Deborah J. Anderson (Boston University School of Medicine & Harvard Medical School) *for discovering that Coca-Cola is an effective spermicide,* and to Chuang-Ye Hong (Taipei Medical University, Taiwan) et al *for discovering that it is not.*

BIOLOGY · Marie-Christine Cadiergues, Christel Joubert, and Michel Franc (École Nationale Vétérinaire de Toulouse, France) *for discovering that the fleas that live on a dog can jump higher than the fleas that live on a cat.*

ECONOMICS · Geoffrey Miller, Joshua Tybur and Brent Jordan (University of New Mexico, USA) *for discovering that professional lap dancers earn higher tips when they are ovulating.*

PEACE · The Swiss Federal Ethics Committee on Non-Human Biotechnology and the citizens of Switzerland *for adopting the legal principle that plants have dignity.* [Source: improb.com]

——— DARWIN AWARDS ———

The Darwin Awards commemorate *'those who improve our gene pool by accidentally removing themselves from it'*. In 2008, the award was 'won' by a Brazilian Catholic priest, Adelir Antonio de Carli, who was lost at sea after an ill-advised trip tied to a number of helium party-balloons. The priest had been attempting to break the world record for a clustered balloon flight, but soon found himself over the Atlantic and unable to inform rescuers of his location since he didn't know how to use his GPS.

——————————— DARWIN'S ANNIVERSARIES ———————————

2009 marked the 200th anniversary of Charles Robert Darwin's birth (12/2/1809), and the 150th anniversary of the publication of *On the Origin of Species by Means of Natural Selection* (24/11/1859). To celebrate, the UK hosted more than 300 events and activities, including major museum exhibitions and festivals. Though he is now considered one of the most significant thinkers of all time, Darwin met with significant scepticism when he first proposed his theory of evolution. Below is a selection from some of the original book reviews that greeted *The Origin of Species*:

GUARDIAN (8/2/1860) · *If an anonymous author ... were to propound the startling theory, that all the various tribes of living creatures ... are descended from some four or five progenitors ... a busy man would be justified in turning from the unread volume with a smile of incredulity.* ❦ NEW YORK TIMES (28/3/1860) · *A series of arguments and inferences so revolutionary as, if established, to necessitate a radical reconstruction of the fundamental doctrines of natural history.* ❦ THE TIMES (26/12/1859) · *This hypothesis may or may not be sustainable hereafter ... but its sufficiency must be tried by the tests of science alone, if we are to maintain our position as the heirs of Bacon and the acquitters of Galileo.*

❦ THE GEOLOGIST (1860, v.3) · *Why should it be thought irreligious to believe the Maker of all things in His first designs should have foreseen the necessity of future modifications to future altered conditions?* ❦ QUARTERLY REVIEW (1860, v.108) · *To find that [species] are all equally the lineal descendants of the same aboriginal common ancestor, perhaps of the nucleated cell of some primaeval fungus, this, to say the least of it, is no common discovery ... if Mr Darwin can ... demonstrate to us our fungular descent, we shall dismiss our pride, and avow, with the characteristic humility of philosophy, our unsuspected cousinship with the mushrooms.* [Source: *The Complete Work of Charles Darwin Online*, darwin-online.org.uk.]

——————————— BIGGEST ANIMALS EVER ———————————

In 2009, scientists writing in *Nature* claimed to have found fossils from the largest snake species ever. *Titanoboa cerrejonensis*, which lived about 58m years ago (just after the extinction of the dinosaurs) in the tropics of South America and South-east Asia, weighed 1,135 kg and stretched 13 metres – longer than a double-decker bus. The creature lived mostly in the water and munched on ancestors of the modern crocodile, though scientists speculated that it would happily have eaten humans, were any around. Below are some other creatures nominated as the 'largest ever':

Rodent .... *Josephoartigasia monesi*, a rat weighing >1 ton; lived 2–4m years ago
Penguin .... *Icadyptes salasi*, 1·5 metres high; lived 35m years ago in the desert
Bird .... *phorusrhacid* (also called terror birds), 3 metres tall; lived 15m years ago
Fish .... *leedsichthys problematicus*, 22 metres long; lived 155m years ago
Insect . *Jaekelopterus rhenaniae*, a sea scorpion 2·5 metres tall; lived 390m years ago
Primate ..... *Gigantopithecus blackii*, an ape 3 metres tall; lived >100,000 years ago

All dates are approximate, and statuses contested. [Source: *National Geographic*, MSNBC, others.]

———————————— CLIMATE HACKING ————————————

'Geoengineering' projects are technological schemes designed to manipulate the climate and mitigate global warming. Although such ideas (dubbed 'climate hacking' by the media) were once dismissed by scientists, the global failure to slow the growth of emissions has pushed geoengineering from the fringes of science into its mainstream[†]. Indeed, a poll of 80 climate scientists conducted by *The Independent* in January 2009 found that 54% agreed with the need to develop a geoengineering 'Plan B', while only 35% disagreed. In response to such interest, the Royal Society launched a working group to study the feasibility of several geoengineering proposals. In September 2009, the group concluded that such technologies are 'very likely to be technically possible', though uncertainties remain regarding their effectiveness, costs, and environmental impacts. Some geoengineering proposals include:

Fertilising the ocean with iron to grow algae that will absorb CO_2
Adding ground limestone to the ocean to help absorb CO_2
Planting artificial trees to capture CO_2 and store it underground
Burning agricultural waste to turn it into charcoal ('biochar') and burying it
Planting vast new forests
Spraying sulphur dioxide aerosols into the stratosphere to reflect solar rays
Injecting salt spray into clouds in the lower atmosphere to increase reflectivity
Genetically modifying crops to increase their reflectivity
Placing gigantic mirrors in orbit between the Sun and the Earth
Painting all the roofs in the world white

The Royal Society report concluded that capturing CO_2 from the ambient air was the geoengineering proposal with the most potential, though cost-effective techniques to do so have not yet been developed. Biochar, ocean fertilisation, and painting roofs white were all found to be ineffective.
[†] Global CO_2 emissions now exceed the worst-case scenario projected by the Intergovernmental Panel on Climate Change in 2001. According to the International Energy Agency, if current trends continue, CO_2 concentration in the atmosphere will exceed 1,000 parts per million by the end of this century – a level at which scientists believe catastrophic and irreversible climate changes will take place.

———————————— UNUSUAL HEALTH RESEARCH ————————————

The Bill and Melinda Gates Foundation annually awards a number of $100,000 (£65,000) grants to fund novel projects that address global health issues. Unlike most funding bodies, the Gates' foundation requires little in the way of preliminary research, and focuses primarily on creative, if unproven, methods to prevent and treat infectious diseases. Some of the projects the foundation funded in 2009 include:

A handheld device that uses a magnet to detect malaria, by a University of Exeter team · *A scheme to infect mosquitoes with a fungus that dulls their sense of smell (making prey harder to find)*, by a Pennsylvania State University scientist · *A plan to develop nanoparticles that attach to tuberculosis-infected cells and deliver drugs*, by a Council for Scientific and Industrial Research in South Africa scientist · *A tomato that delivers antiviral drugs when eaten*, by a State University of New Jersey scientist.

—— SOME NOTABLE SCIENTIFIC RESEARCH · 2008–9 ——

{OCT 2008} · University of Arizona researchers reported in *Nature* that HIV first began spreading among humans in *c*.1990. The scientists arrived at this date by tracing the development of the disease back to its earliest strains, which were found in Africa in 1959. ❧ The Mars rover *Opportunity* located elemental iron on the surface of the red planet, left by collisions with iron-rich meteorites. Since iron can be used to manufacture steel, scientists suggested that any future bases on Mars could be built from materials already on the planet. {NOV} · Researchers at Villanova University in Pennsylvania reported that violent video games played with motion controls – like those on the Nintendo Wii – did not increase measurable levels of hostility any more than violent games played using traditional controls. ❧ US and Russian researchers reconstructed 80% of the genome of a woolly mammoth using hair samples from a carcass preserved in the Siberian permafrost [see p.74]. ❧ Researchers at the US National Institutes of Health discovered that injecting the proteins NAP and SAL into mice pregnant with pups carrying a Down's syndrome-like condition helped the pups develop normally after birth. The results raised hopes for a similar treatment for humans. ❧ Researchers in the Netherlands reported that the presence of graffiti or rubbish made people significantly more likely to litter, trespass, or steal on any given street. The researchers came to this conclusion after observing the behaviour of pedestrians on streets they had 'staged'. ❧ A Canadian study found that male college students who scored highly on a test of psychopathic personality traits were better able to remember the faces and details of sad-looking women than of other subjects. The researchers theorised that psychopathy may be associated with a form of 'predatory memory'. ❧ Two teams of astronomers independently captured the first images of planets outside our solar system. One team, led by Californian researchers, took shots of a planet named Fomalhaut b that is 25 light years away, while a second team, led by Canadian astronomers, took pictures of three planets surrounding the star HR8799, which is 130 light years away. {DEC} · Israeli psychologists found that Wikipedia contributors scored lower on tests of agreeableness, openness, and conscientiousness when compared to other Israelis of the same age and 'internet intensity'. ❧ In a sample of 425 former soldiers, researchers at the UK's Institute of Psychiatry found a small but statistically significant link between higher intelligence test scores and increase in the quantity, concentration, and mobility of sperm. ❧ Researchers in Stockholm were able to 'trick' people into perceiving another body as their own, by using goggles which broadcast images from the perspective of a mannequin. Subjects wearing the goggles said that they felt the mannequin's body 'belonged' to them, and some even began sweating when the mannequin's body was threatened with a knife. ❧ Neuroscientists reported in *Current Biology* on the case of a man left blind by a stroke who was nevertheless able to navigate a cluttered obstacle course. The researchers concluded that the man relied on 'blindsight' – a visual processing system in the brain that is entirely subconscious. {JAN 2009} · A study by

— SOME NOTABLE SCIENTIFIC RESEARCH · 2008–9 cont. —

Cambridge University's autism research centre linked high levels of testosterone in the amniotic fluid of pregnant women to autistic traits found in their children prior to the age of eight. The study raised the possibility of a prenatal screen to detect autism, and catalysed a debate on the ethics of such a test, should one ever be developed. ❦ Experiments run by Oxford University researchers found that volunteers who played the computer game *Tetris* after watching disturbing videos were less likely to report flashbacks of the videos over the course of a week, compared to those who had not played the game. The researchers theorised that playing *Tetris* interfered with the brain's ability to process new sensory stimuli, and suggested that computer games could ameliorate post-traumatic stress disorder. {FEB} · Researchers at Newcastle University found that dairy farmers who named their cows were rewarded with higher yields of milk: up to 500 extra pints per year. ❦ Doctors in Berlin managed to rid an American patient of HIV by performing a bone marrow transplant from a donor with a gene resistant to the virus. The patient, who underwent the transplant to cure his leukaemia, has remained virus-free for two years without antiretroviral drugs. {MAR} · A University of Virginia scientist found that brain speed, spatial visualisation, and reasoning begin to decline around the age of 27, and that peak performance on common brain agility tests occurs around 22. ❦ Psychiatrists at New York's Columbia University discovered that people whose parents or grandparents suffered from depression showed a significant thinning of the brain's right cortex – a region associated with reasoning, planning, and mood. {APR} · Psychologists at the University of Ulster asked 571 people aged 17–25 about their life experiences, and discovered that those with at least one sister were more likely to report feeling happy and balanced than only children or those with brothers. ❦ Researchers in Iowa found that mutations in the CATSPER1 gene, which affects sperm movement, was linked to male infertility in two Iranian families. The scientists said the discovery raised hopes for the creation of a male contraceptive. {MAY} · Researchers from University College London showed that a series of injections of a novel drug (CPHPC) under the skin can remove an abnormal protein linked to Alzheimer's disease from the spinal fluid. They suggested that this might be a useful new approach to treating the degenerative disease. {JUN} · Chinese geneticists discovered a gene marker for 'werewolf syndrome' (congenital generalised hypertrichosis terminalis) which can cause excessive hair growth and facial deformity. {JUL} · Edinburgh psychologists found that wallets containing baby photos were the most likely to be returned: 88% of those planted on city streets were mailed back. Return rates were much lower for other types of pictures, and lowest for no pictures at all. ❦ Canadian researchers found that people with low self-esteem who repeated the mantra 'I am a lovable person' actually felt worse about themselves afterwards. {AUG} · Taiwanese scientists reported that a compound harvested from the coral *Capnella imbricata* might be effective in treating certain sorts of pain which do not respond to the usual analgesics.

———————————— THE CHEMICAL ELEMENTS ————————————

All matter in the universe is comprised of chemical elements, substances that cannot be reduced by chemical means into simpler substances. The atoms that make up a chemical element each have the same number of protons in their nuclei, which gives the element its distinctive 'atomic number'. The elements are frequently listed in order of atomic number, as in the chart below. Information for each element includes its name, its atomic number, symbol, atomic weight and year of discovery:

Hydrogen†	*Aluminium*	*Iron*†	*Strontium*	*Tin*
1 · H · 1.0079	13 · Al	26 · Fe · 55.845	38 · Sr · 87.62	50 · Sn
1776	26.9815 · 1825	ancient	1790	118.71
Helium	*Silicon*	*Cobalt*	*Yttrium*	ancient
2 · He · 4.0026	14 · Si	27 · Co	39 · Y	*Antimony*
1895	28.0855 · 1824	58.9332 · 1735	88.9059 · 1794	51 · Sb
Lithium	*Phosphorus*†	*Nickel*	*Zirconium*	121.76
3 · Li · 6.941	15 · P	28 · Ni	40 · Zr	ancient
1817	30.9738 · 1669	58.6934 · 1751	91.224 · 1789	*Tellurium*
Beryllium	*Sulphur*†	*Copper*†	*Niobium*	52 · Te
4 · Be · 9.0122	16 · S · 32.065	29 · Cu	41 · Nb	127.6
1797	ancient	63.546	92.9064 · 1801	1782
Boron	*Chlorine*‡	ancient	*Molybdenum*†	*Iodine*
5 · B · 10.811	17 · Cl	*Zinc*†	42 · Mo	53 · I
1808	35.453 · 1774	30 · Zn · 65.38	95.94 · 1781	126.9045
Carbon†	*Argon*	ancient	*Technetium**	1811
6 · C · 12.0107	18 · Ar	*Gallium*	43 · Tc · 98	*Xenon*
ancient	39.948 · 1894	31 · Ga	1937	54 · Xe
Nitrogen†	*Potassium*†	69.723 · 1875	*Ruthenium*	131.293
7 · N	19 · K	*Germanium*	44 · Ru	1898
14.0067	39.0983 · 1807	32 · Ge · 72.64	101.07 · 1844	*Caesium*
1772	*Calcium*†	1886	*Rhodium*	55 · Cs
Oxygen†	20 · Ca	*Arsenic*	45 · Rh	132.9055
8 · O · 15.9994	40.078 · 1808	33 · As	102.9055	1860
1771	*Scandium*	74.9216	1803	*Barium*
Fluorine	21 · Sc	ancient	*Palladium*	56 · Ba
9 · F · 18.9984	44.9559 · 1879	*Selenium*	46 · Pd	137.327 · 1808
1886	*Titanium*	34 · Se · 78.96	106.42 · 1803	*Lanthanum*
Neon	22 · Ti	1817	*Silver*	57 · La
10 · Ne	47.867 · 1791	*Bromine*	47 · Ag	138.9055
20.1797 · 1898	*Vanadium*	35 · Br	107.8682	1839
Sodium‡	23 · V	79.904 · 1826	ancient	*Cerium*
11 · Na	50.9415 · 1830	*Krypton*	*Cadmium*	58 · Ce
22.9897	*Chromium*	36 · Kr	48 · Cd	140.116
1807	24 · Cr	83.798 · 1898	112.411 · 1817	1803
Magnesium†	51.9961 · 1797	*Rubidium*	*Indium*	*Praseodymium*
12 · Mg	*Manganese*†	37 · Rb	49 · In	59 · Pr
24.305	25 · Mn	85.4678	114.818	140.9077
1755	54.938 · 1774	1861	1863	1885

———— THE CHEMICAL ELEMENTS cont. ————

Neodymium	Lutetium	Lead	Neptunium*	1968
60 · Nd	71 · Lu	82 · Pb	93 · Np · 237	Seaborgium*
144.242 · 1885	174.967	207.2	1940	106 · Sg · 266
Promethium*	1907	ancient	Plutonium*	1974
61 · Pm · 145	Hafnium	Bismuth	94 · Pu · 244	Bohrium*
1945	72 · Hf	83 · Bi	1940	107 · Bh · 264
Samarium	178.49	208.9804	Americium*	1981
62 · Sm	1923	· 1753	95 · Am · 243	Hassium*
150.36 · 1879	Tantalum	Polonium	1944	108 · Hs · 277
Europium	73 · Ta	84 · Po · 209	Curium*	1984
63 · Eu	180.9479	1898	96† · Cm · 247	Meitnerium*
151.964	1802	Astatine*	1944	109 · Mt · 268
1901	Tungsten	85 · At · 210	Berkelium*	1982
Gadolinium	74 · W	1940	97 · Bk · 247	Darmstadtium*
64 · Gd	183.84 · 1781	Radon	1949	110 · Ds · 271
157.25 · 1880	Rhenium	86 · Rn · 222	Californium*	1994
Terbium	75 · Re	1900	98 · Cf · 251	Roentgenium*
65 · Tb	186.207 · 1925	Francium*	1950	111 · Rg · 272
158.9253	Osmium	87 · Fr · 223	Einsteinium*	1994
1843	76 · Os	1939	99 · Es · 252	Ununbium*
Dysprosium	190.23 · 1803	Radium	1952	112 · Uub
66 · Dy · 162.5	Iridium	88 · Ra · 226	Fermium*	285 · 1996
1886	77 · Ir	1898	100 · Fm	Ununtrium*
Holmium	192.217 · 1803	Actinium	257 · 1952	113 · Uut · 284
67 · Ho	Platinum	89 · Ac · 227	Mendelevium*	2004
164.9303	78 · Pt	1899	101 · Md	Ununquadium*
1878	195.084 · 1735	Thorium	258 · 1955	114 · Uuq
Erbium	Gold	90 · Th	Nobelium*	289 · 1998
68 · Er	79 · Au	232.0381	102 · No · 259	Ununpentium*
167.259	196.9665	1828	1958	115 · Uup
1842	ancient	Protactinium	Lawrencium*	288 · 2004
Thulium	Mercury	91 · Pa	103 · Lr · 262	Ununhexium*
69 · Tm	80 · Hg · 200.5	231.0359	1961	116 · Uuh · 292
168.9342	ancient	1913	Rutherfordium*	2000
1879	Thallium	Uranium	104 · Rf · 261	Ununoctium*
Ytterbium	81 · Tl	92 · U	1964	118 · Uuo
70 · Yb	204.3833	238.0289	Dubnium*	294
173.04 · 1878	1861	1789	105 · Db · 262	2002

Key: * = *not found naturally on Earth.* † = *essential to most living organisms.* ‡ = *essential to animals.*

The Intl Union of Pure and Applied Chemistry (IUPAC) has assigned temporary names to elements 113, 114, 115, 116, and 118 (117 has yet to be discovered). The IUPAC assigns these names by translating each digit of the element's atomic number into Latin or Greek, then adding the suffix '-ium'. Discoverers may propose a final name based on a myth, mineral, place, or scientist. In June, the IUPAC officially confirmed element 112; its discoverers proposed the name 'copernicium', after Nicolaus Copernicus.

———————————— SPACE JUNK ————————————

On 10 February 2009, the defunct Russian military communications satellite *Cosmos 2251* crashed into the American commercial satellite *Iridium 33*. This was the first-ever collision between two intact satellites. The impact, which occurred as both machines travelled at *c.*22,000mph some 491 miles over Siberia, produced >600 pieces of debris that may eventually threaten the International Space Station and the Hubble telescope. While the risk of such collisions is extremely low, the incident caused scientists to express concern over the increasing quantity of 'space junk' orbiting the planet – including obsolete satellites and objects lost by space crews (e.g., the $100,000 tool bag accidentally discarded by a US astronaut during her November 2008 spacewalk†). The US military currently tracks *c.*19,000 man-made objects orbiting the Earth, although a total of *c.*300,000 objects bigger than 1cm are said now to circle the globe – the majority of which are not tracked. The February collision spurred calls for stricter adherence to the Inter-Agency Space Debris Coordination Committee's 'space debris mitigation guidelines', created in 2002. Among other requests, these guidelines ask that space programmes remove from densely populated and useful orbits all spacecraft which have completed their missions – lest a cascade of collisions leaves these regions too dangerous for space exploration.

† Some other objects lost in space include: *a glove*, lost in 1965 by Ed White, the first American on a spacewalk; *pliers*, lost by an astronaut fixing a solar array on the International Space Station in November 2007; *a spatula*, lost in 2006 during a mission by the space shuttle *Discovery*; *a 'very expensive' camera*, lost by an astronaut in June 2007 while repairing another solar array on the Space Station.

———————————— ANIMALS IN SPACE ————————————

Four teddy bears flew into space in December 2008, launched on a weather balloon as part of a stunt by the Cambridge University space club to encourage youth interest in science. The 'teddy-nauts' soared 30km above Earth on their two-hour journey, and were kept warm in special suits designed by Year 8 pupils from nearby schools. Below are some of the other (real) animals that have been sent into space:

1783	*a sheep, cockerel, and duck, on a balloon test flight by the Montgolfier brothers*
1948–49	*rhesus monkeys Albert I, II, and IV, by the US space programme*
1951	*the monkey Yorick, by the US (first animal to survive a space flight)*
1951–52	*the dogs Dezik and Tsygan, by the USSR (first dogs in suborbital space)*
1957	*the dog Laika, by the USSR (first dog to reach orbit)*
1960	*a grey rabbit, 40 mice, 2 rats, dogs Belka and Strelka, by the USSR*
1961	*Ham, by NASA (first chimp in space)*
1963	*Felix the cat, by the French*
1968	*turtles, wine flies, and mealworms, by the Russians*
1969	*Bonnie, a pig-tailed monkey, by the USSR*
1973	*Anita and Arabella, common Cross spiders, by NASA*

[Source: NASA, BBC, *The Times*.] Although animals and insects are still sometimes sent into space for biological experiments, they generally receive less attention than the brave pioneers listed above.

———————— KEY SPACE MISSIONS OF 2009 ————————

HERSCHEL & PLANCK · In May 2009, the European Space Agency (ESA) launched two telescopes – Herschel and Plank – on a single Ariane 5 rocket. Herschel, the largest and most powerful telescope ever sent into space, will scan far-infrared and sub-millimetre wavelengths of light to observe the formation of stars and galaxies. Planck will survey the sky to measure the Cosmic Microwave Background (light left over from 380,000 years after the Big Bang), which will help elucidate the age and shape of the cosmos.

GOCE · ESA's Gravity field and steady-state Ocean Circulation Explorer (GOCE), launched in March 2009, is currently orbiting the Earth to create a detailed map of the subtle variations in the Earth's gravitational field. This knowledge will help scientists create more accurate measurements of ocean circulation and sea level change.

KEPLER · Launched in March 2009, NASA's Kepler telescope will rove in an extended solar orbit for 3½ years, monitoring the brightness of 100,000 stars to gather information on the structure of other planetary systems, and to look for planets that could be similar to Earth.

SERVICING MISSION 4 · In May 2009, NASA launched the final trip to the Hubble telescope in order to repair several instruments and install a new camera. The Hubble was sent into space in 1990, and will be retired in 2010.

LUNAR RECONNAISSANCE ORBITER (LRO) · NASA launched the LRO into a low polar orbit around the Moon in June 2009. The satellite's mission is to create a comprehensive atlas of the Moon's features, which will help prepare for another manned mission to the Moon and a future lunar outpost.

20 July 2009 marked the 40th anniversary of the first human to land on the moon: the *Eagle* landed at 20:17 GMT on 20 July 1969. At 2:65 GMT on 21 July, Neil Armstrong stepped onto the moon's surface and uttered his famous words: 'That's one small step for man, one giant leap for mankind'. Although debate still surrounds whether he said 'a man' or just 'man'.

———————— PLANETARY EVENTS 2010 ————————

3 January.....................*Perihelion: Earth is at orbital position closest to the Sun*
15 January...................*Annular solar eclipse: visible in parts of Africa and Asia*
29 January................................*Mars at opposition: closest approach to Earth*
20 March......... *Equinox: the Sun passes northward over the equator at 17:32 GMT*
22 March...*Saturn at opposition*
21 June...........*Solstice: the Sun directly above the Tropic of Cancer at 11:28 GMT*
26 June..*Partial lunar eclipse: visible in E Asia, Australia, the Pacific & W Americas*
6 July.......................*Aphelion: Earth is at orbital position farthest from the Sun*
11 July......... *Total solar eclipse: visible in S Pacific, parts of S Chile and Argentina*
23 September .....*Equinox: the Sun passes southward over the equator at 3:09 GMT*
21 December.........*Solstice: Sun directly above Tropic of Capricorn at 23:38 GMT*
21 December......*Total lunar eclipse: visible in E Asia, Australia, the Pacific Ocean,*
                                                            the Americas and Europe

─────── SOME INVENTIONS OF NOTE · 2008–9 ───────

{OCT 2008} A Japanese games manufacturer released a piece of software that turns mobile phones into musical instruments. Users can choose their preferred instrument and melody and then 'play' songs by waving their phones in the air. Several phones can be synchronised to form a telephonic 'orchestra'. {DEC} · Australian researchers demonstrated a novel implant to release a drug from inside the body. The 'biobattery' is constructed from materials which create a current as they degrade, reversing the electrostatic charges that keep the drug contained. ❦ In its 'Best of 2008' issue, *Popular Science* magazine highlighted the CellScope – a camera/phone/microscope that can take images of blood and skin in the field and transmit them to a lab for diagnosis. ❦ *The Guardian* reported on a retired Oxford professor who has invented glasses that can be changed by the wearer to fit any prescription. The glasses rely on clear fluid-filled sacs inside the lenses, which can be expanded (for stronger prescriptions) or contracted (for weaker ones) with an attached syringe. The professor hopes to send the spectacles to a billion of the world's poorest people by 2020. ❦ University of Utah researchers developed a car key that uses Bluetooth technology to send the user's mobile into a 'safe' mode, preventing talking and texting. The researchers hope to develop commercial applications targeting the parents of teenagers. {JAN 2009} · *The Journal of Micromechanics and Microengineering* reported on the creation of a motor only twice the size of a human hair. The motor could one day power surgical robots inside the body. ❦ Scientists at the Ministry of Defence unveiled an ultra-hard steel vehicle armour called Super Bainite, which uses a 'string vest' of holes to deflect enemy bullets. {MAR} · A car that can turn into an aeroplane completed its maiden voyage at Plattsburgh International Airport, New York. The $194,000 Terrafugia is small enough to fit into a driveway, but has retractable wings that extend in 30 seconds; it can fly at 115mph. ❦ Researchers at the University of Strathclyde developed a thin film that turns pink when exposed to UV rays for an extended period of time. The developers said they planned to create a wearable device that would alert sunbathers when they had spent too much time outdoors. {APR} · American designer James Pierce created a series of domestic objects designed to increase our sense of attachment to them, thereby discouraging their replacement. The series included a table with a counter that records the number of heavy objects placed on it, and a clock that occasionally displays the wrong time – before saying it was only joking. {MAY} Inventors funded by the US Defense Department unveiled a bionic arm vastly more functional than its predecessors. The arm, nicknamed 'Luke' (after Luke Skywalker) can perform a range of tasks from picking up a grape to operating power tools. {JUN} A research team at the University of New South Wales created a stem-cell enhanced contact lens which can restore sight in damaged corneas. {AUG} The Technical University of Dortmund created a material to help keep beer fresh in bottles for longer. The material screens out the riboflavin that causes beer to change flavour when exposed to light.

———————————— ROBOT ETHICS ————————————

In February 2009, scientists at California State Polytechnic University released a report on the ethics of using robots in the military. Sponsored by the US Navy's Office of Naval Research, the report examined the benefits and risks of using autonomous robots (those operating without any form of external control) in battle and in other military capacities. While autonomous robots are not yet a reality, they are increasingly a legitimate possibility. Development in the field has been accelerated by US Congressional mandates requiring a third of all deep-strike aircraft to be unmanned by 2010, and a third of all ground combat vehicles to be unmanned by 2015. While the use of robots may reduce military casualties, there are also significant risks, not least concerning how robots assess battlefield threats and distinguish between friend and foe. In light of such concerns, the report focused on the need to develop an Artificial Moral Agent (AMA) for robots, which may take the form of a built-in 'warrior code'. Famously, the science fiction writer Isaac Asimov proposed the 'Three Laws of Robotics' in his 1942 short story *Runaround* – these laws are:

[1] *A robot may not injure a human being or, through inaction, allow a human being to come to harm.* [2] *A robot must obey orders given to it by human beings, except where such orders would conflict with the First Law.* [3] *A robot must protect its own existence as long as such protection does not conflict with the First or Second Law.*

The report noted that Asimov's laws are unlikely to be useful in a military context which, by definition, can require causing harm to humans. Yet hope remains that an AMA based on international treaties and national military codes can be developed.

South Korea is reportedly at work on a 'Robot Ethics Charter' to govern robot development and use. ❦ In April 2009, scientists at Cambridge and Aberystwyth universities announced the first scientific discoveries made by a robot. The robot, named 'Adam', consists of a room of lab equipment, supplies, and machinery designed to examine the function of genes in yeast cells. With basic commands, Adam was able to devise and test 20 of his own hypotheses (12 proved correct). ❦ In July 2009, makers of the Energetically Autonomous Tactical Robot (EATR) felt obliged to correct reports that their creation would feed on human flesh. EATR is designed to keep itself supplied with fuel on long-range military missions by foraging for and 'digesting' available organic materials; some had feared that fallen soldiers or civilians might be on the menu. The robot's developers assured the public that EATR is 'strictly vegetarian'.

———————————— IBM & JEOPARDY ————————————

IBM is developing a computer system to compete against human beings on a future episode of the US game show *Jeopardy*, the company revealed in April 2009. The main challenge for the programme (nicknamed 'Watson' after IBM founder Thomas J. Watson Sr), will be to understand *Jeopardy* questions, since these often rely on puns, jokes, and double meanings that are easy for humans to understand but difficult for computers. If Watson succeeds, scientists say it could represent a remarkable step forward in building machines able to interact with mankind. While no date for the battle has yet been set, *Jeopardy* executives said they were considering pitting Watson against contestant Ken Jennings, who won 74 consecutive times in 2004.

─────────── SCI, TECH, NET WORDS OF NOTE ───────────

TWERD · a Twitter nerd. *Also* TWEET-UP · a real-world meeting with friends made on Twitter. *Also* TWUP · a (sexual) pick-up on Twitter. *Also* TWOOSH · a message of exactly 140 characters. *Also* TWITITION · a Twitter petition. (In the US, AT&T was forced to modify its iPhone upgrade policy in response to a popular online TWITITION.) *Also* TWITTURGY · Twittered prayers, &c.

PORN COPS · Facebook employees who remove inappropriate images.

CARROTMOB · a promised 'flashmob' of new customers for eco-friendly businesses. As Jeremy Caplan explained in *Time*, 'instead of steering clear of environmentally backward stores, why not reward businesses with mass purchases if they promise to use some of the money to get greener?'

A-SPACE · a social networking site established by the US government for the nation's intelligence agencies, allowing spooks to share news, links, and videos regarding security threats.

GALLISTICLE · online articles in the form of a list ('LISTICLES') with picture galleries that require repeated clicking, thus boosting page view figures (one measure of web traffic).

KOOGLE · A 'kosher' search engine, designed for Orthodox Jews, that filters out inappropriate material (kugel is a type of Jewish pudding).

NOT-SPOT · An area without broadband or wifi service; not a 'hot spot'.

CYBERGEDDON · the potentially catastrophic effect of a major internet attack on a state like China or the US.

MUSEOMICS · sequencing DNA from museum specimens.

HACKTIVISM · hacking into websites for political or ideological reasons. For instance, in early 2009, Palestinian hackers defaced websites belonging to the US military, NATO, and an Israeli bank, replacing pages with propaganda.

BANGOVER · the physical consequences of (excessive) head-banging, i.e., violently shaking one's head in time to the beat of heavy/hard metal/rock music.

RANGE ANXIETY · the fear of being stranded in an electric car because of insufficient battery performance.

THIRD-HAND SMOKE · cigarette-smoke contaminants that linger on clothing, hair, and other materials, posing potential health risks long after a cigarette has been extinguished.

DARK FLOW · a mysterious force discovered in 2008 pulling galaxy clusters in a particular direction; possibly the gravitational force of other universes.

GREEN LINING · an eco silver lining · the environmental upside to an otherwise disagreeable occurrence, e.g., the recession causing a fall in car usage.

AIRPORT MALARIA · malaria contracted in or near an airport, transmitted by mosquitoes that have been carried by planes from malarial regions.

WED SITES · websites that allow couples to share their wedding with others.

PHARMASCOLDS · those critical of the relationship between the pharmaceutical industry and academic research.

———————— SCI, TECH, NET WORDS OF NOTE cont. ————————

GREENFINGER · a person or nation that launches a geoengineering scheme without global consensus [see p.191].

ECOMODDING · making mechanical and aerodynamic modifications to cars to boost mileage, whether for financial or ecological reasons. Sometimes combined with HYPERMILING – i.e., driving techniques used to save fuel.

GOLDILOCKS ZONE · the zone around stars that is neither too hot nor too cold to support life. NASA's Kepler satellite, launched in March 2009, will spend at least three and a half years searching for planets in this 'habitable zone' [see p.197].

WARCRAFT WIDOWS · the romantic partners of *World of Warcraft* obsessives.

SPITTERATI · those who attend SPIT PARTIES, where saliva is harvested for personalised gene sequencing services.

HARMONISE · Chinese slang for internet censorship – a reference to President Hu Jintao's vision of a 'harmonious society'. The term gained prominence in June 2009 during efforts to censor posts about the 20th anniversary of the Tiananmen Square protests [see p.81].

BING · Microsoft's new search engine – nicknamed, 'But It's Not Google'.

———————— SCIENTIFIC NAMES OF NOTE ————————

The scientific naming system used for plants and animals allows for a flexibility that occasionally produces curious results. For example, in March 2009, a new species of whitebeam tree discovered in North Devon was named *Sorbus admonitor*, or 'No Parking Whitebeam', because of the 'No Parking' sign nailed to the tree for many years (*admonitor* is Latin for 'admonish'). Other unusual recent species names include:

Danionella dracula · a tiny transparent fish discovered in Burma and documented in 2009; named after Count Dracula, because of pieces of bone that poke through its mouth like fangs. *Caloplaca obamae* · lichen discovered in California and documented in 2009; named for President Obama, to show appreciation for his 'support of science and science education'. *Histiophryne psychedelica* · frogfish discovered in Indonesia and documented in 2009; named for its vibrant peach-and-white stripes and erratic swimming style. *Materpiscis attenboroughi* · ancient fish whose fossil was discovered in Australia and documented in 2009; named after Sir David Attenborough, who drew attention to the fossil's site in his 1979 TV series *Life on Earth*. *Diamphipnoa colberti* · stonefly found in Chile and documented in 2008; named after the comedian Stephen Colbert†. *Beelzebufo ampinga* · ancient giant horned toad whose fossil was found in Madagascar and documented in 2008; named after Beelzebub, an ancient god and a nickname for the devil.

† In April 2009, US comedian Stephen Colbert's name was the winning entry in an online poll held by NASA to name a new room at the International Space Station. Despite the legions of fans who voted for Colbert, NASA retained the right to make the final pick, and chose the somewhat more banal runner-up 'Tranquillity'. However, NASA gamely agreed to name a new treadmill at the Space Station the 'Combined Operational Load Bearing External Resistance Treadmill' – or, COLBERT.

———————— ONLINE ACTIVITIES WORLDWIDE ————————

In December 2008, market researchers TNS released the results of their *Digital World, Digital Life* survey, which asked 18–55-year-old internet users in 16 countries a variety of questions about their online activities. On average, respondents said they spent 30% of their leisure time online, though this varied widely by country:

% leisure time spent online			
Italy............31	France........28	Sweden.......18	
US.............30	UK............28	Finland.......16	
China.........44	Spain.........29	Germany.....23	Denmark.....15
Korea.........40	Australia......29	Norway.......22	
Japan.........38	Canada.......28	Netherlands..19	(World.......30)

Not surprisingly, the amount of online leisure time varied with occupational status:

% leisure time online		
Student...............39	Not working.........33	[UK housewives spent 47%
Housewife............36	Working part-time...31	of their leisure time online,
	Working full-time....28	compared to 38% in the US.]

The survey also asked people about the importance of the internet in their lives. Below are the average scores given to the question, 'How much would not having the internet affect your daily routine and personal activities?'. Scores were given on a scale of 1–10, where 1 is 'would not impact at all', and 10 is 'would impact hugely':

China........7·7	Italy..........6·7	US............5·9	Sweden......5·2
Japan........7·3	Germany....6·4	Canada......5·8	Denmark....5·0
Korea........7·1	UK...........6·1	Spain........5·7	Norway.......4·3
France.......6·9	Netherlands.5·9	Australia.....5·4	Finland......4·2

In addition, the survey asked people to name the activities they had engaged in on the internet within the past month. The top ten activities around the world were:

Activity % of total respondents	
Used a search engine.................81	Visited a brand/product site.........61
Looked up the news 76	Paid bills...............................56
Used online banking.................74	Watched a video clip.................51
Looked up the weather..............65	Used a price comparison site........50
Researched a product/service........63	Listened to an audio clip............44

Around the world, the average person had 13 friends whom they had first met online. In the United Kingdom, the average was 17. The survey also revealed that in the UK:

58% .... *had met up with a friend they made on the internet*
45% .... *had telephone conversations with someone they met online*
37% ....*said they could not be sure of an online friend's identity*
25% .... *of the average respondent's friends were 'online-only friends'*
23% .... *of the average respondent's online-only friends were American*
17% .... *of the average respondent's online-only friends were Australian*

———————————————— E-WASTE ————————————————

The average EU citizen discards an astonishing 25kg of 'e-waste' each year, in the form of old computers, mobile phones, TVs, radios, and other electronic gadgets and household goods. The UN Environmental Program (UNEP) estimates that e-waste is now the fastest-growing component of municipal solid waste in Europe, and is projected to increase by 3–5% per annum. In total, the world produces 20–50m tonnes of e-waste every year. Below is the UNEP global breakdown of e-waste types:

Type of material	% of e-waste	Type of goods	% of e-waste
Refractory oxides†	30·2	Other household appliances‡	30
Plastics	30·2	Refrigerators	20
Copper	20·1	DVD players, VCRs, stereos, &c.	15
Iron	8·1	Computers, phones, faxes, printers	15
Tin	4·0	Televisions	10
Lead	2·0	Monitors	10
Aluminium	2·0		
Nickel	2·0	† Oxides with a high melting point, such as	
Zinc	1·0	aluminium oxide and silicon dioxide, which	
Silver	0·2	are prized in electronics manufacturing.	
Gold	0·1	‡ Washers, dryers, vacuum cleaners, &c.	

According to Greenpeace, only 25% of all the e-waste produced in Europe is safely recycled. The remainder ends up in incinerators (where burning can release dangerous heavy metals) or landfill (where toxic chemicals can leach into the groundwater). Environmental groups have also discovered that e-waste is routinely exported to developing countries, where scavengers mine the refuse for precious metals, often at great personal risk to their health. Greenpeace estimates that 23,000 tonnes of e-waste were illegally exported from the UK in 2003. Such exports are banned within the EU, but nonetheless flourish due to a lack of policing. According to the UN and Greenpeace, the main e-waste dumps in the developing world are:

Guiyu, CHINA · New Delhi, Sher Shah, Mumbai, and Chennai, INDIA
Lagos, NIGERIA · Accra, GHANA · Karachi, PAKISTAN

Approved recycling services for electronic waste can be found at: wastedirectory.netregs.gov.uk

———————————————— GAMING SALES ————————————————

UK sales of videogames hit an all-time high in 2008, reaching a total of 82·8m units, and a value of £4·03bn, according to the Entertainment and Leisure Software Publishers Association (ELSPA). Further details on 2008 gaming sales are below:

Sales of	value £		
Games	1·9bn	Nintendo Wii software	481m
Consoles	1·4bn	Microsoft Xbox 360 software	443m
Peripherals	549m	Nintendo DS software	366m
		Sony Playstation 3 software	334m

—— DANGEROUS CODE ——

In January 2009, a group of international cyber-security organisations, led by the US National Security Agency, released a list of the 25 most dangerous computer programming errors that could leave software vulnerable to hackers. This list (unranked, but in categories) also illustrates how little the average user knows about the systems upon which they place so much faith:

INSECURE INTERACTION
BETWEEN COMPONENTS
Improper input validation
Improper encoding or escaping of output
Failure to preserve SQL query structure
Failure to preserve web page structure
Failure to preserve OS
command structure
Cleartext transmission of sensitive data
Cross-site request forgery
Race condition
Error message information leak

RISKY RESOURCE MANAGEMENT
Failure to constrain operations within
the bounds of a memory buffer
External control of critical state data
External control of file name or path
Untrusted search path
Failure to control generation of code
Code download without integrity check
Improper resource shutdown or release
Improper initialisation
Incorrect calculation

POROUS DEFENCES
Improper access control (authorisation)
Broken or risky cryptographic algorithm
Hard-coded password
Insecure permission assignment
for critical resource
Use of insufficiently random values
Execution with unnecessary privileges
Client-side enforcement of
server-side security

—— WIKI VANDALISM ——

In January 2009, Alan Titchmarsh found himself the target of a Wikipedia attack, after vandals modified his biography on 'the free encyclopedia that anyone can edit' to claim (falsely) that he was writing a guide to the *Kama Sutra*. Titchmarsh is far from alone in suffering from 'Wiki-vandalism'. The site maintains a list of entries with 'extraordinarily high vandalism', which includes:

Adolf Hitler · Asian American · Ass
Axl Rose · Borat · Cancer
Chuck Norris · Elizabeth I · Hemingway
Ford Mustang · Halo 2
Hurricane Katrina · Iraq · Jew
Kazakhstan · Leet · Beethoven · Liver
Manchester United · Nipple · Obesity
Pakistan · PM of Canada · Rapping
Stingray · Texas · Uzbekistan

In August 2009, Wikipedia said changes to entries on living people would soon be subject to review by experienced editors before going live.

—— 2009 WEBBY AWARDS ——

Celebrity	*omg.yahoo.com*
Charity	*nature.org*
Community	*flickr.com*
Education	*smarthistory.org*
Fashion	*red-issue.com*
Games	*clubpenguin.com*
Guides/reviews	*veryshortlist.com*
Humour	*theonion.com*
Lifestyle	*bbc.co.uk/bloom*
Magazine	*theatlantic.com*
Music	*npr.org/music*
News	*bbc.com/news*

Webby Award acceptance speeches are limited to 5 words. In 2009, Arianna Huffington's (for Best Politics Site) was, 'I didn't kill newspapers, okay?' [see p.135]. Trent Reznor's (for Artist of the Year) was, 'Wait, we didn't charge anything?'

—————————— STN SIGNIFICA ——————————

Some (in)significa(nt) Sci, Tech, Net footnotes to the year. ❧ Burger King launched a US promotion called 'Whopper Sacrifice', in which those who agreed to delete 10 of their Facebook friends received a free 'Angry Whopper' sandwich. *The New York Times* noted that, given the burger's retail value of $3·69, Facebookers who agreed to the deal valued each of their digital friendships at *c.*37 cents (*c.*24 pence). ❧ Prankster(s) in Austin, Texas, hacked into a digital road sign and changed the display to read 'Zombies Ahead'. Soon afterwards, hackers on Australia's Gold Coast followed suit, posting the message, 'Nobody has ever loved you'. ❧ A University of California team that hijacked a (real) spam network to send out its own (fake) messages concluded that spam typically enjoys a response rate of 0·00001%. ❧ The Indian space programme asked food scientists to create a 'space curry' that astronauts could eat while in orbit on the nation's first manned space mission in 2015. The move followed South Korea's successful 2008 attempt to engineer a 'space kimchi'. ❧ During Barack Obama's inauguration ceremony, Facebook reported *c.*4,000 status updates per minute [see p.267]. ❧ The Egyptian health ministry issued a statement denying the existence of a 'killer text message', amid reports that a man south of Cairo died of a brain haemorrhage immediately after receiving a text message containing a mysterious string of numbers. ❧ Several UK political leaders succumbed to a Facebook game asking people to list '25 random things' about themselves. John Prescott admitted that he'd seen the film *Billy Elliot* six times; Scottish

MP Tom Harris said he'd been to see Eurovision-winning group Bucks Fizz twice; and Nick Clegg revealed that he'd once eaten fried bees. ❧ A study sponsored by NASA found that after six months in the weightless environment of the International Space Station, the muscles of a young astronaut wasted to match those of a typical 80-year-old. ❧ A teenager, inspired by a TV programme on Google Earth, managed to paint a 60ft cartoon of a penis on the roof of his family's home near Hungerford, Berks. The painting remained in place for a year, until a pilot spotted it and tipped off a newspaper. ❧ A New Zealand court allowed legal papers to be served via Facebook to a man who fled the country after allegedly embezzling funds from a family business. (Despite fleeing, the man continued to post updates to his Facebook page.) ❧ Users of the text-to-voice feature on the Kindle 2 e-reader were surprised to discover that the device mispronounced the name 'Barack Obama' as a phrase that sounded like 'Black Alabama'. ❧ A website called ScenicOrNot, modelled on the popular site HotOrNot, asked visitors to rate the 'scenicness' of snapshots of England, Scotland, or Wales, with the aim of producing a map of the most beautiful spots in the UK. ❧ Wikipedia announced that its page on Michael Jackson received more hits in the hours after his death than any other entry in the site's history. ❧ The Cloud Appreciation Society began lobbying to add *Undulatus asperatus* to the World Meteorological Organization's International Cloud Atlas. If they are successful, the dark, roiling clouds would be the first added to the *Cloud Atlas* since 1951.

SI PREFIXES

Below are the SI prefixes and symbols for the decimal multiples and submultiples of SI Units from 10^{24} to 10^{-24}.

10^{24}	yotta	Y	1 000 000 000 000 000 000 000 000
10^{21}	zetta	Z	1 000 000 000 000 000 000 000
10^{18}	exa	E	1 000 000 000 000 000 000
10^{15}	peta	P	1 000 000 000 000 000
10^{12}	tera	T	1 000 000 000 000
10^{9}	giga	G	1 000 000 000
10^{6}	mega	M	1 000 000
10^{3}	kilo	k	1 000
10^{2}	hecto	h	100
10	deca	da	10
1			1
10^{-1}	deci	d	0.1
10^{-2}	centi	c	0.01
10^{-3}	milli	m	0.001
10^{-6}	micro		0.000 001
10^{-9}	nano	n	0.000 000 001
10^{-12}	pico	p	0.000 000 000 001
10^{-15}	femto	f	0.000 000 000 000 001
10^{-18}	atto	a	0.000 000 000 000 000 001
10^{-21}	zepto	z	0.000 000 000 000 000 000 001
10^{-24}	yocto	y	0.000 000 000 000 000 000 000 001

SOME USEFUL CONVERSIONS

A	A *to* B *multiply by*	B *to* A *multiply by*	B
inches	25.4	0.0397	millimetres
inches	2.54	0.3937	centimetres
feet	0.3048	3.2808	metres
yards	0.9144	1.0936	metres
miles	1.6093	0.6214	kilometres
acres	0.4047	2.471	hectares
square feet	0.0929	10.76	square metres
square miles	2.5899	0.3861	square kilometres
UK pints	0.5682	1.7598	litres
UK gallons	4.546	0.2199	litres
cubic inches	16.39	0.0610	cubic centimetres
ounces	28.35	0.0353	grams
pounds	0.4536	2.2046	kilograms
stones	6.35	0.157	kilograms
miles/gallon	0.3539	2.825	kilometres/litre
miles/US gallon	0.4250	2.353	kilometres/litre
miles/hour	1.609	0.6117	kilometres/hour

°C – °F

°C	°F		°C	°F
			49	120.2
100	212		48	118.4
99	210.2		47	116.6
98	208.4		46	114.8
97	206.6		45	113
96	204.8		44	111.2
95	203		43	109.4
94	201.2		42	107.6
93	199.4		41	105.8
92	197.6		40	104
91	195.8		39	102.2
90	194		38	100.4
89	192.2		37	98.6
88	190.4		36	96.8
87	188.6		35	95
86	186.8		34	93.2
85	185		33	91.4
84	183.2		32	89.6
83	181.4		31	87.8
82	179.6		30	86
81	177.8		29	84.2
80	176		28	82.4
79	174.2		27	80.6
78	172.4		26	78.8
77	170.6		25	77
76	168.8		24	75.2
75	167		23	73.4
74	165.2		22	71.6
73	163.4		21	69.8
72	161.6		20	68
71	159.8		19	66.2
70	158		18	64.4
69	156.2		17	62.6
68	154.4		16	60.8
67	152.6		15	59
66	150.8		14	57.2
65	149		13	55.4
64	147.2		12	53.6
63	145.4		11	51.8
62	143.6		10	50
61	141.8		9	48.2
60	140		8	46.4
59	138.2		7	44.6
58	136.4		6	42.8
57	134.6		5	41
56	132.8		4	39.2
55	131		3	37.4
54	129.2		2	35.6
53	127.4		1	33.8
52	125.6		0	32
51	123.8		-1	30.2
50	122		-2	28.4

Normal body temp.
= 37°C (98.6°F)
range 36.1–37.2°C
(97.7–98.9°F)

Travel & Leisure

*The wisdom of a learned man cometh by opportunity of leisure: and he that
hath little business shall become wise. How can he get wisdom that holdeth
the plough, and that glorieth in the goad, that driveth oxen, and is occupied
in their labours, and whose talk is of bullocks?* – ECCLESIASTICUS 38:24–25

——CAR PRODUCTION & THE 'SCRAPPAGE' SCHEME——

The impact of the recession severely tested the British car industry in 2009, as jobs
were shed across the sector, including: 1,200 at Nissan in Sunderland, 600 at the
Aston Martin plant in Warwickshire, and >450 at various Jaguar Land Rover sites. ❦
According to the Society of Motor Manufacturers and Traders (SMMT), more than
800,000 are employed in the UK automotive sector, from manufacture through
to sales. Below are the sixteen car manufacture companies operating in Britain:

Manufacturer	location
Aston Martin	Gaydon
Bentley	Crewe
BMW (Mini)	Oxford
Caterham†	Dartford
Honda	Swindon
Jaguar	Birmingham, Halewood
Land Rover	Halewood, Solihull
Lotus	Norwich
LTI‡	Coventry
MG Motors	Longbridge
Mercedes-Benz	MTC Woking
Morgan	Malvern
Nissan	Sunderland
Rolls-Royce	Goodwood
Toyota	Burnaston, Deeside
Vauxhall	Ellesmere Port

† Maker of the Seven kit car. ‡ Manufacturer
of purpose-built 'black cab' taxis.

Car production fell by 58·7% in January 2009, as the credit crunch forced many
manufacturers to shut down assembly lines over Christmas. To counteract a precipitous fall in sales, the Chancellor introduced a car 'scrappage' scheme in his April
2009 Budget [see p.234]. This scheme allows consumers to scrap an old car (so long
as it is >10 years old) and receive £2,000 towards the cost of a new ('greener') car. In
September 2009, the SMMT announced that 100,000 new cars had been registered
under the scheme, and 100,000 more were on order. After 15 consecutive months
of decline in new car sales, the scrappage scheme increased demand with year-
on-year growth in July and August 2009. ❦ The most popular cars in 2008 were:

Top five models produced in the UK			Top five car producers in the UK	
Make	*model*	*No. of cars*	*Make*	*No. of cars*
BMW	Mini	234,461	Nissan	386,555
Nissan	Qashqai	224,989	BMW (Mini)	234,461
Honda	CR-V	120,150	Honda	230,423
Toyota	Avensis	110,741	Toyota	213,329
Honda	Civic	110,273	Land Rover	184,831

———————————— TRANSLATING DRIVING TESTS ————————————

The Driver and Vehicle Licensing Agency spent £120,900 in 2008–09 translating documents into languages other than English, according to data released by the Department for Transport under the Freedom of Information Act. Below are the number of driving theory tests taken in a language other than English in 2008–09:

Language	No. tests				
Urdu	18,959	Tamil	4,352	Pushto	457
Kurdish	10,295	Portuguese	2,717	Mirpuri	283
Polish	9,757	Gujurati	2,436	Welsh†	20
Bengali	6,229	Cantonese	2,308	Kashmiri	5
Farsi	5,356	Dari	1,256		
Punjabi	5,102	Spanish (Castillian)	985		
Arabic	4,434	Hindi	582		
		Albanian	508		

† The latest (2001) census revealed that 20·8% of people in Wales speak Welsh.

———————————— CARS ON THE ROAD BY AGE ————————————

There were 31,105,988 cars on UK roads in 2007, according to the Society of Motor Manufacturers and Traders. Below is a breakdown of cars by age of vehicle:

Age of vehicle (years)	No. on road
<3	7,159,203
3–6	7,727,679
6–9	6,717,831
9–12	5,142,739
>12	4,358,536

[Source: SMMT · Motor Industry Facts 2008]
The average motorist drove 90 fewer miles in 2008 than 2007, the first decline for 30 years.

———————————————— ROADKILL ————————————————

The number of hedgehogs in Britain is decreasing, according to the 2008 Roadkill Survey by the People's Trust for Endangered Species. Although hedgehogs are the second most likely animal to be crushed underwheel, the numbers found dead have fallen by 7·5% since the research began in 2001. The roadkill survey is conducted by volunteers each year between July and September: dead and living animals are counted by drivers across the country, and an estimate of the population is extrapolated. Below is a breakdown of the animals killed on Britain's roads in 2008:

Road casualty	%				
Rabbit	58	Fox	4	Small mustelid†	1
Hedgehog	16	Badger	3		
Grey squirrel	4	Rat	2		
		Deer	1		

† Includes stoats, weasels, polecats, and minks.

Tests carried out by Royal Holloway, University of London, suggested that hedgehogs have less road sense than rabbits. Researchers observed that rabbits tend to flee when vehicles are 161 metres away – giving them 6 seconds to hop from a car approaching at 60mph. Hedgehogs, however, are slower off the mark, reacting to vehicles when they are just 8 metres away, leaving them little chance of escape.

———————————— TOP ENERGY SOURCES ————————————

Electricity generated by wind turbines and captured in batteries is the cleanest and safest source of energy for cars and trucks, according to a 2008 study by Stanford University professor Mark Jacobson. The study, published in *Energy & Environmental Science*, ranked 12 combinations of energy sources and vehicle technologies according to their ability simultaneously to solve climate, air pollution, and energy security problems. The various combinations were ranked as follows:

1 .. *Wind-powered battery-electric vehicles [BEVs]*.....least pollution & impact, safest
2 .. *Wind-powered hydrogen fuel cell vehicles*.................as above, but less efficient
3 .. *Concentrated-solar-powered BEVs* ..low emissions & safe, but use more resources
4 .. *Geothermal-powered BEVs*............. low impact, but poor resource availability
5 .. *Tidal-powered BEVs*.........low impact from technology, secure but unreliable
6 .. *Solar-photovoltaic-powered BEVs*...............abundant resource but unreliable
7 .. *Wave-powered BEVs*............................... small footprint but unreliable
8 .. *Hydroelectric-powered BEVs*.............big footprint, disruptive, though reliable
9 .. *Nuclear-powered BEVs* ....thermal pollution, waste, risk of mortality
= .. *Coal-with-carbon-capture-powered BEVs*.......thermal pollution, high emissions
11. *Corn-E85 vehicles*...................polluting, uses costly resources, high impact
12. *Cellulosic-E85 vehicles*........... as corn, but larger footprint & more pollution

According to the study, as of 2007 the US could theoretically replace all cars and trucks with battery-electric vehicles powered by energy from 73,000–144,000 wind turbines. Doing so would cut US carbon emissions by 32%, and eliminate *c.*15,000 vehicle-related air pollution deaths by 2020. 2·2–3·6m turbines could theoretically replace the power generated by all fossil fuels in the world.

———————————— UNUSUAL FUELS ————————————

The race to replace fossil fuels has led companies to devise ever more innovative and unusual methods of energy production. Below are some recent examples of note: In February 2008, Virgin Atlantic flew a 747 from London to Amsterdam with a tank partially powered by fuel made from coconuts and Brazilian babassu nuts. ❦ In November 2008, scientists from the University of Nevada described producing diesel fuel from used coffee grounds collected at Starbucks. ❦ Also in November 2008, Professor Gary Strobel of Montana State University announced the discovery of a fungus (*Gliocladium roseum*) growing in trees in the Patagonian rainforest that naturally produces a diesel-like gas. ❦ In December 2008, Air New Zealand flew a 747 partially powered by oil derived from the poisonous tropical shrub jatropha. ❦ In January 2009, Continental Airlines sent a Boeing 737 on a two-hour journey over the Gulf of Mexico with one engine partially powered by oil derived from algae (yes, it was green). ❦ Also in January 2009, the inaugural Zayed Future Energy Prize was awarded by the Crown Prince of Abu Dhabi to Bangladeshi company Grameen Shakti for projects transforming cattle and poultry waste into usable fuel. ❦ In May 2009, Warwick University unveiled a 125mph Formula 3 racing car made from sustainable materials. The steering wheel was fashioned from carrots, the bodywork from potatoes, and the engine ran on waste chocolate and vegetable oil.

———————————— MOST CONVICTED DRIVERS ————————————

12·6% of all UK drivers have penalty points on their licence, according to figures compiled in February 2009 by Admiral Insurance. An analysis of 1·6m motor insurance policies revealed the professions most and least likely to have penalty points:

Reckless professions	*% with points*	*Cautious professions*	*% with points*
Lawyers	20·1	Hairdressers/beauticians	8·9
Doctors	18·7	Retired	9·6
Religious leaders	16·4	Waiting/bar staff	9·6
Police	15·8	Sales assistant	10·4
Education	13·9	Administrator	10·5

Drivers aged 16–34 are most likely to receive a parking ticket, according to DfT statistics released in May 2009. 32% of drivers aged 16–34 had received a parking ticket in the preceding 12 months, compared to 18% of 35–44-year-olds, 11% of 45–54-year-olds, 18% of 55–64-year-olds, and 5% of those aged 65 or over. Of all those who had been issued a parking ticket in the last 12 months, 59% received one ticket, 28% received two, and 13% received three or more parking tickets. 37% of those who had received a parking ticket in the last 12 months did not accept that they had parked illegally.

———————————— MOST POPULAR CAR COLOURS ————————————

SMMT's *Motor Industry Facts 2008* revealed the most popular UK car colours:

1997	*cars*	2007	*cars*
Red	6,733,640	Blue	7,522,576
Blue	6,284,838	Silver	7,345,841
White	3,561,778	Red	4,497,237
Green	2,275,329	Black	3,975,773
Silver	2,068,196	Green	2,948,959

———————————— BICYCLE THEFTS ————————————

The insurance company More Than deliberately abandoned unsecured shiny new bicycles in some of Britain's biggest cities to test how long it would take for the bikes to be stolen. The results of this experiment, published in June 2009, exposed London Bridge railway station as the home of the country's speediest thieves. The time taken for the bikes to be pilfered from various locations around Britain is below:

Location	*time until stolen*		
London Bridge Station	17m	Exchange St, Norwich	2h 34m
Buchanan St, Glasgow	1h 30m	Market St, Manchester	2h 57m
Edgbaston St, Birmingham	1h 55m	East St, Bristol	3h 15m
Queen St, Cardiff	2h 10m	Matthew St, Liverpool	3h 52m
Albert Rd, Portsmouth	2h 12m		
Percy St, Newcastle	2h 25m		

Figures from 2007 revealed that a bicycle is stolen in England every 71 seconds.

---------------------------- QUEUING ----------------------------

The average British adult spends 67 hours a year queuing, confirming the cliché that the Brits can't resist standing in line. The survey by online auction site madbid.com revealed that, during their lifetime, adults will queue for an average of 169 hours (5 months, 2 weeks, 5 days). Britons spend longest queuing at the following locations:

Location average queuing mins./month	
Supermarket..................................53	Clothes shops 33
Waiting for bus/train 43	Bank/post office.....................27
At the bar 35	Cash machine........................25
	Customer service desk..............17

82% of respondents thought queuing was a British tradition, although 25% hated having to wait for anything. 88% revealed that they had abandoned their place after queuing for an especially long time.

-------- DEATHS FROM MOTOR ACCIDENTS · EUROPE --------

Below are the standardised death rates (SDR), per 100,000 population, for motor vehicle traffic accidents in some selected European countries (latest data from 2005):

Deaths per 100,000	♂	♀		♂	♀
Lithuania†	36·3	10·1	Spain	16·0	4·0
Cyprus	28·7	5·2	France	12·6	4·0
Latvia	28·5	9·1	Germany	9·0	3·0
Greece	24·1	6·4	Ireland	8·5	3·7
Poland	21·1	5·5	UK	8·2	2·2
Italy	17·3	4·1	Sweden	6·7	2·2
			Netherlands	6·4	2·1

[Source: World Health Organisation] † Lithuania also has the highest suicide rate in the world. 68·1 males kill themselves per 100,000 population every year, compared to 10·4 male suicides in the UK. The WHO estimates that China, India, and Japan account for 40% of all suicides worldwide.

------------------ WHERE TO SIT ON A BUS ------------------

Dr Tom Fawcett of Salford University carried out an observational study of bus passengers in January 2008, and concluded that passengers' personalities could be deduced from where on a bus they chose to sit. Dr Fawcett proposed seven groups:

Choose to sit — personality traits
Front of lower deck....................................*gregarious, meeters-and-greeters*
Middle of lower deck..*strong communicators*
Back of lower deck..... *risk-takers, choose elevated seats to make them feel important*
Front of top deck ....*forward thinkers*
Middle of top deck ....*independent thinkers, most likely to read or listen to music*
Back of top deck............*rebellious types, dislike their personal space to be invaded*
Anywhere...*chameleons, can fit in anywhere*

PUBLIC TRANSPORT

Bus and light rail use is increasing in England, according to the Department for Transport. Between 2000 and 2007/08, bus and light rail use rose by 19%, and in 2007/8, bus use rose 1·3% on the previous year, largely due to a 4·8% growth in use among Londoners. Since the introduction of free off-peak concessionary fares for the disabled and over 60s, in April 2008, 970m concessionary bus journeys have been made. A breakdown of public transport boardings during 2007/08 is below:

Transport	% share of boardings
Local buses	67
National Rail	16
London Underground	14
Light rail†	3

† The DLR accounts for 35% of all light rail boardings, followed by Tyne & Wear with 21%.

The Bus Passenger Satisfaction Survey revealed the experiences of bus passengers:

Had a seat	97%
Sat upstairs [see p.211]	27
Sat downstairs [see p.211]	73
At bus stop: had a shelter	78
· had a countdown screen	16
Bus: double deck	45
· single deck	55

A greater proportion sit upstairs on buses in London (32%). [Figures for England · 2007–08]

The punctuality of buses fluctuates over the course of the day, as shown by the following 2007–08 figures for the percentage of buses running late by time of day:

Time	% late				
07:00–07:59	4	11:00–11:59	9	16:00–16:59	18
08:00–08:59	19	12:00–12:59	9	17:00–17:59	14
09:00–09:59	17	13:00–13:59	15	18:00–18:59	14
10:00–10:59	11	14:00–14:59	12		
		15:00–15:59	13	Overall	13

The average age of the bus fleet across Britain, as of March 2008, was 8·3 years old. 93% of UK adults live within 13 miles of a bus stop, and 80% said there was at least an hourly bus service. 40% of British adults described themselves as regular bus users, and 27% used buses at least once a week.

TRAFFIC ON THE ROADS

Van mileage fell by 2% in the first quarter of 2009 – the first such drop in fifteen years, according to figures released by the Department for Transport in May. Compared to the same period in 2008, car traffic on motorways was down by 4%, and heavy goods vehicle traffic by 12% – a sign that the recession was causing a fall in the demand and delivery of goods. Below is a breakdown of traffic in 2008:

Vehicle	% of all 2008 traffic
Cars	78
Light vans	14
Heavy goods vehicles	6
Other	2

According to the RAC, the number of cars on the road has increased by 30% in the last decade.

―――――――――――――――――― MEGASHIPS ――――――――――――――――――

Megaships are defined as those that regularly carry more than 3,000 passengers. In December 2009, the largest megaship ever built was scheduled to set sail from Fort Lauderdale, Florida. The 220,000-ton *Oasis of the Seas*, part of the Royal Caribbean cruise line, is four times larger than the *Titanic* – but, fortunately, will be sailing in the Caribbean which tends to be iceberg-free. The ship has berths for 5,400 people, 16 decks, seven themed 'neighbourhoods', a high-wire act, the first dedicated aquatic amphitheatre, and a carousel. Before the *Oasis*, the largest megaships were the *Freedom* class of cruise ships from Royal Carribean; these included:

Freedom of the Seas	*Liberty of the Seas*	*Independence of the Seas*
Maiden voyage: 2006	Maiden voyage: 2007	Maiden voyage: 2008
Gross tonnage: 160,000	Gross tonnage: 160,000	Gross tonnage: 154,407
Passengers: 3,634	Passengers: 3,634	Passengers: 3,634
Features: rock-climbing wall, waterpark, geysers, ice skating rink.	Features: wave generator for surfing, whirlpools over the sea.	Features: golf course, cabaret, and three-storey theatre.

Prior to the launch of the *Freedom of the Seas*, the world's largest passenger ship was Cunard's *Queen Mary 2*. The 151,400-tonne ship first set sail in 2004, and included room for 3,056 passengers, 13 decks, 10 restaurants, a casino, and onboard lecturers.

―――――――――――――――― BUSIEST BRITISH PORTS ――――――――――――――――

There are 52 major ports in Britain; the top ten ports by tonnage in 2008 were:

Port	million tonnes		
Grimsby & Immingham	65·3	Milford Haven	35·9
London	53·0	Liverpool	32·2
Tees & Hartlepool	45·4	Felixstowe	25·0
Southampton	41·0	Dover	24·3
Forth	39·1	Medway	15·0

Below is a breakdown of major port traffic, by cargo type: [Source: DfT, 2008 data]

Liquid bulk	44%	Roll-on/roll-off cargo (Ro-Ro)	18
Dry bulk and general cargo	27	Lift-on lift-off containers (Lo-Lo)	11

Below is the Department for Transport's breakdown of the mode of travel of UK residents leaving Britain, and foreign residents entering: [2008 data, released in 2009]

UK residents' trips abroad		Mode	Overseas residents' trips to UK	
1980	2007		1980	2007
61	81	Air	59	77
39	12	Sea	41	14
–	7	Channel Tunnel	–	10

———————————— AIRCRAFT NOISE ————————————

In January 2009, the government announced that a third runway would be built at Heathrow airport. The runway will increase the area of Heathrow by 2km², and require the demolition of 700 houses and the loss of 230 hectares of greenbelt. Environmental groups vowed to continue their protests against the expansion, and local residents expressed concerns that aircraft noise would significantly increase. ❦ The Department for Transport (DfT) measures aircraft noise using 'equivalent continuous sound level' (L_{eq}), which quantifies sound levels that fluctuate over time. To allow for the fact that the human ear cannot detect all frequencies of sound with equal efficiency, noise is also measured using an A-weighted decibel scale (dB(A)). The combination of these measurements ensures that sound readings allow both for intensity of noise and for the ebb and flow of noise over the course of a day. Therefore, a reading of '24h of 63 L_{eq}' indicates the fluctuating sound level is equivalent to a constant sound of 63dB(A) for 24 hours. The DfT has identified a level of 16h of 57dB(A) L_{eq} as the level at which sound can cause 'significant community annoyance'[†]. Maps showing the contours of noise from airports are usually drawn showing those exposed to ≥57dB(A) L_{eq} between 7am–11pm. According to the DfT, in 2007 the number of people affected by airport noise at this level was:

Airport	aircraft movements (thousands)	area (sq km) within 57 L_{eq} contour	population within 57 L_{eq} contour
Heathrow	475·79	119·6	251,900
Gatwick	258·9	49·0	4,800
Stansted	191·5	30·8	2,500
Manchester	206·5	37·5	36,800
Birmingham[‡]	108·7	16·8	26,800
Luton	83·3	15·4	4,400

† The level at which 'significant community annoyance' is said to occur was set by the 1985 report: *United Kingdom Aircraft Noise Index Study* (ANIS). In 2001, the DfT commissioned a further study to investigate if the growth in aviation and the development of quieter aircraft had affected sensitivity to aircraft noise. *Attitudes to Noise from Aviation Sources in England* (ANASE), published in 2007, concluded that although modern aircraft were significantly quieter than their predecessors, levels of annoyance were unchanged. A level of 57 L_{eq} was therefore retained. ‡ 2006 figures for Birmingham airport.

————— WORLD'S BUSIEST INTERNATIONAL AIRLINES —————

IATA figures below reveal the busiest international airlines in the world as of 2007:

Airline	passengers carried (2007)
Ryanair	49,030,000
Lufthansa	41,322,000
Air France	31,549,000
Easyjet	30,173,000
British Airways	28,302,000
KLM	23,165,000
American Airlines	21,479,000
Emirates	20,448,000
Singapore Airlines	18,957,000
Cathay Pacific	17,695,000

America's Southwest Airlines was the busiest domestic airline, with 101,911,000 passengers.

CARBON OFFSETTING FLIGHTS

Although green groups state that total abstention from flying is the best way to cut personal travel carbon consumption, a number of businesses and individuals use carbon offsetting to assuage their guilt and replenish the environment. One of the simplest forms of offsetting flights involves planting trees. Below is a guide, provided by carbonfootprint.com, to the trees that must be planted to offset a return flight:

Trip type	example	tonnes CO_2 emitted	no. trees to offset
Short haul	London–Malaga	0·48	1
Medium haul	London–Chicago	1·46	2
Long haul	Edinburgh–Perth	3·38	4

An internet survey conducted by Dr Lorraine Whitmarsh and Dr Saffron O'Neil of the University of East Anglia in September 2008 revealed that 29% of Britons said they had offset their carbon emissions. Flight offsetting accounted for 70% of all offsets. Profiling suggested that those most likely to offset carbon had a high level of science education and considered themselves to live a green lifestyle, yet these people tended to fly much more often than respondents who did not choose to offset their carbon emissions. ❦ *The Telegraph* reported that under the Government Carbon Offsetting Fund the Royal Household is expected to offset 2,587 tonnes of carbon during 2008–09, at a cost of £46,000.

CO₂ & AIRPORTS

The projected levels of carbon dioxide (CO_2) emissions at UK airports by 2030 are:

Source	million tonnes CO_2	%			
Heathrow	23·6	41	Freight	2·2	4
Other UK airports	15·9	27	Luton	0·8	1
Residual	8·7	15	London City	0·5	1
Gatwick	4·3	7			
Stansted	2·6	4			

[Source: DfT · By 2030, with a 3rd runway/6th terminal Heathrow will have 122m passengers.]

OUT-OF-TOWN AIRPORTS

Airport	approximate distance to city centre
Schiphol	7 miles from Amsterdam
Athens International	17 miles from Athens
Chicago O'Hare	17 miles from Chicago
Rome Fiumicino	19 miles from Rome
Brussels Charleroi	29 miles from Brussels
Milan Malpensa	30 miles from Milan
London Luton	32 miles from London
Tokyo Narita	40 miles from Tokyo
Paris Beauvais	50 miles from Paris
Stockholm Vasteras	54 miles from Stockholm
Stockholm Skavsta	59 miles from Stockholm

—————————— BUSIEST UK TRAIN STATIONS ——————————

Below are the busiest UK railway stations in 2007–08, based on entries and exits:

Station	entries & exits
Waterloo	100,306,690
Victoria	77,462,118
London Liverpool St.	57,789,977
London Bridge	54,124,745
Charing Cross	39,063,680
Euston	29,341,183

Paddington	29,224,721
King's Cross	24,629,269
East Croydon	22,583,906
London Cannon St	22,177,066

The top ten account for 22% of entries and exits in the UK. [Source: Office of Rail Regulation]

———— THE DEFINITION OF AN OVERCROWDED TRAIN ————

During the last decade, train passenger numbers increased by 50% while the number of trains rose only by *c*.20%. A train used to be classed as overcrowded if more than 10 people were forced to stand for every 100 seats. However, in October 2008, the Department of Transport moved the goalposts. The 'acceptable loading of passengers on trains', which applies nationally, now mandates that a train is not considered overcrowded unless it has >30 standing passengers for every 100 seats.

———————————— TRAIN PUNCTUALITY ————————————

Network Rail announced in May 2009 that more trains were arriving on time than at any other period since punctuality records began in 1992. Punctuality has steadily improved since it reached a low of 78% in 2001/2 in the wake of speed restrictions enforced after the Hatfield crash. Biennial punctuality figures are below:

Year	operator	% on time
1992/3	British Rail	86·7
1994/5	British Rail	86·6
1996/7	Railtrack	89·8
1998/9	Railtrack	87·9

Year	operator	% on time
2000/1	Railtrack	79·1
2002/3	Railtrack/NR	79·2
2004/5	Network Rail	83·6
2006/7	Network Rail	88·1
2008/9	Network Rail	90·6

———————— LONDON STATION DESTINATION GUIDE ————————

Charing Cross	*serves* South & South-east
Euston	Midlands, North-west of England & Scotland
King's Cross	Midlands, North of England & Scotland
Liverpool Street	East of England & East Anglia · Stansted Express
Marylebone	Chilterns
Paddington	West of England & Wales · Heathrow Express
St Pancras	East Midlands & Yorkshire · Eurostar
Victoria	South & South-east · Gatwick Express
Waterloo	South & South-west

——————— SATISFACTION & RAIL TICKET PRICES ———————

Many UK rail fares are twice as expensive as those in Europe, according to a Passenger Focus study, published in February 2009. The report also uncovered varying levels of satisfaction with service and value for money in the South-east, viz:

Company	% satisfied value for money	overall			
c2c	47	90	London Midland	46	80
Chiltern	54	90	London Overground	59	77
First Cap. Connect	36	77	Nat. Exp. East Anglia	33	77
First Great Western	51	80	South West Trains	42	83
Heathrow Express	35	93	Southeastern	37	80
			Southern	42	83
			London & SE average	41	82

The report also noted that customers found searching for the cheapest rail tickets to be complicated and time-consuming. Passenger Focus recommended that the fare structure be simplified to make it more equitable, since the current system makes flexibility very expensive. Tabulated below are the proportions of passengers travelling for less than the fully flexible, full-price ticket on some selected journeys:

Route	full price fare	75% pay	50% pay	25% pay
London–Cardiff	£79	≤£40	≤£30	≤£20
London–Manchester	£115	≤£45	≤£35	≤£25
London–Edinburgh	£126	≤£55	≤£40	≤£30

The cost of rail tickets is particularly high in the UK compared to the rest of Europe:

Cost of … (£)	UK	France	Germany	Spain
Annual season ticket (11–15 miles)	1,860	990	944	788
Unrestricted day return fare (3–10 miles)	7	2	5	3
Unrestricted day return fare (26–50 miles)	24	7	15	8

The report also listed passengers' top five priorities for the rail network in 2007:

[1] Price of train tickets offers excellent value for money
[2] Sufficient train services at times I use the train
[3] At least 19 out of 20 trains to arrive on time
[4] Passengers are always able to get a seat on the train
[5] Passengers are kept informed of delays

A total of 1,232m journeys were taken by train in 2007–08; 833m (67·6%) were made in London and the South-east. 294m (23·9%) journeys were regional, and 104m (8·4%) were long distance. According to the Office of Rail Regulation, 89·9% of all trains ran 'on-time' in 2007–08. Complaints made per 100,000 journeys fell by 17·8% between 2006–07 and 2007–08. 42% of all complaints related to 'train service performance'; the second most common complaint category (18% of all complaints) was 'fares, retailing, and refunds'. Total passenger revenue in 2007–08 was £5·6bn – a 10·8% increase since 2006–07; this rise was reflected by the increase in passenger journeys – up 7·1% since 2006–07 to 1·2bn; the largest increase in passengers numbers took place in London and the South-east.

———————————— THE LURE OF THE MINIBAR ————————————

Britons spend *c.*£526m a year on items from hotel minibars, according to a March 2009 survey by Hotels.com. 46% of Brits regularly raid their hotel minibar, even though 84% think minibars are overpriced. 60% of men like beer in their minibar; 25% like massage oil. Women are more interested in chocolate (43%), or a good book or magazine (38%). Below is the average minibar spend, by nationality:

Nationality	*average spend (£)*		
Irish	22	British	15
Swedish	16	French	12
		Norwegian	10

6% admitted to 'minibar meddling': replacing minibar goods with cheaper shop-bought alternatives.

———————————— TOP VISITOR ATTRACTIONS BY REGION ————————————

32·6m tourists visited Britain in 2007, spending *c.*£16bn, according to VisitBritain. Below are the most popular attractions, by region, in 2007 [with millions of visitors]:

Top FREE attraction	*region*	top CHARGED attraction
Bishop Auckland Town Hall [0·3]	North-east	*Alnwick Garden* [0·6]
Blackpool Pleasure Beach [5·5]	North-west	*Windermere Lake Cruises* [1·3]
Xscape Castleford [3·7]	Yorkshire	*Flamingo Land* [1·3]
Markeaton Craft Park [1]	E Midlands	*Bradgate Country Park* [0·9]
Malvern Hills [1]	W Midlands	*Cadbury World* [0·5]
River Lea Country Park [4·5]	East	*Woburn Safari Park* [0·5]
British Museum [5·4]	London	*Tower of London* [2]
Xscape Milton Keynes [6·7]	South-east	*Canterbury Cathedral* [1]
Ashton Court Estate [1·7]	South-west	*Eden Project* [1·1]

———————————— MOST INFLUENTIAL BRITISH PLACE NAMES ————————————

The Times Universal Atlas of the World identified the most influential British place names by plotting how many namesakes appear in other countries. The data, released in December 2008, revealed Richmond to be the most popular place name, possibly due to the colonial influence of the Dukes of Richmond[†]. The top ten were:

Place name	*No. of global namesakes*		
Richmond	55	Wellington	35
London	46	Bristol	35
Oxford	41	Springfield	34
Manchester	36	Arlington	31
		Newcastle	29

† Charles Lennox, the 4th Duke of Richmond, accounts for at least three of the Richmonds in Canada. He fought in the Napoleonic wars and was made Governor General of Upper Canada in 1818. Richmond, Ontario; Richmond, Quebec; and Richmond County, Nova Scotia are named after him.

MOST DISAPPOINTING TOURIST ATTRACTION

A 2008 survey by Virgin Travel Insurance listed the destinations deemed most disappointing by British travellers. The underwhelming sites abroad and at home are:

Most disappointing · Worldwide	*Most disappointing · UK*
1 ....The Eiffel Tower, Paris	1 ....Stonehenge
2 ... The Mona Lisa, The Louvre, Paris	2 ....The Angel of the North
3 .... Times Square, New York	3 .... Blackpool Tower
4 ....Las Ramblas, Barcelona	4 .... Land's End
5 ..... The Statue of Liberty, New York	5 ... Princess Diana memorial fountain
6 ....The Spanish Steps, Rome	6 .... The London Eye
7 . The White House, Washington DC	7 ....Brighton Pier
8 ....The Pyramids, Egypt	8 .... Buckingham Palace
9 .... The Brandenburg Gate, Berlin	9 ....The White Cliffs of Dover
10 .... The Leaning Tower of Pisa	10 ....Big Ben

Respondents suggested that the following UK destinations would not disappoint: Alnwick Castle, Northumberland; Carrick-a-Rede Rope Bridge, County Antrim; The Royal Crescent, Bath; Shakespeare's Globe Theatre, London; The Backs, Cambridge; Holkham Bay, Norfolk; Lyme Regis and the Jurassic Coast; Tate St Ives; The Isle of Skye, Scotland; The Eden Project, Cornwall.

HAPPIEST EXPATS

86% of British expatriates questioned for a June 2009 NatWest International Banking survey claimed their lives were better than before they emigrated; 87% were financially better off since emigration, and 92% were happier. New Zealand was named the best location for émigrés. The countries with the happiest expats are:

1 .... New Zealand	6 ....Portugal	The main reason given for
2 .... Canada	7 ....Spain	leaving the UK was a feeling
3 .... Australia	8 ....South Africa	of dissatisfaction. Nearly all
4 ....France	9 ....USA	respondents said emigrating
5 .... UAE	10 ....China	had been the right decision.

'GERMIEST' TOURIST ATTRACTION

TripAdvisor surveyed their users in June 2009 to identify the world's 'germiest' tourist attractions. The top five most 'unhygienic' places to visit are listed below:

Rank attraction   hygiene issue
1 .....Blarney Stone, Ireland .... *400,000 people kiss the stone each year*
2 .....Seattle's Wall of Gum ...... *Market Theatre wall covered in used chewing gum*
3 .....Oscar Wilde's tomb, Paris...... *lipstick prints left by fans kissing the tombstone*
4 .....St Mark's Square, Venice................*hordes of bedraggled and pesky pigeons*
5 .....Grauman's Chinese Theatre, Hollywood... *fondling of handprints of the stars*

THE NATIONAL TRUST

The National Trust cares for 215 houses and gardens, 76 nature reserves, 43 pubs and inns, 40 castles, 12 lighthouses, and 6 World Heritage sites. In addition, the Trust and its staff of conservationists look after a myriad of objects and artefacts, including the national collection of lawnmowers, 19 paintings by Turner, and the Oscar awarded to George Bernard Shaw. The National Trust is a charity financed through membership, donations, and revenue accrued from commercial operations. The Trust has 3·5m members, and >50m people visited an open-air Trust property in 2007. The National Trust's top ten most visited properties in 2007–08 were:

Property	location	visitors	description
Wakehurst Place	W Sussex	477,173	*botanic garden, Millennium seed bank*
Waddesdon Manor	Bucks	386,544	*French-style château*
Stourhead House	Wiltshire	382,271	*Palladian mansion, landscaped grounds*
Fountains Abbey	N Yorks	348,725	*World Heritage site, Cistercian abbey*
Polesden Lacey	Surrey	258,310	*Regency country house*
Larrybane	County Antrim	222,613	*limestone cliffs with rope bridge*
Penrhyn Castle	Gwynedd	212,727	*C19th fantasy castle*
Belton House	Lincs	212,256	*Restoration country house*
St Michael's Mount	Cornwall	203,798	*rocky island, medieval church & castle*
Sheffield Park	E Sussex	202,940	*'Capability' Brown landscaped garden*

NEWLY INSCRIBED WORLD HERITAGE SITES · 2009

Cultural sites: Cidade Velha, Historic Centre of Ribeira Grande, Cape Verde
The Tower of Hercules, Spain · Mount Wutai, China
Stoclet House, Belgium · Shushtar, Historic Hydraulic System, Iran
Sulaiman-Too Sacred Mountain, Kyrgyzstan
La Chaux-de-Fonds/Le Locle, watchmaking, town-planning, Switzerland
The Ruins of Loropéni, Burkina Faso · The Sacred City of Caral-Supe, Peru
The Royal Tombs of the Joseon Dynasty, South Korea
Pontcysyllte Aqueduct and Canal, United Kingdom
Natural sites: The Wadden Sea, Germany/The Netherlands · The Dolomites, Italy

The following sites were added to the World Heritage in Danger list in 2009:

Site	risks to the site
Belize barrier reef reserve system, Belize	*mangrove cutting, excessive development*
Los Katios national park, Colombia	*illegal extraction of timber*
Historical monuments of Mtskheta, Georgia	*deterioration of stonework & frescoes*

As of July 2009, there were 890 World Heritage sites. In June 2009, for only the second time in its history, the Committee removed a site from the World Heritage list. Germany's Dresden Elbe Valley was removed 'due to the construction underway of a four-lane bridge in the heart of the cultural landscape'. The first site to be deleted was the Arabian Oryx Sanctuary in Oman, which was removed from the list in 2007 when the Omani government announced that the sanctuary would be cut in size by 90%.

────────────── BRITISH NATIONAL PARKS ──────────────

In March 2009, the Environment Minister Hilary Benn announced that the South Downs would become Britain's 15th national park – though he warned that, because of consultations over boundary disputes, the park was unlikely to be formally created until 2011. (The Downs were first proposed as a national park in the 1940s, and campaigners have been working ever since to have the area recognised.) Tabulated below are the specifications of all of Britain's 15 national parks:

National park	year of designation	area (sq. mi)	scheduled monuments	conservation areas	visitor days/year
Brecon Beacons	1957	519	–	–	7m
Broads	1989	117	13	18	5.5m
Cairngorms	2003	1467	60	4	1.5m
Dartmoor	1951	368	1208	23	4m
Exmoor	1954	267	208	16	1.4m
Lake District	1951	885	>200	21	22m
Loch Lomond	2002	720	60	7	4.1m
New Forest	2005	220	61	18	–
Northumberland	1956	405	196	1	1.5m
North York Moors	1952	554	846	42	9.5m
Peak District	1951	555	457	109	22m
Pembrokeshire Coast	1952	240	–	13	4.7m
Snowdonia	1951	840	359	14	10.5m
South Downs	2009	1020	741	165	39m
Yorkshire Dales	1954	685	203	37	9m

The 3,468 sq. mile Yellowstone National Park in America was the world's first national park, established in 1872. ❦ A survey by the carmaker Vauxhall, released in April 2009, found that the average Briton sees only 2% of Britain's town and cities, visiting just 28 towns in their lifetime. The research also estimated that >1 million Britons have never left their home town or city, even for a holiday.

────────────── BRITAIN'S BEST PICNIC SPOT ──────────────

Sewerby Hall and Gardens in Bridlington, East Yorkshire, was voted Britain's best picnic spot in a June 2009 online poll by the family bakers Warburtons. Below are the other nine locations ideal for eating *al fresco*, *en plein air*, or just 'outside':

Richmond Park, London	Tanfield Railway, Co Durham
Southsea Common, Portsmouth	Loch an Eilein, Cairngorms
Uphill, Somerset	Ironbridge Gorge, Shropshire
Milton Country Park, Cambridge	Rhossili Bay and Worm's Head,
Stanley Park, Blackpool	Rhossili Downs, Gower

Ordnance Survey listed its favourite picnic foods in June 2009. The top 5 were: [1] Chicken drumsticks; [2] Chunky Brussels pâté with crusty bread; [3] Scotch eggs; [4] Brie, Cheddar, Camembert, Stilton, Gouda, Stinking Bishop, red Leicester, Wensleydale (with pickle on the side); [5] Pork pies.

—————————————————— VISAS TO ENTER UK ——————————————————

2·5m foreigners applied for a visa to travel to Britain in 2007–08, compared to 2·8m who applied in 2006–07. >50% of all visa applications were for visits (not including family visits), and the refusal rate for all applications was 18%, down 1% on 2006–07. Below is the global demand for UK visas, by category, in 2007–08:

Visa category	applications		
Visit	1,269,885	Work permit	89,445
Family visit	458,675	Settlement	88,075
Student	343,095	Working holiday	53,000
Other non-settlement	143,020	Transit	41,885
		EEA Family permit	26,235

South Asia accounted for most (20%) of all visa applications, followed by the Gulf states (10%), and Russia (10%). Most visa refusals (45%) originated from West African applicants. The top ten nationalities applying for UK visas in 2007–08 were:

Nationality	issued	refused	%				
Indian	408,465	80,595	20	Philippine	47,410	6,235	13
Pakistani	121,105	83,875	69	Saudi	51,035	535	1
Nigerian	112,630	87,880	78	Bangladeshi	28,075	18,670	67
Chinese	170,800	16,135	9	Thai	42,230	4,705	11
Russian	152,110	8,295	5				
Turkish	80,965	6,000	7				

Applicants from NE Asia & Australasia were most likely (93%) to have their visas approved.

[Source: UK Border Services Visa Statistics 2007–08]

— DESTINATIONS REQUIRING VISAS FOR UK CITIZENS —

Many countries allow UK visitors to enter for a short holiday ($c.\leq30$ days) without a visa. The countries below require UK nationals to apply for a visa before any visit:

Afghanistan · Algeria · Angola · Armenia · Australia · Azerbaijan · Bangladesh
Belarus · Benin · Bhutan · Burkina Faso · Burma · Cambodia · Cameroon
Cape Verde · Central African Rep · Chad · China (not Hong Kong) · Comoros
Congo · Cuba · Djibouti · Dominican Rep · DR Congo · Egypt
Equatorial Guinea · Eritrea · Ethiopia · Gabon · Ghana · Guinea
Guinea-Bissau · India · Indonesia · Iran · Iraq · Ivory Coast · Jordan · Kazakhstan
Kenya · Kuwait · Kyrgyzstan · Laos · Lebanon · Liberia · Libya · Madagascar
Mali · Mauritania · Mongolia · Mozambique · Nauru · Nepal · Niger · Nigeria
North Korea · Pakistan · Qatar · Russia · Samoa · São Tomé & Principe
Saudi Arabia · Sierra Leone · Sudan · Suriname · Syria · Tajikistan · Tanzania
Togo · Turkmenistan · Uganda · USA† · Uzbekistan
Vietnam · Yemen · Zambia · Zimbabwe [source: fco.gov.uk]

This information changes regularly, and travellers are advised to check with the embassy before travel.
† Since January '09, tourists are required to register online before travel: see https://esta.cbp.dhs.gov

—— POPULAR FOREIGN HOLIDAY DESTINATIONS ——

Tabulated below are the holiday destinations that have experienced the greatest percentage growth among visitors from the United Kingdom, between 2003–07:

Destination	% growth
Latvia	1,164
Slovakia	957
Poland	719
Other North Africa†	296
Estonia	239
Lithuania	217
Slovenia	149
Hong Kong (China)	148
Other China	136
Israel	133

† Includes Algeria, Libya, Morocco, & Sudan.
[Source: International Passenger Survey, ONS]

———— TOP UK HOLIDAY DESTINATIONS ————

32% of Britons planned to holiday at home in 2009, according to a June survey by Travelodge. 27% holidayed abroad in 2009, compared to 33% who did so in 2008. In a sign that the economic downturn was changing holiday habits, respondents revealed they expected to spend an average of £567 in 2009, down from £631 in 2008. 40% planned to head for the seaside, 24% the countryside, and 18% planned a theme-park holiday. The top ten UK holiday destinations in 2009 were:

1	Cornwall	6	London
2	Lake District	7	Isle of Wight
3	Yorkshire Dales	8	Devon
4	Scottish Highlands & Islands	9	Norfolk Broads
5	Edinburgh	10	South Wales

——— PLACES TO SEE BEFORE THEY DISAPPEAR ———

A timely guidebook listing endangered destinations to visit before they are lost to climate change or development was published in October 2008. Frommer's *500 Places To See Before They Disappear* includes locations where endangered animals can be seen, unique habitats exist, and unspoilt landscapes survive. The book includes locations as diverse as Fraser Island in Australia, which is threatened by rising sea-levels, and the (now diseased) chestnut tree in Amsterdam which inspired Anne Frank as she hid from the Nazis. Some of the locations in the UK include:

Location	at risk from
Hadrian's Wall	too many visitors; erosion
Jurassic Coast, Dorset	oil spills
Sherwood Forest	logging; agriculture; industrial development
Strawberry Hill, London	lack of funding for renovation
Bluebell woods in East Anglia	global warming
Tower of London	rising water-levels
Holderness coast, East Yorkshire	climate change; rising sea-levels

————— GNOMES & THE CHELSEA FLOWER SHOW —————

The opening of the 2009 Chelsea Flower Show was enlivened by rumours of dissent after a number of exhibitors were alleged to be flouting the regulation prohibiting the display of gnomes. The Royal Horticultural Society enforces strict rules over what may be included in a show garden, and gnomes are at the top of the black list. Organisers vowed to search out and remove any offending items before the judging began; in response, competitors warned that they might resort to concealing their contraband gnomes in deep foliage. The list of items banned by the RHS includes:

No garden gnomes	No peat
No balloons	No coloured tents
No bunting	No side walls or fences above 1·2m
No flags	No children under 5
No brightly coloured creatures	No plastic bags

The Gold & Best in Show winner was *The Daily Telegraph* garden by Ulf Nordjfell.

————————— THE WORLD'S UGLIEST PLANT —————————

In June 2009, the RHS asked *Telegraph* readers to vote for the world's ugliest plant:

Corpse flower (*Amorphophallus titanum*) · Stinky squid (*Pseudocolus fusiformis*)
Vegetable sheep (*Raoulia eximia*) · Tree tumbo (*Welwitschia mirabilis*)
Elephant's trunk (*Pachypodium namaquanum*) · Monkey cups (*Nepenthes*)
Sea onion (*Bowiea volubilis*) · Thorn of the cross (*Colletia paradoxa*)
Bastard cobas (*Cyphostemma juttae*) · Birthworts (*Aristolochia gigantea*)

————————————— TOY OF THE YEAR —————————————

Since 1965, the Toy of the Year Award has been presented by the Toy Retailers Association to celebrate the top market performers. In 2008, the overall winner was Bandai's Ben 10 action figures. Other notable winners in 2008 included:

Category	winner		
Boys' range	Ben 10	Creative	Cup Cake Maker
Girls' range	Sylvanian Families	Innovative	Elmo Live
Collectable	Go Go Crazy Bones	Pre-school range	*In The Night Garden*
		Construction	Lego

Research published in December 2008 by Becky Francis, professor of education at Roehampton University, highlighted a tendency towards gender stereotyping in toys. Francis asked parents of children aged 3–5 years to record what they thought was their child's favourite toy. Francis noted that parents tended to say their sons liked construction or action toys and that their daughters liked dolls or nurturing toys, suggesting that some parents steered their children towards 'gender suitable' toys. Professor Francis noted that many of the sons in the study likely slept with a teddy, yet these toys were rarely mentioned. Francis concluded that most of the girls' toys on the market had very little educational benefit, raising concerns that gender specific toys might limit a child's potential.

RECIPES KNOWN BY HEART

The average Briton can cook ten recipes from memory, according to an April 2009 survey by UKTV Food. Respondents made an average of four home-cooked meals a week, and owned five recipe books. The dishes most can make without a recipe are:

Dish % need no recipe		
Spaghetti Bolognese[†] 65	Lasagne............... 41	Macaroni cheese 32
Roast dinner 54	Cottage/shep. pie 38	Toad in the hole 30
Chili con carne....... 42	Meat or fish stir fry .. 38	† In Italy, the dish is more
	Beef casserole........ 34	often served with tagliatelle.

(Only two people know the recipe for the famous Scottish drink Irn-Bru and, in 2009, one of them, company chairman Robin Barr, retired. Mr Barr will continue to mix the essences for Irn-Bru once a month in a sealed room at the company HQ in Cumbernauld, but he plans to pass on the secret recipe to his daughter Julie. Irn-Bru's formula was created in 1901 by Barr's great-grandfather and has not been altered since. The only other living person to know the recipe remains secret, but Barr revealed they never flew on the same plane and that a copy of the formula is hidden in a bank vault.)

CAR LITTER

In July 2009, Keep Britain Tidy launched a campaign against car litter. The public were asked to report every time they saw someone throw rubbish from a car. After just two weeks, Keep Britain Tidy were informed of >2,700 instances of car littering. The most sightings were in the South-east (452), followed by the North-west (424) and London (366). Cigarettes were the items most likely to be tossed from a car window (616 instances), followed by fast-food packaging (341), and sweet wrappers (243). People in cars were the most frequent litterers (1,910 instances; the car was most likely to be blue in colour), followed by vans (220), and lorries (45). One especially keen-eyed respondent reported an incident of littering from a hot air balloon.

BRITAIN'S SMELLIEST CHEESE

Britain's first Smelliest Cheese Championship was held at The Royal Bath and West Show in Somerset in May 2009. The judges were joined by a team of 10 and 11-year-olds from a local school to sniff out the most mephitic cheese. The top three were:

[1] Stinking Bishop[†] (*made by* Martell & Son)
[2] Driftwood (Whitelake Cheeses) [3] St Oswald (Gorsehill Abbey)

† Stinking Bishop is a soft washed-rind cheese made by Charles Martell since 1972. Martell formulated the cheese (from a recipe based on one traditionally used by local Cistercian monks) with milk from his rare Gloucester breed of cattle. The name derives from the pear perry of the same name that is used to wash the cheese. The perry was traditionally produced by the local Bishop family, and earned its nickname 'Stinking Bishop' after one especially unpopular member of the family. The cheese increased in popularity after Gromit used a slice of the reeking cheese to revive an unconscious Wallace in the 2005 Oscar-winning film *Wallace & Gromit: The Curse of the Were-Rabbit*.

———————————— FOOD ISSUES OF CONCERN ————————————

A February 2009 survey conducted by the Food Standards Agency (FSA) revealed that the following food issues were of the greatest concern to the British public:

Issue	% concerned about		
Food poisoning	53	Quantity of saturated fat	36
Quantity of salt in food	43	Conditions animals are raised in	35
Quantity of sugar in food	41	Use of additives	34
Quantity of fat in food	40	Use of pesticides	32
Food prices	40	Feed given to livestock	28
		Genetically modified foods	26

77% of respondents to another February 2009 survey by the FSA said that their household food bill had risen in comparison to the previous year. Listed below are the changes made to shopping behaviour as a result of food price increases:

Change to shopping habits	%		
Buying foods on special offer	30	Making more meals from scratch	19
Buying fewer luxury goods	29	Buying more foods in bulk	15
Eating out less/fewer takeaways	26	Eating more basic food	14
Buying value food brands	25	Changing food shops	12
		Buying less meat	11

———————————— BRITISH FOOD EXPORTS ————————————

The export of British food has soared in recent years, thanks in part to the allure of British chocolate, which, aside from alcoholic drinks, is Britain's most popular food export. Analysis of export figures by Leatherhead Food International, released in June 2009, revealed the top ten fastest-growing UK export markets in 2008:

Country	% change '07–'08	total value	
Bulgaria	160·6	£5·5m	
Hungary	74·3	£40·2m	
Croatia	72·4	£6·4m	
Denmark	69·7	£220·7m	
Norway	61·1	£116·8m	
Abu Dhabi	60·5	£6·7m	

Country	% change '07–'08	total value
Vietnam	56·5	£12·1m
Poland	53·6	£116·4m
Nigeria	53·1	£58·3m
Jordan	52·8	£8·9m

Ireland is the UK's biggest food export market, followed by France.

The top ten most popular UK food and non-alcoholic drink exports are below:

Product	value '08 (£m)		
Chocolate	361	Lamb	263	Beef	213
Breakfast cereals	353	Fresh fish	241	Sweet biscuits	204
Cheese	282	Crustaceans	238	Milk & cream†	203
		Poultry	215	† not concentrated or sweet

One of the best overseas markets for British cheese is America, where sales of Cheddar increased 20% in 2007–08, to £8·9m, and sales of regional cheeses such as Wensleydale, Cheshire, and Lancashire rose by 11%. If alcohol is included, Britain's most popular food and drink export is Scotch Whisky.

———————— NEW UK MICHELIN STARS · 2009 ————————

The 2008 Michelin Guide bestowed 26 new 1-star awards to restaurants in the UK, and four new 2-star awards. Below are the UK restaurants that won stars in 2008:

* *Michael Wignall at The Latymer*.. Bagshot, Surrey...............modern European
* *The Terrace at Montagu Arms* .... Beaulieu, Hampshire...........modern British
* *Fraiche*............................ Birkenhead, Mersey ....modern French
* *Purnell's*.......................... Birmingham ....modern French
* *Turners*............................ Harbone, Birmingham.........modern French
* *The Burlington*..................... Bolton Abbey, N Yorkshire......modern British
* *Lords of the Manor* .... Bourton-on-the-Water, Glos. ..modern French
* *Casamia* .... Westbury on Trym, Bristol...............Italian
* *Manor House Hotel*................. Castle Combe, Wiltshire.......modern British
* *The Neptune* .... Hunstanton, Norfolk..........modern British
* *La Bécasse*......................... Ludlow, Shropshire.................... French
* *The Nut Tree*....................... Murcott, Oxon ....modern British
* *Auberge du Lac* .... Welwyn Garden City, Herts .... French
* *The Hambrough* .... Ventnor, Isle of Wight.......modern European
* *Plumed Horse*...................... Leith, Edinburgh.............modern European
* *Sangster's*......................... Elie, Fife ....modern British
* *The Albannach*..................... Lochinver, Highlands ....modern Scottish
* *Boath House* .... Nairm, Highlands ....modern Scottish
* *Chapter One*....................... Bromley, Kent ....modern European
* *St John*............................ Islington, London .... British
* *Ambassade de L'Ile*................. South Kensington, London............. French
* *Hélène Darroze The Connaught*.. Mayfair, London.............modern French
* *Murano* .... Mayfair, London..................... Italian
* *Kai*................................ Mayfair, London....................Chinese
* *Semplice*........................... Mayfair, London..................... Italian
* *L'Autre Pied*....................... Regent's Park, London .....modern European
** *The Dining Room*................. Whatley Manor, Wiltshire ..modern European
** *Alain Ducasse The Dorchester* ... Mayfair, London.............modern French
** *Hibiscus*.......................... Mayfair, London.............modern French
** *L'Atelier de Joël Robuchon* .... Covent Garden, London ......modern French

———————— THE WORLD'S BEST RESTAURANTS ————————

2009 was a bad year for British restaurants, at least according to *Restaurant* magazine which had only 4 British eateries in its April list of the world's top 50 establishments. (The ranking is compiled by chefs, writers, and critics.) The top 10 were:

1 .. *El Bulli*......Roses, near Barcelona	6 .. *Per Se*.....................New York
2 .. *The Fat Duck*....... Bray, Berkshire	7 .. *Bras*.............. Laguiole, France
3 .. *Noma*..................Copenhagen	8 .. *Arzak*........San Sebastián, Spain
4 .. *Mugaritz* .....San Sebastián, Spain	9 .. *Pierre Gagnaire*................ Paris
5 .. *El Celler de Can Roca*.......Girona	10 . *Alinea* .... Chicago

THE BBC, CRUFTS & 'AT-RISK' BREEDS

A BBC *Panorama* documentary broadcast in August 2008 alleged that the inbreeding of pedigree dogs had caused some animals serious health and welfare problems. As a result of these concerns, the BBC asked that 14 breeds identified as 'at risk' by the Kennel Club, due to breeding practices, be withdrawn from Crufts. The Kennel Club declined, and the BBC announced it would suspend broadcasting from Crufts in 2009. Below are the breeds that the Kennel Club deemed most at-risk:

Clumber spaniel · Basset hound · Bloodhound · Dogue de Bordeaux · Mastiff
Neapolitan mastiff · Pekinese · Shar-pei · Chow chow · German shepherd
Bulldog · St Bernard · Cavalier King Charles spaniel · Rhodesian ridgeback

In January 2009, the Kennel Club introduced new breeding standards in an attempt to ensure that 'all dogs are healthy, of good temperament and fit for their original function'. These standards actively discourage the practice of breeding 'exaggerated traits' which can impede mobility, restrict breathing, or damage a dog's sight. The Kennel Club also banned the breeding of close relatives.

CRUFTS BEST IN SHOW · 2009

A rare Sealyham terrier[†], *Efbe's Hidalgo at Goodspice* (or Charmin to his friends), triumphed as Crufts Best in Show in March 2009. Although allegations of damaging breeding practices [see above] had dented sponsorship and halted TV coverage, *c.*22,000 dogs were shown in the 4-day event, proving that the contest remains the most important dog show in Britain, at least for breeders. 4-year-old Charmin and his owner Marjorie Good travelled from Pennsylvania, USA, to compete. On accepting the prize, Good said, 'I'm just going to kiss this dog till the end of time!'

[†] The Sealyham terrier is on the Kennel Club's register of most endangered breeds; only 43 puppies were born in Britain in 2008. That said, Charmin's victory will no doubt boost the breed's popularity.
[✤] Researchers from Barnard College, New York, suggested that the 'guilty look' owners often claim to see in the face of a misbehaving hound is a figment of their imagination. The research, published in *Behavioural Processes* in June 2009, tested dog owners by giving them misleading information about whether their dog had stolen a treat. The results indicated that many dog owners claimed to see the 'guilty look' on the face of their hound, regardless of whether the beast had actually done anything wrong.

THE SUPREME CAT SHOW · 2008

The annual Supreme Cat Show is organised by the Governing Council of the Cat Fancy (GCCF). To be eligible, a cat must have qualified by winning a certificate at an ordinary GCCF championship show. A knock-out competition selects the Supreme Kitten, the Supreme Adult, and the Supreme Neuter, who then battle it out to be crowned Supreme Exhibit. The 2008 Show was held at Birmingham's NEC on 22 November where >1,000 pussies were shown. The Supreme Exhibit was awarded to Imperial Grand Premier DAIRYMAINE SARNIA CHERIE, a female neutered Tortie Tabby Maine Coon owned by Miss S. Rabey, and bred by Mrs J. M. Haynes.

'A BUTTERFLY IS AN EVENT'

The wet summers of 2007 and 2008 caused a serious decline in butterfly numbers, according to a 2009 Butterfly Conservation report. Loss of habitat and intensification of farming have also contributed to this declivity – some species, such as high brown fritillaries, now exist in just 50 colonies across Britain. Below is the percentage increase or decrease in butterfly numbers in Britain between 2007–08:

Butterfly	% ±		
Northern brown argus	+91	Pearl-bordered fritillary	−56
Large heath	+66	Black hairstreak	−65
Common blue	+51	Wood white	−66
Small tortoiseshell	−45	Clouded yellow†	−90
High brown fritillary	−49		
Green hairstreak	−54		

† Migrates from Europe into southern Britain for the summer. (Title quote: Alan Bennett)

ATTITUDES TO THE COUNTRYSIDE

53% of adults thought the British countryside was 'boring' because 'there is nothing to do or see there', according to a March 2009 Travelodge survey. The survey also illustrated a worrying ignorance about our green and pleasant land, for example: only 17% claimed to know the Countryside Code; a cavalier 10% thought that it was safe to eat *all* berries and fungi found growing in the wild; and 24% thought they had the right to pick wild flowers. When respondents were shown images of Britain's flora and fauna the results were equally disturbing: 32% could not identify a pheasant; 42% were blank when it came to otters; and 22% did not recognise a hare (one in ten thought it was a deer). 12% mistook a stag for a reindeer, and 10% could not even recognise a sheep. 83% didn't know what a bluebell looked like; 44% could not point out an oak tree; and 71% could not identify a pine tree.

MOST COMMON GARDEN BIRDS

The results of the RSPB's Big Garden Birdwatch were released in March 2009. Nearly half a million people took part in the annual survey, counting some 8·5m birds in gardens across Britain during the weekend of 24–25 January 2009. Despite the presence of house sparrows and starlings at the top of the list, these breeds are both in serious decline – house sparrow numbers have dropped by 65% since the survey began in 1979, and starlings by 73%. The most common garden birds are:

1	house sparrow	5	chaffinch	9	robin
2	starling	6	woodpigeon	10	long-tailed tit†
3	blackbird	7	collared dove		
4	blue tit	8	great tit	† first appearance in top ten.

The cuckoo was added to the Red List [see p.75] of the world's most endangered species in May 2009. The Red List revealed that 20% of the 246 bird species regularly seen in the UK are endangered.

ANIMALS IN THE NEWS · 2009

Some of the year's more unusual animal stories. ❧ An unidentified rooster was arrested in Benton, Illinois, US, after a woman called the police to complain about the animal's aggressive behaviour. The rooster was briefly incarcerated outside the town prison. ❧ In Arkansas, a Silver Asian carp leapt from a lake and broke the jaw of a 15-year-old boater, rendering him unconscious. Local officials confirmed that the lake's carp population had been growing, and said that they were increasingly concerned about carp 'jumping behaviour'. ❧ *Current Biology* reported on a sulphur-crested cockatoo named Snowball who demonstrated a remarkable ability to dance, even synching his moves in time to his favourite music (the Backstreet Boys). ❧ Peru's 'Friends of the Hairless Dog Association' offered President Barack Obama a 4-month old Viringo puppy nicknamed 'Ears'. Viringos are entirely bald and almost toothless, which makes them ideal pets for those, like Obama's daughter Malia, who are allergic to fur and dander. The Obamas declined this offer, and adopted a Portuguese Water Dog named Bo. ❧ The Attorney General of Tasmania warned a parliamentary hearing that the country was experiencing a problem with wallabies breaking into opium fields and running around in circles while high. ❧ A Polish politician criticised a local zoo's adoption of Ninio the elephant, after the pachyderm refused to mate with females: 'We didn't pay 37 million zlotys for the largest elephant house in Europe to have a gay elephant live there', the politician was quoted as saying. ❧ Conservationists were delighted to discover 6,000 Irrawaddy dolphins in Bangladesh, since previous estimates had put the entire population of the endangered mammals at a few hundred. ❧ A restaurant in New York yielded to animal rights activists and released into the ocean a 140-year-old lobster that had spent weeks displayed in a tank. ❧ A 23-year-old Australian man was arrested at Melbourne airport on arrival from Dubai, after two pigeons were discovered in his trousers: the birds had been wrapped in padded envelopes and strapped to the man's legs within a pair of tights. ❧ The journal *Biology* reported on the case of a Swedish chimp who had been hoarding stones in order to hurl them at zoo visitors. ❧ The journal *Science* reported on claims that climate change had begun shrinking Scottish Soay sheep, since warmer winters had allowed smaller specimens to survive. ❧ An Australian dog who had been lost overboard was reunited with its owners after four months. The hound had survived a swim through shark-infested waters and, alighting on an island, lived off baby goats before being rescued. ❧ An orangutan named Bonnie, who lives at the National Zoo in Washington, DC, astonished her keepers when she began to whistle in apparent imitation of her custodians. (Other orangutans have been trained to whistle, but Bonnie is the first known to do so spontaneously.) ❧ A dead shark was found dumped in the middle of a Miami street one evening, after two men failed to sell the animal to local markets. (It was unclear how the men had obtained the shark in the first place.) ❧ A man in a Munich park began swinging a swan at another man whose E German accent he found offensive. Fortunately, both the swan and the man escaped serious injury.

Money

Not even a collapsing world looks dark to a man who is about to make his fortune.
—E. B. WHITE, *Intimations*, in *One Man's Meat*, 1944

CONSUMER CONFIDENCE

The GfK NOP 'consumer confidence barometer' gives a sense of the public mood:

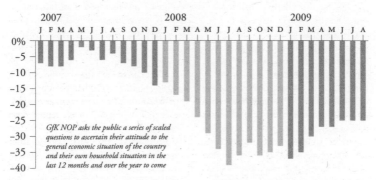

GfK NOP asks the public a series of scaled questions to ascertain their attitude to the general economic situation of the country and their own household situation in the last 12 months and over the year to come

---

NATIONAL SAVINGS & THE FLIGHT TO SAFETY

During the financial turmoil of autumn 2008 [see p.22], savers rushed to deposit their money in 'safe havens'. Traditionally these have been gold, US dollars, and, in the UK, National Savings. Unlike deposits in high street banks, which are guaranteed only up to £50,000[†], all monies invested in National Savings are guaranteed by HM Treasury. Charted below are the 'gross inflows' deposited in National Savings since 2005:

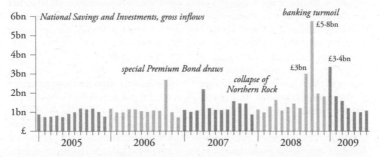

† The UK Financial Services Authority raised the compensation limit for bank deposits from £35,000 to £50,000 on 7/10/08, in the wake of Ireland's announcement of an unlimited deposit guarantee.

———————— WORDS OF THE RECESSION ————————

GD2 · the worst-case scenario of the recession: Great Depression Two.

THE CREDIT MUNCH · recession-prompted comfort eating. *Also* · taking home-prepared food to work. *Also* FOUR FOOD GROUPS OF THE APOCALYPSE · cheap foodstuffs that characterise a disaster. As Frank Rich wrote in *The New York Times*: 'What are Americans still buying? Big Macs, Campbell's soup, Hershey's chocolate and Spam – the four food groups of the apocalypse.' *Also* COMFORT CULTURE · the cultural equivalent of comfort eating.

HE-CESSION · the observation that male-dominated industries have, thus far, been hit hardest in the recession.

SIT-DOWN-LOOK · a Nigerian expression, meaning to passively observe, now used to describe the developing world's quiescent role in the global recession.

RECESSION FLU · maladies caused or exacerbated by the economic crisis.

ZIRP · Zero (%) Interest Rate Policy. *Also* YEAR ZERO · British nickname for the 2009 financial year, in anticipation of (near to) 0% interest rates [see p.238].

THE COPING CLASSES · a description of the 'law-abiding, hard-working, tax-paying' middle class.

BAB · a novel City acronym (Bonuses Are Back) describing the re-emergence of sizeable post-recession payouts [see p.31]. *Also* BANKSTER · banker + gangster.

BOSSNAPPING · the disturbing trend (popular in France) of workers kidnapping their managers in protest against pay cuts or redundancies.

BONFIRE OF THE BILLIONAIRES · the abbreviation of billionaires on *The Sunday Times* 2009 'Rich List' [see p.239].

LA CRISI DEI FORMAGGI · *The cheese crisis* · the serious effect of the recession on Italy's parmigiano industry.

FREDs · Oxfam's dubious acronym for the new poor: [F]orgotten by those in power; [R]ipped off by taxes and the benefits system; [E]xcluded from opportunities; [D]ebt-ridden because they can't afford to get by.

GOOD JOB · a Get Out Of Debt job.

BABYGLOOMERS · baby boomers struggling to support their children and their parents. *Also* KIDDERS · [K]ids [I]n [D]ebt, [D]iligently [E]roding [R]etirement [S]avings.

ECONOCIDE · suicide seemingly catalysed by the economic crisis.

UNPLANDLORDS · property owners forced to rent real estate they can't sell. *Also* FORCED DOWNSIZERS · those forced to move to cheaper properties.

CHEZ MA TANTE · a French euphemism for an item that has been secretly pawned; literally, 'at my aunt's'. (In March 1898, *The New York Times* gave a more detailed account of the origin of this phrase: 'When the Prince de Joinville was very young his mother, the Queen, wife of King Louis Philippe, gave him a gold watch. One day the Queen, not seeing it, asked the young Prince where it was. "Oh," he replied, "*elle est chez ma tante.*" ["it is at my aunt's."] They ran to the Princess Adelaide's palace, but no trace was found of the watch. The Prince finally confessed that he had visited the *mont-de-piété* (the State pawnbroker). The phrase "*chez ma tante*" soon became popular.')

NAYCATION · rejecting any form of vacation; the ultimate STAYCATION.

—————————— WORDS OF THE RECESSION cont. ——————————

KURZARBEIT · a German scheme ('*short work*') under which companies reduce their working week rather than make workers redundant. In return, the government contributes to the wages.

SHOVEL READY · infrastructure projects (roads, bridges, schools, hospitals, &c.) that require only (government stimulus) funding to begin. *Also* PETRI DISH READY · scientific research projects seeking government stimulus.

PESSIMISM PORN · Hugo Lindgren mused on the thrill of titillatingly bleak media reports, in *New York* magazine: 'My wife busted me again the other day. I had slipped away from her and the kids and into the fantasy world of the web. But not the kind of fantasy you're probably thinking of. This was pessimism porn. A friend had turned me on to a futurist named Gerald Celente, who anticipated the Asian financial crisis and other calamities. Now, Celente says, the US is heading for a middle-class tax revolt, food riots, and a Central Park engulfed by shantytowns.'

GLOBAL FORECLOSURE · Niall Ferguson's term for a boom in distressed assets and bankrupt companies.

COSTA FORTUNE · the latest nickname for the Costa del Sol, where many British expats who rely on sterling denominated savings and pensions have been hit by the collapse of the pound.

REYKJAVIK-ON-THAMES · the doom-laden comparison between London and the capital of Iceland [see p.31].

TAXODUS · the threat that high taxes will cause an exodus of rich individuals and profitable companies.

EXTRAVA-GAPPERS · city workers taking (expensive) career breaks during the recession. *Also* FUNEMPLOYED · the happily unemployed, who don't miss the stress of work (or need an income).

SUGOMORI · a Japanese term for 'nesting', used to describe the trend of staying at home to save money.

DEPRESSION ECONOMICS · Paul Krugman defined this term thus: 'A state of affairs like that of the 1930s in which the usual tools of economic policy – above all, the Federal Reserve's ability to pump up the economy by cutting interest rates – have lost all traction. When depression economics prevails, the usual rules of economic policy no longer apply: virtue becomes vice, caution is risky and prudence is folly'.

STEALTH WEALTH · shopping discreetly (STEALTH SPENDING) or buying unbranded products (HIDDEN LUXURY) in an attempt to make ones consumption less conspicuous during a recession. *Also* AFFLUENT THRIFT · low-cost luxury for the newly frugal. *Also* POORGEOISIE · those who conceal their affluence with a (carefully crafted) down-at-heel look. *Also* LOOK-HEAVY-WEIGH-LESS JEWELLERY · an Indian trend in gold wedding bling that looks more valuable than it is.

SUMMER OF RAGE · recession-spurred civil disorder anticipated by the British police, but which failed to materialise.

FINANCIAL ZUD · a Mongolian term for the recession; *Zud* is a local word to describe an unusually severe winter.

MALUS · the opposite of a bonus; a financial penalty for poor performance.

———————— BUDGET 2009 · KEY POINTS ————————

Alistair Darling's second Budget, on 22 April 2009, was a disheartening affair, reflecting the impact of the world economic downturn and the predicament of Britain's finances. The headlines were dominated by two announcements. First, public-sector net borrowing would reach £175bn in 2009 (*c.*12·4% of GDP) – and would then be £173bn in 2010, £140bn in 2011, £118bn in 2012, and £97bn in 2013. Second, that a new 50% band of income tax would be introduced from April 2010 on those earning >£150,000, breaking Labour's manifesto promise. A number of commentators [see over] argued that this was a nakedly political Budget devised to put pressure on the Tories to reject the new 50% tax rate. Some of Darling's key decisions are below (others are detailed elsewhere in this section).

Forecasts	British economy to shrink by 3·5% in 2009; growth forecast for 2010, 1·25%; and from 2011, 3·5% a year
Income tax	no income tax increases in 2009; a new 50% rate for those earning >£150,000 from April 2010; personal tax allowance of those earning >£100,000 to be withdrawn from April 2010
UK net debt	59% in 2009; 68% in 2010; rising to 79% by 2013–14
Inflation target	remains at 2%
VAT	15% rate will continue until December 2009
Employment	from January 2010, everyone under 25 and out of work for 12 months will be offered a job or training
Car scrappage	from May 2009 until March 2010 motorists will get £2,000 discount on new cars if they trade in cars more than 10 years old
Child tax credit	to rise by £20 by 2010; child trust funds for disabled children to rise by £100 a year, £200 a year for the severely disabled
Grandparents	of working age who care for their grandchildren will have that work count towards the basic state pension entitlement
State pension	will be increased by at least 2·5%, regardless of inflation
Fuel duty	to increase by 2p per litre in September and then by 1p a litre above indexation each April for 4 further years
Public services	£5bn further efficiency savings in public services, rising to £9bn in 2013/14
ISAs	savings tax free limit raised to £10,200 (£5,100 in cash) for over-50s in 2009, and for everyone in 2010
Pension tax relief	to be restricted for those earning >£150,000 from April 2011; and then tapered to the standard 20%
Stamp duty	holiday on homes <£175,000 extended until end of 2009
Statutory redundancy pay	to increase from £350 to £380 a week
Carbon budget	UK committed to reduce emissions by 34% by 2020
Tobacco & alcohol duties	2% rise
Housing industry	£500m extra support promised
Armed forces housing	£50 million for modernisation
Tax avoidance	promise to close loopholes that could save £1bn over 3 years
Business capital allowance rate	main rate doubled to 40%
Offshore wind projects	£525m promised over two years
Combating climate change	£1bn promised

———— BUDGET 2009 · PRESS & POLITICAL REACTION ————

The reaction of the headline writers was, in the main, bleak: *Financial Times* 'Darling gambles on growth' · *Guardian* 'Darling's great squeeze' · *Times* 'Red all over' · *Daily Mail* 'Alistair in Wonderland' · *The Herald* '£703bn – A decade of debt' · *Mirror* 'Robin Good' · *Daily Express* 'They've ruined Britain' · *Daily Star* 'Gord help us all' · *Daily Telegraph* 'Return of class war' · *Sun* 'At least it's sunny'. The reaction from commentators and critics was bleaker still:

David Cameron · The fundamental truth is that all Labour governments run out of money. The last Labour government gave us the Winter of Discontent. This Labour government has given us the Decade of Debt. The last Labour government left the dead unburied. This one leaves the debts unpaid. They sit there, running out of money, running out of moral authority, running out of time. You have to ask what on earth is the point of another 14 months of this government of the living dead?

Nick Clegg · This Budget is a political supermarket sweep, a trolley full of random promises, without even a hint of a plan or any real likelihood the promises are ever going to be put into practice.

Guardian · Alistair Darling yesterday revealed the astronomical bill that Britain must pay for financial crisis. And while his figures are plausible, his plans for repaying this mountain of debt are highly suspect.

Times · In the past year we tumbled into recession, bailed out the banks and funded a fiscal stimulus. Yesterday we looked to the Chancellor to say how it would be paid for. The orchestra assembled. The audience settled expectantly. The conductor tapped his baton on his music stand. A hush fell. And from the stage came the shrill, thin sound of a penny whistle.

Independent · Radical, exciting, visionary, this Budget was not. Workmanlike is the word that comes to mind; workmanlike, but strangely old-fashioned and finely attuned to the concerns of voters who might be tempted to stay at home at the next general election.

Andrew Smith, chief economist, KPMG · Even though Mr Darling insists that the end of the recession is in sight, we are still looking at eye-watering budget deficits and a doubling of public debt. And if the Chancellor's growth forecasts again prove over-optimistic, the public finances will turn out even worse.

Iain Dale · This was a cheap Budget delivered in a manner unworthy of a man with the title of Chancellor. There was no strategy, just a series of cheap and recycled announcements. It was a political Budget in that he shamelessly appealed to the Labour Party's happy little band of envy warriors.

Nick Robinson, BBC · The age of abundance is over. Welcome to the age of austerity. For years politicians have argued about how to spend the proceeds of growth. For years to come they will have to argue about what should be cut.

Daily Mirror · Alistair Darling made the best of a bad job in what was a historic Budget for the wrong reasons. ... The fortunes of the country and Labour rest on his forecasts being accurate.

─────────────── INCOME TAX 2009–10 ───────────────

Income tax was first levied in 1799 by Pitt the Younger as a 'temporary measure' to finance the French Revolutionary War. The initial rate was 2 shillings in the pound. The tax was abolished in 1816, only to be re-imposed in 1842 by Robert Peel (again temporarily) to balance a fall in customs duties. By the end of the C19th, income tax was a permanent feature of the British economy. The current rates are:

Income tax allowances	2008–09	2009–10
Personal allowance	6,035	6,425
Personal allowance (65–74)†	9,030	9,490
Personal allowance (>75)†	9,180	9,640
Income limit for age-related allowances	21,800	22,900
Married couple's allowance (born before 6·4·1935)†	6,535	– ‡
Married couple's allowance (aged ≥75)‡	6,625	6,965
Minimum amount of married couple's allowance	2,540	2,670
Blind person's allowance	1,800	1,890

The rate of relief for married couple's allowance remains 10%. † These allowances are reduced by £1 for every £2 of income that exceeds the income limit. ‡ In the 2009–10 tax year all claimants in this category will turn 75, thus entitling them to claim the higher amount of married couple's allowance reserved for those aged ≥75.

Income tax rates	*threshold*	%
Basic rate	£0–£37,400	20
Higher rate	>£37,400	40

Additionally, there is a 10% starting rate for savings income only, with a limit of £2,440. Where an individual has non-savings income in excess of this limit, the 10% savings rate will not be applicable. The tax rates for dividends remain unchanged at 10% for income up to the basic rate limit, and 32·5% thereafter.

─────────────── STAMP DUTY ───────────────

The thresholds below (in £) represent the 'total value of consideration' of the deal. The rate that applies to any given transfer applies to the whole value of that deal.

rate *%*	*Residential* not *in a disadvantaged area*	*Residential in a disadvantaged area*	*Non-residential*
0	0–125,000†	0–150,000	0–150,000‡
1	125,001–250,000	150,001–250,000	150,001–250,000
3	250,001–500,000	250,001–500,000	250,001–500,000
4	>500,001	>500,001	>500,001

The rate of stamp duty on the transfer of SHARES and SECURITIES is set at 0·5%.
† Until 31 December 2009 buyers will pay no stamp duty on properties <£175,000.
‡ Stamp duty of 1% is levied where the annual rent of a property is ≥£1000.

——————— NATIONAL INSURANCE · 2009–10 ———————

Although National Insurance dates from 1911, modern funding of social security was proposed by Beveridge and established by the National Insurance Act (1946).

Lower earnings limit, primary Class 1	£95/w
Upper earnings limit, primary Class 1	£844/w
Primary threshold	£110/w
Secondary threshold	£110/w
Employees' primary Class 1 rate	11% of £110–£844/w · 1% >£844/w
Employees' contracted-out rebate	1·6%
Married women's reduced rate	4·85% of £110–£844/w · 1% >£844/w
Employers' secondary Class 1 rate	12·8% on earnings above £110/w
Employers' contracted-out rebate, salary-related schemes	3·7%
Employers' contracted-out rebate, money-purchase schemes	1·4%
Class 2 rate	£2·40/w
Class 2 small earnings exception	£5,075/y
Special Class 2 rate for share fishermen	£3·05/w
Special Class 2 rate for volunteer development workers	£4·75/w
Class 3 rate	£12·05/w
Class 4 lower profits limit	£5,715/y
Class 4 upper profits limit	£43,875/y
Class 4 rate	8% of £5,715–£43,875/y · 1% >£43,875/y

——————— CAPITAL GAINS TAX ———————

Annual exemptions 2009–10   Individuals &c. = £10,100 · Other trustees = £5,050

Capital Gains Tax will continue to be charged at 18% in 2009–10. Capital gains arising on disposal of a 'principal private residence' remain exempt from charge.

——————— INHERITANCE TAX ———————

Annual exemptions 2009–10   Individuals = £325,000 · Couples &c. = £650,000

Inheritance Tax is charged at 40% on the value of estates over the allowance threshold. The exemption allowance for individuals was increased by £13,000 in 2009–10. 2% of estates are expected to be liable to pay inheritance tax in 2009–10.

——————— CORPORATION TAX ON PROFITS ———————

2009–10	£ per year
Small companies' rate: 21%	0–300,000
Marginal small companies' relief	300,001–1,500,000
Main rate: 28%	≥1,500,001

—— BANK OF ENGLAND INTEREST RATES & THE MPC ——

Since 1997, the Monetary Policy Committee (MPC) has been responsible for
setting UK interest rates. Charted below are the base rate changes since May 2007:

Date	change	rate						
05·03·09	−0·50	0·50%	04·12·08	−1·00	2·00%	07·02·08	−0·25	5·25%
05·02·09	−0·50	1·00%	06·11·08	−1·50	3·00%	06·12·07	−0·25	5·50%
08·01·09	−0·50	1·50%	08·10·08	−0·50	4·50%	05·07·07	+0·25	5·75%
			10·04·08	−0·25	5·00%	10·05·07	+0·25	5·50%

———————— INCOME TAX PAYABLE · 2008–09 ————————

Annual income (£)	No. of taxpayers (000s)	Total tax liability (£m)	Average rate of tax (%)	Average amount of tax (£)
6,035–7,499	1,440	184	1·9	128
7,500–9,999	2,900	1,270	5·0	439
10,000–14,999	6,390	6,690	8·4	1,050
15,000–19,999	4,930	10,000	11·7	2,030
20,000–29,999	6,910	23,700	14·0	3,430
30,000–49,999	5,810	34,900	15·8	6,000
50,000–99,999	2,010	30,700	23·3	15,300
100,000–199,999	470	19,000	30·1	40,500
200,000–499,999	143	14,000	33·8	97,800
500,000–999,999	26	6,330	35·4	242,000
≥1,000,000	11	8,390	35·9	776,000
ALL INCOMES	31,000	155,000	17·9	5,000

———————— THE RECESSION & ATTITUDES TO MONEY ————————

25% of Britons admitted to questioning their personal values since the economic
crisis began, according to a 2009 survey by the Charities Aid Foundation. The
survey asked Britons what effect they thought the recession would have on society:

34% .... think society will become more caring and compassionate
37% .... think people will place less importance on possessions
43% .... think money will become more important
44% .... think people will be more driven at work
45% .... think there will be greater concern about world affairs

77% of respondents said they were still giving the same amount to charity despite the downturn.
8% said they were now giving more. ❦ A July 2009 survey by unltdworld.com revealed that of 16
nationalities polled, the British were most likely to give to charity – 83% said they had donated in
the last year compared to 44% of Americans. Britons were most likely to donate to health charities.

———————— SUNDAY TIMES RICH LIST · 2009 ————————

No.	billionaire (UK)	£ billion	activity	'08
1	Lakshmi Mittal and family†	10·8	steel	1
2	Roman Abramovich	7·0	oil, industry	2
3	The Duke of Westminster	6·5	property	3
4	Ernesto and Kirsty Bertarelli	5·0	pharmaceuticals	6
5	Hans Rausing and family	4·0	packaging	7
6	Sir Philip and Lady Green	3·8	retailing	9
7	Charlene and Michel de Carvalho	3·0	inheritance, brewing	13
8	Sammy and Eyal Ofer	2·7	shipping, property	15
9	David and Simon Reuben	2·5	property	10
9	Joe Lewis	2·5	investment	19
9	John Fredriksen	2·5	shipping	8
9	Kirsten and Jorn Rausing	2·5	inheritance, investment	14

† Mittal topped this year's rankings despite losing *c.*£16·9bn in the collapse of the steel market. According to the list, Britain's thousand wealthiest individuals collectively lost £155 billion (more than a third of their wealth) during the recession; in the top 100, only three saw their wealth increase.

———— THE WORLD'S MOST ADMIRED COMPANIES · 2009 ————

According to *Fortune,* Apple was the world's most admired company in 2009. Apple topped the list for the second year in a row and proved that, despite the worldwide recession, the demand for iPods, iPhones, and Macs continues to rise. Warren Buffett's holding company, Berkshire Hathaway, ranked second, and Toyota, third.

———————— FORBES MAGAZINE RICH LIST · 2009 ————————

Billionaires were not immune from the financial crisis, according to the *Forbes* rich list released in March 2009. Warren Buffett, who headed the list in 2008, lost $25bn (and the top spot) in 2009, and 355 people dropped off the list altogether, leaving just 793 billionaires still living the high-life. Britain went from 35 (dollar) billionaires in 2008, to 25 in 2009. The top ten richest people in the world are:

No.	billionaire	nationality	$bn 2009	business	$bn 2008	(±$bn)
1	William Gates III	American	40·0	software	58·0	(−18)
2	Warren Buffett	American	37·0	investing	62·0	(−25)
3	Carlos Slim Helu	Mexican	35·0	telecoms	60·0	(−25)
4	Lawrence Ellison	American	22·5	software	25·0	(−2·5)
5	Ingvar Kamprad & family	Swedish	22·0	retail (IKEA)	31·0	(−9)
6	Karl Albrecht	German	21·5	retail (Aldi)	27·0	(−5·5)
7	Mukesh Ambani	Indian	19·5	petrochemicals	43·0	(23·5)
8	Lakshmi Mittal	Indian	19·3	steel	45·0	(25·7)
9	Theo Albrecht	German	18·8	retail (Aldi, &c.)	23·0	(4·2)
10	Armancio Ortega	Spanish	18·3	retail (Zara)	20·2	(1·9)

ETHICAL CONSUMERISM

Each household in the UK spent, on average, £707 on ethical goods or services in 2007, according to the Co-operative 2008 Ethical Consumerism Report published in November 2008. A snapshot of ethical consumerism 2006–07 is tabulated below:

Sales of ... (£m)	'06	'07	growth				
Organic food	1,737	1,911	+10%	Efficient light bulbs	26	41	+58
Fairtrade	285	458	+61	Green energy	127	174	+37
Free range eggs	259	314	+21	Rchg'ble batteries	42	75	+79
Free range poultry	116	130	+12	Green cars	96	223	+132
Farmers' markets	225	220	–2	Public transport	377	475	+26
Freedom foods	18	28	+56	Ethical clothing	52	89	+71
Sustainable fish	55	70	+27	Real nappies	4	4	0
				Green funerals	22	26	+18

SKILLS SHORTAGES

The government maintains a National Shortage Occupation List that details the professions in which there is a shortage of workers in the UK. If a job appears on this list, employers can recruit skilled workers from outside the European Union, without having to fulfil the 'resident labour market test' by advertising the position in the UK. Some of the occupations on this shortage list in June 2009 included:

audiological scientist · geologist · contaminated land engineer
geoenvironmentalist · civil engineer · intensive care doctor · paediatrician
orthodontist · clinical psychologist · pharmacist · veterinary surgeon
secondary education teacher of maths or science · quantity surveyor
social worker · ship & hovercraft officer · skilled ballet dancer
high integrity pipe welder · skilled chef · skilled sheep shearer

FLEXIBLE WORKING PATTERNS

As of April 2009, all parents of children <16 had the legal right to request flexible working hours. Figures from the Labour Force Survey show the percentage of workers with flexible working patterns, by sex and type of employment, in 2008:

Full-time employees %	♂	♀	all	Part-time employees	♂	♀	all
Flexible hours	10·4	14·7	12·0	Flexible hours	7·7	10·0	9·5
Annualised hours†	4·5	4·9	4·6	Annualised hours	3·1	4·6	4·3
4·5 day week	1·2	0·8	1·1	Term-time working	4·1	11·5	9·9
Term-time working	1·3	6·2	3·2	Job sharing	1·2	3·1	2·7
9 day fortnight	0·5	0·4	0·4	Any flexible pattern	18·1	30·1	27·6
Any flexible pattern	18·3	27·7	21·9				

† In this arrangement, the number of hours an employee has to work are calculated over a full year, allowing for longer hours to be worked over certain periods of the year and shorter hours at others.

―――――――― COMPLEMENTARY CURRENCIES ――――――――

In 2008, the east Sussex town of Lewes launched its own 'complementary currency' – complementary in that it runs alongside sterling. The Lewes Pound is designed to encourage people to spend their money locally, boosting the local economy and avoiding the 'leaky bucket' effect where locally created wealth is spent elsewhere. At the currency's launch, 8,500 Lewes Pounds were released into the local economy, and holders were able to exchange £1 for 1 Lewes Pound. The notes, decorated with an image of Lewes Castle, are not legal tender – so shopkeepers are free to decline them – however they are legal vouchers (like Book Tokens) and can be redeemed in participating stores. Shops participating in the scheme are encouraged to keep the Lewes Pounds in circulation by passing them in change or using them to pay staff or local suppliers. Some other complementary currencies include:

WIR · founded in 1934, in the aftermath of the 1929 stockmarket crash, the WIR is a Swiss complementary currency with no physical notes, predominantly used by local businesses to trade with each other. Users have WIR bank accounts and spend their money using cheques or credit cards. It is a hugely successful complementary currency, with a circulation of 1·6bn.

TORONTO DOLLAR · scheme to aid the local community, created in 1998. Locals can purchase 1 Toronto dollar for 1 Canadian dollar – 90 cents of which goes into a reserve fund, the remaining 10 cents goes to the Toronto Dollar Community Projects Fund. Participating businesses pay $25 to register for the scheme. Toronto dollars can be redeemed for 90 cents.

THE EKO · launched in 2002, in the ecovillage of Findhorn, Scotland. The notes come in denominations of 1, 5, and 20 Ekos, and are on a par with sterling. 15–20,000 notes are now in permanent circulation.

CHIEMGAUER · a community currency launched in 2003 in Bavaria, Germany. Businesses accepting the notes can convert them back to euros for a small fee – the profits from which go towards local charities. To encourage spending, the notes are a depreciative currency, so that every 3 months the Chiemgauer loses 2% of its value and holders must purchase a coupon to top it up. 90,000 notes are currently in use, which raise c.£2,500 for charity every month.

BERKSHARES · launched in 2006, Berkshares are used in the S Berkshire region of Massachusetts, USA. Users pay $95 for $100 worth of Berkshares, which can be purchased from 12 banks in the area. 370 local merchants are now part of the scheme, and >$1·5m Berkshares are in circulation.

TOTNES POUND · launched in 2007, the notes display a sepia depiction of the town centre. 20,000 notes have been issued and are currently accepted by c.70 local businesses.

Complementary currencies are a form of scrip – a currency substitute that is often used as a form of credit. Historically, scrip was used in remote US mining or logging communities where actual money was scarce. Employees were paid in scrip that they could only spend in the company-owned stores. More recently, scrip is used as gift tokens and in online games. ❦ As listeners to *The Archers* will know, complementary currencies are not always easy to administer, especially with Joe Grundy about.

──────── FINANCIAL SNAP-SCHOTT · 2009 ────────

Item (£)	09·2008	09·2009
Church of England · marriage service (excluding certificate)	247·00	254·00
– funeral service (excluding burial and certificate)	96·00	99·00
Season ticket · Arsenal FC (2009/10; centre, E & W upper tiers)	1,825·00	1,825·00
– Grimsby Football Club (2009/10; Upper Findus)	323·00	299·00
Annual membership · MCC (full London member)	358·00	373·00
– Stringfellows, London	600·00	600·00
– Groucho Club, London (+35; London member)	550·00	595·00
– Trimdon Colliery & Deaf Hill Workmen's Club	4·50	8·50
– The Conservative Party (>22)	25·00	25·00
– The Labour Party (banded by income from 2009)	36·00	19–132·00
– The Liberal Democrats (minimum required)	10·00	10·00
– UK Independence Party	20·00	20·00
– Royal Society for the Protection of Birds (adult)	34·00	36·00
Annual television licence[†] · colour	139·50	142·00
– black & white	47·00	48·00
Subscription, annual · *Private Eye*	28·00	28·00
– *Vogue*	29·90	46·80
– *Saga Magazine*	17·95	24·95
New British Telecom line installation (subject to survey)	124·99	122·50
Entrance fee · Thorpe Park (12+ purchased on the day)	33·00	35·00
– Buckingham Palace State Rooms (adult)	15·50	16·50
– Eden Project, Cornwall (adult, day)	15·00	16·00
'Pint of best bitter' · Railway Inn, Honiton, Devon	2·70	2·80
– Railway Inn, Banff, Scotland	2·60	2·70
– Railway Inn, Trafford, Manchester	1·90	1·90
– Railway Inn, Coleshill, Birmingham	2·50	2·65
– Railway Inn, Putney, London, SW15	2·10	2·15
Fishing rod licence · Salmon and Sea Trout (full season)	68·00	70·00
List price of the cheapest new Ford (Ford Ka Studio 'on the road')	7,645·00	8,595·00
British naturalisation (includes ceremony fee)	655·00	720·00
Manchester United home shirt (2009/10 season)	39·99	42·99
Tea at the Ritz, London (afternoon, per person)	37·00	37·00
Kissing the Blarney Stone (admission to Blarney Castle) [€10 in both years]	7·30	8·90
Hampton Court Maze (adult)	3·50	3·50
Ordinary London adult single bus ticket (cash)	2·00	2·00
Mersey Ferry (adult return)	2·30	2·40
Passport · new, renewal, or amendment (3-week postal service)	72·00	77·50
Driving test (practical + theory; cars, weekday)	86·50	93·00
Driving licence (first · car, motorcycle, moped)	50·00	50·00
NHS dental examination (standard)	16·20	16·50
NHS prescription charge (per item)	7·10	7·20
Moss Bros three-piece morning suit hire (weekend, basic 'Lombard')	45·00	45·00
FedEx Envelope (≤0·5kg) UK–USA (International First)	74·40	70·58

† The blind concession is 50%. Those ≥75 may apply for a free licence.

——————————— RPI & CPI ———————————

Some 2009 changes to the RPI basket:

items removed · frozen imported lamb loin; imported cheddar; large eggs; small fromage frais; fresh single cream; peaches; chilled ready meal for one; 1–2l cider; box of wine; hire domestic wallpaper steamer; MP3 player; can cat food; DVD film rental; watch repair, clean & service

items added · rotisserie cooked hot whole chicken; parmesan cheese; large free range eggs; fresh double cream; small individual yoghurt; plums; peaches/nectarines; chilled ready-meal, meat based; chilled ready-meal, fish/vegetable based; cider (500–750ml); hire of domestic carpet cleaner; hardwood floor; freeview box; MP4 player; Blu-ray disc; internet-based DVD rental; TV rental; watch battery replacement; cat food pouch; rosé wine

CPI & RPI % change over 12 months:

Year	month	CPI	RPI
2009	Aug	1·6	−1·3
	Jul	1·8	−1·4
	Jun	1·8	−1·6
	May	2·2	−1·1
	Apr	2·3	−1·2
	Mar	2·9	−0·4
	Feb	3·2	0·0
	Jan	3·0	0·1
2008	Dec	3·1	0·9
	Nov	4·1	3·0
	Oct	4·5	4·2
	Sep	5·2	5·0
	Aug	4·7	4·8
	Jul	4·4	5·0
	Jun	3·8	4·6
	May	3·3	4·3
	Apr	3·0	4·2
	Mar	2·5	3·8
	Feb	2·5	4·1
	Jan	2·2	4·1
2007	Dec	2·1	4·0

——————— COST OF LIVING WORLDWIDE ———————

Tokyo is the most expensive city in the world, according to the Economist Intelligence Unit, whose February 2009 list is based on price data adjusted for exchange-rate movements. The most and least expensive cities in the world are:

Most expensive cities		*Cheapest cities*	
1 .... Tokyo	6 .... Zürich	1 .... Karachi	6 .... Tripoli
2 .... Osaka Kobe	7 ...... Frankfurt	2 .... Tehran	7 .... Manila
3 .... Paris	= .... Helsinki	3 .... Mumbai	8 .... Kiev
4 ... Copenhagen	9 .... Geneva	4 ..... New Delhi	= ...... Asuncion
5 .... Oslo	10 ..... Singapore	5 .... Kathmandu	10 ...... Pretoria

An alternative list of the world's most expensive cities produced by Mercer in July 2009 also ranked Tokyo and Osaka as the two most expensive cities. The rest of Mercer's top ten were: Moscow, Geneva, Hong Kong, Zürich, Copenhagen, New York, Beijing, and Singapore. London was ranked 16th, down from 3rd in 2008. ❦ According to the Global Property Guide, the most expensive places to own a home in 2009 are: Monte Carlo (average price $47,578 per m²), Moscow, London, Tokyo, Hong Kong, New York, Paris, Singapore, Rome, and Mumbai.

———————— MATERIAL DEPRIVATION ————————

The Department for Work and Pensions developed a number of questions in a bid to gauge the extent of material deprivation among families with children. Since 2005–06, these questions have been included in the Family Resource Survey, a report used to measure income. The list of questions from the latest survey, and the percentage of UK families that can or cannot afford the item or service, are below:

% families that can	can you afford to ...	% families that cannot
77	decorate home	18
58	pursue a hobby/leisure activity	17
57	holiday away from home	38
74	insure the contents of home	18
63	have friends round for drink/meal once a month	15
55	make savings of ≥£10 a month	40
89	have 2 pairs of all-weather shoes for each adult	9
59	replace worn-out furniture	30
71	replace broken electrical goods	22
65	spend money on self each week	32
91	keep house warm	8

[Source: DWP · Family Resource Survey · Households Below Average Income 2006/07] The gap between rich and poor families in Britain in 2007–08 continues to be high, according to statistics released by ONS in July 2009. The income of the richest fifth of the population before tax and benefits was £72,600 – that is 16 times greater than the £4,700 earned by the poorest fifth of the population. When tax and benefits are taken into account, the income for the top fifth of the population fell to £52,400, and the income of the poorest fifth of the population was boosted to £14,300.

———————— THE BANK OF MUM & DAD ————————

66% of young adults (aged 18–25) claim to be completely financially independent while still receiving financial support from their parents, according to February 2009 research by The Children's Mutual. The report suggested that many young people accept handouts from their parents that they never expect to pay back – just 8% said they would pay their parents back for their university education. Young people admitted to receiving the following financial support from their parents:

Financial support (%)	♂	♀		Pay bills	18	16
University fees	28	28		Pay holidays	18	20
Reduced or no rent	43	40		Pay wedding	7	14
Rent support	21	24		Mortgage deposit	6	6
Living costs	39	41		Trust fund	6	14
Pay off debts	12	6		Inheritance	5	7

47% of young people still financially dependent on their parents cited the cost of university as a barrier to their independence; 35% blamed the high cost of renting. The authors of the report nicknamed these youths the 'bungee brood' generation.

———————— POSTAL PRICING IN PROPORTION ————————

Category	size (mm)	thickness (mm)	weight (g)	1st	2nd
Letter	≤240×165	≤5	0–100	39p	30p
Large Letter	≤353×250	≤25	0–100	61p	47p
			101–250	90p	76p
			251–500	124p	104p
			501–750	177p	151p
Packet	>353 long or >250 wide	or >25	0–100	128p	108p
			101–250	162p	141p
			251–500	214p	185p
			501–750	265p	224p
			751–1,000	325p	270p
			1,001–1,250	445p	—

Items >1,250g cost an extra 70p for each additional 250g or part thereof, up to 2,000g.
Recorded Signed For = postage + 75p · Special Delivery (9am) = £10·85 for up to 100g

————————————— AIRMAIL RATES —————————————

AIRMAIL	Letters Europe	Rest of World
Postcards	0·56	0·62
≤10g	0·56	0·62
≤20	0·56	0·90
≤40	0·81	1·35
≤60	1·05	1·82
≤80	1·28	2·31
≤100	1·52	2·80
≤120	1·77	3·26
≤140	2·02	3·75

To find a postcode call
09063 021 222 peak or
08457 111 222 off-peak
For further information see
royalmail.com

Small packets / Printed papers	
Europe	RoW
1·21	1·68
1·31	1·93
1·45	2·19

A universal stamp can be used to send letters up to 40g to Europe (60p), or worldwide (£1·12).

————————— ROYAL MAIL STAMPS OF 2009 —————————

13 Jan ....British Design Classics	1 Sep ....The Fire Service
22 Jan ....Robert Burns	17 Sep ....Royal Navy Uniforms
12 Feb...........................Darwin	8 Oct.....................Best of British
26 Feb...............Celebrating Wales	3 Nov...................Christmas 2009
10 Mar .... Pioneers of the	
Industrial Revolution[†]	
21 Apr.................. House of Tudor	
19 May...........................Plants	
16 Jun ....Mythical Creatures	
18 Aug.......................Postboxes	

† Marked the 250th anniversary of the foundation of Josiah Wedgwood's Staffordshire pottery works, the commencement of James Brindley's Bridgewater Canal from Worsley to Manchester, and Matthew Boulton's bicentenary.

———————————— PONZI SCHEMES ————————————

Banks and investors around the world lost *c.*$65bn, when it was revealed in December 2008 that Wall Street banker Bernard Madoff had perpetuated a Ponzi scheme con. Ponzi schemes are pyramid-selling frauds, in which investors (theoretically) receive unusually high returns funded by the deposits of subsequent investors rather than genuine business activity. Madoff's scheme was exposed when the credit crunch caused new investors to dry up, and existing customers attempted to withdraw their money. The fraud is named after the Italian Charles Ponzi who, although not the first to use pyramid selling, made millions from the scam in 1920s America. Ponzi arrived in the US in 1903 with just $2·50 to his name after he lost his life's savings gambling during the voyage. He travelled across the US and Canada taking odd jobs and spending time in jail for cheque fraud and people-smuggling, before eventually settling in Boston. In 1919, Ponzi received a letter from Spain containing an International Postal Reply Coupon (IRC) – a voucher that could be redeemed for stamps. He noticed that because the coupons were negotiated at a fixed rate, his coupon had cost his Spanish correspondent one-sixth of what it was now worth in stamps in the USA. Ponzi realised the money-making potential of this disparity and set up a company to buy and sell IRCs. Ponzi claimed that this would allow investors a profit of 40% in 90 days. Tempted by this amazing rate of return, many locals began to invest, and initially Ponzi paid out generous returns, encouraging re-investment. As word spread, more and more people clamoured to pledge their money to Ponzi and he quickly became both a millionaire and a local celebrity. However, instead of legitimately trading in IRCs, Ponzi had been using the deposits of new customers to make phoney interest payments and line his own pocket. Ponzi's rags to riches story provoked the *Boston Post* to investigate his wealth and uncover his scam. Ponzi was arrested and in November 1920 was sentenced to 5 years in prison. He was later deported, and died in poverty in 1949.

———————————— BIGGEST BANKS ————————————

The past decade has brought about a radical shift in the location of the world's biggest banks. In 1999, the top five banks (judged by market capitalisation) were located in the United States or United Kingdom. In 2009 the top three were in China:

No.	bank	location	market capitalisation ($m)
1	Indus. & Comm. Bank of China	China	257,004·4
2	China Construction Bank	China	182,186·7
3	Bank of China	China	153,080·5
4	HSBC	UK	143,285·8
5	JP Morgan Chase†	US	128,224·8
6	Wells Fargo†	US	114,141·3
7	Banco Santander	Spain	97,919·7
8	Bank of America†	US	84,519·1
9	Mitsubishi UFJ Financial	Japan	72,194·8
10	BNP Paribas	France	69,214·4

† Government bailout. As of 30/6/2009. [Source · *Financial Times*]

——————— HISTORICAL ECONOMIC INDICATORS ———————

Indicator	2008	2007	2006	2005	2004	2003	2002	2001	2000	1999	1998
FTSE 100 share index	5,357	6,425	5,941	5,168	4,520	4,030	4,566	5,541	6,348	6,313	5,667
Dow Jones Industrial Average	11,253	13,170	11,409	10,548	10,317	8,994	9,226	10,189	10,735	10,465	8,626
CBI business optimism survey	-4.3	-1.5	-8.0	-18.5	6.5	-7.5	-3.2	-27.0	-3.0	-7.0	-33.8
RPI inflation (% year-on-year)	4.0	4.3	3.2	2.8	3.0	2.9	1.6	1.8	2.9	1.6	3.4
Real GDP (% year-on-year)	2.6	2.6	2.9	2.2	3.0	2.8	2.1	2.5	3.9	3.5	3.6
Average mortgage rate (%)	6.90	7.44	6.51	6.53	6.15	5.47	5.65	6.81	7.58	6.97	8.64
Number of taxpayers (million)	32.3	31.8	31.1	30.3	28.5	28.9	28.6	29.3	27.2	26.9	26.2
Highest rate of income tax (%)	40	40	40	40	40	40	40	40	40	40	40
Employment rate (%)	74.5	74.6	74.5	74.7	74.7	74.6	74.5	74.4	74.4	74.0	73.4
Unemployed (millions)	1.78	1.65	1.67	1.47	1.42	1.49	1.53	1.49	1.59	1.73	1.79
Unemployment rate (%)	5.7	5.3	5.4	4.9	4.8	5.1	5.2	5.1	5.4	6.0	6.3
Growth in consumer credit (% year-on-year)	6.3	6.0	7.6	12.5	14.2	14.9	15.9	13.4	14.5	15.8	17.2
Credit cards in issue (millions)	67.4	68.2	67.7	70.6	71.4	66.4	60.4	53.9	49.7	43.5	40.1
Outstanding credit card balance (£bn)	65.3	65.7	66.4	67.5	63.8	54.2	47.5	40.7	35.6	29.7	24.6
Mortgage loan approvals (thousands)	1,285	1,246	1,223	1,196	1,260	1,363	1,425	1,262	1,123	1,146	1,036
Housing transactions (thousands)	916	1,619	1,666	1,531	1,793	1,345	1,588	1,458	1,431	1,470	1,347
Halifax house price (% change year-on-year)	-8.4	9.4	8.3	5.7	18.3	22.4	17.4	8.5	9.8	7.2	5.4
Change in average earnings (%)	3.7	3.6	3.7	3.9	4.2	3.6	4.0	4.9	4.5	3.6	4.7
GfK consumer confidence aggregate	-7	-7	-5	-3	-3	-5	3	1	0	2	-1
UK current account balances ($bn)	-53.5	-105.0	-83.3	-58.9	-46.1	-30.0	-27.9	-30.4	-38.9	-35.4	-5.3
New car registrations (thousands)	2,116	2,390	2,340	2,444	2,599	2,646	2,682	2,578	2,337	2,242	2,262
US Dollar/GB Pound ($/£)	1.83	2.00	1.84	1.82	1.83	1.63	1.50	1.44	1.51	1.62	1.66
Euro/GB Pound (€/£) [pre-1999 estimated]	1.25	1.46	1.47	1.46	1.47	1.44	1.59	1.61	1.64	1.52	(1.48)
Gold price per Troy ounce (£)	472	347	328	245	223	222	206	188	184	172	177
Oil US Dollar/barrel (Brent futures close)	98.5	72.7	66.1	55.2	38.0	28.5	25.0	24.9	28.5	18.0	13.3

[Sources: Bank of England; ONS; Halifax Building Society; Department of Transport; HM Treasury; British Bankers' Association · Many figures have been rounded]

————————————— BRITISH STANDARDS —————————————

The world's first standardisation body, British Standards, started life in 1901 when the Engineering Standards Committee was created to regulate the production of iron and steel for use on railways, bridges, and in shipping. By 1929, the Committee had been granted a Royal Charter, and in 1930 the organisation was renamed the British Standards Institution (BSI). In 1946, the BSI became the founder member of the International Organisation for Standardisation (ISO). ❦ The BSI now oversees 27,000 standards. *c*.1,700 new or revised standards are added each year, and although most of these do not impose formal regulations, certain products (e.g., motorcycle helmets) are required to comply with the relevant standards before they can be sold in Britain or the EU. The BSI also oversees the granting of Kitemarks – a symbol attached to a service or product that attests its quality. Kitemarks were introduced in 1903, and can be used alongside British, European, or international standards. ❦ The creation of new standards is managed by a committee that canvasses opinion from interested parties. Most standards take 12–15 months to be finalised, and *c*.6,000 standards are in development at any one time. ❦ Although modern standards address innovations like web accessibility and stem cell research, the oldest British Standard still in use was created in 1927: BS275 regulates the dimension of rivets. Splendidly, BS0 sets the standard for writing a British Standard.

————————————— COLOUR ECONOMIES —————————————

The 'green economy' made headlines in 2009, as Europe and the United States sought to jolt themselves out of their economic doldrums with a renewed focus on sustainable technologies, low-emission vehicles, and eco-friendly household goods. Other colours that have been linked with various sectors of the economy include:

Black economy........................ *trade in illegal goods or through illegal channels*
White economy...................... *the 'legitimate' economy; or, the voluntary sector*
Grey economy.................*trade in legal commodities through unofficial channels*
Red economy ....*the South Korean economy after the 2002 World Cup*†
Blue economy..........*ocean and waterway industries, including fishing and tourism*
Purple economy.................. *the subsidy of religious organisations via tax breaks*‡
Pink economy.................. *goods and services sold to (or provided by) homosexuals*
Silver economy..................*goods and services sold to (or provided by) the elderly*
Yellow economy.. *that which relates to illegal sex-related activities (e.g., prostitution)*§
Brown economy................. *the pre-green (i.e., polluting, wasteful, &c.) economy*

† South Koreans were exuberant after co-hosting the 2002 World Cup, which saw an unprecedented showing by their soccer team, the Red Devils. After supporters thronged the streets wearing red, some in the press nicknamed the euphoria 'red fever'. The term 'red economy' was used to describe the related rise in commercial activity, as banks lowered interest rates and sales increased. A 2002 report from the Hyundai Research Institute created a dubious backronym: 'Resilient, Enthusiastic, and Dynamic'. ‡ Max Wallace, Director of the Australian National Secular Association, defined the purple economy as 'the wealth generated by the eternal mass-exemption from taxation of religious organizations, their subsidiaries and their charitable arms'. § In China, according to the economist Yang Fan.

—————————— STOCK EXCHANGES WORLDWIDE ——————————

The world's first stock exchange was established in Antwerp in 1460. The London Stock Exchange was founded in 1773, to replace informal trading at coffee-houses, notably Jonathan's Coffee House in Change Alley. Below is a snapshot of the world's top stock exchanges as of 7/09, based on their domestic market capitalisation[†]:

NYSE Group · *New York Stock Exchange & NYSE Arca*
Est. 1792 · 11 Wall St, NYC
Listed companies · 3,149
Domestic market capitalisation
$9,828,785m
Value of share trading · $1,340,581m

TSE · *Tokyo Stock Exchange*
Est. 1878 · 2–1 Nihombashi
Kabutocho, Chuo-ku, Tokyo
Listed companies · 2,353
Domestic market capitalisation
$3,330,556m
Value of share trading · $350,386m

NASDAQ · *National Association of Securities Dealers Automated Quotation*
Est. 1971 · 165 Broadway, NYC
Listed companies · 2,879
Domestic market cap. · $2,372,696m
Value of share trading · $1,468,533m

SSE · *Shanghai Stock Exchange*
Est. 1990 · 528 South Pudong Road, Shanghai
Listed companies · 866
Domestic market cap. · $2,724,188m
Value of share trading · $691,519m

LSE · *London Stock Exchange*
Est. 1773 · 10 Paternoster Square, London
Listed companies · 2,902
Domestic market cap. · $2,415,949m
Value of share trading · $278,995m

EURONEXT
Est. 2000 · 5 locations across Europe
Listed companies · 1,169[‡]
Domestic market cap. · $2,196,994m[‡]
Value of share trading · $153,435m[‡]

HKEx · *Hong Kong Exchanges*
Est. 2000 · One and Two Exchange Square, Central, Hong Kong
Listed companies · 1,278
Domestic market cap. · $2,051,955m
Value of share trading · $150,088m

TSX · *Toronto Stock Exchange* and *TSX Venture Exchange*
Est. 1861 · 130 King St W, Toronto
Listed companies · 3,729
Domestic market cap. · $1,481,473m
Value of share trading · $101,507m

BME · *Bolsas y Mercados Españoles*
Est. 2002 · Plaza de la Lealtad 1, Madrid
Listed companies · 3,518
Domestic market cap. · $1,210,553m
Value of share trading · $181,587m

Deutsche Börse Group (Frankfurt Stock Exchange)
Est. 1997 · Börsenplatz 4, Frankfurt/Main
Listed companies · 810
Domestic market cap. · $1,194,695m
Value of share trading · $158,832m

‡ Euronext data are as of June 2009

† Domestic market capitalisation is a measure frequently used to gauge the size of a stock exchange: it is the total number of outstanding shares from domestic companies multiplied by their respective prices. The volume of share trading is for the month of July 2009, except where noted. The number of listed companies does not include investment funds. [Source for page: World Fed. of Exchanges]

Parliament & Politics

I am not made for politics because I am incapable of wishing for,
or accepting the death of my adversary. – ALBERT CAMUS, *The Rebel*, 1951

———— HOUSE OF COMMONS · STATE OF THE PARTIES ————

TOTAL [as at September 2009] 646	Independent 5
Labour 349	Independent Conservative 1
Conservative 193	Independent Labour 1
Liberal Democrat .63	Ulster Unionist 1
Scottish National Party 7	Respect 1
Plaid Cymru 3	Speaker (John Bercow, see p.254) 1
Democratic Unionist 9	Deputy Speakers 3
Sinn Féin [seats not taken] 5	Vacant [Michael Martin's Glasgow NE seat] 1
Social Democratic & Labour 3	GOVERNMENT MAJORITY 62

———— ATTITUDES TOWARDS THE EXPENSES SCANDAL ————

A May 2009 BBC/Ipsos MORI poll taken at the height of 'Expensegate' [see p.18] found that 71% of Britons were dissatisfied with the way the Commons operated – as illustrated by the response, from various years, to the following question:

Which of these statements best describes your opinion on the present system of governing Britain? (%)	1973	1995	2003	2009
Works extremely well/could not be improved	5	3	2	1
Could be improved in small ways but mainly works well	43	19	34	23
Could be improved quite a lot	35	41	42	38
Needs a great deal of improvement	14	35	18	37
Don't know	4	3	4	1

The 2009 poll revealed that 52% believed that MPs should put the country's interests first, and 43% thought they should put their constituents' interests first. However, 62% of respondents in 2009 thought that MPs actually put their own interests first. Respondents were asked if they agreed with the following statements:

Most MPs make a lot of money by using public office improperly			*Most MPs have a high personal moral code*		
Year	% agree	% disagree	Year	% agree	% disagree
1985 . . . . 46 31			1985 . . . . 42 35		
1994 . . . . 64 22			1994 . . . . 28 59		
2009 . . . . 68 28			2009 . . . . 37 58		

—— POLITICAL BLOGGING & 'SMEARGATE' ——

It is possible that 2009 marked the year that British blogging entered the political mainstream; it was certainly the year that the political bloggers bagged their first major prey. ❦ The political blogosphere in Britain is currently dominated by a handful of sites, the majority of which (and the most widely read) have right-of-centre or libertarian leanings. According to a July 2009 *Total Politics* poll, the ten best British political blogs are:

Paul Staines a.k.a. *Guido Fawkes*

1 .... *Guido Fawkes*	6 .... *Dizzy Thinks*
2 .... *Iain Dale's Diary*	7 .... *Paul Waugh*
3 ..*Spectator Coffee House*	8 .... *Tom Harris MP*
4 ..... *Conservative Home*	9 .... *Devil's Kitchen*
5 .... *Political Betting*	10 . *Daniel Hannan MEP*

Partisanship is the norm for many of these blogs, and even the most serious stories are leavened with flippancy. *Guido Fawkes* is subtitled 'Tittle tattle, gossip, and rumours'; *Iain Dale* promises 'Politics, Gossip, Humour, Commentary'. This mix makes attacks from bloggers hard to repel: too serious a response is derided as po-faced, but simply dismissing bloggers is recklessly to underestimate their power. ❦ The blogging story of the year centred around Labour's desire to wrest control of the blogosphere from the Right. In January, Gordon Brown's special adviser Damian McBride emailed a series of smear stories to Derek Draper, allegedly for inclusion in a proposed anti-Tory 'attack blog' called *Red Rag*. (Draper, a former Peter Mandelson aide and disgraced lobbyist, had returned to politics, and edited the pro-Labour blog *LabourList*.) Draper responded to McBride's email, which included lurid and vile fictions about senior Conservatives and their families, with the words, 'Absolutely totally brilliant Damian'. In April, it was revealed that these emails had been obtained by Paul Staines (a.k.a. 'Guido Fawkes') who passed them to *The Sunday Times* and *The News of The World* for publication. The 'Smeargate' scandal resulted in the resignation of McBride and Draper, a (much-delayed) apology from Brown, and an exacerbation of the public's revulsion towards politics. The blogosphere, led by Staines, gloated at having struck so close to the heart of government. ❦ The rise of political blogging comes at a time when many are sceptical of the symbiosis between political reporters and those they cover. (After McBride quit, some journalists expressed a lack of surprise at the actions of the man known as 'McPoison'.) The 'lobby system' may have opened up recently – No. 10 now publishes summaries of press briefings online. Yet, for the most part, political correspondents remain willing to launder into news unattributable briefings, gossip, and (wittingly or not) smears. As Alice Miles noted in *The Times*: 'It is only through the collusion of journalists that underhand and anonymous attacks on political colleagues can have any effect'. Bloggers represent an insurgency to mainstream media and political parties: since they require no 'access' or favours, bloggers need not 'play the game'. ❦ Smeargate was something of a feedback loop: bloggers blogging about bloggers. (Although, as *Private Eye* noted, Staines chose to give his scoop to the 'dead tree press' rather than publish it first online.) That said, the scandal is likely to establish political blogs in Britain, just as *The Drudge Report*'s exposé of the Monica Lewinsky affair established such blogs in America.

—————— POLITICAL WORDS & PHRASES OF NOTE ——————

SAVED THE WORLD · an embarrassing slip by Gordon Brown who, at PMQs in December 2008, instead of saying, 'We not only saved the banks …', said 'We not only saved the world …'

HAIR DRYER TREATMENT · Downing St. slang for Brown's alleged 'in-your-face' explosions of rage [see p.253].

POWER REVEALS · Mayor of London Boris Johnson's reply when asked whether he thought 'power corrupted'.

PRESBYTERIAN CONSCIENCE · when asked about Expensegate by Andrew Marr in May, Brown bizarrely said, 'To be honest, what I've seen offends my Presbyterian conscience'.

VOODOO *or* UNDEAD MPs · Fraser Nelson's term for MPs who announced their resignation in the wake of Expensegate, but held on until the election, (presumably) to maximise their pay-off (*c.*£120,000) and avoid a potentially embarrassing by-election.

MIDDEN · term for a dung-heap, used by a Lib Dem MP to describe the scandal-ridden Commons.

THE FISH ROTS FROM THE HEAD · an Italian phrase, used by Damian Green to criticise the government's handling of allegations against him [see p.32].

NORWAY DEBATE · after the Speaker attempted to secure his position by apologising for his and Parliament's role in Expensegate, the senior Tory MP Sir Patrick Cormack shocked the Commons by comparing the mood of the House to the May 1940 'Norway Debate' that precipitated the resignation of Neville Chamberlain.

THE SELF-RIGHTEOUS BROTHERS · Alan Johnson's term for Cameron and Nick Clegg who, he claimed, had been given an 'easy ride' over Expensegate.

GOD · The Whitehall nickname for Cabinet Secretary Sir Gus O'Donnell.

HOTMAIL PLOT · press nickname for a failed backbench coup against Brown in June, which Labour MPs were asked to join by emailing *signonnow@hotmail.co.uk*. [The plotters later moved to texts sent to pay-as-you-go mobiles.]

LABOUR WAGs · 'Women Against Gordon' · the SISTERHOOD of former BLAIR BABES who failed to oust Brown during what the *Daily Mail* called THE NIGHT OF THE LONG STILETTOS [see p.21]. When Hazel Blears resigned on the day of the local elections, she wore a brooch with the provocative slogan ROCKING THE BOAT.

TALIBROWN · (fanatical) supporters of Brown – akin to the Blairite ULTRAS.

SQUEAKER BERCOW · see p.254.

LIAR · during a debate over spending cuts, Cameron stopped short of calling Brown a liar, but claimed 'there is a THREAD OF DISHONESTY running through this premiership'. Seemingly in response, Peter Mandelson claimed that George Osborne had told a DELIBERATE UNTRUTH in claiming that the Tories had been denied access to government public spending data.

ZERO PER CENT RISE · another embarrassing slip by Brown who told the Commons during PMQs in July that there would be a 'zero per cent rise' in total spending during 2013–14.

—————— GORDON BROWN'S 'NEWS SANDWICH' ——————

Gordon Brown's stumbling premiership [see p.21] could not have been helped by a stream of media reports commenting on his bitten-to-the-quick fingernails, his curious habit of smiling at inappropriate moments, his haggard appearance†, and his alleged displays of anger and frustration. Two days after Darling's controversial Budget [see p.234], Bloomberg (not an organisation given to hyperbole) reported that the recession and the collapse in Labour's polling may have increased Brown's anxiety:

> *The strain shows, say current and former Brown aides: Among other things, it has inflamed a temper that has always been the subject of gallows humour among those who work with him, they say. The prime minister, 58, has hurled pens and even a stapler at aides, according to one; he says he once saw the leader of Britain's 61 million people shove a laser printer off a desk in a rage. Another aide was warned to watch out for 'flying Nokias' when he joined Brown's team‡.*

Bloomberg said that Brown's advisers employed a novel form of news management:

> *One staffer says a colleague developed a technique called a 'news sandwich' – first telling the prime minister about a recent piece of good coverage before delivering bad news, and then moving quickly to tell him about something good coming soon.*

† In May, *The Sun* published Brown's make-up regimen which, it said, had been left in the back of a taxi by an aide: [1] Transparent Brush. Foam all over. [2] Small pot under eyes, dimple, creases, blend in. [3] Clinique. Super balanced make-up. All over again, like painting a wall, and ears. Shut eyes over lids then with make-up pad smooth over liquid. [4] Powder (dark brush) terracotta Guerlain, all over. ‡ In July, Kevin Maguire leapt to the Prime Minister's defence, writing in *The Daily Mirror*, 'For the record, Brown doesn't throw mobile phones. No. 10 officials say he's more of a sweeper, clearing tables with a swing of his arm, or pushing chairs across the floor, when the red mist comes down'.

—————— LOCAL GOVERNMENT JARGON ——————

To improve communication with the public, the Local Government Association (LGA) proposed a list of 200 words and phrases that should be banned. The LGA sent the list to councils across the country in March 2009. Some examples are below:

Jargon to be avoided	*alternative*		
Actioned	do	Going forward	in the future
Baseline	starting point	Income streams	money
Benchmarking	measuring	Interface	talking to each other
Blue sky thinking	thinking up ideas	Outsourced	privatised
Bottom-up	listening to people	Procure	buy
Can do culture	get the job done	Quick hit	success
Citizen empowerment	people power	Reconfigured	reform
Cross-fertilisation	spreading ideas	Robust	tough
Facilitate	help	Slippage	delay
Fast-track	speed up	Symposium	meeting
		Upward trend	getting better

THE FALL OF SPEAKER MARTIN

On 19/5/2009, Michael Martin MP announced he would resign as the 156th Speaker of the Commons on 21/6. In so doing, he became the first Speaker to step down under pressure since Sir John Trevor was forced out in 1695 for taking a bribe. ❦ Martin's election to the Speakership in 2000 was notable for two reasons: it broke the convention that the post alternate between the main parties (Betty Boothroyd, his predecessor, was also a Labour MP); and Martin became the first Roman Catholic Speaker since the Reformation. ❦ Few considered Martin's Speakership an unalloyed success. Some questioned his political neutrality and others his intellectual rigour. In 2001, *The Independent*'s Simon Carr assessed his media reception: *The Sun* [described him] as coming from the same chimp farm as Two Jags [John Prescott]; Simon Hoggart, in *The Guardian*, compared him to a supply teacher in a sink school; Matthew Parris, of *The Times*, the most thoughtful and considered of the sketchwriters, saw him simply as "a drongo". *The Independent*'s sketch had his face "red and throbbing like a haemorrhoid"'. However, it was the nickname 'Gorbals Mick' – bestowed by *The Daily Mail* – that stuck, despite being criticised by Martin's defenders as insensitive (he was not born in the Gorbals, but in Glasgow's Anderston region), and sectarian ('Mick' can be a slur for Catholic). To some, the name 'Gorbals Mick' exemplified a snobbery that objects to a man with Martin's background or accent holding a great office of State. ❦ While popular with some MPs, Martin's authority was dented by procedural gaffes, the resignation of key staff members, and questions about his expenses. In 2008–09, the arrest of Damian Green [see p.32], and Expensegate [see p.18] added further pressure. In his handling of these crises, Martin was said to be too rigid a defender of the status quo. Soon, MPs' private doubts were publicly expressed to the media and in the Chamber. By the time a motion of no confidence had been tabled, few thought Martin could survive. And, despite a last-ditch attempt to pacify the House, he didn't. ❦ The 157th Speaker was selected from a field of 10, for the first time by secret ballot:

Candidate / Round	1st	2nd	3rd
Margaret Beckett	74	70	·
Sir Alan Beith	55	46	·
JOHN BERCOW	179	221	322
Sir Patrick Cormack	13	·	·
Parmjit Dhanda	26	·	·
Sir Alan Haselhurst	66	57	·
Sir Michael Lord	9	·	·
Richard Shepherd	15	·	·
Ann Widdecombe	44	30	·
Sir George Young	112	174	271

Although a Tory, Bercow's politics had evolved substantially from right to left, and his close ties to Labour MPs dismayed many of his colleagues. Indeed, so unpopular was Bercow on his own benches, commentators interpreted his victory as a Labour ploy to spite (and spike) the Tories. ❦ In his acceptance speech, Bercow pledged impartiality (to some mirth), and promised reform. But within hours of being dragged to the Speaker's chair (a more than usually ironic show of symbolic reluctance), speculation was rife that his tenure might not last beyond the next general election. His *Daily Mail* nickname – 'Squeaker Bercow' – may not bode well.

—————————— THE CABINET ——————————

Few recent Cabinet reshuffles have had the drama of Brown's 5/6/09 attempt to cling to power – set, as it was, against the turmoil of the disastrous (for Labour) local and European elections [see p.20], and the wave of resignations that preceded and succeeded them. (Europe Minister Caroline Flint quit in the middle of Brown's post-reshuffle press conference, later to be replaced by Glenys Kinnock.) According to a wealth of reports, Brown's most significant decision – to keep Alistair Darling as Chancellor – was forced upon him by Darling, who was said to have resisted an attempt to replace him with the 'über-Brownite' Ed Balls. Brown's claims that he had never planned to replace his Chancellor were met with incredulity by the press, who reacted with similar surprise to Peter Mandelson's rapid promotion to First Secretary of State, making him deputy PM in all but name [see p.38]. Eyebrows were also raised at Brown's failure to promote more women, his decision to allow Europe, business, and transport to be run from the Lords, and his ennoblement of the pugnacious businessman Sir Alan Sugar to become 'Enterprise Tsar'. Despite these controversies, and a pervasive atmosphere of chaos, the reshuffle achieved its central purpose: to staunch the flow of resignations and secure Brown's premiership until May 2010.

Prime Minister; First Lord of the Treasury	Gordon Brown
Leader of the Commons; Lord Privy Seal	Harriet Harman
SoS for Business, &c., First Secretary of State	Peter Mandelson
Chancellor of the Exchequer	Alistair Darling
SoS Foreign & Commonwealth Affairs	David Miliband
SoS Justice; Lord Chancellor	Jack Straw
SoS the Home Department	Alan Johnson
SoS Environment, Food, & Rural Affairs	Hilary Benn
SoS International Development	Douglas Alexander
SoS Communities & Local Government	John Denham
SoS Children, Schools, & Families	Ed Balls
SoS Energy & Climate Change	Edward Miliband
SoS Health	Andy Burnham
SoS Northern Ireland	Shaun Woodward [unpaid]
Leader of the Lords; Chancellor of the Duchy of Lancaster	Baroness Royall
Minister for the Cabinet Office, & Olympics; Paymaster General	Tessa Jowell
SoS Scotland	Jim Murphy
SoS Work & Pensions	Yvette Cooper
Chief Secretary to the Treasury	Liam Byrne
SoS Wales	Peter Hain
SoS Defence	Bob Ainsworth
SoS Transport	Lord Adonis
SoS Culture, Media, & Sport	Ben Bradshaw
Also attending · Minister for Africa, Asia, & the UN	*vacant*
Minister of State for Employment & Welfare Reform	Jim Knight
Minister of State for Dept. Business, Innovations, & Skills	Pat McFadden
Minister for Housing	John Healey
Minister for Science and Innovation	Lord Drayson [unpaid]
Parliamentary Secretary to the Treasury and Chief Whip	Nicholas Brown

THE SCOTTISH PARLIAMENT

The current state of parties (as at 18 September 2009)

Number of MSPs	Constituency	Regional	Total
Scottish National Party	21	26	47
Scottish Labour	37	9	46
Scottish Conservative	3	13	16
Scottish Liberal Democrat	11	5	16
Scottish Green Party	0	2	2
Independent	0	1	1
Presiding Officer (Alex Fergusson)	1	0	1

Scotland's first Muslim MSP, Bashir Ahmad, died on 6 February 2009; he was a regional list MSP for the Scottish National Party and was replaced by the next member on the list, Anne McLaughlin.

THE NATIONAL ASSEMBLY FOR WALES

The current state of parties (as at 18 September 2009)

Number of AMs	Constituency	Regional	Total
Labour	24	2	26
Plaid Cymru	7	8	15
Conservative	5	7	12
Liberal Democrat	3	3	6
Independent	1	0	1
Presiding Officer (Lord Dafydd Elis-Thomas)	1	0	1

In September 2009, the Welsh Conservatives said that official car use figures showed members had travelled almost as far as the moon in 2008, undermining the Assembly's environmental policies.

THE NORTHERN IRELAND ASSEMBLY

The current state of parties (as at 18 September 2009)

DUP...............36	SDLP...............16	Green Party...........1
Sinn Féin............28	Alliance...............7	Independent...........1
Ulster Unionists......18	PUP...................1	Speaker: William Hay

THE LONDON ASSEMBLY

The current state of parties (as at 18 September 2009)

Conservative.........11	Liberal Democrat.....3	British Nat. Party.....1
Labour...............8	Green.................2	(May 2008 turnout, 45·3%)

THE HOUSE OF LORDS

State of the parties (as at 21 July 2009)

Conservative	193	Bishops	26
Labour	215	Other	17
Liberal Democrat	71	Total	724
Crossbench	202		

Excludes 12 Members who are on leave of absence, 2 who are suspended and 1 disqualified as an MEP.

Archbishops and Bishops..26 [0]
Life Peers under the Appellate Jurisdiction Act 1876.........................23 [1]
Life Peers under the Life Peerages Act 1958...........................598 [146]
Peers under the House of Lords Act 1999...................................92 [2]

[Numbers within brackets indicate the number of women included in the figure.]

TOP TEN MOST FANCIABLE MPs

Below are the 'most fanciable' members of parliament, according to *Sky News*'s political editor Adam Boulton, who publishes a list on his blog each Valentine's Day:

#	Name (age)	Party
1	Andy Burnham (39)	Lab
2	Lynne Featherstone (57)	Lib Dem
3	Adam Afriyie (43)	Con
4	Ed Vaizey (40)	Con
5	Julia Goldsworthy (30)	Lib Dem
6	Ed Miliband (39)	Lab
7	Caroline Flint (47)	Lab
8	Nick Clegg (42)	Lib Dem
9	David Miliband (43)	Lab
10	Jacqui Smith (46) [see p.18]	Lab

No Cabinet members made the list in 2008; in 2009, all Labour MPs listed are in the Cabinet.

WESTMINSTER DOG OF THE YEAR · 2008

The Westminster Dog of the Year contest, organised by the Kennel Club, has been running since 1992; it is open to all MPs and Lords, and, since 2005, parliamentary journalists. In October 2008, UKIP MP Bob Spink's greyhounds, Jessie and Fozzy Bear, fought off competition from 11 other political pooches to win first prize. Second place was awarded to an 18-month-old Newfoundland named Lollie, belonging to Conservative MP Roger Gale. Third place also went to a Conservative Party hound – Andrew Rosindell's Staffordshire Bull Terrier, Buster.

In September 2008, the dog welfare charity Dogs Trust withdrew its support from all Kennel Club events – including the Westminster Dog of the Year competition. The charity described this boycott as the 'strongest signal' it could send to urge the Kennel Club to take action to 'ensure that the health and well-being of pedigree dogs is ranked over appearance and artificial breed standards' [see p.228]. ❦ On 28 July 2009, the Chancellor's spokesman reported that Alistair Darling's cat Sybil had passed away. Sybil entered Downing Street on 11 September 2007, when she accompanied the Darlings from Edinburgh. However, the political limelight did not suit Sybil, who was transferred to an undisclosed London location after just six months. Sybil followed in the illustrious paw prints of other famous Downing Street cats, including Humphrey (1989–2006) and Wilberforce (1970–88).

——PARLIAMENTARY SALARY & ALLOWANCES——

Members of Parliament

Members' Parliamentary salary	£64,766 (from 1·4·2009)
Staffing expenditure (maximum)	£103,812
Administrative and Office Expenditure (AOE)	£22,393
Communications expenditure (maximum)	£10,400
London costs allowance†	£7,500
Personal Additional Accommodation Expenditure (PAAE)‡	£24,222
Winding up expenditure	£42,068
Car mileage, first 10,000 miles	40p per mile
– thereafter	25p per mile
Motorcycle allowance	24p per mile
Bicycle allowance	20p per mile

† Replaces the London supplement. Any member can claim this allowance provided they do not claim the Personal Additional Accommodation Expenditure. ‡ Replaces the additional cost allowance.

Position

Prime Minister†	£132,923 (from 1·04·2009)
Cabinet Minister†	£79,754
Cabinet Minister (Lords)	£108,253
Minister of State†	£41,370
Minister of State (Lords)	£84,524
Parliamentary Under Secretary†	£31,401
Parliamentary Under Secretary (Lords)	£73,617
Government Chief Whip†	£79,754
Government Deputy Chief Whip†	£41,370
Government Whip†	£26,624
Leader of the Opposition†	£73,617
Leader of the Opposition (Lords)	£73,617
Opposition Chief Whip†	£41,370
Speaker†	£79,754
Attorney General (Lords)	£113,248
Lord Chancellor†	£79,745

[† Ministers in the Commons additionally receive their salaries as MPs, as above.]

Backbench Peers

Subsistence	Day £86·50 · Overnight £174·00
Office secretarial allowance	£75·00 per sitting day and <40 additional days
Travel	as for MPs
Spouses/children's expenses	6 return journeys per year

Lords Ministers and paid office holders

Ministers' night subsistence allowance	£38,280 for those with a second home in London
London supplement	£2,916 except those with official residence, &c.
Secretarial allowance	£5,658
Spouses/children's expenses	15 return journeys per year

──── SALARIES FOR DEVOLVED LEGISLATURES &c. ────

Scottish Parliament (from 1·04·2009)	*total salary*
Member of the Scottish Parliament (MSP)	£56,671
First Minister	£138,099
Cabinet Secretary	£98,914
Scottish Minister	£83,131
Presiding Officer	£98,914
Solicitor General	£96,577

National Assembly for Wales (from 1·4·2009)	*total salary*
Assembly Member (AM)	£53,108
Assembly First Minister	£132,862
Assembly Minister	£94,478
Presiding Officer	£94,478
Leader of the largest non-cabinet party	£94,478
AMs who are also MPs or MEPs	£17,703

Northern Ireland Assembly (from 1·4·2009)	*total salary*
Members of the Legislative Assembly (MLA)	£43,101
Presiding Officer	£80,902

European Parliament (from 14·7·2009)	*total salary*
UK Members of the European Parliament	as MPs or *c.*€7,000/month[†]

† Since July 2009, MEPs receive a common salary. UK MEPs elected before June 2009 may choose to receive this flat rate or opt to receive the same remuneration as an MP, as they did previously.

Members of Parliament who are also members of a devolved legislature receive their full parliamentary salary [see above] and one-third of the salary due to them for their other role. Since 2004, Westminster MPs are ineligible to serve additionally as MEPs. The devolved legislatures control their own expenses and allowances.

London Assembly (from 1·4·2009)	*total salary*
Member of the London Assembly (MLA)	£52,910
Mayor of London	£143,911
Deputy Mayor	£127,784

──── CELEBRITY PRIME MINISTER ────

Below are the 'celebrities' that Britons would most like to see as Prime Minister:

1 .... Simon Cowell	6 .... Russell Brand	† Price stood for election in
2 .Joanna Lumley [see p.36]	7 .... Katie Price[†]	2001 on a platform advocating
3 ...... Trevor McDonald	8 .... Fern Britton	free breast implants and more
4 .... Chris Moyles	9 .... Will Young	nudist beaches. [Source: MSN
5 .... Cheryl Cole	10 .... Delia Smith	Entertainment, May 2009]

—————— THE CONSTITUTIONAL 'GOLDEN TRIANGLE' ——————

In British parliamentary terms [see also p.76], the 'Golden Triangle' is a nickname for the three senior British civil servants who advise the British monarch on forming a government in the event of an uncertain election result. These 'three wise men' are: the Prime Minister's principal private secretary, the Cabinet Secretary, and the Monarch's private secretary. With opinion polls suggesting that the next general election might not produce a clear-cut result, *The Guardian* reported in January 2009, 'As part of their preparations for a hung parliament, the three senior mandarins will be briefed by the permanent secretaries of Whitehall's departments on the Tories' and Liberal Democrats' plans for government. The civil service will ensure they are versed in the main sticking points if Labour or the Tories embark on coalition talks with the Lib Dems'. ❦ Sir Kenneth Stowe, principal private secretary to Harold Wilson, Jim Callaghan, and Margaret Thatcher, enumerated three principles to resolve the uncertainty of forming a government: [1] The Queen's government must be carried on; [2] The PM appointed by the sovereign must be able to command a majority in the House of Commons; [3] The PM must be confident of leading or commanding the support of the majority party in the Commons.

————————————— CLEVEREST VOTERS —————————————

Voters with the highest IQ in childhood tend to vote Green or Liberal Democrat, according to research published in the journal *Intelligence* in November 2008. The researchers compared childhood intelligence (recorded by the 1970 British Cohort Study) with how, as 34-year-old adults, they voted in the 2001 general election. The results of the study suggested that those with higher childhood intelligence were more likely to be engaged by politics, take part in rallies or demonstrations, and sign petitions. The average childhood IQ score for 2001 voters by party was:

Party	average IQ		
Green	108·3	Plaid Cymru	102·5
Liberal Democrat	108·2	Scottish National	102·2
Conservative	103·7	UK Independence	101·1
Labour	103·0	British National Party	98·4
		Did not vote/none of the above	99·7

————————— THINK TANK OF THE YEAR · 2008 —————————

In 2008, *Prospect* gave its 'Think Tank of the Year' award to the Royal United Services Institute, whose slogan is 'Independent thinking on defence and security'. The judging panel noted: 'this think tank combines strong focus with global reputation ... Once aligned with the political right, this think tank has moved to the centre ground, deploying expertise, research and a new rigour in an impressive set of publications and policy interventions'. The award was presented by the Shadow Chancellor, Tory MP George Osborne, who wryly observed that the RUSI was the only think tank whose members genuinely 'think about tanks'. ❦ *Prospect's* runner-up think tank was the respected economic analyst, The Institute for Fiscal Studies.

———————— DEVOLUTION & PUBLIC OPINION ————————

The English view of devolution was probed by the NatCen *British Social Attitudes* report published in January 2009. Respondents living in England were asked about their identity; the results show that, since 1997, the English have felt less British:

National identity (%)	1997	1999	2000	2001	2003	2007
English not British	7	17	18	17	17	19
More English than British	17	14	14	13	19	14
Equally English and British	45	37	34	42	31	31
More British than English	14	11	14	9	13	14
British not English	9	14	12	11	10	12

When asked about the economic relationship between England and Scotland, 28% of the English strongly agreed that Scotland should pay for its own services out of local taxes, since the country had its own parliament. Below are further responses:

Compared with other parts of the UK, Scotland's share of government spending is:	% of the English agreeing		
	2000	2003	2007
... much more than its fair share	8	9	16
... little more than its fair share	13	13	16
... pretty much its fair share	42	45	38
... little less than its fair share	10	8	6
... much less than its fair share	1	1	1
Don't know	25	25	22

When asked about the 'West Lothian' question, 61% agreed that Scottish MPs should *not* be allowed to vote on legislation that only concerned England. However, 55% said that the existence of the Scottish parliament had made no difference to how Britain is governed, and 58% said the same about the Welsh Assembly.

———————— THE SPECTATOR PARLIAMENTARIAN AWARDS ————————

Newcomer of the year .... Lord Mandelson [see p.38] [Lab]
Minister to watch .... Ed Miliband [Lab]
Speech of the year† .... Diane Abbott [Lab]
Inquisitor of the year .... Frank Field [Lab]
Peer of the year .... Baroness Manningham-Buller [Crossbench]
Resignation of the year .... David Davis [Con]
Campaigner of the year‡ .... Ben Wallace [Con]
Politician of the year .... Boris Johnson [Con]
Parliamentarian of the year .... Vincent Cable [Lib Dem]
Readers' Representative Award .... Nadine Dorries [Con]

† In her winning speech, Abbott opposed proposals to extend the terror detention limit to 42 days.
‡ Wallace was awarded the Campaigner of the Year accolade for becoming the first MP to publish full details of his expenses; *The Spectator* called him 'arguably the bravest man in Westminster'.

———————— THINGS THROWN AT POLITICIANS ————————

The classic cream-pie-in-the-kisser manoeuvre was refreshed in March 2009, when Lord Mandelson had a cup of green custard tossed in his face by a protestor upset at the plans for Heathrow's third runway. The activist, Leila Deen, claimed her attack was a 'lighthearted way of making a very serious point'. Lord Mandelson responded pithily, 'I suppose in a democracy people are entitled to have their say but I would rather people said it to my face rather than throw it'. 'Pieing', which dates to the early days of slapstick, was first used on politicians in the 1970s by American 'Yippies' – an anarchic umbrella group of anti-war and pro-freedom-of speech activists. Other notable efforts to embarrass politicians with missiles include:

Year	item	thrown at	protestor's cause
1970	*cream pie*	Chair, US Cmsn on Obscenity & Pornography	*censorship*
1972	*pot of ink*	PM Edward Heath	*anti-European Economic Community*
1984	*egg, fruit*	German Chancellor Helmut Kohl	*anti-Kohl policies*
1998	*ice water*	Deputy PM John Prescott	*striking Liverpool workers*
2000	*cream pie*	Victoria, Australia Premier Steve Bracks	*police brutality*
2000	*custard pie*	Shadow Home Sec. Ann Widdecombe	*pro-asylum*
2000	*choc. éclair*	Agriculture Minister Nick Brown	*pro-environment*
2001	*custard pie*	Intl Dev. Sec. Clare Short	*anti-globalisation*
2001	*tomato*	PM Tony Blair	*British sanctions on Iraq*
2001	*cream pie*	Canadian PM Jean Chrétien	*social policies*
2001	*eggs*	Deputy PM John Prescott	*pro-countryside*
2004	*eggs*	Deputy PM John Prescott	*pro-hunting*
2004	*purple flour*	PM Tony Blair (and other MPs in the Commons)	*Fathers 4 Justice*
2004	*shoes*	Former Iraqi Pres. Iyad Allawi	*Iraqi politics*
2004	*slurry*	MEP Robert Kilroy-Silk	*respect for Islam*
2006	*eggs*	Education Sec. Ruth Kelly	*Fathers 4 Justice*
2008	*custard pie*	Immigration Minister Phil Woolas	*pro-immigration*
2008	*pair of shoes*	US President George W. Bush†	*the invasion of Iraq*
2009	*shoe*	Chinese Premier Wen Jiabao	*human rights*
2009	*shoe*	Iranian Pres. Mahmoud Ahmadinejad	*a prior injury*
2009	*shoe*	Indian Home Minister P. Chidambaram	*1984 Sikh killings*
2009	*shoe*	Indian MP Naveen Jindal	*Indian political system*
2009	*shoe*	Indian PM candidate Lal Krishna Advani	*personnel matter*

[All titles are at the time of attack.] † At Bush's last news conference in Iraq, in December 2008, journalist Muntadar al-Zaidi flung one of his shoes at the President while shouting, in Arabic, 'This is a gift from the Iraqis; this is the farewell kiss, you dog!' He then flung his other shoe with the words, 'This is from the widows, the orphans, and those who were killed in Iraq!'. Bush managed to duck both shoes. Al-Zaidi was arrested, beaten, and served time in prison, but he became a hero to some in the Arab world. A Turkish firm that claimed to have manufactured Al-Zaidi's shoes reported they had hired 100 extra staff to keep up with demand for Model 271, or, the 'Bye Bye Bush Shoe'. In many parts of Asia, shoes and feet are equated with uncleanliness, and throwing a shoe at someone is a dramatic way of saying they are no better than dirt. In 2009, Indians inspired by al-Zaidi also began hurling shoes at politicians; some villagers even attended shoe-throwing classes to better their aim. In India, feet are also associated with the lower castes [see p.296]. Sources: *Telegraph*; BBC; *Slate*; *LA Times*.

GENERAL ELECTION BREAKDOWN 1979–2005

Date	3·5·79	9·6·83	11·6·87	9·4·92	1·5·97	7·6·01	5·5·05
Winning party	Con	Con	Con	Con	Lab	Lab	Lab
Seat majority	43	144	102	21	179	167	67
PM	Thatcher	Thatcher	Thatcher	Major	Blair	Blair	Blair
Leader of Op.	Callaghan	Foot	Kinnock	Kinnock	Major	Hague	Howard
Lib (Dem) leader	Steel	Steel	Steel	Ashdown	Ashdown	Kennedy	Kennedy

Conservative

Seats	339	397	375	336	165	166	198
Votes (m)	13·70	13·01	13·74	14·09	9·60	8·36	8·78
Share of votes (%)	43·9	42·4	42·2	41·9	30·7	31·7	32·4
% of seats	53·4	61·1	57·8	51·6	25·0	25·2	30·5

Labour

Seats	268	209	229	271	418	412	355
Votes (m)	11·51	8·46	10·03	11·56	13·52	10·72	9·55
Share of votes (%)	36·9	27·6	30·8	34·4	43·2	40·7	35·2
% of seats	42·4	32·2	35·2	41·6	63·6	62·7	55·2

Liberal Democrat (&c.)

Seats	11	23	22	20	46	52	62
Votes (m)	4·31	7·78	7·34	6·00	5·24	4·81	5·99
Share of votes (%)	13·8	25·4	22·6	17·8	16·8	18·3	22·0
% of seats	1·7	3·5	3·4	3·1	7·0	7·9	9·6

Monster Raving Loony

Candidates	–	11	5	22	24	15	19
Average vote (%)	–	0·7	0·7	0·6	0·7	1·0	–
Lost deposits	–	11	5	22	24	15	19

Women MPs	19	23	41	60	120	118	127
– as %	3·0	3·5	6·3	9·2	18·2	17·9	19·7

Turnout (%)	76·0	72·7	75·3	77·7	71·4	59·4	61·4
– England (%)	75·9	72·5	75·4	78·0	71·4	59·2	61·3
– Wales (%)	79·4	76·1	78·9	79·7	73·5	61·6	62·6
– Scotland (%)	76·8	72·7	75·1	75·5	71·3	58·2	60·8
– N. Ireland (%)	67·7	72·9	67·0	69·8	67·1	68·0	62·9

Postal vote (%)	2·2	2·0	2·4	2·0	2·3	5·2	14·6
Spoilt ballots (%)	0·38	0·17	0·11	0·12	0·30	0·38	0·7
– av./constituency	186	79	57	61	142	152	291
Deposit to stand	£150	£150	£500	£500	£500	£500	£500
– threshold (%)	12½	12½	5	5	5	5	5

Some figures (e.g., that of a winning party's majority) are disputed. Source: House of Commons.

BRITISH PRIME MINISTERS

Prime Minister	date of birth	star sign	position in family	siblings	child of MP	at Eton	at Harrow	at Oxbridge	in the forces	party as PM	age when first PM	time as PM	Admins.	date of death	age at death
Gordon Brown	20-02-1951	♓	2nd of 3	2b	·	·	·	·	·	Lab	56y 129d		1	—	—
Tony Blair	06-05-1953	♉	2nd of 3	1b 1s	·	·	·	O	·	Lab	43y 361d	10y c.55d	3	—	—
John Major	29-03-1943	♈	4th of 4	2b 1s	·	·	·	·	·	Con	47y 245d	6y 154d	2	—	—
Margaret Thatcher	13-10-1925	♎	2nd of 2	1s	·	·	·	O	·	Con	53y 204d	11y 209d	3	—	—
James Callaghan	27-03-1912	♈	2nd of 2	1s	·	·	·	·	◆	Lab	64y 9d	3y 29d	1	26-03-2005	92
Edward Heath	09-07-1916	♋	1st of 2	1b	·	·	·	O	◆	Con	53y 335d	3y 259d	1	17-07-2005	89
Harold Wilson	11-03-1916	♓	2nd of 2	1s	·	·	·	O	·	Lab	48y 219d	7y 279d	4	24-05-1995	79
Alec Douglas-Home	02-07-1903	♋	1st of 7	4b 2s	·	◆	·	O	·	Con	60y 109d	363d	1	09-10-1995	92
Harold Macmillan	10-02-1894	♒	3rd of 3	2b	·	◆	·	O	◆	Con	62y 335d	6y 281d	1	29-12-1986	92
Anthony Eden	12-06-1897	♊	4th of 5	3b 1s	·	◆	·	O	◆	Con	57y 299d	1y 279d	1	14-01-1977	79
Clement Attlee	03-01-1883	♑	7th of 8	4b 3s	·	·	·	O	◆	Lab	63y 205d	6y 92d	2	08-10-1967	84
Winston Churchill	30-11-1874	♐	1st of 2	1b	◆	·	◆	·	◆	Con	65y 163d	8y 240d	3	24-01-1965	90
Neville Chamberlain	18-03-1869	♓	3rd of 6	1b 4s	◆	·	·	·	·	Con	68y 71d	2y 348d	1	09-11-1940	71
Ramsay MacDonald	12-10-1866	♎	only child	0	·	·	·	·	·	Lab	57y 102d	6y 289d	4	09-11-1937	71
Stanley Baldwin	03-08-1867	♌	only child	0	·	·	◆	C	·	Con	55y 292d	7y 82d	4	13-12-1947	80
Andrew Bonar Law	16-09-1858	♍	4th of 7	3b 3s	·	·	·	·	·	Con	64y 37d	209d	1	30-10-1923	65
David Lloyd George	17-01-1863	♑	3rd of 4	1b 2s	·	·	·	·	·	Lib	53y 325d	5y 317d	2	26-03-1945	82
Herbert Henry Asquith	12-09-1852	♍	2nd of 5	1b 3s	·	·	·	O	·	Lib	55y 198d	8y 244d	4	15-02-1928	75
Henry Campbell-Bannerman	07-09-1836	♍	6th of 6	1b 4s	·	·	·	C	·	Lib	69y 89d	2y 122d	1	22-04-1908	71
Arthur James Balfour	25-07-1848	♌	3rd of 8	4b 3s	·	◆	·	C	·	Con	53y 352d	3y 145d	1	19-03-1930	81
Earl of Rosebery	07-05-1847	♉	3rd of 4	1b 2s	·	◆	·	O	·	Lib	46y 302d	1y 109d	1	21-05-1929	82
Marquess of Salisbury	03-02-1830	♒	5th of 6	3b 2s	◆	◆	·	O	·	Con	55y 144d	13y 252d	4	22-08-1903	73
William Ewart Gladstone	29-12-1809	♑	5th of 6	3b 2s	◆	◆	·	O	·	Lib	58y 340d	12y 126d	4	19-05-1898	88
Benjamin Disraeli	21-12-1804	♐	2nd of 5	3b 1s	·	·	·	·	·	Con	63y 68d	6y 339d	2	19-04-1881	76
Viscount Palmerston	20-10-1784	♎	1st of 5	1b 3s	◆	·	◆	C	·	Lib	71y 109d	9y 141d	2	18-10-1865	81
Earl of Aberdeen	28-01-1784	♒	1st of 7	5b 1s	·	·	◆	C	·	Con	68y 326d	2y 42d	1	14-12-1860	76

—————————— BRITISH PRIME MINISTERS cont. ——————————

Prime Minister	date of birth	star sign	position in family	siblings	child of MP	at Eton	at Harrow	at Oxbridge	in the forces	party as PM	age when first PM	time as PM	Admins.	date of death	age at death
Earl of Derby	29-03-1799	♈	1st of 7	2b 4s	◈	◈	·	O	·	Con	52y 331d	3y 280d	3	23-10-1869	70
Lord John Russell	18-08-1792	♌	3rd of 7	6b	◈	·	·	C	·	Lib	53y 316d	6y 11d	2	28-05-1878	85
Robert Peel	05-02-1788	≈≈	3rd of 11	5b 5s	◈	·	◈	O	·	Con	46y 308d	5y 57d	2	02-07-1850	62
Lord Melbourne	15-03-1779	✶	2nd of 6	3b 2s	·	◈	·	C	·	Whig	55y 123d	6y 255d	2	24-11-1848	69
Earl Grey	13-03-1764	✶	2nd of 9	6b 2s	·	◈	·	C	·	Whig	66y 254d	3y 229d	1	17-07-1845	81
Duke of Wellington	01-05-1769	♉	6th of 9	6b 2s	◈	◈	·	·	◈	Tory	58y 266d	2y 320d	2	14-09-1852	83
Viscount Goderich	01-11-1782	♏	2nd of 3	2b	·	·	◈	C	·	Tory	44y 305d	130d	1	28-01-1859	76
George Canning	11-04-1770	♈	2nd of 13	7b 5s	·	◈	·	O	·	Tory	57y 1d	119d	1	08-08-1827	57
Earl of Liverpool	07-06-1770	♊	1st of 3	1b 1s	◈	·	·	O	·	Tory	42y 1d	14y 305d	1	04-12-1828	58
Spencer Perceval	01-11-1762	♏	5th of 9	2b 6s	◈	·	◈	C	·	Tory	46y 338d	2y 221d	1	11-05-1812	49
Lord Grenville	24-10-1759	♏	6th of 9	3b 5s	◈	◈	·	O	·	Whig	46y 110d	1y 42d	1	12-01-1834	74
Henry Addington	30-05-1757	♊	4th of 6	1b 4s	·	·	·	O	·	Tory	43y 291d	3y 54d	1	15-02-1844	86
William Pitt	28-05-1759	♊	4th of 5	2b 2s	◈	·	·	C	·	Tory	24y 205d	18y 343d	2	23-01-1806	46
Duke of Portland	14-04-1738	♈	3rd of 6	1b 4s	◈	◈	·	O	·	Whig	44y 335d	3y 82d	2	30-10-1809	71
Earl of Shelburne	02-05-1737	♉	1st of 5	1b 3s	◈	·	·	O	◈	Whig	45y 63d	266d	1	07-05-1805	68
Lord North	13-04-1732	♈	1st of 6	1b 4s	◈	◈	·	O	·	Tory	37y 290d	12y 58d	1	05-08-1792	60
Duke of Grafton	28-09-1735	♏	2nd of 3	2b	◈	·	·	C	·	Whig	33y 16d	1y 106d	1	14-03-1811	75
Earl of Chatham	15-11-1708	♉	4th of 7	1b 5s	◈	◈	·	O	◈	Whig	57y 257d	2y 76d	1	11-05-1778	69
Marquess of Rockingham	13-05-1730	♉	8th of 10	4b 5s	◈	◈	·	C	·	Whig	35y 61d	1y 113d	2	01-07-1782	52
George Grenville	14-10-1712	♎	2nd of 7	5b 1s	◈	◈	·	O	·	Whig	50y 184d	2y 85d	1	13-11-1770	58
Earl of Bute	25-05-1713	♊	2nd of 8	2b 5s	·	◈	·	·	·	Tory	49y 1d	317d	1	10-03-1792	78
Duke of Devonshire	1720	?	2nd of 7	3b 3s	◈	·	·	·	·	Whig	c.36	225d	1	02-10-1764	c.44
Duke of Newcastle	21-07-1693	♋	8th of 11	2b 8s	◈	·	·	C	·	Whig	60y 238d	7y 205d	2	17-11-1768	75
Henry Pelham	26-09-1694	♎	9th of 11	2b 8s	◈	·	·	C	·	Whig	48y 336d	10y 191d	1	06-03-1754	59
Earl of Wilmington	?1673	?	5th of 5	3b 1s	·	·	·	O	·	Whig	c.69	1y 136d	1	02-07-1743	c.70
Robert Walpole	26-08-1676	♍	5th of 17	9b 7s	◈	◈	·	C	·	Whig	44y 107d	20y 314d	1	18-03-1745	60

—————— POLITICAL BOOK BOOSTS ——————

In 2009, one of the first historical novels ever written became an unlikely symbol of opposition to French President Nicolas Sarkozy. *The Princess of Cleves*, a romantic French tale written in 1679, first rose to political prominence in 2006, when Sarkozy criticised the inclusion of questions about the book in an employment exam, saying: 'A sadist or an idiot, up to you, included questions about *The Princess of Cleves* in an exam for people applying for public sector jobs'. This remark was only the first of several in which the President dismissed the book as irrelevant. In response, Sarkozy's opponents began championing *The Princess* as a symbol of traditional French values, and an emblem of dissent against Sarkozy's policies. Sales of *The Princess* surged, and the novel became the surprise hit of the 2009 Paris Book Fair, where badges proclaiming 'I am reading *The Princess of Cleves*' were the accessory to have. ❧ Several other political leaders unexpectedly boosted book sales in 2009. In April, Venezuelan President Hugo Chávez presented the 1971 tome *Open Veins of Latin America*, by Uruguayan journalist Eduardo Galeano, to Barack Obama at the Summit of the Americas in Trinidad. The book quickly jumped from 54,295 on Amazon.com's sales chart to number 2. *Open Veins* was not the first book to

Nicolas Sarkozy

get a boost from Chávez: in 2006, he delivered a scathing anti-American speech to the UN that plugged Noam Chomsky's 2003 text *Hegemony and Survival*. Overnight, sales of Chomsky's book soared from number 160,722 on Amazon.com's chart to number 7. ❧ In early 2009, Japanese PM Taro Aso boosted language textbook sales in his country after making a series of reading blunders in public. Aso's mistakes came from misreading *kanji* – Chinese characters that form the basis of written Japanese. These characters (of which there are thousands) prove difficult for many Japanese, and Aso is no exception: in late 2008 he accidentally described Sino-Japanese exchanges as 'cumbersome' (he meant 'frequent'), and offered to 'stench' an apology for WWII. Aso's mistakes boosted language textbook sales across the board and led one book – *Chinese Characters that Look Readable but are Easily Misread* – to top the best-seller chart in February. ❧ A memorable boost from an unlikely source came in January 2006, when Osama bin Laden declared, via audiotape, 'If Bush declines but to continue lying and practising injustice [against us], it is useful for you to read the book of *The Rogue State*'. Within 24 hours William Blum's *Rogue State: a Guide to the World's Only Superpower* had surged from 205,000 on Amazon's chart to 21.

In July 2009, Radio 4's *World At One* asked its political panel which books they planned to read during the summer recess. International Development secretary Douglas Alexander said he would read *The Storm* by Vince Cable, *Facts are Subversive* by Timothy Garton Ash, and, for his children, *The Utterly Otterleys* by Mairi Hedderwick. Tory MP Richard Benyon said he would read *The End of the Line* by Charles Clover, as well as 'some unutterable trash'. The Lib Dem foreign affairs spokesman Ed Davey said he would also read *The Storm*, in addition to Bob Woodward's *The War Within: A Secret White House History 2006–08*, and Mark Leonard's *What Does China Think?* ❧ Elsewhere it was reported that Gordon Brown would spend his summer watching videotapes of sporting events he had missed.

———————————— OBAMA'S INAUGURATION ————————————

Barack Obama was sworn in as the 44th President of the United States a few minutes after noon on Tuesday, 20 January, 2009. His oath as the nation's first African-American President was heralded as deeply significant, and millions of Americans flooded into an ice-cold Washington DC to witness history in the making. Obama himself remained characteristically sober and even downbeat during his 18-minute address, noting the 'gathering clouds and raging storms' of war and recession. He vowed to confront such challenges, and to remake America by the light of its best ideals: 'hard work and honesty, courage and fair play, tolerance and curiosity, loyalty and patriotism'. Below is the programme of the day's swearing-in ceremony:

11:30am EST · *Arrival* of Bushes & Obamas at West Front Lawn, Capitol
Building · *Call to order & welcoming remarks* by Sen. Dianne Feinstein
Invocation by Pastor Rick Warren · *My Country 'Tis of Thee* by Aretha Franklin

11:50am · *Oath of Office* by Vice President Joseph R. Biden, Jr administered by
Associate Justice of the Supreme Court John Paul Stevens · *Air and Simple Gifts*
by John Williams (composer/arranger), Itzhak Perlman (violin), Yo-Yo Ma (cello),
Gabriela Montero (piano), and Anthony McGill (clarinet)

11:56am[†]· *Oath of Office* by President Barack Obama using Abraham Lincoln's
inaugural Bible, administered by Chief Justice of the US John G. Roberts, Jr[‡]

12:05pm · Obama's inaugural address · *Praise Song for the Day* by Elizabeth
Alexander · *Benediction* by Rev. Dr Joseph E. Lowery · *National Anthem*
by The United States Navy Band Sea Chanters

† Scheduled time; the ceremony ran *c*.5 minutes late. By law, Obama became President at noon, as *Air and Simple Gifts* was performed. ‡ Obama and Roberts both stumbled over the 35-word oath, interrupting each other and misplacing the word 'faithfully'. These minor slips led some to question whether the swearing-in was binding. So, displaying what the White House called 'an abundance of caution', Obama re-took the oath the next day. Yet, because this second oath was not sworn on a Bible, some (erroneously) questioned its validity, and others (absurdly) questioned Obama's Christianity.

———— ADDRESSING BOTH US HOUSES OF CONGRESS ————

In March 2009, Gordon Brown beat both Nicolas Sarkozy and Angela Merkel to become the first European[†] leader to meet President Obama in the White House. During his visit to Washington, Brown became only the fifth British Prime Minister to address both houses of the United States legislature; below are the other four:

Winston Churchill (1941, 1943, 1952) · Clement Attlee (1945)
Margaret Thatcher (1985) · Tony Blair (2003)

† Japanese Prime Minister Taro Aso was the first foreign leader to visit Obama in the White House. Queen Elizabeth II addressed both US houses in 1991, becoming the first British monarch so to do.

—————— INTERNATIONAL SPY AGENCIES OF NOTE ——————

The Security Service [MI5]
UNITED KINGDOM
(est. 1909 · c.3,500 staff)
Protects against 'covertly organised
threats to national security', such as
'terrorism, espionage and the prolifera-
tion of weapons of mass destruction'.

Secret Intelligence Service
[SIS or MI6†]
UNITED KINGDOM
(est. 1946 · Staff numbers classified)
'Tasked by the British Government
to collect intelligence worldwide
in support of its security, defence,
foreign and economic policies'.

Central Intelligence Agency [CIA]
UNITED STATES
(est. 1947 · c.20,000 staff‡)
Collects information on adversaries,
provides analysis, and conducts covert
action 'to preempt threats or achieve
US policy objectives'.

Ministry of State Security
CHINA
(est. 1983 · Staff numbers classified)
Safeguards national security by
working to combat foreign espionage,
sabotage, and conspiracies.

*Directorate-General for
External Security* [DGSE]
FRANCE
(est. 1982 · 4,000 staff‡)
Collects information on terrorism,
organised crime, espionage and
other threats to French interests;
carries out clandestine operations.

GERMANY
Federal Intelligence Service [BND]
(est. 1956 · c.6,050 staff)
Collects and analyses intelligence on
foreign threats to German interests.

Ministry of Intell. & Security [MOIS]
IRAN
(est. 1983 · Staff numbers classified)
Tasked with the 'gathering, procure-
ment, analysis, and classification of
necessary information inside and
outside the country'.

*Institute for Intelligence and
Special Assignments* [Mossad]
ISRAEL
(est. 1950 · 1,200 staff‡)
'Appointed by the State of Israel to
collect information, analyse intelligence, and perform special covert
operations beyond its borders'.

Directorate for Inter-Services Intel. [ISI]
PAKISTAN
(est. 1948 · 25,000 staff‡)
Reportedly collects foreign and
domestic intelligence, coordinates
intelligence functions of the military,
conducts surveillance, and organises
covert offensive & wartime operations.

Foreign Intelligence Service [SVR]
RUSSIA
(est. 1991 · 15,000 staff‡)
Russia's primary foreign intelligence
agency. Responsible for counter-
terrorism, intelligence-gathering,
and protecting Russian commercial
interests abroad.

† MI6 is a colloquial term and no longer in official use. For a breakdown of the various British
Military Intelligence units, see *Schott's Original
Miscellany*. ‡ Reported estimate; actual figures
are classified. Summary of activities taken from
agency websites and news reports. ❦ The CIA
is reportedly known to staff as 'the Company',
MI6 as 'the firm', and MI5 as 'the office'. (The
British Royal family is also said to call itself 'the
firm'.) The headquarters of the KGB were also
once reportedly called 'the office'.

THE HAGUE

The Hague (*Den Haag* in Dutch) is the third largest city in the Netherlands and the capital of the province of South Holland. In 2008, its population was 475,904. The origins of the city lie with a castle built between 1230–80, by Count William II of Holland, which served as a hunting lodge and meeting place for local aristocrats. In 1586, The Hague was chosen as the seat of the Dutch parliament, and over the next few centuries it became an intellectual and cultural centre as well as a neutral meeting ground for the European powers. In 1899, the city hosted a major international peace conference at which 26 nations agreed to one of the first modern codifications of the laws of war: the Hague Convention. This conference also established the Permanent Court of Arbitration (PCA) – the first court ever established to settle international disputes. Both of these agreements entrenched The Hague as a centre of international law and diplomacy, and today the city is home to scores of international organisations, including the judicial bodies below:

International Court of Justice (ICJ) · Founded in 1945 as the primary judicial body for the UN, the ICJ settles legal disputes between nations and gives advisory opinions to international organisations. Decisions are made by 15 judges elected by the UN General Assembly and Security Council.

International Criminal Court (ICC) · The world's first permanent war crimes tribunal, founded by international treaty in 2002. A 'court of last resort', the ICC prosecutes individuals charged with the gravest international crimes. At the time of writing, the court had taken up four cases, all from Africa.

International Criminal Tribunal for the former Yugoslavia (ICTY) · A UN body established by Security Council Resolution 827 in 1993 to prosecute perpetrators of war crimes in the former Yugoslavia. Among others, the court indicted former Yugoslavian President Slobodan Milošević, in 1999.

Iran-United States Claims Tribunal (IUSCT) · Created by the 1981 Algiers Accords as a third-party court to deal with the disbursement of Iranian funds frozen by the US in the 1979 Iranian Embassy hostage crisis. While the deadline for filing new private claims was 1982, several major cases between Iran and the US remain outstanding.

Permanent Court of Arbitration (PCA) · Established in 1899, the PCA is no longer a court in the usual sense, but provides a framework of services for resolving international disputes that may involve states, intergovernmental organisations, and private parties.

Special Court for Sierra Leone (SCSL) · An independent judicial body created by the UN and Government of Sierra Leone to try those who committed war crimes and crimes against humanity in Sierra Leone after 30 November 1996.

Special Tribunal for Lebanon (STL) · Established by an agreement between the UN and Lebanon to try those suspected of the 2005 attack that killed former Lebanese PM Rafiq Hariri. No suspects have yet been named.

Images of storks are found throughout The Hague, including on the city's logo and coat of arms. The animals nested around the city in the Middle Ages, and were seen as omens of luck and prosperity.

———————————— THE EUROPEAN UNION ————————————

The European Union (EU) has its roots in the European Coal & Steel Community (ECSC), formed in 1951 between Belgium, France, Germany, Italy, Luxembourg, and the Netherlands, who united to co-operate over production of coal and steel: the two key components of war. Since then, through a series of treaties, Europe as an economic and political entity has developed in size, harmonisation, and power. For some, the expansion in EU membership [see below] and the introduction of the euro (in 2002) are welcome developments in securing co-operation and peace; for others, the growth of the EU is a threat to the sovereignty of member nations.

MAJOR EU INSTITUTIONS

European Parliament · the democratic voice of the people of Europe, the EP approves the EU budget; oversees the other EU institutions; assents to key treaties and agreements on accession; and, alongside the Council of Ministers, examines and approves EU legislation. The EP sits in Strasbourg and Brussels, and its members are directly elected every 5 years.

Council of the EU · the pre-eminent decision-making body, the Council is made up of ministers from each national government. The Council meets regularly in Brussels to decide EU policy and approve laws, and every three months Presidents and PMs meet at European Councils to make major policy decisions.

European Commission · proposes new laws for the Council and Parliament to consider, and undertakes much of the EU's day-to-day work, such as overseeing the implementation of EU rules. Commissioners are nominated by each member state, and the President of the Commission is chosen by the national governments. It is based in Brussels.

European Court · ensures EU law is observed and applied fairly, and settles any disputes arising. Each state sends a judge to the Court in Luxembourg.

EU MEMBERSHIP

Country	entry	members
Belgium		
France		
Germany	1952	6
Italy		
Luxembourg		
Netherlands		
Denmark		
Ireland	1973	9
UK		
Greece	1981	10
Portugal	1986	12
Spain		
Austria		
Finland	1995	15
Sweden		
Cyprus		
Czech Rep.		
Estonia		
Hungary		
Latvia	2004	25
Lithuania		
Malta		
Poland		
Slovakia		
Slovenia		
Romania	2007	27
Bulgaria		
Turkey		
Croatia	*in accession talks*	
Macedonia		
Serbia		
Bosnia-Herzegovina	*potential candidates*	
Montenegro		
Albania		

———————————THE EUROPEAN PARLIAMENT———————

In June 2009, the 27 countries of the European Union went to the polls [see p.20]. Across Europe, voters swung to the right, ensuring that the centre-right European People's Party (EPP) continued to hold the majority of parliamentary seats. Left-wing parties in Britain, France, Spain, and Germany all suffered heavy defeats, and turnout hit its lowest-ever level, suggesting growing voter apathy. (The lowest turnouts were in Slovakia, 19·6%, and Lithuania, 20·9%). Turnouts since 1979 are below:

Year turnout (%)	1984 59	1994 57	2004 45
1979 62	1989 58	1999 50	2009 43

736 MEPs were elected in June 2009, 49 fewer than the 785 elected in 2007 (the total number of MEPs had temporarily increased after the accessions of Romania and Bulgaria). MEPs are allocated to each country through a system known as 'degressive proportionality', which assigns more MEPs to larger countries while avoiding strictly proportional representation. There are seven official parties in the parliament, to which MEPs align themselves depending on the policies of their national party. A breakdown by party grouping after the 2009 elections is below:

Party grouping	party name	abbreviation	MEPs
Conservatives	... *European People's Party*	EPP	265
Socialists	*Progressive Alliance of Socialists & Democrats*	S&D	184
Liberals	*Alliance of Liberals & Democrats for Europe*	ALDE	84
Greens	*The Greens–European Free Alliance*	Greens–EFA	55
Anti-federalists ..	*European Conservatives & Reformists*	ECR	55
Leftwing	*European United Left–Nordic Green Left*	GUE–NGL	35
Eurosceptics	*Europe of Freedom & Democracy*	EFD	32
Not aligned	—	—	26

The number of MEPs elected to represent each of the member nations is below:

Country	MEPs				
Germany	99	Czech Republic	22	Ireland	12
France	72	Greece	22	Lithuania	12
Italy	72	Hungary	22	Latvia	8
UK	72	Portugal	22	Slovenia	7
Poland	50	Sweden	18	Cyprus	6
Spain	50	Austria	17	Estonia	6
Romania	33	Bulgaria	17	Luxembourg	6
Netherlands	25	Denmark	13	Malta	5
Belgium	22	Finland	13		
		Slovakia	13	TOTAL	736

British MEPs are aligned thus: S&D – Labour (13 MEPs); ALDE – Lib Dems (11); EFA – Green Party (2); Scottish National Party (2); Plaid Cymru (1); ECR – Conservatives (26); GUE-NGL – Sinn Féin (1); EFD – UKIP (13); Not aligned – BNP (2); DUP (1). The Tories left the EPP in May 2009 and set up the anti-federalist ECR because the EPP opposed a referendum on the Lisbon Treaty. The BNP failed to find a party grouping that would accommodate its extremist tendencies.

———————————— LIVING IN EUROPE ————————————

Tabulated below are Eurostat data on the number of British nationals living in other European states, and the number of European nationals living in Britain:

UK nats living in EU states[†]		EU nats living in UK[‡]
97,300	Ireland	369,700
600	Poland	110,000
Unavailable	France	100,300
105,000	Germany	100,300
24,700	Italy	88,400
19,800	Portugal	84,600
322,800	Spain	60,900
40,300	Netherlands	45,500
100	Lithuania	26,100
15,100	Sweden	25,700
700	Slovakia	24,300
7,800	Austria	19,800
300	Romania	17,600

13,200	Denmark	16,500
Unavailable	Greece	13,500
26,200	Belgium	12,200
Unavailable	Bulgaria	12,200
Unavailable	Cyprus	10,500
2,900	Finland	9,700
2,900	Czech Rep.	6,700
Unavailable	Malta	5,600
1,900	Hungary	5,200
300	Latvia	4,400
Unavailable	Estonia	3,600
4,900	Luxembourg	600
200	Slovenia	Unavailable
687,000	TOTAL	1,173,900

† Figures 2007. ‡ Figures 2005, except Belgium, which are 2003. [Source: Social Trends 39, 2009]

—— TRENDS IN UK OPINION ON THE EUROPEAN UNION ——

The European Commission biannually produces the Eurobarometer, which seeks to measure attitudes towards the European Union across the 27 member states. The latest statistics, published in February 2009, reveal trends in UK opinion of the EU:

% of UK citizens who ...	2004	2005	2006	2007	2008
Trust in the EU	35	25	26	25	25
Trust in the European Commission	39	26	25	22	27
Trust in the European Parliament	39	27	25	25	27
Trust in national government	32	33	24	30	29
Support the euro	31	28	29	24	28
Support EU enlargement	50	43	36	36	40

The survey asked what the number one issue of concern was in the UK. In 2004 and 2006 it was immigration, in 2005 and 2007 it was crime, but in 2008 it was the economic situation. British respondents were also asked about EU membership:

Membership of the EU ... (% agreeing)	2004	2005	2006	2007	2008
Is a good thing	38	34	34	34	32
Has brought benefits	39	37	39	37	39

All statistics from the Autumn editions of the survey. 67% of British respondents thought decisions about terrorism policy should be taken jointly at EU level. [Source: Eurobarometer, Autumn 2008]

———————— OFFENSIVE EU ARTWORK ————————

The Czech Republic was forced to apologise in January 2009 after it was revealed that a sculpture commissioned to celebrate the Czech presidency of the EU was a hoax. Artist David Cerny was to be awarded £350,000 of EU funding to create a giant sculpture representing Europe, with the assistance of 27 up-and-coming artists, one from each EU state. However, the final work, *Entropa*, was a collection of parodic stereotypes, created by Cerny and two friends. Parts of the sculpture, housed in the atrium of the European Council building in Brussels, had to be hidden with a sheet after member states complained at their savage depiction. The Czech Deputy PM offered this apology: 'This piece of art has never been meant as the Czech presidency vision of the EU or member states. It is not how the Czech government views the EU. *Entropa* is a provocation of a kind and I understand some feel offended and I would like to apologise to them'. Cerny also apologised, and returned all the public money he received. Some of the stereotypes are listed below:

Austria..........*smoking nuclear reactor*
Belgium ....*half-eaten box of chocolates*
Bulgaria .....*Turkish-style 'squat' toilets*
Denmark.................*made of Lego*
Estonia ....*hammer and sickle*
Finland.................*a drunken man*
France ....*banner saying 'strike!'*
Greece.................*a burnt-out forest*
Ireland............*self-playing bagpipes*
Italy.......*masturbating football players*

Latvia............*mountains* [it has none]
Lithuania......*series of urinating figures*
Luxembourg..............*a 'for sale' sign*
Netherlands ...*totally flooded with some minarets peeping above the water*
Romania......... *a Dracula theme park*
Spain ....*totally concreted over*
Sweden..........*flat-pack furniture box*
UK......*nothing, signifying that Britain did not want to be part of Europe*

———————— NUMBER OF WOMEN PER 100 MEN · EU ————————

Longer female life expectancy is thought to explain why none of the 27 EU states has more men than women in their overall population, although Ireland has parity between the sexes. Below are the number of women per 100 men in 2007:

Country ♀ *per 100* ♂			
Estonia ....117·1	France ....105·8	Spain ....102·7
Latvia.............117·1	Austria.............105·6	Netherlands ......102·2
Lithuania.........114·6	Romania..........105·2	Denmark.........102·0
Hungary..........110·6	Czech Rep........104·7	Luxembourg......102·0
Poland............106·9	Belgium ....104·3	Greece............101·9
Portugal ....106·6	Finland............104·2	Sweden...........101·5
Bulgaria ....106·4	Germany ....104·2	Malta.............101·3
Slovakia..........106·0	UK.................103·9	Ireland............100·0
Italy...............105·9	Slovenia ....103·7	
	Cyprus............103·1	EU-27 average ...104·9

[Source: Eurostat] According to the European Commission, 77% of women in Europe think that men dominate the political scene, 83% agreed that more women in politics would lead to different decision making, and 48% would like women to make up ≥50% of all members of the European Parliament.

Establishment & Faith

Kings are like stars – they rise and set, they have
The worship of the world, but no repose.
— PERCY BYSSHE SHELLEY (1792–1822)

────────────────── THE SOVEREIGN ──────────────────

ELIZABETH II
by the Grace of God, of the United Kingdom of Great Britain
and Northern Ireland and of her other Realms and Territories Queen,
Head of the Commonwealth, Defender of the Faith

Born at 17 Bruton Street, London W1, on 21 April, 1926, at *c.*2:40am
Ascended the throne, 6 February, 1952 · Crowned, 2 June, 1953

The Queen was named as the most trusted public figure in Britain in an April 2009 YouGov survey.

────────────────── PRINCE PHILIP AS CONSORT ──────────────────

On 18 April, 2009, Prince Philip, Duke of Edinburgh, Earl of Merioneth and Baron Greenwich, became the longest-serving royal consort in British history – surpassing the record of 57 years and 70 days set by Queen Charlotte, the wife of George III. ❦ Princess Elizabeth and Prince Philip first met in 1934 at the wedding of Prince Philip's cousin, Princess Marina of Greece, to the Duke of Kent, who was an uncle of Princess Elizabeth. Their engagement was announced on 9 July, 1947, and they were married in Westminster Abbey at 11:30 am, on 20 November. Philip became the monarch's consort on 6 February, 1952, when Princess Elizabeth ascended the throne on the death of her father, George VI. ❦ The last public statement the Queen made about her husband was during the celebrations for their golden wedding anniversary in 1997: 'He is someone who doesn't take easily to compliments … He has, quite simply, been my strength and stay all these years, and I, and his whole family, and this and many other countries, owe him a debt greater than he would ever claim or we shall ever know.' Other long-serving consorts include:

Consort	consort to	served	Consort	consort to	served
Charlotte	George III	57y70d	Anne of Denmark‡	James VI&I*	29y99d
Philippa	Edward III	41y202d	Mary of Teck	George V	25y259d
Eleanor of Provence	Henry III	36y306d	Henrietta Maria	Charles I	23y231d
Eleanor of Aquitaine†	Henry II	34y254d	Catherine of Braganza	Charles II	22y261d

* King of Scotland (1567–1625) & England (1603–25)

† Before marrying her second husband, Henry II, Eleanor of Aquitaine was Queen consort of France.
‡ Queen consort of Scotland (1589–1619) and, following the union of the crowns, England (1603–19).

———— ROYAL PREROGATIVE POWERS ————

Prerogative powers are those reserved by the Crown which are exercised either directly by the monarch or on her behalf by her Ministers – often without the need for parliamentary approval. In 2003, as part of a report on the impact of the prerogative on ministerial accountability, the Public Administration Select Committee (PASC) published a memo from the Treasury Solicitor's Department which, for the first time, publicly itemised 'the sweeping but little-understood powers enjoyed by ministers under the ancient Royal Prerogative'. Below are the prerogative powers 'which have been consistently recognised by the courts' outlined in this memo:

DOMESTIC AFFAIRS
The appointment and dismissal of Ministers
The summoning, prorogation and dissolution of Parliament
Royal assent to Bills
The appointment and regulation of the civil service
The commissioning of officers in the armed forces
Directing the disposition of the armed forces in the UK
The appointment of Queen's Counsel
The prerogative of mercy†
The granting of honours

The issue and withdrawal of UK passports
The creation of corporations by Charter
The Monarch can do no wrong
(i.e., the Queen cannot be prosecuted in her own courts)

FOREIGN AFFAIRS
The making of treaties
The declaration of war
The deployment of the armed forces on operations overseas
The recognition of foreign states
The accreditation and reception of diplomats

† Used to correct sentencing errors rather than, as originally, to save people from the death penalty.

———— THE ROYAL ORDER OF SUCCESSION ————

Sovereign · The Prince of Wales · Prince William of Wales · Prince Henry of Wales · The Duke of York · Princess Beatrice of York · Princess Eugenie of York · The Earl of Wessex · Viscount Severn · The Lady Louise Windsor · The Princess Royal · Mr Peter Phillips · Miss Zara Phillips · Viscount Linley · The Hon Charles Armstrong-Jones · The Hon Margarita Armstrong-Jones · The Lady Sarah Chatto · Master Samuel Chatto · Master Arthur Chatto · The Duke of Gloucester · The Earl of Ulster · Lord Culloden · The Lady Davina Lewis · The Lady Rose Windsor · The Duke of Kent · The Lady Amelia Windsor · The Lady Helen Taylor · Master Columbus Taylor · Master Cassius Taylor · Miss Eloise Taylor · Miss Estella Taylor · The Lord Frederick Windsor · The Lady Gabriella Windsor · Princess Alexandra, the Hon. Lady Ogilvy · Mr James Ogilvy · Master Alexander Ogilvy · Miss Flora Ogilvy · Miss Marina Ogilvy · Master Christian Mowatt · Miss Zenouska Mowatt · The Earl of Harewood

The eldest son of the monarch is heir to the throne followed by his heirs, after whom come any other sons of the monarch and their heirs, followed by any daughters of the monarch and their heirs. Roman Catholics are barred from succession under the Act of Settlement (1701).

———————— 'INTERVIEW WITHOUT COFFEE' ————————

The *News of the World*'s January 2009 revelation that Prince Harry, as a 21-year-old officer cadet on exercise in Cyprus in 2006, used the terms 'Paki' and 'raghead' to describe two of his comrades was greeted with a degree of anger and embarrassment. The Prince issued a formal apology for his behaviour and – according to the *Guardian* – the Army planned to deal with the incident in its usual way: 'Prince Harry faces the prospect of what in polite army circles is called an interview without coffee – and in less polite ones "a bit of a bollocking".' According to the Army Rumour Service website, an 'interview without coffee' is less severe than a 'carpet parade', which for officers is 'normally preceded by the words "Your hat, my office"', and for privates with the words 'Soldier-and-Escort, by-the-right, Quick-MARCH ...' Apparently, the Royal Air Force's equivalent of an interview without coffee is being called to a 'meeting with tea and no biscuits, or even no tea and no biscuits, depending on the gravity of your crime'.

During 2009, Princes William and Harry learned to fly helicopters at RAF Shawbury in Shropshire. Prince William is training to become an RAF search and rescue pilot, and Prince Harry is set to become an Army helicopter pilot. Harry hopes to be redeployed to Afghanistan once he is qualified.

———————— ROYAL FAMILY ENGAGEMENTS · 2008 ————————

Mr Tim O'Donovan annually compiles a list of official engagements undertaken by the Royal family during the year – as reported in the pages of the Court Circular – which is subsequently published as a letter to *The Times*. Below is 2008's listing:

	Official visits, openings, &c.	Receptions, lunches, dinners, &c.	Other, e.g., investitures, meetings	Total official engagements UK	Total official engagements abroad
The Queen	101	59	213	373	44
Duke of Edinburgh	129	120	52	301	53
Prince of Wales	166	95	193	454	106
Duchess of Cornwall	104	37	14	155	62
Duke of York	82	53	79	214	293
Earl of Wessex	156	66	32	254	75
Countess of Wessex	27	16	13	56	7
Princess Royal	299	109	74	482	52
Duke of Gloucester	155	40	39	234	68
Duchess of Gloucester	60	20	20	100	44
Duke of Kent	142	44	17	203	4
Princess Alexandra	64	29	25	118	2

Prince William carried out 24 official engagements and Prince Harry 17, including 2 overseas.

———————— NEW ROYAL HOUSEHOLD ————————

In January 2009, it was announced that the Queen had 'graciously agreed to the creation of a joint Household for Prince William and Prince Harry', which 'lays the basis for the Princes' lives in the future as they progress their public, military, and charitable activities'. The Household of His Royal Highness Prince William of Wales and His Royal Highness Prince Henry of Wales is headed by Jamie Lowther-Pinkerton, advised by Sir David Manning, the former British Ambassador to the US, and has offices within St James's Palace. Listed below are the other Royal Households:

Household of The Queen
Household of The Prince Philip, Duke of Edinburgh
Household of The Prince of Wales and The Duchess of Cornwall
Household of The Duke of York
Household of The Earl and Countess of Wessex
Household of The Princess Royal
Household of The Duke and Duchess of Gloucester
Household of The Duke of Kent
Household of Prince and Princess Michael of Kent
Household of Princess Alexandra, the Hon. Lady Ogilvy

In terms of precedence, the Household of Prince William and Prince Harry falls between that of the Prince of Wales and the Duchess of Cornwall and the Household of the Duke of York. According to Buckingham Palace, 'Royal Households support Members of the Royal Family in their official and private lives. Households primarily comprise office and support functions, and where a Household is based is not necessarily where the Member of the Royal Family lives'.

———————— ROYAL FINANCES ————————

The Queen receives income from public funds to meet expenditure that relates to her duties as Head of State and the Commonwealth. This derives from 4 sources:

Source (year ending 31 March)	2008	2009
The Queen's Civil List†	£12·7m	£13·9m
Parliamentary Annuities	£0·4m	£0·4m
Grants-in-Aid	£22·0m	£22·6m
Expenditure met directly by Government Departments and the Crown Estate	£4·9m	£4·6m
TOTAL	£40·0m	£41·5m

† Figures are for 2007–08. ❦ The monarchy 'cost' each UK citizen 69p in 2009, an increase of 3p since 2008. This figure does not include the cost of royal security, which is estimated at £50m a year. Reports that the security bill for Princess Eugenie's 'gap year' could exceed £100,000 prompted discussions about how much protection junior royals, in particular, should receive. In June 2009, the Metropolitan Police Commissioner asked the government to provide more funding for royal protection, stating that officers were 'overstretched'. The *Daily Telegraph* attributed increased security costs to providing junior royals with protection for gap years, ski trips, and nights out in London.

──────── THE QUEEN'S CHRISTMAS BROADCAST · 2008 ────────

'Christmas is a time for celebration, but this year it is a more sombre occasion for many. Some of those things which could once have been taken for granted suddenly seem less certain and, naturally, give rise to feelings of insecurity. People are touched by events which have their roots far across the world. Whether it is the global economy or violence in a distant land, the effects can be keenly felt at home. Once again, many of our service men and women are serving on operations in common cause to bring peace and security to troubled places. In this ninetieth year since the end of the First World War, the last survivors recently commemorated the service and enormous sacrifice of their own generation. Their successors in theatres such as Iraq and Afghanistan are still to be found in harm's way in the service of others. For their loved ones, the worry will never cease until they are safely home. ... Over the years, those who have seemed to me to be the most happy, contented and fulfilled have always been the people who have lived the most outgoing and unselfish lives; the kind of people who are generous with their talents or their time. There are those who use their prosperity or good fortune for the benefit of others whether they number among the great philanthropists or are people who, with whatever they have, simply have a desire to help those less fortunate than themselves. ... They tend to have some sense that life itself is full of blessings, and is a precious gift for which we should be thankful. When life seems hard, the courageous do not lie down and accept defeat; instead, they are all the more determined to struggle for a better future. I think we have a huge amount to learn from individuals such as these. And what I believe many of us share with them is a source of strength and peace of mind in our families and friends. Indeed, Prince Philip and I can reflect on the blessing, comfort and support we have gained from our own family in this special year for our son, the Prince of Wales. ... Through his charities, the Prince of Wales has worked to support young people and other causes for the benefit of the wider community, and now his sons are following in his footsteps. ... We can surely be grateful that, two thousand years after the birth of Jesus, so many of us are able to draw inspiration from his life and message, and to find in him a source of strength and courage. I hope that the Christmas message will encourage and sustain you too, now and in the coming year. I wish you all a very happy Christmas.'

> *When life seems hard, the courageous do not lie down and accept defeat; instead, they are all the more determined to struggle for a better future.*

When the Queen's Christmas broadcast is entered into Microsoft Word's 'Auto Summarise' feature and is condensed down to two sentences, the result is:

> *At Christmas, we feel very fortunate to have our family around us.*
> *Countless millions of people around the world continue to celebrate his birthday at Christmas, inspired by his teaching. I wish you all a very happy Christmas.*

ROYAL COLOURS

The colour purple has enjoyed associations with royalty since antiquity, but it is not the only shade reserved for sovereigns. Below is a brief guide to the royal rainbow:

PURPLE · Often dubbed 'the royal colour', purple's privileged associations stem from the ancient Mediterranean. There, a prized dye, perhaps of a deep raspberry, was once created using sea snails of the genus *Murex* and *Purpura*. Since each snail produced only a few drops of ink, cloth so-coloured was extremely expensive and restricted to the wealthy and powerful. In ancient Rome, purple was reserved (sometimes on pain of death) for the garb of the emperor, senior magistrates, and military commanders. Precise rules about who could wear purple varied by reign, though Nero is said to have been among its most zealous protectors. Byzantine emperors also favoured the shade, restricting its use – and it is from such rulers that we get the phrase 'born in the purple'†. Purple continued its association with royalty through the Middle Ages, and only truly lost its exclusive lustre when the first synthetic mauve dye was created in 1856.

RED · Crimson has long been the regal colour of England, an association that derives from the uniforms of British soldiers and the use of red in the Cross of St George. Red has also been the royal colour of Korea and Malaysia.

ROYAL BLUE · Blue was adopted by the kings of medieval France as a colour of sacred authority, supposedly because the high priests of ancient Israel wore robes of this shade. Of note is a hyacinth-blue robe dotted with gold *fleurs-de-lis* that was given to the French king as part of his coronation ceremony. Subsequently, the colour became associated with royalty throughout Europe, leading to the term 'royal blue'.

GREEN · Green was the royal colour of the Chinese Ming dynasty (1368–1644), when it was reserved for imperial use. Interestingly, green is today the royal colour among Guatemalan weavers, because the ancient Maya (who once ruled the region) reserved the Quetzal bird's blue-green feathers for royal use.

IMPERIAL YELLOW · A sunshine yellow called *ming huang* was adopted as the colour of China's imperial family in the 1650s during the Qing dynasty, which lasted until 1912. The colour was supposed to represent the celestial nature of the royal bloodline, and its use was restricted to the imperial family. During the reign of Emperor Qianlong (1736–96), at the height of the dynasty, *ming huang* was worn only by the Emperor, Empress, and Empress Dowager, though different yellows were reserved for other court members. *Jin huang*, a golden yellow, was worn by the Emperor's sons and second and third degree imperial consorts; *xiang se*, an incense yellow, by the two lowest degrees of imperial consorts, the daughters of the Emperor, and the wives of his sons; and *xing huang*, an apricot yellow, by the Crown Prince and his consort.

† Children born to Byzantine emperors were said to be 'born in [or to] the purple', apparently after the porphyry lining the birthing rooms (porphyry is a purple stone). In the UK, 'purple airspace' once referred to a special air zone around royal flights, in which other aircraft were not permitted to fly. ❦ Naturally, a degree of debate and speculation surrounds a number of these entries.

———————————— WHO'S NEW IN WHO'S WHO ————————————

Published annually since 1849, *Who's Who* is one of the world's most respected bio-graphical reference books. Below are some of the 846 new entries in the 2009 *Who's Who* (those who have died during the year enter the companion *Who Was Who*):

Tomma Abts .... *artist*
Monica Ali .... *writer*
Simon Beaufoy. *screenwriter & director*
Jacqueline Beech .... *judge*
Graham Bell............... *TV presenter*
Mary Berry.. *TV cook & cookery writer*
Mark Billingham... *writer & comedian*
Daniel Cohen.... *controller, BBC Three*
Clive Cookson .... *science editor, FT*
Daniel Craig .... *actor*
Christine Davies .... *physicist*
Linda de Cossart............... *surgeon*
Thomas Delay .... *Chief Executive, Carbon Trust*
Timothy Donohoe.............. *chemist*
Joanne Elvin ....*editor, Glamour*
David Farmer ....*oceanographer*
François Fillon ....*French PM*
Jonathan Freeman-Attwood............ *Principal, Royal Academy of Music*
David Gilmour... *musician, Pink Floyd*
Daisy Goodwin ..... *producer & writer*
(Albert) Cecil Graham... *paediatrician*
Philippa Harris................*producer*
Roger Highfield.. *editor, New Scientist*
Anya Hindmarch ......*fashion designer*
Toomas Ilves .... *Estonian President*
Ben Kelly.............*interior designer*
Siân Kevill.............*editorial director, BBC World*
John Lanchester................. *writer*

Robin Leatherbarrow *chemical biologist*
Robert Martienssen.....*plant geneticist*
Natalie Massenet..*Net-a-Porter founder*
Thomas Meagher .... *plant biologist*
Dmitry Medvedev ... *Russian President*
Fiona Millar................. *journalist*
Henrietta Moore...*social anthropologist*
Anne Nightingale....... *radio presenter*
Barack Obama..... *American President*
Steven Osborne .... *pianist*
Ian Owens...................... *ecologist*
Douglas Perkins.. *Specsavers co-founder*
Sophie Raworth........*BBC journalist*
Fredrik Reinfeldt.......... *Swedish PM*
(Frances) Alice Rogers ..*mathematician*
John Sauven.......... *executive director, Greenpeace*
Simon Sebag-Montefiore..... *historian*
Martin Siegert............... *geoscientist*
Kate Silverton..........*BBC journalist*
Mriganka Sur ....*neuroscientist*
(Alice) Elspeth Talbot Rice.........*QC*
David Tang.................*entrepreneur*
Mark Urban ....*BBC journalist*
Cherry Vann ....*archdeacon*
Jimmy Wales........ *Wikipedia founder*
Elizabeth Wiener........*ITN journalist*
Henry Winter................*journalist*
Oliver Wright .... *news editor, The Independent*
Caroline Wyatt..........*BBC journalist*

A few recreations – MARK BILLINGHAM 'trying to smuggle examples of Victorian taxidermy into the house' · JONATHAN FREEMAN-ATTWOOD 'lots of Bach, playing cricket, French wine châteaux, Liverpool FC, reading, singing to the dog' · DAISY GOODWIN 'collecting books with Daisy in the title, avoiding meetings, knitting, reading poetry and classic crime' · ROGER HIGHFIELD 'watching bad TV, cooking, dodgy DIY, Wii boxing' · BEN KELLY 'looking at the colour orange' · ELSPETH TALBOT RICE 'playing polo enthusiastically but badly, playing lacrosse increasingly slowly, playing the French horn occasionally, cooking and eating' · DAVID TANG 'reading, collecting art, the roulette' · HENRY WINTER 'singing out of tune' · OLIVER WRIGHT 'walking, failing newspaper shorthand examinations'.

SOME HONOURS OF NOTE · 2009

New Year Honours

KNIGHT BACHELOR
Chris Hoy......................cyclist
Terry Pratchett..................author

DBE
Jenny Abramsky........BBC Executive
Anne Owers...Chief Inspector Prisons

CBE
Ben Ainslie.......................sailor
Dave Brailsford.........British cycling
Earl Cameron.....................actor
Michael Chance........... opera singer
Peter Jones.................entrepreneur
Courtney Pine ....jazz musician
Robert Plant .... singer, songwriter
Bradley Wiggins ....cyclist

OBE
Rebecca Adlington...........swimmer
Diana Athill.............editor, author
Sarah Ayton.......................sailor
Iain Percy..........................sailor
Michael Sheen ....actor
Howard Shelley.....pianist, conductor
Sarah Webb ....sailor

MBE
Tim Brabants ....canoeist
Edward Clancy...................cyclist
Nicole Cooke ....cyclist
James Degale.....................boxer
Paul Goodison ....sailor
Lewis Hamilton.............. F1 driver
Anya Hindmarch .....fashion designer
Kelly Hoppen........interior designer
Jason Kenny......................cyclist
Paul Manning....................cyclist
David Miles............... banjo player
Christine Ohuruogu........... athlete
Victoria Pendleton..............cyclist
Zac Purchase.....................rower
Rebecca Romero ....cyclist
Eleanor Simmonds...........swimmer

Queen's Birthday Honours

KNIGHT BACHELOR
Nick Faldo .... golfer
Christopher Lee..................actor
Andrew Motion...................poet

DBE
Mitsuko Uchida................ pianist

CBE
Jeff Banks.............fashion designer
Lindsay Duncan ....actor
Alastair Lansley ....architect
Jonathan Pryce....................actor
Delia Smith ....cookery writer

OBE
Peter Dickinson................. author
Sue Johnston......................actor
Kay Mellor.......................writer
Elaine Morgan .... author
John Sherlock.................sculptor
Billy Williams........ cinematographer

MBE
Christopher Bailey. designer, Burberry
James Bolam ....actor
Charlotte Edwards............ cricketer
Gail Emms.........badminton player
Bernardine Evaristo............. author
Graeme Hick................. cricketer
Chinwe Chuckwuogo-Roy.......artist
Anna Wing.......................actor

966 people were honoured in the New Year Honours list, 378 (39%) of whom were women. 6% of those honoured were from ethnic minorities. 70% were rewarded for work in their local community. In the Queen's Birthday Honours 984 people were rewarded, 42% of whom were women. 7·7% came from ethnic minorities. 10% of rewards went to those working in education, including 16 head teachers. Industry and the economy accounted for 14% of the awards. Sport made up 4% of the total.

———————————— CITY LIVERY COMPANIES ————————————

Livery companies are trade associations, based in the City of London, that trace their roots to medieval craft guilds. Their traditional role was to regulate trade, set wages, train apprentices, and ensure quality control. Some of the 108 livery companies that remain in existence in the City of London still carry on this regulatory role (e.g., the Fishmongers, whose Fishmeter inspectors ensure that the fish sold at Billingsgate Market is fit for human consumption). And most livery companies perform charitable functions, including supporting their profession through scholarships and prizes. Some of the livery companies associated with obsolete trades have found modern equivalents with which to associate: the Fanmakers, for instance, now embrace mechanical fan-makers and those concerned with air-conditioning. In 1515, after many years of wrangling, an order of precedence for the then 48 livery companies was established, reflecting the economic and political power of each association. The top companies became known as the Great Twelve:

The Worshipful Company of …	*rank*
Mercers (general merchants)	1
Grocers	2
Drapers (wool/cloth merchants)	3
Fishmongers	4
Goldsmiths	5
Merchant Taylors (tailors)	6/7†
Skinners (fur traders)	7/6†
Haberdashers	8
Salters (salt traders)	9
Ironmongers	10
Vintners (wine merchants)	11
Clothworkers	12

† The Merchant Taylors and the Skinners have long disputed their position in this order of precedence. Consequently the two companies change places each Easter – a curious arrangement which might explain the phrase 'at sixes and sevens'. ❦ The company currently occupying the 108th (or last) place in the precedence is the Worshipful Company of Security Professionals. Formed as a Guild in 1999, the Court of Aldermen allowed the security professionals to form a City Livery Company in 2008. ❦ Members of all the companies also vote to elect the Lord Mayor of London.

———————————— THE ELIZABETH CROSS ————————————

The Ministry of Defence announced in July 2009 that the Queen would lend her name to the Elizabeth Cross – a new award to be granted from August 2009 to the next of kin of UK Armed Forces personnel who have died on operations, or as a result of terrorism, since 1948 (or September 1945, in the case of service in Palestine). The MOD stated that the award 'is not a posthumous medal for the fallen but an emblem demonstrating tangible national recognition for Service families for their loss'. Made of hallmarked silver, in the form of a cross with a laurel wreath passing between the arms, the arms of the Cross bear floral symbols representing England (rose), Scotland (thistle), Ireland (shamrock), and Wales (daffodil). The Cross will be accompanied by a Memorial Scroll, signed by the Queen. (The Elizabeth Cross is the first award to which a reigning monarch has lent their name since the George [VI] Cross in 1940 for acts of bravery by civilians or military personnel. Queen Victoria was the first to create an award in her name; the Victoria Cross was introduced in 1856 for acts of gallantry by the Armed Forces.) The Queen said: 'This seems to me a right and proper way of showing our enduring debt to those who are killed while actively protecting what is most dear to us all'.

———————————— POLITICAL GIFT-GIVING ————————————

The British press excoriated American President Barack Obama for the gifts he gave Gordon and Sarah Brown when the couple paid their first official visit to the Obama White House in March 2009. While Brown gave Obama a pen holder fashioned from the timbers of the Victorian anti-slave ship HMS *Gannet*, a framed commission for the HMS *Resolute*†, and a first edition of Sir Martin Gilbert's biography of Winston Churchill, Obama presented Brown with a DVD set of 25 classic American films. The President's gift was seen by some to lack style or significance: 'We do have television and DVD stores on this side of the Atlantic,' pointed out the *Telegraph*'s Iain Martin. Obama's gift-giving skills were again criticised in April 2009, when he gave the Queen a video iPod on his visit to London for the G20 summit. Other recent gifts given to world leaders that have caused comment include:

In March 2009, US Secretary of State Hillary Clinton gave Russian Foreign Minister Sergey Lavrov a plastic button printed with what was supposed to be the Russian word for 'reset' (symbolising a new beginning for Russo–American relations). By mistake, the word actually printed translated as 'overload'. ❦ When former US Secretary of State Condoleezza Rice visited Libya in 2008, Moammar Gadhafi gave her gifts worth >$212,000, including a diamond ring, a musical instrument, and a locket that contained a photograph of himself. (In 2007, Gadhafi expressed his admiration for Rice by calling her 'my darling black African woman'.) ❦ In the summer of 2007, Gordon Brown was given a leather-and-fur-trimmed bomber jacket by the then President George Bush; commentators felt that this Top Gun look was a little unlikely given Brown's saturnine suit-and-tie demeanour. ❦ In 2004, Argentine President Nestor Kirchner gave George Bush 136kg of raw lamb meat.

According to etiquette experts interviewed at the time of Obama's 'giftgate' kerfuffle, while gifts to heads of state need not be expensive, they should show effort, and ideally bear some relationship to the recipient's interests. Cultural sensitivity is also of the utmost importance. Below are some tips on giving gifts around the world:

INDIA · Do not give gifts made from cows, as the animals are sacred. Avoid giving alcohol to Muslims, Hindus, Buddhists, or Sikhs. ❦ JAPAN · If visiting Japan, wait for your host to give you a gift first, or they will lose face. Do not give gifts in a set of four, since the Japanese word for four rhymes with the word for death. Do not wrap gifts in white, black, or blue; these colours are associated with funerals. ❦ CHINA · Do not include anything like a knife or sword, which may symbolise severing the relationship. (The same rule applies throughout much of Latin America.) ❦ ISLAMIC COUNTRIES · Do not give alcohol, pork products, a copy of the Koran, or art that depicts natural scenes or people (this violates the Islamic edict that people should not try to represent what God has made). ❦ MEXICO · Do not give Mexican silver, red roses (these symbolise romance), or anything in a group of 13.

† The President's desk is carved from timbers of HMS *Resolute*, a sister ship to HMS *Gannet*. In 1854, the British abandoned the ship after it became embedded in Arctic ice. A year later, a US crew saved it and returned it to Britain. Queen Victoria presented the desk to President Hayes in 1880.

AN ELEMENTARY GUIDE TO FORMS OF ADDRESS

Personage	envelope	start of letter	verbal address
The Queen	The Queen's Most Excellent Majesty†	Madam/May it please your Majesty	Your Majesty/Ma'am
The Duke of Edinburgh	HRH The Duke of Edinburgh†	Sir	Your Royal Highness/Sir
The Queen Mother	Her Majesty Queen —— The Queen Mother†	Madam	Your Majesty/Ma'am
Royal Prince	HRH The Prince —— (The Prince of ——)†	Sir	Your Royal Highness/Sir
Royal Princess	HRH The Princess (of) ——†	Your Royal Highness	Your Royal Highness/Madam
Royal Duke	HRH The Duke of ——†	Your Royal Highness	Your Royal Highness/Sir
Royal Duchess	HRH The Duchess of ——†	Your Royal Highness	Your Royal Highness/Madam
Duke	His Grace The Duke of ——	My Lord Duke/Dear Duke	Your Grace/Duke
Duchess	Her Grace The Duchess of ——	Dear Madam/Dear Duchess	Your Grace/Duchess
Marquess	The Most Honourable The Marquess of ——	My Lord/Dear Lord	My Lord/Lord
Marchioness	The Most Honourable The Marchioness of ——	Madam/Dear Lady	Madam/Lady
Earl	The Rt Hon. The Earl of ——	My Lord/Dear Lord	My Lord/Lord
Earl's wife	The Rt Hon. The Countess of ——	Madam/Dear Lady	Madam/Lady
Countess	The Rt Hon. The Countess of ——	Madam/Dear Lady	Madam/Lady
Viscount	The Rt Hon. The Viscount ——	My Lord/Dear Lord	Lord
Viscount's wife	The Rt Hon. The Viscountess ——	Madam/Dear Lady	Lady
Baron	The Rt Hon. Lord ——	My Lord/Dear Lord	Lord
Baron's wife	The Rt Hon. Lady ——	My Lady/Dear Lady	Lady
Baroness	The Rt Hon. The Lady (*or* The Baroness) ——	My Lady/Dear Lady	Madam/Lady
Baronet	Sir Bertie Wooster Bt (*or* Bart)	Dear Sir Bertie	Sir Bertie
Baronet's wife	Lady ——	Dear Madam/Dear Lady	Lady
Knight of an Order	Sir Bertie Wooster (*and order*)	Dear Sir Bertie	Sir Bertie
Knight Bachelor	Sir Bertie Wooster	Dear Sir Bertie	Sir Bertie
Knight's wife	Lady ——	Dear Madam/Dear Lady	Lady ——
Dame	Dame ——	Dear Madam/Dear Dame	Dame ——

—— AN ELEMENTARY GUIDE TO FORMS OF ADDRESS cont. ——

Personage	envelope	start of letter	verbal address
Life Peer	The Rt Hon. Lord —— (of ——)	My Lord/Dear Lord ——	Lord ——
Life Peeress	The Rt Hon. The Lady (*or* Baroness) —— (of ——)	My Lady/Dear Lady ——	Lady ——
Archbishop	The Most Rev. & Rt Hon. The Lord Archbishop of ——	Dear Archbishop	Your Grace/Archbishop
Bishop	((The Rt Rev.) (and Right Hon.)) The Bishop of ——	Dear Bishop	Bishop
Lord Chancellor	The Rt Hon. The Lord Chancellor	*by rank*	*by rank*
Prime Minister	The Rt Hon. The Prime Minister PC MP	Dear Prime Minister	Prime Minister/Sir
Deputy PM	The Rt Hon. The Deputy Prime Minister PC MP	Dear Deputy Prime Minister	Deputy Prime Minister/Sir
Chancellor of the Exchequer	The Rt Hon. The Chancellor of the Exchequer PC MP	Dear Chancellor	Chancellor/Sir
Foreign Secretary	The Rt Hon. The SoS for Foreign & Comwth Affairs	Dear Foreign Secretary	Foreign Secretary/*by rank*
Home Secretary	The Rt Hon. The SoS for the Home Department	Dear Home Secretary	Home Secretary/*by rank*
Secretary of State	The Rt Hon. The SoS for ——	Dear Secretary of State	Secretary of State/*by rank*
Minister	(The Rt Hon.) Bertie Wooster Esq. (PC) MP	Dear Minister	Minister/*by rank*
MP‡	Bertie Wooster Esq. MP	Dear Mr Wooster	Mr Wooster
MP Privy Councillor	The Rt Hon. Bertie Wooster PC MP	Dear Mr Wooster	Mr Wooster
Privy Councillor	The Rt Hon. Bertie Wooster PC	Dear Mr Wooster	Mr Wooster
High Court Judge	The Hon. Mr Justice ——	Dear Sir ——/Dear Judge	Sir/My Lord/Your Lordship
Ambassador (British)	His Excellency —— HM Ambassador to ——	*by rank*	Your Excellency
Lord Mayor	The Rt Hon. The Lord Mayor of ——	My (Dear) Lord Mayor	Lord Mayor
Mayor	The Worshipful Mayor of ——	(Dear) Mr Mayor	Mr Mayor

It is hard to overstate the complexity of 'correct' form which (especially in the legal and clerical fields, as well as chivalry) can become extremely rococo, and is the subject of considerable dispute between sources. Consequently, the above tabulation can only hope to provide a very elementary guide. ❧ Readers interested in the correct formal styling of the wives of younger sons of earls, for example, are advised to consult specialist texts on the subject. † It is usual to address correspondence to members of the Royal family in the first instance to their Private Secretary. ‡ A similar styling is used for Members of the European Parliament [MEP]; Scottish Parliament [MSP]; National Assembly for Wales [AM]; and Northern Ireland Assembly [MLA]. From the moment Parliament is dissolved there are no Members of Parliament, and consequently the letters MP should not be used. By convention medical doctors are styled Dr ——, whereas surgeons use the title Mr ——; many gynaecologists, although surgeons, are styled Dr ——.

———————————— COMPOSITION OF THE JUDICIARY ————————————

The figures below show the gender and ethnic composition of the judiciary in England and Wales – based on figures released by the Judicial Database in 2008:

Position	(%)	♂	♀	white	ethnic	No.
Heads of Division		100	0	100	0	5
Lords of Appeal in Ordinary		92	8	100	0	12
Lord Justices of Appeal		92	8	100	0	37
High Court judges		90	10	97	3	110
Circuit judges		87	13	97	3	653
Recorders		85	15	95	5	1,305
Judge advocates		100	0	100	0	9
Deputy judge advocates		92	8	100	0	12
District judges (county courts)		78	22	95	5	438
District judges (magistrates' courts)		77	23	98	2	136
Deputy district judges (county)		73	27	96	4	773
Deputy district judges (magistrates)		76	24	93	7	167
District/cost judges, &c. (Family Division)		77	23	98	2	48
Deputy masters, &c. (Family Division)		66	34	96	4	115
All		81	19	96	4	3,820

The legal year is traditionally divided into four terms. Circuit judges are expected to sit for a minimum of 210 days, district judges for 215. The law terms in 2010 are:

HILARY.............. 11 Jan – 31 Mar		TRINITY................8 Jun – 30 Jul
EASTER.............. 13 Apr – 28 May		MICHAELMAS .... 1 Oct – 21 Dec

———————————— OFFENDERS SENTENCED ————————————

The type of sentence handed down to offenders, by court, in the years 2005–07:

Court (% of those sentenced)	fine	community sentence	immediate custody	other sentence
Magistrates' court · 2005	73	13	4	10
2006	71	13	4	12
2007	70	14	4	12
Crown Court · 2005	3	30	58	9
2006	3	23	56	19
2007	3	18	54	24
All courts · 2005	69	14	7	10
2006	68	13	7	12
2007	67	14	7	13

There were c.10·1m crimes against adults living in private households in 2007/08, according to the British Crime Survey. 5·0m crimes were recorded by the police, 1·4m of these were detected, and 1·78m offenders were found guilty. [Source: Criminal Statistics: England & Wales 2007 · Nov 2008]

CORONERS & INQUESTS

The office of coroner was established in 1194 with a loosely defined role that included gathering taxes and investigating deaths. However, by the early C19th concern was voiced that murders were going undetected and deaths during epidemics were going unreported. In 1836, the Births and Deaths Registration Act ensured that the recording of deaths was more accurate, and, in 1887, the Coroners Act delineated the duties of a modern coroner: to investigate sudden, unexpected, or unnatural deaths. Nowadays, coroners are independent judicial officers who must have worked as a lawyer or doctor for at least five years. There are currently more than 120 coroners in England and Wales. They are employed by local councils, and most of them perform their coronal duties alongside their usual jobs – although there are 32 full-time coroners who bear the heaviest case loads. A doctor will report a death to a coroner if the death occurs in the following circumstances:

after an accident or injury	*if* the death was sudden
following an industrial disease	and unexplained
during surgery	*if* the patient was not seen by the
before recovery from an anaesthetic	doctor issuing the medical certificate
if the cause of death is unknown	after he/she died, or during the 14
if the death was violent or unnatural	days before the death

Once a coroner has been notified, a death cannot be registered until the coroner's investigation is complete. If the coroner is unable to establish that a death resulted from natural causes, then a post-mortem is held. If, after a post-mortem, the death still cannot be ascribed to natural causes, an inquest is held. An inquest is not a trial, but is instead concerned with establishing facts, including: *who* died, *when* and *where* they died, and *how* the death occurred. A jury may be summoned if: the death occurred in prison; the death was caused in circumstances that may affect the health and safety of the public; the death needed to be reported to a government department; or if the coroner so decides. No speeches are given during an inquest, but witnesses may be called and interested parties (e.g., the family of the deceased) may ask questions. According to the Dept for Constitutional Affairs, 229,600 deaths were reported to a coroner in 2006 – 45.7% of all registered deaths. Inquests were held into 29,300 of these deaths; the verdicts are below:

Male deaths (18,855)	*verdict*	*Female deaths* (8,692)
31%	ACCIDENT/MISADVENTURE	40%
23	NATURAL CAUSES	28
13	SUICIDE	9
12	INDUSTRIAL DISEASE	2
2	DRUG RELATED	1
9	OPEN VERDICTS†	8
9	ALL OTHER	12

Coroners also have responsibility for treasure trove – any precious metal which was originally hidden and where the owner cannot now be found. In Scotland, the Procurator Fiscal holds responsibilities similar to those of a coroner. † Open verdicts are recorded when there is insufficient evidence.

MILITARY BANDS

There are 23 regular bands in the British Army and 20 Territorial Army bands. Three special composite bands, the British Army Brass Band, the Army Big Band, and the Corps Sinfonietta, are composed of members from all the regular bands and perform across the country. The Foot Guards Household Division Bands and the Royal Artillery Band have 49 musicians; the other bands have 35. Military bands can be hired for special events. Notable military bands include: [Source: MOD]

Band of	*notable for*
The Life Guards	mounted band; most members play two instruments
The Blues & Royals	mounted band; they also have a symphonic concert band
Heavy Cavalry & Cambrai	includes a wind ensemble called 'Baroque & Roll'
Light Cavalry	one of two Royal Armoured Corps bands
Royal Artillery	has key role at ceremonial events such as Changing of the Guard
Royal Corps of Signals	works alongside the Motorcycle Display Team
Coldstream Guards	recently completed 3-month tour of the USA
Scots Guards	most members are 'double-handed' – able to play wind & string
Welsh Guards	includes a Salon Orchestra that plays during State investitures
Prince of Wales' Divisions	the only Welsh male voice choir in the army
Brigade of Gurkhas	march at a faster pace than other bands
Royal Electrical & Mechanical Engineers	includes a German 'oompah' band
The Rifles	specialise in bugle playing

UK SOVEREIGN BASE AREAS

The UK's Sovereign Base Areas (SBAs) comprise two military bases on the island of Cyprus over which the United Kingdom retains sovereignty. The bases at Akrotiri and Dhekelia remained under UK control after the Republic of Cyprus gained independence from the British in 1960. Akrotiri and Dhekelia cover roughly 3% of the land area of Cyprus (98 mi^2); 60% of this land is privately owned, 20% is owned by the Ministry of Defence, and the remaining 20% is SBA Crown Land. The boundaries of the bases were drawn to include large UK military installations but avoid towns and villages, although a large number of Cypriots now work within the SBAs, and currently *c.*7,000 Cypriots and *c.*7,800 British service personnel and their families live on the bases. The constitutional character of the SBAs is unique, since they are part of the UK but are classed as military bases and not 'colonial' territory. (Their status is defined by Appendix O of the 1960 Treaty of Establishment, which states that the UK government must use the SBAs only as military bases, must not set up customs posts between an SBA and the Republic, and must ensure full cooperation with the Cypriot government.) Unlike traditional British overseas territories which are headed by a Governor, SBAs are overseen by an Administrator (since April 2006, Air Vice-Marshal Richard Lacey), who reports directly to the MOD, rather than the Foreign & Commonwealth Office. SBAs have their own police and courts (separate from the UK and Cypriot judiciary) to deal with criminal and civil matters. As of 1 January 2008, the SBAs became the only UK territory to join the euro, when they adopted the currency alongside the Republic of Cyprus.

UK SERVICE RANKS

service	ROYAL NAVY	ROYAL MARINES†	ARMY	ROYAL AIR FORCE	NATO
OFFICERS	Admiral of the Fleet	—	Field Marshal	Marshal of the RAF	OF-10
	Admiral	General	General	Air Chief Marshal	OF-9
	Vice Admiral	Lieutenant General	Lieutenant General	Air Marshal	OF-8
	Rear Admiral	Major General	Major General	Air Vice-Marshal	OF-7
	Commodore	Brigadier	Brigadier	Air Commodore	OF-6
	Captain	Colonel	Colonel	Group Captain	OF-5
	Commander	Lieutenant Colonel	Lieutenant Colonel	Wing Commander	OF-4
	Lieutenant Commander	Major	Major	Squadron Leader	OF-3
	Lieutenant	Captain	Captain	Flight Lieutenant	OF-2
	Sub-Lieutenant	Lieutenant/2nd Lieutenant	Lieutenant/2nd Lieutenant	Flying Officer/Pilot Officer	OF-1
	Midshipman	—	Officer Cadet	Officer Designate	OF-(D)
OTHER RANKS	Warrant Officer Class 1	Warrant Officer Class 1	Warrant Officer Class 1	Warrant Officer	OR-9
	Warrant Officer Class 2	Warrant Officer Class 2	Warrant Officer Class 2	—	OR-8
	Chief Petty Officer	Colour Sergeant	Staff Sergeant	Flight Sergeant/Chief Technician	OR-7
	Petty Officer	Sergeant	Sergeant	Sergeant	OR-6
	Leading Rate	Corporal	Corporal	Corporal	OR-4
		—	Lance Corporal		OR-3
	Able Rating	Marine	Private (Class 1–3)	Junior Technician/ Leading & Senior Aircraftman	OR-2
		—	Private (Class 4)/Junior	Aircraftman	OR-1

[Source: DASA] The Naval rank of Warrant Officer Class 2 was introduced in 2004. † The Royal Marines were established in 1664 as a corps of sea soldiers to be raised and disbanded as required. In 1755, they became a permanent part of the Navy, trained as soldiers and seamen to fight and to maintain discipline on ships. The Royal Marines gained their tough fighting reputation during the capture of Gibraltar in 1704, and have since played a decisive role in military deployments across the world.

CHELSEA PENSIONERS

Women were finally admitted as Chelsea Pensioners in March 2009, when Dorothy Hughes (85) and Winifred Philips (82) donned the distinctive scarlet coat and took up residence at the Royal Hospital in Chelsea. The famous army retirement home was established in 1682, at the behest of Charles II, 'for the succour and relief of veterans broken by age and war'. Prior to this, retired soldiers had no official provisions for their care, although many were looked after by monastic infirmaries until the Dissolution of 1536. Sir Christopher Wren was appointed to design and build the Royal Hospital in 1682, but, due to a funding crisis, the grounds were not ready to accept soldiers until 1692, when the first 476 moved in. The beautiful buildings and grounds have seen a few changes over time, not least after bombing during the two World Wars, but the original three-quadrangle design and iconic cupola remain. For a soldier to qualify for admission to the Royal Hospital Chelsea he (and now she) must receive an army pension, be aged ≥65, and have no dependent partner. On becoming an In-Pensioner, veterans must surrender their army pension in return for food, lodging, and medical care. (Out-Pensioners are former soldiers who receive a pension but live away from the hospital.) Chelsea Pensioners wear a blue uniform within the grounds of the hospital but may wear civilian clothes outside. The famous scarlet coats and tricorne hats are worn at all official functions. Each pensioner has an individual 2·7m × 2·7m berth, although meals are taken communally in the large dining hall. The Hospital also has two lounges, bars, a handicraft centre, library, bowling green, cybercafé, and allotments. There are currently 290 male and two female In-Pensioners.

AVERAGE AGE OF THE ARMY

According to the DASA *Age Distribution of UK Regular Forces* report, as of April 2009:

Average (median) age of males in the UK armed forces .... 29 years
Average (median) age of females in the UK armed forces .... 27 years
Percentage of UK army personnel under the age of 18 .... 2·5%
Percentage of UK army personnel over the age of 50 .... 2·2%

HM ARMED FORCES TOYS

In May 2009 it was announced that the Ministry of Defence had agreed a deal with the Character Group to manufacture a series of action figures based on the armed forces. 32 toys are planned for the range, which will be launched with 10" figures representing each branch of the armed forces: the Army infantryman will come with a Kevlar flak-jacket and a SA80A2 assault rifle; the Royal Marine commando will sport the famous green beret; and the Royal Air Force fast jet pilot will wear a flying helmet with oxygen mask and natty white leather flying gloves. As well as earning a royalty from the sale of these figures, the MOD hopes to boost the public image of the armed forces. Over time, the range will include various military vehicles and equipment, as well as a female soldier, a Gurkha, and a generic 'baddie'.

———————————— DARWIN & RELIGION ————————————

In a March 2009 survey to mark the 200th anniversary of Charles Darwin's birth, theological think-tank Theos revealed that 80% of Britons reject the theory of creationism. Below is a breakdown of respondents' views on the origins of human life:

Humans evolved by a process of evolution which removes any need for God......37%
*Humans evolved by a process of evolution which can be seen
as part of God's plan*...28%
Humans were created by God sometime within the last 10,000 years............17%
*Humans evolved through evolution which required the special intervention
of God, or a higher power, at key stages*...11%

Respondents' views of God, and God's relationship (if any) to the universe, were:

God designed and created the universe and remains involved with it............34%
*God is an invention of human minds and has nothing to do with the
creation of the universe*..31%
God is like an impersonal power or force within the universe...................11%
God and the universe are really the same...9%
God designed and created the universe but has no further involvement with it....8%

When asked about the relationship between faith and science, it was clear that most Britons felt belief in one did not negate the other: 47% agreed that science challenges religious beliefs but that they can co-exist; 26% said science neither supports nor undermines religious belief; 12% felt that science positively supported religious belief; and just 10% said that science totally undermined religious belief. The relationship between evolution and Christianity was also examined:

Evolution presents challenges to Christianity but it is possible to believe in both..42%
Evolution and Christianity are totally disconnected subjects......................24%
Evolution and Christianity are totally incompatible..............................16%
Evolution and Christianity are wholly compatible................................14%

The survey suggested that some people were unclear as to Darwin's literary output. 5% believed he penned *A Brief History of Time* (by Stephen Hawking), 3% thought he wrote *The God Delusion* (by Richard Dawkins), and 1% believed he was responsible for *The Naked Chef* (by Jamie Oliver).

———————— RELIGIOUS VALUES & PUBLIC LIFE ————————

63% agree that laws 'should respect and be influenced by' Britain's traditional Christian values, according to a February 2009 poll by the BBC. The percentages who agreed that religion 'has an important role to play in public life' are below:

Religion	% agreeing	Hindu	...100	Other	...66
Christian	...73	Sikh	...74	No religion	...36
Muslim	...91	Jewish	...33	ALL	...62

———————————————— RELIGION & WEALTH ————————————————

In 2009, a Pew Global Attitudes survey showed that members of the lower[†] class were more likely to say that religion was important to them than members of the middle[†] class, at least in 13 countries. The percentages of lower and middle class respondents who reported that religion was 'very important' in their lives are below:

Lower	% very important	Middle			
42	Argentina	30	86	Malaysia	60
78	Brazil	73	48	Mexico	33
15	Bulgaria	8	46	Poland	32
49	Chile	39	16	Russia	14
64	Egypt	63	79	South Africa	78
72	India	60	26	Ukraine	22
			39	Venezuela	34

† The 'middle class' was defined as those earning ≥$4,286 per year in 'standardized international dollars' – a World Bank threshold for defining the middle class. People whose incomes did not meet this threshold were classified as 'lower class'. ❦ Previous Pew studies have shown that poorer nations are, on the whole, more religious than wealthier ones. A Pew 2007 Global Attitudes Survey created an index of religiosity by asking people in 47 nations three questions: whether faith in God was necessary for morality; how important religion was in their lives; and whether they prayed at least once a day. The survey found that people in the poorest nations scored the highest (Senegal came top), while wealthy Western European countries scored the lowest (Sweden was at the bottom). Both the United States and Kuwait, however, were considerably more religious than their GDPs might suggest.

———————————— SEVEN DEADLY SINS OF THE SEXES ————————————

Men and women sin in different ways, according to a study of confessional data by 96-year-old Jesuit priest Roberto Busa[†]. The results, published in the Vatican newspaper *L'Osservatore Romano* in February 2009, also revealed that 30% of Catholics no longer considered confession to be necessary. The most common sins by sex are:

♂ · Lust	1	♀ · Pride	Envy	6	Avarice
Gluttony	2	Envy	Avarice	7	Sloth
Sloth	3	Anger			
Anger	4	Lust	† Renowned for his 30-year-in-the-making		
Pride	5	Gluttony	computerised study of St Thomas Aquinas.		

———————————————— THE TEMPLETON PRIZE ————————————————

French physicist and philosopher of science Bernard d'Espagnat was awarded the £820,000 Templeton Prize in March 2009. D'Espagnat was recognised for his 'explorations of the philosophical implications of quantum physics', that have 'opened new vistas on the definition of reality and the potential limits of knowable science'. ❦ Sir John Templeton founded his eponymous prize in 1972, 'to encourage and honour the advancement of knowledge in spiritual matters'.

DEBAPTISM

In 2009, a London man attempted to become the first Christian in Britain to officially cancel his baptism. John Hunt, baptised in 1953 at the St Jude and St Aidan parish church in Southwark, made headlines in March after he wrote to the diocese asking to be removed from its baptismal roll. Hunt claimed that, at five months old, he was too young to consent to his christening, and that he no longer believed in God. However, the diocese refused to remove Hunt's name, arguing that a baptism is a matter of public record that cannot be undone. 'It's a bit like trying to expunge Trotsky from the photos,' the Bishop of Croydon, the Right Reverend Nick Baines, told the BBC. The diocese informed Hunt that if he wished, he could place an announcement revoking his baptism in the *London Gazette*, considered a journal of record. Hunt complied. Notably, he also availed himself of the 'Certificate of Debaptism' on the National Secular Society website. The certificate, which the Society says has been downloaded by 100,000 people over five years, reads, in part:

> *In the name of human reason, I reject all [the Church's] Creeds and all other such superstition, in particular, the perfidious belief that any baby needs to be cleansed by Baptism of alleged original sin, and the evil power of supposed demons.*

Hunt's case prompted Church of England officials to note that baptism is not considered a formal sign of church membership, which effectively lapses with non-attendance. However, the Roman Catholic Church does view baptism as incorporation into the Church. Those who wish to renounce Catholic baptism may write to their place of baptism and request that a note confirming they have left the Church be added to the records in the margin alongside their baptismal entry. Catholic debaptism movements reportedly exist in Spain, Italy, and Argentina; Germans can renounce their baptism, in part to avoid payment of a 'church tax'.

PRAYERS FOR THE FINANCIAL CRISIS

The Church of England released a series of special prayers in January 2009 in response to the global economic downturn. For those worried about debt, one prayer included a plea for help with setting up a household budget: 'Help us to learn to let no debt remain outstanding, except the debt to love one another'. Another prayer aimed to help workers deal with the stress of remaining employed after colleagues had been sacked. Below is 'The Prayer on Being Made Redundant':

> *'Redundant' – the word says it all – 'useless, unnecessary, without purpose, surplus to requirements'. Thank you, Heavenly Father, that in the middle of the sadness, the anger, the uncertainty, the pain, I can talk to you. Hear me as I cry out in confusion, help me to think clearly, and calm my soul. As life carries on, may I know your presence with me each and every day. And as I look to the future, help me to look for fresh opportunities, for new directions. Guide me by your Spirit, and show me your path, through Jesus, the way, the truth and the life. Amen.*

The recession wiped £1·3bn from the Church of England's portfolio, according to May 2009 accounts.

THE SPIRITUAL BAROMETER

or, A Scale of The Progress of Sin & Grace – quoted by William Collier, 1810

70	GLORY	70
–	Dismission from the body.	–
–	↑	–
–	↑	–
60	Desiring to depart, to be with Christ.	60
–	Patience in tribulation.	–
–	Glorying in the Cross.	–
–	↑	–
50	Ardent love to the souls of men.	50
–	Following hard after God.	–
–	Deadness to the world by the cross of Christ.	–
–	↑	–
40	Love of God shed abroad in the heart.	40
–	Frequent approach to the Lord's table.	–
–	Meetings for prayer and experience.	–
–	↑	–
30	Delight in the people of God.	30
–	Looking to Jesus.	–
–	↑	–
–	↑	–
20	Love of God's house and word.	20
–	Vain company wholly dropped.	–
–	Daily perusal of the Bible with prayer.	–
–	↑	–
10	Evangelical light.	10
–	Retirement for prayer and meditation.	–
–	Concern for the Soul. Alarm.	–
–	↑	–
0	*Indifference*	0
–	Family worship only on Sunday evenings.	–
–	Private prayer frequently omitted.	–
–	Family religion wholly declined.	–
10	Levity in conversation. Fashions, however indecent, adopted.	10
–	↓	–
–	↓	–
–	↓	–
20	Luxurious entertainment.	20
–	Free association with carnal company.	–
–	↓	–
–	↓	–
30	The theatre, Vauxhall, Ranelagh, &c.	30
–	Frequent parties of pleasure. House of God forsaken.	–
–	Much wine, spirits, &c.	–
–	↓	–
40	Love of novels, &c.	40
–	Scepticism. Private prayer totally declined.	–
–	Deistical company prized.	–
–	↓	–
50	Parties of pleasure on the Lord's day.	50
–	Masquerades; Drunkenness; Adultery.	–
–	Profaneness, lewd songs.	–
–	↓	–
60	Infidelity; jesting at religion.	60
–	Sitting down in the chair of the scorner.	–
–	↓	–
–	↓	–
70	Death.	70
	† PERDITION †	

——— RELIGIOUS TOLERANCE & INTEGRATION ———

77% of British Muslims say they identify 'extremely strongly' or 'very strongly' with their country, compared to 50% of non-Muslim Britons who say the same. According to the Gallup Coexist Index, released in May 2009, only 52% of French Muslims and 40% of German Muslims identified as strongly with their country. One of the more surprising findings of the survey was the notably conservative views of British Muslims compared to their European counterparts. None of the 500 British Muslims questioned thought homosexuality was 'morally acceptable' – in contrast to the 35% of French Muslims, 19% of German Muslims, and 58% of the general British public who did. Sex before marriage was deemed 'morally acceptable' by only 3% of the British Muslims questioned, compared to 82% of the general British public, 48% of French Muslims, and 27% of German Muslims. 42% of the British public think it necessary to 'tone down' religious observances in order to better integrate. Respondents were asked which actions they thought might be necessary to facilitate further integration into British society: the results are below:

% agreeing it is necessary to ...	British public	British Muslims		
Remove headscarf	32	3	Remove the turban 18 3	
Remove face veil	53	12	Remove visible crosses 17 2	
Remove the yarmulke[†]	24	1	89% of the British public felt learning the language aided integration. † Jewish skullcap.	

Gallup also tested opinions about the place of religion, in countries around the world: below is the percentage agreeing that religion is an important part of life:

Country	%				
Bangladesh	99	Ethiopia	91	Canada	45
Senegal	98	Brazil	88	Germany	44
Pakistan	98	South Africa	82	Belgium	37
Afghanistan	97	India	79	Netherlands	33
Tanzania	96	Italy	72	UK	29
Malaysia	94	USA	67	France	25
		Israel	50	Norway	20

——————— MALE-FRIENDLY HYMNS ———————

A survey of churchgoing men in May 2009 by *Sorted* magazine revealed that nearly 60% enjoyed singing hymns in church, although most preferred powerful and anthemic pieces to more emotional and sensitive songs. The survey suggested that men were uncomfortable with 'girly' decor in church, since 60% said they disliked flowers and embroidered banners. 72% of men questioned said their favourite part of a service was the sermon. *Sorted* suggested the following male-friendly hymns:

Onward Christian Soldiers · And Can It Be · Guide Me O Thou Great Redeemer
All People That on Earth do Dwell · Be Thou My Vision · How Great Thou Art
Amazing Grace · Eternal Father, Strong to Save (For Those in Peril on the Sea)
Our God Reigns · Dear Lord and Father of Mankind

—————————— INDIA'S CASTE SYSTEM ——————————

Traditionally, Indian society has been influenced by the caste system – a method of stratifying people into classes based on birth, marriage, and occupation. The term caste derives from the Portuguese *casta* (borrowed from the Latin *castus*, for 'race' or 'clan'), which the Portuguese used to describe Indian society after arriving in the C16th. While discrimination on the basis of caste has been illegal in India since 1949, the system remains embedded in some areas, and continues to affect some social interactions. ❦ The Hindu *varnas* ('colours') are an over-arching division of society first mentioned in a creation myth about the first being in the sacred Sanskrit *Rig Veda*:

> *When they divided Purusha, how many portions did they make? The Brahmin was his mouth, and from both his arms the Kshatriya was made. His thighs became the Vaishya, and from his feet the Shudra was produced.* – The Rig Veda X:90

The four *varnas* correspond to the following (historically hereditary) occupations:

Brahmins	*priests and teachers*	Vaishyas	*farmers and merchants*
Kshatriyas	*nobles and warriors*	Shudras	*peasants and labourers*

A fifth class, now called the Dalit, is said to exist outside of the *varna* system. Once called the 'untouchables', this group performed the lowest types of labour, including anything to do with waste, death or violence, which are considered polluting†.

Origins · Some trace the roots of the system to an Aryan invasion of N India *c*.1500 BC, when the conquerors used the caste system to legitimise their own rule while placing the region's aboriginal populations on the lowest rungs.

Colours · Traditionally, Brahmins were associated with the colour white, Kshatriyas red, Vaishyas brown, and Shudras black. Some have thus proposed a racialised division, but genetic analysis has produced varying results.

While *varna* exists as a symbolic division of society, it is *jati* that today principally structures the caste system. A *jati,* literally meaning 'birth', is a kinship group that is (historically) responsible for a particular craft or occupation. There are thousands of *jati*, which vary geographically, and can each be roughly fitted into a particular *varna*. Notions of *jati* are governed by rules of ritual purity and pollution. Thus the bodily substances and secretions of each *jati* are prohibited from mixing with those of others, and to work, marry or dine below one's *jati* is to pollute oneself. Such transgressions require participation in cleansing activities – which may include bathing, purifying rites, or the payment of fines, depending on the severity of the offence. ❦ Traditionally, movement across castes was quite limited. However, lower castes could sometimes improve their standing by adopting the practices of higher castes. Today the lower castes are the subject of affirmative action. Globalisation, migration, urbanisation, and the introduction of new, caste-free occupations (such as computer programming) are also responsible for weakening the hierarchy.

† Mahatma Gandhi named this class the *Harijans*, or God's children. More recently this group has claimed the term *Dalit*, meaning oppressed, and led campaigns demanding rights and recognition.

—————————— BANNED RELIGIOUS GROUPS ——————————

In May 2009, the Church of Scientology went on trial in France accused of organised fraud – charges it vigorously denies. The case centres on a former Scientologist who claims that the Church manipulated her into spending large sums on spiritual services and vitamins. A verdict, expected in October 2009, could see the organisation banned in France. (Scientology was founded by the science fiction writer L. Ron Hubbard in 1954. It is officially considered a religion in the UK and US, but has been banned in Greece and declared 'unconstitutional' in Germany.) Tabulated below is a sample of other religious groups banned in certain countries:

Falun Gong · a blend of Taoism, Buddhism, meditation, and traditional Chinese exercise banned in China since 1999 as an 'evil cult'. China also officially bans *Guan Yin* (the Way of the Goddess of Mercy), *Zhong Gong* (based on *qigong* exercise), and a variety of Christian groups.

Jehovah's Witnesses · a Christian sect founded in the US in the late C19th, whose controversial practices (like rejecting blood transfusions and military service) have led to bans in Singapore since 1972, Moscow since 2004, and Tajikistan since 2007. In 1964, Syria banned Jehovah's Witnesses as a 'politically motivated Zionist organisation'.

Salafism · a branch of Islamic thought that venerates the earliest generations of Muslims. Tajikistan's Supreme Court banned Salafism in February 2009 because of a perceived threat to national order. The Tajik government has also banned *Hizbut Tahrir*, a fundamentalist Islamic organisation, on the grounds that it is an extremist group. (Hizbut Tahrir is also banned in Russia, but not the US or most of the EU.)

Baha'i Faith · a monotheistic religion founded in Persia in the C19th that emphasises spiritual unity. Egypt banned Baha'i activity in 1960, Iraq in 1970, and Iran in 1983, because the group are considered apostates from Islam.

Unified Buddhist Church of Vietnam · A C20th branch of Buddhism banned in Vietnam in 1981 for refusing to join the official Vietnam Buddhist Church. *Tin Lanh Dega*, Dega Protestantism, practised by ethnic minorities in Vietnam's Central Highlands, is also banned because of claims that supporters seek political autonomy.

In areas with one state-sanctioned religion, such as Saudi Arabia, all other groups are banned.

—————————— CHILDREN & RELIGION ——————————

'Beatbullying' questioned >250 London youths (aged 11–16) in November 2008 about their experience of faith and religious tolerance. The main findings are below:

48% .... have religious belief	15 .... discussed religion at school
38 .... have no religious belief	6 .... discussed religious issues at home
37 .... practise a religion	48 .... never talked about religion
19 .... mainly had friends of	23 .. were bullied because of their faith
the same religion	19 .... suffered racist bullying

Sport

My aim is to become a legend. I don't think about records. I don't put myself.
under pressure. I know what to do and I go and execute. — USAIN BOLT

—— WORLD CHAMPIONSHIP ATHLETICS · BERLIN ——

Jamaican sprinter Usain 'Lightning' Bolt dominated coverage of the August 2009 World Championship Athletics in Berlin, as he smashed his own 100m and 200m world records. This supreme athletic ability, matched with a gregarious personality, ensured that Bolt was never far from the media's adoring gaze. S African middle-distance runner Caster Semanya caught the crueller aspect of this gaze when the IAAF clumsily revealed it was subjecting the 18-year-old to a gender test, after questions were asked of her sudden improvement in form. The manner in which Semanya's privacy had been breached was widely criticised, as was the tone of much of the media's reporting. At the time of writing, public sympathy seemed firmly with Semanya, regardless of the test's conclusions. Selected competition results are below:

Men	event	Women
Usain Bolt [JAM] 9·58s WR	100m	Shelly-Ann Fraser [JAM] 11·06s
Ryan Brathwaite [BAR] 13·14s	110/100m hurdles	B. Foster-Hylton [JAM] 12·51s
Usain Bolt [JAM] 19·19s WR	200m	Allyson Felix [USA] 22·02s
LaShawn Merritt [USA] 44·06s	400m	Sanya Richards [USA] 49·00s
Mbulaeni Mulaudzi [RSA] 1:45·29s	800m	Caster Semenya [RSA] 1:55·45s
Yusuf Saad Kamel [BRN] 3:35·93s	1,500m	M. Yusuf Jamal [BRN] 4:03·74s
Kenenisa Bekele [ETH] 13:17·09s	5,000m	Vivian Cheruiyot [KEN] 14:57·97
Yaroslav Rybakov [RUS] 2·32m	high jump	Blanka Vlašic [CRO] 2·04m
Dwight Phillips [USA] 8·54m	long jump	Brittney Reese [USA] 7·10m
Andreas Thorkildsen [NOR] 89·59m	javelin	Steffi Nerius [GER] 67·30m
Phillips Idowu [GBR] 17·73m	triple jump	Yargeris Savigne [CUB] 14·95m
Steven Hooker [AUS] 5·90m	pole vault	Anna Rogowska [POL] 4·75m
Trey Hardee [USA] 8,790pts	dec-/heptathlon	Jessica Ennis [GBR] 6,731pts
Jamaica 37·31s	4×100m relay	Jamaica 42·06s
USA 2:57·86s	4×400m relay	USA 3:17·83s

Team GB enjoyed its best result since 1999, taking 6 medals in total (exceeding the target of 5). Phillips Idowu and Jessica Ennis secured gold in the triple jump and heptathlon respectively. Silver medals were won by Lisa Dobriskey in the 1,500m, and the men's 4×400m relay. Bronzes were earned by Jenny Meadows in the 800m, and the men's 4×100m relay. Team GB's haul came despite the absence of some top names (Paula Radcliffe pulled out of the marathon due to injury), and the disappointing performance of others (Christine Ohuruogu failed to defend her 400m Olympic title). With 20 Britons making finals and 11 personal bests set, hope was expressed that Team GB might reach (or exceed) its London 2012 target of 8 medals.

TWENTY20 WORLD CUP · 2009

The second Twenty20 Cricket World Cup was hosted by England in June 2009. The high quality and fast pace of play made the tournament a resounding success and brought a wider audience to this previously derided (by some) abbreviated version of the game. By scheduling the men's and women's tournaments concurrently, the ICC introduced a larger crowd to women's cricket and created a format that might encourage other competitions to take the women's game more seriously. South Africa were favourites in the men's competition, and they produced some outstanding play, mainly thanks to Jacques Kallis. Yet it was Sri Lanka and the creative batting of Tillakaratne Dilshan that looked unstoppable as they coasted their way to the final, unbeaten. England proved inconsistent. They lost to the Netherlands in their opening match, yet beat Pakistan – the eventual and deserving winners of the tournament. In the women's contest no other team came close to England who remained unbeaten as they claimed yet another trophy (they also hold the Ashes and the 50-over World Cup). ❦ The results of the semi-finals and finals are below:

Women's competition	*Men's competition*
SEMI-FINAL 1 · Trent Bridge	SEMI-FINAL 1 · Trent Bridge
New Zealand......................145/5	Pakistan 149/4
India................................ 93/9	South Africa......................142/5
New Zealand won by 52 runs	Pakistan won by 6 runs
SEMI-FINAL 2 · The Oval	SEMI-FINAL 2 · The Oval
Australia...........................163/5	Sri Lanka..........................158/5
England 165/2	West Indies.................101 all out
England won by 8 wickets	Sri Lanka won by 57 runs
THE FINAL · Lord's	THE FINAL · Lord's
New Zealand.................85 all out	Sri Lanka..........................138/6
England ....86 for 4	Pakistan 139/2
England won by 6 wickets	Pakistan won by 8 wickets

After a nervous performance in their semi-final against Australia, England tightened their game to inflict a devastating defeat on New Zealand. Swing bowler Katherine Brunt excelled, taking 3 wickets for 6 runs as the Kiwis were bowled out for just 85. Faced with such an easy target, the English batswomen were able to play safe and ensure victory. Claire Taylor, who was later named player of the tournament, hit the winning runs – hitting a four in an unbeaten 39 from 32 balls to seal victory. The result confirmed England's domination of women's cricket.

The confidence of pre-match favourite Sri Lanka was dented early on when the team's star batsman Tillakaratne Dilshan was dismissed in the first over. Pakistan's accurate bowling then restricted Sri Lanka to 138/6. With a legion of cheering fans behind them, an exuberant Pakistan batted their way to glory. Showman Shahid Afridi led the way, hitting 54 (not out) from 40 balls. With the future of Pakistani international cricket in doubt (after the March 2009 terrorist attack on the Sri Lankan team in Lahore), Pakistan's victory came as a welcome boost to their supporters.

THE PREMIERSHIP · 2008/09

Team	won	drew	lost	goals for	goals against	goal difference	points
Manchester Utd	28	6	4	68	24	44	90
Liverpool	25	11	2	77	27	50	86
Chelsea	25	8	5	68	24	44	83
Arsenal	20	12	6	68	37	31	72
↑ CHAMPIONS LEAGUE ↑							
Everton	17	12	9	55	37	18	63
Aston Villa	17	11	10	54	48	6	62
Fulham	14	11	13	39	34	5	53
↑ UEFA CUP ↑							
Tottenham	14	9	15	45	45	0	51
West Ham	14	9	15	42	45	–3	51
Manchester City	15	5	18	58	50	8	50
Wigan	12	9	17	34	45	–11	45
Stoke City	12	9	17	38	55	–17	45
Bolton	11	8	19	41	53	–12	41
Portsmouth	10	11	17	38	57	–19	41
Blackburn	10	11	17	40	60	–20	41
Sunderland	9	9	20	34	54	–20	36
Hull City	8	11	19	39	64	–25	35
↓ RELEGATION ↓							
Newcastle	7	13	18	40	59	–19	34
Middlesbrough	7	11	20	28	57	–29	32
West Brom	8	8	22	36	67	–31	32

Chelsea's Nicolas Anelka was the league's top scorer with 19 goals, followed by Manchester United's Cristiano Ronaldo with 18. Steven Gerrard of Liverpool was in third place with 16 goals.

OTHER DIVISIONS – UP & DOWN

Up	2008/09	Down
Wolves, Birmingham City Burnley	*Championship*	Norwich, Southampton Charlton Athletic
Leicester City, Peterborough Scunthorpe	*League One*	Northampton, Crewe Cheltenham, Hereford
Brentford, Exeter Wycombe, Gillingham	*League Two*	Chester Luton†
Burton Albion Torquay	*Conference National*	Woking, Northwich Victoria Weymouth, Lewes

† Luton started the 2008–09 season with a –30 point deficit after the FA deducted 10 points for paying agents via a third party, and 20 points for failing to comply with the League's insolvency rules.

———————— THE FA CUP FINAL· 2009 ————————

30/5/2009 · Wembley Stadium
Attendance: 89,391
CHELSEA – 2 (Drogba 21, Lampard 72), EVERTON – 1 (Saha 1)
Referee: Howard Webb

Everton's Louis Saha claimed the fastest goal in FA Cup Final history when he scored after just 25 seconds. Chelsea quickly re-grouped and were soon dominating the field of play, with Florent Malouda and Nicolas Anelka both finding plenty of space to menace the Everton defence. Chelsea's guile paid off after 21 minutes when Malouda's soaring cross was met by the head of Didier Drogba. The heat began to tell, especially on the Toffees, who were making all the running. The second half began as a more open affair, as Everton manager David Moyes's tactical tinkering paid off. Frank Lampard, however, had other ideas and scored the winning goal with his unfavoured left foot. Controversy came when a great shot by Malouda hit the bar and bounced close to the line. Referee Howard Webb ruled no goal as the TV pundits endlessly showed replays proving that the ball had indeed crossed the line. The matter was soon forgotten when the final whistle went, and Chelsea rejoiced in their first silverware since Jose Mourinho left the club two years earlier.

Ashley Cole became the first player of the modern era to win five FA Cup winner's medals. The last player to do so was Jimmy Forrest of Blackburn Rovers, who won his fifth medal in 1891.

———————— THE CHAMPIONS LEAGUE FINAL· 2009 ————————

27/5/2009 · Stadio Olimpico, Rome
Attendance: 72,700
BARCELONA 2 (Eto'o 10, Messi 70), MANCHESTER UNITED 0
Referee: Massimo Busacca [SUI]

Manchester United entered the final as the dominant side, confident that they would make history by becoming the first club successfully to defend the Champions League. However, their lead in the first ten minutes proved to be anomalous. Barcelona scored with their first attack – Samuel Eto'o broke free of Nemanja Vidic and hit home a goal that Edwin van der Sar should have saved. From then on, Barcelona's impressive midfield – Andrés Iniesta and Xavi – ensured that Manchester United struggled to gain any meaningful possession. Sir Alex Ferguson tried to regain the initiative by repeatedly shifting formation, bringing on both Carlos Tevez and Dimitar Berbatov, but neither exerted any real influence. The second Barcelona goal came from a Xavi cross that was expertly (and somewhat surprisingly) headed in by the diminutive Lionel Messi. Sir Alex's hopes of the double were dashed. Instead it was Barcelona's rookie manager, Pep Guardiola, who added to his trophy cabinet (Barcelona also won La Liga and the Spanish Cup).

Lionel Messi was the top scorer of the whole Champion's League competition, scoring 9 goals. Steven Gerrard of Liverpool was joint second with Miroslav Klose of Bayern Munich, on 7 goals.

PREMIERSHIP WAGE BILL

The Premiership spent £1·2bn on player wages in 2007/08, up 23% from 2006/07. Deloitte's Annual Review of Football Finance, published in June 2009, uncovered the soaring wage bill in the top flight of football, with British clubs far outspending the leagues of Italy, Spain, Germany, and France. The Premiership made £1·93bn in 2007/08, but the huge debts of Chelsea (£711m), Manchester United (£649m), Arsenal (£318m), and Liverpool (£300m) raised questions as to whether current wage rates are sustainable. The wage bills for Premiership teams in 2007/08 were:

Team	2007/08 wages £	Team	2007/08 wages £
Chelsea	172,096,000	Blackburn Rovers	39,661,000
Manchester Utd	121,080,000	Fulham	39,344,000
Arsenal	101,302,000	Bolton Wanderers	39,033,000
Liverpool	90,438,000	Wigan Athletic	38,351,000
Newcastle Utd	74,562,000	Sunderland	37,091,000
Portsmouth	54,680,000	Middlesbrough	34,761,000
Manchester City	54,222,000	Reading	33,123,000
Tottenham Hotspur	52,921,000	Birmingham City	26,624,000
Aston Villa	50,447,000	Derby County	26,109,000
Everton	44,480,000	Premiership average	59,800,000

SOME FOOTBALL AWARDS OF NOTE · 2008/09

FIFA world player of the year	Cristiano Ronaldo [Man. Utd]
European footballer of the year	Cristiano Ronaldo [Man. Utd]
Prof. Footballers' Assoc. player of the year	Ryan Giggs [Man. Utd]
PFA young player award	Ashley Young [Aston Villa]
Football Writers' Assoc. player of the year	Steven Gerrard [Liverpool]
FA women's football awards: players' player of the year	Fara Williams [Everton]
LMA manager of the year	David Moyes [Everton]

WORLD RECORD FOOTBALL TRANSFERS

Real Madrid paid £80m to Manchester Utd for Cristiano Ronaldo in June 2009, breaking the world record for the largest-ever transfer fee. The deal is expected to earn Ronaldo £9·5m in the first year. The previous top five highest signings were:

Year	player	from	to	transfer fee
2009	Kaká	AC Milan	Real Madrid	£56m
2001	Zinedine Zidane	Juventus	Real Madrid	£46m
2000	Luis Figo	Barcelona	Real Madrid	£37m
2000	Hernan Crespo	Parma	Lazio	£35·5m
1999	Christian Vieri	Lazio	Inter Milan	£32m

The costliest transfer of a British player was the £29·1m paid by Man Utd for Rio Ferdinand in 2002.

——— GOLF MAJORS · 2009 ———

♂	course		winner	score
MASTERS	Augusta, Georgia		Angel Cabrera [ARG]	−13
US OPEN	Bethpage, New York		Lucas Glover [USA]	−4
THE OPEN	Turnberry, Scotland		Stewart Cink† [USA]	−2
USPGA	Chaska, Minnesota		Yang Yong-eun [KOR]	−8
♀				
KRAFT NABISCO	Mission Hills, California		Brittany Lincicome [USA]	−9
LPGA	Havre de Grace, Maryland		Anna Nordqvist [SWE]	−15
US OPEN	Bethlehem, Pennsylvania		Eun-Hee Ji [KOR]	E
BRITISH OPEN	Royal Lytham, England		Catriona Matthew [SCO]	−3

† Cink beat 59-year-old Tom Watson (winner of five previous Opens) in a dramatic play-off. ❦ 2009 was the first year since 2004 that Tiger Woods failed to win any of the major golf tournaments.

——— BRITISH & IRISH LIONS TOUR OF SOUTH AFRICA ———

The British and Irish Lions tour of South Africa in June–July 2009 was an exciting and closely fought contest that resulted in a 2–1 defeat for the Lions. During the warm-up matches the Lions beat a series of local sides with ease, giving the tourists plenty to cheer about. However, World Cup holders South Africa proved a more challenging opponent. The first Test set the scene for the series, as first one side then the other proved dominant. The Springboks took the advantage in the first half before the Lions mounted a stirring second-half comeback, only to fall short of victory. The series hinged on the second Test which started controversially when Schalk Burger† appeared to gouge the eyes of Lions wing Luke Fitzgerald, yet was only sent to the sin-bin. What followed was a tense, close-run match until an agonising last-minute penalty by South Africa's Morne Steyn put a series victory beyond the Lions' grasp. Yet, even with the series effectively over, the Lions ended on a high, producing a passionate display to beat the Springboks by some margin.

1st Test · Kings Park, Durban · SOUTH AFRICA 26–21 LIONS
SA – *tries*: Smit, Brussow · *cons*: Pienaar (2) · *pens*: Pienaar (3), Steyn
Lions – *tries*: Croft (2), Phillips · *cons*: Jones (3)

2nd Test · Loftus Versfeld, Pretoria · SOUTH AFRICA 28–25 LIONS
SA – *tries*: Pietersen, Habana, Fourie · *con*: M. Steyn (2) · *pens*: F. Steyn, M. Steyn (2)
Lions – *tries*: Kearney · *con*: S. Jones · *pens*: S. Jones (5) · *drop goal*: S. Jones

3rd Test · Ellis Park, Johannesburg · SOUTH AFRICA 9–28 LIONS
SA – *pens*: M. Steyn (3)
Lions – *tries*: S. Williams (2), Monye · *cons*: S. Jones (2) · *pens*: S. Jones (3)

† Burger was later banned for eight weeks by the International Rugby Board. South African coach Peter de Villiers said eye gouging did not belong in the game, yet argued that rugby will always have collisions, and asked ironically, 'why don't we all go to the nearest ballet shop, get some nice tutus...'.

—————————— RUGBY UNION SIX NATIONS · 2009 ——————————

After 61 years, in a thrilling match against Wales, Ireland completed the Grand Slam and with it took the Six Nations championship. The Welsh were just 2 minutes from winning the match and the Triple Crown, but Ronan O'Gara's last-ditch drop goal secured an Irish victory. Six Nations 2009 results and the final table are below:

Date		result		venue
07·02·09	Ireland	30–21	France	Croke Park
07·02·09	England	36–11	Italy	Twickenham
08·02·09	Scotland	13–26	Wales	Murrayfield
14·02·09	Wales	23–15	England	Millennium Stadium
14·02·09	France	22–13	Scotland	Stade de France
15·02·09	Italy	9–38	Ireland	Stadio Flaminio
27·02·09	France	21–16	Wales	Stade de France
28·02·09	Scotland	26–6	Italy	Murrayfield
28·02·09	Ireland	14–13	England	Croke Park
14·03·09	Scotland	15–22	Ireland	Murrayfield
14·03·09	Italy	15–20	Wales	Stadio Flaminio
15·03·09	England	34–10	France	Twickenham
21·03·09	England	26–12	Scotland	Twickenham
21·03·09	Italy	8–50	France	Stadio Flaminio
21·03·09	Wales	15–17	Ireland	Millennium Stadium

FINAL TABLE 2009						TOTAL HONOURS EVER		
points	w	d	l	pd	country	triple crowns	grand slams	titles
10	5	0	0	48	Ireland	10	2	11
6	3	0	2	54	England	23	12	25
6	3	0	2	23	France	n/a	8	16
6	3	0	2	19	Wales	19	10	24
2	1	0	4	–23	Scotland	10	3	14
0	0	0	5	–121	Italy	n/a	0	0

——————— HEINEKEN EUROPEAN CUP FINAL · 2009 ———————

LEICESTER 16–19 LEINSTER
23·05·09 · Murrayfield, Edinburgh

LEICESTER – *tries:* Woods; *cons:* Dupuy; *pens:* Dupuy (3) · LEINSTER – *tries:* Heaslip; *cons:* Sexton; *pens:* Sexton (2); *drop goals:* O'Driscoll, Sexton

——— INTERNATIONAL RUGBY BOARD AWARDS · 2008 ———

International player of the year .... Shane Williams [WAL]
International team of the year... New Zealand
International coach of the year................................ Graham Henry [NZL]
International sevens player of the year............................ D. J. Forbes [NZL]

———————— THE RUGBY LEAGUE WORLD CUP · 2008 ————————

New Zealand amazed Australia in the final of the Rugby League World Cup in November 2008, winning by 13 points to take the trophy for the first time. Australia hosted the competition and, having held the trophy since 1975, were supremely confident of victory. Underlining their dominance, Australia beat New Zealand 30–6 in their opening match and then routed England, the other main threat (on paper at least), 52–4. ❦ England did not fulfil their potential during the contest and were criticised for not playing with the heart manifested by 'minnows' such as Papua New Guinea and Fiji. England's high hopes ended in the semi-finals with an error-strewn 22–32 defeat to New Zealand. ❦ Australia began the final fiercely, racing to a 10–0 lead. Yet the Kiwis were not daunted, and Jeremy Smith got them off the mark with a powerful try. Luck was with the Kiwis as video referee decisions went their way, and the Aussies began to make mistakes. With momentum on their side, New Zealand propelled themselves to a truly impressive victory.

AUSTRALIA 20–34 NEW ZEALAND
22·11·08 · SUNCORP STADIUM, BRISBANE

Australia – *tries*: Lockyer (2), Williams, Inglis · *goals*: Thurston (2)
New Zealand – *tries*: Smith, Ropati, Hohaia, Marshall, penalty try, Blair.
goals: Luke (3), Marshall (2)

———————————— MAN OF STEEL · 2008 ————————————

England and St Helens prop James Graham was awarded the 2008 Man of Steel prize, in October 2008. Sports journalists selected a St Helens player for the prize for the fourth year in a row. Graham received a cheque for £5,000, and a trophy.

———————— RUGBY LEAGUE CHALLENGE CUP · 2009 ————————

HUDDERSFIELD GIANTS 16–25 WARRINGTON WOLVES
29·8·08 · WEMBLEY STADIUM

Huddersfield – *tries*: Lunt, B. Hodgson, D. Hodgson · *goals*: B. Hodgson (2)
Warrington – *tries*: Mathers, Monaghan, Hicks, V. Anderson
goals: Bridge (4) · *drop goals*: Briers

Warrington Wolves triumphed in a fast-paced final against Huddersfield Giants to lift the Challenge Cup for the first time since 1974. Warrington's success was largely attributed to coach Tony Smith who had transformed the underachieving club since taking over in March 2009. The Wolves started in style, scoring three impressive tries in the first fourteen minutes. The Giants responded but had two tries ruled out, leaving them 18–10 down at half-time. The second half was slightly more sedate before a Vinnie Anderson try and conversion by Chris Bridge put the Wolves 14 points ahead. Victory was secured with a last-minute drop goal by Lee Briers.

———————— TOUR DE FRANCE · 2009 ————————

Alberto Contador secured his second overall Tour de France victory in 2009, after seeing off a challenge from his Astana team-mate, and returning Tour legend, Lance Armstrong. British eyes were firmly fixed on the sight of Mark Cavendish sailing across the finishing line in first place in Paris, having achieved his sixth stage win and confirming his position as one of the fastest road race sprinters. Brit Bradley Wiggins also demonstrated his potential as a future Tour winner by taking fourth place overall, equalling Robert Millar's 1984 best British performance. After years of scandal and intrigue, public enthusiasm for the Tour was re-ignited and c.15m spectators watched the race from the roadside. Much of this renewed interest was due to the return of Lance Armstrong who proved that, even aged 37, he was still a force to be reckoned with. Contador was open about his rivalry with Armstrong, explaining that, 'He was tough to cope with because he wanted to win the Tour too – that just doesn't work, having two guys who want to win in the same team'. Armstrong was quick to confirm that he would return to the Tour in 2010, but leading a different team. Below are the final standings in the 2009 Tour de France:

1	Alberto Contador [ESP]	Astana	85 hours 48 mins 35s
2	Andy Schleck [LUX]	Team Saxo Bank	+4 min 11s
3	Lance Armstrong [USA]	Astana	+5 min 24s
4	Bradley Wiggins [GBR]	Garmin-Slipstream	+6 min 1s

Green Jersey (sprint points) – Thor Hushovd [NOR], Cervelo Test Team, 280pts | Polka Dot Jersey (King of the Mountains) – Franco Pellizotti [ITA], Liquigas, 210pts. | White Jersey (best young rider) – Andy Schleck [LUX], Team Saxo Bank, 85:52:46 | Team – Astana, 256:02:58. ❦ Mark Cavendish's hopes of winning the Green Jersey were dashed when he was disqualified from the 14th stage of the Tour for not staying on the racing line and edging rival Thor Hushovd into a barrier.

———— CYCLING WORLD TRACK CHAMPIONSHIP · 2009 ————

Great Britain failed to realise their high hopes at the Track Cycling World Championships in Pruszków, Poland, in March 2009. The usually dominant Team GB was missing triple Olympic gold medallist Chris Hoy and double Olympic gold medallist Bradley Wiggins. Australia topped the table with a total of 10 medals – 4 of which were gold. Great Britain took 9 medals, the details of which are below:

	Event	*medallist*	*medal*
♀	Women's sprint	Victoria Pendleton	G
♀	Team pursuit	Great Britain	G
♂	Men's team pursuit	Great Britain	S
♀	Individual pursuit	Wendy Houvenaghel	S
♀	Team sprint	Victoria Pendleton & Shanaze Reade	S
♀	Women's scratch	Elizabeth Armitstead	S
♂	Men's point race	Chris Newton	B
♀	Women's points race	Elizabeth Armitstead	B
♀	500m time trial	Victoria Pendleton	B

———————FORMULA ONE TEAMS & DRIVERS · 2009———————

McLaren Mercedes.............. Lewis Hamilton [GBR] & Heikki Kovalainen [FIN]
Renault...Fernando Alonso [ESP] & N. Piquet Jr replaced by Romain Grosjean [FRA]
Ferrari .... Felipe Massa† [BRA] & Kimi Räikkönen [FIN]
Brawn .... Rubens Barrichello [BRA] & Jenson Button [GBR]
BMW Sauber ....Nick Heidfeld [GER] & Robert Kubica [POL]
Toyota.......................................Timo Glock [GER] & Jarno Trulli [ITA]
RBR-Renault..........................Sebastian Vettel [GER] & Mark Webber [AUS]
Williams.............................Kazuki Nakajima [JAP] & Nico Rosberg [GER]
Toro Rosso .Sebastien Buemi [SWI] & S. Bourdais replaced by Jaime Alguersuari [ESP]
Force India..........................Giancarlo Fisichella [ITA] & Adrian Sutil [GER]

† Massa was seriously injured during the Hungarian GP. Michael Schumacher was to stand in but
an old injury forced him out. Luca Badoer and then Giancarlo Fisichella temporarily took the wheel.

———FORMULA ONE WORLD CHAMPIONSHIP · 2009———

Date	Grand Prix	track	winning driver	team
29·03·09	Australian	Albert Park	Jenson Button	Brawn
05·04·09	Malaysian	Sepang	Jenson Button	Brawn
19·04·09	Chinese	Shanghai Int.	Sebastian Vettel	RBR-Renault
26·04·09	Bahrain	Sakhir	Jenson Button	Brawn
10·05·09	Spanish	Catalunya	Jenson Button	Brawn
24·05·09	Monaco	Monte Carlo	Jenson Button	Brawn
07·06·09	Turkish	Istanbul	Jenson Button	Brawn
21·06·09	British	Silverstone	Sebastian Vettel	RBR-Renault
12·07·09	German	Nürburgring	Mark Webber	RBR-Renault
26·07·09	Hungarian	Budapest	Lewis Hamilton	McLaren
23·08·09	European	Valencia	Rubens Barrichello	Brawn
30·08·09	Belgian	Spa	Kimi Räikkönen	Ferrari
13·09·09	Italian	Monza	Rubens Barrichello	Brawn
27·09·09	Singaporean	Singapore		
04·10·09	Japanese	Suzuka		
18·10·09	Brazilian	São Paulo		
01·11·09	Abu Dhabi	Yas Marina		

———————SUPERBIKES, RALLY & MOTORSPORT———————

Isle of Man TT (Superbike) [2009] .... John McGuinness (Honda)
Isle of Man TT (Senior TT final standing) [2009] .... Steve Plater (Honda)
Moto GP [2008].. Valentino Rossi (Yamaha)
British Superbikes [2008].......................................Shane Byrne (Ducati)
World Superbikes [2008].. Troy Bayliss (Ducati)
World Rally [2008] .... Sébastien Loeb (Citroën)
Le Mans [2009].............David Brabham, Marc Gené, Alexander Wurz (Peugeot)

——————— WOMEN'S CRICKET 50-OVER WORLD CUP ———————

England's women won the Cricket World Cup in March 2009 for the first time since 1993. England beat New Zealand by 4 wickets in Sydney, Australia, to secure the title. 27-year-old vice-captain and all-rounder Nicki Shaw was the hero of the hour, taking 4 for 34 as the Kiwis were dismissed for 166. England suffered a small setback when Claire Taylor (who was named Player of the Tournament after scoring 324 runs during the competition) was caught out by Aimee Mason, leaving England on 109 for 2. But the English side soon rallied, and the confident pairing of Colvin and Shaw led the tourists to a well-deserved victory [see also p.299].

——————— WISDEN CRICKETER OF THE YEAR ———————

In 2009, the Wisden Cricketers of the Year (awarded to the players who exerted the greatest influence on the English season in 2008) were Claire Taylor† [ENG], James Anderson [ENG], Dale Benkenstein [RSA], Mark Boucher [RSA], and Neil McKenzie [RSA]. The Wisden Leading Cricketer in the World was Virender Sehwag [IND].

† The first female cricketer to be rewarded by Wisden since the awards were introduced in 1889. Taylor scored nearly 800 international runs in 2008, and helped England's women retain the Ashes.

——————— TWENTY20 CUP FINAL DAY · 2009 ———————

Sussex won their first Twenty20 Cup when they beat Somerset by 63 runs at Edgbaston in August 2009. Sussex scored 172 – led by Dwayne Smith's 59 from 26 balls. Somerset's Marcus Trescothick scored a promising 33 before the Sussex bowlers took control. Chasing Sussex's imposing score Somerset collapsed to 109 all out.

Semi-final 1	Sussex (137–3) *bt* Northampton (136–6) by 7 wickets
Semi-final 2	Somerset (146–3) *bt* Kent (145–5) by 7 wickets
Cup Final	Sussex (172–7) *bt* Somerset (109 all out) by 63 runs

——————— INDIAN PREMIER LEAGUE ———————

The Indian Premier League moved to South Africa in 2009 after the Indian government warned it could not provide sufficient security for the event because of the general election. The move did not diminish the quality of the play, and the tournament was again deemed a major success for world cricket. The Deccan Chargers beat Bangalore Royal Challengers by six runs in the final. English players Andrew Flintoff and Kevin Pietersen joined the league for the first time, but both failed to live up to their price tags. The most expensive players to join the league in 2009 were:

Player	team	cost ($)	Player	team	cost ($)
K. Pietersen [ENG]	Bangalore	1·55m	J. P. Duminy [RSA]	Mumbai	950k
A. Flintoff [ENG]	Chennai	1·55m	T. Henderson [RSA]	Rajasthan	650k
			M. Mortaza [BAN]	Kolkata	600k

PAMPLONA BULL RUN

On 10 July 2009, a 27-year-old Spanish man, Daniel Jimeno Romero, was gored to death during the annual running of the bulls in Pamplona; three others were seriously injured. ❦ Pamplona is the ancient Basque city in northern Spain famed for the annual 'running of the bulls', which takes place 7–14 July as part of the festival celebrating St Fermín – the city's patron saint. The purpose of the run is to transfer to the bullring each morning the six bulls destined to fight that afternoon. For decades, hundreds of foolhardy folk have dared to run along the narrow streets in front of these bulls – the aim being to see how close they can get to the animals without being trampled or gored. Runners must enter the fenced area of the run by 7·30am, after which they sing a song three times – at 7·55am, 7·57am, and 7·59am:

A San Fermín pedimos, por ser nuestro patrón, nos guíe en el encierro, dándonos su bendición.

We ask for San Fermín, who is our Patron, to guide us through the Bull Run, and give us his blessing.

Then, at precisely 8·00am, a rocket is launched to announce that the gates of the Santo Domingo enclosure [A] are open; a second rocket indicates that all the bulls have left the enclosure and are running down Santo Domingo [B] towards the Plaza Consistorial [C]. A sharp turn takes the bulls up Mercaderes towards [D] where they turn into the long and narrow Estafeta. The bulls tend to slow down along this section until they exit the street [E], and enter the fenced funnel, Teléfonica [F], which herds them up the narrow Callejón [G] and into the Plaza de Toros [H]. A third rocket indicates all the bulls have entered the bullring, and a final rocket is fired when the event is over. The 848·6m run lasts, on average, just 4 minutes.

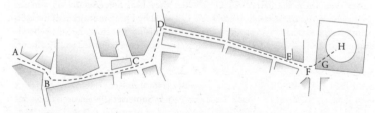

At least 15 runners have died in Pamplona since records were first kept in the 1920s, though reports vary. This latest death – at the horns of a 'rogue' light-brown bull named Capuchino – once again focused public attention on this curious 'sport'.

PUNCICATE

Prior to the Champions League final in Rome, the BBC described a curious form of Italian soccer hooliganism – *puncicate* – i.e., stabbing one's opponents in the buttocks. *Puncicate* dates back to medieval duels, when to wound someone in the back was a sign of skill; nowadays *puncicate* is associated with a group of *ultra* Roma fans. In *The Times*, Tony Evans criticised UEFA's decision to hold the final in Rome, noting that dozens of British football fans have suffered stabbings in 'the only city in Europe where visiting supporters are routinely and specifically targeted with blades'.

—————————— LONDON MARATHON · 2009 ——————————

Millions were raised for charity when >35,000 runners set off in balmy sunshine for the 29th London Marathon in April 2009. The key results are listed below:

♂ race results	♂ wheelchair race results
S. Wanjiru [KEN] 2h 5m 10s	K. Fearnley [AUS] 1:28:56
T. Kebede [ETN] 2:05:20	D. Weir [GBR] 1:28:57
J. Gharib [MAR]................2:05:27	E. Van Dyk [RSA]...............1:28:59

♀ race results	♀ wheelchair race results
I. Mikitenko [GER] 2:22:11	A. McGrory [USA] 1:50:39
M. Yamauchi [GBR]............2:23:12	S. Graf [SWI]...................1:50:40
L. Shobukova [RUS]............2:24:24	D. Roy [CAN]..................1:50:41

– OTHER MARATHONS OF NOTE · 2008/09 –

BERLIN...................*first run* 1974	NEW YORK..............*first run* 1970
2008 · 28 Sep ....fine, mild	2008 · 2 Nov.....................windy
♂ ......H. Gebrselassie [ETH] · 2:03:59	♂ ....M. dos Santos [BRA] · 2:08:43
♀.........I. Mikitenko [GER] · 2:19:18	♀...........P. Radcliffe [GBR] · 2:23:56
Purse..........................$340,000	Purse.......................>$600,000

CHICAGO................*first run* 1977	BOSTON ....*first run* 1897
2008 · 12 Oct..............hot, humid	2009 · 20 Apr......................cool
♂ ....E. Cheruiyot [KEN] · 2:06:25	♂ ....D. Merga [ETH] · 2:08:42
♀........L. Grigoryeva [RUS] · 2:27:17	♀.........S. Kosgei [KEN] · 2:32:16
Purse..........................$485,000	Purse..........................$796,000

—————————— EUROPEAN TEAM CHAMPIONSHIPS ——————————

The inaugural European Team Championships were held in Leiria, Portugal, in June 2009. The competition replaced the old European Cup, and now allows national men's and women's teams to compete as a whole. Dwain Chambers (100m & 200m), Emily Freeman (100m), Mo Farah (5,000m), David Greene (400m hurdles), Tim Benjamin (400m), and Andy Turner (110m hurdles) all won their events, helping Britain to finish a creditable third. The 2009 results are below:

1 .....Germany.............*points* 326·5	7 .....Ukraine......................265·5
2 .....Russia.........................320	8 .....Spain..........................257
3 .....GB & N. Ireland............303	9 .....Greece ....216·5
4 .....France........................301	10....Czech Rep.................213·5
5 .....Poland 289	11....Portugal......................200
6 .....Italy..........................278	12....Sweden......................138

The bottom three teams – Czech Republic, Portugal, and Sweden – were relegated to the lower league for 2010. Finland, Belarus, and Norway secured promotion into the top league for 2010.

--------- WORLD BOXING CHAMPIONS · AT 14·9·2009 ---------

Weight	WBC	WBA	IBF	WBO
Heavy	V Klitschko [UKR]	Valuev [RUS]	W Klitschko [UKR]	W Klitschko [UKR]
Cruiser	Fragomeni [ITAL]	Jones [PAN]	Adamek [POL]	Ramirez [HUN]
Light heavy	Pascal [CAN]	Campillo [SPA]	Cloud [USA]	Erdei [HUN]
Super middle	Froch [GBR]	Kessler [DEN]	Bute [CAN]	Stieglitz [GER]
Middle	Pavlik [USA]	Sturm [GER]	*vacant*	Pavlik [USA]
Light middle	Martinez [ARG]	Santos [PUR]	Spinks [USA]	Dzinziruk [UKR]
Welter	Berto [USA]	Mosley [USA]	Hlatshawayo [RSA]	Cotto [PUR]
Light welter	Alexander [USA]	Khan [GBR]	Urango [COL]	Bradley [USA]
Light	Valero [VEN]	Marquez [MEX]	*vacant*	Marquez [MEX]
Super feather	Soto [MEX]	Linares [VEN]	Guerrero [USA]	Martinez [PUR]
Feather	Aoh [JPN]	John [INA]	Cruz [MEX]	Luevano [USA]
Super bantam	Nishioka [JPN]	Dunne [IRE]	Caballero [PAN]	Lopez [PUR]
Bantam	Hasegawa [JPN]	Moreno [PAN]	Agbeko [GHA]	Montiel [MEX]
Super fly	Darchinyan [AUS]	Darchinyan [AUS]	Darchinyan [AUS]	Sonsona [PHI]
Fly	Naito [JPN]	Kaovichit [THA]	*vacant*	Narvaez [ARG]
Light fly	Sosa [MEX]	Reveco [ARG]	Viloria [USA]	Calderon [PUR]
Straw	Sithsamerchai [THA]	González [NIC]	Garcia [MEX]	Nietes [PHI]

The Ring magazine, the self-proclaimed 'bible of boxing', ranks the best boxers across all weight divisions, which many fans regard as an authoritative source of the best 'pound-for-pound' boxers. At 14/9/2009, *The Ring* top 10 were: [1] *Manny Pacquiao* (PHI; Light Welterweight); [2] *Juan Manuel Marquez* (MEX; Lightweight); [3] *Bernard Hopkins* (USA; Light Heavyweight); [4] *Shane Mosley* (USA; Welterweight); [5] *Israel Vazquez* (MEX; Super Bantamweight); [6] *Rafael Marquez* (MEX; Super Bantamweight); [7] *Nonito Donaire* (USA; Super Flyweight); [8] *Miguel Cotto* (PUR; Welterweight); [9] *Celestino Caballero* (PAN; Super Bantamweight); [10] *Paul Williams* (USA; Welterweight). · In February 2009, Joe Calzaghe retired from boxing undefeated. Nicknamed the 'Pride of Wales', Calzaghe enjoyed a long and illustrious career in which he held the WBO super middleweight title for over ten years. Calzaghe retired with a professional fighting record of 46 wins and no losses.

----------------- THE LAUREUS AWARDS · 2009 -----------------

The Laureus World Sporting Academy encourages the 'positive and worthwhile in sport', presenting awards to athletes in all disciplines. Some 2009 winners were:

World sportsman of the year.....................................Usain Bolt (sprinter)
World sportswoman of the year......................Yelena Isinbayeva (pole vault)
World team of the year.......................................Chinese Olympic team
World breakthrough of the year....................Rebecca Adlington (swimming)
Comeback of the year ....· Vitali Klitschko (boxing)
World Sportsperson of the Year with a Disability........Daniel Dias† (swimming)
World Action Sportsperson of the Year.........................Kelly Slater (surfer)

† 20-year-old Brazilian Daniel Dias won 4 golds, 4 silvers, and 1 bronze medal in the pool at Beijing 2008. Dias started swimming aged 16 and mastered all four swimming styles in just 2 months.

WIMBLEDON 2009

Roger Federer was hailed as the best tennis player in history as he won his sixth Wimbledon title and took his fifteenth grand slam [see p.313], breaking Pete Sampras's record of 14 titles. Federer's victory was hard-won in a gruelling five-set match against Andy Roddick (who had lost two previous Wimbledon finals to the Swiss). The 4h18m match boasted the most games (77) of any grand slam final, and Federer finally wrested victory 16–14 in the fifth set. In the women's contest the Williams sisters once again proved their incredible dominance, as Serena took her third Wimbledon title after again facing her sister Venus in the final. ❦ Throughout Wimbledon fortnight Britain was preoccupied with three things – Andy Murray, Centre Court's new (retractable) roof, and the (surprisingly clement) weather. All three came together when a light shower prompted officials to close the roof on Centre Court, allowing Andy Murray's epic match against Stan Wawrinka to play on late into the night. 12·6m viewers watched Murray finally secure victory at 10·38pm. Murray was ultimately beaten in the semi-finals by Andy Roddick, but his run generated plenty of hype and enthusiasm for the future. ❦ The results were:

MEN'S SINGLES
Roger Federer [SUI]
bt Andy Roddick [USA]
5–7, 7–6 (8–6), 7–6 (7–5), 3–6, 16–14

———

*'I'm staggered, to be honest, that
I have done this.'* – ROGER FEDERER

LADIES' SINGLES
Serena Williams [USA]
bt Venus Williams [USA]
7–6 (7–3), 6–2

———

*'I feel like I shouldn't be holding the
trophy, like I'm holding Venus's trophy.'*
– SERENA WILLIAMS

MEN'S DOUBLES
Daniel Nestor [CAN]
& Nenad Zimonjic [SRB]
bt Mike Bryan [USA]
& Bob Bryan [USA]
7–6 (9–7), 6–7 (3–7), 7–6 (7–3), 6–3

LADIES' DOUBLES
Venus Williams [USA]
& Serena Williams [USA]
bt Rennae Stubbs [AUS]
& Samantha Stosur [AUS]
7–6 (7–4), 6–4

MIXED DOUBLES
Mark Knowles [BAH]
& Anna-Lena Groenefeld [GER]
bt Leander Paes [IND]
& Cara Black [ZIM]
7–5, 6–3

BOYS' SINGLES
Andrey Kuznetsov [RUS]
bt Jordan Cox [USA]
4–6, 6–2, 6–2

GIRLS' SINGLES
Noppawan Lertcheewakarn [THA]
bt Kristina Mladenovic [FRA]
3–6, 6–3, 6–1

BOYS' DOUBLES
Pierre-Hugues Herbert [FRA]
& Kevin Krawietz [GER]
bt Julien Obry [FRA]
& Adrien Puget [FRA]
6–7 (3–7), 6–2, 12–10

GIRLS' DOUBLES
Noppawan Lertcheewakarn [THA]
& Sally Peers [AUS]
bt Kristina Mladenovic [FRA]
& Silvia Njiric [CRO]
6–1, 6–1

———————— FEDERER'S FIFTEEN GRAND SLAMS ————————

Year	tournament	beat	score
2003	Wimbledon	Mark Philippoussis [AUS]	7–6, 6–2, 7–6
2004	Australian Open	Marat Safin [RUS]	7–6, 6–4, 6–2
2004	Wimbledon	Andy Roddick [USA]	4–6, 7–5, 7–6, 6–4
2004	US Open	Lleyton Hewitt [AUS]	6–0, 7–6, 6–0
2005	Wimbledon	Andy Roddick [USA]	6–2, 7–6, 6–4
2005	US Open	Andre Agassi [USA]	6–3, 2–6, 7–6, 6–1
2006	Australian Open	Marcos Baghdatis [CYP]	5–7, 7–5, 6–0, 6–2
2006	Wimbledon	Rafael Nadal [ESP]	6–0, 7–6, 6–7, 6–3
2006	US Open	Andy Roddick [USA]	6–2, 4–6, 7–5, 6–1
2007	Australian Open	Fernando Gonzalez [CHI]	7–6, 6–4, 6–4
2007	Wimbledon	Rafael Nadal [ESP]	7–6, 4–6, 7–6, 2–6, 6–2
2007	US Open	Novak Djokovic [SRB]	7–6, 7–6, 6–4
2008	US Open	Andy Murray [GBR]	6–2, 7–5, 6–2
2009	French Open	Robin Soderling [SWE]	6–1, 7–6, 6–4
2009	Wimbledon	Andy Roddick [USA]	5–7, 7–6, 7–6, 3–6, 16–14

———————— TENNIS GRAND SLAM TOURNAMENTS · 2009 ————————

Event	month	surface	♂	winner ♀
Australian Open	Jan	Plexicushion	Rafael Nadal	Serena Williams
French Open	May/Jun	clay	Roger Federer	Svetlana Kuznetsova
Wimbledon	Jun/Jul	grass	Roger Federer	Serena Williams
US Open	Aug/Sep	DecoTurf	Juan Martin del Potro	Kim Clijsters

———————————— THE DAVIS CUP ————————————

6–8 March · Group 1, Europe/Africa 2nd Round, *Braehead Arena, Glasgow*
Ukraine *bt* Great Britain 4–1
Illya Marchenko [UKR] *bt* Josh Goodall [GBR] 7–6 (7–2), 7–6 (7–5), 7–6 (7–5)
Sergiy Stakhovsky [UKR] *bt* Chris Eaton [GBR] 6–3, 3–6, 6–3, 6–4
Sergei Bubka & Sergiy Stakhovsky [UKR]
bt Colin Fleming & Ross Hutchins [GBR] 6–4, 3–6, 6–3, 5–7, 6–4
Ivan Sergeyev [UKR] *bt* Josh Goodall [GBR] 7–6 (7–3), 6–3
Chris Eaton [GBR] *bt* Illya Marchenko [UKR] 6–3, 6–4, 7–6 (7–5)

18–20 Sept · Group I, Europe/Africa, Play-Offs, *Echo Arena, Liverpool*
Poland *bt* Great Britain 3–2 (GBR relegated to Euro-African Group 2)
Andy Murray [GBR] *bt* Michal Przysiezny [POL] 6–4, 6–2, 6–4
Jerzy Janowicz [POL] *bt* Daniel Evans [GBR] 6–3, 6–3, 7–6 (7–5)
Mariusz Fyrstenberg & Marcin Matkowski [POL]
bt Andy Murray & Ross Hutchins [GBR] 7–5, 3–6, 6–3, 6–2
Andy Murray [GBR] *bt* Jerzy Janowicz [POL] 6–3, 6–4, 6–3
Alexander Peya [AUT] *bt* Michal Przysiezny [POL] 6–2, 6–1, 7–5

THE SPORTING POWER TOP TWENTY

In January 2009, *The Times* compiled its Sporting Power 100. Contenders were judged in five categories – their influence on their sport; their knock-on effect on other sports; their effect at grass-roots level; their crowd-pleasing ability; and the esteem in which they are held by their peers and the general public. The top 20 were:

1. Sir Alex Ferguson[†] *manager, Man U*
2. Lord Coe...*chairman, London 2012*
3. Sheikh Mansour...*owner, Man City*
4. Jeremy Darroch...*chief exec, Sky TV*
5. Dave Brailsford........*performance director, British Cycling*
6. Roman Abramovitch *owner, Chelsea*
7. David Beckham............*footballer*
8. Fabio Capello.... *manager, England*
9. Simon Fuller.............. *chief exec, 19 Entertainment*
10. Richard Scudamore....... *chief exec, Premier League*
11. Lewis Hamilton....... *racing driver*
12. Lord Triesman........*chairman, FA*
13. Bernie Ecclestone........ *chief exec, Formula One*
14. Pini Zahavi........... *football agent*
15. Roger Mosey...*director, BBC Sport*
16. Andy Murray.......... *tennis player*
17. Jonny Wilkinson.......*rugby player*
18. John Varley......*chief exec, Barclays*
19. Malcolm Glazer.....*owner, Man U*
20. Sepp Blatter.........*president, Fifa*

† Ferguson has won more trophies than any other manager in the English game. He has managed Manchester Utd for 22 years.

EXERCISE & FOOD

Food cravings might be dictated by exercise, according to preliminary research by Dr David Stensel of Loughborough University first publicised in February 2009. Dr Stensel analysed levels of the hormones *ghrelin* (which stimulates hunger) and *peptide YY* (which suppresses appetite) in people undertaking different types of exercise. He noted that the appetite of those who spent 60 minutes running on a treadmill was temporarily suppressed, whereas swimming in cold water appeared to boost levels of *ghrelin* and therefore appetite. In his initial findings, Dr Stensel suggested types of exercise that might boost cravings for the following foods:

Form of exercise	*possible craving*	
Long-distance run	....fruit	Gentle walk ......no effect on appetite
Weight-lifting	....junk food	Swimming in cold water................ biscuits or chocolate

SPORTSWOMEN OF THE YEAR

Some of the winners of the 2009 Sunday Times Sportswomen of the Year awards:

Sportswoman of the year ....Nicole Cooke · road cyclist
Team of the year....................................... England women's cricket team
UK Sport Olympian of the year ....Rebecca Adlington · swimmer
Paralympian of the year ....Eleanor Simmonds · swimmer
Young sportswoman of the year...............................Laura Robson · tennis

—— BBC SPORTS PERSONALITY OF THE YEAR · 2008 ——

'After the year I've had and the whole team has had, to be crowned Sports Personality of the Year, it just means so much. This is the big one and this is just unbelievable'.
– CHRIS HOY, BBC Sports Personality of the Year 2008

Sports personality of the year .... Chris Hoy, cyclist
Team of the year .... British Cycling
Overseas personality .... Usain Bolt
Coach of the year.................................. Dave Brailsford, British Cycling
Lifetime achievement.. Sir Bobby Charlton
Young personality .... Eleanor Simmonds (paralympic double gold swimmer)
Unsung hero .... Ben Geyser (Dorchester Amateur Boxing Club founder)
Helen Rollason award 'for courage and achievement in the face of adversity' ..... Alastair Hignell

————————————— WOMEN & SPORT —————————————

55% of women would exercise more if sports facilities were of better quality, according to November 2008 research by the Women's Sport and Fitness Foundation. Other incentives that women said would encourage them to do more sport include:

	% agreeing		
Private changing cubicles	82	Ability to try before you buy	45
Hair-dryers in changing rooms	56	Wide choice of activities	42
Clean changing rooms	52	Providing space to socialise	32
Discounts for repeat visits	47	Full-length changing room mirrors	28
		Free towels	23

————————— CHILDREN'S ATTITUDE TO SPORT —————————

Just 13% of boys and 4% of girls said winning was the most important part of playing sports – although it is notable that three times as many boys as girls said winning was important to them personally. The April 2009 research by the Cricket Foundation and the MCC asked children (aged 8–16) what was most important to them when participating in sports. The results, by gender, are tabulated below:

Most important %	♂	♀		♂	♀
Having fun	49	50	Helping teammates	6	5
Doing my best	21	23	Not getting hurt	3	3
Winning	13	4	Never giving up	2	2
Getting fit	4	10	Not losing	2	2
			Other	0	1

When children were asked what they thought was most important to their fathers when they took part in sport, 37% of boys and 31% of girls said 'doing their best'. This was followed by 19% of boys and 23% of girls who said 'having fun', and 18% of boys and 14% of girls who said 'winning'. ❦ 80% of girls and 64% of boys said they would not cheat at sport even if they really wanted to win; 31% of boys and 18% of girls would consider cheating, and 5% of boys and 2% of girls would cheat.

——————— DARTS · PDC ———————

World number one, Phil 'The Power' Taylor, cruised to his 14th world title in January 2009, crushing Raymond 'Barney' van Barneveld 7–1 at Alexandra Palace. Taylor's metronomic three-dart average of 110·94 was the highest ever in a PDC World Championship final, and it proved the key to his ultimate success. Although The Power stormed to a 2–0 lead in less than 20 minutes, the Dutchman refused to capitulate and clawed his way back to 2–1. Barney's window of opportunity was soon slammed shut as Taylor hit a double four to take the lead to 3–1. The Power, now fully in control, took the last few sets with aplomb, checking out with an impressive 81. Van Barneveld was magnanimous in defeat: 'I don't know what to do to beat this man. I practise ten hours a day and it is not good enough. He is the greatest ever.'

——————— DARTS · BDO ———————

Ted 'The Count' Hankey overcame his nerves to clinch the BDO World Championship at Lakeside with a closely fought 7–6 victory over Tony 'Silverback' O'Shea. The Count looked in control as he took an early 3–1 lead with relative ease. But then the nerves began to bite, and Hankey suffered a series of wobbles which saw him miss key shots and with them the chance to take his second BDO world title. The Silverback, sensing an opportunity, fought back from 6–4 down to level the match at 6–6. In the deciding set, The Count showed his mettle and scooped the £95,000 title with a double ten. 'Count Chuckula' admitted that his success was due, in part, to a change in his pre-match routine – instead of drinking his usual 13 pints before stepping up to the oche, he now imbibes a more modest three.

——————— WORLD SNOOKER CHAMPIONSHIP ———————

John Higgins won his third World Snooker Championship when he beat Shaun Murphy at the Crucible in May 2009. (Higgins joined Stephen Hendry, Steve Davis, Ray Reardon, John Spencer, and Ronnie O'Sullivan in the select group of players who have won three or more World titles.) Yet Higgins's victory was by no means a foregone conclusion. Murphy worked hard early in the match to even the score, before Higgins found a second wind and ended the first day with an 11–5 lead. Higgins remained focused on day two and, despite Murphy's best efforts, the Scotsman did not deviate in securing his twentieth world-ranking tournament.

THE FINAL · FRAME-BY-FRAME
John Higgins [SCO] 18–9 Shaun Murphy [ENG]

DAY ONE					
Frame	tally	49–63..........3–4	82–0..........10–5	76–43.........14–6
83–0..........1–0		69–3..........4–4	128–6 (128)...11–5	28–70.........14–7
85–6..........2–0		98–1..........5–4		49–79.........14–8
79–20.........3–0		12–87.........5–5	DAY TWO	94–26.........15–8
7–83..........3–1		70–51.........6–5	Frame tally	80–59.........16–8
50–96.........3–2		95–11.........7–5	64–42.........12–5	106–21........17–8
4–114 (109)....3–3		70–45.........8–5	0–91..........12–6	0–78..........17–9
		132–0 (128)....9–5	60–49.........13–6	105–0.........18–9

—————— WORLD SWIMMING CHAMPIONSHIP · 2009 ——————

All eyes were on the clock at the August 2009 World Swimming Championship in Rome, as record after record fell. The increasing speed of the swimmers was largely due to the widespread use of polyurethane 'super suits'. The first such suit was the Speedo LZR, introduced in 2008 and worn by Michael Phelps. Thereafter, a host of 'super suits' were developed, each with greater body coverage and a higher proportion of polyurethane. Since this swimwear revolution, 158 world records have been broken, prompting questions to be asked about the place of technology in the sport. FINA, swimming's governing body, first banned these suits (in May 2009), and then reinstated them (in June 2009) on appeal. Finally, in August 2009, FINA declared that from 1/1/2010 all suits must be textile only and cut as shorts for men and from shoulder to knee for women. Since Rome 2009 was the last major competition to allow polyurethane suits, many of the 43 records broken there might remain untested for years to come. This sartorial controversy aside, the championship proved a success for Great Britain. The team produced their best ever result to claim 7 medals in the pool (2 golds, 3 silvers, and 2 bronzes). Additionally, 15-year-old Tom Daley won gold in the 10m platform dive event, and Keri-Anne Payne took gold in the 10km open water race. Selected results from Rome are below:

	Event	winner	record	time
♂	50m backstroke	Liam Tancock [GBR]	WR	24·04s
♂	100m butterfly	Michael Phelps† [USA]	WR	49·82s
♂	200m butterfly	Michael Phelps [USA]	WR	1:51·51s
♂	200m freestyle	Paul Biedermann [GER]	WR	1:42·00s
♀	100m backstroke	Gemma Spofforth [GBR]	WR	58·12s
♀	50m freestyle	Britta Steffen [GER]	WR	23·73s
♀	100m freestyle	Britta Steffen [GER]	WR	52·07s
♀	200m freestyle	Federica Pellegrini [ITA]	WR	1:52·98s

† Phelps won 5 gold medals at the championship, including 3 in the relay; he also won a silver.

———————— WORLD ROWING CHAMPIONSHIP ————————

The British rowing team achieved an impressive haul of 9 medals at the World Rowing Championship in Poznan, Poland, in August 2009. British boats made 11 of the 14 Olympic-class finals which offered encouragement for success in London 2012. Golds were secured in the men's four, the paralympic men's arms-only single skulls, and paralympic mixed coxed four. Despite coming a creditable third in the medals table, Britain recognised that there was room for improvement – the number of silver medals indicated that a few British rowers had been inched out of a gold. The top of the medals table (including all five paralympic events) is below:

Country	gold	silver	bronze	total
Germany	4	1	4	9
New Zealand	4	0	1	5
Great Britain	3	5	1	9

——— READY RECKONER OF OTHER RESULTS · 2008/09 ———

AMERICAN FOOTBALL · Superbowl   Pittsburgh Steelers 27–23 Arizona Cardinals
ANGLING · National Coarse Ch. Div.1   Dave Trafford 12·340kg
BASEBALL · World Series [2008]   Philadelphia Phillies 4–1 Tampa Bay Rays
BASKETBALL · NBA finals   Los Angeles Lakers 4–1 Orlando Magic
   BBL Trophy final   Newcastle Eagles 83–71 Guildford Heat
THE BOAT RACE   Oxford *bt* Cambridge [by 3·5 lengths, in 17m 0s]
BOG SNORKELLING   ♂ Conor Murphy [NI] ♀ Laura Smith [GBR]
BOWLS · World Matchplay   Mervyn King [ENG] *bt* David Gourlay [SCO] 9–8, 12–7
CHEESE ROLLING · Cooper's Hill   ♂ Christopher Anderson [ENG]
     ♀ Michelle Kokiri [NZL]
CHESS · British Championship   ♂ GM David Howell ♀ IM Jovanka Houska
   FIDE World Championship [2008]   Vishwanathan Anand
COMPETITIVE EATING · Int. Hot Dog Eating   Joey 'Jaws' Chestnut [USA] [68 in 10 mins]
   World Nettle Eating Championship   Mike Hobbs [ENG] 48 ft of raw leaves
CRICKET · Test series – England *vs* India (in India)   India *bt* England 1–0
   One day series (in India)   India *bt* England 5–0
   Test series – England *vs* West Indies (in W Indies)   West Indies *bt* England 1–0
   One day series (in W Indies)   England *bt* West Indies 3–2
   Test series – England *vs* West Indies   England *bt* West Indies 2–0
   One day series   England *bt* West Indies 2–0
   Women's Test   England *vs* Australia match drawn
   Women's One day series   England *bt* Australia 4–0
   Friends Provident Trophy   Hampshire *bt* Sussex by 6 wickets
   County Championship [2008]   Durham
CROQUET · World Championship   Reg Bamford [RSA]
CYCLING · Tour de France   Alberto Contador [ESP] [see p.306]
   Tour of Britain   Edvald Boasson Hagen [NOR] (Team Columbia)
DARTS · Ladbrokes W. Ch. [PDC]   Phil Taylor *bt* Raymond Van Barneveld [see p.316]
   Lakeside World Championship [BDO]   Ted Hankey *bt* Tony O'Shea [see p.316]
ELEPHANT POLO · Kings' Cup   Audemars Piguet 7–1 SOCO International
ENDURANCE RACES · Marathon des Sables   ♂ Mohamad Ahansal [MAR] 16:27·26
     ♀ Touda Didi [MAR] 23:30·44
   Devil o' the Highlands   ♂ Craig Stewart 5:34·39 · ♀ Helen Johnson 6:51·27
EQUESTRIANISM · Badminton   Flint Curtis *ridden by* Oliver Townend [GBR] 44·5 pen
   Burghley   Carousel Quest *ridden by* Oliver Townend [GBR] 43·0 pen
FOOTBALL · FA Cup Women's   Arsenal 2–1 Sunderland
   UEFA Cup   Shakhtar Donetsk 2–1 Werder Bremen
   Community Shield   Chelsea 2–2 Manchester Utd (AET; 4–1 penalties)
   Carling Cup   Manchester Utd 0–0 Tottenham Hotspur (AET; 4–1 penalties)
   Women's European Championship   Germany 6–2 England
   Premier League   Manchester United
   Championship   Wolverhampton Wanderers
   League 1   Leicester City
   League 2   Brentford
   Scottish Premier League   Rangers
   Scottish Cup   Rangers 1–0 Falkirk

— READY RECKONER OF OTHER RESULTS · 2008/09 cont. —

FORMULA ONE · World Drivers' Champion [2008]   Lewis Hamilton [GBR] · McLaren
  World Constructors' Championship [2008]   Ferrari [ITA]
GOLF · Solheim Cup   USA
  Mission Hills World Cup [2008]   Sweden
GREYHOUND RACING · Blue Square Greyhound Derby   Kinda Ready
HOCKEY · EuroHockey Nations   ♂ England 5–3 Germany
                                                 ♀ Netherlands 3–2 Germany

HORSE RACING
  Grand National   Mon Mome *trained by* Venetia Williams *ridden by* Liam Treadwell
  Vodafone Epsom Derby   Sea The Stars *trained by* John Oxx *ridden by* Mick Kinane
  Cheltenham Gold Cup   Kauto Star *trained by* Paul Nicholls *ridden by* Ruby Walsh
  1,000 Guineas   Ghanaati *trained by* Barry Hills *ridden by* Richard Hills
  2,000 Guineas   Sea The Stars *trained by* John Oxx *ridden by* Mick Kinane
  The Oaks   Sariska *trained by* Michael Bell *ridden by* Jamie Spencer
  St Leger   Mastery *trained by* Saeed bin Suroor *ridden by* Ted Durcan
ICE HOCKEY · Stanley Cup   Pittsburgh Penguins 4–3 Detroit Red Wings
MOBILE PHONE THROWING · World Champ.   Pauli Kosunen [FIN] 79·6m
NETBALL · Superleague title   TeamBath
RUGBY LEAGUE · Super League [2008]   Leeds Rhinos
  Challenge Cup   Huddersfield Giants 16–25 Warrington Wolves
  League Leaders' Shield   St Helens
  World Club Challenge   Manly Warringah Sea Eagles 28–20 Leeds Rhinos
RUGBY UNION · Guinness Premiership   Leicester Tigers [top of table]
  Guinness Premiership Championship   Leicester Tigers 10–9 London Irish
  EDF Energy Anglo-Welsh Cup   Gloucester 12–50 Cardiff Blues
  Magners Celtic League   Munster
  Heineken Cup   Leicester 16–19 Leinster
  European Challenge Cup   Northampton Saints 15–3 Bourgoin
  Varsity Match [2008]   Oxford 33–29 Cambridge
RUNNING · Great North Run   ♂ Martin Lel [KEN] 0:59·32
                                            ♀ Jessica Augusto [POR] 1:09·08
SNOOKER · UK Championship [2008]   Shaun Murphy [ENG] *bt* Marco Fu [HKG] 10–9
SQUASH · British Open Rachael Grinham [AUS] *bt* Madeline Perry [NI] 11–6, 11–5, 12–10
            Nick Matthew [GBR] *bt* James Willstrop [GBR] 8–11, 11–8, 7–11, 11–3, 12–10
SUDOKU · World Sudoku Championship   Jan Mrozowski [POL]
TENNIS · Australian Op. R. Nadal [ESP] *bt* R. Federer [SUI] 7–5, 3–6, 7–6 (7–3), 3–6, 6–2
                    Serena Williams [USA] *bt* Dinara Safina [RUS] 6–0, 6 3
  French Open   Roger Federer [SUI] *bt* Robin Söderling [SWE] 6–1, 7–6 (7–1), 6–4
                    Svetlana Kuznetsova [RUS] *bt* Dinara Safina [RUS] 6–4, 6–2
  US Open J. M. del Potro [ARG] *bt* R. Federer [SUI] 3–6, 7–6 (7–5), 4–6, 7–6 (7–4), 6–2
                    Kim Clijsters [BEL] *bt* Caroline Wozniacki [DEN] 7–5, 6–3
  Fed Cup [2008]   Russia *bt* Spain 4–0
  Davis Cup [2008]   Spain *bt* Argentina 3–1
TRIATHLON · European Championships   ♂ Javier Gomez [ESP] 1:44·14
                                        ♀ Nicola Spirig [SUI] 1:55·42
World Championship series   ♂ Alistair Brownlee [GBR] ♀ Emma Moffatt [AUS]

Ephemerides

*Scarcely anything is more familiar to the eyes of an Englishman than
an almanack of some sort or other* – ROBERT KEMP PHILLIP, 1889

——————————— 2010 ———————————

Roman numerals................ MMX	Indian (Saka) year...... 1932 (22 Mar)
English Regnal year[1] .....58th (6 Feb)	Sikh year ... 542 Nanakshahi Era (14 Mar)
Dominical Letter[2].................... C	Jewish year .... 5771 (9 Sep)
Epact[3] XIV	Roman year [AUC] ...... 2763 (14 Jan)
Golden Number (Lunar Cycle)[4] ..XVI	Masonic year................6010 AL[5]
Chinese New Year. Tiger 4708 (14 Feb)	Knights Templar year........ 892 AO[6]
Hindu New Year...... 2066 (16 Mar)	Baha'i year...............167 (21 Mar)
Islamic year.............1432 (7 Dec)	Queen bee colour.................blue

[1] The number of years from the accession of a monarch; traditionally, legislation was dated by the Regnal year of the reigning monarch. [2] A way of categorising years to facilitate the calculation of Easter. If January 1 is a Sunday, the Dominical Letter for the year will be A; if January 2 is a Sunday, it will be B; and so on. [3] The number of days by which the solar year exceeds the lunar year. [4] The number of the year (1–19) in the 19-year Metonic cycle; it is used in the calculation of Easter, and is found by adding 1 to the remainder left after dividing the number of the year by 19. [5] Anno Lucis, the 'Year of Light' when the world was formed. [6] Anno Ordinis, the 'Year of the Order'.

— TRADITIONAL WEDDING ANNIVERSARY SYMBOLS —

1st ....Cotton	10th ....Tin	35th ....Coral
2nd ....Paper	11th ....Steel	40th ....Ruby
3rd..............Leather	12th ....Silk, Linen	45th .... Sapphire
4th.......Fruit, Flowers	13th ....Lace	50th .... Gold
5th................ Wood	14th ....Ivory	55th ....Emerald
6th................Sugar	15th ....Crystal	60th .... Diamond
7th....... Wool, Copper	20th ....China	70th ....Platinum
8th...............Pottery	25th ....Silver	75th .... Diamond
9th...............Willow	30th .... Pearl	*American symbols differ.*

——————————— BRITISH SUMMER TIME ———————————

BST starts and ends at 1am on these Sundays (*'spring forward – fall back'*):
2010.......... clocks forward 1 hour, 28 March · clocks back 1 hour, 31 October
2011.......... clocks forward 1 hour, 27 March · clocks back 1 hour, 30 October

RED-LETTER DAYS

Red-letter days are those days of civil and ecclesiastical importance – so named because they were marked out in red ink on early religious calendars. (The Romans marked unlucky days with black chalk, and auspicious days with white.) When these days fall within law sittings, the judges of the Queen's Bench Division sit wearing elegant scarlet robes. The Red-letter days in Great Britain are tabulated below:

Conversion of St Paul	25 Jan	St Barnabas	11 Jun
Purification	2 Feb	Official BD HM the Queen†	12 Jun
Accession of HM the Queen	6 Feb	St John the Baptist	24 Jun
Ash Wednesday†	17 Feb	St Peter	29 Jun
St David's Day	1 Mar	St Thomas	3 Jul
Annunciation	25 Mar	St James	25 Jul
BD HM the Queen	21 Apr	St Luke	18 Oct
St Mark	25 Apr	SS Simon & Jude	28 Oct
SS Philip & James	1 May	All Saints	1 Nov
St Matthias	14 May	Lord Mayor's Day†	13 Nov
Ascension†	13 May	BD HRH the Prince of Wales	14 Nov
Coronation of HM the Queen	2 Jun	St Andrew's Day	30 Nov
BD HRH Duke of Edinburgh	10 Jun	(† *indicates the date varies by year*)	

ON RECEIVING A FAVOUR

Pride combined with feeling + a favour .... smarts under it
Senseless arrogance + a favour .... takes it as a due
Stupidity + a favour .... does not perceive it
Levity + a favour .... forgets it
A broken spirit + a favour .... is surprised and humbled by it
Suspicion + a favour .... misinterprets it
Crafty selfishness + a favour .... seeks for more
A generous spirit + a favour .... feels it without humiliation

— RICHARD WHATELY, D.D., Archbishop of Dublin

KEY TO SYMBOLS USED OVERLEAF

[★ BH]	UK Bank Holiday	[§ *patronage*]	Saint's Day
[◑]	Clocks change (UK)	[WA 1900]	Wedding Anniversary
[❦]	Hunting season (traditional)	●	New Moon [GMT]
[ND]	National Day	☺	Full Moon [GMT]
[NH]	National Holiday	[☄]	Annual meteor shower
[ID 1900]	Independence Day	[UN]	United Nations Day
[BD1900]	Birthday	[◉]	Eclipse
[†1900]	Anniversary of death	[£]	Union Flag to be flown (UK)

Certain dates are subject to change, estimated, or tentative at the time of printing.

JANUARY

Capricorn [♑]   *Birthstone* · GARNET   *Aquarius* [♒]
(Dec 22–Jan 20)   *Flower* · CARNATION   (Jan 21–Feb 19)

1★................New Year's Day [★BH] · E. M. Forster [BD1879].................F
2...............St Munchin [§ *Limerick*] · Isaac Asimov [BD1920].................Sa
3...............St Genevieve [§ *Paris*] · J. R. R. Tolkien [BD1892].................Su
4...............Quadrantids [⚵] · Jakob Grimm [BD 1785]...................M
5...............Twelfth Night · Amy Johnson [†1941].....................Tu
6...............Epiphany · St Joan of Arc [BD 1412]........................W
7.............. Catherine of Aragon [†1536] · Nicholas Cage [BD 1964]............Th
8.............Galileo Galilei [†1642] · David Bowie [BD1947]...............F
9............Richard Nixon [BD1913] · Katherine Mansfield [†1923].............Sa
10.................Rod Stewart [BD1945] · Coco Chanel [†1971]................Su
11.............. Thomas Hardy [†1928] · Arthur Scargill [BD1938] ....M
12..............................Des O'Connor [BD1932]..............................Tu
13..............St Hilary of Poitiers [§ *snake-bites*] · Wyatt Earp [†1929]...............W
14..............Cecil Beaton [BD1904] · Richard Briers [BD1934].............Th
15.............. ☺ · Molière [BD1622] · Aristotle Onassis [BD1906]...............F
16...............André Michelin [BD1853] · Eric Liddell [BD1902]................Sa
17..........St Anthony of Egypt [§ *basket-makers*] · Vidal Sassoon [BD1928]..........Su
18.........USA – Martin Luther King Day · A. A. Milne [BD1882]...........M
19...........................Paul Cézanne [BD1839].........................Tu
20.........St Sebastian [§ *archers, soldiers & athletes*] · Tom Baker [BD1934].........W
21................Louis XVI [†1793 *executed*] · Lenin [†1924]....................Th
22............Francis Bacon [BD1561] · Queen Victoria [†1901]...............F
23................ St John the Almsgiver · Salvador Dali [†1989]................Sa
24................ St Francis de Sales [§ *journalists*]..........................Su
25......Scotland – Burns' Night · Conversion of St Paul · St Dwyn [§ *lovers*]......M
26............Australia – Australia Day [NH] · Paul Newman [BD1925]...........Tu
27.............Holocaust Memorial Day · Thomas Crapper [†1910].............W
28..... St Thomas Aquinas [§ *universities and students*] · Sir Thomas Bodley [† 1613].....Th
29............ Anton Chekhov [BD1860] · Tom Selleck [BD1945]................F
30.......................... ☺ · Phil Collins [BD1951]...........................Sa
31............ Tallulah Bankhead [BD1902] · Norman Mailer [BD1923]...........Su

French Rev. calendar......*Nivôse* (snow) | Dutch month ......*Lauwmaand* (frosty)
Angelic governor...............*Gabriel* | Saxon month.......*Wulf-monath* (wolf)
Epicurean calendar.....*Marronglaçaire* | Talismanic stone ....*Onyx*

❦ The Latin month *Ianuarius* derives from *ianua* ('door'), since it was the opening of the year. It was also associated with *Janus* – the two-faced Roman god of doors and openings who guarded the gates of heaven. Janus could simultaneously face the year just past and the year to come. ❦ *If January Calends be summerly gay,'Twill be winterly weather till the calends of May.* ❦ *Janiveer – Freeze the pot upon the fier.* ❦ *He that will live another year, Must eat a hen in Januvere.* ❦ On the stock market, the *January effect* is the trend of stocks performing especially well that month. ❦

─────── FEBRUARY ───────

Aquarius [♒]   *Birthstone* · AMETHYST   *Pisces* [♓]
(Jan 21–Feb 19)   *Flower* · PRIMROSE   (Feb 20–Mar 20)

1 .... Partridge & pheasant shooting season ends [☙] .... M
2 .... Candlemas · Groundhog Day, USA · James Joyce [BD1882] .... Tu
3 .... St Blaise [§ *sore throats*] · Felix Mendelssohn [BD1809] .... W
4 .... Sri Lanka [ID 1948] · Charles Lindbergh [BD1902] .... Th
5 .... St Agatha [§ *bell founders*] · Sir Robert Peel [BD1788] .... F
6 ... Accession of HM Queen Elizabeth II [£] · New Zealand – Waitangi Day .. Sa
7 .... Grenada [ID 1974] · Sir Thomas More [BD1478] .... Su
8 .... Mary Queen of Scots [†1587 *beheaded*] · James Dean [BD1931] .... M
9 .... J. M. Coetzee [BD1940] · Carmen Miranda [BD1909] .... Tu
10 ...... Queen Victoria & Prince Albert of Saxe-Coburg Gotha [WA 1840] ...... W
11 .... Scottish salmon fishing season opens [☙] .... Th
12 .... Lady Jane Grey [†1554 *beheaded*] · Charles Darwin [BD1809] .... F
13 .... St Modomnoc [§ *bee-keepers*] · Oliver Reed [BD1938] .... Sa
14 .... ● · St Valentine [§ *lovers*] · Kevin Keegan [BD1951] .... Su
15 .... Galileo Galilei [BD1564] .... M
16 .... John McEnroe [BD1959] · Kim Jong-il [BD1942] .... Tu
17 .... Paris Hilton [BD1981] .... W
18 .... Nepal [ND] · Bloody Mary I [BD1516] .... Th
19 .... Prince Andrew [BD1960] [£] · Nicolaus Copernicus [BD1473] .... F
20 .... Robert Altman [BD1925] · Mike Leigh [BD1943] .... Sa
21 .... Int. Mother Language Day [UN] · Malcolm X [†1965 *assassinated*] .... Su
22 .... Feast of Chair of St Peter · Julie Walters [BD1950] .... M
23 .... Brunei [ND] · César Ritz [BD1850] .... Tu
24 .... Estonia [ID 1918] · Charles V [BD1500] .... W
25 .... Sir Christopher Wren [†1723] · Pierre Auguste Renoir [BD1841] .... Th
26 .... Victor Hugo [BD1802] · Buffalo Bill [BD1846] .... F
27 .... Dominican Republic [ID 1844] · Elizabeth Taylor [BD1932] .... Sa
28 .... ☺ · Hind stalking season closes [☙] · Vincente Minelli [BD1903] .... Su

French Rev. calendar ..... *Pluviôse* (rain)	Dutch month *Sprokelmaand* (vegetation)
Angelic governor .... *Barchiel*	Saxon month .... *Solmonath* (Sun)
Epicurean calendar .... *Harrengsauridor*	Talismanic stone .... *Jasper*

❧ Much mythology and folklore considers February to have the most bitter weather: *February is seldom warm.* ❧ *February, if ye be fair, The sheep will mend, and nothing mair; February, if ye be foul, The sheep will die in every pool.* ❧ *As the day lengthens, the cold strengthens.* ❧ That said, a foul February is thought to predict a fine year: *All the months in the year, Curse a fair Februeer.* ❧ The word *February* derives from the Latin *februum* – which means cleansing, and reflects the rituals undertaken by the Romans before spring. ❧ Having only 28 days in non-leap years, February was known in Welsh as *y mis bach* – the little month. ❧ February is traditionally personified in pictures either by an old man warming himself by the fireside, or as 'a sturdy maiden, with a tinge of the red hard winter apple on her hardy cheek'. ❧

─────────────────────MARCH─────────────────────

Pisces [♓]   *Birthstone* · BLOODSTONE   *Aries* [♈]
(Feb 20–Mar 20)   *Flower* · JONQUIL   (Mar 21–Apr 20)

1 .... St David [§ *Wales*] · Trout fishing season begins [♥] .... M
2 .... St Chad [§ *medicinal springs*] · D. H. Lawrence [†1930] .... Tu
3 ....Alexander Graham Bell [BD1847] · Hergé [†1983] .... W
4 .... Antonio Vivaldi [BD1678] .... Th
5 .... St Piran [§ *tin-miners*] · Elaine Paige [BD1948] .... F
6 .... Ghana [ID 1957] · Michelangelo [BD1475].................... Sa
7 ....Piet Mondrian [BD1872] · Brett Easton Ellis [BD1964] .... Su
8 .... Women's Rights & Int. Peace Day [UN] · King William III [†1702] ...... M
9 ....St Dominic Savio [§ *wrongly accused*] · Yuri Gagarin [BD1934] .... Tu
10............. Prince Edward [BD1964] [£] · Zelda Fitzgerald [†1948] .... W
11...............Sir Henry Tate [BD1819] · Harold Wilson [BD1916]................ Th
12............... Jack Kerouac [BD1922] · Yehudi Menuhin [†1999] .... F
13............Susan B. Anthony [†1906] · L. Ron Hubbard [BD1911] .... Sa
14........... St Matilda [§ *parents with large families*] · Albert Einstein [BD1879] .... Su
15............. 😊 · Hungary [ND] · Julius Caesar [†44BC *assassinated*]............... M
16....... St Urho [§ *Finnish immigrants in America*] · Bernardo Bertolucci [BD1941] ...... Tu
17......... St Patrick's Day [§ *Ireland*] · Rudolf Nureyev [BD1938] .... W
18...........Neville Chamberlain [BD1869] · Wilfred Owen [BD1893]............ Th
19........ St Joseph [§ *fathers and carpenters*] · Edgar Rice Burroughs [†1950]........... F
20...........First Day of Spring · Tunisia [ID 1956] · Spike Lee [BD1957] .... Sa
21................. J. S. Bach [BD1685] · Brian Clough [BD1935] .... Su
22...........World Day for Water [UN] · Marcel Marceau [BD1923].............. M
23............World Meteorological Day [UN] · Pope Julius III [†1555] ....Tu
24............. St Dunchad [§ *Irish sailors*] · Alan Sugar [BD1947] .... W
25..... Annunciation Day · Greece [ID 1821] · Sarah Jessica Parker [BD1965] .....Th
26............... Bangladesh [ID 1971] · Noël Coward [†1973].................. F
27...................... Mariah Carey [BD1970] .... Sa
28.............[●] · Dirk Bogarde [BD1921] · Neil Kinnock [BD1942]............. Su
29........... Lord Norman Tebbit [BD1931] · John Major [BD1943]........... M
30............. ☺ · Eric Clapton [BD1945] · Celine Dion [BD1968] ....Tu
31................ St Balbina [§ *scrofulous diseases*] · John Donne [†1631]............... W

French Rev. calendar..... *Ventôse* (wind)	Dutch month ..*Lentmaand* (lengthening)
Angelic governor.............*Machidiel*	Saxon month.....*Hrèth-monath* (rough)
Epicurean calendar.... *Oeufalacoquidor*	Talismanic stone .... *Ruby*

❦ The first month of the Roman year, March is named for Mars, the god of war but also an agricultural deity. ❦ The unpredictability of March weather leads to some confusion (*March has many weathers*), though it is generally agreed that March *comes in like a lion, and goes out like a lamb*. Yet, because March is often too wet for crops to flourish, many considered *a bushel of Marche dust* [a dry March] *is worth a ransom of gold*. ❦ March hares are 'mad' with nothing more than lust, since it is their mating season. ❦ The *Mars* bar is named after its creator, Frank Mars. ❦

APRIL

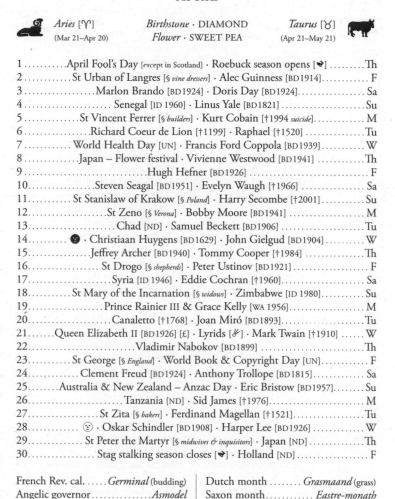

Aries [♈]   *Birthstone* · DIAMOND   **Taurus [♉]**
(Mar 21–Apr 20)   *Flower* · SWEET PEA   (Apr 21–May 21)

1 ....April Fool's Day [except in Scotland] · Roebuck season opens [♥] ....Th
2 ....St Urban of Langres [§ *vine dressers*] · Alec Guinness [BD1914]........... F
3 ....Marlon Brando [BD1924] · Doris Day [BD1924]................ Sa
4 .... Senegal [ID 1960] · Linus Yale [BD1821] ....Su
5 ....St Vincent Ferrer [§ *builders*] · Kurt Cobain [†1994 *suicide*]............ M
6 ....Richard Coeur de Lion [†1199] · Raphael [†1520] ....Tu
7 .... World Health Day [UN] · Francis Ford Coppola [BD1939]...........W
8 ....Japan – Flower festival · Vivienne Westwood [BD1941] ....Th
9 ....Hugh Hefner [BD1926] .... F
10............Steven Seagal [BD1951] · Evelyn Waugh [†1966] .... Sa
11............ St Stanislaw of Krakow [§ *Poland*] · Harry Secombe [†2001]...........Su
12............St Zeno [§ *Verona*] · Bobby Moore [BD1941] ....M
13.............. Chad [ND] · Samuel Beckett [BD1906] ....Tu
14......... ◕ · Christiaan Huygens [BD1629] · John Gielgud [BD1904].........W
15..........Jeffrey Archer [BD1940] · Tommy Cooper [†1984] ....Th
16.............. St Drogo [§ *shepherds*] · Peter Ustinov [BD1921]................. F
17..................Syria [ID 1946] · Eddie Cochran [†1960]....................Sa
18..........St Mary of the Incarnation [§ *widows*] · Zimbabwe [ID 1980]..........Su
19..........Prince Rainier III & Grace Kelly [WA 1956]...................M
20...................Canaletto [†1768] · Joan Miró [BD1893]...................Tu
21......Queen Elizabeth II [BD1926] [£] · Lyrids [☄] · Mark Twain [†1910] ......W
22.........................Vladimir Nabokov [BD1899] ....Th
23........ St George [§ *England*] · World Book & Copyright Day [UN]........... F
24............ Clement Freud [BD1924] · Anthony Trollope [BD1815]............Sa
25......Australia & New Zealand – Anzac Day · Eric Bristow [BD1957].......Su
26...................Tanzania [ND] · Sid James [†1976].......................M
27................St Zita [§ *bakers*] · Ferdinand Magellan [†1521].................Tu
28............ ☺ · Oskar Schindler [BD1908] · Harper Lee [BD1926] ....W
29......... St Peter the Martyr [§ *midwives & inquisitors*] · Japan [ND] ....Th
30................ Stag stalking season closes [♥] · Holland [ND]................ F

French Rev. cal. ......*Germinal* (budding)	Dutch month .... *Grasmaand* (grass)
Angelic governor...............*Asmodel*	Saxon month............ *Eastre-monath*
Epicurean calendar........*Petitpoisidor*	Talismanic stone .... *Topaz*

❦ April, T.S. Eliot's 'cruellest month', heralds the start of spring and is associated with new growth and sudden bursts of rain. ❦ Its etymology might derive from the Latin *aperire* ('to open') – although in Old English it was known simply as the *Eastre-monath*. ❦ *April with his hack and his bill, Plants a flower on every hill.* ❦ The custom of performing pranks and hoaxes on April Fool's Day (or *poisson d'avril*, as it is known in France) is long established, although its origins are much disputed. ❦ *If it thunders on All Fools' day, it brings good crops of corn and hay.* ❦ Cuckoos used to appear in letters to *The Times* c.8 April; the last was on 25 April, 1940. ❦

———————————————————MAY———————————————————

Taurus [♉]   *Birthstone* · EMERALD   *Gemini* [♊]
(Apr 21–May 21)   *Flower* · LILY OF THE VALLEY   (May 22–Jun 21)

1 ....May Day · David Livingstone [†1873] .... Sa
2 ....Leonardo da Vinci [†1519] · J. Edgar Hoover [†1972] ....Su
3 ....World Press Freedom Day [UN] · St James the Lesser [§ *hatmakers*].........M
4 ....St Florian [§ *invoked against fire & water*] · Diana Dors [†1984] ....Tu
5 ....Eta Aquarids [☄] · Michael Palin [BD1943]...................W
6 ....Orson Welles [BD1915] · Marlene Dietrich [†1992]................Th
7 ....Johannes Brahms [BD1833] ....F
8 ....VE Day · Jack Charlton [BD1935].......................Sa
9 ....Europe Day – European Union [£] · Howard Carter [BD1874] ....Su
10 ....St Catald [§ *invoked against plagues, drought & storms*] · Fred Astaire [BD1899].......M
11 ....William Pitt the Elder [†1778] · Salvador Dali [BD1904]............Tu
12 ....Dante Gabriel Rossetti [BD1828] · Burt Bacharach [BD1928].........W
13 ....Stevie Wonder [BD1950] · Chet Baker [†1988]..................Th
14 .... ☻ · St Matthias [§ *alcoholics & carpenters*] · Frank Sinatra [†1998] ....F
15 ....International Day of Families [UN] · St Isidore [§ *rural life*]............Sa
16 ....Pierce Brosnan [BD1953]...........................Su
17 ....Norway [ND] · Dennis Hopper [BD1936]...................M
18 ....International Museum Day · Fred Perry [BD1909]...............Tu
19 ....St Yves [§ *lawyers & Brittany*] · Victoria Wood [BD1953]............W
20 ....Cameroon [ND] · Christopher Columbus [†1506] ....Th
21 ......St Eugene de Mazenod [§ *dysfunctional families*] · Elizabeth Fry [BD1780] ....F
22 ....International Day for Biological Diversity [UN] · George Best [BD1946]....Sa
23 ....Captain William Kidd [†1701] · Heinrich Himmler [†1945 *suicide*].......Su
24 ....Jean-Paul Marat [BD1743] · Bob Dylan [BD1941]...............M
25 ....Miles Davis [BD1926] · Ian McKellen [BD1939].................Tu
26 ....Georgia [ID 1918] · Michael Portillo [BD1953]..................W
27 .... ☽ · Cilla Black [BD 1943] · Pat Cash [BD1965] ....Th
28 ....Azerbaijan [ND] · Thora Hird [BD1911]......................F
29 ....International Day of United Nations Peacekeepers [UN]............Sa
30 ....St Walstan [§ *agriculture*] · Joan of Arc [†1431]..................Su
31 .....The Visitation of the Blessed Virgin Mary · Clint Eastwood [BD1930] ....M

French Rev. calendar... *Floréal* (blossom)	Dutch month ...... *Blowmaand* (flower)
Angelic governor...............*Ambriel*	Saxon month....... *Trimilchi* [see below]
Epicurean calendar...........*Aspergial*	Talismanic stone .... *Garnet*

❦ Named after *Maia*, the goddess of growth, May is considered a joyous month, as Milton wrote: 'Hail bounteous May that dost inspire Mirth and youth, and warm desire'. ❦ However, May has long been thought a bad month in which to marry: *who weds in May throws it all away.* ❦ Anglo-Saxons called May *Trimilchi*, since in May cows could be milked three times a day. ❦ May was thought a time of danger for the sick; so to have *climbed May hill* was to have survived the month. ❦ Kittens born in May were thought weak, and were often drowned. ❦

———————————————————JUNE———————————————————

Gemini [Ⅱ]	Birthstone · PEARL	Cancer [♋]
(May 22–Jun 21)	Flower · ROSE	(Jun 22–Jul 22)

1 .... Samoa [ID 1962] · Helen Keller [†1968] .... Tu
2 ...... Coronation of Elizabeth II [1953] [£] · Johnny Weissmuller [BD1904]..... W
3 .... St Kevin [§ *blackbirds*] · Josephine Baker [BD1906]................. Th
4 .... Tonga [ID 1970] · Angelina Jolie [BD1975] .... F
5 ....World Environment Day [UN] · Pancho Villa [BD1878] .... Sa
6 .... D Day · Diego Velázquez [BD 1599] · Carl Jung [†1961]............ Su
7 ....Malta [ND] · Paul Gauguin [BD1848] · Tom Jones [BD1940]........... M
8 .... St Medard [§ *good weather, prisoners & toothache*] · Bonnie Tyler [BD1951]........ Tu
9 .... Charles Saatchi [BD1943] · Charles Dickens [†1870] .... W
10 .... HRH Prince Philip [BD1921] [£] · Les Dawson [†1993] ....Th
11 .... Gene Wilder [BD1933] · John Wayne [†1979]................. F
12 .... ◉ · Anthony Eden [BD1897] · George Bush Snr [BD1924]............ Sa
13 ...St Anthony of Padua [§ *horses, mules, & donkeys*] · Alexander the Great [†323 BC] .. Su
14 ....Emmeline Pankhurst [†1928] · John Logie Baird [†1946]........... M
15 .... St Vitus [§ *epileptics*] · Noddy Holder [BD1946]...................Tu
16 .... Freshwater fishing season opens [♥] · Enoch Powell [BD1912]......... W
17 ....St Botulph [§ *agricultural workers*] · Barry Manilow [BD1943] ....Th
18 ....Seychelles [ND] · Roald Amundsen [†1928 *lost in the Arctic*]............. F
19 ....Prince Edward & Sophie Rhys-Jones [WA 1999] .... Sa
20 .... Longest Day · First Day of Summer · Johnny Morris [BD1916] .... Su
21 ....St Aloysius Gonzaga [§ *youth*] · Prince William [BD1982] .... M
22 .... Esther Rantzen [BD1940] · Judy Garland [†1969]................Tu
23 ....Midsummer Eve · Luxembourg [ND] · Vespasian [† 79] .... W
24 .... Midsummer Day · Juan Manuel Fangio [†1911]................Th
25 .... Mozambique [ID 1975] · Eddie Large [BD1941]................. F
26 ..... ☺ · United Nations Charter Day [UN] · Joseph Montgolfier [†1810]..... Sa
27 .... Djibouti [ID 1977] · John Entwhistle [†2002]................. Su
28 .... Archduke Ferdinand of Austria [†1914 *assassinated*]............... M
29 .... St Paul [§ *authors*] · Paul Klee [†1940]...................Tu
30 ....St Theobald [§ *bachelors*] · Sir Stanley Spencer [BD1891].............. W

French Rev. calendar.. *Prairial* (meadow)	Dutch month ...*Zomermaand* (Summer)
Angelic governor................ *Muriel*	Saxon month......... *Sere-monath* (dry)
Epicurean calendar....... *Concombrial*	Talismanic stone ....*Emerald*

❦ *June* is probably derived from *iuvenis* ('young'), but it is also linked to the goddess *Juno*, who personifies young women. In Scots Gaelic, the month is known as *Ian t-òg-mbìos*, the 'young month'; and in Welsh, as *Mehefin*, the 'middle'. ❦ According to weather lore, *Calm weather in June, Sets corn in tune*. ❦ To 'june' a herd of animals is to drive them in a brisk or lively manner. ❦ Wilfred Gowers-Round asserts that 'June is the reality of the Poetic's claims for May'. ❦ In parts of South Africa the verb 'to june-july' is slang for shaking or shivering with fear – because these months, while summer in the north, are mid-winter in the south. ❦

─────────────── JULY ───────────────

🦀   *Cancer* [♋]   *Birthstone* · RUBY   *Leo* [♌]   🦁
     (Jun 22–Jul 22)   *Flower* · LARKSPUR   (Jul 23–Aug 23)

1 .... Canada – Canada Day [NH] · Amy Johnson [BD1903] .... Th
2 .... Amelia Earhart [†1937 *disappeared over the Pacific*] .... F
3 .... St Thomas [§ *architects*] · Tom Stoppard [BD1937] .... Sa
4 .... USA – Independence Day [NH] · Calvin Coolidge [BD1872] .... Su
5 .... Algeria [ID 1962] · P.T. Barnum [BD1810] .... M
6 .... Frida Kahlo [BD1907] · Louis Armstrong [†1971] .... Tu
7 .... Sir Arthur Conan Doyle [†1930] .... W
8 ....Christiaan Huygens [†1695] · Vivien Leigh [†1967].............Th
9 .... David Hockney [BD1937] · Barbara Woodhouse [†1988]............ F
10 ....George Stubbs [†1806] · Mel Blanc [†1989]................... Sa
11 ...[◉]· ● · World Population Day [UN] · St Benedict [§ *inflammatory diseases*]... Su
12 .... Kiribati [ID 1979] · Jennifer Saunders [BD1958] .... M
13 .... St Henry [§ *the childless*] · Jean-Paul Marat [BD1793]...............Tu
14 .... France – Bastille Day · Billy the Kid [†1881] .... W
15 ....St Swithin's Day · Iris Murdoch [BD1919]....................Th
16 .... Feast of Our Lady of Mount Carmel · Hilaire Belloc [†1953].......... F
17 .... Duchess of Cornwall [BD1947] [£] · Donald Sutherland [BD1935] .... Sa
18 ...... William Makepeace Thackeray [BD1811] · W. G. Grace [BD1848] .... Su
19 ....George Degas... Edgar Degas [BD1834] · Brian May [BD1947] .... M
20 ....St Wilgefortis [§ *difficult marriages*] · Guglieimo Marconi [†1937]..........Tu
21 .... Belgium [ND] · Ernest Hemingway [BD1899].................. W
22 .. St Mary Magdalene [§ *hairdressers & repentant women*] · William Spooner [BD1844] ..Th
23 .... Graham Gooch [BD1953] .... F
24 .. Simón Bolívar Day – Venezuela & Ecuador · Alexandre Dumas [BD1802] .. Sa
25 .... St James [§ *labourers*] · Nicole Farhi [BD1946] .... Su
26 .... ☽ · St Ann [§ *women in labour*] · Aldous Huxley [BD1894] .... M
27 ....St Pantaleon [§ *physicians*] · Bob Hope [†2003].................Tu
28 .... Delta Aquarids (South) [☄] · Beatrix Potter [BD1866] .... W
29 ......St Martha [§ *cooks*] · Prince Charles & Lady Diana Spencer [WA 1981] .....Th
30 ....Emily Brontë [BD1818] · Kate Bush [BD1958]................... F
31 .... St Ignatius of Loyola [§ *those on spiritual exercises*] · Franz Liszt [†1886] .... Sa

French Rev. calendar.. *Messidor* (harvest)	Dutch month ....*Hooymaand* (hay)
Angelic governor............... *Verchiel*	Saxon month....*Mæd-monath* (meadow)
Epicurean calendar........... *Melonial*	Talismanic stone .... *Sapphire*

❦ July was originally called *Quintilis* (from *Quintus* – meaning 'fifth'), but it was renamed by Mark Antony to honour the murdered Julius Caesar, who was born on 12 July. ❦ *A swarm of bees in May is worth a load of Hay; A swarm of bees in June is worth a silver spoon; But a swarm of bees in July is not worth a fly.* ❦ *If the first of July be rainy weather, 'Twill rain mair or less for forty days together.* ❦ *Bow-wow, dandy fly – Brew no beer in July.* ❦ July used to be known as the thunder month, and some churches rang their bells in the hope of driving away thunder and lightning. ❦

AUGUST

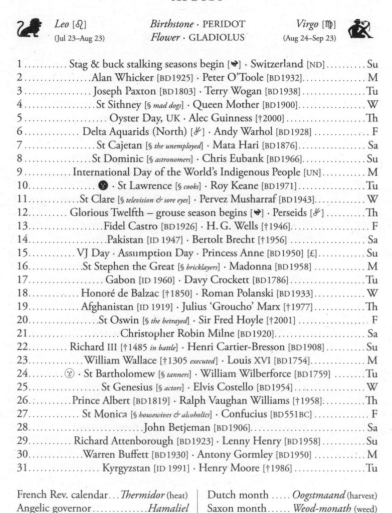

Leo [♌]
(Jul 23–Aug 23)

Birthstone · PERIDOT
Flower · GLADIOLUS

Virgo [♍]
(Aug 24–Sep 23)

1 .... Stag & buck stalking seasons begin [❦] · Switzerland [ND].......... Su
2 ....Alan Whicker [BD1925] · Peter O'Toole [BD1932]................ M
3 .... Joseph Paxton [BD1803] · Terry Wogan [BD1938] .... Tu
4 ....St Sithney [§ *mad dogs*] · Queen Mother [BD1900]................ W
5 .... Oyster Day, UK · Alec Guinness [†2000] .... Th
6 .... Delta Aquarids (North) [♆] · Andy Warhol [BD1928] .... F
7 ....St Cajetan [§ *the unemployed*] · Mata Hari [BD1876]................ Sa
8 ....St Dominic [§ *astronomers*] · Chris Eubank [BD1966]................ Su
9 .... International Day of the World's Indigenous People [UN].......... M
10 .... ● · St Lawrence [§ *cooks*] · Roy Keane [BD1971]................ Tu
11 ....St Clare [§ *television & sore eyes*] · Pervez Musharraf [BD1943]............ W
12 .... Glorious Twelfth – grouse season begins [❦] · Perseids [♆] .... Th
13 ....Fidel Castro [BD1926] · H. G. Wells [†1946]................... F
14 ....Pakistan [ID1947] · Bertolt Brecht [†1956]............... Sa
15 .... VJ Day · Assumption Day · Princess Anne [BD1950] [£]............. Su
16 ....St Stephen the Great [§ *bricklayers*] · Madonna [BD1958].............. M
17 .... Gabon [ID1960] · Davy Crockett [BD1786].................... Tu
18 ....Honoré de Balzac [†1850] · Roman Polanski [BD1933]............. W
19 ....Afghanistan [ID1919] · Julius 'Groucho' Marx [†1977]............ Th
20 ....St Oswin [§ *the betrayed*] · Sir Fred Hoyle [†2001] .... F
21 ....Christopher Robin Milne [BD1920]........................ Sa
22 .... Richard III [†1485 *in battle*] · Henri Cartier-Bresson [BD1908].......... Su
23 ....William Wallace [†1305 *executed*] · Louis XVI [BD1754].............. M
24 .... ☽ · St Bartholomew [§ *tanners*] · William Wilberforce [BD1759] .... Tu
25 .... St Genesius [§ *actors*] · Elvis Costello [BD1954] .... W
26 ....Prince Albert [BD1819] · Ralph Vaughan Williams [†1958]............ Th
27 .... St Monica [§ *housewives & alcoholics*] · Confucius [BD551BC] .... F
28 ....John Betjeman [BD1906]............................ Sa
29 .... Richard Attenborough [BD1923] · Lenny Henry [BD1958]............ Su
30 ....Warren Buffett [BD1930] · Antony Gormley [BD1950] .... M
31 .... Kyrgyzstan [ID1991] · Henry Moore [†1986] .... Tu

French Rev. calendar... *Thermidor* (heat)	Dutch month ..... *Oogstmaand* (harvest)
Angelic governor..............*Hamaliel*	Saxon month...... *Weod-monath* (weed)
Epicurean calendar............*Raisinose*	Talismanic stone .... *Diamond*

❦ Previously called *Sextilis* (as the sixth month of the old calendar), August was renamed in 8BC, in honour of the first Roman Emperor, Augustus, who claimed this month to be lucky, as it was the month in which he began his consulship, conquered Egypt, and had many other triumphs. ❦ *Greengrocers rise at dawn of sun, August the fifth – come haste away, To Billingsgate the thousands run, Tis Oyster Day! Tis Oyster Day!* ❦ *Dry August and warme, Dothe harvest no harme.* ❦ *Take heed of sudden cold after heat.* ❦ *Gather not garden seeds near the full moon.* ❦ *Sow herbs.* ❦

—————————— SEPTEMBER ——————————

 Virgo [♍]
(Aug 24–Sep 23)

Birthstone · SAPPHIRE
Flower · ASTER

Libra [♎]
(Sep 24–Oct 22)

1 ....Partridge shooting season opens [❦] · St Giles [§ *cripples, lepers, & nursing mothers*] .. W
2 .... Baron Pierre de Coubertin [†1937] .... Th
3 .... E. E. Cummings [†1962] · Charlie Sheen [BD1965] .... F
4 ....St Ida of Herzfeld [§ *widows*] · Georges Simenon [†1989] .... Sa
5 ....George Lazenby [BD1939] · Douglas Bader [†1982] .... Su
6 .... Swaziland [ID 1968] · Tim Henman [BD1974] .... M
7 ....Brazil [ID 1822] · Catherine Parr [†1548] .... Tu
8 ..... ☻ · International Literacy Day [UN] · Nativity of Blessed Virgin Mary ... W
9 .... William the Conqueror [†1087] · Captain William Bligh [BD1754] ......Th
10 .... St Nicholas of Tolentino [§ *sick animals*] · Karl Lagerfeld [BD1938] .... F
11 .... New Year – Ethiopia · Georgi Markov [† 1978 *assassinated*] .... Sa
12 .... John F. Kennedy & Jacqueline Bouvier [WA 1953] .... Su
13 .... St John Chrysostom [§ *orators*] · Roald Dahl [BD1916] .... M
14 .... Exaltation of the Holy Cross · Isadora Duncan [†1927] ....Tu
15 ....Battle of Britain Day · Agatha Christie [BD1890] .... W
16 ....International Day for the Preservation of the Ozone Layer [UN] ....Th
17 .... Stirling Moss [BD1929] · Des Lynam [BD1942] .... F
18 ....Chile [ID 1810] · Greta Garbo [BD1905] .... Sa
19 ....St Januarius [§ *blood banks*] · George Cadbury [BD1839] ....Su
20 ....Alexander the Great [BD 356BC] · Sir James Dewar [BD1842]........... M
21 .... International Day of Peace [UN] · St Matthew [§ *accountants*] ....Tu
22 .... First Day of Autumn · Dame Christabel Pankhurst [BD1880]........ W
23 .... ☺ · Mickey Rooney [BD1920] · Julio Iglesias [BD1943].............Th
24 ....Guinea-Bissau [ID 1973] · Jim Henson [BD1936] .... F
25 ....St Cadoc of Llancarvan [§ *cramps*] · Christopher Reeve [BD1952] .... Sa
26. St Cosmas & St Damian [§ *pharmacists & doctors*] · Olivia Newton-John [BD1948]. Su
27 .... St Vincent de Paul [§ *charitable societies*] .... M
28 ....Thomas Crapper [BD1836] · Brigitte Bardot [BD1934] ....Tu
29 ....Michaelmas Day · Sebastian Coe [BD1956]................... W
30 .... Botswana [ID 1966] · James Dean [†1955]................... Th

French Rev. calendar....*Fructidor* (fruit)	Dutch month .... *Herstmaand* (Autumn)
Angelic governor................... *Uriel*	Saxon month...... *Gerst-monath* (barley)
Epicurean calendar............*Huîtrose*	Talismanic stone ....*Zircon*

❦ September is so named as it was the seventh month in the Roman calendar. ❦ *September blows soft, Till the fruit's in the loft. Forgotten, month past, Doe now at the last.* ❦ *Eat and drink less, And buy a knife at Michaelmas.* ❦ To be 'Septembered' is to be multihued in autumnal colours, as Blackmore wrote: 'His honest face was Septembered with many a vintage'. ❦ *Poor Robin's Almanack* (1666) states: 'now *Libra* weighs the days and nights in an equal balance, so that there is not an hairs breadth difference betwixt them in length; this moneth having an R in it, Oysters come again in season'. ❦ The Irish name *Meán Fómhair* means 'mid-autumn'. ❦

———————————OCTOBER———————————

Libra [♎]   *Birthstone* · OPAL   *Scorpio* [♏]
(Sep 24–Oct 22)   *Flower* · CALENDULA   (Oct 23–Nov 22)

1 ......Int. Day of Older Persons [UN] · Pheasant shooting season opens [❧] ..... F
2 ....Trevor Brooking [BD1948] · Sting [BD1951]...................Sa
3 ....Germany [ND] · Gore Vidal [BD1925]......................Su
4 ....St Francis of Assisi [§ *animals & birds*] · Ann Widdecombe [BD1947]........M
5 ....International Teacher's Day [UN] · Louis Jean Lumière [BD1864] ......Tu
6 ....Habitat Day [UN] · Melvyn Bragg [BD1939] ....W
7 ....😐 · St Sergius [§ *Syria*] · Desmond Tutu [BD1931]................Th
8 ....Clement Attlee [†1967] .... F
9 ....Brian Blessed [BD1937] · John Lennon [BD1940] ....Sa
10..................Fiji [ID 1790] · Edith Piaf [†1963] ....Su
11........St Gummarus [§ *glove-makers*] · Eleanor Roosevelt [BD1884]...........M
12..................Spain [ND] · Magnus Magnusson [BD1929]...................Tu
13..................Claudius [†54] · Paul Simon [BD1941] ....W
14...............Cliff Richard [BD1940] · Roger Moore [BD1927] ....Th
15.........St Teresa of Avila [§ *headache sufferers*] · Chris de Burgh [BD1948]..........F
16....................World Food Day [UN] · St Hedwig [§ *brides*] ....Sa
17....Int. Day for the Eradication of Poverty [UN] · Rita Hayworth [BD1918]....Su
18...............St Luke [§ *artists & doctors*] · Charles Babbage [†1871] ....M
19...........................Philip Pullman [BD1946] ....Tu
20.....St Acca [§ *learning*] · Jacqueline Kennedy & Aristotle Onassis [WA 1968].....W
21..................St I Iilarion [§ *hermits*] · Orionids [☄] ....Th
22..................Vatican [ND] · Derek Jacobi [BD1938].......................F
23.........😊 · St John of Capistrano [§ *jurors*] · Anita Roddick [BD1942] ....Sa
24................United Nations Day [UN] · Zambia [ID 1964]..................Su
25................Kazakhstan [ND] · Pablo Picasso [BD1881]....................M
26..........................Alfred the Great [†899] ....Tu
27............Turkmenistan [ID 1991] · John Cleese [BD1939]...............W
28...............St Simon the Zealot [§ *sawyers*] · Czech Republic [ND]..............Th
29...................Turkey [ND] · Joseph Pulitzer [†1911].....................F
30.. St Marcellus the Centurion [§ *conscientious objectors*] · Michael Winner [BD1935].. Sa
31.................[●] · Hallowe'en · Sir Jimmy Savile [BD1926] ....Su

French Rev. cal. ... *Vendémiaire* (vintage)	Dutch month .... *Wynmaand* (wine)
Angelic governor................*Barbiel*	Saxon month....... *Win-monath* (wine)
Epicurean calendar.........*Bécassinose*	Talismanic stone ....*Agate*

❧ October was originally the eighth month of the calendar. ❧ *Dry your barley land in October, Or you'll always be sober.* ❧ October was a time for brewing, and the month gave its name to a 'heady and ripe' ale: 'five Quarters of Malt to three Hogsheads, and twenty-four Pounds of Hops'. Consequently, *often drunk and seldom sober falls like the leaves in October.* ❧ In American politics, an *October surprise* is an event thought to have been engineered to garner political support just before an election. ❧ Roman Catholics traditionally dedicated October to the devotion of the rosary. ❧

NOVEMBER

 Scorpio [♏]
(Oct 23–Nov 22)

Birthstone · TOPAZ
Flower · CHRYSANTHEMUM

Sagittarius [♐]
(Nov 23–Dec 21)

1 ....All Saints' Day · Hind and doe stalking season opens [❦]...........M
2 ....All Souls' Day · Marie Antoinette [BD 1755] ....Tu
3 ....St Martin de Porres [§ *barbers*] · Ian Wright [BD 1963] ....W
4 ...St Charles Borromeo [§ *learning and the arts*] · Wilfred Owen [†1918 *killed in action*]..Th
5 ....Guy Fawkes Night · Taurids [✦] · Vivien Leigh [BD 1913]............F
6 ...... ● · St Leonard of Noblac [§ *against burglars*] · Colley Cibber [BD 1671]......Sa
7 ....Marie Curie [BD 1867] · Leon Trotsky [BD 1879]..................Su
8 ....Bram Stoker [BD 1847] · Margaret Mitchell [BD 1900]..............M
9 ....Cambodia [ID 1953] · Dylan Thomas [†1953]...................Tu
10 ....St Tryphon [§ *gardeners*] · Richard Burton [BD 1925]................W
11 ....Remembrance Day · USA – Veterans Day · Angola [ID 1975] ....Th
12 ....François Auguste Rodin [BD 1840] · Elizabeth Gaskell [†1865]..........F
13 ....St Homobonus [§ *clothworkers*].........................Sa
14 ....Prince Charles [BD 1948] [£] · Boutros Boutros-Ghali [BD 1922] ....Su
15 ....St Albert the Great [§ *scientists*] · William Pitt the elder [BD 1708] ....M
16 ....Int. Day for Tolerance [UN] · King Henry III [†1272] ....Tu
17 ....Leonids [✦] · Peter Cook [BD 1937]........................W
18 ....St Odo of Cluny [§ *rain*] · Margaret Atwood [BD 1939] ....Th
19 ....Monaco [ND] · Jodie Foster [BD 1962].......................F
20 ....Queen Elizabeth II & Prince Philip [WA 1947] [£] ....Sa
21 .... ☺ · Presentation of the Blessed Virgin Mary in the Temple........Su
22 ....Benjamin Britten [BD 1913] · John F. Kennedy [†1963 *assassinated*] ....M
23 ....St Felicity [§ *martyrs*] · Roald Dahl [†1990] ....Tu
24 ....Scott Joplin [BD 1868] · Ian Botham [BD 1955].................W
25 .....St Catherine of Alexandria [§ *philosophers*] · Andrew Carnegie [BD 1835] .....Th
26 ....St John Berchmans [§ *altar boys & girls*] · Tina Turner [BD 1939]...........F
27 ....Ernie Wise [BD 1925] · Bruce Lee [BD 1940] ....Sa
28 ....East Timor [ND] · Enid Blyton [†1968].....................Su
29 ....Giacomo Puccini [†1924] · Graham Hill [†1975]...............M
30 ....St Andrew [§ *Scotland & Russia*] · Oscar Wilde [†1900] ....Tu

French Rev. calendar.....*Brumaire* (fog)	Dutch month .. *Slaghtmaand* [see below]
Angelic governor.............*Advachiel*	Saxon month......*Wind-monath* (wind)
Epicurean calendar.......*Pommedetaire*	Talismanic stone ....*Amethyst*

❦ Originally the ninth (*novem*) month, November has long been associated with slaughter, hence the Dutch *Slaghtmaand* ('slaughter month'). The Anglo-Saxon was *Blotmonath* ('blood' or 'sacrifice month'). ❦ A dismal month, November has been the subject of many writers' ire, as J.B. Burges wrote: 'November leads her wintry train, And stretches o'er the firmament her veil Charg'd with foul vapours, fogs and drizzly rain'. ❦ Famously, Thomas Hood's poem *No!* contains the lines 'No warmth, no cheerfulness, no healthful ease ... No shade, no shine, no butterflies, no bees, No fruits, no flowers, no leaves, no birds —— November!' ❦

DECEMBER

 Sagittarius [♐]   *Birthstone* · TURQUOISE   **Capricorn** [♑]
(Nov 23–Dec 21)   *Flower* · NARCISSUS   (Dec 22–Jan 20)

1 . . . . World AIDS Day [UN] · Dr George Birkbeck [†1841]. . . . . W
2 . . . . United Arab Emirates [ID 1971] · Marquis de Sade [†1814]. . . . . Th
3 . . . . International Day of Disabled Persons [UN] · Eamonn Holmes [BD1959]. . . . F
4 . . . . St Ada [§ *nuns*] · Ronnie Corbett [BD1930]. . . . . Sa
5 . . . . ☻ · Thailand [ND] · Sir Henry Tate [†1899] . . . . Su
6 . . . . St Nicholas [§ *bakers & pawnbrokers*] · Anthony Trollope [†1882] . . . . M
7 . . . . USA – Pearl Harbor Day · St Ambrose [§ *protector of bees & domestic animals*] . . . . . . Tu
8 . . . . The Immaculate Conception · Mary Queen of Scots [BD1542] . . . . W
9 . . . . John Milton [BD1608] · John Malkovich [BD1953] . . . . Th
10 . . . . Nobel Prizes awarded · Human Rights Day [UN] . . . . F
11 . . . . St Damasus [§ *archaeologists*] · Willie Rushton [†1996] . . . . Sa
12 . . . . Lionel Blair [BD1931] · Frank Sinatra [BD1915]. . . . . Su
13 . . . . St Lucy [§ *the blind*] · Wassily Kandinsky [†1944]. . . . . M
14 . . . Geminids [☄] · St Agnellus [§ *invoked against invaders*] · Nostradamus [BD1503]. . . Tu
15 . . . . USA – National Bill of Rights Day · Jean Paul Getty [BD1892]. . . . . W
16 . . . . Ludwig van Beethoven [BD1770] · Jane Austen [BD1775]. . . . . Th
17 . . . . Bhutan [ND] · Kerry Packer [BD1937] . . . . F
18 . . . . International Migrants Day [UN] · Betty Grable [BD1916] . . . . Sa
19 . . . . Sir William Edward Parry [BD1790] · Grace Mildmay [BD1900]. . . . . . . Su
20 . . . . . . St Ursicinus of Saint-Ursanne [§ *against stiff neck*] · Uri Geller [BD1946]. . . . . . M
21 . . . . . . ☿ · Shortest Day · First Day of Winter · Thomas Becket [BD1118]. . . . . . Tu
22 . . . . Noel Edmonds [BD1948] . . . . W
23 . . . . Ursids [☄] · St Dagobert [§ *kings, orphans & kidnap victims*] . . . . Th
24 . . . . Christmas Eve · Ava Gardner [BD1922]. . . . . F
25 . . . . Christmas Day [NH] · Annie Lennox [BD1954]. . . . . Sa
26 . . . . Boxing Day [NH] · St Stephen [§ *stonemasons & horses*]. . . . . Su
27 . . . . St John [§ *Asia Minor*] · Janet Street-Porter [BD1946]. . . . . M
28 . . . . Childermass · Woodrow Wilson [BD1856] . . . . Tu
29 . . . . William Gladstone [BD1809] · Grigori Rasputin [†1916 *murdered*] . . . . W
30 . . . . Our Lady of Bethlehem · Bo Diddley [BD1928] . . . . Th
31 . . . . New Year's Eve · Scotland – Hogmanay · Anthony Hopkins [BD1937] . . . . . F

French Rev. calendar. . . . *Frimaire* (frost)	Dutch month . . . *Wintermaand* (Winter)
Angelic governor . . . . *Hanael*	Saxon month. . . . . . *Mid-Winter-monath*
Epicurean calendar. . . . . *Boudinaire*	Talismanic stone . . . . *Beryl*

❦ *If the ice will bear a goose before Christmas, it will not bear a duck afterwards.* ❦ Originally the tenth month, December now closes the year. ❦ *If Christmas Day be bright and clear there'll be two winters in the year.* ❦ The writer Saunders warned in 1679, 'In December, Melancholy and Phlegm much increase, which are heavy, dull, and close, and therefore it behoves all that will consider their healths, to keep their heads and bodies very well from cold'. ❦ Robert Burns splendidly wrote in 1795 – 'As I am in a complete Decemberish humour, gloomy, sullen, stupid'. ❦

———— TELEGRAPHY & TWITTER ————

The 140-character limit of Twitter posts was guided by the 160-character limit established by the developers of text messaging. Yet, there is nothing new about new technology imposing restrictions on articulation. During the C19th telegraphy boom, some carriers charged extra for words >15 characters and for messages >10 words. Thus, the cheapest telegram was often limited to 150 characters. ❦ Concerns for economy and desires for secrecy fuelled a boom in code books that reduced common and complex phrases into single words. Dozens of different codes were published; many catered to specific occupations and all promised efficiency. ❦ The phrases below are from the 3rd edition of *The Anglo-American Telegraphic Code* (1891):

ACESCET	*Has met with a trifling accident.*
ACUATE	*You will accomplish but little.*
ADFLUXION	*The account is full of errors.*
ADJUTORY	*Accumulate no debts.*
ALAND	*Advertise liberally but economically.*
ALOOFNESS	*Agent is dead.*
AMPHIMACER	*You must send my allowance immediately.*
ANDALUSITE	*You seem to be annoyed.*
ANTALGIC	*Application was received, acted upon, and rejected.*
APSE	*The sheriff will not arrest.*
ARBORIST	*A libelous article.*
BABYLONITE	*Please provide bail immediately.*
BALLOTER	*Returned from the bank 'no good'.*
BANISHER	*Forced into bankruptcy.*
BARRACAN	*A battle is reported to have begun.*
BLACKTAIL	*You have made a blunder.*
BLOCKISH	*Allow for a liberal bonus.*
BLOWZED	*Borrow as little as possible.*
BOUTADE	*Business is declining.*
CAPRIPED	*Cattle are scarce.*
CASSOCKED	*His character as to honesty, bad.*
CAUSSON	*Give liberally for charitable purposes.*
CELLAR	*The cheaper the better.*
COGWARE	*Compliments of the season.*
COMMITTER	*Compulsion must be used if necessary.*
CONFORMER	*Condemn the entire thing.*
CONFUTER	*The prisoner(s) will probably be condemned.*
CRISP	*Can you recommend to me a good female cook?*
CUISH	*A crisis seems to be approaching.*
DECEMVIR	*Has been dead a long time.*
DESERTLESS	*Denial is useless.*
DEWS	*Destroyed by a cyclone.*
EDUCT	*A large amount has been embezzled.*
EMICATION	*The epidemic has broken out again.*
EMPLOY	*Take every precaution against escape.*
ENRINGED	*The news causes great excitement.*
EVIDENTIAL	*A gunpowder explosion occurred.*
EXPEDITE	*You can go to any extreme.*
FLANK	*A fire is raging here. Please send engine.*
GEYSER	*Do not pay in gold.*
HABERDASH	*A writ of habeas corpus cannot be issued.*
HEMSTICH	*Hindered by ill health.*
HORTYARD	*There is little hope.*
HUB	*Can you recommend to me (us) a competent housemaid?*
HURST	*The hunting expedition will not set out.*
ILLITERAL	*A panic is thought to be imminent.*
INSIDIATOR	*How much is your life insured for?*
KAVASS	*A large number were killed.*
LAMBATIVE	*Employ a good lawyer.*
MAHOGANY	*Malaria prevails extensively.*
MANNITE	*The market should be manipulated.*
MESSET	*Energetic means must be adopted.*
NOTED	*A notorious character.*
ORANGEMAN	*What is the opinion on the street?*
ORGANISM	*Taxation is oppressive.*
PANEL	*Stocks have reached panic prices.*
PHANTASTIC	*Physician gives very little hope.*
PORY	*It would establish a bad precedent.*
RELEASER	*The mistake cannot be rectified.*
ROLLABLE	*Your request is unreasonable.*
ROSELITE	*Resistance is useless.*
RUSSET	*Bank just robbed.*
SCHOTTISH	*The wet season now prevails.*
SLANK	*Sick of the entire matter.*
SLOKE	*Snow impedes operations.*
TITMOUSE	*I (we) accept with pleasure your invitation for the theatre tomorrow evening.*
WASTAGE	*War is inevitable.*
WREAKFUL	*Writ of execution.*

KEEP CALM & CARRY ON

The psychological impact of the economic downturn, and the consequent rise in uncertainty, unemployment, and insolvency, were neatly encapsulated by the popularity of a poster slogan designed in 1939 to placate the populace on the eve of World War Two:

KEEP CALM AND CARRY ON

Set in bold white sans serif type against a blood-red background, this injunction carried the imprimatur of authority by being set under the crown of King George VI. ❧ It seems that the man responsible for reviving the *Keep Calm* poster was Stuart Manley, the owner of Barter Books in Alnwick, Northumberland, who discovered an original copy among an auction lot of old books. He hung the poster in his shop window, and was soon overwhelmed by the public response: 'Lots of people saw it and wanted to buy it. We refused all offers but eventually we decided we should get copies made for sale.' According to the BBC, 'Sales remained modest until 2005, when it was featured as a Christmas gift idea in a national newspaper supplement. "All hell broke loose", says Mr Manley. "Our website broke down under the strain, the phone never stopped ringing and virtually every member of staff had to be diverted into packing posters".' ❧ The ubiquity of the *Keep Calm and Carry On* poster during 2008–09 was remarkable. The slogan was transferred to all manner of media – from mugs and mouse mats to key fobs and deck chairs – and a slew of celebrities were seen sporting the slogan on T-shirts. (Notably, Katie 'Jordan' Price was snapped in such a garment after her very public break-up from husband Peter Andre.) Inevitably, the success of this sixty-year-old slogan prompted a host of parodies, including *Get Excited and Make Things*; *Eat Candy and Regret Decision*; *Keep Calm and Have a Cupcake*, and *Now Panic and Freak Out.* ❧ In his book *Propaganda in War, 1939–1945*, the historian Michael Balfour noted that *Keep Calm and Carry On* was one of three slogans penned by a committee of political advisors and ad-men and approved by the government. (The other two were *Freedom Is In Peril* and *Your Courage, Your Cheerfulness, Your Resolution Will Bring Us Victory*.) However, although *c.*2·5 million copies of the *Keep Calm* poster were originally printed, only a handful were ever seen by the public because, as Balfour pointed out, in the absence of any immediate German threat, the slogan was 'too obviously inappropriate to the actual conditions'. Balfour stated that the original poster campaign was 'greeted with disdain' by the public, and served only to prove that governments were no match for the advertising industry in creating effective and timely campaigns. ❧ It is curious that a poster created to reassure the populace on the eve of war, albeit never used, chimed so deeply during a recession some sixty years later. The unemotional and authoritative tone of its wording, the simplicity and elegance of its design, and the presence of a royal crest (as opposed to a governmental logo) all combined to give the poster a bygone charm akin to that of early 'Received Pronunciation' radio broadcasts. More than half a century after it was written, and in very different circumstances, people found the slogan *Keep Calm and Carry On* strangely calming.

EIGHT RULES FOR CHILDREN

Work quickly
Sing sweetly
Step lightly
Write neatly
Sing softly

Walk sprightly
Speak gently
And politely.

– Emma L. Eldridge, 1911

MARKS OF SUSPICION

'Always suspect a man who affects great softness of manner, an unruffled evenness of temper, and an enunciation studied, slow and deliberate. These things are all unnatural, and bespeak a degree of mental discipline into which he that has no purposes of craft or design to answer, cannot submit to drill himself. The most successful knaves are usually of this description, as smooth as razors dipped in oil, and as sharp. They affect the innocence of the dove, which they have not, in order to hide the cunning of the serpent, which they have.' Charles Caleb Colton, *c.*1825

ANNIVERSARIES OF 2010

25th Anniversary (1985)
The Rainbow Warrior was sunk by French secret service agents. ❦ Mikhail Gorbachev became leader of the Soviet Union.

50th Anniversary (1960)
John F. Kennedy won the US Presidential election. ❦ Lady Chatterley's Lover was published in the UK – the book sold out in one day. ❦ Betting shops were legalised in Great Britain. ❦ Harold Macmillan made his Wind of Change speech, condemning apartheid.

75th Anniversary (1935)
Nylon was invented by Wallace Carothers. ❦ The Chinese Communist Party's 'Long March' ended.

100th Anniversary (1910)
Japan annexed Korea. ❦ Pablo Picasso painted Le Guitariste. ❦ George V ascended the throne. ❦ The Egyptian PM Boutros Ghali was assassinated.

150th Anniversary (1860)
Rubber manufacturer Frederick Walton invented linoleum. ❦ Robert Bunsen and Gustav Kirchhoff discovered caesium. ❦ George Eliot's The Mill on the Floss was published. ❦ The Second Opium War ended.

200th Anniversary (1810)
Beethoven composed his Bagatelle in A minor (Für Elise). ❦ Colombia declared independence from Spain. ❦ George III was pronounced insane.

250th Anniversary (1760)
The Afghans defeated the Marathas at the Battle of Barari Ghat.

500th Anniversary (1510)
A German locksmith, Peter Henlein, invented the pocket watch. ❦ The *Mary Rose* was completed.

800th Anniversary (1210)
Genghis Khan conquered the kingdom of Xi Xia.

―――――― NOTABLE CHRISTIAN DATES · 2010 ――――――

Epiphany · *manifestation of the Christ to the Magi*..................................... 6 Jan
Presentation of Christ in the Temple (Candlemas).......................... .2 Feb
Ash Wednesday · *1st day of Lent*... 17 Feb
The Annunciation · *when Gabriel told Mary she would bear Christ* .... .25 Mar
Good Friday · *Friday before Easter; commemorating the Crucifixion* .... .2 Apr
Easter Day (Western churches) · *commemorating the Resurrection* .... .4 Apr
Easter Day (Eastern Orthodox) · *commemorating the Resurrection* .... .4 Apr
Ascension Day · *commemorating the ascent of Christ to heaven*....................... 13 May
Rogation Sunday · *the Sunday before Ascension Day*................................. .9 May
Pentecost (Whit Sunday) · *commemorating the descent of the Holy Spirit* .... 23 May
Trinity Sunday · *observed in honour of the Trinity*................................. 30 May
Corpus Christi · *commemorating the institution of the Holy Eucharist*................... .3 Jun
All Saints' Day · *commemorating all the Church's saints collectively*..................... 1 Nov
Advent Sunday · *marking the start of Advent*.................................... .28 Nov
Christmas Day · *celebrating the birth of Christ*.................................. .25 Dec

A few other terms from the Christian Calendar:

Bible Sunday...................2nd in Advent	Palm Sunday...................before Easter
Black/Easter Monday ..... the day after Easter	Passion Sunday................. 5th in Lent
Collop/Egg Monday......... first before Lent	Plough Monday.............. after Epiphany
Egg Saturday..... day prior to Quinquagesima	Quadragesima.............1st Sunday in Lent
Fig/Yew Sunday.................Palm Sunday	Quinquagesima .... Sunday before Lent
Holy Saturday.................before Easter	Refreshment .... 4th Sunday in Lent
Holy Week ....before Easter	Septuagesima .... 3rd Sunday before Lent
Low Sunday .... Sunday after Easter	Sexagesima ....2nd Sunday before Lent
Maundy Thursday.............before Easter	Shrove Tuesday ('pancake day').... before Lent
Mothering Sunday.............. 4th in Lent	Shrovetide.............period preceding Lent
	St Martin's Lent.....................Advent
	Tenebrae .... last 3 days of Holy Week

―――――― CHRISTIAN CALENDAR MOVEABLE FEASTS ――――――

Year	Ash Wednesday	Easter Day	Ascension	Pentecost	Advent Sunday
2010	17 Feb	4 Apr	13 May	23 May	28 Nov
2011	9 Mar	24 Apr	2 Jun	12 Jun	27 Nov
2012	22 Feb	8 Apr	17 May	27 May	2 Dec
2013	13 Feb	31 Mar	9 May	19 May	1 Dec
2014	5 Mar	20 Apr	29 May	8 Jun	30 Nov
2015	18 Feb	5 Apr	14 May	24 May	29 Nov
2016	10 Feb	27 Mar	5 May	15 May	27 Nov
2017	1 Mar	16 Apr	25 May	4 Jun	3 Dec
2018	14 Feb	1 Apr	10 May	20 May	2 Dec
2019	6 Mar	21 Apr	30 May	9 Jun	1 Dec
2020	26 Feb	12 Apr	21 May	31 May	29 Nov
2021	17 Feb	4 Apr	13 May	23 May	28 Nov

—————— NOTABLE RELIGIOUS DATES FOR 2010 ——————

HINDU

Makar Sankrant · *Winter festival* ....14 Jan
Vasant Panchami · *dedicated to Saraswati and learning* ....20 Jan
Maha Shivaratri · *dedicated to Shiva* ....12 Feb
Holi · *spring festival of colours dedicated to Krishna* ....28 Feb
Varsha Pratipada (Chaitra) · *Spring New Year* ....16 Mar
Hindu New Year & Ramayana Week ....16 Mar
Rama Navami · *birthday of Lord Rama* ....24 Mar
Hanuman Jayanti · *birthday of Hanuman, the Monkey God* ....30 Mar
Raksha Bandhan · *festival of brotherhood and love* ....24 Aug
Janmashtami · *birthday of Lord Rama* ....2 Sep
Ganesh Chaturthi · *birthday of Lord Ganesh* ....11 Sep
Navarati & Durga-puja · *celebrating triumph of good over evil* ....*starts* 8 Oct
Saraswati-puja · *dedicated to Saraswati and learning* ....*starts* 14 Oct
Dassera (Vijay Dashami) · *celebrating triumph of good over evil* ....17 Oct
Diwali (Deepvali) · *New Year festival of lights* ....5 Nov
New Year ....6 Nov

JEWISH

Purim (Feast of Lots) · *commemorating defeat of Haman* ....28 Feb
Pesach (Passover) · *commemorating exodus from Egypt* ....30 Mar
Shavuot (Pentecost) · *commemorating revelation of the Torah* ....19 May
Tisha B'Av · *day of mourning* ....20 Jul
Rosh Hashanah (New Year) ....9 Sep
Yom Kippur (Day of Atonement) · *fasting and prayer for forgiveness* ....18 Sep
Sukkoth (Feast of Tabernacles) · *marking the time in wilderness* ....23 Sep
Simchat Torah · *9th day of Sukkoth* ....1 Oct
Chanukah · *commemorating re-dedication of Jerusalem Temple* ....2 Dec

ISLAMIC

Milad Al-Nabi · *birthday of Muhammad* ....26 Feb
Ramadan · *the month in which the Koran was revealed* ....*starts* 12 Aug
Eid al-Fitr · *marks end of Ramadan* ....10 Sep
Eid al-Adha · *celebrating the faith of Abraham* ....17 Nov
Al Hijra (New Year) ....7 Dec
Ashura · *celebrating Noah leaving the Ark, the saving of Moses, & Hussein's martyrdom* .....16 Dec

SIKH

Birthday of Guru Gobind Singh · *founder of the Khalsa* ....5 Jan
Sikh New Year (Nanakshahi calendar) ....13 Apr
Vaisakhi (Baisakhi) · *founding of the Khalsa* ....13 Apr
Hola Mahalla · *festival of martial arts* ....14 Apr
Birthday of Guru Nanak (founder of Sikhism) ....14 Apr
Martyrdom of Guru Arjan ....16 Jun
Diwali · *festival of light* ....5 Nov
Martyrdom of Guru Tegh Bahadur ....24 Nov

—————— NOTABLE RELIGIOUS DATES FOR 2010 ——————

BAHA'I

Nawruz (New Year) .... 21 Mar	Day of the Covenant .... 26 Nov
Ridvan .... 21 Apr	Ascension of Abdu'l-Baha ..... 28 Nov
Declaration of the Báb .... 23 May	*World Religion Day* .... 18 Jan
Ascension of Baha'u'llah ...... 29 May	*Race Unity Day* .... 14 Jun
Martyrdom of the Báb .... 9 July	*International Day of Peace* ...... 21 Sep
Birth of the Báb .... 20 Oct	*In addition, the eve of each of the*
Birth of Baha'u'llah .... 12 Nov	*nineteen Baha'i months is celebrated.*

JAIN

Mahavira Jayanti · *celebrates the day of Mahavira's birth* .... 28 Mar
Paryushan · *time of reflection and repentance.* .... 5 Sep
Diwali · *celebrated when Mahavira gave his last teachings and attained ultimate liberation* ... 5 Nov
New Year .... 6 Nov
Kartak Purnima · *time of pilgrimage* .... Oct/Nov

BUDDHIST

Parinivana Day · *marks the death of the Buddha* .... 8 Feb
Losar · *Tibetan New Year* .... 14 Feb
Sangha Day (Magha Puja Day) · *celebration of Buddhist community* .... 30 Mar
Wesak (Vesak) · *marks the birth, death, & enlightenment of the Buddha* .... 27 May
Dharma Day · *marks the start of the Buddha's teaching* .... 26 Jul

RASTAFARIAN

Ethiopian Christmas .... 7 Jan	Birthday of Marcus Garvey ..... 17 Aug
Ethiopian Constitution .... 16 Jul	Ethiopian New Year's Day ...... 11 Sep
Haile Selassie birthday .... 23 Jul	Crowning of Haile Selassie ...... 2 Nov

PAGAN

Imbolc · *fire festival anticipating the new farming season* .... 2 Feb
Spring Equinox · *celebrating the renewal of life* .... 20 Mar
Beltane · *fire festival celebrating Summer and fertility.* .... 1 May
Summer Solstice (Midsummer; Litha) · *celebrating the sun's power.* .... 21 Jun
Lughnasadh · *harvest festival.* .... 1 Aug
Autumn Equinox (Harvest Home; Mabon) · *reflection on the past season* .... 23 Sep
Samhain (Halloween; All Hallows Eve) · *Pagan New Year.* .... 31 Oct
Winter Solstice (Yule) · *celebrating Winter.* .... 21 Dec

CHINESE LUNAR NEW YEAR · 14 Feb

[Every effort has been taken to validate these dates. However, readers should be aware that there is a surprising degree of debate and dispute. This is caused by the interplay of: regional variations; differing interpretations between religious authorities; seemingly arbitrary changes in dates when holidays conflict; avoidance of days considered for one or other reason inauspicious; as well as the inherent unpredictability of the lunar cycle. Many festivals, especially Jewish holidays, start at sundown on the preceding day.]

PUBLIC & BANK HOLIDAYS

England, Wales, & N. Ireland	2010	2011
New Year's Day	1 Jan	3 Jan
[NI *only*] St Patrick's Day	17 Mar	17 Mar
Good Friday	2 Apr	22 April
Easter Monday	5 Apr	25 April
Early May Bank Holiday	3 May	2 May
Spring Bank Holiday	31 May	30 May
[NI *only*] Battle of the Boyne	12 Jul	12 Jul
Summer Bank Holiday	30 Aug	29 Aug
Christmas Day	27 Dec	26 Dec
Boxing Day	28 Dec	27 Dec

Scotland	2010	2011
New Year's Day	1 Jan	3 Jan
2nd January	4 Jan	4 Jan
Good Friday	2 Apr	22 Apr
Early May Bank Holiday	3 May	2 May
Spring Bank Holiday	31 May	30 May
Summer Bank Holiday	2 Aug	1 Aug
Christmas Day	27 Dec	26 Dec
Boxing Day	28 Dec	27 Dec

These are the expected dates of holidays; some are subject to proclamation by the Queen.

A MAN'S CHOICE THINGS

His house free from wet.
His farm compact.
His land pleasant.
His bed soft.
His wife chaste.
His food wholesome.
His drink small and brisk.
His fire bright.
His clothes comfortable.
His neighbourhood peaceful.
His servant diligent.
His maid handy.
His son sincere.
His daughter accomplished.
His friend faithful.
His companion without deceit.
His horse gentle.

His hound swift.
His hawk full of avidity.
His oxen strong.
His cows of one colour.
His sheep of kindly breed.
His swine long.
His household moral.
His home orderly.
His bard learned.
His harper fine of feeling.
His mill near.
His church far.
His lord powerful.
His King just.
His spiritual father discreet.

AND HIS GOD MERCIFUL.

This was addressed by Catwg the Wise to his father, Gwynlliw Vilwr.

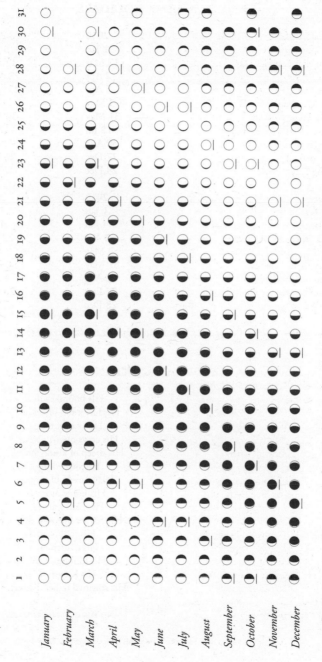

PHASES OF THE MOON · MMX

Key: ● New Moon · ◑ First Quarter · ○ Full Moon · ◐ Last Quarter · Dates are based on Universal Time (Greenwich Mean Time)

A MORAL & PHYSICAL THERMOMETER

DR JOHN COAKLEY LETTSOM (1744–1815)

or, A Scale of the Progress of Temperance and Intemperance.
Liquors, with their Effects, in the Usual Order.

TEMPERANCE

70 — 1	WATER		
60 — 2	MILK & WATER		Health, Wealth. / Serenity of Mind. / Reputation, / Long life, & Happiness.
50 — 3	SMALL BEER		
40 — 4	CYDER & PERRY		
30 — 5	WINE		Cheerfulness, / Strength & Nourishment / when taken only at Meals / and in moderate Quantities.
20 — 6	PORTER		
10 — 7	STRONG BEER		

INTEMPERANCE

		VICES	DISEASES	PUNISHMENTS
10 — 9	PUNCH	Idleness	Sickness & Puking & Tremors of the hands in the morning	Debt
20 — 10	TODDY & CRANK	Peevishness	Jaundice	Black eyes
		Quarrelling & Fighting	Bloatedness	Rags
30 — 11	GROG AND BRANDY & WATER	Lying	Inflamed eyes / Red nose & face	Hunger
40 — 12	FLIP & SHRUB	Swearing	Sore & swelled legs	Hospital
		Obscenity	Pains in the limbs & burning in the palms of the hands and soles of the feet	Poorhouse
50 — 13	BITTERS INFUSED IN SPIRITS; USQUEBAUGH HYSTERIC WATER	Swindling		Jail
		Perjury	Dropsy	Whipping
60 — 14	GIN, ANISEED, RUM, BRANDY, & WHISKEY IN THE MORNING	Burglary	Epilepsy / Melancholy	The Hulks
70 — 15	AS ABOVE, DURING THE DAY AND NIGHT	Murder	Madness / Apoplexy	Botany Bay
		SUICIDE	DEATH	GALLOWS

THE TWO ALMANACKS · A FABLE

Upon a desk it chanced one day,
Two almanacks together lay —
One of the present year, and one
With date of the old year, just gone;
When slightly raising up his head,
The latter to his neighbour said:
'Dear neighbour for what crime have I
Deserved my altered destiny?
My master used to honour me,
Each moment of the day would he
Turn over and consult my page:
But now, alas! in my old age,
Dishonoured, to the dust I'm thrown,
While he hath eyes for thee alone.'
The other then, in page and rim:
Quite fresh and new, thus answered him:
'Thou art not of this age, my friend,
And of thine own there is an end
Sunday, with us, as thou mayest see,

Is only Saturday with thee.
Thou art, poor friend, a day too late:
Thou must blame nothing but thy date;
And if, thanks to my own, I'm now
What thou wert once, yet I must bow
To the same lot, to have lived my time
Of twelve months more, my only crime.'
Thus all things change and pass away
In this frail world. To outlive our day
Is to be dead: nothing is wrong
And men are charmed, just so long
As we can serve them. Let us lose
Our usefulness, and we abuse
And call them ingrates. Be content,
Men of bygone age, of power spent;
Old servants, veterans, human flowers
Of withered beauty; lovers ye,
Who mourn your mistress' perfidy
— ALL ARE OLD ALMANACKS

– ANON, ? *The Courrier de L'Europe*, c.1889

AN ESTIMATE OF HUMAN LIFE

What is the fleeting life of mortal man?
Its date extended, measures but a span:

⁂

A *Dream* – that leaves no memory behind,
A *Bubble* – blown away by every wind;
A *Glass* that's broke, and scarcely lasts a day,
As *Ice*, which quickly melts in tears away,
A *Flower* that fades as soon as in the bloom,
A *Tale* i' th' morning told, forgotten e're 'tis noon
As *Grass* cut down, and wither'd in an hour,
A *Shadow* – that has no continuance in its power,
As *Dust* that's driven by the whirling storm,
A *Point* that knows no substance, parts, or form,
A *Voice*, which nothing but a sound can boast,
A *Sound* that in surrounding air is lost,
A *Vapour*, toss'd about by ev'ry breath,
A *Nothing!* – Such is man,
the sport of
TIME and DEATH.

– ANON, *Tickler, or, Monthly Compendium of Good Things*, 1818

AN ALPHABET OF GOOD COUNSEL

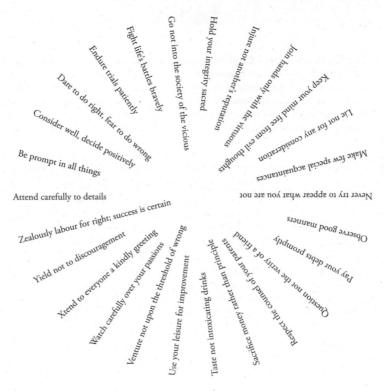

Attend carefully to details
Be prompt in all things
Consider well, decide positively
Dare to do right, fear to do wrong
Endure trials patiently
Fight life's battles bravely
Go not into the society of the vicious
Hold your integrity sacred
Injure not another's reputation
Join hands only with the virtuous
Keep your mind free from evil thoughts
Lie not for any consideration
Make few special acquaintances
Never try to appear what you are not
Observe good manners
Pay your debts promptly
Question not the veracity of a friend
Respect the counsel of your parents
Sacrifice money rather than principle
Taste not intoxicating drinks
Use your leisure for improvement
Venture not upon the threshold of wrong
Watch carefully over your passions
Xtend to everyone a kindly greeting
Yield not to discouragement
Zealously labour for right; success is certain

– from *Godey's Magazine*, 1878, quoted variously including in *The Meyer Brothers Druggist*, 1914

A WEEK'S WORK

SUNDAY – Church doors enter in,
Rest from toil, repent of sin,
Strive a heavenly rest to win.
MONDAY – To your calling go:
Serve the Lord, love friend and foe;
to the tempter, answer, 'No'.
TUESDAY – Do what good you can;
Live in peace with God and man;
Remember, life is but a span.
WEDNESDAY – Give away and earn;
Teach some truth, some goodness learn;
Joyfully good for ill return.
THURSDAY – Build your house upon

Christ, the mighty Corner stone;
Whom God helps, his work is done.
FRIDAY – For the truth be strong;
Own your fault, if in the wrong,
Put a bridle on your tongue.
SATURDAY – Thank God and sing,
Tribute to His treasure bring;
Be prepared for Terror's King!
THUS your hopes on Jesus cast,
THUS let all your weeks be passed,
And you shall be saved at last.

– ANON, *widely quoted*

Index

I confess there is a lazy kind of learning which is only indical when scholars (like adders which only bite the horse's heels) nibble but at the tables, which are *calces librorum*, neglecting the body of the book. But though the idle deserve no crutches (let not a staff be used by them, but on them), pity it is the weary should be denied the benefit thereof, and industrious scholars prohibited the accommodation of an index, most used by those who most pretend to condemn it. – THOMAS FULLER

―――――― A(H1N1) – BBC ――――――

CRIME – FRED GOODWIN

—————— FREUD, CLEMENT – MAY, EPHEMERIDES ——————

─────── McBRIDE, DAMIAN – PRESS, AWARDS ───────

───── SCI, TECH, NET SIGNIFICA – YOU TUBE ─────

KEITH WATERHOUSE
6·2·1929–4·9·2009 (80)

Waterhouse was a Fleet Street legend – and the journalists' journalist. A prolific columnist for the *Mirror* and the *Mail*, Waterhouse was also a talented author, playwright, and drinker. Additionally, Waterhouse was responsible for the best (only?) joke about indices: 'Should not the Society of Indexers be known as Indexers, Society of, The?'

——————————— ERRATA, CORRIGENDA, &c. ———————————

In keeping with many newspapers and journals, *Schott's Almanac* will publish in this section any significant corrections from the previous year. Below are some errata from *Schott's Almanac 2009* – many of which were kindly noted by readers.

[p.28 *of the 2009 edition*] The date of the Henley by-election was incorrect; it was held on 26/6/08, as was correctly stated on p.55. [p.62] A reader suggested that the obituary of Jeremy Beadle should have included a reference to his indefatigable charity work, for which he was made an MBE in 2001. [p.179] *Joseph and the Amazing Technicolor Dreamcoat* was erroneously called *Joseph and his Amazing Technicolor Dreamcoat*. [p.225] An entry on the 'cost of culture' around the world stated that entrance to the Statue of Liberty was free. However, as a reader noted, 'unless you fancy a swim, the only way to get there is the ferry that costs $12, so there is a cost involved to get in'. [p.277] Following the Union, Scotland and England remained separate states until 1707, when the United Kingdom was formed. The three lions have traditionally symbolised England, and not the UK. [p.297] Jacques Rogge is President, not chairman, of the International Olympic Committee. [p.319] The Epsom Oaks was won by Look Here, trained by Ralph Beckett and ridden by Seb Sanders. [p.337] Ascension Day was incorrectly stated as 21 April; it was in fact 21 May. This year it is 13 May, as updated on p.337. [p.338] A reader noted that the Islamic holiday of Ashura has different meanings for Sunni and Shi'a Muslims: for the former it marks the day Noah left the Ark and the day that Moses was saved from the Egyptians; for the latter it commemorates the martyrdom of Hussein, the grandson of Muhammad, in 680 CE. This entry has now been amended, again on p.338.

——————————— ACKNOWLEDGMENTS ———————————

The author would like to thank:

Pavia Rosati · Jonathan, Judith, Geoffrey, & Oscar Schott, Anette Schrag
Richard Album, Joanna Begent, Catherine Best, Martin Birchall,
Keith Blackmore, Julia Clark, Andrew Cock-Starkey, James Coleman,
Aster Crawshaw, Iain Dale, Jody & Liz Davies, Will Douglas, Mary Duenwald,
Stephanie Duncan, Jennifer Epworth, Kathleen Farrar, Minna Fry,
Alona Fryman, Tobin Harshaw, Mark & Sharon Hubbard, Nick Humphrey,
Max Jones, Amelia Knight, Alison Lang, Annik Le Farge, John Lloyd,
Ruth Logan, Chris Lyon, Mark Lotto, Jess Manson, Michael Manson,
Susannah McFarlane, Sara Mercurio, David Miller, Polly Napper, Nigel Newton,
Sarah Norton, Alex O'Connell, Cally Poplak, Dave Powell, Alexandra Pringle,
Natalie Sandison, Leanne Shapton, Bill Swainson, Caroline Turner,
Greg Villepique, & Rett Wallace